Time Out

Havana

timeout.com/havana

Penguin Books

PENGUIN BOOKS

Published by the Penguin Group
Penguin Books Ltd, 80 Strand, London WC2R ORL, England
Penguin Books USA Inc., 375 Hudson Street, New York, New York 10014, USA
Penguin Books Australia Ltd, 250 Camberwell Road, Camberwell, Victoria 3124, Australia
Penguin Books Canada Ltd, 10 Alcorn Avenue, Toronto, Ontario, Canada M4V 3B2
Penguin Books (NZ) Ltd, cnr Rosedale and Airborne Roads, Albany, Auckland, New Zealand

Penguin Books Ltd, Registered Offices: Harmondsworth, Middlesex, England

First published 2001

Second edition 2004
10 9 8 7 6 5 4 3 2 1

Colour reprographics by Icon, Crowne House, 56-58 Southwark Street, London SE1 1UN
Printed and bound by Cayfosa-Quebecor, Ctra. de Caldes, Km 3 08 130 Sta, Perpètua de Mogoda, Barcelona, Spain

Edited and designed by
Time Out Guides Limited
Universal House
251 Tottenham Court Road
London W1T 7AB
Tel + 44 (0)20 7813 3000
Fax + 44 (0)20 7813 6001
Email guides@timeout.com
www.timeout.com

Editorial

Editor Ismay Atkins
Deputy Editor Ros Sales
Listings checker Karen McCartney
Proofreader Tamsin Shelton
Indexer Anna Raikes

Editorial/Managing Director Peter Fiennes
Series Editor Ruth Jarvis
Deputy Series Editor Lesley McCave
Guides Co-ordinator Anna Norman
Accountant Sarah Bostock

Design

Art Director Mandy Martin
Acting Art Director Scott Moore
Acting Art Editor Tracey Ridgewell
Senior Designer Averil Sinnott
Designers Astrid Kogler, Sam Lands
Digital Imaging Dan Conway
Ad Make-up Charlotte Blythe

Picture Desk

Picture Editor Jael Marschner
Deputy Picture Editor Kit Burnet
Picture Researcher Alex Ortiz

Advertising

Sales Director Mark Phillips
International Sales Manager Ross Canadé
International Sales Executive James Tuson
Advertising Assistant Sabrina Ancilleri

Marketing

Marketing Manager Mandy Martinez
US Publicity & Marketing Associate Rosella Albanese

Production

Guides Production Director Mark Lamond
Production Controller Samantha Furniss

Time Out Group

Chairman Tony Elliott
Managing Director Mike Hardwick
Group Financial Director Richard Waterlow
Group Commercial Director Lesley Gill
Group Marketing Director Christine Cort
Group General Manager Nichola Coulthard
Group Art Director John Oakey
Online Managing Director David Pepper

Contributors

Introduction Ismay Atkins. **History** Christine Ayorinde. **Havana Today** Claudia Lightfoot (*Europe: friend or foe?* Sebastian Doggart). **Havana Tomorrow** Giles Tremlett. **Where to Stay** Mike Fuller, Karen McCartney (*New for old* Karen McCartney; *Casas particulares* Anna Papadopoulos; *So long, wise guys* Mike Fuller). **Sights Introduction** Karen McCartney. **La Habana Vieja** Susan Hurlich (*Urban refit* Juliet Barclay; *Statuary rites* Karen McCartney). **Centro Habana** Mike Fuller (*Beat it* Anna Papadopoulos). **Vedado** Susan Hurlich (*Just like starting over* Karen McCartney). **Miramar & the Western Suburbs** Karen McCartney. **Eastern Bay & the Coast** (*Keeping the faith* Christine Ayorinde). **Eating & Drinking** Mike Fuller, Fiona Murphy, Lucia Newman, Matt Pickles (*Chinatown* Fiona Murphy; *Herbivore Havana* Karen McCartney; *Menu reader* Beatriz Llamas). **Shops & Services** Karen McCartney (*Getting agro* Anna Papadopoulos; *Peso shops* Karen McCartney). **Festivals & Events** Laura Burns. **Children** Cecilia Vaisman. **Film** Laura Burns. **Galleries** Holly Block, Rolando Milian. **Gay & Lesbian** Joseph Mutti. **Music & Nightlife** Robert Mann (*Bienvenue, willkommen, welcome* Robert Mann; *Generation rap* Pablo Herrera, Ardath Whynacht). **Performing Arts** Sebastian Doggart (*Remember my name, High-density dance* Sebastian Doggart; *Havana laugh* Solitaire Faber). **Sport & Fitness** Gregory Biniowsky, Martin Hacthoun (*Esquina caliente* Gregory Biniowsky; *The Blues* Martin Hacthoun). **Beyond Havana: Getting Started** Ismay Atkins, Karen McCartney; **Pinar del Río** Laura Burns; **Varadero** Ismay Atkins, Jake Duncombe; **The Central Provinces** Ismay Atkins; **Santiago de Cuba** Robert Mann. **Directory** Rolando Correa, Sue Herrod, Karen McCartney (*US citizens travelling to Cuba* Emily Wasserman; *Specialist travel packages* Anna Papadopoulos). **Consultants** Juliet Barclay, Gregory Biniowsky, Laura Burns, Jake Duncombe, Mike Fuller, Orlando Galloso, Beatriz Llamas, Claire Losada, Karen McCartney, Anna Papadopoulos, Matt Pickles, Mariley Reinoso. **Additional listings checking** Rolando Correa, Orlando Galloso, Hiram Gonzáles, Sue Herrod, Claire Losada, Anna Pertierra, William Sullivan.

Maps JS Graphics (john@jsgraphics.co.uk). Maps based on material supplied by Apa Publications GmbH & Co, Verlag KG (Singapore branch).

Photography Lydia Evans, except: pages 6, 10 AKG-images; pages 13, 15, 19, 28 Associated Press; pages 12, 30 Getty Images; page 133 Axiom; page 173 Corbis; pages 208, 210 South American Pictures. The following photograph was supplied by the featured artists/establishments: page p135, 161.

The Editor would like to thank: Sol Meliá, Gran Caribe, the Cuban Tourist Board, Stalin Mainer and John Warr.

Contents

Introduction 2

In Context 5

History 6
Havana Today 21
Havana Tomorrrow 28

Where to Stay 31

Where to Stay 32

Sightseeing 47

Introduction 48
La Habana Vieja 50
Centro Habana 64
Vedado 72
Miramar & the Western Suburbs 82
Eastern Bay & the Coast 88

Eat, Drink, Shop 95

Eating & Drinking 96
Shops & Services 116

Arts & Entertainment 131

Festivals & Events 132
Children 137
Film 140
Galleries 145
Gay & Lesbian 150
Music & Nightlife 153
Performing Arts 166
Sport & Fitness 176

Beyond Havana 183

Getting Started 184
Pinar del Río Province 186
Varadero 191
The Central Provinces 196
Santiago de Cuba 206

Directory 213

Getting Around 214
Resources A-Z 218
Vocabulary 231
Further Reference 232
Index 234

Maps 239

Cuba 240
Havana Overview 241
Street Index 243
Playas del Este 246
Miramar & the Western Suburbs 248
The City 250
La Habana Vieja 252

Introduction

Cuba is deliciously different. It provides travellers tired of mass homogenised culture with something to get their anti-imperialist teeth into. Irresistibly romantic recent history plays a principal role; handsome bearded rebels armed with a vision of national independence and social equality deliver small country from US domination (and withstand extreme hostility from the most powerful nation in the world for over 40 years as a result). Then there's the nostalgic appeal; Cuba is one of the last places on earth untainted by Coca-Cola billboards. Rebel status is an undeniable part of its allure but Cuba, in particular Havana, has much more to offer than a glimpse of life without McDonald's. Politics just happen to hog the limelight.

Arguably Latin America's best-preserved colonial city, Havana is one of the oldest, grandest and safest cities in the Americas, and packs a cultural punch well beyond its size and certainly beyond its economic status. Centuries of Spanish and African interaction have made it a hotbed of culture, and the vibrancy of Cuban music and dance alone make it worth the trip. Add in palm trees and a tropical climate, not to mention the egg-timer appeal of a country teetering on the brink of massive change, and you have a potent cocktail. Ice-cream shaded colonial buildings, cool squares and waves lapping against the crumbling sea wall make it visually bewitching, while smart, charismatic *habaneros* take care of the rest.

The city's inherent allure isn't something that has escaped the attention of the Cuban government. In an ironic U-turn, it began to welcome international tourists (or more accurately the hard currency in their money belts) with wide open arms in the early 1990s. Following the collapse of the Soviet Union, and Cuba's subsequent economic meltdown, the tourist industry hasn't looked back. But then, frankly, who could blame it? Tourists just can't seem to get enough of Cuba (and all things Cuban), titillated by its exoticism and intrigued by its eccentricities. Undeterred by poor standards of service at inflated prices, human rights fiascos and the US agenda, visitors keep pouring through the gates of Havana's international airport, eager to catch a glipse of the twilight years of the Cuban Revolution.

But don't come expecting picture postcard revolutionary utopia. Havana comes with plenty of grit, gripes and, as any Cuban you let bend your ear will tell you, its share of inequalities. The dual economy (the country is run in hard currency, while its inhabitants suffer on worthless peso wages) is a constant trial for Cubans.

One word of advice: the Cuban government happily channels tourists down a rose-tinted highway, lined with dollar-gobbling, air-conditioned hotels and plenty of privileges. Be sure to off-road.

ABOUT THE TIME OUT CITY GUIDES

The *Time Out Guide to Havana & the best of Cuba* is one of an expanding series of Time Out City Guides, now numbering over 45, produced by the people behind London and New York's successful listings magazines. Our guides are all written and updated by resident experts who have striven to provide you with all the most up-to-date information you'll need to explore the city or read up on its background, whether you're a local or a first-time visitor. The guide contains detailed practical information, plus features that focus on unique aspects of the city.

THE LOWDOWN ON THE LISTINGS

Above all, we've tried to make this book as useful as possible. Addresses, telephone numbers, websites, opening times, admission prices and, for hotels, credit card details, are included in our listings. And, as far as possible, we've given details of facilities, services and events. However, owners and managers can change their arrangements at any time. Also, in Havana and the rest of Cuba, shops, bars and, in particular, *paladares*, don't keep precise opening times, and may close earlier or later than stated. Similarly, arts programmes are often finalised very late. If you're going out of your way to visit a particular venue, we'd advise you whenever possible to phone first. While every effort has been made to ensure the accuracy of this guide, the publishers cannot accept responsibility for any errors it may contain.

There are two things to remember in Havana: everything will take longer than you are expecting, and everything will cost more than you are expecting. The golden rule is to take a sense of humour with you, wherever you go.

PRICES AND PAYMENT

The prices given in this guide should be treated as guidelines, not gospel. We have listed prices

in US dollars ($) throughout, and also in Cuban pesos where relevant. Credit cards are generally only accepted in hotels in Havana. (Although other establishments may claim to accept them, in practice, credit card machines are often broken.) We have used the following abbreviations: **MC** for MasterCard and **V** for Visa. Note that American Express and cards issued by US banks (or even its subsidiaries outside the US) are not accepted in Cuba.

THE LIE OF THE LAND

To make the book (and the city) easier to navigate, we have divided Havana into areas and assigned each one its own chapter in our **Sightseeing** section (pages 47-93). Although these areas are a simplification of Havana's geography, we hope they will give you a useful means of understanding the city's layout and finding its most interesting sights. The areas are used in addresses throughout the guide. See page 48 for a summary of these areas.

Though distances within Havana can be big, many tourists choose to avoid the hassle and crush of the city buses and opt instead for a taxi (ranging from 1950s 'yank-tanks' to air-conditioned tourist taxis), a pedal-powered *bicitaxi*, or a cheeky little orange three-wheeled *cocotaxi*.

TELEPHONE NUMBERS

Havana's phone system can be extremely frustrating and is prone to breakdown. Phone numbers within the city tend to have between five and seven digits. To call Havana from abroad, dial your international access code, then 53 for Cuba and 7 for Havana. Phone codes for places outside Havana are listed in full (if dialling from outside Cuba, drop the 0), for example, in the **Beyond Havana** chapters (pages 184-212).

ESSENTIAL INFORMATION

For all the practical information you might need for visiting Havana, including emergency phone numbers and details of local transport, turn to the **Directory** chapter at the back of the guide. It starts on page 214.

MAPS

We provide a map reference for all places listed in central Havana, indicating the page and grid reference at which an address can be found on our street maps. These are located at the back of the book (pages 240-252), and include a map of Cuba (page 240), an overview map of Havana (page 241) and detailed street maps of the city (pages 246-252). To make the maps easier to navigate, there is also a street index (pages 243-245). Street maps for towns in the Beyond Havana section of the guide (pages 184-212) are included in the relevant chapter.

LET US KNOW WHAT YOU THINK

We hope you enjoy the *Time Out Guide to Havana & the best of Cuba*, and we'd like to know what you think of it. We welcome tips for places that you consider we should include in future editions and take note of your criticism of our choices. There's a reader's reply card at the back of this book for your feedback – or you can email us at guides@timeout.com.

Advertisers

We would like to stress that no establishment has been included in this guide because it has advertised in any of our publications and no payment of any kind has influenced any review. The opinions given in this book are those of *Time Out* writers and entirely independent.

There is an online version of this guide, and guides to over 45 international cities, at **www.timeout.com**.

In Context

History 6
Havana Today 21
Havana Tomorrow 28

Features

The Padilla Affair 11
Special times 16
Key events 20
Europe: friend or foe? 22

Spanish observation post, **Spanish-American War**, 1898. *See p11.*

History

Spanish colony, US playground, socialist utopia: Cuba's story is compelling, and the plot keeps getting thicker.

The written history of the Caribbean begins with the arrival of Christopher Columbus (Cristóbal Colón in Spanish). However rich and varied life in pre-Columbian Cuba may have been, there is no evidence that the indigenous peoples possessed a written language. Our knowledge of these times, therefore, is based on archaeological excavations and the writings of Spanish explorers.

The island was first inhabited by the Siboney (or Ciboney) and the Guanahatabey, groups that probably migrated (somewhat ironically) from Florida and spread throughout the Caribbean. The archaeological evidence indicates that they were hunter-gatherers, living in small groups near the shoreline or close to rivers and streams. They were followed by the more technologically savvy Taíno, an Arawak people from South America. The Taíno were excellent farmers, boat builders and fishermen. Men cleared and defended the village, while women cultivated crops and produced manufactured goods. Seafood was the main source of protein, so most Taíno settlements were located within easy reach of the sea.

TROUBLE IN PARADISE

Christopher Columbus first set foot on Cuban soil on 27 October 1492. Convinced that he had reached Asia by sailing westwards, he returned home to Spain in the following year, leaving half his men behind on the neighbouring island of Hispaniola. Apart from another fleeting visit by Columbus the following year, Cuba was at this point little more than a staging post for further colonisation as explorers busied themselves discovering other parts of the Caribbean. It wasn't until 1508, when Sebastián de Ocampo circumnavigated Cuba, that the Spanish realised that their new discovery was actually an island.

The pace of life changed dramatically in 1511, when Diego Columbus (Christopher's son) decided to 'settle' the island and appointed Diego Velázquez as its first governor. The new lords of Cuba quickly set about enslaving or killing all but a handful of the indigenous Taíno. One early rebel was Hatuey, a chief from Hispaniola who fled to Cuba where he fought the Spaniards but was captured and burnt at the stake.

Until recently, the conventional view has been that the Spaniards totally exterminated the Taíno in Cuba through the imaginative and diligent application of disease, cruelty (in the form of slavery and torture) and murder. The most recent evidence, while not detracting from the conquistadors' formidable skills as psychopaths, indicates that a few scattered pockets of Taíno society did survive, no doubt overlooked in the general butchery. When the Spaniards began to exploit the island's mineral and agricultural resources, the penny soon dropped that by wiping out the locals, they had also destroyed their only convenient source of labour. This little gaffe was easily remedied, however, when the first African slaves arrived in Cuba from 1513 onwards.

THE SPANISH GET SETTLED

Meanwhile, the settlement of Cuba was progressing at a frenetic rate. Seven towns were founded across the island (Baracoa, Santiago de Cuba, Bayamo, Sancti Spíritus, Trinidad, San Cristóbal de la Habana and Puerto Príncipe – now Camagüey). Pánfilo de Narváez established the westernmost of these in 1514, and named it San Cristóbal de La Habana (said to be after a prominent local Indian chief, Habaguanex, though this is disputed). Havana was originally located about 50 kilometres (31 miles) south of its current location, near the present-day town of Batabanó, but this region was found to be marshy and plagued with mosquitoes, so the city was relocated to its current home in 1519.

The same year, after setting off from Santiago de Cuba, conquistador Hernán Cortés and his fleet had stopped for supplies in Havana harbour en route to Mexico on his notorious mission to convert the Aztecs into a historical footnote. The knock-on effect of this expedition meant that Havana rapidly became an important hub for Spanish activities in the Caribbean. Its large, sheltered harbour provided an ideal anchorage for vessels en route to Spain, laden with silver and gold plundered from Central and South America.

When Spanish galleons opened the Philippines for trade in 1564, Havana's fortune was made. All the riches of the New World and the Orient passed through the city en route for Seville. For all its wealth, Havana also had the drawbacks associated with a boom town. It was filthy with sewage and rotten produce; drunks, cut-throats, and whores roamed the mud streets, and during hot weather yellow fever epidemics were frequent. Inevitably, Havana's growing prosperity attracted the attention of English, Dutch and French pirates. The city was extensively plundered or burned with monotonous regularity, until in 1558, the *habaneros* began the construction of the Castillo de la Real Fuerza as a defensive bastion on the edge of the bay (it was completed in 1577). Another two fortresses – Castillo de Los Tres Reyes del Morro and Castillo San Salvador de La Punta – on either side of the harbour entrance, were completed in 1630. A heavy chain was stretched across the harbour mouth and could be lifted into place to block the entrance. The pirates responded by simply plundering Spanish ships on the open seas instead of in the harbour.

By the late 16th century, Caribbean piracy had become big business and was well organised. English and French pirates were often licensed by their governments to prey on Spanish shipping, as a means of weakening Spain's hold on the New World. The destruction of the Spanish Armada in the English Channel in 1588 further increased the vulnerability of its colonies to piracy.

Despite these setbacks, Havana grew in power and significance throughout the 16th century. In 1592 Philip II gave Havana its title of 'city'; this was also the year that the Zanja Real, the first aqueduct in the Americas, was built to bring the waters of the Río Almendares to the city. As the 'key to the Indies' it became the pre-eminent city of the New World (even though Mexico City and Lima were larger), and the Cuban capital was officially moved from Santiago de Cuba to Havana in 1607. Trade (legal and illegal) made residents rich. Like the nouveaux riches of any era, affluent *habaneros* flaunted their wealth. Stonemasons and craftsmen were brought from Spain to build vast mansions (*palacios*), full of columns and arches, grand staircases and tiled courtyards. In 1674 work began on the massive walls that would take the best part of a century to build, ultimately enclosing the city within a protective ring of stone ten metres (35 feet) high.

FIRST STIRRINGS OF REVOLUTION

Despite Cuba's growing wealth, political and economic power remained firmly in Spanish hands. This was reinforced by a trade monopoly. When gold supplies began to run down, Spain began to look for other sources of income and tobacco became Cuba's most important export. In 1717 Spain created an agency known as the Factoría, which purchased all Cuban tobacco at a (low) fixed price and had exclusive rights to sell it abroad. The tobacco growers tried to rebel but were brutally suppressed. In 1740, the Real Compañía de Comercio was founded to control all imports to and exports from the port of Havana. The resulting extortionate customs duties and restricted supply of goods caused great

discontent among the populace. A black economy quickly sprang up, and Havana became the smuggling centre of the Caribbean.

This was all to change when a British expeditionary force under the Earl of Albemarle breached Havana's defences in June 1762. The new masters removed trading restrictions and the city prospered under the brief British rule. The British ceded control of the city back to Spain in 1763 in return for Spanish-held territories in Florida, but Cuban landowners and merchants had got a taste of the economic potential of free trade. Things would never be the same again.

After regaining control, the Spanish undertook an extensive programme of renewal and modernisation in Havana: streets were cobbled and gas lighting installed; sewers and drains were built; architectural styles were harmonised; parks and grand avenues were built. Havana was Spain's showpiece in the New World, a great city of 55,000 inhabitants.

In 1791, revolution in neighbouring Haiti destroyed its sugar industry. Cuba replaced it as the region's main supplier and large amounts of capital were poured into creating new production capacity. Trade between Cuba and the newly established United States rapidly became an important source of revenue for the island. Although Spain signed a treaty with Britain to end the slave trade in 1817, Cuba's fast-growing economy was heavily reliant on slave labour. The trade simply moved underground and continued to grow.

A period of relative peace on the European continent after the Napoleonic Wars prompted Spain to lessen the financial drain on its colonies. Discontent over crippling taxation and heavy-handed leadership had been growing for a number of years throughout the New World. In an effort to calm tensions, the Factoría tobacco monopoly in Cuba was abolished in 1817. The gesture was too little, too late. The fires of revolution were already burning throughout Spanish America.

THE YANKS ARE COMING

By 1824 all of Spain's chickens had come home to roost. Years of poor leadership, greed, arrogance and military ineptitude had cost it the bulk of its great American empire, which at one time had spanned nearly all of South and Central America and much of what is now the western United States. All that remained were two islands – Puerto Rico and Cuba – and the Spanish were determined to hold on to these vestiges of their former greatness. The USA, on the other hand, felt that these islands would make a lovely addition to its young nation. The United States articulated a sweeping policy concerning the Americas that would have repercussions for Cuba right up to the present day. The Monroe Doctrine, named after President James Monroe, claimed the western hemisphere as a US sphere of influence and warned Europe not to interfere in the affairs of any of the newly independent American nations.

Meanwhile, revolutionaries from newly liberated Spanish America joined forces with disaffected Cubans in a number of unsuccessful plots aimed at freeing the island from colonial rule. The US feared that independence would end Cuba's participation in the slave trade (a major source of labour for the southern United States). US policy at that time was to try to distance Cuba and Puerto Rico from other Latin American countries, increase their reliance on the US and thereby hasten their ultimate incorporation into the US itself. The policy was very effective and, helped in no small measure by continued Spanish mismanagement, US influence in Cuba grew quickly and it became the island's main trading partner.

'The US made numerous attempts to either buy Cuba from Spain or to forcibly annex it.'

After the Mexican War of 1847, the US annexed Texas, California and New Mexico. In 1848 President Polk felt that Cuba had become a US colony in all but name and offered Spain $100 million for its territory. The Spanish government turned him down. For the next 20 years the US made numerous attempts to either buy Cuba from Spain or forcibly to annex it. Some Cubans also regarded this as a better option than a Haitian-style revolution or the untimely ending of the slave trade on which the economy depended. This cat-and-mouse game continued until the end of the US Civil War, when the abolition of slavery diminished Cuba's value to the USA.

By the mid 19th century Cuba's once relatively diversified agricultural base had been almost completely turned over to the production of a single crop: sugar. Whatever the long-term negative economic and political ramifications of Cuba's emergence as a monocrop economy, it led to a short-term period of prosperity in the 1860s, resulting in new affluent neighbourhoods springing up outside the city walls. The colonial city centre became a congested slum as Havana's rich fled the old city for leafy suburbs like the Cerro and later Vedado. In 1863 the city walls were torn down to accommodate Havana's explosion into the surrounding countryside.

Slaves for sale in the 19th century.

THE TEN YEARS WAR

Spain once again demonstrated its feeble grasp of political reality by failing to respond to Cuban calls for political reform and imposing new taxes in 1866. This was in addition to the extortionate duties already levied on imported and exported goods, which had pushed Cubans to the brink of revolt several times in the recent past. An economic recession followed.

Wealthy plantation owners on the west of the island, who benefited from the huge profits from sugar, were reluctant to rise up against Spain for fear of triggering a slave uprising. Small-scale planters from the eastern region were badly affected by the recession and thus had less to lose. On 10 October 1868 landowner Carlos Manuel de Céspedes issued what was to become known as the Grito de Yara, a proclamation of Cuban independence. Others responded to the call and the revolutionary war that followed lasted a decade. The Ten Years War officially ended in 1878 when the rebels accepted Spanish peace terms.

While the goal of independence was not achieved, the war had three effects. First, it gave Cuba the revolutionary heroes it needed to rally the populace to the cause of independence. Carlos Manuel de Céspedes, Máximo Gómez and Afro-Cubans Antonio Maceo (known as the Bronze Titan) and Guillermón Moncada have inspired generations of Cuban freedom fighters. Secondly, the war instilled a revolutionary spirit into the Cuban people that they possess to this day. Finally, it destroyed large amounts of agricultural land and bankrupted many Cuban sugar planters, thereby opening the door to a virtual monopoly of the Cuban sugar industry by US interests. These countervailing forces would shape much of the island's later history.

The terms of the treaty signed in February 1878 were hardly satisfactory from the Cuban perspective. The Pacto de Zanjón (Treaty of Zanjón) freed any slaves who had fought on either side during the war, but left the institution of slavery in place. More alarmingly, Cuba would remain subject to Spanish rule, though its people were given some limited representation in the Spanish Cortés (parliament). Some of the Cuban military leaders, including General Antonio Maceo, decided to reject the treaty at what became known as the Protest of Baraguá. Fighting continued until they were eventually forced to give up and go into exile.

The combination of the war and the ending of slavery in 1886 severely affected sugar production. Competition from European sugar beet caused a fall in world prices and resulted in the loss of some of Cuba's markets. US capital began to flow into the sugar, mining and tobacco industries. By 1884 the United States was buying most of Cuba's exports. This further increased Cuban dependency on its big brother.

I HAVE A DREAM...

One important figure to emerge at this period was José Martí. He articulated the programme for a Cuba that would be 'economically viable and politically independent'. Responsible for organising Cuban exiles in the US, together with the generals Máximo Gómez and Antonio Maceo, Martí planned an uprising for early 1895. The uneasy peace came to an end in April with the outbreak of a new War of Independence. Martí was killed in the revolution but his vision remains at the centre of Cuban political life. Unfortunately, it is yet to be achieved.

The War of Independence was brutal and bloody. Once again, the shadow of US interests fell across the proceedings, with American public opinion (and business interests) firmly on the side of the Cuban rebels. When the battleship USS *Maine* mysteriously exploded and sank in Havana harbour on 15 February 1898, it provided a pretext for the US to enter the conflict and signalled the beginning of the Spanish-American War. The war lasted barely three months; just enough time for Havana to be blockaded and the Spanish fleet to be defeated at Santiago de Cuba. With US help, the rebels had won. Cuba was free.

NO SUCH THING AS A FREE COUNTRY

The first hint the Cubans got that they had been conned was their exclusion from the peace table. The United States and Spain negotiated terms for the withdrawal of Spanish forces and agreed the means by which control of the island would pass to the US. For the next four years the island was run by a military government under General Leonard Wood. The US occupation had two principal objectives: firstly to rebuild the physical infrastructure that had been destroyed by the war; and secondly to ensure that the new Cuban political and constitutional framework was shaped in a way favourable to US business interests. This goal was assisted in large part by the imposition of the Platt Amendment, an appendix to the Constitution that gave the US the right to intervene in Cuban affairs if order or stability (in other words, US interests) were threatened. It also granted the leasing of areas of Cuban territory for US military bases (one of which was the now notorious Guantánamo Bay). The first in a long and distinguished line of US laws, this had the effect of making life for Cubans as unpleasant as possible.

In 1902, the Republic of Cuba was created, with the pro-American former schoolmaster Tomás Estrada Palma as its first president.

The Padilla Affair

Heberto Padilla (1932-2000) was one of the finest Cuban poets of his generation, but he is better known throughout the world for his controversial arrest in 1971. The 'Padilla Affair' was widely publicised internationally and became symbolic of the limitations on artistic freedom in Revolutionary Cuba.

During the heady early days of the Revolution, characterised by creative experimentation and exuberance, Padilla, like many other young Cubans, was an enthusiastic supporter of the new politics. However, after hardline communists lobbied to have the *Lunes de Revolución* literary supplement, of which he was an editor, closed down in November 1961, he began to take a more critical view. Unlike others, he began to express this in his writing.

Things eased slightly in the mid 1960s when a cooling-off in Cuban-Soviet relations led Castro and others to assert Cuba's ideological independence by cultivating left-leaning intellectuals in Europe and Latin America. Capitalist imports such as Fellini's *La Dolce Vita* offered Cuban filmgoers a welcome respite from ideologically driven Bulgarian and Czech features. But worsening economic conditions soon forced a return to the socialist camp. The timing was unfortunate for Padilla. In October 1968 an international jury voted unanimously to award the 36-year-old poet the Cuban Writers and Artists Union (UNEAC) annual poetry prize for his collection of verse, *Fuera del Juego* (*Out of the Game*), in which a political critique was barely veiled. UNEAC directors immediately denounced Padilla's poetry as counter-Revolutionary and, when the jury protested, the book *was* published but with an appendix criticising the poet and his work.

In March 1971 Padilla was arrested. He was released five weeks later in a scandal in which he had to put his name to a 4,000-word public 'confession' of his counter-Revolutionary 'crimes'. A letter of protest signed by various intellectuals with international clout, including Jean-Paul Sartre, Simone de Beauvoir, Gabriel García Márquez and Susan Sontag, was sent to Castro. He responded in a speech attacking what he called 'pseudo-leftist bourgeois intellectuals'. The Padilla episode marks the time when many writers in Latin America and elsewhere broke with Castro and the Cuban Revolution. The notable exception is Gabriel García Márquez, who has remained a renowed supporter of the Revolution.

Padilla remained under virtual house arrest until 1980 when Senator Edward Kennedy persuaded the government to allow him to move to the US. He taught literature at universities in Princeton, New York, Miami and Alabama until his death in 2000.

Holding out for a hero: **Che Guevara** in Revolutionary times.

When Estrada was elected to a second term the opposition Liberal Party accused him of fraud and launched a protest in 1906. This ushered in a second period of US occupation. President Teddy Roosevelt appointed Charles Magoon as Governor of Cuba. Hated by Cubans (regardless of political stripe), Magoon served until 1909 when José Miguel Gómez was elected Cuban president. The troops returned twice more (in 1912 and 1917) when it seemed as if outbreaks of unrest might threaten US property.

The early republican period saw huge foreign investment, especially from the US, and also large-scale immigration from the former mother country, Spain. Whole industries were rebuilt and manufacturing output returned quickly to levels reached before the War of Independence. The fact that these revitalised industries were now largely American-owned was not lost on the more alert observers of the time. Renewed industrial expansion fuelled rapid growth in Havana's population (which trebled between 1900 and 1930). Neo-classical mansions were built along wide avenues in Miramar and other new communities west of the Almendares river. Electrification spread across the extended city. Sewage and drainage systems were modernised, and Havana at last lost its characteristic reek. The goal of all this renewal and expansion was to attract tourism. In the short space of 15 years, Havana transformed itself from a war-ravaged hellhole into an irresistible magnet for foreign visitors.

Outside of the tourist areas and affluent neighbourhoods, however, it was a different story. Housing for lower-income families was generally poor and cramped. Sanitation was non-existent and disease a constant threat. Discontent among the poor and dispossessed, who felt that they had gained little from Cuba's independence, fuelled much of the violence and protest that became an integral part of mid 20th-century political life on the island.

World War I was a time of great prosperity in Cuba. The war destroyed European sugar beet production and the Cuban sugar industry enjoyed enormous profitability. The period was known as 'the dance of the millions' and was accompanied by a building boom in Havana.

Havana's ambition to become the premier tourist destination in the Caribbean was helped immensely in 1919 when the US implemented Prohibition laws. As the Stateside moral crusade gained momentum, holidaymakers flocked to Havana. Sun, sea, sex, drink, drugs, gambling – who could ask for anything more? For those who did ask there was opera, baseball, deep-sea fishing, golf and ballroom dancing.

ECONOMIC GLOOM

As sugar prices began to plummet in the 1920s, the economy fell to its knees. More Cuban property passed into US hands. Nationalism was once again at the forefront of the Cuban political agenda. Gerardo Machado ran for president in 1924 on a nationalist ticket and won easily (he may even have done so without vote rigging). The Cubans thought they had finally elected a president who was committed to real independence. The Americans thought their business interests were at last in safe hands. They were both wrong. Machado's regime set new standards in brutality and corruption, inadvertently giving the Communist Party (founded by Julio Mella in 1925) and other leftist organisations their first significant measure of popular support. The public's loathing of Machado became intertwined with a more general dissatisfaction with Cuba's dependency on the US and the hated Platt Amendment. The Wall Street Crash of 1929 and the subsequent worldwide Great Depression tied a bow on the whole sorry situation.

THE RISE OF BATISTA

Through manipulation of both the Cuban electorate and the US government, Machado managed to get his term of office extended. In 1933 a general strike forced his resignation and flight into exile. The temporary government that replaced him was ousted in September when a number of non-commissioned officers seized power in an action known as the Revolt of the Sergeants. They installed a governing committee chosen by the student movement and with Dr Ramón Grau San Martín as president.

Meanwhile, one of the revolting sergeants (so to speak), Fulgencio Batista, was busy forging the personal and business relationships that were to define the shape of Cuban politics and society for the next 25 years. He formed a friendship with mobster and gambling boss Meyer Lansky, as well as with one of President Franklin Roosevelt's closest advisers, Ambassador Sumner Welles, who became a stout supporter of Batista.

The new revolutionary government established fair working practices, granted land to peasant farmers, enfranchised women and denounced the Platt Amendment. The US, predictably, felt that such reforms bordered on communism, and so refused to recognise the new government. In January 1934 there was another coup, led by Batista. Grau was forced to resign and Batista replaced him with the pro-American Colonel Mendieta. The US immediately recognised the new government and acceded to Cuban demands to revoke the Platt Amendment, though it continued leasing Guantánamo Bay.

Although other men held the title of president between 1934 and 1940, it was Batista who held the real power in Cuba. The Batista regime was concerned with creating the appearance of good government, if not its substance. In 1938 the Communist Party (later known as the Partido Socialista Popular) was legalised. After six years as the power behind the throne, Batista had himself properly elected to the post in 1940

Camilo Cienfuegos and **Fidel Castro** before the Revolutionaries take Havana. *See p15.*

and a Cuban constitution was adopted that was a model of social justice. When, in a more-or-less democratic election in 1944, the candidate Batista had groomed for the presidency lost to the veteran politician Grau, Batista graciously took himself off to 'retirement' in Florida.

Behind the scenes, however, it was a different story: political opponents were eliminated, student and labour groups repressed and political dissent harshly punished. It wasn't just Batista, though: the two presidents in power from 1944 to 1952 (Grau and his protégé, Carlos Prío Socarrás) presided over regimes that were, if anything, more corrupt than Batista's. In 1952 Batista reappeared as a candidate for the presidency but, fearing defeat in the elections, he seized power in a bloodless coup. His new government was once again immediately recognised by the US. This launched an era of political authoritarianism and repression during which he suspended the Constitution, kept a tight rein on the unions and outlawed the Communist Party.

Batista spent most of the 1940s cosying up to US organised crime and big business interests. Cuba quickly became a mecca for gambling, drug trafficking and prostitution. These businesses operated with impunity for a decade (until they were shut down after the 1959 Revolution). By the mid to late 1950s, tourism had done much to eliminate the reliance of the Cuban economy on sugar production. Batista was beginning to plough some of this money into urban renewal projects, aimed at improving living conditions throughout Havana. Unfortunately, his time had nearly run out.

THE REVOLUTION IS COMING

By this point, the Cuban peasantry and working class had endured a bellyful of bad government. For more than 450 years they had been ruled by one mendacious incompetent after another. Worse, their destiny seemed to be as a perennial pawn in someone else's game, whether that of the Spanish, the British, the Americans, or some homegrown despot. The US ownership of many Cuban industries and its domination of the market hindered development and the economy was on a course to total collapse. This deepened a sense of frustration and, from 1953 onwards, various revolutionary groups, including that led by Fidel Castro, opposed the regime. Revolution had twice failed to secure Cuba's independence. Maybe it would be third time lucky.

The Revolution got off to a very bad start. On 26 July 1953 Fidel Castro, a 26-year-old lawyer, led a revolt in which 150 people attacked the Moncada army barracks near Santiago de Cuba. The attack was a failure; Castro and his brother Raúl were arrested, and around 70 of his followers were killed. During the subsequent trial Castro made his famous 'History Will Absolve Me' speech, outlining his vision for a radically reformed Cuban society. At the end of the trial, Castro was sentenced to 15 years in prison. He was released and exiled to Mexico less than two years later as part of an amnesty instituted by Batista to curry favour with an increasingly hostile Cuban populace. During his exile, a Revolutionary force, named the 26th of July Movement (Movimiento 26 de Julio in Spanish, often shortened to M-26-7), was created to mobilise the uprising against Batista.

> **'Fidel and Raúl Castro, Che Guevara and a handful of others managed to escape to the Sierra Maestra.'**

Batista soon had cause to wonder if releasing the Castro brothers had been a mistake. Together with 82 men they set off from Mexico on a leaky 60-foot yacht named *Granma* in miserable weather, landing in the eastern Cuban province of Oriente (now renamed, aptly enough, Granma). Fidel and Raúl Castro were back, and this time they had brought with them an Argentinian doctor named Ernesto 'Che' Guevara. Che described the Revolutionaries' arrival as 'less of a landing, more of a shipwreck'. There was worse to come.

The invasion was intended to be part of a general anti-Batista uprising orchestrated by leftist political parties, student activists and labour unions in Cuba. Unfortunately, Fidel and co landed on 2 December 1956, two days after the planned uprising in Santiago on 30 November. To add insult to injury, Batista's forces were tipped off about the invasion and attacked Castro's small force as it headed for the mountains. In the ensuing firefight, most of the Revolutionaries were either killed or captured, but Fidel and Raúl Castro, Che Guevara and a handful of others managed to escape to the Sierra Maestra. The Cuban Revolution had not made the most auspicious entrance on to the world stage.

Batista was returned for a second term of office in 1954. From their mountain base, the Revolutionaries began to build an army with which they would wage guerrilla war against Batista for the next two years. Against all the odds, Batista was unable to defeat the guerrillas. Their campaign was given new momentum in 1958, when the US government, as if by magic, woke up to the fact that Batista was not a beacon of democracy at all, but a murdering megalomaniac. Worse, he was bad for business.

With alacrity, an embargo was placed on arms shipments to Batista's forces, which rather hampered his ability to suppress the Revolution.

In a last-ditch attempt to quieten political opposition, Batista called a presidential election for November 1958. The voters stayed away in droves, the result was clearly rigged, and the US finally withdrew its support of the regime. Ever the astute operator, Batista did not intend to hang around and see how it all turned out, and on 31 December 1958 he beat a hasty retreat to self-imposed exile in the Dominican Republic.

On 2 January 1959 Che Guevara and Camilo Cienfuegos led their rebel army into Havana. Castro marched his army across the island, entering the city on 8 January. Within a month, the new government had reinstated the 1940 Cuban Constitution. Recognition by the US quickly followed. The Revolution was over and Cuba was finally an independent country. It was not to last.

CUBA LIBRE?

What became known as the 'triumph' of the Revolution had been achieved through the combined efforts of a number of movements that apparently had little in common other than a wish to liberate Cuba. But one thing was clear: if Cuba was to be a truly independent country, it would need to eliminate its almost total economic dependency on the United States. Castro's tool for achieving this was simple: he implemented a programme to nationalise key industries and services. An Agrarian Reform Law was passed in May 1959. In 1960 US-owned properties on the island were nationalised. The reaction in the US was one of horror and it retaliated by suspending its sugar quota. The US could see its Caribbean jewel, for so long just tantalisingly out of reach, suddenly disappear over the horizon.

America's hostile stance was driving Cuba firmly into the arms of the Soviet Union. The USSR agreed to purchase five million tonnes of Cuban sugar over a five-year period and in return would supply Cuba with oil, iron, grain, fertiliser, machinery and $100 million in low-interest loans.

In an attempt to destabilise Cuba, the US government launched a large-scale propaganda campaign, embargoed oil exports to the island, indefinitely extended the 1958 arms embargo, and formed a paramilitary army of Cuban exiles, ready to take the island by force. On 19 October 1960 US-Cuban relations had deteriorated to the extent that the US imposed an economic embargo on Cuba that permitted only food and medicine to be imported to the island. On 3 January 1961 Cuba and the US officially broke off diplomatic relations and in April, Castro declared the Revolution was socialist. In June 1961 all teaching centres were nationalised and a National Literacy Campaign began. While it may have alarmed the US and members of the Cuban bourgeoisie, the Revolution's commitment to social justice ensured its support by the masses.

It is tempting to argue that, but for a few inflammatory actions by the Revolutionary government and subsequent overreaction by the US, Cuban history in the second half of the 20th century might have been very

Goodbye to all that: the **Mariel** boatlift. *See p18.*

Special times

The end of the Cold War was welcomed in many quarters, but it was a disaster for Cuba. More than 80 per cent of the country's trade disappeared along with COMECON, and in July 1990 the government was forced to declare a so-called 'special period in peacetime', a polite way of introducing a series of harsh measures. Already stretched to the limit after decades of sacrifice, ordinary Cubans were asked to tighten their belts still further. The Soviet Union had supplied two-thirds of the island's food, nearly all its oil and 80 per cent of its machinery and spare parts, and the resulting shortages affected everyone; rationing was extended and the huge drop in fuel imports meant longer waits for public transport as well as frequent power cuts.

To avoid total economic collapse, the government was forced to turn to an old standby, tourism, and it soon overtook sugar as the largest earner of foreign exchange. The desperate attempt to shore up the Revolution created the conditions for a Cuban-style glasnost, a tentative and limited opening-up in economic, political and intellectual spheres. Some foreign investment and limited market reforms were permitted; travel restrictions for Cuban citizens were eased and contact with *gusanos* (worms, the word used for exiled relatives) was no longer condemned; and, in August 1993, with inescapable irony, it became legal for Cubans to shop at the dollar stores. Individuals were also permitted to set up small businesses such as *paladares* (private restaurants) or *casas particulares* (renting rooms).

By the mid 1990s the worst of the crisis was over. But this came at a cost. Mass tourism and the decriminalisation of the dollar created a new class system of sorts. Greater contact with the capitalist world has fuelled discontent and the standard of living for those with access to the dollar economy contrasts sharply with the impoverished conditions of the majority. Social problems eradicated in the early years of the Revolution re-emerged, notably crime and prostitution. Even Cuba's achievements in education and health have been eroded by shortages of paper, equipment and medication. Despite the government's expressed determination to cling to the socialist model, the Special Period clearly marked the beginning of the transition towards certain, still tightly controlled, brands of capitalism.

different. This view, however, ignores the resentment felt by the Cuban people at 60 years of American interference, and the need for Castro's government to maintain popular support by being seen to deliver quickly on its Revolutionary promises.

WORLD ON A KNIFE-EDGE

The open hostility culminated in the 17 April 1961 invasion of the Bay of Pigs, or Playa Girón, by US-trained and supported Cuban exiles. Unfortunately for them, President Kennedy decided not to deploy US air power while it was under way. Denied significant air or naval support, the insurgents were easy prey for the Cuban Army and Air Force. Of the 1,400 men who landed at the Bay of Pigs, 1,197 were captured, and the rest killed in the fighting.

After the Bay of Pigs debacle, Castro realised that there was little hope of re-establishing normal relations with an increasingly paranoid US. What he urgently needed was a powerful ally who would help him resist US pressure. The obvious candidate was America's sworn enemy and Cuba's most important trading partner, the USSR. In December 1961 Castro became a Marxist-Leninist. His transformation from vaguely left-wing nationalist to committed communist was now complete.

The low point in the tense relations between Cuba and the US began on 14 October 1962, when US Intelligence discovered that the Soviet Union was installing nuclear missile bases in Cuba. President Kennedy warned that any missile launched from Cuba at a target in the western hemisphere would be viewed by the US as an attack by the Soviet Union. An intense game of brinksmanship ensued and the two superpowers edged towards nuclear war in what came to be known as the Cuban Missile Crisis. Finally, and without Castro's knowledge, Soviet Premier Khrushchev agreed to dismantle the Cuban missile sites and return all weapons to the USSR on the condition that the United States would guarantee not to intervene militarily in Cuba. Once again, two foreign powers had decided Cuba's fate without having the decency to include it in the discussion.

Unfortunately, the Cuban government was not in a position to do anything about the situation, as the Soviet Union was the only friend that Castro had. Cuba was driven to replace earlier years of dependence on the US with dependence on the Soviet Union.

THE ACCIDENTAL COMMUNIST

Throughout the 1960s the US embargo deepened. All trade between Cuba and the US was banned. America applied pressure to its NATO partners and to Latin American countries to join its embargo, and they obediently complied. In 1963 US citizens could no longer travel to Cuba. While there is some evidence that President Kennedy intended restoring normal relations with Cuba (as a hedge against growing Soviet influence on the island, if for no other reason), he was assassinated before he could do anything about it. Some conspiracy theorists assert that the assassination may have been a plot by either Cuban exiles or organised crime bosses opposed to Kennedy's softening approach to the Castro government. Whatever the truth, after Kennedy's death the stalemate resumed.

Not all US attempts to overthrow Castro were as overt as economic sanctions and amphibious invasions. Between 1961 (after the Bay of Pigs fiasco) and officially 1962 (but in practice it continued until 1965), as part of a destabilisation programme code-named Operation Mongoose, the CIA attempted to kill Castro eight times. On at least one occasion, the Mafia was hired to do the job; other attempts involved poisoned drinking glasses and exploding cigars, but none so much as injured Castro. When they failed to kill him, CIA attention turned to trying to discredit him in the eyes of the world.

Cuban economic policy during the 1960s was aimed at reducing the country's reliance on sugar. A rapid programme of industrialisation began to build self-sufficient socialism. The programme failed due to a number of factors: economic mismanagement, the exodus of skilled personnel and the embargo. Cuba ended up more reliant on sugar (and on imports from the USSR) than ever, and the basic necessities of life grew increasingly scarce. Rationing was introduced in 1962 and has remained ever since. For many Cubans, the deprivation proved too much and there was a mass exodus; almost 200,000 had left by the end of 1962.

The large-scale migration to the US deprived Havana of many of its professionals. In addition, the Revolutionary government diverted resources away from Havana towards rural areas and the city began to deteriorate. It is estimated that, at the peak of this policy of malign neglect, 150 colonial-era buildings collapsed in the city each year. They were replaced by Soviet-style high-rises of poor design and unsafe concrete construction.

RAPPROCHEMENT... OR NOT

With huge subsidies from the USSR and rises in the world price of sugar, the 1970s saw some improvement in living standards. In 1974 the US government conducted secret normalisation talks with Cuban officials. Apparently, excellent progress was made, but the talks collapsed when Cuba became involved in the Angolan civil war later that year. Cuban foreign policy in the 1970s had shifted from the ideal of exporting Revolution abroad to the more practical goal of offering other third-world countries military and civilian assistance. This further confirmed American opinion that Castro was a loose cannon and must be stopped. Throughout the remainder of the decade, attempts by various Cuban and US politicians to relax the embargo were blocked.

Rapprochements were made from other quarters, however. In 1975 the Organisation of American States voted to end sanctions against Cuba. In 1977 the US travel ban was dropped, the two countries signed a fishing rights agreement and opened Interests Sections (an

Statue honouring **Antonio Maceo.** *See p10.*

intermediate step on the way to establishing diplomatic relations) in each other's capitals. In comparison with the previous 15 years, relations were positively balmy.

In December 1975 the First Congress of the Communist Party was held. The following year Cuba adopted a new constitution and a Soviet-style economic management and planning system. Later in the year, Castro was elected president of the State Council, consolidating the roles of president, prime minister and commander of the armed forces.

In 1980 the Revolution was 20 years old, but for many, the hoped-for improvements in living standards had yet to arrive. Many Cubans had had enough and wanted out. Castro responded by allowing free emigration from the port of Mariel, west of Havana. Within days, a flood of migrants was sailing out of Cuba for the US. By September 125,000 Cubans had left.

The improvement in relations with the US came to an abrupt end when Ronald Reagan became president in 1981 and instituted what was probably the most hostile Cuba policy since the early 1960s. Despite conciliatory signals from Cuba, the US administration tightened the embargo, reinstated the travel ban and allowed the 1977 fishing treaty to lapse. Around the same time, Miami exile Jorge Mas Canosa founded the Cuban-American National Foundation (CANF), which quickly emerged as the most powerful anti-Castro pressure group in the US. This group's relentless political lobbying would largely determine US Cuba policy for the next decade.

THE SPECIAL PERIOD

Meanwhile, conditions in Eastern Europe were changing. Perestroika was announced in the Soviet Union in March 1985. In 1989 the Berlin Wall fell and within two years Soviet communism vanished from the world stage. This was a disaster for Cuba. At a stroke, the island lost the subsidies and other monetary support it had previously received from the USSR. The ensuing decade of severe scarcity and deprivation was called, with an Orwellian flourish, the 'Special Period'.

Of major concern to the Cuban government was the loss of the country's protector. Without the Soviet Union, how would Cuba defend itself against its rapacious neighbour to the north? Sensing easy prey, the US stepped up the pressure. In 1992 Congress passed the Cuban Democracy Act (CDA), also known as the Torricelli bill after the New Jersey senator who presented it. Designed to 'wreak havoc on the island', the act promised to impose sanctions against any countries found to be 'assisting' Cuba. It further restricted humanitarian aid in the form of food, medicine or medical supplies; it prohibited vessels that had been to Cuba within the previous 180 days from entering any US port; and it banned US Cubans from making remittances to their relatives back home. It was anticipated that the act would bring about the collapse of Castro's regime 'within weeks'. While it is certain that the CDA caused additional hardship to Cubans, the US had severely underestimated Castro's ability to turn a situation to his political advantage.

In 1994, in response to riots in Havana, Castro again announced an open migration policy, giving Cubans free licence to leave the island if they wished. Almost immediately a new boatlift began and 30,000 migrants left Havana for Florida. This time however, the arms of America were not so welcoming, and the Coast Guard was dispatched to prevent the seaborne immigration. The US had learnt its lesson from the Mariel boatlift and was unwilling to allow more Cubans to arrive unimpeded into Florida. The US policy since this time has been to repatriate any Cubans found at sea or in the air, but to admit those who make it to landfall in the US (after a detailed background check).

'Bush denounced Cuba as one of the seven states of the "axis of evil".'

In 1996 the US gave Cuba another bloody nose in the form of the Cuban Liberty and Democratic Solidarity Act (better known as the Helms-Burton law). This introduced a raft of measures aimed at tightening the embargo still further. The international reaction was immediate. The United Nations, the European Union, the Organisation of American States, and many other countries condemned it outright. Aside from its manifest shortcomings from a human rights standpoint, the Helms-Burton law walks all over the concept of national sovereignty and gives the United States sole authority to determine other countries' rights to trade with Cuba. Not surprisingly, most nations have chosen to do little more than pay lip service to it, and Canada and Mexico have gone so far as to enact opposing legislation, making it an offence for their residents to abide by any provision of Helms-Burton. It seemed that, at long last, the US had lost international support for its relentless campaign against Cuba.

As the relationship with the US continued to nosedive, the Cuba's relationship with religion in general and the Catholic Church in particular began to thaw. The '90s was a period

Castro welcomes **Pope John Paul II**, 1998.

of religious revival in Cuba – perhaps brought on by the hardships of the Special Period. The state responded by allowing freedom of worship for all faiths. In 1991 the Communist Party abandoned its commitment to atheism and admitted believers to its ranks. Pope John Paul II visited in 1998 and in the same year Christmas was restored as a holiday.

LOOKING TO THE FUTURE

US-Cuban relations seemed less tense in 2000 after the return of the Elián González – the six-year-old boy picked up in the Straits of Florida and 'kidnapped' by his Miami relatives. In October the US Senate approved a bill that would lift restrictions on the sale of food and medicine to Cuba. Things took a downward turn in 2001, however, when George W Bush was inaugurated as president. A recount of votes from Florida assured Bush's victory and he is naturally keen to cultivate this constituency, which also happens to be home to many Cuban-Americans. Old hostilities flared up again as the 'War on Terror' filled the vacuum left by the end of the Cold War and Bush denounced Cuba as one of the seven states of the 'axis of evil', that he deems to be set on acquiring chemical, nuclear and biological weapons. Further fanning the flames, the US military used the base at Guantánamo Bay to house prisoners from the Afghanistan war.

Surprisingly, things took an upward turn in 2002 when US business interests, keen to establish a foothold on the island, lobbied for an end to the embargo. There were several visits to the island by US official delegations, including one headed by former president Jimmy Carter in May. However, in July, after the US House of Representatives voted to loosen both trade and travel restrictions, Bush administration officials stepped in to scupper further moves towards engagement with Cuba.

In 2003 Cuba appeared to play right into the hands of its enemies when the government arrested some 70 dissidents and executed three men who had attempted to hijack a ferry. International condemnation followed. Cuba's response was to claim that the head of the US Interests Section in Havana was helping dissidents to organise an opposition party. It also accused the US of not taking enough steps to discourage illegal immigration from Cuba.

On this occasion, Cuba's actions have not only exacerbated tensions with the US but have also put a strain on its relationship with Canada and some EU countries. Not for the first time in its 44 years, the Revolution appears to be teetering on the brink. The still-charismatic (though presumably not immortal) figure of Fidel Castro is fighting what can only be a losing battle to maintain state socialism alongside an economy heavily dependent on Western tourism and remittances from exiles. Change appears inevitable. How and when remains to be seen. Miraculously, and despite attempts to topple them, both Castro and his Revolution have outlived many of those who predicted their downfall decades ago.

Key events

AD 1-1000 Some time during this period, the Taino replace Cuba's Ciboney inhabitants.

TROUBLE IN PARADISE
1492 Christopher Columbus lands on Cuba, kicking off a period of Spanish occupation that would last for four centuries.
1513 First slaves arrive on the island.

THE SPANISH GET SETTLED
1519 San Cristóbal de la Habana officially founded on its present site.
1558-9 Three castles are built in Havana to protect the city from attack, though this does little to reduce piracy in the harbour.
1607 Capital of Cuba moved from Santiago de Cuba to Havana.

FIRST STIRRINGS OF REVOLUTION
1762 British expeditionary force takes control of Havana, though their occupation lasts less than a year: in 1763 they hand the country back to the Spanish.

THE YANKS ARE COMING
1825 First direct intervention in Cuban affairs by the US, when it prevents Mexico and Venezuela from liberating Cuba from Spanish rule.
1848 US President Polk offers to sell Cuba to Spain for $100 million. The offer is rejected.

THE TEN YEARS WAR
1868-78 Ten Years War: although Cuba loses to Spain, the Cuban people have taken their first steps towards independence.
1886 Slavery formally abolished in Cuba.

I HAVE A DREAM...
1895-8 War of Independence. Spanish rule ends, only to be replaced with interference by the US, who intervene in the war when the USS *Maine* explodes in Havana harbour.

NO SUCH THING AS A FREE COUNTRY
early 1900s Havana prospers, attracting American tourists escaping Prohibition in US. Sugar becomes an increasingly lucrative crop.
1902 Republic of Cuba created. Tomás Estrada Palma is elected first president.

ECONOMIC GLOOM
1924 Regime of newly elected President Gerardo Machado represses the working classes and ignites feelings of rebellion in the Cuban population.

THE RISE OF BATISTA
1934 President Batista, endorsed by the US, begins repressive 25-year rule.

THE REVOLUTION IS COMING
26 July 1953 Castro and his army try unsuccessfully to storm the Moncada Barracks near Santiago de Cuba. Castro and his brother Raúl sentenced to 15 years in jail but released after less than two. They go to Mexico, where they plan to overthrow Batista.
1956 Castro, Raúl, Che Guevara and fellow Revolutionaries arrive by boat in eastern Cuba to launch another attack but are forced to hide in the mountains.
31 December 1958 Batista flees. The following day, Guevara marches into the capital, followed six days later by Castro, who declares the triumph of the Revolution.

CUBA LIBRE?
1960 Cuba's relationship with USSR grows, and the two sign a trade agreement. The US imposes a trade embargo with the island.

WORLD ON A KNIFE-EDGE
17 April 1961 Hundreds of US-backed anti-Castro exiles die when President Kennedy aborts an invasion of Cuba at the Bay of Pigs.
14 October 1962 Kennedy discovers that Cuba has Soviet missiles aimed directly at USA. Nuclear war averted at the last minute.

THE ACCIDENTAL COMMUNIST
October 1965 First official boatlift to the US takes 3,000 Cubans to Miami.

THE SPECIAL PERIOD
1989 Collapse of Soviet bloc shrivels Cuba's economy overnight. The following year, Castro declares the 'Special Period'.
1994 In response to riots, Castro allows people to leave for Florida. 30,000 do so.
1996 Helms-Burton Act imposes rigid conditions on trade by the US with Cuba.

LOOKING TO THE FUTURE
October 2000 Senate approves the easing of certain parts of the US blockade on Cuba. Food and medicine can be traded between the two countries, but with cash, not on credit.
2001 US President George Bush names Cuba as part of the 'axis of evil'.
2003 Castro sparks international outrage by arresting some 70 dissidents and executing men who attempted to hijack a ferry.

Havana Today

A complex bundle of paradoxes makes Havana unfathomable to most visitors – therein lies its allure.

At first sight, Havana, like the rest of Cuba, seems to be trapped in a time warp, where life has been more or less on hold for several decades. Relatively speaking, this impression is pretty accurate. Yet, Havana is, in fact, in the throes of considerable change: the advent of mass tourism and the legalisation of limited private enterprise are having a profound effect on the social and economic infrastructure of the city.

To start with, there's a surprising amount of money splashing around on the quiet, thanks to tourism, remittances from the US and the success of *negocio* – the city's favourite pastime of wheeling and dealing in and out of the formal economy. On an individual level people are painting their houses, throwing up padlocked cages to protect their new cars, and breeding large expensive dogs. The easy traffic flow still seems like a dream compared with other capital cities but for residents it's clear that the number of cars on the road is increasing, as the familiar '50s clunkers are being joined by brand new Peugots and Audis. It used to be that there was no money and nothing to buy. These days, the centres that pass for shopping malls in Havana are full of everything you could need, from winking Christmas lights to centrifugal vegetable juicers.

These signs of improvement in the lives of certain individuals have been around for a while; what is new is that public buildings are slowly beginning to get the treatment too. Some blocks of flats are getting thorough facelifts, and the street lights along the Malecón are extending steadily westwards, illuminating the treacherous potholes that nobody has yet got round to mending. Schools have been spruced up and issued with videos and computers and, strangest of all, the Focsa building – the 32-storey concrete monolith that dominates the Vedado skyline, which has been spectacularly falling to bits for years – is being done up with state funding. These signs of spending can puzzle in the context of the constant cry of poverty and the blaming of the embargo for all Cuba's economic ills.

POLITICS AND POLEMICS

Politics is in the air you breathe in Cuba. It is impossible to avoid, and in Havana even more so. People have lived with rhetoric for so long that they barely even ponder the issues any more, though they dutifully turn out for marches and flag-wave when required. Many people's private politics have developed out of a healthy degree of cynicism and disappointment at the reality of their lives. Publicly, however, the political stakes have been raised several notches in this past year and there has been such a feverish atmosphere that older people are reminded of the early days of the Revolution. Maybe partly because the eyes of the world's press have been upon it.

Cuba entered the new millennium in a state of heightened polemical excitement, induced by the case of the child Elián González, who was picked up in the Straits of Florida, 'kidnapped'

Europe: friend or foe?

Cuba's destiny has been tied to Europe ever since Christopher Columbus set foot on Cuban sand in 1492. Even after nominal independence from Spanish rule in 1898, Europe continued to provide the lead for Cuban architecture, music, arts – even its political thinking.

The 1959 Revolution sought to move away from cultural, economic and political dependency on Europe and the US. It has achieved much in this direction, but transatlantic links remain strong. In the arts, Cuban films have been co-produced with European collaboration, and Cuban dancers regularly appear on European stages. Meanwhile, Cuba has held a Siren-like lure for European writers, including Anaïs Nin, Simone de Beauvoir, Jean-Paul Sartre, Federico García Lorca, Winston Churchill and Graham Greene.

On a personal level, it seems as if there is a mutual fan-club between Cubans and Europeans. Perhaps it's the appeal of the Other: Europeans like the sensual exoticism of the Caribbean island, while Cubans are drawn to the promise of economic security in Europe. Thousands of marriages have resulted from this synergy between the Old World and the New.

Economically, the EU's relationship with Cuba has deepened since the collapse of the Soviet Union. By 2003, when the EU opened smart new offices in Miramar, Europe was Cuba's chief economic partner, accounting for over 40 per cent of trade, as well as much of its foreign investment, and some $16.5 million a year in development aid.

But divisions have been widening recently in this cross-cultural marriage. Politically, the EU has combined a condemnation of the US trade embargo with measured criticism of the Castro administration. In 1996, it stated that further economic co-operation was dependent on Castro taking steps towards democratisation and improving Cuba's human rights record. This carrot has not lured Castro to change his ways, and if anything tensions have grown. By awarding the 2002 Sakharov human rights prize to leading Cuban dissident Oswaldo Paya, the EU aggravated Castro into announcing he had no interest in any involvement with Europe. A year later, relations nosedived again: the EU condemned Castro for executing three ferry hijackers and imprisoning a group of dissidents. The EU cancelled plans to include Cuba in the Cotonou Agreement – a trade and aid pact with former European colonies – and publicly backed dissidents who were still free.

Castro retaliated again by arranging demonstrations by hundreds of thousands of Cubans outside the embassies of Spain and Italy. He denounced Spain's prime minister, José María Aznar, as 'a little Führer', called Silvio Berlusconi 'a fascist' and accused both countries of pushing the European Union into a 'fascist-imperialist alliance with America'. Shortly afterwards, Castro closed down the Spanish embassy's cultural centre on the Malecón. He soon reopened the centre under his own management team, promising it would be 'completely dedicated to promoting the best values of Spanish culture in our country'.

It is highly unlikely that these gestures will provoke the EU to follow the US with a full-scale embargo. There is widespread consensus in Brussels that such a policy is counter-productive, internationally illegal and anachronistic. At the same time, there is evidence that European investment is slowing. Many private investors have had their fingers burned by Cubans reneging on contracts, and Cuba has defaulted on many of its short-term loans. In addition, Europeans are getting wise to Cuba's new national sport, fleecing foreigners.

Not so pretty in pink: a *camello* bus. *See p26.*

by his Miami relatives to huge and constant protest in Cuba, and finally returned to his home country. Elián was a gift to the propaganda machines on both sides of the water. It was during this time that one of Havana's most prominent landmarks was built: the imposing square, officially named the Tribuna Abierta Anti-Imperialista, but known on the street as the '*protestodromo*', went up defiantly in front of the US Interests Section to replace the Plaza de la Revolución as the main focus of protest. The space is dominated by a heroic statue of José Martí, the apostle of the nation, holding a child in his arm and pointing accusingly at the US Interests Section. Along with this new landmark, two political traditions were established that have now become part of everyday life (and the butt of many jokes): the weekly *tribuna abierta*, a political rally that rotates around the country, and the *mesa redonda*, a round table 'discussion' on a political topic televised to universal tedium every week.

No propaganda tool can be quite as good as a six-year-old floating in shark-infested waters. Still, Elián has been replaced in government iconography by five men, imprisoned in the US for spying, known officially in Cuba as the '*cinco heroes*' (five heroes). The five don't have quite the same appeal, being burly and moustachioed, but they are featured on T-shirts and posters and would surely be on car stickers if those had reached Cuba yet.

So, the political game is daily fare in Havana. But the game took a nasty and shocking turn earlier this year with two separate events. First, the little launch that shuttles people across the bay to Regla was hijacked for the 14th time in its history and taken some way out to sea, laden down with workers, bicycles and a couple of tourists, before being retaken. To worldwide horror and condemnation, the perpetrators were tried and executed within four days. Suddenly, politics went beyond the familiar posturing.

While the world was still reeling from the executions, 75 dissidents were condemned to an average of 20 years' imprisonment each for expressing ideas contrary to official policy and allegedly receiving foreign money for doing so. The world reacted again. Most European countries withdrew trade and aid. The Italians, who had been helping to fund the restoration in La Habana Vieja, and the Spanish, who were funding similar work on the Malecón, pulled out and were publicly vilified in Cuba as a result.

Fidel led a protest march down Avenida 5ta in Miramar, enclave of embassies. Left-wing intellectuals, long-time supporters of Cuba, withdrew their support publicly. There was disquiet and unrest in Havana and, for a while, there was a feeling of real fear, not helped by the fact that the main source of information in Cuba is hearsay.

Things have calmed down now and people have gone back to the main business of life: daily survival. But still the fact remains that relations with the rest of the world are at a low point and are particularly fragile with the US, which is in stick-shaking mode. But the visitor will feel no signs of animosity. In fact, the worsening political situation has had some oddly beneficial side-effects for Havana's economy, as thousands of US citizens have come over on 'last chance' holidays via third countries before George Bush imposes his promised crackdown on travel here.

STRUCTURE OF A CITY

Havana has both suffered from, and been saved by, neglect. Before the early 1980s the city was left to crumble, very few buildings went up and even fewer repairs were made. The housing stock and infrastructure rotted away, while ugly

210
CRISTAL

new pre-fabricated workers' settlements were erected in other parts of the country. The 1982 UNESCO declaration of La Habana Vieja as a World Heritage Site was the first sign of the massive restoration programme to come. By the time the tourist phenomenon caught up with the city in the '90s, there was both good and bad news. The good news was that what was left of the city had been saved from the ravages of '60s and '70s urbanisation by dint of neglect; the bad news was that much of it had simply fallen down. The main restoration work has been directed towards La Havana Vieja, the old colonial heart of the city. It's the best-preserved colonial town in the Americas and a testament to the work of the City Historian's Office, headed by the charismatic Eusebio Leal. The work being carried out in Old Havana is a clever mixture of cultural, artistic and social regeneration, funded by carefully managed and profitable state-owned companies. For more on the restoration project, *see p52* **Urban refit**. Beyond Old Havana, the city is in a precarious state. Buildings frequently just collapse, especially in Centro Habana.

ENTER THE DOLLAR

The Cuban economy was left in serious crisis after the collapse of the Eastern bloc. The government responded by the stringent belt-tightening euphemistically dubbed the 'Special Period' (*see p16* **Special times**) and a simultaneous reluctant economic liberalisation. The country was at its lowest ebb in 1993 and looking back at those dark days, it really does seem nothing short of miraculous how Cuba has managed to turn itself around. That year, the dollar was legalised. The decision was taken to target all the country's scant resources at the embryonic tourist industry in an effort to save the economy. The policy has worked and tourism has long outstripped sugar production as Cuba's main source of income. In 2002, half the country's sugar mills were finally closed.

Havana didn't need to try hard to sell itself on the tourism front, and visitors flocked in. The problem was more how to build enough hotels and other facilities to cater for the numbers wanted to come. The city has risen to the challenge and the areas most attractive to tourists have been rapidly and beautifully restored. Hotels have shot up in the western areas of Miramar and new fleets of taxis seem to appear every month. Boutique hotels are opening with frequency in Old Havana in response to changing tastes (*see p35* **New for old**).

As part of the same drive, the government also permitted a limited amount of free enterprise: *cuenta propistas* (self-employed people) are allowed to rent out rooms, open *paladares* (private restaurants) and hire themselves out as taxi drivers – though not all at once. In fact, *habaneros* had every advantage to make the most of the new possibilities, leaving the rest of the country far behind economically.

The opportunities for *habaneros* to earn dollars, legally or otherwise, are increasing all the time. Life in the city is largely organised around the scramble for *fula*, slang for dollars. If you aren't fortunate enough to land a dollar-paid job with a foreign employer, or become a legal *cuenta propista*, there are ever more ways of generating dollars in the informal sector.

'It's no longer a question of being able to get better things in the dollar shops, it's now the only option.'

The laws do keep changing with mind-boggling frequency, however, as the government constantly tries to avoid creating a wealthy class – the impossible balancing act of generating wealth for the country without overly benefiting the individual. Whole businesses are built up around taking commission from *paladares* and *casas particulares* for delivering punters, and more tourists mean more sales for sex and cigars.

HAVES AND HAVE NOTS

It's much more comfortable being a foreigner in Havana these days. You're not such a rarity and the tourist apartheid is nowhere near as extreme as it was a few years ago. Generally speaking, there is more money flowing around among *habaneros*. But the government isn't so happy, because – guess what? – class is back. The growing class of nouveaux riches, gold-chain-sporting, even mobile-phone-using Cubans to be seen at the city's pools and discos is a thorn in the official flesh. Every now and again there are crackdowns and several of the city's discos are closed for no apparent reason.

The last couple of years have seen a new phenomenon in Havana: the appearance of a group of gilded youth. These are the sons and daughters of the new rich, the restaurateurs and property owners and government officials with access to plenty of dollars. These kids are dressing in the right labels and flaunting them at a few select venues around the city. A couple of hundred of them can turn up to party at the 1830 restaurant (*see p108*), spilling out on to that corner of the Malecón. A $10 dollar entry is not a problem for them. This group is also developing a new, healthier relationship with foreigners; as they are self-sufficient, they're not so interested in hunting down foreign connections.

LA LUCHA

There's considerably more money in Havana than in the rest of the island, but still, not all of Havana's two million-odd inhabitants have easy access to dollars. There are plenty of have-nots and life is a struggle for most. A common answer to the question 'How are you?' is '*en la lucha*' (meaning 'in the struggle'). *La lucha* doesn't spare any area of human activity; it is all a struggle. The insidious double economy gets worse as wages are virtually frozen in pesos and more goods are available only for dollars. It's no longer a question of being able to get better things in the dollar shops, it's now the only option. The ration book, *la libreta*, which guarantees some basic supplies, is still crucial. However, every month less food seems to arrive. Typically, *habaneros* can count on six pounds of rice, three pounds of split peas and eight eggs a month. Apart from *la libreta*, food can only be bought in the dollar shops, the *agromercados* and on the black market. With the average monthly wage at 350 Cuban pesos, or $15, most of these options are out of the question. The *agromercado* may look cheap to a foreigner, but a pound of onions at ten pesos represents a significant chunk of a monthly salary. Not surprisingly, *habaneros* are obsessed with food. They talk about it all the time and feel constantly deprived, partly because their taste runs to enormous quantities of meat and fried foods, and both meat and cooking oil are very expensive.

Public transport is one of the most nightmarish elements of *la lucha* in Havana. Fuel and spare part shortages mean that buses are few and far between, and are unpleasantly crowded. The colourful converted trucks with two humps, known as *camellos* (camels), are quite a sight but are an uncomfortable experience. Queues are interminable so hitching a ride at the traffic lights is a common way to get around; this can be disconcerting to anyone from more cautious cultures, especially as it is often quite young schoolchildren begging a ride with a polite '*compañero, por favor*'. Bicycles are still widely used and seem to be completely unregulated. The silent, unlit bike coming at top speed with no brakes out of a side street is a daily hazard.

La vivienda (housing) is another major preoccupation. Broken-down, dangerous, crumbling houses shored up with makeshift wooden supports abound. Houses, in particular in Centro Habana and La Habana Vieja, collapse regularly, sometimes even killing passers-by. Havana has no shantytowns but there are *solares* (multi-family homes) and *ciudadelas* (large mansions turned into multiple dwellings). And the housing laws mean that there is no escape. *Habaneros* can't just move house even if there were any empty ones to move to. The only legal way to move house is by exchange, *la permuta*. An expanding family in a one-room apartment might find an elderly couple willing to exchange a larger one. But as ever, the poorest are caught because a *permuta* to a larger place always involves a few thousand clandestine dollars as part of the deal. Also, those trapped in the worst housing will never find anyone willing to exchange. People unable to raise the cash or living in very bad housing are stuck and have been for years. Meanwhile, they do their best with cardboard partitions and breezeblock extensions and *barbacoas* (literally barbecues) – platforms thrown up to create an extra floor. The housing situation has caused real suffering for many families. Even in a society like this, with a tradition of extended family, the pressure on human relationships is enormous. There is no privacy, no escape, and it is very common for divorced couples to go on living together for years, sometimes in tight-lipped silence, because they have no choice.

La lucha in all its manifestations occupies a large part of every day and is met with ingenuity and a certain dose of self-pity. Cubans think they are the hardest done by in the world… nobody suffers like a Cuban. On the other hand, nobody rises above their circumstances with more invention and humour. Huge amounts of energy are given to problem-solving and the phrases most often heard are '*no es fácil*' (it's not easy), followed by '*hay que resolver*' (you've got to find a solution) or '*hay que inventar*' (you've got to be inventive). The skills of resolving and inventing take on surreal proportions as people duck and dive around the black market, barter goods and services, throw up extensions, add two-stroke engines to their bikes, recycle spare parts or pirate CDs and videos.

MAYBE IT'S BECAUSE I'M A *HABANERO*

There are 2.2 million *habaneros* spread throughout the 15 *municipios* and the one thing they all have in common is that they all love their city and 'know' it is the best in the world. There's a whole body of literature and music based on the city. One salsa song belted out to great delight at large public gatherings calls out in praise of each area of the city in turn.

When the Revolution triumphed, Havana was not at the forefront of planned change. Not only did the new government prioritise agrarian reform, but Fidel mistrusted the capital. Despite the mass exodus of the professional middle classes, he was left with a largely Americanised city and *capitalinos* who were sharp, sophisticated and represented possible dissent. He was right. *Habaneros* are feisty and independent. His solution was to encourage people to pour in from the eastern provinces to fill the gaps the exiles had left. The city's demographics changed fast and it is a blacker and more working-class city than it was in 1959. Despite the fact that so many of the city's inhabitants came from the east, *orientales*, known derogatorily as '*palestinos*', are still the butt of wickedly sharp humour.

The *habanero* lives with paranoia, paradox, humour and curiosity. Everything is a tragedy and a huge joke; humour is a way to deal with the contradictions of everyday life. Cubans have internalised the absurdities and stresses of their lives into a value system incomprehensible to anyone else. Just when you think you have made sense of the psyche, another face appears and you realise you haven't even begun to fathom this complicated mindset. Anyone judging *habaneros* by other paradigms, even Latin American ones, is heading for a fall.

SEX AND SHOPPING

What do *habaneros* do for R&R when they are not engaged in *la lucha*? Despite the increasing amount of money in the city, there still aren't many exciting ways of spending it. Cubans spend a lot of time at home, rocking on the porch, playing dominoes or watching the soaps. There are a few clubs, bars and restaurants that charge in both dollars and pesos, but not many given the size of the city – one reason for *habaneros* to make their own entertainment. This is a city of music-making and spontaneous parties; a bottle of rum and a boom box is all you need and the legendary Cuban exuberance does the rest.

Bodies are a free source of fun; sexual activity starts young and goes on to a full and interesting (often promiscuous) adult sex life. The climate favours body culture, and sport, in one form or another, is almost as popular as sex. Shopping is an option for some nowadays and there are many more options than there were, with designer clothes available for those who can afford them.

Habaneros have a lot to teach the world about taking pleasure in life despite the odds. Hundreds of thousands of them dream of escape and would leave tomorrow if they could, but that doesn't stop them from enjoying life with gusto. Everyone is playing the waiting game: everyone knows change will come but exactly when or in what form, no one knows. Some are so desperate that any change would be welcome; others, more cautious, realise that change doesn't automatically mean improvement.

It is a fascinating time to be in Havana. The transition is unfolding before our eyes but no one's sure of the outcome. One of the most imaginative aspects of the Spanish language is that it allows for many possible futures. Where English says 'in the future…', Spanish will allow '*en un futuro*…' ('in *a* future…').

Between two flags: marching in Miami's Little Havana.

Havana Tomorrow

The 64,000-peso question: what happens next?

Fidel Castro's exceptional career as the master of Cuba can be summed up in one indisputable fact: the 'comandante en jefe' has held power longer than any other current world leader, with the exception of Thailand's largely ceremonial King Bhumibol Adulyadej. When Castro and his bearded rebels took over on 1 January 1959, Eisenhower was US president and Macmillan was British prime minister. The Berlin Wall still had not gone up, let alone come down and, as Fidel likes to boast, he has held off ten US presidents, including George W Bush.

For years observers have speculated about what would happen when he went, only to see his potential successors – and those dedicated to his overthrow – come and go, while Fidel has stayed. But Castro is no youngster. Born in 1926, his end is now, surely, in sight and speculation about a future without Fidel is no longer pointless. Anybody who saw Oliver Stone's benign 2003 documentary *Comandante* knows that he is remarkably sprightly and lucid for his age. Diplomats who visit him say his concentration has dimmed but, when he needs to be, he is still as sharp as a needle. State officials, on the other hand, get testy about foreign journalists describing Castro as 'ageing' – a sure sign that it now really matters.

In 2001, aged 75, Castro fainted at the end of a speech. Cubans were suddenly, sharply reminded of his mortality. The long-standing question of how the Fidel era might end looked increasingly likely to be settled by what is known as the 'biological solution' or, in other word's, Castro's death. And, still, the question arises: 'What happens when Fidel goes?' The short answer is that, officially, one Castro will be replaced by another. Fidel's youngest brother Raúl, a seventysomething himself, is his designated successor.

Currently, both first vice-president and defence minister, Raúl does not, at first sight, look set to restyle Cuban politics. A veteran of the Revolution, he went to jail with his elder brother in the 1950s and has warned the US that it has a better chance of reaching a deal with his big brother than with him. But some observers detect, surprisingly, a potential liberal. As defence minister he oversees – among other things – the burgeoning Gaviota tourism-to-taxis empire and other army-owned industries, farms and businesses. These have been among the most successful enterprises in the land. The officer class, having been forced to find ways of feeding and financing the army, is now, in one of those delightful contradictions that Castro's Cuba constantly throws up, well versed, even enthusiastic, about the theories of a number of American business gurus, including Peter Drucker and W Edwards Deming.

'This does not look like a country waiting to be taken over by the US, or anyone else for that matter.'

Raúl, some observers suggest, has picked up a regard for capitalist enterprise over the years. He has also overseen a slimming down of the military. With his Revolutionary credentials unquestioned, and his moral, political and military authority not in doubt, he may be a surprise candidate to lead, or at least spark, some sort of transition away from Castro-style state socialism in Cuba. Or not, of course. Nothing, in Cuba, is that easy.

Other scenarios: what if Raúl himself dies, or the regime simply crumbles without Fidel there to head it? Will, as Castro likes to warn Cubans, the Miami Cuban contingent sweeps across the Straits of Florida and try to take over? There is little doubt that many would like to. Forty years of plots, campaigns, invasions and hard lobbying in the US are not likely to be forgotten as soon as the man that militant Miami Cubans have demonised finally dies.

Some Miami Cubans have considerable wealth, be they the family of Jorge Mas Santos – son and heir to Cuban American National Foundation founder Jorge Mas Canosa – or Leopoldo Fernández Pujals, who made his millions making pizzas for Spaniards. These multi-millionaires, and others besides, have declared an intense interest in the political future of the island.

But the very nature of their success in the US and elsewhere may be their biggest impediment to gaining political power in Cuba. Not all Miami Cubans are militant, pro-embargo anti-Castroists. And ordinary Cubans living in Cuba have been fed on a diet of anti-American propaganda for as long as most can remember. The trade embargo and the violence of anti-Castroist groups have made it easy for them to believe that the US, and those who live there, simply wish them ill. The national hero remains José Martí, who fought for independence from the Spanish at the end of the 19th century. This does not look like a country waiting to be taken over by the US, or anyone else for that matter.

So what about the other opposition, the one that dares to stay and confront Fidel Castro on his own territory? Every Sunday, a group of women gather at a Catholic church in Havana's Miramar district. Dressed in white, their presence is a silent protest against the imprisonment of 76 dissidents – some of them husbands of the women – in a crackdown on people suspected of 'serving a foreign power' early in 2003. Condemned by Amnesty International and other human rights groups, the prison sentences of up to 26 years were followed, in a clear sign that the regime was ready to play tough, by the execution of three men who had hijacked a ferry and tried to take it to Florida.

The church gathering is, in fact, the only regular protest against Castro's regime. Protected by the Roman Catholic establishment, these 'women in white' include Blanca Reyes, wife of poet Raúl Rivero, Claudia Márquez, wife of Cuban Liberal Democratic Party leader Osvaldo Alfonso Valdés, and Gisela Delgado, wife of dissident economist Hector Palacios. Castro's secret agents, many of whom had infiltrated the human rights and 'independent journalist' groups to which the 76 dissidents belonged, claimed the men had all been working for the US – a claim vigorously denied by their wives. But 40 of them were also co-organisers of what has been the most effective protest movement against Castro in recent times, the so-called Varela Project.

Led by Oswaldo Paya, another devout Catholic and church protégé, the Varela Project is a peaceful attempt to bring change via a petition in which ordinary, named Cubans call on Castro to hold a referendum on reforms. Paya delivered a first copy of the petition, with 11,000 signatures on it, to the Havana parliament in 2002. Mr Paya argued that, under the terms of the country's constitution, a referendum was compulsory if more than 10,000 people back it. The request was, nevertheless, turned down. But Castro was rattled. He responded by organising his own massive, popular petition calling for a constitutional amendment, later approved by law-makers, ratifying Cuba's socialist system as 'untouchable'.

Then the arrests came. Mr Paya, however, was not among those locked up. He had

Fidel Castro at Che Guevara's funeral, with **Raúl Castro** and **Carlos Lage**. But who's next up?

steered clear of involvement with the American quasi-embassy in Havana, the American Interests Section, which had openly backed and helped many of those jailed – and was also being looked after by the Church. He and others, such as Dagoberto Valdés in Pinar del Río, keep a timid light of opposition shining. Within a few months of the arrests, Mr Paya reappeared with a further 14,000 signatures – names and addresses attached. Mr Paya and his followers are the most attractive proponents of change to many, especially to European countries, who awarded him the EU's Sakharov Prize for freedom of thought. But they seem to have little support among ordinary Cubans, who had hardly heard of the project until the trials – and then took good note of the lengthy prison sentences handed down to those involved.

A more eccentric option appeared on the scene in 2003 when Eloy Gutiérrez-Menoyo, a 68-year-old former Revolutionary who had fought by Castro's side – then broke with him and tried to rally support against him in 1964 at the head of an armed faction called Alpha 66 – came to Cuba on a visit. Instead of boarding a flight home he declared, to the surprise of his own wife and children, that he was staying in Cuba to seek peaceful change. His family flew back to the US; Gutiérrez-Menoyo stayed. His anti-Castro credentials are squeaky clean: he was captured in 1965 and jailed for 30 years, but released in 1986. The former rebel, who is Spanish-born, had then returned to Spain but moved to Miami a few years later, where he set up a moderate opposition movement called Cambio Cubano. Now in Cuba, it remains unclear how, exactly, he plans to lobby for peaceful change from within.

Another, less spectacular, less visible path to change in Cuba also exists. The last time the Spanish-speaking world waited for a comparable 'biological solution', it was that brought about by the death of another long-standing, all-powerful leader of Galician origin: Spanish dictator General Francisco Franco. Few would have guessed that, within three years of his death, Spain would be a fully democratic country. Still fewer would have expected the change to be orchestrated by those who, as he lay dying, swore unfailing loyalty. Yet it was senior regime members who oversaw a peaceful, relatively untraumatic transition in which, crucially, those whose livelihoods depended on state patronage did not lose out and all ideas of revenge were forgotten.

Two men are well placed to bring about such a transition: Ricardo Alarcon, head of the national congress, and Carlos Lage, another vice-president. Both, of course, profess eternal loyalty to Fidel and his legacy. Both may also mean it.

Nobody can predict how things will go. But there is one thing everybody agrees on. Nothing will be the same without Fidel.

Where to Stay

Where to Stay **32**

Features

The best Hotels 32
New for old 35
Casas particulares 39
So long, wise guys 44

Where to Stay

1950s mob hangouts, spruced-up colonial gems, international high-rises or a private home. You decide.

The year 2003 is destined to go down in Cuban history as the turning point in the country's endeavour to haul itself out of economic slump, using tourism as its lifeline. Tourist number two million, since the beginning of the year, is scheduled to arrive before the year is out, signalling Cuba as a key player in the Caribbean market. But, regardless of this gleaming new statistic, the effects of mass tourism have been apparent for years, not only in the island's social and economic make-up, but also in the growing quantity and quality of its accommodation. The hotel industry in Havana – and indeed the rest of Cuba – is an area of massive development, with new hotel conversions springing up, former hotels coming back to life and existing hotels getting makeovers.

Standards are rarely guaranteed in Cuba, but it is now possible at least to choose from a broad range of accommodation – from a beautifully restored colonial building, through to a modern international-style hotel. While the latter are in no short supply these days (and are generally as devoid of character as you might expect, but deliver on services), many of Havana's hotels tell fascinating tales of Cuba's extraordinary history.

NAMES AND CHAINS

Since Cuba started welcoming foreign investment (mostly in the form of joint ventures) in the early 1990s, many of Cuba's mid-range to upmarket hotels are at least part-owned by foreign companies. The most widespread is the Spanish chain **Meliá**.

Some of the most interesting hotels in Havana are run by **Habaguanex** (*see p35* **New for old**), the commerical division of the City Historian's Office. These characterful, historical small hotels have filled a gap in the market for high-quality, original accommodation. **Izlazul**, **Rumbos** and **Horizontes** are all Cuban companies offering cheap to mid-range accommodation, as is **Gran Caribe**, specialising in mid-range and upmarket hotels.

STAYING COOL (WHEN THE AIR-CON'S BROKEN)

How you react to the inevitable inconveniences that are part and parcel of hotel accommodation in Cuba is entirely up to you. Standards vary enormously, but complaints tend to revolve around the same issues: mechanical failures (the air-conditioning or lifts); insipid food; drab decor; slow, inefficient or rude service and poor communications services. It will be a relief to know that you would be extremely unlucky to come up against all of these problems in one stay but most visitors will encounter at least one. Before kicking up a fuss (rarely a successful route) it's worth remembering that tourism is a relatively new development in Cuba and that the island forms part of the developing world, so resources are scarce. Unfortunately, these factors are not taken into account when prices are set, and the added niggle of having paid hand over fist will do little to increase your tolerance.

The best Hotels

For gourmet feeds
Hotel Occidental Miramar (*see p45*).

For architectural genius
Hotel Raquel (*see p35*).

For gangster territory
Hotel Capri (*see p43*); **Hotel Habana Riviera** (*see p41*); **Hotel Nacional de Cuba** (*see p42*).

For illustriousness
Hotel Nacional de Cuba (*see p42*).

For discerning budgeteers
Casa del Científico (*see p40*); **Hostal Valencia** (*see p37*).

For originality and atmosphere
Any of the Habaguanex hotels, particularly **Hostal Los Frailes** (*see p37*) and **Hotel Santa Isabel** (*see p36*).

For peace and quiet
Hostal Los Frailes (*see p37*).

For business travellers
Hotels Habana Libre (*see p41*); **Habana Riviera** (*see p41*); **Meliá Habana** (*see p45*); **Meliá Cohiba** (*see p41*) and **Occidental Miramar** (*see p45*).

Hotel Armadores de Santander. See p34.

PESO HOTELS

Some hotels, mainly those belonging to the Islazul and Horizontes chains, reserve a set number of rooms for Cuban guests, who pay in pesos. Otherwise, Cubans go to *campismos* – bungalow or cabin-style accommodation – by beaches or rivers for their holidays. These venues charge in pesos, though as a foreigner you will have to pay in dollars (normally a disproportionate number), even if you're in the company of Cuban friends. Paying in pesos is no longer a viable option for foreigners, so travellers should drop all hopes of getting bargain accommodation at local rates.

SECURITY AND SECURITY

Guests in Havana hotels will sooner or later fall prey to the more distasteful repercussions of tourism – the hustlers (*jineteros*) patrolling the surrounding streets in search of business. For this reason the security in hotel lobbies tends to be strict; Cubans are questioned on entering a hotel and under no circumstances will they be allowed up to your room. From the government's point of view, Cuba cannot afford to acquire a name for itself as a sex tourism destination. You may not like this policy, often criticised as a form of segregation, but the reality is if you want to avoid an unpleasant scene, don't invite a Cuban to your hotel room.

You may even be asked by officials to produce evidence that you are a guest, so hang on to your guest card (*tarjeta de huésped*), issued on arrival. You may need it to get in and out of the hotel, to access the dining room or ride in the lift.

It's wise to use the hotel safe deposit box (sometimes chargeable) for your valuables. (If you are in a *casa particular*, lock them in your suitcase and lock your room). Also, while packing to leave, be sure to check that your cleaner has not 'tidied away' any of your belongings in a place that you are unlikely to check. But if you feel that staff have provided a satisfactory service, consider leaving a tip or some toiletry items. Your room maid, and indeed all hotel personnel, earn extremely low wages, in line with the rest of the population.

RATES AND SEASONS

Hotel room rates go up during high season (December to April) and particularly around Christmas and Easter. Rates also tend to be higher during July and August, when Cubans are on holiday. You should also book in advance if your visit is likely to coincide with a major event in the city, such as the film festival in December. For details of Havana's main festivals and events *see pp132-36*. During busy periods it is wise to pay for your accommodation for up to a few days in advance to ensure it is not given to someone else – even after you've checked in!

THE OFFICIAL WORD

Visitors to Cuba are officially required to have two nights' accommodation pre-booked. Always fill in the 'address in Cuba' section of your tourist card when you enter the country, whether it's an official *casa particular* or a hotel. For more on tourist cards and visas, *see pp214-33*.

STAR RATINGS AND CREDIT

All 'tourist' hotels in Cuba (as opposed to peso hotels) are either state-run or joint ventures with foreign companies, and are classified on a star system from one to five. This is no guarantee of quality, however. Four- and even five-star hotels in Cuba are often only equivalent to three-star hotels elsewhere, although the prices are likely to be just as high. Price is normally a more reliable indicator as to how many services the hotel offers.

Note that US credit cards (or even American Express cards issued by a bank outside the US) are not accepted in Cuban hotels and that *casas particulares* only ever accept cash.

DISABLED VISITORS

People with disabilities are strongly advised to contact their chosen hotel or *casa particular* before going to Havana to find out which, if any, disabled services are offered.

La Habana Vieja

Expensive hotels

Hostal Conde de Villanueva

Calle Mercaderes #202, entre Lamparilla y Amargura (862 9293/9294/fax 862 9682/ www.habaguanex.com). **Rates** $80-$90 single; $130-$150 double; $220-$240 suite. **Credit** MC, V. **Map** p252 E15.

Dating from the 18th century, and once the home of an 18th-century aristocrat who brought railways to Cuba, this building is now a discreet, sober hotel renovated in a style that successfully incorporates the old and the new. The enchanting courtyard, with abundant plants and peacocks, is overlooked by first-floor stained-glass windows and turquoise wooden beams and shutters. The nine rooms (three of them suites) – decorated conservatively in masculine colours – are each named after varieties of tobacco plant. The cigar theme continues with an excellent cigar shop in the mezzanine, a cigar tasting room and photos of famous cigar smokers, including Nat King Cole and Ernest Hemingway.

Hotel services *Bars (2). Café. Conference facilities. Garden. Laundry. Restaurant.* **Room services** *Air-conditioning. Minibar. Room service (24hrs). TV (satellite).*

Hostal del Tejadillo

Calle Tejadillo #12, esquina San Ignacio (863 7283/fax 863 8830/www.habaguanex.com). **Rates** $62-$72 single; $100-$120 double; $77-$87 single suite; $130-$150 double suite. **Credit** MC, V. **Map** p252 D15.

This charming 18th-century house, well located in a pleasant niche of Old Havana, opened as a 32-room *hostal* in 2000. Time lingers in the downstairs rooms at the Tejadillo; with no windows, history seems trapped within the centuries-old walls. For some, this makes up for the lack of view. Others may prefer a second- or third-floor room; north-facing rooms overlook the cathedral. Breakfast is served in the courtyard or adjoining restaurant. Rooms are decorated in light, pretty colours, and the two beautifully tended courtyards also lend the *hostal* a fresh feel.

Hotel services *Air-conditioning. Babysitting. Bar. Laundry. Restaurant.* **Room services** *Minibar. Safe. TV (cable).*

Hotel Ambos Mundos

Calle Obispo #153, esquina Mercaderes (860 9530/ fax 860 9532/www.habaguanex.com). **Rates** $70-$80 single; $110-$130 double. **Credit** MC, V. **Map** p252 E15.

Hemingway fans will know the Ambos Mundos as the place where the writer penned much of *For Whom the Bell Tolls*. His room, No.511, is maintained much as if the writer never checked out, complete with adjustable table at which Hemingway used to write, standing up. Ernie aside, the pinky coloured Ambos Mundos has a classically designed lobby, which manages to retain an air of calm despite the bustle on its doorstep. There's an impressive original lift, which is fun to ride in – provided you're not in a hurry, that is. The verdant rooftop cocktail bar contributes to the hotel's significant charm.

Hotel services *Babysitting. Bars (2). Conference rooms. Laundry. Parking. Restaurant.* **Room services** *Air-conditioning. Minibar. Room service (24hrs). TV (satellite).*

Hotel Armadores de Santander

Calle San Pedro #4, esquina Luz (862 8000/ fax 862 8080/www.habaguanex.com). **Rates** $80-$90 single; $130-$150 double; $105-$115 junior suite (single); $180-$200 junior suite (double); $300 special suite. **Credit** MC, V. **Map** p252 F15.

It's impossible not to be wowed by Armadores de Santander: a stunning blue and white floor competes with an ornate cream and gold ceiling, and a majestic marble staircase climbs from the lobby flanked by wrought iron railings... and that's just the entrance. This majestic three-storey building was the headquarters for Havana's main shipbuilders during the 19th century, and has been restored with a vaguely nautical theme (think luxury cruiser). All rooms are exquisitely furnished, some with spacious terraces (south-facing rooms have the best views of the bay). The 'special' suite, with fine sea views, king-size bed and jacuzzi, is fine territory for a splurge.

Hotel services *Bar. Billiards room. Restaurant. Roof terrace.* **Room services** *Air-conditioning. Minibar. Safe. TV (cable).*

Hotel Florida

Calle Obispo #252, esquina Cuba (862 4127/ fax 862 4117/www.habaguanex.com). **Rates** $80-$90 single; $130-$150 double; $105-$115 single suite; $180-$200 double suite. **Credit** MC, V. **Map** p252 E15.

The magnificent entrance of the Florida, which opens directly on to bustling Calle Obispo, draws the gaze of hundreds of passers-by every day. The entrance features a lady in marble and the staircase is overarched by a beautiful stained-glass roof created to celebrate the hotel's reopening in 1999. First inaugurated as a hotel in 1885, the building is a splendid example of the restoration work taking place in Old Havana. The 25 well-furnished rooms have Italian marble floors, high ceilings and balconies and the atmosphere is one of unabashed sophistication. Located in the thick of Old Havana's restaurants, bars and sights.

Hotel services *Bars (2). Business services. Laundry. Parking. Restaurant. Shop.* **Room services** *Air-conditioning. Minibar. Room service (24hrs). Safe. TV (satellite).*

Hotel Raquel

Calle San Ignacio #103, esquina Amargura (860 8280/fax 860 8275/www.habaguanex.com).
Rates $105-$115 single; $180-$200 double; $130-$140 single suite; $230-$250 double suite. **Credit** MC, V. **Map** p252 E15.

The Raquel is the Habaguanex chain's newest hotel and it seems that the company's architects and interior designers have put their hearts and souls into the project. Since it opened its doors in June 2003 the hotel has generated much interest, and deservedly so. Its design – primarily art nouveau with eclectic elements – is harmonious. Light pours into the lobby through amber, pale yellow and orange stained glass in the roof; and original columns stretch up from a marble floor to the roof. The ornate three-storey building dates back to 1908, originally designed as offices. Its 25 rooms (four suites) are tastefully furnished in period style. The decor has been chosen to reflect the hotel's theme: the Old Testament. Right in the heart of what was once the Jewish quarter, Raquel isn't far from Sinagoga Adath Israel de Cuba (*see p63*), Cuba's oldest synagogue. All the rooms have biblical names and the Garden of Eden restaurant serves kosher-style dishes. The cupola on the hotel terrace, with its eye-catching mosaic tiled roof, offers a picturesque view of the surrounding area. Pricey, but well worth it.

Hotel services *Bar. Parking. Restaurant.* **Room services** *Air-conditioning. Laundry. Minibar. Safe. TV.*

Hotel San Miguel

Calle Cuba #53, esquina Peña Pobre (862 7656/ 863 4029/fax 863 4088/www.habaguanex.com).
Rates $80-$90 single; $130-$150 double. **Credit** MC, V. **Map** p252 D15.

With only ten bedrooms, the appeal of the San Miguel – originally built in the 19th century but modified in the early 20th century by Antonio San Miguel y Segalá – lies in its intimate and hospitable atmosphere. Downstairs is a cosy, atmospheric bar (which would be even more atmospheric if the television were removed), while a grandiose marble staircase sweeps up to the upper floors. The soft beige and pale yellow rooms are furnished in tasteful period style. The third-floor roof terrace and some of the bedroom balconies have unrivalled views over the Bay of Havana, the Morro Castle and La Cabaña fortress.

New for old

In 1994 the Hostal Valencia shut down its peso cash register, keeping its doors open only to bearers of hard currency. Since then, a further 15 hotels belonging to the same chain, Habaguanex, have been inaugurated at an astonishing pace, given the meticulous restoration work that reopening the hotels has involved. Another two, the Saratoga and Palacio Cueto, are planned for 2004.

The company deserves full marks for its performance since its inception as part of the City Historian's Office project (*see p52* **Urban refit**) to resuscitate Havana's colonial core. It takes a sustainable development approach: rescue work on centuries-old buildings for dollar-generating commercial use has gone hand in hand with community development projects – schools, maternity homes, day care centres – aimed at raising living standards in a desperately run-down area.

Anyone returning to Old Havana, even after a relatively short absence, will appreciate the visual impact of the restoration work. Sadly dilapidated buildings – which all Habaguanex hotels and restaurants were before the company set to work – have been miraculously restored to their original glory, raising the area's architectural spec.

From a visitor's point of view, the Habaguanex initiative is great news. The hotels are original, well run and of a high quality, characteristics that were painfully lacking in Havana's hotelscape. The policy of the City Historian's Office's extends to preserving culture as well as architecture, so many of the hotels are themed to reflect Cuba's historical diversity. Themes include the island's Jewish heritage (**Raquel**, *see above*), the shipping industry (**Armadores de Santander**, *see p34*) and religious life (**Los Frailes**, *see p37*). Staff, trained at the company's own school, are refreshingly attentive and committed to the project. In the long run it can only be hoped that the jaded attitudes and looks of boredom so prevalent in the Cuban tourist industry will not creep in through the back doors, or indeed the ancient cellars, of Habaguanex hotels.

Habaguanex hotels offer a ten per cent discount on selected Habaguanex restaurants and free entrance to the main museums in Old Havana. The hotels are listed in the La Habana Vieja section of this chapter, *see pp34-8*. Note that nearly all restaurants in Old Havana are also owned by Habaguanex; for reviews, *see pp96-115*.

Hotel Sevilla. *See p38.*

Hotel services *Bar. Parking. Restaurant. Terrace.* **Room services** *Air-conditioning. Laundry. Minibar. Safe. TV (cable).*

Hotel Santa Isabel

Calle Baratillo #9, entre Obispo y Narciso López (860 8201/fax 868391/www.habaguanex.com). **Rates** $160 single; $200 double; $180 junior suite (single); $300 junior suite (double); Santovenia suite (double) $400. **Credit** MC, V. **Map** p252 E16.

Guests, waiters, receptionists and even porters seem-like actors in a well-cued film at the refined Santa Isabel. Originally the palace of the Count of Santovenia, this magnificent 19th-century building is now arguably the best hotel in Havana, and directly on the charming Plaza de Armas to boot. Photos of the count and his family, together with works of art by top Cuban painters, adorn the walls of the lobby, while furnishings exude discretion and finesse. The 27 rooms (ten suites) are subtley decorated in pastel pink and very comfortably fitted with antique furniture and wrought iron double beds. Most rooms have their own balcony overlooking the Plaza de Armas, the best of these being situated on the third floor. The *pièce de resistance,* the Santovenia Suite, was occupied by former US president Jimmy Carter during his visit to Cuba in 2002. Robert Plant and Jack Nicholson have also stayed at the Santa Isabel. Despite the hotel's official address, the entrance is actually on the Plaza de Armas (eastern side).

Hotel services *Babysitting. Bars (2). Business services. Car rental. Laundry. Parking (free). Restaurant. Tourist services.* **Room services** *Air-conditioning. Minibar. Room service (24hrs). Safe. TV (satellite).*

Palacio O'Farrill

Calle Cuba #102, esquina Chacón (860 5080/ fax 860 5083/www.habaguanex.com). **Rates** $80-$106 single; $130-$182 double; $105-$181 junior suite (single); $180-$232 junior suite (double). **Credit** MC, V. **Map** p252 D15.

This 18th-century neo-classical palace once belonged to Don Ricardo O'Farrill, a Cuban with origins in – you guessed it – Ireland. And palace is the key word; Don Ricardo was head of one of the most prosperous families in Cuba during colonial times, (thanks to the slave trade), and the splendour of this three-storey residence, with its 38 bedrooms, gives an indication of the extent of his wealth. The Palacio reopened in 2002 and the design of each floor reflects a different period: the first floor is 18th-century in style; the second incorporates 19th-century elements; and the third-floor rooms have a modern, 20th-century look. The most spacious rooms are located on the second floor. There's jazz in the courtyard every night (from 7pm), very apt as Don Ricardo O'Farrill was the great-great grandfather of the famous jazz pianist Chico O'Farrill, who died in Miami in 2002.

Hotel services *Bar. Laundry. Parking. Restaurant. Terrace.* **Room services** *Air-conditioning. . Minibar. Safe. TV (cable).*

Mid-range hotels

Hostal el Comendador

Calle Obrapía, esquina Baratillo (867 1037/fax 860 5628/www.habaguanex.com). **Rates** $57-$78 single; $90-$132 double; $100-$125 suite. **Credit** MC, V. **Map** p252 E16.

This 18th-century Hispanic-Moorish style residence has an appealing air of tranquillity and seclusion that contrasts with the more ebullient atmosphere of its neighbour, the Hostal Valencia (*see p37*). In keeping with Habaguanex's policy of promoting the most valuable historical aspects of its projects, the Comendador has an archaeological excavation site on the ground floor, which has spookily turned up human remains. It is supposed that these belonged to servants or slaves, since they weren't buried in coffins. The Comendador's three suites feature stained-glass decoration and reproduction antique-style baths. Breakfast is served in the Bodegón Onda (*see p99*), which also offers Spanish tapas.

Hotel services *Babysitting. Bar. Laundry.* **Room services** *Air-conditioning. Minibar. Room service (noon-11pm). Safe. TV (satellite).*

Hostal Los Frailes

Calle Brasil (Teniente Rey) #8, entre Mercaderes y Oficios (862 9383/9510/fax 862 9718/www.habaguanex.com). **Rates** $57-$67 single; $90-$110 double; $77-$87 single suite; $130-$150 double suite. **Credit** MC, V. **Map** p252 E15.

Just a few steps away from the St Francis monastery, the Frailes has become something of a tourist attraction since it reopened as a hotel in 2001, such is the success of its design. A copper sculpture of a hooded friar stands outside the main entrance of what used to be the residence of the Marquis Don Pedro Claudio Duquesne in the 19th century. Inside, the polished terracotta floor, beige leather sofas, stucco walls and stone courtyard (complete with fresh-water spring and hanging plants) are awe-inspiring. Staff, dressed as friars (a tough call in the heat), take real pride in the originally decorated 22 rooms (four mini suites), all equipped with antique-style bathrooms, period furnishings and thick wooden beds. Beware: ground-floor rooms have no windows. Breakfast is served in the nearby Café Taberna. This hotel prides itself on its quiet, meditative atmosphere – a rarity in Old Havana's noisy streets. Deep breaths, now…

Hotel services *Bar (open 24hrs, serves light snacks).* **Room services** *Air-conditioning. Minibar. TV (cable).*

Hotel Beltrán de Santa Cruz

Calle San Ignacio #411, entre Muralla y Sol, near the Plaza Vieja (860 8330/fax 860 8383/www.habaguanex.com). **Rates** $57-$78 single; $90-$132 double. **Credit** MC, V. **Map** p252 E15.

The Hotel Beltrán's neat, colourful exterior distinguishes it from the sadly dilapidated buildings surrounding it. Blue and yellow predominate throughout this painstakingly restored 18th-century building, opened as a hotel in 2002. Count Don Juan de Juruco, the first owner, received some of Havana's most illustrious visitors here, including the esteemed German scientist Alejandro de Humboldt. All rooms are doubles, with a private bathroom. Breakfast is served in the central courtyard or in the lobby bar. Nearby Plaza Vieja is home to several art galleries.

Hotel services *Bar. Laundry. Parking.* **Room services** *Air-conditioning. Minibar. Safe. TV (cable).*

Budget accommodation

Hostal Valencia

Calle Oficios #53, esquina Obrapía (867 1037/fax 860 5628/www.habaguanex.com). **Rates** $40 single; $60 double; $85 suite. **Credit** MC, V. **Map** p252 E15.

A private home in the 18th century, the Valencia now offers unpretentious *parador*-style accommodation, with 12 rooms (without air-conditioning) featuring brightly painted shutters and leather Spanish furniture. A bohemian feel emanates from the *hostal*'s Bar Nostalgia, where photographs on the walls pay homage to 1950s singers. All in all, the bags of style at low prices and the relaxed atmosphere mean that the Valencia is often fully booked.

Hotel services *Babysitting. Bars (2). Laundry. Restaurant.* **Room services** *Ceiling fans. Minibar. Safe. TV (satellite).*

Mesón de la Flota

Calle Mercaderes #257, entre Amargura y Brasil (Teniente Rey) (863 3838/www.habaguanex.com). **Rates** $40 single; $60 double. **Credit** MC, V. **Map** p252 E15.

Every night flamenco brings the crowds to the Mesón, a 19th-century inn that hosted sailors from Spanish galleons during the colonial period (for those worried about the noise, performances end at 11pm). A modest hotel, with five en suite rooms, it has successfully conserved the ambience of a Spanish tavern: posters of well-known Spanish bullfighters hang from the original stone walls and wine barrels stand beside the stone arches. All rooms are named after ships that once docked at the port, and the reception desk doubles up as a bar. Great value.

Hotel services *Bar. Restaurant.* **Room services** *Air-conditioning. Safe. TV (satellite).*

Residencia Académica

Convento de Santa Clara, Calle Cuba #610, entre Luz y Sol (613335/fax 335696). **Rates** (per person) $25 dormitories; $35 suite. **No credit cards**. **Map** p252 E15.

Santa Clara was once an abattoir, Havana's first. Then, in 1644, it was handed to the silent order of the Poor Clares, who ran it as a convent until 1922, when it lost its religious status and subsequently passed into the hands of several public organisations. These days, it offers eight rooms consisting of four- or five-bed dormitories. The management assured us that, while groups are preferred, no one is expected to share a room with strangers. Avoid staying here in summer months unless you have practised sleeping in a sauna first, as there's no air-conditioning.

Hotel services *Babysitting. Bar/café. Garden. Laundry. Parking.*

Casas particulares

Casa de Eugenio y Fabio

Calle San Ignacio #656, entre Jesús María y Merced (862 9877). **Map** p252 F15.

Antique collectors and art enthusiasts will love this beautifully clean colonial-style home, decorated with precious and delicate objects. The bedrooms lead on to a lovely interior courtyard. English spoken.

Room services *Air-conditioning. Fans. Fridge.*

Casa de Jesús y María

Aguacate # 518, entre Sol y Muralla (861 1378/jesusmaria2003@yahoo.com). **Map** p252 E15.

Three modern doubles, all with their own bathroom and an extra single bed, open on to a pretty Andalusian-style tiled courtyard with wrought iron furniture. A delightful oasis.

Room services *Air-conditioning. Fridge.*

Casa de Migdalia Caraballe Martín

Calle Santa Clara #164, 1er piso, apto F, entre Cuba y San Ignacio (tel/fax 861 7352/casamigdalia@yahoo.es). **Map** p252 E15.

Reasonably spacious, clean rooms (one with en suite bathroom) furnished with double and single beds, overlooking the bustling street below. The owner is helpful and enthusiastic. Some English spoken.

Room services *Air-conditioning. Fans.*

Rafaela y Pepe

Calle San Ignacio #454, entre Sol y Santa Clara (867 5551). **Map** p252 E15.

All rooms have balconies (one has no fewer than three) at this exquisitely preserved colonial-style home, with antique ornaments and mosaic floors.

Room services *Air-conditioning. Fans. Fridge.*

Centro Habana

Expensive hotels

Hotel Inglaterra

Paseo de Martí (Prado) #416, entre San Rafael y San Miguel (860 8595-7/fax 860 825). **Rates** $75-$80 single; $100-$120 double; $126-$150 triple. **Credit** MC, V. **Map** p252 D14.

The Inglaterra was founded in 1875, making it the oldest hotel in Cuba. And it's showing in parts; the lobby is in dire need of an overhaul and the rooms are rather tired-looking. On the plus side, the hotel is full of original features: crystal chandeliers, ornate ceilings and intricately designed Andalusian ceramic wall tiles dating back to the 19th century, when they were brought from Seville by Spanish galleons. Plans are afoot to replace the elevators and refurbish the lobby leaving these lovely features intact. Café El Louvre, in pole position for people-watching, has tabletops made up of ceramic tiles designed by renowned Cuban artists. The best of the Inglaterra's 83 rooms have good views over Parque Central. Traditional music is played nightly on the open-air rooftop bar/grill, from where guests can enjoy impressive views of Parque Central.

Hotel services *Babysitting. Bars (3). Car rental. Laundry. No-smoking rooms (2). Parking (free). Restaurants (2). Tourist services.* **Room services** *Air-conditioning. Minibar. Room service (24hrs). TV (satellite).*

Hotel NH Parque Central

Calle Neptuno, entre Martí (Prado) y Zulueta (860 6627/6628/fax 860 6630). **Rates** $205 single; $270 double; $330 suite. **Credit** MC, V. **Map** p251/p252 D14.

Formerly the Golden Tulip, the Parque Central was taken over by the Spanish Navarra Hoteles chain in 2001. The hotel's vast range of services remains, though internet connections have been expanded. Located near the boundary between Centro Habana and La Habana Vieja, the hotel's modern architecture is in stark – not to mention controversial – contrast to many of the colonial-era buildings in the vicinity. The modest-sized rooftop swimming pool, with adjacent jacuzzi, has stunning views over the city. Incredibly, all rooms have only 220v sockets. One of Havana's slickest hotels.

Hotel Plaza

Calle Agramonte (Zulueta) #267, esquina Neptuno (860 8583-9/fax 860 8869/www.gran-caribe.com). **Rates** $80 single; $120 double; $161 triple; $96 suite (1 person); $144 suite (2 people). **Credit** MC, V. **Map** p252 D14.

This hotel was first opened in 1909 and subsequent renovations have aimed at conserving the original feel and decor. To a large extent these efforts have been successful, particularly in the vibrant lobby, where guests tread on a colourful mosaic tiled floor and streams of coloured light pour in from the glass roof. It's a different story in the top-floor modern restaurant (where buffet breakfast is served), which suffers from a distinct lack of character. Rooms (some noisy) are decorated in a colonial style, but are also looking tatty in parts.

Hotel services *Babysitting. Bars (3). Business services. Laundry. No-smoking rooms (10). Restaurants (3).* **Room services** *Air-conditioning. Minibar. Room service (24hrs). Safe. TV (satellite).*

Hotel Sevilla

Calle Trocadero #55, entre Martí (Prado) y Agramonte (860 8560/fax 860 8582). **Rates** $120 single; $164 double; $195 triple. **Map** p251 D13.

The Spanish-Moorish style of the Sevilla's façade is fabulously ornate, in keeping with a hotel that was one of Havana's leading turn-of-the-20th-century hotels. The Moorish style, so prevalent in Andalusia, is continued throughout, with brightly coloured ceramic tiles, intricate mosaics and Moorish arches. Refurbishment work to the whole hotel was completed in 2003 (and it's now under the French chain Accor) and the standard of accommodation has improved immeasurably. The attractive El Patio Sevillano bar is open 24 hours a day should you need a mojito at four in the morning, while the fine Roof Garden restaurant (*see p104*) has great views. The hotel pool, one of few in the area, is a pleasant chill-out zone. Graham Greene's *Our Man in Havana* is set here and the immediate vicinity – compulsory reading for those planning a stay here.

Hotel services *Babysitting. Bars (2). Business services. Car rental. Guided tours. Gym. Laundry. Medical services (24hr). Parking. Restaurants (2). Shop. Spa. Swimming pool. Tourist services.* **Room services** *Air-conditioning. Minibar. Room service (24hrs). Telephone. TV (satellite).*

Hotel Telegrafo

Paseo de Martí (Prado) #408, esquina Neptuno (861 1010/fax 861 4741/www.habaguanex.com). **Rates** $80-$90 single; $130-$150 double. **Credit** MC, V **Map** p252 D14.

Originally opened in 1860, this historic hotel moved to its present location beside the Hotel Inglaterra (*see above*) in 1911 (it reopened in 2001). In those days it

was considered to be one of the best hotels in Latin America, and was unique in having telephones not only in every room but at each table in the restaurant. Today, relics of the antique phones, together with a section of the underwater cable that formed part of the first telephonic link established between New York and Havana in the 1880s, are on display beside the lifts. Design is the thing here these days: the ultra-modern lobby, with overhead spotlights and hardwood panelling, leads on to a courtyard bar with ancient half-arch porticos and sections of the original brick wall exposed. The first two floors are decorated in 19th-century style, while the top floor reflects contemporary tastes. The 63 rooms are unusually spacious, decorated in warm colours and equipped with double-glazed windows as well as period shutters (a definite plus, given the busy road below). Of all the newly renovated Habanaguex hotels, the Telegraph has the most contemporary feel.
Hotel services *Car rental. Disabled: adapted room. Laundry. No-smoking bedrooms (3). Parking. Restaurant. Shop. Snackbar (24hrs). Tourist office.*
Room services *Air-conditioning. Babysitting. Minibar. Room service (24hrs). Safe. TV (satellite).*

Casas particulares

Cuba's complexities and perplexities are difficult to understand at the best of times, let alone if you're staying in a five-star hotel that's virtually cordoned off to the majority of the local population. One of the best ways to get to know Cubans on their own turf, and get to grips with the realities of daily life, is to stay in a licensed private home, known as a *casa particular.*

HOW IT WORKS

As with the other (still relatively few) areas of private enterprise permitted by the state, *casas particulares* are strictly regulated, along similar lines to *paladares* (private restaurants). The *dueña* or *dueño* (landlord or landlady) is required to register with the authorities in order to obtain a licence: rooms for rent have to meet with certain standards and all transactions must be entered in the official register.

The first illusion to dispose of is that the Cuban hosts involved are raking it in. The taxes levied are phenomenal: the landlord/lady has to pay on average $100 per month for every registered room (due to go up by $30 in 2004), regardless of whether he or she receives clients. In addition, at the year's end, a further tax deduction is due (25 to 30 per cent), calculated according to business recorded.

PAPERWORK AND ETIQUETTE

When booking into a registered *casa*, you will be required to show your passport and the details will be entered into a register. This procedure is the most certain way of knowing whether your landlord has a licence to rent. Prices vary according to the area and standard of the accommodation but generally fall between $20 and $35 a night. It's worth trying to negotiate on price for longer stays, or by paying up front. Most hosts will prepare meals and do laundry by arrangement. Many landlords don't speak much English, so have a few relevant phrases to hand.

Finally, you should talk directly to the owners unaccompanied by taxi drivers, intermediaries or hustlers. These people will demand to be paid commission, which usually works out at $5 per day, which will be added to your bill.

LISTINGS

The *casas* chosen in this guide have been selected on the basis of quality, cleanliness, security and tranquillity, and all are legally registered. A sign with blue and white chevrons saying *arrendador inscripto* is displayed on the doors of these homes. It should be noted that these are by no means typical Cuban homes in terms of the level of comfort or amenities.

Web directories are still few and far between but **Havana Rentals** (www.havana-rentals.com) and **Casa Particular Organisation** (www.casaparticularcuba.org) both provide booking services.

Pictured above: **Casa de Dr José Ma Parapar de la Riestra** (*see 46*).

Hotel services *Babysitting. Bars (3). Business services (internet access). Car rental. Concierge. Conference rooms. Currency exchange (24hrs). Gym. Jacuzzi. Laundry. Medical services (24hrs). No-smoking rooms. Parking (free). Restaurants (2). Shops. Swimming pool. Tourist services.* **Room services** *Air-conditioning. Minibar. Room service (24hrs). TV (pay movies/satellite).*

Mid-range

Hotel Park View

Calle Colón #101, entre Prado y Morro (861 3293/ fax 863 6036/www.habaguanex.com). **Rates** $45-$50 single; $70-$80 double; $99-$114 triple. **Credit** MC, V. **Map** p252 D15.

Built in 1928, the Park View was a prestigious hotel in its day. Now, after a full renovation care of Habaguanex, it's back in business. A quiet, centrally located establishment, with modest-sized but modern rooms, Park View is excellent value for money. If you want a balcony, ask for a room on the first or fourth floor. The lobby bar, which is decorated in two-tone green, like the exterior of the hotel, is a pleasant spot for a cocktail, though you may want a jacket as the air-conditioning can be fierce. The Prado restaurant on the top floor has an interesting view of the surrounding, sadly neglected, but nevertheless beautiful colonial buildings.

Hotel services *Bar (24hrs). Café. Car rental. Business services. Restaurant.* **Room services** *Air-conditioning. Minibar. TV.*

Budget hotels

Casa del Científico

Paseo de Martí (Prado) #212, esquina Trocadero (862 4511/863 8103/3591/fax 860 0167/ hcientif@ceniai.inf.cu). **Rates** *2nd floor* $25 single; $31 double; $37 triple. *3rd floor* $41 single; $55 double; $64 triple. *Both* Breakfast $2. **No credit cards. Map** p251 D13.

Time has bypassed the Casa del Científico. This hotel was the home of José Miguel Gómez – second president of the Republic of Cuba – between 1914 and 1924, and now offers strictly unrefurbished accommodation. Everything – down to the private chapel – is as it was in Gómez's time. These days, though, the marble staircases are worn in places, and the magnificent crystal chandeliers have gathered dust, as has the early 20th-century furniture. Managed by the Cuban company Cientur, the hotel is open to the public, though priority is given to scientists attending events in the area (so book early). Some rooms have only cold water but their prices are adjusted accordingly. A beautiful winding marble staircase with a stained-glass roof leads upstairs to a pleasant restaurant.

Hotel services *Bar. Business services. Café. Laundry. Restaurant. Shuttle service. Tourist services.* **Room services** *Air-conditioning. Minibar. Room service (7.30am-9.30pm). Safe. TV (satellite).*

Hotel Habana Libre. *See p41.*

Hotel Caribbean

Paseo de Martí (Prado) #164, esquina Colón, Centro Habana (860 8233/8210/fax 860 7994/ rel.pub@caribean.hor.tu.cu). **Rates** $33-$38 single; $48-$56 double. Breakfast à la carte. **Credit** MC, V. **Map** p252 D14/15.

This modest 38-room hotel, remodelled in 1998, has a functional but friendly air, and isn't a bad option for budget travellers. All rooms have en suite bathrooms, and breakfast is served in the snack bar.

Hotel services *Air-conditioning. Bar. Laundry. Parking.* **Room services** *Safe (free). TV (cable).*

Hotel Lincoln

Avenida de Italia (Galiano) #164, esquina Virtudes (338209). **Rates** $30-$39 single; $40-$46 double. **Credit** MC, V. **Map** p251 D13.

If the striking building ever gets the complete makeover that it really deserves, this 135-room hotel will be a big success. The architecture is attractive, though the pink and white façade is crumbling, and the hotel has innate character. Unfortunately, refurbishments under way seem half-hearted: tacky bedspreads, matching curtains and Formica furniture give the rooms a sad – or worse – seedy feel. Staff hinted that the fifth floor is probably the nicest, so go for east-facing rooms on that floor, overlooking Galiano. Room 810 is preserved as a museum recording the kidnapping of the Argentinian world champion racing driver Juan Manuel Fangio by Revolutionary forces in February 1958 (he was released unharmed after two days). The top floor has a roof terrace bar with a superb view of the area.

Hotel services *Bars (2). Business services. Medical services (9am-6pm). Parking. Restaurants (3).* **Room services** *Air-conditioning. Minibar (some rooms). Safe. TV (satellite).*

Casas particulares

Casa de Evora Rodríguez García
Paseo del Prado #20 (penthouse), entre San Lazaro y Cárcel (tel/fax 861 7932/mgilc@hotmail.com).
Map p251 C15.
A very classy apartment with a magnificent view over La Punta, the entrance to the Bay of Havana. The double rooms are well furnished, light and pleasant, each with an adjoining bathroom.
Room services *Air-conditioning. Fridge. TV.*

Casa de Gladys Cutido
Calle Soledad #272 (bajos), entre Concordia y Virtudes (873 7838/30renta-gladys@yahoo.es).
Rates $25-$30. **Map** p250 C12.
The top two floors in this three-storey home, modern and in immaculate condition, have been attractively made over for the exclusive use of guests. Two kitchens, one on each floor, are open to guests. Gladys's endearing personality provides a final touch.
Room services *Air-conditioning. Fridge. TV.*

Casa de Mercedes
Calle Concordia #151, piso 6, apto 10, esquina San Nicolás (863 5816). **Map** p251 D14.
Accommodation here consists of a well-decorated double bedroom, with its own balcony, in a spacious and thoughtfully designed apartment. The six flights of stairs may not appeal to any but fitness obsessives, and the lift wasn't working at the time of writing, but we hope it's repaired soon.
Room services *Fans.*

Casa de María Del Carmen Villafaña
Malecón #51, esquina Cárcel, piso 3 (861 8125).
Map p251 C15.
This vast, elegant but homely apartment has a fantastic seafront location, with large airy doubles with en suite bathrooms; furnishings are antique. The entrance is via the car park in San Lázaro.
Room services *Air-conditioning. TV.*

Casa de Raúl Diaz Macaya
Calle Marina #113, apto 4F, entre Príncipe y Vapor (878 7075/rauldiaz20022002@yahoo.es).
Map p250 C12.
The two double bedrooms, adjoining bathroom and lounge have been redecorated in this spotless modern apartment. The experienced and professional owner has rented to visitors for over ten years. The location is very central, and privacy is guaranteed.
Room services *Air-conditioning. Fridge. TV.*

Vedado & Nuevo Vedado

Expensive hotels

Hotel Habana Libre
Calle L, entre 23 y 25 (554011/fax 333141/www.solmelia.com). **Rates** $140 single; $160 double; $250 junior suite. **Credit** MC, V.
Map p250 B11.
After the Nacional, the Habana Libre is probably Cuba's most famous hotel, not least because you just can't miss it: it towers Vedado's liveliest junction. Opened in 1958 as part of the Hilton hotel chain, it was nationalised and used as the new Revolutionary government's headquarters for the first three months of 1959. Between 1960 and 1963, Fidel Castro himself stayed regularly in the Castellana suite on the 22nd floor, the only rooms that retain the original '50s furnishings.

In 2000 the Spanish Meliá group took over the hotel. Its 572 rooms are remarkable for their spaciousness, and the hotel has a functional, busy feel that won't appeal to all. However, you couldn't want for a better location, on the cusp of lively La Rampa. The Pico Turquino nightclub on the top floor has fantastic views of Havana's skyline (and a retractable roof). The lobby area probably looked great in the '70s but it could maybe do with a facelift now.
Hotel services *Airline offices (5). Babysitting. Bank. Bars (4). Beauty salon. Business services. Café. (24hrs). Car rental. Gym. Laundry. Medical services. No-smoking floors. Parking. Restaurants (4). Shops. Spa. Swimming pool.* **Room services** *Air-conditioning. Minibar. Room service (24hrs). Safe. TV (satellite).*

Hotel Habana Riviera
Malecón, esquina Paseo (334051/fax 333739/www.gran-caribe.com). **Rates** $72-$102 single; $96-$154 double; $137-$219 triple; $140-$157 junior suite; $300-$317 presidential suite. **Credit** MC, V. **Map** p250 A9.
The vast reception area of the Hotel Habana Riviera has probably changed little since it was built in the 1950s by Mafioso Meyer Lansky (*see p44* **So long, wise guys**), as part of a plan to establish a network of casino hotels in Cuba. Those shady days are long gone, and today the Riviera is now a respectable and pleasant place to stay. And yet… call us fanciful but we can't help feeling that the spirit of the bad old days still resonates in the corridors. The salt water swimming pool, complete with diving boards (a rarity in Havana), is a big attraction. Curiously, the pool is coffin-shaped – one of Meyer Lanksy's architectural suggestions or pure coincidence? The buffet breakfast has one major defect in common with so many hotels in Cuba: the morning coffee is dreadful. Renovations in progress at press time.
Hotel services *Babysitting. Bars (2). Business services. Car rental. Laundry. Parking. Restaurants (2). Swimming pool. Tourist services.* **Room services** *Air-conditioning. Minibar. Room service (24hrs). TV (satellite).*

Hotel Meliá Cohiba
Paseo, entre 1ra y 3ra (333636/fax 334555/www.solmelia.com). **Rates** $175 single; $225 double; $265 junior suite; $300 suite; $365 senior suite. Breakfast $15. *Servicio real* (incl breakfast) $225 single; $275 double; $365 suite; $475 junior suite; $685 senior suite. **Credit** MC, V. **Map** p250 A9.
Vedado's most modern hotel was opened in 1995. Facilities and standards of service make it an appealing option for business people, but holidaymakers

may find it rather soulless. If money is no object, try the 'royal' service (*servicio real*), available on four floors. This offers express check-in and check-out, an all-day buffet (7am-11pm) and an exclusive lift, plus butler service, morning coffee in your room and free use of the gym and sauna. Otherwise, there are no fewer than five restaurants to choose from. Unlike many hotels in Havana, the swimming pool is only open to guests (and their guests), so it tends to be quieter than is usual.

Hotel services *Babysitting. Bars (5). Beauty salon. Business services. Gym. Internet access. Laundry. Massage. No-smoking rooms. Parking ($8 per day). Restaurants (5). Shops. Squash court. Swimming pool.* **Room services** *Air-conditioning. Minibar. Room service (24hrs). Safe. TV (pay movies/satellite).*

Hotel Nacional de Cuba

Calle O, esquina 21 (873 3564/3567/reservations 855 0294/fax 873 5171/www.gran-caribe.com).
Rates *Standard* $120 single; $170 double; $210 triple; $215 junior suite; $390 senior suite; $400 special suite; $450 royal suite; $1,000 presidential suite. *Executive floor supplement* $21-$30 per night.
Credit MC, V. **Map** p250 B12.

Elegance reigns at the Hotel Nacional, declared a national monument in 1998. Built in 1930, it has effortlessly withstood the test of time, remaining sophisticated, refined and subtly stylish. Clearly, the marvellous location, twin-towered building, spacious gardens and magnificent views are part of the magic; but there's also something about cruising through the lobby in the knowledge that you're following in the footsteps of so many famous names (visit the Hall of Fame) that gives the place a special aura. The standard rooms aren't particularly exciting, but the views over the Malecón or the hotel gardens are impressive.

Hotel services *Babysitting. Bars (5). Beauty salon. Business centre. Café. Car rental. Concierge. Garden. Gym. Internet access. Laundry. Parking. Restaurants (2). Shops. Swimming pools. Tennis court. Tourist services.* **Room services** *Air-conditioning. Minibar. Room service (24hrs). Safe. TV (satellite).*

Hotel Presidente

Calle Calzada #110, esquina Presidentes (G) (551801/551804/fax 333753/www.hotelesc.com).
Rates $90 single; $140 double; $130 single suite; $220 double suite. 20% supplement 22 Dec-2 Jan.
Credit MC, V. **Map** p250 A10.

This seductively elegant, tranquil hotel was fully restored in 1999, with subtle 1920s-style decor, care of the Spanish Hoteles C company. The lobby is furnished with antiques and the delicate overhead lighting makes for an intimate ambience. Services have recently been expanded to cater for 21st-century demands, and there's now 24-hour internet and fax access. The two tenth-floor suites, featuring Louis XV-style furnishings are particularly grand, and there's a lovely swimming pool and bar area out back.

Hotel services *Bars (3). Business services. Concierge. Laundry. Parking (free). Restaurants (2). Swimming pool.* **Room services** *Air-conditioning. Minibar. Room service (10am-midnight). Safe. TV (satellite).*

Hotel Habana Riviera. See p41.

Mid-range hotels

Hotel Capri

Calle 21, entre N y O (333747/www.horizontes.cu). **Rates** call for details. **Credit** call for details. **Map** p250 B12.

This 1950s hotel with heavy mob connections was closed at press time for an overhaul. And it really was about time; last time we checked it was looking pretty rough around the edges. But if Horizontes does a good job on it, it could be a decent, well-located hotel.

Hotel St John's

Calle O #206, entre 23 y 25 (333740/fax 333561/ www.horizontes.cu). **Rates** $50-$63 single; $67-$80 double; $90-$104 mini suite. **Credit** MC, V. **Map** p250 B12.

The Hotel St John's is ideally located just off La Rampa. It was fully refurbished in the late 1990s, but it's already beginning to weather, particularly in the corridors and the lobby. The modest-size swimming pool on the top floor, beside the café-bar, becomes the Pico Blanco nightclub at 10.30pm. Request a room on the seventh floor or higher for a view of the city (as opposed to the wall of the neighbouring building).

Hotel services *Bars (2). Business services. Parking. Restaurant. Swimming pool.* **Room services** *Air-conditioning. Room service (24hrs). Safe. TV (satellite).*

Hotel Victoria

Calle 19 #101, esquina M (333510/fax 333109/ www.gran-caribe.com). **Rates** $49-$63 single; $70-$90 double; $130 mini suite. **Credit** MC, V. **Map** p250 B11.

The genteel Victoria was a popular spot with the '30s generation of Spanish and Latin American poets and writers, who gathered here for their literary soirées. A decade or so later wealthy Americans, such as Marlon Brando and Errol Flynn, joined the list of distinguished guests. These days the furnishings are discreet, if a little motelish in parts. The real bonus at the Victoria is experienced, hospitable staff and a rare personal touch. There's a cute swimming pool at the back too.

Hotel services *Bar. Business services. Currency exchange. Laundry. Parking. Restaurant. Swimming pool.* **Room services** *Air-conditioning. Internet. Minibar. Room service (7am-midnight). Safe. TV (satellite).*

Budget hotels

Hotel Vedado

Calle O #244, entre 23 y 25 (334072/fax 334186/ www.horizontes.cu). **Rates** $50-$63 single; $67-$80 double. **Credit** MC, V. **Map** p250 B12.

First impressions of the Hotel Vedado – the gloomy, pokey lobby area – aren't encouraging. The rooms aren't particularly attractive either. But the big advantage of the Vedado is that it's well placed for exploring the area. Request a room on the seventh floor or above if you want a view.

Hotel services *Bars (2). Cafés. Currency exchange. Guided tours. Gym. Laundry. Parking. Restaurants (2). Swimming pool. Tourist services.* **Room services** *Air-conditioning. Room service (7am-midnight). Safe. TV (satellite).*

So long, wise guys

One of the first tasks undertaken by the fledgling Cuban Revolution was to purge paradise of US meddling, and that included organised crime. It got tough on mobsters and racketeers, shutting down casinos, brothels and drug operations, and the men who ran them. One wise guy was told he had 24 hours to leave the country while he was doing a few rounds at the golf course at a posh Havana country club. In addition, Cuba's new social planners had their hands full looking for ways to keep busy the suddenly unemployed casino workers, prostitutes and con artists.

The euphoria was pervasive; there's some sense of the atmosphere in the shots of the trashed casinos hanging in the lobby of Centro Habana's **Hotel Sevilla** (*see p38*), whose **Roof Garden** restaurant (*see p104*) once rung with spinning roulette wheels and slot machines.

Meyer Lansky – pal of celeb gangsters Benjamin 'Bugsy' Siegel and Charles 'Lucky' Luciano, and former boss of many of the newly jobless – was known, in his Havana days, to take chauffeured drives along the Malecón. He would slip out of a secret tunnel from the **Hotel Nacional** (*see p42*), whose Vista al Golfo bar exhibits photos from those times (hotel staff claim Sinatra and Corleone also dined there). Lansky was also a regular customer at the still outrageously kitsch restaurant **Monseigneur** (*see p107*) in Vedado, where – according to Cuban writer Enrique Cirules – the elegant grey-clad mobster would pick at his favourite dish: boiled shrimp with lemon.

Havana was crawling with many more goons like Anastasia, Costello and Genovese... Check out the barbershop hidden under the Cuban Institute of Radio and Television (ICRT), with its entrance on Calle M between 21 and 23; made men are known to have nipped in for a trim in pre-Revolutionary times.

Lansky took a dive when the bearded rebels made a sting, and in 1960 lost his beloved **Hotel Habana Riviera** (*see p41*). For a decade afterwards the poor chump lammed around Israel, Europe and a bunch of bohunk Latin American countries, one kick ahead of the G-men, and finally croaked in Miami.

Florida Mafia figure Santos Trafficante Jr also hid out in Cuba, but the victorious guerrillas took him down along with Lansky's brother, packing them off to jail in the summer of 1959. Seething with revenge after his release, he allegedly teamed up with Chicago's Sam Giancana and the CIA, planning to poison one of Castro's soft drinks.

Other Mafia hot spots included the **Hotel Capri** (*see p43*) (where movie star George Raft had a penthouse) and the **Plaza Carlos III** shopping mall (*see p120*), formerly one of the city's biggest brothels.

Casas particulares

Casa de Ana

Calle F #107, entre 5ta y Calzada (bajos) (832 2360/831 2344). **Map** p250 A10.

A spacious and tastefully decorated colonial building with large double bedrooms, each with a modern en suite bathroom, to let to visitors. There's a lounge for guests and a roof patio. Ana is a charming and professional host.

Room services *Air-conditioning. Fridge. Safe.*

Casa Belkis

Calle 19 #1259, entre 20 y 22 (833 8628/hostalbelkis@yahoo.com). **Map** p249 C7.

This home, which is set in a quiet, pleasant street, is at the upper end of the *casa particular* market. It offers modern, well-equipped double bedrooms, each with their own bathroom, and comfortable orthopaedic beds with linen sheets. A cosy atmosphere makes it worth the trek.

Room services *Fridge. Safe. TV.*

Casa de Carlos Y Julio

Calle E #609 (altos), entre 25 y 27 (832 7203/carnel@cubarte.cult.cu). **Map** p250 C10.

This period home is beautifully preserved and tastefully furnished. Two doubles (one en suite).

Room services *Air-conditioning. Fridge.*

Casa de Esther Fonseca

Calle 25 #359, Apto A, piso 2, entre L y K (832 0120). **Map** p250 B11.

This apartment is in a perfect location, seconds away from La Rampa. It's in pristine condition too, and subtly decorated. Esther offers guests double bedrooms with an en suite or adjoining bathroom.

Room services *Air-conditioning. Fridge. TV.*

Casa de Irma

Avenida de los Presidentes (G) #159, piso 2, entre Calzada y 9 (832 7721). **Map** p250 A10.

Don't be disheartened by the slightly dilapidated entrance to this second-floor flat. Inside lie clean, modern rooms. A terrace overlooks the *avenida*.

Room services *Air-conditioning. Fridge. Minibar.*

Miramar

Expensive hotels

Hotel LTI-Panorama

Calle 3ra, esquina 70 (204 0100/4969/www.lti.de). **Rates** $95 single; $120 double; $143 single suite; $180 double suite; $300 presidential suite. **Credit** MC, V. **Map** p248 B2.

Opened in December 2002, this German concern has a slick, modern exterior. In fact, it looks more like an office block than a hotel. Once inside, however, the combination of bright, Caribbean colours and enthusiastic staff should dispel any initial fears. The enormous space created by the lobby, extending the whole way up to the roof, is particularly impressive. Rooms at the back of the hotel have sea views; others overlook the unsubtle Russian embassy. The 11th-floor bar should not be missed; the decor is superb, as are the mojitos. Good service at affordable prices – we approve.

Hotel services *Babysitting. Bars (2). Beauty salon. Car rental. Concierge. Currency exchange. Garden. Gym. Internet access. Laundry. No-smoking rooms. Parking (free). Restaurants (2). Shuttle service (free). Spa. Squash courts. Swimming pool.* **Room services** *Air-conditioning. Jacuzzi (suites only). Minibar. Room service (24hrs). Safe. TV (pay movies/satellite).*

Hotel Meliá Habana

Avenida 3ra, entre 76 y 80 (204 8500/fax 204 8505/ www.solmelia.com). **Rates** *Standard* $175 single; $225 double; $265 junior suite. Breakfast $15. *Servicio real* (incl breakfast) $225 single; $275 double; $365 junior suite; $525 suite. **Credit** MC, V. **Map** p248 B1.

This plush hotel, opened in 1998 by Fidel Castro, has had a number of heads of state and famous names among its guests. It's popular with business guests, given its location in the hub of business development in Cuba and its vast array of services. The impressive cream marble lobby, with its central pool, is an ideal spot to enjoy piano music in the early evening. Restaurants, bars and cafés abound. Don't miss the swimming pool, reputedly the largest in Cuba.

Hotel services *Babysitting. Bars (5). Beauty salon. Business services. Concierge. Garden. Gym. Internet access. Laundry. No-smoking rooms. Parking (free). Restaurants (4). Shuttle bus (free). Spa. Swimming pool. Tennis court.* **Room services** *Air-conditioning. Dataport (servicio real only). Minibar. Room service (24hrs). Safe (servicio real only). Turndown (servicio real only). TV (pay movies/satellite).*

Hotel Occidental Miramar

Avenida 5ta, entre 72 y 76 (204 3584/fax 204 3583). **Rates** $110 single; $150 double; $180-$205 triple; $210 junior suite; $300 senior suite. **Credit** MC, V. **Map** p248 B2.

In June 2003 this modern hotel, previously the Novotel, passed into Spanish hands. The same staff remain, which is good news given that service here has a reputation for excellence. Rooms have a cheerful blue and yellow motif, while the lobby manages to combine comfort and formality. There's a free shuttle service into the centre. The food is very good here.

Hotel Services *Bar. Conference facilities. Hairdresser. Internet access. Laundry. Parking. Shuttle service. Shopping gallery. Restaurants (2). Swimming pool. Tennis & squash courts. Tourist office.* **Room services** *Air-conditioning. Fridge. Room service (24hrs). Safe. TV (satellite).*

Mid-range hotels

Hotel Comodoro

Avenida 3ra, esquina 84 (204 5551/fax 204 2089/ www.cubanacan.cu). **Rates** *Hotel* $65-$80 single; $90-$110 double; $130-$160 triple; $135-$155 suite. *Bungalow apartments* $89-$248. Breakfast $7. **Credit** MC, V. **Map** p248 B1.

This hotel, opened in 1952, was formerly a school for art instructors and was later used by the central committee of the Communist Party as its headquarters. Today, it is an attractively designed Cubanacán hotel with a choice of rooms in the main building or bungalows in the hotel gardens, some with their own kitchen. The hotel has recently set up facilities for scuba diving and will take qualified divers out to the nearest coral reefs. Alternatively, you could go for a dip in one of the nine, yes nine, swimming pools on site. Home to one of Havana's best shopping complexes (*see p118*).

Hotel Nacional de Cuba. *See p42.*

Hotel services *Bars (5). Business services. Concierge. Garden. Laundry. Nightclub. Parking (free). Restaurants (3). Swimming pools.* **Room services** *Air-conditioning. Kitchenette (most bungalow rooms). Minibar. Room service (24hr). Safe. TV (satellite).*

Hotel Copacabana

Avenida 1ra #4404, entre 44 y 46 (204 1037/fax 204 2846/www.gran-caribe.com). **Rates** $75-$85 single; $110-$120 double; $157-$172 triple; $132 suite; $148 junior suite. **Credit** MC, V. **Map** p248 B3.

One look at the lobby reveals that the Copacabana is well past its sell-by date, though plans are apparently afoot to redecorate the rooms. Dreary decor aside, guests will enjoy the relaxed atmosphere of this place, which is more popular with families than business people (business services are available). At the back of the hotel, behind the regular pool, is a fabulous saltwater pool – an entirely natural walled-off area where the coral seabed and marine life will keep snorkellers happy.

Hotel services *Babysitting. Bars (3). Beauty salon. Business services. Cafés (3). Car rental. Conference services. Gym. Laundry. Massage. Medical services. Parking (free). Restaurants (3). Shops. Shuttle service. Swimming pools (2). Tennis & squash courts. Tourist services.* **Room services** *Air-conditioning. Minibar. Room service (24hrs). TV (satellite).*

Budget hotels

Hotel Mirazul

Avenida 5ta #3603, entre 36 y 40, Miramar (tel/fax 204008). **Rates** $40 single; $50 double. Breakfast $3. **Credit** MC, V. **Map** p248 B4.

This tiny hotel, marked only by a blue awning on Quinta Avenida, has recently had a facelift. There's no pool, but the charm of this hotel lies in its quiet, intimate atmosphere. Business people will be attracted by facilities that include three conference rooms.

Hotel services *Bar. Business services. Garden. Laundry. Parking (free). Restaurant. Sauna.* **Room services** *Air-conditioning. Minibar. Room service (7am-midnight). Safe. TV (satellite).*

Casas particulares

Casa de Dr José Ma Parapar de la Riestra

Calle 70 #912, entre 9 y 11 (203 7269/ jparapar@infomed.sld.cu). **Map** p248 C2.

Crossing the threshold of this elegant mansion is like stepping back to 1948, the year it was built. The furniture, decor and even the artwork remain intact, as they were half a century ago. Attentive owner and very private. Highly recommended.

Room services *Air-conditioning. TV.*

Casa de Marta

Calle 28 #106, piso 3, apto 3, entre 1ra y 3ra, Miramar (203 8380). **Map** p249 B5.

A comfortable and modern apartment where the friendly hosts have obviously thought carefully about guests' comfort and privacy. A separate entrance leads into a recently redecorated lounge, with adjoining terrace and magnificent sea view.

Room services *Air-conditioning. Fridge.*

Casa de Mayra

Calle 3ra #8, entre 0 y 2, Miramar (209 1947). **Map** p249 A7.

Mayra has two modern en suite doubles for rent in this spacious house. There's a state-of-the-art kitchen and a dining room, together with a lounge and porch that guests are invited to use. The location, close to Vedado and two blocks from the coast, makes this an ideal choice.

Room services *Air-conditioning. Fridge.*

Raúl Campos Alfonso

Calle 12A, entre 1ra y Mar, Miramar (209 3066/ raulniva1@hotmail.com). **Map** p249 A6.

Luxurious accommodation is available in this immense, modern seafront villa with its own saltwater swimming pool, gym and terrace overlooking the sea. All rooms have en suite bathrooms. Owner Raúl is a lively, outgoing character who will ensure that your stay is nothing short of eventful.

Room services *Air-conditioning. Fridge. TV.*

Playas del Este

Mid-range

Hotel Tropicoco

Avenida de las Terrazas, Santa María del Mar (971371/fax 971389/www.horizontes.cu). **Rates** $40 single; $70 double. **Credit** MC, V. **Map** p246 A21.

This Horizontes hotel was restored in 2001, and if you get a feeling of déjá vu as you walk into the lobby, that's probably because the stark post-Revolutionary-style architecture is repeated in several other Cuban hotels. The hotel has plenty of rooms with sea views and airy common spaces.

Hotel services *Restaurants (2). Bar (3). Pool.* **Room services** *Air-conditioning. Safe. TV.*

Villa Los Pinos

Avenida de las Terrazas, Santa María del Mar (897 1361/fax 897 1524). **Rates** 2-, 3- & 4-room houses $120-$250. Breakfast $5. **Credit** MC, V. **Map** p246 A20.

A relaxed, relatively upmarket constellation of small villas in a semi-wooded area right next to the beach. Each unit has lockable bedrooms (with en suite bathrooms), a kitchen and a living room, some also have swimming pools. No visitors are admitted inside the houses, so don't plan on throwing any bashes at your beach pad.

Hotel services *Bars (2). Café. Babysitting. Car rental. Laundry. Medical services. Restaurant. Tennis court. Watersports. Sauna. Swimming pool.* **Room services** *Air-conditioning. Minibar. Safe ($2 per day). TV (satellite).*

Sightseeing

Introduction	**48**
La Habana Vieja	**50**
Centro Habana	**64**
Vedado	**72**
Miramar & the Western Suburbs	**82**
Eastern Bay & the Coast	**88**

Features

The best Sights	48
Urban refit	52
Statuary rites	60
Beat it	66
Alley of bones	70
Just like starting over	76
Along Río Almendares	80
Treasure island	85
Open for business	86
Keeping the faith	91

Introduction

Enigmatic Havana will woo you just as you're walking down the street.

Havana glories in its history, has a dynamic cultural life and thrives on the gregarious personality of its inhabitants, *los habaneros*. This is a city pulsing with energy that will sweep you up and hold you captive until long after your visit has ended.

Most visitors head straight for **La Habana Vieja** (Old Havana) – the historical core of the city – and rightly so; it has over 500 years of history to offer. Every plaza, street, museum, art gallery and building reveals a secret of Cuba's past. Since the old city was declared a UNESCO World Heritage Site in 1982, a pacy programme of renovation, co-ordinated by the City Historian's Office (*see p52* **Urban refit**), has given parts of Old Havana a much-needed facelift. A word of warning: *jineteros* (hustlers) tend to favour the tourist-intensive arteries in this area.

However little time you have in Havana, make sure you venture outside La Habana Vieja. Havana's various *barrios* (neighbourhoods) all have their own story to tell: **Centro Habana** is a vibrant, urban onslaught to the west of the colonial core, beyond the former city walls; leafy **Vedado**, still further west, is a cultural and commercial hub; spacious, sometimes swanky **Miramar** and the western suburbs beyond have few official sights but reveal Cuba's little-seen upmarket side. Across the bay, there are imposing fortresses, seaside towns and the **Playas del Este**, a handy beach escape.

TIPS FOR VISITORS

- A small number of museums and historic sites do not charge admission fees (most charge $1-$2) but they do appreciate a donation that will be used for maintenance costs.
- If you would like a guided tour in English, it would be wise to call the museum or site beforehand to make a reservation, as bilingual guides may not be available if you turn up on

The beautiful south

Just over 20 kilometres (12 miles) to the south of La Habana Vieja is the city's largest recreational area, comprising the **Jardín Botánico**, **Parque Lenin**, **Parque Zoológico Nacional** and **ExpoCuba**. Take bus No.88 from the Víbora neighbourhood, or hire a taxi (around $15).

ExpoCuba

Carretera del Rocío km3.5, El Globo, Calabazar, Boyeros (578284). **Open** *Jan-Aug* 9am-5pm Tue-Sun. Closed Sept-Dec, except for special events. **Admission $1.**

25 pavilions at Cuba's largest exhibition area are given over to self-congratulatory displays on the achievements of the Revolution. ExpoCuba also houses a 500-seat amphitheatre, an amusement park and a restaurant.

Jardín Botánico Nacional

Carretera del Rocío km3.5, El Globo, Calabazar, Boyeros (539364/549170). **Open** 8am-5pm (last entry 3.30pm) daily. **Admission** $1; $1.50 concessions. *Train ride with guide* $4.

Easily accessible from Parque Lenin, these gardens feature around 150,000 examples of 4,000 different species of trees and bushes from around the world; the best way to see it all is from the seat of the dinky little 'train'. It's worth sacrificing your street cred for a ride, since it covers most of the garden, way too much to tackle on foot. Don't miss the delightful Japanese garden, next to Cuba's best vegetarian restaurant, El Bambú (*see p107*).

Parque Lenin

Calle 100, esquina Cortina de la Presa, Arroyo Naranjo (403026). **Open** 9am-5pm Wed-Sun. **Admission** free.

Every Sunday throngs of *habaneros* flock to this beautiful site conceived by Celia Sánchez Manduley, Fidel Castro's close companion, and opened in 1969. Some 160,000 trees have been planted in this green, undulating landscape spanning 6.7 square kilometres (three square miles). A narrow-gauge railway can take you on a tour of the park, with its artificial lake, freshwater aquarium,

spec. If your guide was informative and pleasant, consider tipping him or her (even though the entrance fee is almost always higher for those who request a guided tour).

● Many of the sights listed have special rules for cameras and video cameras, which tend to change often and without notice. Check before you start shooting or snapping, as the extra cost may be quite hefty.

● Be prepared to be confronted with monolingual (Spanish) explanatory texts in many museums and historic sites. Few places have English translations.

● Children, particularly those under 12, are often allowed free admission.

● Cubans, rightly or wrongly, are known for their lack of punctuality, but there tends to be no tardiness when it comes to shutting up shop. Indeed, 5pm may even mean 4.45pm.

● Street names, particularly in La Habana Vieja and Centro Habana, can be confusing. Most people use the old pre-Revolutionary names, while some maps and street signs use a modern name. We have tried to give both in listings; *see p218* for a list of old and new street names.

amphitheatre, amusement park, cafés and restaurants, plus popular Equestrian Centre ($12-$15 per hour). Pony trekking is a less expensive option. Naturally, the huge bust of Lenin, carved in 1982 by Soviet sculptor L E Kerbel, is a focal point. You'll see why when the rugged beauty of the white marble piece captures your gaze.

Parque Zoológico Nacional

Entrance 1: Avenida de la Independencia (Rancho Boyeros), esquina 243, Fontana, Boyeros. Entrance 2: Avenida Soto, esquina Zoo Lenin, Boyeros (447613). **Open** 9.30am-3.30pm Wed-Sun. **Admission** $3; $2 concessions (incl optional guide).

The national zoo was set up in 1984 on the grounds of 11 abandoned farms, and is now home to 1,000 animals and 110 species. Tour buses (included) wind their way through the 243 hectares that have been transformed into African prairie land roamed by giraffe, zebra, antelopes and rhinoceros, hippos and lions. There's also a children's zoo.

Top five Sights

Castillo San Salvador de la Punta

Centro Habana's 17th-century castle has opened the lid on its colonial treasure chest after extensive renovation. *See p67.*

Museo de Bellas Artes

Beautifully renovated, world-class museum dedicated – in two buildings – to Cuban and international art. *See p68.*

Museo de la Ciudad

The former Spanish royal palace is now one of the city's most elegant museums. *See p52.*

Plaza de Armas

One of Latin America's finest squares – in the heart of Old Havana – is your first port of call. *See p50.*

Real Fábrica de Tabacos Partagás

Cuba's celeb cigar factory lets you experience a day in the life of a *habano* cigar. *See p70.*

La Habana Vieja

The city's core combines history with a tangible contemporary energy.

Map p252

Plaza de Armas. 3pm. 'You wan' restaurant?', 'Private house?', 'Where you fron?', 'You wan' sex?', '*Gramna!*', '*Rebelde!*'. Despite its many historical charms, UNESCO World Heritage Site status and phenomenally extensive renovation programme, it would be hard to describe Old Havana as a decorous museum piece. In fact, visitors are as likely to be as excited by the commotion that is Old Havana streetlife as they are by the plethora of museums. The density of museums (many very modest) in Old Havana can be overwhelming, so it's best to be selective and to leave plenty of time for strolling.

A World Heritage Site since 1982 (along with the colonial fortresses), La Habana Vieja, or Old Havana, is usually the first stop on the tourist trail. It's easy to see why: with its five centuries of rich architectural heritage and an impressively high concentration of museums and galleries, there's an enormous amount to do and see. A huge restoration project run by the City Historian's Office is doing much to preserve the fabric of the old city.

San Cristóbal de La Habana (1519), one of the first seven towns founded by the Spanish colonisers in Cuba, was from the start service-oriented. Tagged the 'Key to the New World and Bastion of the West Indies' because of its strategic location, the port of Havana was a stopping point for all Spanish galleons sailing between Spain and its Latin American colonies. The area now known as Old Havana supplied and repaired boats, and its war ships protected them from pirates who craved their rich cargoes of gold and silver. Later, a large defensive system of colonial fortresses along the northern shore and city walls was built to protect the city and the wealth of passing ships.

Note that this guide defines La Habana Vieja as the area that stood within the old city walls. They occupied what are now **Avenida de los Misiones** (Monserrate) and **Avenida de Bélgica** (Egido), encircling La Habana Vieja in an egg shape along the bay to the east. The street names can often be confusing, as maps and common speech use new (official) names and old (popular) names interchangeably. But within La Habana Vieja, it's not hard, with a good map, to find one's way around the grid of narrow streets and small city blocks, nor to get the feel of the early colonial streetscape: a city that radiates out from central squares, characterised by buildings constructed side by side (ventilated mainly through inner courtyards) and an abundance of churches. For more on street names, *see p218*.

On the down side, Old Havana is the area most targeted by *jineteros* (literally 'jockeys', or touts), eager to make a buck by selling fake cigars, guidance to a *paladar* (for a commission) or become your driver for the day. The best strategy is to keep walking – the slightest eye contact can rev them up.

Plaza de Armas

The oldest square in Old Havana and the site where the city was founded, tranquil, palm-filled **Plaza de Armas** is a good place to begin exploring. It's surrounded by centuries of architecture, spanning the 16th to the 20th centuries, with a fascinating juxtaposition of building styles tumbling one on top of the other.

Stand in the middle of **Parque Céspedes** (1834), at the centre of the square, and look around you. To the north-east is the 16th-century, Renaissance-style **Castillo de la Real Fuerza** (*see p51*), the first bastion fortress with triangular bulwarks to be built in the New World; it currently houses the **Museo Nacional de la Cerámica Cubana**. The 17th-century school for orphan girls in the south-west corner is now the popular restaurant La Mina. The **Palacio del Segundo Cabo** to the north and the Palacio de los Capitanes Generales (home to the splendid **Museo de la Ciudad**; *see p51*) to the west are stunning 18th-century baroque buildings. **El Templete** (*see p53*), located next to the Castillo, is a 19th-century, neo-classical folly marking the legendary spot where Havana was founded. The 20th-century eclectic building that housed the former US embassy, on the plaza's south side, is now the **Museo Nacional de Historia Natural** (*see p52*).

Still on the Plaza de Armas, don't miss the central white marble statue of Carlos Manuel de Céspedes, Cuban patriot, initiator of the Ten Years War (*see p10*) against Spanish colonial rule in 1868 and 'Father of the Nation'. Sculpted by Sergio López Mesa, this replaced a statue of Spanish King Fernando VII, which stood in the park until 1955 (it now stands to the right of the Palacio del Segundo Cabo). Four days a week (closed Mon, Tue, Sun & rainy days), Havana's largest and best second-hand **book market** (*see p121*) takes over the park.

The east side of the square is dominated by the 18th-century Casa del Conde de Santovenia, renovated in 1867 as a hotel, and again in 1998 as the elegantly decorated, upmarket **Hotel Santa Isabel** (*see p36*). An often-missed attraction on the Plaza de Armas is **Casa de la Tinaja**, located next to the La Mina restaurant. A *tinaja* is a large jar made of porous stone that is used to filter water for drinking. Since 1544 filtered drinking water has been offered on this spot to pedestrians in La Habana Vieja, and the tradition continues to this day. Stop by for a glass of water – but note that there may only be one glass; neck it without the glass touching your lips, like locals do. Several doors up on Obispo, the **Museo de la Orfebrería** (863 9861), also known as the Casa de la Plata, displays 18th- to early 20th-century gold- and silverwork (*orfebrería*) by Cuban and foreign masters and a tempting little shop sells contemporary jewellery. Closed at press time, it is scheduled to reopen in spring 2004.

Castillo de la Real Fuerza/Museo Nacional de la Cerámica Cubana

Calle O'Reilly #2 (861 6130). **Open** 9am-7pm daily. **Admission** $1 ($2 guided tour); free under-12s. **Map** p252 D16.

One of the oldest European defensive structures in the Americas, the Castillo de la Real Fuerza (1558-77) was the home of the Spanish captains general in Havana for 200 years, until the new palace – the Palacio del Segundo Cabo – was built across the square. Heavy-duty this fort may be (its walls are 6m/20ft thick), but it didn't stand up to invasion from the English, who took Havana in 1762. Crowning its cylindrical tower is a small bronze weathervane in the shape of a woman, with one hand on her hip, holding what was once a palm leaf, and the other holding a cross. A replica of the original (now in the Museo de la Ciudad, *see p51*), it was cast in 1632 by Cuban artist Jerónimo Martín Pinzón. Called 'La Giraldilla', she is believed to represent Doña Inés de Bobadilla, wife of Hernando de Soto and the first and only female governor of Cuba. The image is now reproduced on the Havana Club rum label.

Inside the castle is the Museo Nacional de la Cerámica Cubana, with permanent collections (and some sales) by Cuban ceramicists and international artists. At press time, renovations to the fort were in progress, but the museum remains open for visits. A monument to Cubans who died in World War II stands in the front of the Castillo. It's not a very long list of names – Cuba helped the war effort mainly with sugar and chocolate.

Museo de la Ciudad

Palacio de los Capitanes Generales, Calle Tacón #1, entre Obispo y O'Reilly (861 2876/5779 ext 101). **Open** 9am-6pm daily. **Admission** $3 ($5 incl guided tour in English); free under-12s. **Map** p252 E15.

The Palacio de los Capitanes Generales (1770-91) is now the city's historical museum, and one of Havana's finest sights. To start with, it has without a doubt the grandest and most beautiful courtyard

Book market on **Plaza de Armas**.

in Havana, and rivals the cathedral as the city's finest 18th-century baroque building. Between 1791 and 1898, more than 60 representatives of the Spanish Crown lived here, but it wasn't until the 1999 Ibero-American Summit in Havana that a King of Spain sat in the Royal Chair in the Throne Room. The museum houses historical exhibitions, including displays of old horse-drawn vehicles and artillery, plus funerary and religious art. The Captain General's apartments are furnished in the sumptuous style of their epoch and El Cabildo (the room where the town council used to sit) has an 18th-century portrait of Columbus. Don't miss the his and hers Carrara marble nautilus shell baths.

Sightseeing

Museo Nacional de Historia Natural

Calle Obispo #61, entre Oficios y Baratillo (863 9361/862 9402/www.medioambiente.cu/museo). **Open** 9.30am-5pm Tue-Fri; 9.30am-4pm Sat. **Admission** $3; free under-12s. **Map** p252 E16.

The museum's mammal, bird and reptile exhibitions incorporate a sophisticated video system of animal sounds. Displays also explore the origins of life on Earth and Cuban fauna (Cuban flora awaits renovation of the top two floors). The children's room is a winner, with activities related to nature and prehistory.

Palacio del Segundo Cabo/ Instituto Cubano del Libro

Calle O'Reilly #4, esquina Oficios (switchboard 862 8091/bookshops 863 2244/gallery 862 8091 ext 151). **Open** *Instituto* 8am-4.30pm Mon-Fri. *Bookshops* 10am-5.30pm Mon-Sat; 10am-3pm Sun. *Gallery* 9am-5.30pm daily. *Museum* 10am-5pm Mon-Wed, Fri-Sun. **Admission** *Museum* $1 (incl obligatory guide, English-speaking available); free under-16s. *Gallery* free. **Map** p252 E16.

Originally the royal post office responsible for all postal communication within Spain's Ibero-American colonies, and later the Royal Treasury, the Palacio del Segundo Cabo (1770-91) later became the official residence of the Vice-Captain General of Cuba. Open for visits as a museum, it was one of the earliest civilian buildings to be designed in the Cuban baroque style, with elaborate entrances, arches and windows. It's also worth looking out for Moorish details in the balconies and the courtyard, and the *mudéjar* influence from Andalusia can be discerned in the building's general layout. Today, the Palacio is the home of the Instituto Cubano del Libro (a state-run institution responsible for the promotion of literature) as well as three bookshops (for all, *see p121*). The mezzanine floor of the palace is occupied by Galería Raúl Martínez, which exhibits and sells works by well-known Cuban painters.

Urban refit

Hundreds of Old Havana's key buildings have been restored thanks to a funding system designed by the Oficina del Historiador de la Ciudad (City Historian's Office) in Havana. It's a simple but effective concept: all the profits earned in the restaurants, bars and hotels of La Habana Vieja are invested directly back into the city's restoration. But in addition to the physical renovation of Old Havana's buildings, the organisation hopes to bring about a spiritual renaissance in the life of the old city. Services for visitors are a key financial focus, but the balance between tourism and local rejuvenation is given very careful attention. Alongside upmarket hotels, other projects have included a new public library on the Plaza de Armas, an old people's home, a day-care rehabilitation centre for children with degenerative illnesses and an extensive programme of cultural activities. Housing is Old Havana's most pressing problem; the historical centre has 70,600 inhabitants living in 22,500 'units', most of which are the results of multiple subdivisions of the existing space over more than a century. These appalling conditions constitute an urgent challenge.

In 1981 a planning programme was devised for much-needed restoration work. Each of the 3,500 buildings in the historical centre was assigned a grade of historical/aesthetic importance, a proposed end use and a carefully costed restoration schedule. Restorations have already been completed in large sections of the old city, but the situation is still grave – there are serious structural collapses roughly every three days. You'll notice that *habaneros* instinctively cross to the other side of the street rather than walk too close to a shaky façade or a crumbling balcony.

The north-eastern part of the old city contains the majority of the city's grandest edifices, such as the Renaissance fortress **Castillo de la Real Fuerza** (*see 51*), the 18th-century **Palacio del Segundo Cabo** (*see p52*), the **Catedral de la Habana** (*see p59*), the **Basílica Menor y Convento de San Francisco de Así** (*see p55*) and numerous aristocratic mansions. This section of the city is referred to as the 'golden kilometre' because its grand buildings attract much of the revenue needed for investment in housing in areas less blessed with dramatic architecture.

Palacio del Segundo Cabo. *See 52.*

El Templete
Calle Baratillo, esquina O'Reilly (no phone).
Open 9am-6.30pm daily (ticket booth closes 5.30pm).
Admission $1 (incl guide); free under-12s.
Map p252 E16.
The oldest neo-classical building in Havana, the columned El Templete (1828) marks the spot where, under a legendary ceiba tree (an ancestor of the one currently on the site), Havana was founded in its present location on 16 November 1519, with the first mass and town council. (In fact, the city was originally founded several years earlier on the south coast of the island, but moved later to this strategically stronger location.) Inside the chapel are three paintings by French artist Jean Baptiste Vermay (whose ashes lie in the middle of the room): two represent the mass and *cabildo* (town council) and the huge middle one shows the inauguration of El Templete.

Each year, on 16 November, a procession headed by the city's 16th-century maces – normally kept in the Museo de la Ciudad – makes its way around the Plaza de Armas to the ceiba to commemorate the city's founding. Superstitious *habaneros* (and that means everyone) queue up all evening to walk around the tree and make a wish. The wishes are only meant to work if you haven't spoken all day, a feat quite beyond the average *habanero*, so plenty of money is left between the roots of the tree as an extra insurance policy.

Along Calle Oficios to Plaza de San Francisco

It's only a short three-block walk along Calle Oficios, Havana's oldest street, from the southwest corner of Plaza de Armas to Plaza de San Francisco, but it's packed with sights along the way. Just a few doors down Calle Oficios is the **Casa de los Artistas** (No.6; *see p146*).

Next door, in the 17th-century Casa de Obispo, is the **Museo Numismático** (*see below*), and across the street at No.13 is the **Museo del Automóvil** (*see below*), which exhibits cars dating back to 1905. Halfway down Jústiz, between calles Baratillo and Oficios, is a late 18th-century house known as **Casa de la Comedia** (*see p168*).

Back on Oficios is the former Colegio de San Ambrosio, which provided ecclesiastical studies for children from 1689 to 1774. The building is now the **Casa de los Árabes** (No.16; *see below*). Across the street is the **Gabinete de Conservación y Restauración** of the **City Historian's Office** (No.19, entre Obrapía y Obispo, 861 5846), which holds workshops on restoring items such as colonial furniture, statuary, textiles, documents and ceramics. Though not a museum, visitors are welcome to check out the excellent 'before and after' photo exhibition in the entrance hall (a good way of getting to grips with the extent of renovation taking place in the area) and the 17th- and 18th-century objects in the patio.

Sightseeing

Casa de los Árabes

Calle Oficios #16, entre Obispo y Obrapía (861 5868). **Open** 9am-4.30pm Mon-Sat, 9.30am-12.30pm Sun. **Admission** free. **Map** p252 E15.

Houses modest exhibitions on Islamic textiles, carpets, clothing, weapons, ceramics and furniture. It's also home to Havana's only mosque.

Museo del Automóvil

Calle Oficios #12, esquina Jústiz (861 5062). **Open** 9am-5pm Tue-Sun. **Admission** $1; free under-12s. **Map** p252 E16.

While you needn't be any kind of expert to spot knackered old cars on the streets of Havana, this museum is still worth a visit for its beautifully restored vehicles dating back as far as 1905, plus historically interesting ones, such as Che Guevara's 1960 Chevrolet. There have been talks of this museum moving to the corner of calles Obispo and Aguiar, but plans were unclear at press time.

Museo Numismático

Calle Oficios #8, entre Obispo y Obrapía (861 5811). **Open** 9.15am-4.45pm Tue-Sat; 9am-1pm Sun. **Admission** $1; free under-12s. **Map** p252 E15.

Coins dating from the conquest to the present day, including an early 20 peso coin, the only one still existing of the ten produced, and 20 golden coins. (Note that in 2004, this museum is due to move to Calle Obispo, entre Aguiar y Habana). Unlikely to raise your pulse unless you're a coin enthusiast.

Plaza de San Francisco

Formerly a small inlet covered by the waters of the bay, **Plaza de San Francisco** dates from 1628. From the start it was a commercial centre, and during the colonial period a fair took place here every October with coin and card games, lotteries and cock fights – perhaps an early sign of Havana's future role as a gambling mecca. One of the terminals of the Zanja Real, the first aqueduct in the Americas, the water supply in the square helped to supply victual ships tied up at the wharves that fringed the square. In its day it has also been home to a governor, a mayor and the city jail, and some of the buildings around the square were the residences of some of the city's most wealthy and notable inhabitants.

Today, this spacious, paved square is dominated by the 18th-century basilica on the south side, with its impressive tower, the Lonja del Comercio (1909) on the north side, and the Aduana (1914, Customs House) and Sierra Maestra cruise ship terminal on the east side. More modern additions include Benetton, restaurants – whose tables, chairs and umbrellas are gradually sprawling unattractively into the treeless square – and the **Agencia de Viajes San Cristóbal** (*see p229*), which specialises in cultural tourism in Old Havana. In the centre of the square, the Carrara marble **Fuente de los Leones** was sculpted in 1836 by Italian artist Giuseppe Gaggini. The square is frequently used for girls' 15th birthday celebrations, so you're likely to see bevies of be-crinolined beauties self-consciously feeding the pigeons.

The 42-metre (140-foot) tower – the tallest colonial structure in Cuba after Trinidad's Iznaga Tower (*see pp195-205*) – topping the baroque **Basílica Menor y Convento de San Francisco de Asís** (*see p55*) is the first thing to catch the eye on the square; the convent houses a small museum dedicated to religious art. In front of the basilica is Villa Soberón's endearing bronze statue of **El Caballero de París** (*see p60* **Statuary rites**). Accessible only via the church is the small garden in memory of Mother Teresa. At the southern end of the garden is the **Iglesia de Ortodoxo Griego**, still under construction, to be Cuba's only active Greek Orthodox church.

A huge chunk of the square is taken up by the eclectic **Lonja del Comercio** (Stock Exchange, Calle Amargura #2, esquina Oficios, 866 9587/9588), spruced up by the City Historian's Office in 1996 to provide profitable office space for rent. The addition of an upper floor with a reflective glass façade obstructs the view of the beautiful golden dome crowned by a bronze statue of the god Mercury – a replica of the original work by Flemish artist Jean Boulogne – but visitors can enter the building during working hours to admire the striking cupola (no photos allowed). Exit at the back of the Lonja to see the curious **Jardín Diana de**

Gales (Calle Baratillo, esquina Carpinetti), a garden planted in memory of Princess Diana, with two unattractive abstract sculptures by Cuban artists and an engraved Welsh slate plaque donated by the British ambassador.

Continuing south on Oficios, between the short street Churruca and Muralla is the eclectic early 20th-century **Palacio de Gobierno** (Calle Oficios #211, 863 4352). The Republican Chamber of Representatives was housed here until it moved to the Capitolio in 1929, and the Palacio became home to the Ministry of Education. Today, the main building is a museum, with documents from the Republican period (1902-59), including the first passports ever issued in Cuba; it also houses the tiny **Museo de la Educación**, focusing on the literacy campaign in Cuba (note that Havana's key museum on education is the Museo de Alfabetizacíon in Marianao; *see p87*) and the municipal government of La Habana Vieja.

Just before you get to the palace you'll see a railway carriage, the **Mambí**, parked incongruously on side street Calle Churruca. It was used by successive early 20th-century Cuban presidents on their trips round the island and is worth a visit for the inlaid mahogany furniture, specially designed silver and glass and the ingenious early air-conditioning system.

Adjacent to the Palacio's annex is the leafy **Parque Alejandro de Humboldt**, named after the German naturalist considered by many to be Cuba's 'second discoverer' after Columbus. Across the street is **Casa Alejandro de Humboldt** (*see below*), where he worked during his first visit to Cuba. One block east on Santa Clara takes you to Calle San Pedro and the **Muelle de Luz** (Luz Dock), which has ferries to Regla and Casablanca. One block north on San Pedro at the corner with Sol is the **Fundación Havana Club** (*see below*), a museum about rum-making.

Back on Oficios and west on Brasil (Teniente Rey), will find you at the **Aqvarivm** (No.9; *see below*), a small freshwater aquarium. Continuing on Brasil, you'll come across archaeological sites that show portions of the 16th-century **Zanja Real** (Royal Canal), part of the original aqueduct that provided the city with fresh water from the Río Almendares, the first aqueduct built by the Spaniards in America.

Aqvarivm

Calle Brasil (Teniente Rey) #9, entre Oficios y Mercaderes (863 9493). **Open** 9am-5pm Mon-Sat; 9am-1pm Sun. **Admission** $1; free under-12s. **Map** p252 E15.

Set up by the City Historian's Office, this aquarium is a celebration of the obsession of *habaneros* with keeping freshwater fish in tanks.

Basílica Menor y Convento de San Francisco de Asís

Calle Oficios, entre Amargura y Brasil (Teniente Rey) (862 9683/3467). **Open** 9am-6.30pm daily. **Admission** *Church & museum* $2. *Tower* $1 (closed for renovation until early 2004); free under-12s. **Map** p252 E15.

Built between 1719 and 1738, this was one of Havana's most modish religious sites in its day. The basilica has a central nave and two side aisles, and it originally had a dome and crossing at the eastern end, but they were destroyed by a hurricane in 1846. The east wall of the central nave now boasts an arresting *trompe l'oeil* mural of how the perspective of the church would have appeared before the dome's demise. Today, the main hall of the church, with its excellent acoustics, is one of Havana's finest concert halls, home to the renowned all-female chamber orchestra Camerata Romeu. Chamber and choral music concerts are held every Saturday night and occasionally during the week.

The crypt of the basilica is the final resting place of numerous 17th- and 18th-century aristocrats. Both the basilica and the convent, with its exquisite storeyed cloisters, now house the Museo de Arte Religioso, with paintings by José Nicolás de la Escalera and Vicente Escobar, missals with tortoise shell, ivory and hammered silver covers, polychrome wooden images and early marriage registries (one for whites and the other for *mestizos* and blacks). The armchairs and lectern used by Fidel Castro and Pope John Paul II during the latter's January 1998 visit to the island are also here (*see p19* for picture). The tower, which provides one of the best views of Old Havana, was under renovation at the time of writing and closed to the public.

Casa Alejandro de Humboldt

Calle Oficios #254, esquina Muralla (863 9850). **Open** 9am-4pm Tue-Sat; 9am-noon Sun. **Admission** free. **Map** p252 E15.

In this house, explorer Federico Enrique Alejandro de Humboldt (1769-1859) installed his instruments, and botany and mineral collections, during his first stay in Havana (1800-01). Restored as a museum, there are more than 250 scientific instruments, books, maps and works of art detailing Humboldt's work in Cuba. The museum is also the venue for major cultural, scientific and environmental events.

Fundación Havana Club (Museo del Ron)

Calle San Pedro #262, esquina Sol (861 8051/862 3832). **Open** *Museum* 9am-5pm Mon-Thur; 9am-4pm Fri-Sun. *Shop* 9am-9pm daily. **Admission** *Museum* $5 (incl obligatory guided tour, English-speaking available); free under-16s. **Map** p252 E15.

This promotional centre houses the Museo del Ron, one of the city's newest and snazziest museums, showing the stages of traditional rum production. Displays cover sugar cane harvesting, sugar mills (with a tiny working model of a mill and distillery that children will love) and the processes of fermentation, distillation, filtration, ageing, blending and bottling. Tours happily emerge in the tasting room; you can also buy a liquid souvenir in the gift shop. When you visit, ask about the monthly lottery for a bottle of 25-year-old San Cristóbal rum. The Fundación is also becoming a popular venue for contemporary art, with a gallery on the second floor.

Plaza Vieja

The 16th-century **Plaza Vieja** has always been a residential rather than a military, religious or administrative space, and is surrounded by elegant colonial residences, combined with a few very striking early 20th-century art nouveau buildings. Over the past 150 years, Plaza Vieja has played host to an open-air food market, a park, an outrageously misjudged car park built by Batista in 1952 (now demolished) and an amphitheatre. However, restoration is gradually re-establishing Plaza Vieja's original atmosphere; the white Carrara showpiece fountain at the centre of the square is a replica of the original 18th-century one by Italian sculptor Giorgio Massari that was destroyed by the construction of the car park; and many of the 18th-century residences around the square are now restored with housing on the top floors and commercial establishments, including several small museums and art/photo galleries, on the ground floor. Also on the square is the restaurant **Santo Angel** (*see p103*).

The best place to start in the Plaza Vieja is the intriguing **Cámara Oscura** (*see below*) located atop Edificio Gómez Vila (1933) in the north-eastern corner of the square, providing a bird's eye view of Old Havana and the bay.

The oldest and best-preserved structure in the Plaza Vieja is the Casa del Conde de San Juan de Jaruco (1737) on the south side, restored as the **La Casona** art gallery (*see pp145-9*). On the west side, look out for the original small frescoes on the façade of the mid 18th-century **Casa del Conde de Casa Lombillo** (No.364), restored in 1989. The **Centro de Desarrollo de las Artes Visuales** (862 9295, closed Sun, free), on the plaza's north-west corner, was built in 1805 and has some interesting baroque woodwork. On the eastern side of the square is the 18th-century building that houses the **Fototeca de Cuba** (*see pp145-49*), with photography exhibitions.

The whimsical art nouveau **Palacio Cueto** (1908), on the south-eastern corner, is currently in a state of rack and ruin. Differing in style from the rest of the square, this building was constructed initially as a hotel, was later converted into apartments, and is now being restored to its original role by the City Historian's Office. (In 1988 its façade featured in the Cuban movie *Vals para La Habana.*) On the south side of the square, the former home of historian Martín Félix de Arrate (No.101) now houses the **Museo del Naipe 'Marqués de Prado Ameno'** (Calle Muralla #101, entre San Ignacio y Mercaderes, 860 1534), dedicated to the somewhat specialist subject of playing cards.

There are still more sights in the immediate vicinity of Plaza Vieja. An interesting silkscreen workshop is located one block west of Plaza Vieja. Inside the **Taller de Artes Serigráficas René Portocarrero** (Calle Cuba #513, entre Brasil/Teniente Rey y Muralla, 862 3276, www.artnet.com, closed Sat, Sun) is a small gallery shop. A block north on Calle Cuba, at the corner of Amargura, is the former Iglesia y Convento de San Augustín, now the **Iglesia de San Francisco de Asís** (861 8490), not to be confused with the Basílica y Convento de San Francisco de Asís. Built in 1633 by the Augustinians and later transferred to the Franciscans who renamed it, the convent has assumed various identities in its time. Today, it houses the splendid **Museo Nacional de Historia de las Ciencias Carlos J Finlay** (*see below*).

Cámara Oscura

Calle Brasil (Teniente Rey), esquina Mercaderes (no phone). **Open** 8.30am-6pm daily. **Admission** $1 (incl English-speaking guide); free under-12s. **Map** p252 E15.

Located on the top floor of the Edificio Gómez Vila, 35m (115ft) off the ground, the Cámara Oscura provides a 360-degree panoramic 'moving image' of what's happening in much of La Habana Vieja. The only one of its kind in the Americas, the Cámara Oscura was donated to Cuba by Cádiz, Spain.

Museo Nacional de Historia de las Ciencias Carlos J Finlay

Calle Cuba #460, entre Amargura y Brasil (Teniente Rey) (863 4824/4841/museofin@ceniai.ins.cu). **Open** 9am-5pm Mon-Sat. **Admission** $2 (incl guide, English-speaking available). **Map** p252 E15.

On 14 August 1881, when this former convent was a scientific academy, Cuban scientist Dr Carlos J Finlay presented his ground-breaking work naming the *Aedes aegipti* mosquito as the transmitter of yellow fever. Now a science museum, there are paintings, busts and portraits of erudite scientists from around the world, a panorama of medicine in Cuba and a display of Finlay's work. On the third-floor is a restored 19th-century pharmacy.

Calle Mercaderes

North of Plaza Vieja, the corner of Calles Amargura and Mercaderes is known as the **Cruz Verde** (Green Cross), due to a green-painted cross fastened to an old cornerstone (on a building now known as the Casa de La Cruz

Plaza Vieja: crumbling buildings and smart new paintwork side by side. *See p56.*

Verde). During the 18th and 19th centuries, this was the first stop for the Procession of the Cross (Vía Crucis) on Good Friday, which went from the Basílica Menor y Convento de San Francisco de Asís to the Iglesia del Santo Cristo del Buen Viaje. Restoration of the building will provide flats for local people and the ground floor will house the **Museo del Chocolate**, due to open in late 2003. Opposite, an 18th-century residence is almost fully restored as the future **Museo de Arte Ceremonial Africano** (Mercaderes #27), but there is no clear opening date.

Further north, on the corner of Mercaderes and Lamparilla, sits tiny **Parque Rumiñahui**. The centrepiece of the park is a sculpture given to Fidel Castro by Ecuadorean artist Oswaldo Guayasamín. On the other side of Mercaderes is the luxury **Hostal Conde de Villanueva** (*see p34*), located in the elegant former home of the Conde de Villanueva (1789-1853), who was an key international promoter of Cuban cigars and a leader of Creole society.

Around Parque de Simón Bolívar

Continuing north on Mercaderes, you'll reach **Parque Simón Bolívar** on the corner of Calle Obrapía. In addition to a statue of 'El Libertador' himself, the park has a ceramic mural (1998) by Venezuelan artist Carmen Montilla. South of the park is the **Casa-Museo Simón Bolívar** (*see p58*), popularly known as Casa de México, which was inaugurated in 1993 to commemorate the 210th anniversary of the South American liberator's birth.

Across the street is a small gunsmith's shop, the Armería de Cuba, which played a significant, if unwilling, part in the Revolution. Young Revolutionaries stormed the shop on 9 April 1958, the day of a general strike, to get weapons for the fight in the city. The shop now houses the **Museo Armería 9 de Abril** (861 8080, closed Sun), with displays of old guns. Facing the park on Mercaderes is **Terracota 4**, the studio-galleries of three ceramicists: Amelia Carballo, José Ramón González and Ángel Norniella. Also worth a stop is next-door **Habana 1791** (*see p128*), a boutique that sells Cuban colognes and perfumes.

Facing the park on Obrapía is the Mexican-themed **Casa de Benito Juárez** (*see p58*), and across the street is the 1796 building that houses the **Casa Oswaldo Guayasamín** (*see p58*), named after the Ecuadorean-born 'artist of the Americas', who died in 1999. To the west of the park is the atmospheric **Casa de la Obra Pía** (*see p58*), built in 1665 by a former solicitor general, Captain Martín Calvo de la Puerta y Arrieta. The house (and street) assumed the name Obra Pía (meaning 'pious act') in 1669, when the owner began providing dowries for orphan girls. It was restored as a museum in 1983. On the opposite side of Obrapía, the **Casa de Africa** (Calle Obrapía #157, entre Mercaderes y San Ignacio, 861 5798), located in a 17th-century residence, has displays including a large collection of gifts received by Castro from African countries, and a collection of *santería* icons belonging to famous Cuban ethnographer and expert on Afro-Cuban culture, Fernando Ortiz. Closed for extensive restoration work, it may reopen in early 2004.

Back on Calle Mercaderes, the **Museo del Tabaco** (No.120, entre Obispo y Obrapía, 861 5795, closed Mon) offers a modest display of lithographic prints, old pipes and lighters, early cigar boxes and ashtrays, and a Casa del Habano (862 8472) on its ground floor. In the same building is the **Taller de Papel Artesanal** (no phone), which makes handmade paper using natural fibres and recycled, textured paper from all manner of sources. Across the street is the enthralling **Maqueta de La Habana Vieja** (*see below*), a scale model (1:500) showing some 3,500 buildings located within the 2.14 square kilometres (one square mile) that make up the old city. Opposite is the small but interesting **Casa de Asia** (No.111, entre Obispo y Obrapía, 863 9740, closed Mon), which displays collections from different Asiatic cultures, including silverwork, mother-of-pearl and stone from the Great Wall of China.

Sightseeing

Casa de Benito Juárez/ Casa de México

Calle Obrapía #116, esquina Mercaderes (861 8166/mexico@cultural.ohch.cu). **Open** 9.30am-4.45pm Tue-Sat; 9am-12.45pm Sun. **Admission** free. **Map** p252 E15.

This pink building has an uninspiring permanent display on the Aztecs, collections of silver- and copperwork, ceramics and textiles, plus pre-Columbian and popular handicrafts from Mexico. Two rooms feature rotating exhibitions by contemporary Mexican and Cuban artists.

Casa de la Obra Pía

Calle Obrapía #158, esquina Mercaderes (861 3097). **Open** 9am-4.30pm Tue-Sat; 9.30-11.30am Sun. **Admission** free. **Map** p252 E15.

This eye-catching yellow house has a large courtyard, coloured decorative friezes and a uniquely designed baroque portal made in 1686 in Cádiz, Spain. Its interior is filled with colonial furniture and linen goods typical of those that would have filled the home of 18th-century Havana nobility. A permanent collection of objects belonging to Cuban novelist Alejo Carpentier is also housed here, including the blue Volkswagen he used when he was Cuban ambassador to UNESCO in Paris. The Casa de la Obra Pía is also home to the sisterhood of embroiderers and weavers of Belén, one of the Old Havana guilds that is being revived (*see p128*).

Casa Oswaldo Guayasamín

Calle Obrapía #111, entre Oficios y Mercaderes (861 3843). **Open** 9am-4.30pm Tue-Sat; 9am-noon Sun. **Admission** free. **Map** p252 E15.

Along with work by the late Ecuadorean artist Guayasamín (a friend of Castro in his time), the upper floor has murals painted by renowned 18th-century Cuban painters José Nicolás de la Escalera and José Andrés Sánchez. A small shop sells Guayasamín silkscreens, lithographs, reproductions and jewellery.

Casa-Museo Simón Bolívar

Calle Mercaderes #156, entre Obrapía y Lamparilla (861 3988). **Open** 9am-5pm Tue-Sat; 9am-noon Sun. **Admission** free. **Map** p252 E15.

Simón Bolívar, South American liberator, stayed here when he visited Havana in March 1799. The ground floor has detailed displays on his life and work, and there are also three art galleries with works by Cuban and international artists. The upper floor, with its splendid tinted-glass windows and curved iron and marble banister, has contemporary Venezuelan and Latin American paintings, sculptures and literature.

Maqueta de La Habana Vieja

Calle Mercaderes #116, entre Obispo y Obrapía (no phone; co-ordinate visits through Museo de la Ciudad 861 5001). **Open** 9am-6pm daily. **Admission** $1; $2 with guide. **Map** p252 E15.

This captivating scale model (1:500) of the old city model took three years to build, and is enlivened by an evocative sound and light show.

Plaza de la Catedral & around

Originally named Plaza de la Ciénaga (Swamp Square) because of its muddy terrain, with time the **Plaza de la Catedral** – the last square built inside the walls of the old colonial city – became one of Havana's most important squares. Here, the main conduit of the Zanja Real – the city's first aqueduct, constructed between 1565 and 1592 – entered a cistern to supply the Spanish fleet docking in Havana. Once the square had been drained and paved, buildings were constructed around the central space to create a dry square embellished with porticoes, which provide shade and shelter from tropical rainstorms. In addition to the cathedral, which gives the square its definitive appearance, the other three sides are taken up by the façades of 18th-century aristocratic baroque mansions, all built within a 40-year period and showing a strong architectural harmony.

With its curves and flourishes above doors and windows, the **Catedral de La Habana** (*see p59*) is Havana's finest example of 18th-century Cuban baroque. Baroque was late to arrive in Cuba, and the porous nature of the locally quarried limestone, which was embedded with coral fossils and seashells, handicapped its ornate style. Even so, Cuban writer Alejo Carpentier described the cathedral as 'music made into stone'. On the south side of the square, across from the cathedral, is the Casa del Conde de Casa Bayona (1720), or Casa de Don Luís Chacón, the oldest house in the area and today the **Museo de Arte Colonial** (*see below*).

The mid 18th-century Casa del Conde de Casa Lombillo, on the eastern side of the square, is unusual in having three façades: the main one on Empedrado and the other two facing Mercaderes and the square. Today, it houses the **City Historian's Office** (*see p54*) and two galleries: one displaying 19th-century lithographs of Old Havana and the other a photo exhibition of restoration work in the area.

The **Casa del Marqués de Arcos** (1746) next door is a mansion that became a post office in the mid 19th century, a role it partially maintains to this day (look out for the unusual stone mask postbox in the wall). Restoration work has been hampered by severe subsidence – the square is still very marshy below the surface. The mansion's imposing main entrance is on Calle Mercaderes; stand here to get a good view of the striking mural by Cuban artist Andrés Carillo on the opposite wall, depicting 67 important artistic, literary and intellectual figures from 19th-century Cuba.

Facing these two houses across the square is the Casa del Marqués de Aguas Claras, now restaurant **El Patio** (*see p103*). Built between 1751 and 1775, it boasts an exquisite inner courtyard and elegant original 18th-century stained glass on its upper-storey windows. Next door, the commercial **Galería Victor Manuel** (*see p147*) occupies the former Casa de Baños (public bath house), which was built over the square's cistern in the 19th century.

The north-west corner of the square is occupied by the 18th-century Casa de los Condes de Peñalver, which has at different times served as a post office, a bank and a school. Today, it houses the **Centro de Arte Contemporáneo Wilfredo Lam** (*see p146*), one of Havana's best art galleries. Half a block west up Calle Empedrado is **La Bodeguita del Medio** (*see p100*), the renowned Hemingway haunt that today is more likely to be full of camera-wielding tourists than gravelly writers. A few doors further along is the **Fundación Alejo Carpentier** (Calle Empedrado #215, entre Cuba y San Ignacio, 861 5506, closed Sat, Sun), which promotes the work of one of Cuba's most important 20th-century writers. Another block west on Empedrado is **Parque Cervantes**, with a marble statue (1906) of the great writer himself.

Catedral de La Habana

Calle Empedrado #158, Plaza de la Catedral (861 7771). **Open** 10.30am-3.00pm Mon-Sat; 10.30am-noon Sun. **Mass** 8.15pm Mon, Tue, Thur, Fri; 5.30pm Sat (special mass for children); 10.30am Sun. **Admission** free. **Map** p252 D15.

Construction of the cathedral was begun in 1748 by the Jesuits; though they were expelled from Cuba in 1767, work continued on the building for a further 20 years and in 1787, the Diocese of Havana was established and the church was consecrated as the Catedral de la Virgen María de la Concepción Inmaculada. The two towers, which are different in size, continue to puzzle scholars: some say one is larger to accommodate the small interior staircase, while others argue that the other is narrower to prevent closing the street.

The interior of the cathedral dates from the early 19th century, when the original baroque altars were replaced with neo-classical ones, and the original wood ceilings were plastered over. Its paintings, sculptures and gold- and silverwork were executed by the Italian masters Bianchini and Guisseppe Perovani. The eight large paintings by Jean Baptiste Vermay are copied from originals by Rubens and Murillo. Note that despite the official opening times, the cathedral is often locked, though you can sometimes gain access just before mass.

Museo de Arte Colonial

Casa del Conde de Casa Bayona, Calle San Ignacio #61, Plaza de la Catedral (862 6440). **Open** 9am-6.45pm daily. **Admission** $2; free under-12s. **Map** p252 D15.

This *casa* once accommodated the Havana Club rum company, but became the Museo de Arte Colonial in 1969. Panelled ceilings with elaborate designs complement the collections of opulent colonial decorative art, furniture, glasswork and European porcelain.

Calle Tacón & northern La Habana Vieja

Walking up from Calle Tacón's southern end (from O'Reilly) takes you past several adjoining houses of note. The first, No.4, built in 1759, is where the Havana Architectural Association was founded in 1916. It is now restaurant **Don Giovanni** (*see p101*), but the building was closed at the time of writing for restoration of the interior 17th-century decorative wall friezes, painted by anonymous Italian artists. But you can still enter the foyer to see the large ceramic mural (a copy of Klimt). The oldest house on this stretch is the Casa de Juana Carvajal at No.12, dating from the early 17th century. It is named after a liberated slave who was given this building as an inheritance by her former owner, Lorenza Carvajal. Juana enlarged the house in 1725 and decorated the interior with friezes. In 1988 it was restored as the headquarters of

Statuary rites

Dozens of passers-by are drawn every day to the life-size bronze statue of a humbly dressed man captured mid step by the entrance to the **Basílica Menor y Convento de San Francisco de Asís** (*see p55*). Approach it and you will see something quite remarkable: the extended left hand is smooth and shiny where hundreds of people have touched it. Unlike most statues, it is neither majestic nor regal; it is instead dedicated to Havana's most beloved homeless person, most commonly known around town as the Cabellero de París, the Parisian Gentleman.

Dozens of legends have emerged around this enigmatic figure but a few common threads emerge. His real name was José María López Lledín, a native of Lugo in Spain, where he was born in 1899 into a wealthy family. Some say he lost his mind when, during the trip from Spain to Cuba, the vessel sunk and he lost his family. Others claim that he was accused of a crime he did not commit. Either way, for many years he wandered the streets of Havana, the victim of worsening dementia, with his mane of greying hair, a shaggy beard, long nails and an elegant black cape. With him he carried a portfolio containing his treasures, gifts, pens and coloured pieces of card, which he bestowed on passers-by; he never asked for alms, he only gave. In time, he became a well-known figure in his favourite haunts around the Plaza de Armas in Old Havana and even on Avenida 5ta in Miramar, where the eccentric 'gentleman' would spend hours reciting poetry or recounting tales of another era.

His great-grandson has hinted that he was in love with a young lady he left behind in Spain as a boy. When she didn't appear at the appointed time on the quays in Havana, where he was waiting with a bunch of flowers, he gave the bouquet to a passing woman. Thereafter, he returned to the quays every day in the vain hope that his love would arrive; she never did, and he continued to bestow flowers on passing women.

In 1977 he was admitted to a psychiatric hospital, where he died eight years later, at the age of 85. His remains were exhumed and placed in the Basílica Menor de San Francisco de Asís, his final resting place. The statue is by sculptor José Villa Soberón, who also sculpted John Lennon's statue in Vedado (*see p76* **Just like starting over**).

the **Gabinete de Arqueología** (archeology department of the City Historian's Office).

Across from the brightly coloured umbrellas of the craft market (*see p129*), back on Calle Tacón, is the large and sombre baroque **Seminario de San Carlos y San Ambrosio** (862 6989). It was built in 1774 as a Jesuit seminary – renowned Cuban intellectuals José de la Luz y Caballero and Félix Varela were among its alumni – and still functions as such. It boasts one of the most tranquil courtyards in Havana and a magnificent library, in which visitors are welcome (ring the bell to the right of the entrance). Cross through the park on the other side of Tacón to reach the bay and the white Carrara marble **Fuente de Neptuno** (Neptune Fountain), which dates from 1838.

North of the Seminario is a small castle, built in 1939 as an imitation colonial fortress. Always a police station, today it is the General Command of the Policia Nacional Revolucionaria (PNR). In front of the castle is **Parque Arqueológico de la Maestranza**, which shows the remains of one of the earliest artillery factories in Latin America. To the west is the neighbouring Parque Infantil 'La Maestranza', a small children's amusement area, and at the northern end of the park is the **Parque Anfiteatro**. Inland is the **Palacio de la Artesanía** (*see p128*), a popular stop for handicrafts, books and music. Housed in the palatial late 18th-century home of Mateo Pedroso y Florencia, one of Havana's richest slave traders, the building constitutes a typical example of the spatial distribution common in Havana's 18th-century domestic buildings, with open ground-floor areas suitable for retail, warehousing and stabling, a cramped mezzanine floor that functioned as slave quarters and the high-ceilinged, airy rooms on the top floor in which the family lived in style.

North of here, where the road curves around into Monserrate, is the handsome Casa de Francisco Pons (1906), which now houses the wonderful **Museo Nacional de la Música** (*see p61*). Head south on Compostela to reach the unusual **Iglesia del Santo Ángel Custodio** (861 0469), opposite the Museo de la Revolución (*see p68*). The church's wedding-cake appearance is due to a mixture of 17th-century Gothic and 19th-century neo-Gothic styles. Two of Havana's most outstanding sons, Félix Varela and José Martí, were baptised in

the church, and renowned 19th-century Cuban writer Cirilo Villaverde used it as the setting for the key scene of his famous romantic novel, *Cecilia Valdés*, when the heroine has her lover stabbed on the steps of the church as he is about to marry another woman.

Gabinete de Arqueología de la Oficina del Historiador

Calle Tacón #12, entre O'Reilly y Empedrado (861 4469). **Open** 10.30am-5.30pm Tue-Sat; 9am-1pm Sun. **Admission** $1; free under-12s. **Map** p252 D16.

Dedicated to archaeological studies in Old Havana, inside is a fascinating and often-overlooked exhibition of pre-Columbian art, vessels and textiles, household objects from the 16th to the 19th centuries, and glass and ceramics from early shipwrecks in the bay. One of the rooms, currently awaiting restoration, has 12 unique floor-to-ceiling murals painted by an anonymous 18th-century artist. These murals alone make a visit worthwhile.

Museo Nacional de la Música

Calle Capdevila #1, entre Habana y Aguiar (861 9846). **Open** 10am-5pm Mon-Sat. **Admission** $2; free under-15s. **Map** p252 D15.

Displays include an unusual collection of African drums, string instruments, music boxes, old American phonographs, a Chinese organ and one of the first gramophones (1904) made by the Victor Talking Machine Company. A small store sells CDs, cassettes and magazines about Cuban music.

Calle Obispo & around

One of the first streets to be constructed in La Habana Vieja, and still one of the liveliest in the area, Calle Obispo runs from Plaza de Armas almost as far as Parque Central. This street, in the process of being paved at the time of writing, is great for strolling and bustles with life – courtesy of a blend of tourists and locals (including plenty of hustlers). It's lined with shops offering handicrafts, art and books, plus bars, restaurants and holes-in-the-wall selling cheap pizzas and ice-cream.

The dignified and eclectic 1920s **Hotel Ambos Mundos** (*see p34*) occupies the intersection of Obispo and Mercaderes. Ernest Hemingway stayed here off and on during the 1930s, and began writing *For Whom the Bell Tolls* in room 511. The room has been restored as a mini museum featuring Hemingway's desk and authentic furniture from the period. Across the street is a late 1950s building, notable for being out of character with the surrounding area. An old Dominican convent, which became the Universidad de La Habana in 1728, originally stood on this site, but was knocked down in the early 20th century. In 1958 the present – rather hideous – building of offices and a heliport was constructed and all that remains of the university is the bell. The building, now under reconstruction in an attempt to give it a less aggressive appearance, will have a church-like tower on one side as a tribute to the original tower of the university church of San Juan de Letrán.

The **Farmacia Taquechel** (*see p129*) at No.155, with its floor-to-ceiling cedar and mahogany shelves and 19th-century French porcelain apothecary's jars, is worth a browse, as is **Droguería Johnson** (862 0311), two blocks up the street at the corner with Aguiar, with tall shelves and original counters.

On the corner of Obispo and Calle Cuba is the 1907 Banco Nacional de Cuba, one of the first buildings constructed after the Republic was born in 1902. The Ministerio de Finanzas y Precios and the modest **Museo de las Finanzas** (Calle Obispo #211, esquina Cuba, 867 1800 ext 1007, closed Sun) – check out the magnificent old round vault door – are now located here. In the early 20th century this area was known as Havana's Wall Street because of the concentration of banks.

Back on Obispo, at the corner of Calle Cuba, is the elegant neo-classical **Hotel Florida** (*see p34*). Built in 1836 and a hotel since 1885, it has retained its beautiful inner patio and arches. At the western end of Obispo is a cluster of good bookstores (*see p121*). At the very end of Obispo, where it hits Monserrate, is **El Floridita** (*see p101*), where the daiquiri, king of cocktails, was born. Inside are photographs and a bust of the Floridita's most famous client, Hemingway. On the adjacent *plazuela* (small square) is an exceptionally elegant life-size Carrara marble statue of engineer Francisco de Albear y Lara, sculpted in 1895 by Cuban artist José Vilalta de Saavedra. Albear built an aqueduct, still functioning, which was awarded the Gold Medal for technical and aesthetic excellence at the Paris Exhibition in 1878. Across the street is the luscious, imposing Centro Asturiano (1927), a Spanish Renaissance building, now part of the Bellas Artes complex (*see p68*).

Head a couple of blocks north along Avenida Bélgica (part of the western boundary of Old Havana) to No.261 to see the opulent art deco **Edificio Bacardí** (862 9271). Built in 1930 for the Bacardí company and topped by the company's bat emblem, it's now an office building. For the best view of the building, go to the rooftop terrace of Hotel Plaza located across the street.

Plaza del Cristo

A sleepy little park three blocks south of Obispo on Bernaza, **Plaza del Cristo** was created in 1640 around the Ermita del Humilladero. The hermitage was the final station on the Vía Crucis (procession of the cross; *see also p56*), which took place every year during Lent. The baroque **Iglesia del Santo Cristo del Buen Viaje** (Esquina Teniente Rey y Bernaza, 863 1767) now covers the site of the old hermitage on the north-eastern side of the plaza. Of the original building, only the enclosure and painted wood-panelled ceiling still remain.

A couple of blocks east on Calle Brasil (Teniente Rey), at the corner of Compostela, is **Farmacia Sarrá** (861 0969), the most beautiful old colonial pharmacy in Old Havana. The interiors are extraordinary: one half is Gothic with early Revolutionary decorative additions, the other part is neo-classical. Currently closed for renovation, there are plans to reopen it in early 2004 under the name Farmacia La Reunión, its first name.

Across the road from Farmacia Sarrá on Calle Compostela stands the **Convento de Santa Teresa**. It's destined to be restored for use as a hotel, but work may not start for several years and the building is currently supported by wooden props.

Southern Habana Vieja

A poorer area less frequented by tourists, southern Old Havana offers visitors the chance to enjoy the more natural pace of normal daily life, and to visit some luscious churches and convents. Three blocks south of Farmacia Sarrá, at the junction of Calles Compostela and Luz, is the 1720 baroque **Convento e Iglesia de Nuestra Señora de Belén** (*see 63*).

Along Calle Acosta, one block to the west of Calle Compostela, is the orthodox **Sinagoga Adath Israel de Cuba** (Calle Acosta #357, esquina Picota, 861 3495). The synagogue, recently renovated, had not been reopened at the time of writing; meanwhile, services are held in the room downstairs. From Calle Compostela, two blocks east on Calle Luz is one of Old Havana's must-sees: the exquisite 17th-century **Convento e Iglesia de Santa Clara** (*see below*). South of here, on the corner of Calles Cuba and Acosta, is the **Iglesia del Espíritu Santo** (Calle Cuba, esquina Acosta,

862 3410). Claiming to be the oldest church in Havana, the original hermitage, built in 1638 for freed slaves, no longer exists. Elegant and dignified, this simple church contains murals, stained glass and a wooden ceiling. Two blocks further south is the baroque mid 18th-century **Convento e Iglesia de La Merced** (*see below*). Its plain exterior contrasts sharply with its magnificent interior – well worth a lingering visit.

South-west of here you enter the old working-class neighbourhood of **San Isidro**, one of Old Havana's poorest areas. On the corner of Calle Leonor Pérez (Paula) and Avenida de la Bélgica (Egido) is the **Casa Natal de José Martí** (*see below*), birthplace of Cuba's national hero.

At the eastern end of Calle Leonor Pérez (Paula), overlooking the bay, is the baroque **Iglesia de San Francisco de Paula** (*see below*), unusual for its isolated location in the middle of a busy portside road. The walkway at the front of the church leads to the dockside **Alameda de Paula**, the first promenade to be constructed in La Habana Vieja. Created in 1771, it was originally a dirt track stretching three blocks and bordered by two lines of poplars. In 1805 a tiled pavement and stone seats were added; later, a fountain with a commemorative column was built in honour of the Spanish navy (only the column survives). One block south on Luz to San Pedro takes you to the stately neo-classical **Hotel Armadores de Santander** (*see p34*), built in 1827.

Casa Natal de José Martí

Calle Leonor Pérez (Paula) #314, esquina Avenida de Bélgica (Egido) (861 3778). **Open** 9am-5pm Tue-Sat; 9am-1pm Sun. **Admission** $1 ($2 with guide); free under-12s. **Map** p252 F14.

This modest dwelling, dating from 1810, was where Cuban national icon José Martí was born on 28 January 1853: the Martí family rented the upper storey. Inside are objects relating to Martí's life and work: family belongings, manuscripts, photographs and furniture.

Convento e Iglesia de La Merced

Calle Cuba #806, esquina Merced (863 8873). **Open** 8am-noon, 3-5pm daily. **Mass** 9am Mon-Sat; 9am, noon Sun. **Admission** free. **Map** p252 F15.

Built between 1755 and 1876, La Merced is arguably one Cuba's most beautiful churches. Its lavish robin-eggshell blue interior has high arches and frescoes covering the chapel and cupola. The Capilla de Lourdes (Lourdes Chapel) has an outstanding collection of religious paintings by renowned Cuban artists: Estéban Chartrand, Miguel Melero, Pidier Petit and Juan Crosa, among others. The other chapel has a peaceful grotto. The convent's serene courtyard has interesting statuary.

Convento e Iglesia de Nuestra Señora de Belén

Calle Compostela, entre Luz y Acosta (862 9615/ 861 2846). **Open** 8am-6pm Mon-Fri. **Admission** free. **Map** p252 E15.

Built in 1720 as a Franciscan convent, church and hospital for the poor, Belén was taken over by the Jesuits in the mid 19th century. The church's present appearance is the result of over two centuries of successive renovation and expansion. The unusual vaulted arch, built in 1775 over Calle Acosta to the south, connects the convent with its neighbouring buildings. The original church is now restored and open for visits, but five of the six cloisters are under restoration as an old people's home, a hostel and a junior high school.

More extraordinary is the **Real Observatorio** (Royal Observatory), built in 1858 on top of the tower of the school, and used continuously until 1925. The Jesuits were Cuba's first official weather forecasters and used the observatory for the study of hurricanes and other tropical weather patterns. The observatory was the first of its kind in the Caribbean and, over time, became one of the most important weather stations in the Americas. It's currently under restoration as the future Museo de Meteorología y Astronomía.

Convento e Iglesia de Santa Clara

Calle Cuba #610, entre Sol y Luz (861 5043/3775). **Open** 8.30am-5pm Mon-Fri. **Admission** (incl guide) $2; free under-12s. **Map** p252 E15.

Built between 1638 and 1643, Santa Clara was the city's first nunnery, with its first occupants coming from Cartagena de Indias in Colombia. It remained a working nunnery until 1922, when the nuns sold the church and convent and moved to a new site. Apparently, for the next 40 days, people visited the convent continuously to see what was behind its formerly impenetrable walls.

The simple, stark exterior of the building and its thick, rammed-earth walls bely the surprising richness of the interior, which features ornately carved wooden ceilings and beautiful leafy patios, open for visits. Two of the three cloisters are fully restored: one houses the Centro Nacional de Conservación, Restauración y Museología (CENCREM), the organisation in charge of restoring artefacts from all over Cuba; the other contains a small free-standing building run as a cheap and moderately cheerful Moorish-style *hostal*, **Residencia Académica** (*see p37*).

Iglesia de San Francisco de Paula

Avenida del Puerto, esquina Leonor Pérez (Paula) (860 4210). **Open** 8.30am-7pm daily. **Admission** *Museum* $1; free under-12s. *Concerts* $5/$10. Mass is not held in this church. **Map** p252 F15.

In 1664 a chapel and women's hospital were built on this site; both were destroyed in a hurricane in 1730 and, 15 years later, rebuilt in a baroque style. In the 1940s, despite public protest, the hospital and part of the church were torn down. It has now been restored as a concert hall; the ashes of famous Afro-Cuban violinist Claudio José Domingo Brindis de Salas are preserved here. Inside is a tiny religious art museum.

Centro Habana

Essential sights in the eastern reaches, and plenty of urban overload.

Maps p250 & p251

It is estimated that on any given day there is one person occupying every 7.5 square metres (81 square feet) of Centro Habana, making it Havana's most densely populated neighbourhood. Characterised by jam-packed multi-family buildings (known as *solares*), its shabbiness and lack of green spaces often discourage visitors, who usually only venture to the sprinkling of key sights on its eastern border. Adventurers to the depths of Centro Habana are, however, usually rewarded with a fascinating glimpse of tourist-free Cuba.

Much of Centro Habana's history is related to that of the city walls (*las murallas*), built between 1674 and 1797 to encirce the old city. Shortly after the walls were finished, a grid pattern was superimposed over an earlier haphazard development of Centro Habana, with the wealthy moving to the 'better' streets (Reina and Carlos Tercero, today Avenidas Simón Bolívar and Salvador Allende respectively) and workers settling elsewhere in apartment blocks. However, by 1863 the city had become so overcrowded that the walls began to be demolished to open up land speculation in the bordering areas. From 1880 a huge amount of building was undertaken, with construction controlled by urban ordinances. This was generally a time of effervescence and growth in Havana. Centro Habana's new look was finished in the 1920s, when French urbanist Jean Claude Nicholas Forestier was contracted to landscape the area.

From Capitolio north along El Prado

Paseo del Prado (known as 'El Prado') was the first promenade to be built outside the city walls. Completed in 1772, it was built as a place where city dwellers could stroll, socialise and catch the sea breeze. It become popular with Havana's bourgeoisie, eager to show off their fashionable European gowns and suits. El Prado was remodelled in 1834, and prominent buildings sprang up along its sides. By 1928 Forestier had introduced bronze lions, lamp-posts and marble benches to what was now a pulsing artery. These days it is an essential street for tourists, veritably packed with sights.

The domed **El Capitolio** (*see below*) dominates El Prado's southern end; politically speaking it's a blight on the capital's skyline, but it looks pretty impressive all the same, especially from the Hotel Sevilla's **Roof Garden** restaurant (*see p104*). Across the street from the Capitolio to the east is the **Sala Polivalente 'Kid Chocolate'** (*see p177*), an indoor sports arena named after Cuba's finest ever amateur boxer, winner of two world titles.

El Capitolio

Paseo de Martí (Prado), entre San Martín (San José) y Dragones (860 3411/861 0261). **Open** 8am-8pm daily. **Admission** $3; $5 with camera (incl guided tours in English); free under-12s. **Map** p251 D14.

Look familiar? This smaller clone of Washington's Capitol building was built between 1926 and 1929 by Enrique García Carrera. The 62m (207ft) dome was the highest point in the city until 1958, when it was surpassed by the José Martí monument in the Plaza de la Revolución (*see p75*). The steps up from El Prado are flanked by bronze statues from Italian sculptor Angelo Zanelli, who has another inside the foyer, which at 17.7m (58ft) tall is the world's third largest indoor statue. Although the original was recovered after being stolen long ago, the 24-carat diamond embedded in the floor in front of the statue is a replica, and marks point zero of Cuba's central highway network.

The Capitolio is a cache of pleasant surprises, from original fine art and a vast library to the unusual acoustics that reverse the sound of your footsteps in the Salón de los Pasos Perdidos (Hall of the Lost Steps). The wings on either side of the entrance hall once housed the ornate Senate and Chamber of the House of Representatives, but now governmental offices are at the Plaza de la Revolución.

Parque Central & around

Bordered by El Prado, Zulueta (Agramonte), Obrapía and Neptuno, **Parque Central** was laid out in 1877. At its centre is the 1905 statue of José Martí in Carrara marble, by José Vilalta de Saavedra – the first monument in the country dedicated to the poet, writer, lawyer and fighter for Cuban independence. He obviously inspires locals, who gather in the park under his gaze to debate passionately about baseball (*see p177* ***Esquina caliente***).

Several key hotels border the park, including the **Hotel Inglaterra** (*see p38*), whose sidewalk is paved with tiles glazed with

El Capitolio: one thing Havana and Washington have in common. *See p64.*

images from contemporary artists. Its café was a popular meeting point for youthful *habaneros* rebelling against the Spanish regime, and is still a good place to watch the action on El Prado. Opposite the north-east corner of the park is the **Hotel Plaza** (*see p39*), and on the Neptuno side is the luxury **Hotel NH Parque Central** (*see p39*), a harsh modern effort that stands at odds with its surroundings. The latest arrival is the renovated **Hotel Telegrafa** (*see p39*). On the corner of El Prado and Obrapía is the neo-baroque **Gran Teatro de La Habana** (*see p167*), with its magnificent interior monumental staircase and exterior decoration.

The northern stretch of El Prado

The **Palacio de los Matrimonios** (Prado #306, esquina Ánimas, 862 5781, closed Mon) is one of the most popular places to get married in Havana. The 1914 building is a former Spanish social club, and its upper floor is worth a peek for its deliciously ostentatious ornamentation. East along Trocadero is the stunning Moorish-style **Hotel Sevilla** (*see p39*), built in 1908 and recently restored. Al Capone and his bodyguards are reputed to have taken over the entire sixth floor on a visit here.

North on El Prado, at Trocadero, is the Casa de José Miguel Gómez (1915), once home of the Republic's first president, and now the **Casa del Científico** (*see p40*) – a hotel, restaurant and bar. It has a striking stained-glass window and an observation tower with views of El Prado. Further north, at Calle Colón, is the **Teatro Fausto** (*see p169*), with its interesting art deco-inspired exterior.

La Punta & around

Off El Prado's northern terminus is the **Castillo de San Salvador de la Punta** (*see p67*), finished in 1630. This castle, and its counterpart El Morro across the bay, was built when the Spanish realised that they had to do more to keep out marauders. It has been impressively restored and opened to visitors in 2002.

On the corner of Malecón and El Prado is the **Memorial a los Estudiantes de Medicina**, constructed around the remains of a wall used by colonial firing squads. On 27 November 1871 eight medical students were shot here by loyalist soldiers, after being falsely accused of desecrating the tomb of a Spanish journalist opposed to Cuba's independence (*see p70* **Alley of bones**).

Sightseeing

Beat it

Rumba in Cuba is a dance, as well as a type of music. Confusingly, it has little to do with rumba flamenco, and absolutely nothing to do with Latin ballroom dance. Authentic Cuban rumba is a raw call and response format in song and dance, driven by pulsating African rhythms and tinged with Hispanic influences. A direct legacy of the African slaves brought to Cuba, rumba was born in the docklands of Matanzas and Havana. It incorporates many complex rhythms played out on a range of percussion, including boxes (*cajones*), conga drums and hand-held instruments, among them the all-important *clave* (wooden sticks that beat out the syncopated rhythms). Rumba tended to be played by slaves on their days off, and was a secular manifestation of African religious traditions.

The original rhythms have now been distilled into three main rumba formats, each with its own dance form: *yambú*, the slowest, is a dance for couples in which a game of seduction is acted out but never consummated; *guaguancó*, the most popular form, is more overtly sexual, an interaction in which the man tries to catch the woman unawares; and finally, *columbia*, the most flamboyant form, is predominantly a display of male virtuosity, either a solo or a

To the south-east of the memorial is a further reminder of Havana's brutal colonial past: the remains of the **Cárcel de La Habana** (*see below*). The jail sits on the romantically named **Parque de los Enamorados** (Lovers' Park), in which there's a powerful but deteriorating statue of an Indian couple.

Presiding over the bay is the massive marble and bronze **Monumento a Máximo Gómez**. Designed by sculptor Aldo Gamba and unveiled in 1935, this striking monument honours the Dominican commander-in-chief of Cuba's Liberation Army, a key figure in Cuban independence struggles. A spiralling road leads to the underwater tunnel linking metropolitan Havana with the eastern beaches and bay.

Cárcel de La Habana

Avenida de los Estudiantes, entre Paseo de Martí (Prado) y Agramonte (Zulueta) (no phone). **Open** 9am-2pm Tue-Sat; 9am-1pm Sun. **Admission** free. **Map** p251 C15.

Many Cuban revolutionaries who fought against Spanish colonialism, including José Martí, were imprisoned here. In the early 20th century the original building was demolished except for the chapel and a couple of cells, which today host small art exhibitions. There's a modest display of photos of the cells and torture devices.

Callejón de Hamel.

gladiatorial shoot-out between a succession of male soloists. Within these formats, rumba allows for endless improvisation and other dance elements are often woven in.

Rumba is sometimes an impromptu happening, in the street or in a courtyard. However, as a visitor, your best bet is to find the regular rumba spots in Havana, where the event is more formal but does still attract at least as many Cubans as tourists. The most atmospheric is the **Callejón de Hamel** (*see p156*), where several rumba groups play on the weekends; the best known is Clave y Guaguancó, who also perform regularly at the **UNEAC** (*see p160*). Other good venues are **Centro Cultural El Gran Palenque** (*see p159*), the patio of the **Conjunto Folklórico Nacional de Cuba** (*see p172*), where Los Muñequitos de Matanzas, one of the greatest of all rumba troupes, can occasionally be seen. Folkloric troupe Raices Profundas often plays on the patio of the **Teatro Mella** (*see p169*). Younger rumba troupes Vocal Baobab and Iroso Obbá are also well worth catching. Copious quantities of rum are consumed at rumba gatherings, so things can get rather heated.

Castillo de San Salvador de la Punta

Avenida del Puerto y Paseo de Martí (Prado)(860 3196). **Open** 10am-6pm Wed-Sun. **Admission** $5; free under-12s. **Map** p251 C15.

The fort of San Salvador was designed by Giovanni Baptista Antonelli, who also designed the Castillo de los Tres Reyes del Morro (*see p88*) on the opposite side of the harbour mouth. It was commissioned by Captain General Juan de Texeda, whose name can still be seen cut into a stone in the bulwark to the right of the entrance. Every night for centuries a chain boom used to be raised between the two castles to keep out marauding shipping, and the chain's terminal on the Punta side, three massive upended cannons, can still be seen.

The British invasion in the mid 1700s seriously damaged the fort – walk around to the Morro side to see a British cannonball still embedded in the wall. (If the guards make a fuss, ask to see Echecerría the director; he'll probably escort you and give you a fascinating lecture in English on Havana's fortifications.) Despite the damage, it was still used for defence in the 19th century. By the time the 20th century came around it was anything but a protective bastion, and at one point was even used as a cow barn.

Nevertheless, a trophy restoration, finished in 2002, raised the fortress of San Salvador de la Punta to its original height by clearing out its moat, and unearthed relics spanning five centuries, many of which are exhibited in the historical gallery. On the second floor a ship gallery displays models of historic vessels. This hall also shows the urinal and toilet for troops, both interconnected to the drainage sluice from the main square, an impressive step on the road to modern plumbing.

The Treasure Gallery, unique in Latin America, holds the riches from those 16th- to 19th-century treasure galleons sunk off the Cuban coast, including gold bars, emeralds, pieces of eight and treasure boxes. Wall maps and photos of diving operations show how the booty was retrieved.

Unlike the guards' quarters upstairs, this museum's public lavatory is one of Havana's finest, with polished wooden toilet seats, suspended tanks and pull chains, plus iron-supported thick blue glass washbasins.

Museo Nacional de Bellas Artes & around

The **Museo de la Revolución** (*see below*) and Memorial Granma Palacio Presidencial (behind the museum) are essential visits for anyone wanting to get to grips with the Cuban Revolution. Across from the Granma exhibit is the Cuban wing (Arte Cubano) of the **Museo Nacional de Bellas Artes** (*see below*), which opened in 2001 after an expensive renovation. It is now easily Havana's most impressive museum. Leaving the museum by the main entrance you will see **Real Fábrica de Tabacos La Corona** (*see p69*) to your left.

Museo Nacional de Bellas Artes

Arte Cubano: *Calle Trocadero, entre Zulueta (Agramonte) y Avenida de Bélgica (Monserrate) (861 3858).* Arte Universal: *Calle San Rafael, entre Zuleta (Agramonte) y Avenida de Bélgica (Monserrate) (861 3858).* **Open** *Both* 10am-6pm Tue-Sat; 10am-2pm Sun. **Admission** *Arte Cubano* $5. *Arte Universal* $5. *Both* $8. Free under-12s. **Map** p252 D14/15.

The National Museum of Fine Arts, opened in its current location in 1954, was reopened in 2001 to unanimous applause, following a five-year closure. No expense had been spared on the renovation work, catapulting it straight into the don't-miss category. The art collection – totalling nearly 50,000 works – has been divided into two separate buildings: the Cuban art collection (Arte Cubano), which stayed in the original Palacio de Bellas Artes (1954) on Trocadero, and the international collection (Arte Universal), which was installed in the refurbished Arte Universal wing two blocks down on San Rafael, half a block east of Parque Central in the former Centro Asturiano, a beautiful early 20th-century building.

The Arte Cubano building takes in more than 30,000 works organised into sections: colonial, turn-of-the-last-century, modern and contemporary. This collection incorporates the very best of Cuban art, and is by far the most comprehensive in the country, with works by key artists, such as Amalia Páez, René Portocarrero and Wilfredo Lam, as well as more recent works by Zaida del Río and Roberto Fabelo.

The international collection (Arte Universal) is a passable survey of world art – divided by country of origin, with work ranging from the 16th century to the present – but it blanches when compared to the building itself. Its entry hall is staggering: a cavernous space with a massive staircase crowned on both sides by carved marble lions, while the celestial stained-glass ceiling depicts Columbus's arrival in the Americas. The restoration is the masterpiece of Cuban architect José Linares, a tireless visionary. The largest collections in Arte Universal are Italian, French and Spanish – and these should be the essential stops on any fleeting visit. Those with more time may want to investigate the fourth floor, dedicated to ancient art; it houses mainly Greek, Roman and Egyptian sculpture and artefacts, the most impressive being a Greek amphora from the fifth century BC in remarkably good nick. Other small collections include German, Dutch, Flemish, Latin American and US works.

Museo de la Revolución

Calle Refugio #1, Avenida de las Misiones y Agramonte (Zulueta) (861 3858). **Open** 10am-5pm daily. **Admission** $4 (incl camera); free under-12s. *Tour* $2 (English-speaking available). **Map** p252 D15.

The Museum of the Revolution is located in the elegant Palacio Presidencial, the official residence of 21 Cuban presidents between 1920 and 1965. The Revolutionary government announced its first new laws here in 1959 and continued to use the palace until 1965 when its headquarters moved to the Plaza de la Revolución. The building was turned into a museum dedicated to the Cuban Revolution in 1974.

The palace was designed by Cuban Carlos Maruri and Belgian Paul Belau, with the interior decoration entrusted to Tiffany of New York. Highlights of the interior include the Salón de los Espejos, which is a replica of the Hall of Mirrors in the Palace of Versailles. The Salón Dorado (Golden Hall) is made of yellow marble with gold embossing on the walls, and there are four canvases by Esteban Valderrama and Mariano Miguel González mounted on 18-carat gold sheets. There are permanent exhibitions on the history of Cuban struggles from the 15th century to the present, including Che Guevara's pipe and the uniform of Cuban cosmonaut Arnaldo Tamayo.

One hall is dedicated to the so-called Special Period (*see p16* **Special times**), the emergency plan taken on by Cuba in the early 1990s when the collapse of the Soviet Union took away 85% of the island's trade to devastating effect. Bullet holes from a failed coup carried out by students in 1957 are still visible in the Palacio's main stairway.

Behind the museum (and included in the ticket price) is an exhibit of the *Granma* yacht, in which Fidel and 81 others sailed from Tuxpán, Mexico, to Cuba in December 1956 to launch the Revolution. The boat, displayed behind glass, is surrounded by planes, vehicles and weapons used during the Revolutionary

Museo Nacional de Bellas Artes – the belle of them all. *See p68.*

wars against Batista and in the Battle of Playa Girón (Bay of Pigs). A major overhaul is scheduled in the near future, but the museum won't close.

Real Fábrica de Tabacos La Corona

Calle Agramonte (Zulueta) #106, entre Refugio y Colón (862 6173). **Open** 9am-3pm Mon-Fri. **Admission** (incl tour) $10; free under-12s. **Map** p252 D15.

Built in 1888 by the American Tobacco Company, this factory now offers a behind-the-scenes look at cigar making, and a shop.

South of the Capitolio

The land immediately south of the Capitolio was originally Campo de Marte, an 18th-century drill square. In 1892 it was renamed Parque Cristóbal Colón to commemorate the fourth centennial of the discovery of America, and in 1928 became the **Parque de la Fraternidad**. The new park was designed, in accordance with Forestier's plans, for the sixth Pan-American Conference. A silk cotton tree, the so-called 'Tree of American Fraternity', was planted in the centre of the park with soil from 21 countries of the Americas, and busts were erected of North and South American independence heroes: Abraham Lincoln, Simón Bolívar, Benito Juárez and others. The streets around the park are some of the best spots to see Havana's 'mobile museum' – American cars from the late 1940s and early '50s, now mostly privately operated taxis.

The south-west corner is overlooked by the impressive neo-classical **Palacio de Domingo Aldama** (Calle Amistad #510, entre Reina y Estrella, 862 2076-9, closed Sat, Sun). Built in 1844 by prestigious architect Manuel José Carrera, it is actually two large mansions built together to appear as one grand structure. Visitors are welcome to see the staircases, ironwork and ornamental fountains. North of here, on Calle Industria, is the stunning neo-baroque **Real Fábrica de Tabacos**

Partagás (*see below*). The H Upmann cigar plant on Amistad has now been moved to Vedado (*see p77*). South-east of the Capitolio is the Asociación Cultural Yoruba de Cuba and its **Museo de los Orishas** (*see below*).

Museo de los Orishas

Paseo de Martí (Prado) #615, entre Máximo Gómez (Monte) y Dragones (863 5953). **Open** 9am-5pm daily. **Admission** $6; free under-12s. **Map** p251 E14.

Opened in 2000 by a group of enterprising *babalaos* (experts in divination), this is the first museum in the world dedicated to the *orishas* (gods) of the Yoruba pantheon. Its larger-than-life terracotta *orishas* have large painted backdrops showing the natural environment and attributes connected with each one. Descriptions are (unusually) in Spanish, English and French. Because it's a bona fide NGO, it depends on its income and charges more than state museums. For more on Afro-Cuban religion, *see p91* **Keeping the faith**.

Real Fábrica de Tabacos Partagás

Calle Industria #520, entre Dragones y Barcelona (862 008). **Open** 9.30-11am, 12.30-3pm Mon-Fri. **Admission** (incl tour) $10; free under-12s. **Map** p251 E14.

This factory has been producing fine cigars for more than 150 years, and offers the most insightful cigar tour in Havana. An English-speaking guide is always available, and the cigar shop is one of the most popular in the city.

Southern Centro Habana

Officially part of the Cerro district, but on Centro Habana's southernmost boundary, is the **Cuatro Caminos** (Four Roads) market. The country's largest indoor agricultural market since 1920, it stands at the juncture of four districts.

Mercado Cuatro Caminos

Calle Máximo Gómez (Monte), entre Arroyo (Manglar) y Matadero (860 9608). **Open** 9am-9pm daily. **Map** p250 F12.

The country's largest indoor agricultural market is full of bustle, excitement and smells. *Habaneros* come here to buy live goats and hens, takeaway meals and a tantalising array of tropical fruit and vegetables. An interesting detour. For more on the city's fruit and vegetable markets *see p125* **Getting agro**.

Around Salvador Allende (Carlos III)

The Jesús Rodríguez **chess hall** on Calle Soledad (entre Neptuno y San Miguel) gives a glimpse of Havana's favourite game in action. To the west, on Avenida Reina, lies the neo-Gothic **Convento e Iglesia del Sagrado Corazón de Jesús e Ignacio de Loyola** (*see p71*).

Alley of bones

On the north end of Calle Aramburu, a couple of blocks up from San Lázaro (map p250 C12), is the only remaining section of the **Espada cemetery** (1804). All that is left is a small segment of wall that once housed coffins and the eerie indentations that still remain. This was the Villa de San Cristóbal's (Havana's former name) first cemetery, and the bodies had filled up several city blocks before it was decided to build vertically.

In the middle of the wall fragment, there's a plaque memorial to Georg Weerth, a 'poet of the German proletariat' and friend of Carl Marx and Engels. Mr Weerth came to Cuba in 1853, and decided to stay in Havana, but fell victim to yellow fever in 1856 and was buried in the cemetery in the foreigners' section (the third category after whites and blacks). His body is long gone because no family member came to pick it up when the cemetery relocated to the Colón cemetery (*see p77*) in Vedado in 1908. Local sources say many of the crowded graves were not handled properly during the move and even today, if the tarmac is scraped back, bones can be unearthed. Juan Marino, a Cuban intellectual moved by Weerth's story, erected a memorial in 1963. Every fourth Saturday of the month at 3pm there is a poetry recital and singing in front of the wall where the memorial is, a part of the cemetery now known as Poets' Alley.

The Espada cemetery was also linked to an alleged crime that led to the execution of eight medical students. The students were condemned for desecrating a cemetery tomb, that of Spanish journalist and known agitator Gonzalo Castañon, who had been killed in Key West, Florida, the previous year. The students were executed by a Spanish firing squad in 1871. The **Memorial a los Estudiantes de Medicina** (*see p65*) now stands in their memory. Tragically, ten years after the execution, Castañon's son inspected the site, and signed an affidavit that said the tomb had never been damaged.

Convento e Iglesia del Sagrado Corazón de Jesús e Ignacio de Loyola

Avenida Reina, entre Belascoaín y Gervasio (862 4979/2149/2129). **Open** 8am-noon, 3-6pm daily. *Mass* 8am, 4.30pm Mon-Sat; 8am, 9.30am, 4.30pm Sun. **Admission** free. **Map** p250 D12.

This church was constructed between 1914 and 1923, and is one of Havana's most magnificent. Its tower is over 77m (257ft) tall and topped by a bronze cross, with 32 gargoyles and a variety of statuettes. The inside is lit by 69 spectacular stained-glass windows.

Chinatown

Cuba's Chinatown, or **el barrio chino**, is centred around calles Zanja and Dragones in the heart of Centro Habana, and was once the most economically important in Latin America. The first Asian slaves arrived in 1847 to work in the sugar industry, and at its height Havana's Chinese community numbered 130,000 people. Many Chinese Cubans left the country after 1959. However, the remaining Chinese and their descendants maintain a distinct community and Chinatown is now home to numerous traditional Chinese associations, a Chinese-language newspaper, restaurants (*see p102* **Chinatown**) and a pharmacy (Zanja, entre Manrique y San Nicolás) with natural medicines. Chinese New Year is celebrated here every year, with traditional dragon and lion dances. In 1995 the government approved the creation of a state business entity with the goal of promoting the recovery of Chinese arts and traditions, resulting in a rejuvenation of the district. On the south-western edge of the *barrio* is the charming **Iglesia Nuestra Señora Caridad del Cobre**.

Iglesia Nuestra Señora Caridad del Cobre

Calle Manrique #570, esquina Salud (861 0945). **Open** 7.30am-6pm Tue-Fri; 7.30am-noon Sat; 7.30am-noon, 4-6pm Sun. **Admission** free. **Map** p251 D13.

Built in 1802 and completely restored in the early 1950s, this church has a gold-plated altar, lovely statuary, stained-glass windows and two grottos.

Along the Malecón & Calle San Lázaro

The **Malecón** seaside promenade was constructed between 1901 and 1954 to maximise access to the seafront. Now a 24-hour source of adventure, it gives vital breathing (and kissing) space for *habaneros*. Inland on Trocadero, at the corner of Industria, is the **Casa Museo José Lezama Lima** (863 3774), currently closed but scheduled to reopen in 2004. The poet and novelist lived here from 1929 until his death in 1976.

Moving west will bring you to the *barrio* known as **Cayo Hueso**, roughly bordered by Padre Varela (Belascoaín), Zanja, Infanta and Malecón, and the second community to establish itself outside the city walls. It is said that its name comes from the phonetic corruption of the English 'Key West', spoken by returning Cubans who settled in this neighbourhood. Many of these were former tobacco industry lords who had fled the island in 1857 after the economic crash, but returned after the War of Independence at the turn of the last century.

The recently restored **Parque Maceo**, by the waterfront at the northern end of Calle Padre Varela (Belascoaín), has new fountains and benches, plus lush Chinese grass. In it stands a monument to Lieutenant-General Antonio Maceo, known as the 'Bronze Titan', who survived 24 bullet wounds before he was killed in action in 1896. At the western end of the park is the **Torreón de San Lázaro**, the oldest monument in area, a little circular watchtower built in 1665 to overlook the former cove of San Lázaro (*la caleta*), a frequent landing site for pirates.

The forge where José Martí toiled as a teenager, sentenced to hard labour by the Spanish, is located on . It is now the **Museo Fragua Martiana** (Calle Príncipe #108, esquina Hospital, 870 7338, closed Sat, Sun), and features some of the national hero's belongings, including a revolver, prisoner chains, jail clothes and texts.

On Infanta and San Lázaro is the cement **Parque de los Mártires Universitarios**, created in 1967 to honour university students involved in Cuba's independence struggles. On Infanta, between Neptuno and Concordia, lies the baroque **Convento e Iglesia del Carmen** (878 5168); its tower is topped by a gracious 7.5-metre tall sculpture of *Our Lady of Carmen*, made in Naples in 1886. Also on Infanta is the **Convento y Capilla de la Inmaculada Concepción** (*see below*), with its attractive chapel.

Search the streets south-west of the convent for **Callejón de Hamel** (*see p156*), a small pedestrian street one block south of San Lázaro. Its buildings are covered with murals depicting Afro-Cuban *orishas* and allegories by renowned Cuban artist Salvador González Escalona. This is one of the best places to see rumba in Havana. *See p66* **Beat it**.

Convento y Capilla de la Inmaculada Concepción

Calle San Lázaro #805 (ring bell), entre Oquendo y Marqués González (878 8404). **Open** 8am-5pm Mon-Fri; 5-7pm Sat; 8-11am Sun. **Admission** free. **Map** p252 C13.

A private girls' school until 1961, visitors are these days welcome to visit the patio and chapel, with a delicate wooden ceiling, stained-glass windows and a painted altar.

Vedado

Havana's cultural hotspot is a jewel of urban planning, with leafy boulevards and sumptuous mansions.

Map p250

With its high density of artistic institutions, museums, clubs and theatres, Vedado is a key social and cultural hub. A shame, then, that it's so often overlooked by tourists who make a beeline for La Habana Vieja, missing out on the more cosmopolitan feel of Vedado. In fact, the two areas couldn't be more different – Old Havana is packed tight to bursting, while Vedado boasts grand houses set back from the road with verandas and gardens in front.

Once an area of dense woods and limestone hillocks, in the 17th-century Vedado (meaning 'forbidden zone') became a military area closed to civilians in a drive to defend Old Havana against pirates. By the 19th century, after the limestone outcroppings had practically disappeared as stone for construction, Vedado began slowly to be populated. The economic boom of the early 20th century, when US money (some of which came from US gangsters) flooded in after the end of the Spanish-American wars, led to an explosion in construction that was to make Vedado the neo-classical and eclectic showpiece of Havana.

Today, the area has the highest concentration of high-rises in the city and is an interesting mix of neo-classical and Italian-style mansions and eclectic, art deco and modern buildings. Vedado was the first part of Havana to be developed with a uniform urban plan: grids of measured blocks; tree-lined streets oriented to catch cooling ocean breezes; and numerous parks. It was also the first district to have lettered and numbered streets, making it easy to navigate.

La Rampa

Vibrant and bustling at any time of the day or night, La Rampa – the steep stretch of Calle 23 between Calle L and the Malecón – is the best place to start exploring Vedado. In the 1950s these five blocks replaced the Prado in Centro Habana as the most popular place for Havana high life. Today, La Rampa still buzzes with bars, discos, cinemas, restaurants and hotels, an excellent jazz club, **La Zorra y el Cuervo**, and the city's largest and most popular ice-cream parlour, **Coppelia** (Calle 23, esquina L, closed Mon). Designed by architect Mario Girona in 1966, Coppelia was intended to be the 'ice-cream parlour of the people', and featured in the opening scenes of Tomás Gutiérrez Alea's film *Fresa y Chocolate*. Note that the impossibly long queues are to pay in pesos, but if you want to say you've been to Coppelia but don't want to queue for three days, head for the kiosks outside or the dollar section inside. Nearby is the 27-storey landmark **Hotel Habana Libre** (1958; *see p41*), which was built by an American firm as the Havana Hilton just before the Castro took over. In 1960 it was nationalised and renamed. In fact, immediately after seizing Havana, Fidel and Che took over a whole floor as a command post. Over the front entrance is an immense abstract tiled mural by Cuban artist Amelia Peláez. Along La Rampa, you'll find business offices, ministries and international airline agencies (near the Malecón), plus a *feria artesanal* (crafts fair) between L and M selling handicrafts. Opposite is the **Pabellón Cuba** (Calle N #266, 832 9056/9110, closed Mon), an exhibition hall built in 1963 that hosts cultural activities and exhibitions all year round.

Just off La Rampa, with its grand, palm-lined entrance on Calle O, is one of the most celebrated hotels in the city, the **Hotel Nacional de Cuba** (*see p42*). Built in 1930 to accommodate US tourists attracted by Havana's gambling opportunities, it was once the preferred lodging for Winston Churchill and Mafia king Meyer Lansky (*see p44* **So long, wise guys**). The hotel occupies a commanding position on Taganana Hill, the site of the 18th-century Santa Clara Gun Battery. Two cannons – a German Krupp and an immense Ordonez, once the largest in the world, with a ten-kilometre (six-mile) range – are still here. Non-residents are free to roam the gardens, and its terrace bar is one of the finest places to sip mojitos in town (*see p115*).

At the bottom of La Rampa, two blocks south of the Nacional on Calle O, is the **Casa-Museo Abel Santamaría** (*see below*), and on the ground floor of the same building is a well-stocked peso bookstore.

Casa-Museo Abel Santamaría

Calle 25 #164, entre O e Infanta (870 0417).
Open 10am-5pm Mon-Fri; 10am-1.30pm Sat.
Admission free. **Map** p250 B12.

La Rampa (*see p72*) area, crowned by the twin towers of the Hotel Nacional.

Inside apartment 604 (on the sixth floor; there are two lifts), Fidel Castro and Abel Santamaría spent 14 months planning the 26 July 1953 assault on the Moncada Barracks in Santiago de Cuba. The small apartment, still with its original furnishings, seems an unlikely starting point for events that shaped the history of a nation.

University & around

On Calle L, three blocks south of 23, is the monumental 88-step *escalinata* (staircase) leading up to the **Universidad de La Habana**, sitting atop Aróstegui Hill like an acropolis. The welcoming *Alma Mater* sculpture halfway up the stairs was made in 1919 by Czech artist Mario Korbel. Facing the base of the stairway, in an amphitheatre-like area often used for political rallies, is the **Memorial a Julio Antonio Mella**, which holds the ashes of the young student leader and founder of the University Student Federation (1923) and the Communist Party of Cuba (1925). In 1929 Mella was assassinated while in exile in Mexico. At the bottom of the hill is Calle Infanta, which marks the limit between Vedado and Centro Habana.

Within the university grounds are two unusual museums: the **Museo de Ciencias Naturales Felipe Poey** and the **Museo Antropológico Montané** (for both, *see p74*), both located in the Escuela de Ciencias (Science Department), which has a magnificent, leafy inner courtyard. Two blocks south of the stairway is the eclectic Casa de Orestes Ferrara (1928), which has, since 1961, housed the **Museo Napoleónico** (*see p74*), with its extraordinary collection of Napoleonic and French Revolutionary artefacts. Continuing south past the large **Estadio Universitario Juan Abrahantes** (University Stadium) and on to Calle Zapata is a splendid view to the west of the white chalk sides and shady old jagüey trees of Aróstegui Hill.

After Zapata crosses Avenida de los Presidentes (Calle G), you can glimpse the small 18th-century **Castillo del Príncipe**, built after the British invasion of 1762. This fortress (off-limits to the public) is unique in Cuba for its partially vaulted tunnel, which allowed protected movement about the castle.

North of the castle on Avenida de los Presidentes (Calle G), at Calle 27, is the semicircular Italian marble **Monumento a José Miguel Gómez** (1936). Designed by Italian artist Giovanni Nicolini, the monument has bas-reliefs showing important moments in the life of Gómez, who was president of Republican Cuba from 1909 to 1913.

Back at the castle and east along Avenida Salvador Allende (formerly Avenida Carlos III) is **Quinta de los Molinos** (1837), the summer residence of the captains general of Cuba. Máximo Gómez, general-in-chief of the Liberation Army, also stayed here in 1895. The house, named after the two tobacco mills (*molinos*), is now the **Casa-Museo Máximo Gómez** (879 8850). Currently being restored, there was no reopening date set at press time. The ornamental tropical gardens that front the house were transplanted from an earlier site on El Prado and contain fountains, artificial hillocks, mini waterfalls, pergolas and grottos. To arrange a walk around the grounds, phone 879 8175. One of Havana's key music venues, **La Madriguera** (*see pp153-65*), is also located here, home to the Asociación Hermanos Saíz, which represents young musicians, writers, artists and poets. Musicians can often be heard practising in the gardens.

Museo de Ciencias Naturales Felipe Poey & Museo Antropológico Montané

Facultad de Matemáticas y Cibertica, Escuela de Ciencias, Universidad de La Habana, Avenida de la Universidad, esquina J (879 3488). **Open** 9am-noon, 1-4pm Mon-Fri. Closed Aug. **Admission** $1; free under-12s. **Map** p250 C11.

Downstairs in the handsome Escuela de Ciencias is the Museum of Natural Sciences Felipe Poey (1874); named after an eminent 19th-century naturalist (his death mask is on display), this is the oldest museum in Cuba. Displays include Cuban flora and fauna – plenty of stuffed animals – and a fine collection of multicoloured Polymita snail shells. Upstairs, the Museo Antropológico Montané (1903) has a rich collection of pre-Columbian pottery and idols. Another highlight is a tenth-century Taíno tobacco idol from the Guantánamo Province, used to crush tobacco leaves in religious ceremonies.

Museo Napoleónico

Calle San Miguel #1159, entre Ronda y Masón (879 1460/12). **Open** 10am-5.30pm Mon-Sat. **Admission** $3; $2 tour; free under-12s. **Map** p250 C11.

This is the finest collection of Napoleonic and French Revolutionary memorabilia outside France. Assembled by Orestes Ferrara, adviser to President Gerardo Machado and ambassador to Washington, DC and Rome, the collection includes the emperor's death mask, his gold-handled toothbrush, a lock of hair, Napoleonic art works by famous European artists and a farewell note written by Marie Antoinette to her children on the day of her execution. Also check out the stunning mahogany-panelled dining room and library.

Universidad de La Habana

Avenida de la Universidad, esquina J (878 3231/ authorisation for photos within buildings 832 9844). **Open** 8am-5.30pm Mon-Fri. **Admission** free. **Map** p250 C11.

Built between 1906 and 1940 around a central quadrant, this majestic neo-classical walled complex contains numerous interesting buildings. These include the Aula Magna (Main Hall, 1906-11, usually only open for important events), with its exquisite murals painted in 1910 by Armando Menocal, and the late art deco library (1937). The tranquil shady campus replaced the original university in Old Havana, dating from 1728, which was knocked down during Batista's presidency to make way for a helipad.

Plaza de la Revolución

Rising above the city on Catalanes Hill, the **Plaza de la Revolución** (until 1959, called Plaza Cívica) – measuring one kilometre in length – is Cuba's political centre. Paseo leads directly south on to this bleak square, a huge asphalt wasteland that badly lacks shade. Nevertheless, given its political importance, it's an essential stop on any sightseeing itinerary. It's also a key location for May Day marches and other festivities, and was also where the Pope celebrated a mass during his first visit to Cuba in January 1998.

The first large modern buildings were constructed around the square in the early 1950s under Batista. With the notable exception of the **Teatro Nacional** and the **Biblioteca Nacional** (1957), they are all government buildings, including the ministries of the Interior (1953), Communications (1954), Defence (1960) and Economy and Planning (1960). Most important is the Palacio Presidencial (1958), on the south side of the plaza, which houses the Council of State, the Council of Ministers, the headquarters of the Cuban Communist Party and Castro's Presidential Office.

The awesome **Memorial y Museo a José Martí** (*see below*), constructed during the 1950s to designs by Aquiles Maza and Juan José Sicre, is the centrepiece of the square. Looking west from the top of the memorial you can see **Plaza Organopónico**, a 0.6-hectare (1.5-acre) mini-farm with neat rows of raised beds planted with seasonal vegetables. Located just a few blocks from the towering memorial, city residents buy the day's harvests at the little stand (open 8.30am-5pm daily) on Calle Colón at the corner with Calle Hidalgo.

Attracting as much attention as Martí's memorial is the steel silhouette of **Ernesto 'Che' Guevara** on the façade of the Ministry of the Interior on the north-west side of the square. The world-famous image – and prime photo opportunity – comes from the iconographic photograph of the revolutionary by Alberto 'Korda' Gutiérrez. Nearby is **Teatro Nacional de Cuba** (1958; *see p168*), one of the city's most important venues. The stark, imposing façade conceals two performance spaces, a piano bar and the animated Café Cantante (*see pp153-165*).

The theatre is surrounded by abundant gardens, decorated with ponds, winding paths and sculptures by Cuban artists.

In the otherwise monotonous Ministerio de la Informática y las Comunicaciones on the north-east side of the square is the fabulous **Museo Postal Cubano José Luis Guerra Aguiar** (*see below*), a little-known gem for philately types. Just north is the **Sala Polivalente Ramón Fonst** (1991), a sports centre that houses the **Museo Nacional del Deporte**, closed for repairs until August 2004.

Memorial y Museo José Martí

Plaza de la Revolución (592351/fax 860 5846/ memorial@etecsa.cu). **Open** 9am-5pm Mon-Sat. **Admission** *Museum* (incl optional tour, English-speaking guides) $3; free under-12s. *Mirador* $2. **Map** p250 D/E9.

The heart of this memorial – a gleaming white, 18m (58ft) marble sculpture of a contemplative Martí – was carved on site by Juan José Sicre. The statue sits on a vast base that provides an impressive podium for political rallies. Behind the statue is a soaring grey marble tower, 109m (350ft) high, with a star-shaped base. At the top is a *mirador*, which is the highest viewing point in Havana, allowing visitors an unrivalled panorama of the city. Inside the tower's base is a museum devoted to Martí – writer, anti-colonialist thinker and martyr to Cuban nationalism – and the achievements of the Revolution. The exhibitions, sometimes self-congratulatory but undeniably impressive, include a large collection of photographic material on Martí's life, plus information and resources on the construction of the square, and the historical events that have occurred on it. One room has rotating exhibitions by Cuban artists, and there's also a small concert chamber in the building. Bizarrely, you have to pay for the museum and the *mirador*, even if you only want to see the *mirador* – but not vice versa.

Breaktime at the **Universidad de la Habana**. *See 74.*

Museo Postal Cubano José Luis Guerra Aguiar

Avenida de la Independencia (Rancho Boyeros), esquina 19 de Mayo (881 5551). **Open** 9am-5pm Mon-Fri. **Admission** $1 ($3 with tour in Spanish). **Map** p250 D10.

Displays, with written explanations in Spanish and English, cover Cuba's postal history from 1648 to the present day. Among the highlights: the first books in the world published on philately; a rare 1850 English 'penny black'; the first stamp circulated in Cuba from 1855; the fairly complete remains of the first 'Postal Rocket' – loaded with letters in its nose cone – launched in Cuba (and the world) in 1939; the First Day Cover stamped in space during the 1980 flight of cosmonauts Arnaldo Tamayo (Cuban) and Yuri Romanenko (Russian); plus examples of every Cuban stamp ever printed. The museum's shop sells a wide variety of Cuban stamps.

Sala Polivalente Ramón Fonst/ Museo Nacional del Deporte

Avenida de la Independencia (Rancho Boyeros), entre Bruzón y 19 de Mayo (Sala Polivalente 881 1011/ 4296/4196/museum 881 4696/882 0068/museo@ inder.co.cu). **Admission** $1 sports events; $2 museum (closed at time of writing).

The sports centre is open for basketball, gymnastic and karate and other sporting events. The museum is closed for repairs until August 2004, but until this date smaller exhibitions can be found at the Villa Panamericana (*see p181*), the Ciudad Deportiva (*see p177*), the Hotel Sevilla in Centro Habana (*see p39*) and ExpoCuba (*see p49*).

Calle 23

Calle 23 stretches across Vedado from east to west, a defining artery in terms of character and geography. From the modern-day buzz and '50s high-rises of La Rampa, Calle 23 soon enters a mixture of low-rise apartment buildings, parks

Just like starting over

At the inauguration of a statue of John Lennon in Havana in December 2000, to mark the 20th anniversary of his death, Fidel Castro declared, 'There are vindications that are just.' He was referring, of course, to his sizeable cultural U-turn; in its heyday the Beatles' music was seen by the Cuban authorities as a symbol of youthful rebellion and ideological deviation, and therefore antipathetic to the Revolution. These days veteran leaders on the island cannot but feel uncomfortable when they recall how the Fab Four's music was censored in Cuba until 1966, when a Beatles' song was played for the first time on the radio, signalling the start of an ideological thaw.

Beatlemania was not, however, their sole target; rock fans in general were persecuted for being part of the 1960s youth culture, which was – somewhat ironically considering all those Che Guevara posters hanging on Western walls – viewed as reactionary in Cuba. Men with long hair were stopped by patrols and had their manes sliced off in the nearest barber shop. Then there was the 'lemon test': if the patrol couldn't get a lemon to drop through the leg of your jeans, out came the scissors again, this time for a spot of on-the-spot tailoring. And then it was off to the UMAP (Military Production Support Unit) for 'rehabilitation'.

But by the start of the '90s official attitudes had changed dramatically, to the extent that the UNEAC (National Union of Writers and Artists) felt confident enough to launch a series of colloquiums on the impact of the Beatles' music. Around the same time the first Cuban concert was held in homage to John Lennon, in the very park where his statue is now located.

Since the bronze life-size statue of the former Beatles member was inaugurated in 2000 it has been the focus of continuous attention in this previously quiet and unknown park in Vedado. The Cuban sculptor José Villa Soberón designed the statue in such a way as to invite the viewer to take a seat next to it and even address a few words to Lennon, whose gaze is uncannily commanding.

The artist aimed to perpetuate the memory of John Lennon just as his fans remember him: no marble pedestal, just a natural pose with long hair, jeans, boots and the emblematic glasses. And at his feet is inscribed (in Spanish): 'You may say that I'm a dreamer but I'm not the only one.'

Appropriately enough, the statue was unveiled by the internationally famous Cuban singer-songwriter Silvio Rodríguez, one of the founders of the *nueva trova* movement on the island and a well-known Beatles fan.

While the statue itself is unlikely to be lifted, since it weighs over two tonnes, Lennon's glasses have been stolen twice and this third pair is already loose. There is now round-the-clock vigilance and, while visitors are encouraged to sit by Lennon and to leave flowers on his lap, contact with the statue itself is frowned upon.
Parque Lennon, Calle 17, entre 6 y 8, Vedado. **Map** p250 B9.

and commercial areas along its central stretch. In a small park at 23 and J, Cervantes fans will find an unusual nude and skinny statue of **Don Quixote** mounted on his rail-thin steed Rocinante. A few blocks further west are several reconstruction projects in progress under the City Historian's Office: the future **Casa-Museo de Arquitectura y Mobiliaria** (Calle 23 #864, information 862 1636), between D and E, will contain exhibits on architecture and furniture. The façade and interior show striking examples of elaborate moulded wall reliefs. At the intersection of 23 and B, on the south side, a splendid 1923 mansion is being renovated as a future youth centre.

Further west on 23, at the intersection with Calle 12, is Vedado's second vibrating nerve centre (after 23 and L), with restaurants, cafés, peso shops, art galleries, cinemas and the headquarters of the **Instituto Cubano del Arte e Industria Cinematográficos**. One block south of 23, on Calle 12, is Zapata, where you'll find the main entrance to the **Cementerio Colón** (*see below*), an extraordinary city of the dead on the southern limits of Vedado. Following Zapata west around the periphery of Colón to Calle 26 is the **Cementerio Chino** (*see below*). Following Zapata east to the intersection with Paseo is the often-missed **Memorial a Ethel y Julius Rosenberg**. Sculpted by Cuban artist José Delarra, it honours the American couple who died in the electric chair in Sing Sing prison, New York, in 1953, after being falsely accused of giving the Russians the secret of the atom bomb. Every year, on 19 June – the day of their execution – Cubans gather here for a modest remembrance ceremony.

Back on Calle 23, between 14 and 16, is a new **cigar factory** (yet to be named; 835 1371), which was in the final stages of renovation at the time of writing. You'll easily recognise it as it occupies a full block and is painted a soft yellow colour. The famous old H Upmann cigar company in Centro Habana will be relocating to this site.

The quieter western end of 23 is a residential neighbourhood of large individual properties, which extends as far as Río Almendares, the boundary between Vedado and Miramar.

Cementerio Chino

Calle 26, entre 28 y 33 (to arrange visits 832 1050). **Admission** free. **Map** p249 D7.

Dating from the 19th-century Qing dynasty, this Chinese cemetery has Asian-style lion statues and brightly coloured burial chapels, as well as Western classical and Christian influences. Although not usually open to the public, visits can be arranged (groups only) by contacting the offices of Cementerio Colón.

Cementerio Colón

Calle Zapata y Calle 12 (833 4196). **Open** 9am-5pm daily. **Admission** $1 (incl optional tour); free under-12s. **Map** p250 C9.

A dazzling miniature city of creamy marble, glittering bronze, angels, crosses and rich symbolism, Cementerio Colón was designed by Spanish architect Calixto de Loira and built between 1871 and 1886, on 55 hectares (136 acres) of former farm land. Laid out in a grid divided by *calles* and *avenidas*, with the octagonal **Capilla Central** (central chapel) at its heart, the cemetery has monuments, tombs and statues by outstanding 19th- and 20th-century artists. Plots were assigned according to social class, and soon became a means for patrician families to display their wealth and power with ever more elaborate tombs and mausoleums.

The main entrance is marked by a grandiose gateway decorated with biblical reliefs and topped by a marble sculpture by José Vilalta de Saavedra, *Faith, Hope and Charity*. Some of the most important and elaborate tombs lie between the main gate and the Capilla Central: the **Capilla del Amor** (Chapel of Love) built by Juan Pedro Baró for his beloved wife Catalina Laza; the exquisite **Monumento a los Bomberos** (Firemen's Monument) built by Spanish sculptor Agustin Querol and architect Julio M Zapata to commemorate the 28 firemen who died when a hardware shop in La Habana Vieja caught fire in 1890; and probably the most visited grave in the cemetery, **La Milagrosa** (The Miraculous One), the final resting place for Amelia Goryi de Hoz who died in childbirth in 1901 and was buried here with her stillborn baby at her feet. When her tomb was opened some years later, the dead child was found in Amelia's arms. Ever since, the mother has been the centre of popular myth, and is celebrated as the Miraculous One, symbolising eternal hope.

A huge number of famous Cubans have also found their final resting place here, including General Máximo Gómez, novelist Alejo Carpentier, composer Hubert de Blanck and countless martyrs to the Revolution. Start your visit at the information office (right of the main entrance), where you can enlist the services of an excellent English-speaking guide.

Central Vedado

Running south through the heart of Vedado from the Malecón, **Avenida de los Presidentes** and **Paseo** are like two fancy wide ribbons, with large trees on both sides and down their middle, and bordered by some of the most upmarket mansions in the area. Cutting across these avenues are key east–west streets such as **Línea**, **17** and **23**.

Cuban writer Alejo Carpentier called Calle 17 'the gallery of sumptuous residences', and it's easy to see why. Check out the grand house at No.301 (1915), now the **Instituto Cubano de Amistad con los Pueblos** (ICAP), which was designed by American architect Thomas Hastings. Immediately west, at No.354, is the former residence of banker Juan Gelats. This 1920 building, with its white marble spiral staircase and lovely stained-glass window, is now the base of the **National Union of Writers and Artists of Cuba** (UNEAC). Further west on the corner of Calle 17 and E is the **Museo Nacional de Artes Decorativas** (*see below*), housed in the beautiful Casa de José Gómez Mena (1927). At Calle 19 and B you'll find one of Havana's many typical open-air vegetable markets (*see p126* **Getting agro**).

A couple of blocks west on 19, at the corner of E, is a splendid mansion that is being renovated as the **Casa-Museo Dulce María Loynaz** (1902-97), where one of Cuba's important literary figures lived and wrote. Ranked among the top poets of the Spanish-speaking world, Loynaz's home was also the scene of get-togethers for distinguished Cuban and foreign writers. Renovation work should be completed in early 2004; call 552236 for information.

Just south of the junction of Calle 17 and Paseo is the Casa de Juan Pedro Baró. In 1995 the house became the much-loved **Casa de la Amistad** (*see below*), used for cultural and recreational activities, and housing several eateries. Three blocks further west on Calle 17, at 6, is a neighbourhood park recently renamed **Parque Lennon**. This area was a popular scene for rock and Beatles' fans back in the day, and a life-size statue of John Lennon, made by Cuban sculptor José Villa Soberón, was unveiled here on 8 December 2000, marking the 20th anniversary of his assassination in New York. *See p76* **Just like starting over**. Bordering the park is the **Unión Francesa de Cuba** (Calle 17 #861, esquina 6, 832 4493), a cultural society founded by French immigrants in 1925 and today representing some 600 members. Located in an early 20th-century mansion, the building includes a tiny gallery, restaurants (*see p108*) and a rooftop with fine views of the area.

Mind my wings.
Cementerio Colón. *See p77.*

Casa de la Amistad

Calle Paseo #406, entre 17 y 19 (831 2823/830 3114/3115). **Open** *Casa* 9am-6pm Mon-Sat. *July-Aug* Mon eve, Thu eve. *Restaurants* 11am-midnight Mon-Fri; 11am-2am Sat; 11am-6pm Sun. **Admission** $5 Tue eve, Sat eve; otherwise free. **Map** p250 B9.

Built in 1926 by Don Pedro Baró for his beloved wife Catalina Laza, this mansion – designed by Cuban architects Govantes and Cabarrocas – combines an Italian Renaissance exterior with a modern art deco interior. Sand from the banks of the Nile, crystal from France and Carrara marble from Italy were used in its construction. The former library is now a cigar shop and the lush gardens are one of Vedado's most captivating spots for live music. *See also pp153-65.*

Museo Nacional de Artes Decorativas

Calle 17 #502, esquina E (830 9848/8037/ 832 0924). **Open** 11am-6pm Tue-Sat; 9.30am-1pm Sun. **Admission** $2; $3 tour (English-speaking guides available); free under-12s. **Map** p250 B10.

This beautiful museum, equipped with one of the most attractive staircases to be found in Cuban residential architecture, has interior decoration by

Jansen of Paris and French mahogany carpentry. The first floor has rococo Louis XV period furniture, tapestries, paintings, a Regency-style dining room with walls covered in Italian marble, and paintings by Hubert Robert, among others. The second floor has collections of Chantilly and Meissen porcelain, and Chinese crystal and decorative panels from China.

UNEAC

Casa de Juan Gelats, Calle 17 #354, esquina H (832 4551-3). **Open** 8am-5pm Mon-Fri. *Bookshop* Sept-June 9am-5pm Mon-Fri. July, Aug 9am-5pm Fri, Sun. *Performances* 5pm Wed; 8.30pm-2am Sat (cabaret; no shorts, no children). **Admission** free. *Performances* $5. **Map** p250 B11.

The National Union of Writers and Artists of Cuba is housed in a beautiful converted mansion with leafy grounds. The bookstore is the city's best source for magazines and periodicals on Cuban literature, art and music. Café Hurón Azul and the patio area is a meeting place for writers and artists, and a popular venue for bands and soloists. *See also pp153-165.*

Along the Malecón

On the waterfront in front of the Hotel Nacional is the **Memorial a las Víctimas del Maine** dedicated to the 266 sailors who died when the US battleship *Maine* exploded in Havana harbour on 15 February 1898. Dispatched to Cuba two months earlier to protect US interests during Cuba's independence war with Spain, the Americans blamed Spain for the explosion and used it as the pretext to enter the war under the slogan 'Remember the *Maine*'. However, the possibility that the US sabotaged its own ship, so as to justify entering the war, cannot be ruled out. The heavy iron eagle that originally topped the monument was knocked down by jubilant crowds immediately after the 1959 Revolution, who then carried the pieces triumphantly through the streets. Today, the segments of the eagle's body are on permanent display in the Museo de la Revolución (*see p70*); the head is in the Eagle Bar of the US Interests Section, open only to American and Cuban staff.

Three blocks further west along the Malecón is the **United States Interests Section** (USINT, 1952), the closest Cuba comes to having an American embassy. Of little interest architecturally, the American-designed building is significant as a symbol of what Cuba considers to be hostile American policies. East of USINT, facing it in defiance, is the **Tribuna Anti-Imperialista**, a public square built for protests against American imperialism. On the south side of the square is the much-photographed caricature of a Cuban Revolutionary yelling at Uncle Sam: '*Señores Imperialistas, ¡no les tenemos absolutamente ningún miedo!*', meaning 'Imperialists, we have no fear of you at all!'

West around the headland, at the foot of Avenida de los Presidentes, is the recently spruced-up **Monumento a Calixto García Iñiguez**, in honour of the 19th-century rebel leader of the liberation army in Oriente Province. Made of black granite, its 24 bronze friezes depict scenes from the Wars of Independence. One block south is the beautiful art deco **Casa de las Américas** (*see below*), a cultural centre founded in 1959 to promote, investigate and exhibit Latin American and Caribbean literature and art. International literary figures such as Gabriel García Márquez are regular visitors. Another block south is the ten-storey **Hotel Presidente** (1927, reopened 1999), which combines Spanish Renaissance architecture with eclecticism; when it was built, it was one of the city's tallest buildings. A few blocks west along the Malecón are the eye-catching, multicoloured umbrellas of the *feria artesanal* (crafts fair). Beyond is the 22-storey **Hotel Meliá Cohiba** (1994), a Cuban-built, Spanish-run giant whose startlingly contemporary structure stands out from the traditional architectural streetscape of Paseo. The Cohiba dwarfs the nearby ultra-kitsch **Hotel Riviera** (1957), once the world's largest casino hotel outside Las Vegas. Another kilometre west is the mouth of the Almendares river (*see p80* **Along Río Almendares**) and the tunnel to Miramar.

Casa de las Américas

Avenida de los Presidentes (G), esquina 3ra (552706-9/fax 334554/www.casa.cult.cu). **Open** *Casa* 8am-4.45pm Mon-Fri. *Galería Latinoamericana & Sala Contemporánea* 10am-4.45pm Mon-Fri. **Admission** *Casa* free. *Galería & Sala* $2; free under-12s. **Map** p250 A10.

The Casa's collection of over 6,000 works of art are displayed in four galleries. The main building houses the Galería Latinoamericana, which has rotating exhibitions, and the Sala Contemporánea, where Cuban and Latin American photographs and engravings are exhibited and sold. Also under the Casa's wing are the Galería Haydee Santamaría (Calle G, esquina 5), located one block south, and the nearby Galería Mariano (Calle 15 #607, entre B y C), which houses a mainly popular art collection. The main building also houses Librería Rayuela, which sells books in Spanish and English, records and cassettes. Casa de las Américas is also a publishing house.

Calle Línea & around

Calle Línea was the first east–west thoroughfare through Vedado and one of the main axes along which this part of the city was

Along Río Almendares

Map p249

Called the Casigüagüas river by Cuba's Indians and renamed the Almendares by a visiting 17th-century Spanish bishop, this was the source of fresh water for the tiny colonial population that settled in Old Havana in the 16th century. No longer a water source for Havana, the Río Almendares area is now the city's most important green lung. Over the years, it has suffered deforestation and pollution caused by domestic waste and the factories along its banks.

In the 1920s French landscaper Forestier proposed that a large national park be created in Havana that would include the entrance to Havana Bay and the greenbelt along Río Almendares. This larger dream was never realised but in 1989 a smaller version took shape through a long-term project called **Parque Metropolitano de La Habana** (PMH). Covering an area of seven square kilometres (2.7 square miles) along a 9.5-kilometre (six-mile) stretch of the river from its mouth, the project aims to clean up the river, revitalise agriculture, carry out reforestation and add recreational facilities. Results are already visible: trees are planted; communities are receiving natural water treatment plants; the ceramics factory and limestone quarries have been closed; the carbonic gas factory is recycling its water; and trails have been prepared in the forests.

urbanised. Línea still has a busier, more urban feel than the rest of tranquil, leafy Vedado.

On Calle 17, between M and N, is the unsubtle, 28-storey **Edificio Focsa** (1956), which used to house Russian bureaucrats and students in the years following the Revolution. When built, the Focsa building was among the largest reinforced concrete structures in the world. The tower, which adds another five storeys to the building's height, was formerly the exclusive Club La Torre, for wealthy owners of large companies. Having reached a sorry state of decay, the Focsa's 30 floors, 376 apartments, the restaurant (La Torre) and exterior are finally being renovated and repainted with an anticipated completion date in December 2003. At ground level there's a shopping centre (*see p118*).

Back on the ground and west on Línea, a small square with an eight-metre (26-foot) high memorial honours those Chinese who participated in Cuba's independence wars. At the column's base is written, to the eternal pride of Chinese-Cubans: 'Not one Chinese was a deserter, not one Chinese was a traitor.' Two blocks further west is the **Centro Cultural Bertolt Brecht**, where every last Saturday of every month, at 3pm, a 'Tarde de Creole' takes place. Organised by the Cuban-Haitian group Bannzil Creole Kiba, it offers Haitian music, song and dance. Next door is the **Patronato de la Casa de la Comunidad Hebrea** and **Gran Sinagoga Bet Shalom** (Calle I #241, entre 13 y 15, 832 8953), the biggest of the city's three functioning Jewish centres for religious worship, education, social work and recreation, built in the 1950s. A monumental parabolic dome highlights the main entrance to the synagogue.

At the corner of Calle Línea and Avenida de los Presidentes is the **Museo Nacional de la Danza** (*see p81*), opened in October 1998

Beginning at the river's mouth, on a tongue of land on the eastern side, is the **Torreón de Santa Dorotea de Luna de La Chorrera**, a tower built in 1762 to replace an earlier fort that was destroyed by the British. The spot is now a gastronomic destination, with the Mesón de la Chorrera restaurant and a bar housed in the tower itself, and the swanky restaurant **1830** (*see p107*) in the beautifully restored 1920s mansion next door.

Located on the western banks of the river, at the point where it's crossed by Calle 23, is the delightful **Parque Almendares**. Developed in the late 1950s as a family recreational area for city dwellers, it later fell into disuse. Under the PMH project, the park has been revived, the riverside walkway has new benches and the river is regularly cleared of *malangueta*, a voracious aquatic plant that quickly chokes waterways. Park activities include a children's playground, pony rides, an open-air snack bar and a small amphitheatre for concerts.

From here the road enters the lush, wild **Bosque de La Habana**, 6.2 hectares (15 acroes) of forest, criss-crossed with small footpaths winding through lavish vegetation, where climbing plants tumble from the branches of ancient trees. Tiny Isla Josefina, part of the Bosque, is a protected island. This forest in the middle of the city shelters migratory and Cuban birds, reptiles (mainly lizards) and various types of insects.

Heading south on Avenida 26, and then west on Calzada de Puentes Grandes (also called Avenida 51), takes you to the **Jardines de La Tropical**, with its fantasy architecture and vegetation. Designed by the Tropical brewing company in 1912, the gardens have profuse vegetation, grottos, mazes, cascades, pavilions, an unusual open ballroom and a miniature Swiss chalet (formerly where the gardener lived). Located on a natural terrace, overlooking the garden, is the mansion of the former brewers, with its stark castle-like exterior, with lush Moorish interior decor inspired by the pavillions of Granada's Alhambra. The air of neglect hanging over the gardens only serves to intensify its other-worldly atmosphere.

To find out more about the PMH, meet the specialists and see a scale model (1:2,000) of the project, visit the **Aula Ecológica** (Ciclovía y 26, 881 9979, closed Sat & Sun). Guides – some English-speaking – are available.

Jardines de La Tropical

Avenida Tropical y Rizo (881 8767). **Open** 9am-5pm Tue-Sun. **Admission** free.

Parque Almendares

Calle 47 #1161, entre 24 y 26 (203 8535). **Open** *Jan-June, Sept-Dec* 10am-5pm Tue-Fri; 10am-6pm Sat, Sun. *July-Aug* 10am-5pm Mon-Fri; 10am-6pm Sat, Sun. **Admission** free.

to coincide with the 50th anniversary of the National Ballet of Cuba. Two blocks west on Línea, between E and F, is the **Galería Habana** (1962; *see pp145-49*), which was the first of a national network of galleries set up to disseminate and promote Cuban artists.

The Parroquia del Sagrado Corazón de Jesús, more commonly known as the **Parroquia del Vedado** (Vedado Parish Church, Calle Línea, entre C y D, 832 6807), and conspicuous for the wide shaded park running along its side, is a couple of blocks further on. Built over 100 years ago as the first church in the district, it still retains almost all its original features, including the wooden altar, stained-glass windows and a carved wooden pulpit. One of the smaller stained-glass windows was commissioned by María Teresa Bances – the wife of Cuban nationalist José Martí's son. Her former home is nearby on Calzada #807, at the corner of 4, and is now the **Centro de Estudios Martianos** (Calzada #807, esquina 4, 552297/8, closed Sat, Sun), devoted to the study of Martí. It's not a museum but visits are allowed during working hours; phone first.

Museo Nacional de la Danza

Calle Línea #365, esquina Avenida de los Presidentes (G) (831 2198/musdanza@cubarte.cu). **Open** 11am-6.30pm Tue-Sat. **Admission** $2; $1 tour (call in advance for English-speaking guides); free under-12s. **Map** p250 A10.

Through displays taken mainly from the private collection of Alicia Alonso, Cuba's prima ballerina and the founder of the Ballet Nacional de Cuba, the story of ballet in Cuba is told through photos, costumes, prints, awards, sculptures and sheet music. Treasures include a signed autobiography of Isadora Duncan that she gave to Alonso and a black fur cape belonging to Anna Pavlova. Future plans for the museum include a documentation and information centre on dance.

Miramar & the Western Suburbs

Old Havana's alter ego is commodious, contemporary and chic.

If the sights of Old Havana provide visitors with a unique opportunity to step back in time, then a trip to Miramar, the setting for the most recent historical developments in Cuba, will complete the picture. To leave Havana without seeing Miramar is akin to abandoning a fascinating story just as the plot begins to thicken, for it shows Cuba at its most modern, and affords glimpses of the country's elusive future.

WAY OUT WEST

Historically, Havana has always spread west. The political and economic elite have traditionally moved westward, away from the site where the city was founded in Old Havana, to Centro Habana, Vedado, Miramar, and as far west as Jaimanitas and *punto cero* (point zero), the military code-name for the area where President Fidel Castro is said to reside. The suburbs west of the Almendares river are some of Havana's newest neighbourhoods, and until the Revolution were the exclusive enclave of the fabulously rich. The city jumped the Almendares river and expanded into new terrain in the 1930s and '40s, due to the pressure of population growth and an economic upturn. Initially, the recent arrivals, mainly middle and upper-middle class, were forced to use a drawbridge, the Puente de Pote (1924), to commute from their offices in Old Havana to the green and spacious suburbs of Miramar. However, the completion of the Malecón coastal road, leading into the tunnel going under the Río Almendares, in the 1950s, facilitated the journey.

Today, Miramar and the upmarket suburbs of Siboney and Cubanacán are as fashionable as ever: a number of sports celebs, such as the former 400- and 800-metre world record holder Ana Fidelia Quirot, and musicians Chucho Valdés and Silvio Rodríguez are residents.

Miramar

Maps p248-p249

The journey along Havana's seaside Malecón takes you all the way from Old Havana, via Vedado, into the Almendares tunnel, spitting you out in the spacious elegance of Miramar's Avenida 5ta, known colloquially as **Quinta Avenida**, flanked by state-of-the-art offices and spruced up mansions. This route into Miramar is not only the most direct, it is also the most scenic. In terms of elegance and splendour, Avenida 5ta is said to be unparalleled in Latin America; indeed, it is arguably one of the most magnificent urban thoroughfares in the world. The central part of the avenue is a pedestrian walkway exquisitely landscaped with manicured bushes and other exotic greenery, plus a lawn that appears to have been cut with nail scissors. Here, at first light, joggers and power-walkers engage in a race against time, aware that the rising sun and commuter traffic fumes will turn the crisp dawn air into a thick humid soup by 8am.

As you exit the tunnel, turn your gaze from the picturesque central walkway to the right at the corner of Calle 2. The building you see is known locally as the **Casa de Las Brujas** (Witches' House), on account of its unforgiving façade of grey, black and green, and the fact that a couple of elderly sisters lived here until their demise (refusing the state's numerous attempts to buy their home). This sadly dilapidated house, with its fairytale features, is a prime example of how Miramar's decadent bourgeois past stands – often decaying – alongside its forward-looking present. Miramar is a neighbourhood of contrasts, where architectural trends are above all eclectic, ranging from classical interpretations of colonial architecture to art deco and, particularly from Calle 42 onward, more modern mid to late 20th-century styles.

Moving down Avenida 5ta, there is increasing evidence of recent economic developments and the emergence of a higher-income professional sector, with foreign company offices, international banks, real estate offices, embassies in renovated mansions, modern hotels and retail outlets. *See p86* **Open for business**.

At the junction of Avenida 5ta and Calle 10 is a clock tower, the official symbol of Miramar, known as the **Reloj de Quinta Avenida**, designed by New York architect George Duncan in 1924. Two blocks west along Avenida 5ta is the **Museo del Ministerio del Interior** (*see p84*), housed in an attractively restored building, and a must if you want to see the evidence of a whole range of devious CIA-backed attempts to assassinate Fidel and topple his government.

Two blocks further along Avenida 5ta, at Calle 16, is the **Casa del Habano** (*see p122*), a magnificent mansion and one of the best places to buy cigars in the area. Further along, on the corner of 5ta and 30, is **Le Select** (*see p117*) – another example of the growing number of upmarket retail outlets springing up to cater for the area's wealthier residents, often occupants of the nearby elite residential apartment buildings that have started to appear as a result of increasing foreign investment in the area. One of the most recent examples is the three-storey **Monte Carlo Palace**, on 5ta between 44 and 46, which, like its counterparts, is occupied exclusively by foreign diplomats, and company directors and representatives.

To get a fantastic overview of demographic and architectural trends within the city, ask for a guided tour of the scale model in the **Maqueta de La Habana** (*see p84*) on Calle 28. Two blocks away from the scale model is the charming **Parque Prado**, set between Calles 24 and 26 and split by Avenida 5ta. The park boasts a statue of the early 20th-century Mexican freedom fighter Emiliano Zapata on its southern side, and a bust of Mahatma Gandhi on its northern side. Beside it is **Iglesia de Santa Rita de Casia** (*see p84*), the first of three Catholic churches on Avenida 5ta where people still worship. Further along, on Calle 60, is the Romanesque **Iglesia de San Antonio de Padua** (*see p84*), while several blocks west, to the south side, on the corner of 5ta and 82, is the Romanesque-Byzantine **Iglesia de Jesús de Miramar** (*see p84*) run by the Capuchin order.

Judging by the largely deserted pews and aisles, it's not the churches of Miramar that draw the crowds; it's more likely to be the aquarium. The **Acuario Nacional de Cuba** (*see below*) is a big hit with locals, especially during the summer school break, and its popularity will undoubtedly grow when the new dolphin show is premièred. In 2000 a virus killed all five trained dolphins and the shows were suspended.

Miramar officially ends at Calle 42 but most people consider that it stretches for an extra kilometre or so along the coast. Therefore, if you continue along Avenida 3ra, past the sombre tower of the **Russian Embassy** (corner of Avenida 5ta and Calle 62), you reach the heart of recent business developments in the area – the impressive complex of office blocks known as the **Miramar Trade Center**, located between 76 and 80. The centre is now viewed as the future business core of the city.

Miramar means 'sea view' in Spanish, yet ironically its coastal road **Avenida Primera**, unlike the Malecón, gives little access to the shore – except for rocky swimming areas at the ends of Calles 16 and 66 – as private houses and buildings reserve this area for their own use.

Acuario Nacional de Cuba

Avenida 3ra, esquina a 62 (203 6401-6).
Open 10am-6pm Tue-Sun. **Admission** $5 adults; $3 under-12s. **Map** p248 B3.

This aquarium was founded during the 1960s and was the first of its kind in Cuba. The collection includes over 3,000 sea creatures, representing around 350 species of marine life. There's a somewhat tacky sea lion show three times a day, and five dolphins were, at the time of writing, being trained to perform for the crowds from the end of 2003.

Miramar Trade Center: looking to the future.

Iglesia de Jesús de Miramar

Avenida 5ta #8003, entre 80 y 82 (203 5301). **Open** 9am-noon, 4-6pm daily. *Mass* 5pm Tue-Sat; 9am, 5pm Sun. To visit at other times, enter via the sacristy. **Map** p248 B1.

This is the most architecturally distinguished of the churches located along Avenida 5ta, due to its vast dome, visible for several blocks east and west. Construction work on this, Cuba's second largest church, was completed in 1953. Inside, 14 large paintings of the Stations of the Cross by Spanish artist César Hombrados enhance the solemn atmosphere. In one Station the artist portrays himself as one of the executioners derobing Jesus; in another his wife is shown as the Virgin Mary.

Iglesia de San Antonio de Padua

Calle 60 #316, esquina Avenida 5ta (203 5045). **Open** 7.30-11.30am Mon-Fri; 8.30-11.30am Sat; 8-11.30am, from 4pm Sun (1hr before mass). *Mass* 5pm Mon, Tue, Thur, Sat, Sun; 8.30am Wed, Thur; 9.45am Sun. **Map** p248 B3.

This church belongs to the Franciscan order and is dedicated to St Anthony of Padua, the Portuguese saint of the poor and of true love. Its vast organ, one of the finest in Latin America, is well kept but, sadly, due to a lack of spare parts, cannot be played.

Iglesia de Santa Rita de Casia

Avenida 5ta, esquina 26 (204 2001). **Open** 9am-noon, 2-5pm Mon-Fri; 2pm onward Sat; 9am-noon Sun. *Mass* 5.30pm Tue, Thur, Sat; 8am Wed, Fri; 10.30am Sun. **Map** p249 B5.

The church itself is unremarkable, but if you are keen on the work of renowned Cuban sculptress Rita Longa, you will want to see the statue inside, her interpretation of this 14th-century Italian saint.

Maqueta de La Habana

Calle 28 #113, entre 1ra y 3ra (202 7303/7322). **Open** 9.30am-5pm Tue-Sat. **Admission** $3; $1 under-12s. *Guides* $20-$30. **Map** p249 A5.

This is no ordinary scale model. It reproduces all the buildings (and even trees) in the 144 sq km (54 sq miles) that comprise the metropolitan area of the city on a scale of 1:1,000. Buildings are made out of recycled cigar boxes and colour codes are used to indicate the different historical periods: ochre for the colonial era (16th-19th centuries), yellow for the Republic (1900-58) and cream for post-Revolutionary developments. The model is the work of the Comprehensive Development of the City Group, which has advised city officials on urban planning since 1987. Insightful guided tours are available in English; they are well worth the extra cost, particularly for groups.

Museo del Ministerio del Interior

Avenida 5ta, esquina 14 (203 4432). **Open** 9.30am-5pm Tue-Fri; 9am-4pm Sat. **Admission** $2; $3 with guide; free under-12s. **Map** p249 B6.

The former headquarters of the Ministry of the Interior is now a fascinating museum, with exhibits ranging from gruesome photos of torture victims of the Batista regime to more recent material on the Elián González crisis. The museum also features a range of explosives and weapons included in plans by Miami groups and the CIA to assassinate Fidel Castro; some of the more intriguing are devices made out of a cuddly toy, a Quaker Oats box and a shampoo bottle. Even without English captions, it is well worth a visit.

Cubanacán

The further west you go, the more magnificent the properties become. So, once you reach the end of Avenida 3ra you are moving into what was almost exclusively millionaire terrain less than half a century ago. Cubanacán is the site of the former Havana Country Club, which became the **Instituto Superior de Arte** (*see p85*), Cuba's leading arts academy, thanks to an initiative by Che Guevara. Slightly west, alongside impressive mansions, is the **Palacio**

Marina Hemingway. *See p86.*

Treasure island

Miramar enjoyed very high living standards before the Revolution took hold in 1959. At that time, when Fidel Castro and his guerillas finally drove Batista out, the middle and upper-middle classes had barely established themselves in Miramar in their uniquely designed homes, symbols of their growing prosperity. Angered and disconcerted, to put it mildly, by the pace and nature of the new government's reforms, many of the owners left the country; others held on, convinced that the crisis would blow over. By 1961, with the failure of the Bay of Pigs invasion, their hopes were dashed too and most joined their former neighbours in Miami.

During the early months of the Revolution, Miramar was the scene of a frenetic exodus, with suitcases and trunks, even domestic animals, being piled into taxis leaving for the airport. Most émigrés were convinced that their absence from Cuba would be a short-term measure. They left their servants in charge of the house, stashed their money away and concealed their treasures – some of which are now national and world heritage pieces – in double walls, gardens, garages and even in the sea, at strategic points off the coast. The authorities took immediate measures and changed the money, rendering the wads of Cuban pesos hidden away worthless. Overnight, the owners were turned into virtual paupers. As for the treasures, a hunt began and some, but by no means all, of these items have been recovered by the authorities. Doubtless, some Miramar properties abandoned in the early 1960s still harbour priceless secrets.

Those who remained in their homes fared somewhat better. Whatever money they had in the bank was changed into the new Cuban peso and they were paid some compensation for businesses that were nationalised. They were also allowed to keep one property as their home, while second and third homes became hostels for students from the countryside. But their hopes for growing prosperity quickly vanished and morale plummeted. The smart new properties fell into decay as maintenance costs proved impossible to meet and, to this day, a number of properties still remain as they were on 1 January 1959. Unpainted for decades, these homes stand as crumbling monuments to a bygone era when social class and wealth (as well as skin colour) divided the population along strictly demarcated lines.

A good place to see many of these decaying mansions is on Primera Avenida, which hugs the coast. Look closely and you may notice that a number of these properties are multi-family residences; their current residents (and their descendants) took advantage of the chaos of the immediate aftermath of the Revolution to move in. Today, they still live in homes whose former owners may, even now, be waiting on the other side of the Florida Straits for the crisis to 'blow over'.

de las Convenciones (Calle 146, entre 11 y 13, 202 6011), built in 1979 for the sixth Summit of the Non-Aligned Nations. It becomes the focus of very tight security when the 589-member National Assembly meets here twice a year. In comparison to its neighbours, the architecture of the palace is graceless and unimaginative, but don't lose interest just yet because behind it is the much-talked-about but little-seen area of **El Laguito**, the lakeside site chosen by tycoons to build palaces back in the 1920s and '30s. It is said that the style and undreamed-of luxury of these residences, now known as 'protocol houses', outshine anything else in this opulent neighbourhood. Only visiting heads of state (Mikhail Gorbachev stayed here during his last historic visit to Cuba in 1989), and those willing to fork out $1,000-$2,000 per day in rent are privileged with an invite to this secluded and restricted-access area.

Nearby is the **PABEXPO** (Avenida 17, entre 174 y 190, 271 5513, closed Sat & Sun) exhibition centre, built in 1987, comprising four connecting pavilions used for trade fairs, including the Cubadisco music fair in May (*see p133*).

Instituto Superior de Arte (ISA)

Calle 120 #1110, esquina a 9na (208 8075).

Built between 1961 and 1965 on the grounds of the old Country Club golf course, the Higher Institute of Art is considered to be one of the major architectural feats of the Revolutionary era, and is a work of extraordinary beauty and complexity. Its domed halls, like gigantic mushrooms amid this vast woody landscape, will catch your attention immediately from the adjoining road; they form part of the ISA's five schools, incorporating Catalan vaulted arches, cupolas, inner courtyards and curved passageways. African, Asian and Spanish elements also feature in the design, as do symbols of masculine and feminine sexuality.

Project co-ordinator Ricardo Porro, a Cuban architect, designed the visual arts and modern dance schools, while plans for the rest of the complex were undertaken by the Italian architects Vittorio Garatti (ballet and music) and Roberto Gottardi (dramatic arts). Sadly, only three of the five parkland pavilions are completed, and areas of it are in a sorry state of neglect. Californian architect John Loomis put the spotlight on the ISA in a fascinating book about Cuba's 'forgotten' art shools (*Revolution of Forms: Cuba's Forgotten Arts Schools*) in 1999. Castro has since invited the three original architects to meet to plan the project's completion. Discussions continue apace but the restoration and completion programme hasn't begun. Though overgrown, this awe-inspiring complex stands as a symbol of a period of great energy and optimism in the early days of the Revolution.

Siboney & Jaimanitas

Sightseeing

To the west of Cubanacán is the district of Siboney, the heart of scientific research in Cuba, otherwise known as the *Polo Científico del Oeste* (Scientific Pole of the West). The complex comprises some 30 buildings and research is carried out in the spheres of pharmaceutics, genetic engineering and biotechnology. Some remarkable progress has been made here in the 30 or so years since the initiative was set up and Cuba has now come up with vaccines against meningitis B and C, and hepatitis B, while its work on an AIDS vaccine and cure is being taken very seriously.

Back down on Quinta Avenida and westward in the direction of Jaimanitas, between Calles 188 and 292, you'll see another reminder of the good old, bad old days: **Club Havana** see *p179*), previously known as the Havana Biltmore Yacht and Country Club. Opened in 1928 to cater for the refined tastes of El Laguito residents, this club was so exclusively white and upper class that even dictator Fulgencio Batista was judged not to be 'the right sort' on the grounds of colour. The club now belongs to the coastguard, the former golf course is its training camp. Meanwhile, the plush clubhouse and its private beach are now mainly frequented by foreign diplomats, and entrepreneurs. Plus ça change…

About a kilometre further along Avenida 5ta is the village of Jaimanitas, famously home to **José Fuster**, an astonishingly prolific ceramicist, painter and engraver. His eccentrically decorated home/studio and garden, in a style reminiscent of Gaudí, can be seen from several blocks away and is probably Fuster's best piece of work. *See also p145-p149.*

Jaimanitas is also, in a manner of speaking, Fidel Castro's home, since this is the closest you will come to the area known as *punto cero*, the military zone where all roads leading in are blocked and guarded, so don't come expecting photos or sightseeing tours. At most, you may catch a glimpse of a three-car convoy of identical Mercedes speeding along Quinta Avenida, also called the Presidential Route. The man himself is likely to be in one of them.

About 300 metres (984 feet) along from the main entrance to Jaimanitas, on the north side of Avenida 5ta, is **Marina Hemingway** *see p181*). The marina dates

Open for business

As you enjoy the sights of Miramar, observe the traffic on Avenida 5ta for a moment. Most of the more modern cars will have HK registration plates, indicating that their owners are foreign residents. These people are likely to be employees of the growing number of foreign companies with the foresight to perceive that beyond the beaches, mojitos and hand-rolled cigars, Cuba is a vast, untapped market and a potential gold mine. Or a nickel mine, in the case of the Canadian company Sherrit, involved in the extraction of nickel from one of the largest reserves in the world, in the east of Cuba. Not just mining, but tourism, oil, telecommunications and other sectors have attracted foreign capital from investors willing to flout the 1996 Helms-Burton Law (penalising foreign companies investing in property in Cuba once owned by Americans) and risk the US courts in order to reap the benefits. These benefits tend to be long-term; Cuba offers potential investors a highly skilled workforce but the severe shortage of resources and equipment means that an infrastructure has first to be created before business can really start. In short, there's no chance of making quick cash.

Since Cuba opened itself up to foreign investment in 1993-4, at a time when the economy was in free fall, there has been a slow but steady economic recovery, thanks to the influx of hard currency from Canadian, European and Latin American firms. Foreign companies are encouraged to find a Cuban partner and set up *empresas mixtas* (joint ventures) wherever feasible, or they now have the option of going it alone. Indeed, there are dozens of 100 per cent foreign-owned concerns currently operating on the island. In the meantime, US firms, prohibited from doing business with their communist neighbour, can only watch as this lucrative market is divided up niche by niche.

Do a lap of luxury at **Club Havana**. *See p86*.

back to pre-Revolutionary days, when it was known as Barlovento. It has potential but due to shortage of initiative or resources a lacklustre atmosphere hangs over the place. There's nothing for Hemingway fans here, but scuba divers should check out La Aguja Diving Centre (*see p182*), one of Havana's few diving centres.

Marianao & La Lisa

These two working-class municipalities border Playa to the south and are characterised by generally poor-quality housing and roads that are in an appalling condition. Nevertheless, if you want to get away from swanky hotels and spruced-up World Heritage Sites to get a glimpse of life as it is lived by the majority of *habaneros*, Marianao and La Lisa certainly offer that.

Art deco fans should seek out **Plaza Finlay** (also known as El Obelisco), at the junction of Avenida 31 and Calle 100. On this well-designed art deco square-cum-traffic roundabout, there's also a 32-metre (107-foot) syringe-like obelisk in the centre – a tribute to Dr Carlos J Finlay, who identified the strain of mosquito responsible for transmitting yellow fever. Four curved-façade buildings complete the architectural harmony of the square. For more art deco, stroll another eight blocks along Avenida 31 to the **Hospital Materno Eusebio Hernández** (1938), also known as the Maternidad Obrera. This maternity hospital is one of the most interesting buildings of its genre in Havana. Thousands of babies have been born in this hospital, which, from the air, resembles a vast womb.

Also of interest in Marianao is the immense Ciudad Escolar Libertad educational complex, established on the site of the old Columbia Military Camp, which Fulgencio Batista flew out of in a tremendous hurry in the early hours of 1 January 1959. Located among the schools on the site is the **Museo Nacional de Alfabetización** (*see below*), created in homage to participants in the massive 1961 literacy campaign. Those with even a smattering of Spanish will find the displays compelling.

After dark, Marianao is the place to be if you want to satisfy your curiosity about legendary **Tropicana** (Calle 74 #4504, entre 41 y 45, 267 1717) cabaret. Opened over 70 years ago, Tropicana is still as ostentatious as ever.

To the west, Marianao is bordered by the municipality of **La Lisa**. The area is seriously run-down and has little to offer tourists. Those keen to see the MI-4 helicopter used by Castro the Cessna plane piloted by Che Guevara in the early years of the Revolution should visit the **Museo del Aire** (*see below*).

Museo Nacional de Alfabetización

Ciudad Libertad Escolar, Avenida 29E, esquina 76, Marianao (260 8054). **Open** 8am-3pm Mon-Fri; 8am-noon Sat. **Admission** free.

Exhibits include photos, documents, film footage, personal belongings and letters, which form a testimony of the most successful literacy campaign in history. Over 100,000 people of all ages, one only seven years old, joined brigades formed to eliminate illiteracy in the period between January and December 1961. These days, Cuba's literacy rate is estimated at 96%, the highest in Latin America.

Museo del Aire

Avenida 212, entre 29 y 31, La Coronela, La Lisa (271 0631). **Open** 10am-5pm Wed-Sun. **Admission** $2; $4 with guide.

This open-air exhibition of combat planes, helicopters, rockets and documents charts the history of Cuba's air defence from the early days of the Revolution, through the Soviet era to the present. Also of interest are personal belongings of the first Cuban cosmonaut, Arnaldo Tamayo, and a planetarium.

Eastern Bay & the Coast

Colonial settlements, white sands and an expressive culture on the city's eastern fringes make it worth crossing the bay.

An immense castle and fortress stand watch over the harbour channel, beckoning visitors to venture to the other side. This world apart on the eastern bay – gobbled up by the city as it grew – includes several seaside villages and residential areas. Further east, the palm-fringed white sand of Havana's Playas del Este (Eastern Beaches) provides an easily accessible slice of tropical paradise.

Parque Histórico Militar Morro-Cabaña

Dominating the north-eastern side of the harbour, overlooking La Habana Vieja, are the two fortresses of the Parque Histórico Militar Morro-Cabaña. Key players in the defence of the colonial city, these fortresses are now among Havana's most impressive sights.

The **Castillo de Los Tres Reyes del Morro**, known as 'El Morro', is the oldest structure on the eastern side of the bay, erected in response to the constant threat of pirates. It was designed by Italian military engineer Juan Bautista Antonelli (also responsible for Castillo de San Salvador de la La Punta on the other side; *see p67*) and built by slaves with rocks extracted from the moats between 1589 and 1630. El Morro sits on a steep rocky outcrop, which helped the canted structure withstand siege by the British for several weeks in 1762. The fortress only succumbed when a mine was set off beneath one of the ramparts; the ravine it made is still visible.

Along with a deep moat and two batteries, additional defence was originally provided by an ocean-side tower, replaced in 1844 by a lighthouse called the Faro del Morro. Now a symbol of Havana, it offers one of the finest views of the city, especially at sunset. The history of the lighthouse and castle is explored in the Sala de Historia, while the Sala de Cristobal Colón charts the history of Columbus's journey to the Americas. Another interesting historical feature of the *castillo* is the prisons, which have holes in the back walls through which prisoners were fed to the sharks.

In 1763, at the end of the British occupation, construction began on the **Fortaleza de San Carlos de la Cabaña**, a 15-minute walk south-east of the Morro castle. This 700-metre (2,297-foot) long fortress is the largest in the Americas and has never been attacked. It cost so much that King Carlos III is reputed to have asked for a spyglass to see it, claiming that such an pricey project could surely be observed from Madrid.

It has a luxurious covered entrance leading to cobbled streets, a chapel and various military structures, many of which are now museums, restaurants or shops. There is a historical display with gruesome torture devices and a collection of colonial military paraphernalia. The Comandancia de Ché Guevara displays objects Che used in his military headquarters in the fortress just after the Revolution's triumph.

Nearby is the baroque Capilla de San Carlos, a bijou chapel where soldiers worshipped San Carlos, patron of the fort. On the eastern side of the complex is the Foso de los Laureles (Moat of the Laurels). This is where, during the 19th century and under the Batista regime, dozens of prisoners faced firing squads. (The tables were turned after the Revolution, with the execution of counter-Revolutionaries ordered by Che Guevara.) There are bullet holes and a plaque in the wall behind the palm tree. The area beyond the moat is where Soviet missiles were stored during the missile crisis of October 1962 (*see p17*); disarmed examples are on display.

In the early colonial period, a flagship in the harbour fired regular cannon blasts in the morning and at night to signal the opening or closing of the city gates. Today, a squad attired in 19th-century uniforms continues the Ceremonia del Cañonazo (cannon firing ceremony; *see p132*) at 9pm every evening. It's worth timing your visit to coincide with this attraction.

Parque Histórico Militar Morro-Cabaña

Carretera de la Cabaña, Habana del Este (863 7941). **Open** *Castillo & Fortaleza* 9am-10pm daily. *Faro* 9am-8pm daily. **Admission** *Castillo & Fortaleza* $3 before 6pm; $5 after 6pm; free under-12s; camera $2; video camera $5. *Faro* $2; free under-12s. **Map** p251 C16.

Bayside Havana

As Havana spread out in concentric circles, it swallowed surrounding villages such as **Casablanca**, **Regla** and **Guanabacoa**. The first two communities have always had a close link with the industrial area of eastern and south-eastern Havana Bay, and been inhabited by less well-off *habaneros* dependent on the sea and harbour for their living.

Casablanca

South-east of La Cabaña is Casablanca, a village that climbs out of the sea to a weather station and the **Estatua Cristo de la Habana**. Known by some as the 'Christ with sensuous lips', this 20-metre (70-foot) high marble statue was sculpted in 1958 by Cuban artist Jilma Madera. The statue can be reached by car but more interesting is the 20-minute climb up a staircase from the little park north of the ferry dock, or the road that winds up the hill to the west. Until recently, some of Havana's night-time crowd would blare disco music at the base of the glowing statue, where there were several booths hawking anything from fast food to jewellery. That brief commercial aspect of 'El Cristo' has been swept into local history, and the spot has been returned to its original contemplative state.

The picturesque **Tren Eléctrico de Hershey**, Cuba's only electric train, has its western terminus in Casablanca. Built in 1920 by US chocolate magnate Milton Hershey, this line linked Havana to the Hershey sugar mill in Matanzas, part of the Hershey estates, which covered a huge tract of land in the Matanzas Province. The dinky trains depart from Casablanca at 4.10am, noon, 8.30pm and 9.10pm daily for the pleasant 90-kilometre (56-mile) trip through scenic farming communities. Tickets ($3 for tourists) can be bought at the station at Casablanca.

Regla

The old town of Regla on the south-eastern side of the bay has always been a major fishing and boat repair hub and port for Havana, and was one of the first suburbs established outside city walls. Founded in 1687, by the mid 19th century it was the city's most important economic centre, with the largest sugar warehouses in the Caribbean. The many slaves who settled here bequeathed to the area a strong Afro-Cuban religious culture.

As you exit the ferry at **Muelle Regla** on to Calle Santuario, you'll see the neo-classical **Iglesia de Nuestra Señora de Regla** (*see p90*). A few blocks up, on Calle Martí, is the **Museo Municipal de Regla** (*see p90*). Further up Martí, between Ambrón and La Piedra, is the **Casa de la Cultura** (979905) – home to the Guaracheros de Regla, one of the famous *comparsas* (carnival dance troupes). **Parque Guaycanamar** is Regla's shop-lined central park. A short walk south-west of the park leads to a high metal staircase, which provides quick access to the **Colina Lenin** (*see p90*).

All aboard the **Tren Eléctrico de Hershey**.

Monumento a Ernest Hemingway – the man of the sea remembered in Cojímar. *See p92.*

Colina Lenin

Calzada Vieja, entre Enlase y Rotaria (976899). **Open** *Exhibition* 9am-6pm Tue-Sat; 9am-noon Sun. **Admission** free.

Offering a panoramic view of the harbour, this was one of the first memorials outside the USSR to the communist leader, originally consisting of an olive tree planted by Regla workers in 1924. It has been replaced several times due to its struggle with the tropical climate. An immense bronze relief portrait of Lenin's face, surrounded by cement figures, by Cuban artist Thelma Marin was installed in 1984. There's a small exhibition hall with photos of Lenin, and commemorative ceremonies are held here every 21 January and 22 April, the dates of his birth and death respectively.

Iglesia de Nuestra Señora de Regla

Calle Santuario #11, entre Máximo Gómez y Litoral (976228). **Open** noon-5pm Mon; 7.30am-5.30pm Tue-Sun. **Admission** free.

Built in 1818, this church has a mudéjar panelled ceiling and is the sanctuary of the Virgen de Regla, Havana's patron saint. This black figure, although ostensibly Christian, was used by the slaves to veil their worship of the Yoruban deity Yemayá, goddess of the seas. There are two *santería* museum halls adjacent to the church (free admission). For more on Afro-Cuban religions, *see p91* **Keeping the faith**.

Museo Municipal de Regla

Calle Martí #158, entre Facciolo y la Piedra (976989). **Open** 9am-6pm Tue-Sat; 9am-1pm Sun. **Admission** $2 ($3 with guide); free under-12s.

A small but inspiring museum with exhibitions on the history of Regla, the most important gods in Afro-Cuban religions and the War of Independence, along with many objets d'art. Exhibits include books, maps, photos and artefacts. Helpful staff.

Guanabacoa

Inland from Regla is Guanabacoa, once a pre-colonial community and later a centre for the slave trade. Today, it's a lively town, just within the city boundaries, and is the heart of Havana's Afro-Cuban religions: Regla de Ocha, Palo Monte and Abakuá (*see p91* **Keeping the faith**). The town's historical centre was declared a National Monument in 1999, and has some of the most splendid churches in the region.

Guanabacoa is best reached from Havana by car, on the Vía Blanca highway then the Carretera Vieja, passing the **Ermita del Potosí** (no phone), at press time closed for renovation, on the land of the old cemetery. Built in 1644, making it one of the oldest churches in Cuba, it has a mujédar panelled ceiling and an original stone floor.

Guanabacoa also has two Jewish cemeteries, located on the old highway about three kilometres (two miles) south-east of Potisí: the Ashkenazi **Cementerio de la Comunidad Religiosa Ebrea Adath Israel** (976644) and the Sephardic **Cementerio de la Unión Hebrera Chevet Ahim** (975866). Both have memorials to the six million Jews who perished in Nazi concentration camps, and are open from 7am to 6pm daily.

On one side of the Parque Martí in the city centre is the 1721 **Iglesia de Nuestra Señora de la Asunción** (Calle División #331, entre Martí y Cadenas, 977368), locally called Iglesia Parroquial Mayor. It's worth seeing for the exquisitely painted altar. North-east of the park on Calle Santo Domingo and Lebredo is the **Iglesia de Nuestra Señora de la Candelaria y Convento de Santo Domingo** (977376, closed Mon), a beautiful baroque church built in the mid 1700s, whose convent was used as a barracks during the British occupation in 1762.

Half a block from the park on Calle Pepé Antonio is the **Teatro Carral**. Opened in the early 1800s as a dance hall (and now a cinema), it has a lovely Moorish arch over its entrance. One block west of Parque Martí on Calle Martí is the town's **Museo Histórico de Guanabacoa** (979117, closed Tue), where the Festival de Raices Africanas 'El Wemilere' is held every November (*see p136*). The **Bazar de los Orishas**, two blocks further west (979510, closed Sun), has handicrafts from local artists and hosts monthly Afro-Cuban dance shows.

Keeping the faith

The most widely practised religion in Cuba is *santería*, known also as the *regla de ocha* or Yoruba religion after the *orishas* or gods from western Nigeria. *Orishas* represent forces of nature and archetypal human qualities: **Changó** is the god of thunder, **Yemayá** the goddess of the sea and motherhood, and **Ochún** the goddess of love and fresh water. Most *orishas* have Catholic saint equivalents: Yemayá is also known as the Vírgen de Regla; Ochún is the Vírgen de la Caridad del Cobre, the patron saint of Cuba. Curiously, Changó, the womanising macho man, is linked with **Santa Bárbara**, the virgin martyr.

Those who wish to initiate into the *regla de ocha* must first consult a *babalawo* – an expert in divination – to discover which *orisha* is their 'guardian angel'. Some devotees simply receive the *collares*, a set of beaded necklaces, colour-coded to represent different *orishas*. Others are recommended to enter into a deeper relationship with one *orisha* by taking an initiation called *asiento*. Those who do so must dress completely in white for a year and observe certain taboos. Initiations are costly (around two years' salary) and most people take them for health reasons or in the hope of an improvement in their material circumstances. During the ceremonies in honour of the *orishas*, each one is invoked by using his or her distinctive drum rhythm and dance. Some of the initiated participants may become possessed and assume certain aspects of the *orisha*'s personality.

The annual festivals of the most popular *orishas* draw huge crowds. On 16 December, eve of the feast of San Lázaro or Babalú Ayé, who is renowned for his healing powers, hundreds of thousands of pilgrims make their way to the sanctuary at **El Rincón** in southern Havana. Some of the more devout drag themselves along on their hands and knees, often with large stones tied to their legs.

Membership of Afro-Cuban religions crosses race and class boundaries. Even Fidel Castro is linked in the popular imagination with Changó. Many believe that this accounts for his 40-year reign and miraculous escapes from CIA-backed assassination attempts.

Widely practised throughout Cuba, the **reglas congas**, known also as *palo monte*, originated among the Bakongo peoples of West Central Africa. The term *palo* (stick) refers to the ritual use of trees and plants, which are believed to have magical powers. A *prenda* or *nganga*, normally a three-legged cauldron, is filled with natural elements such as sticks, seeds and earth. It also contains the spirit of a dead person and is used by *paleros* to control supernatural forces. Ritual written symbols called *firmas* are drawn on the ground, the walls or on cloth worn on the body to call down spirits. Because *palo* is more closely associated with magical practices than the *regla de ocha*, *paleros* tend to be more reticent and it is rare for outsiders to be invited to attend ceremonies.

Abakuá is an all-male secret society that came from eastern Nigeria. Ceremonies, called *plantes*, enact the myth of the African princess Sikán, who discovered the secret of the sacred fish Tanze. A drum called *ekue* is used to re-create the mystical voice of the fish. Masked figures or *íremes* represent the ancestors. A system of writing known as *anaforuana* uses symbols to embody religious powers and mark ritual objects. *Abakuá* members' first loyalty is to their brother members and they are required to be *chébere* or brave and defiant; much is often made of the erroneous belief that a new initiate has to kill the first person who crosses his path.

The ferry to **Regla**: it's quicker than swimming (but only just). *See p89.*

Habana del Este

Moving east you will pass the first of a series of commuter belts: the Ciudad Camilo Cienfuegos, built in the 1960s in response to serious housing shortages. Like Cojímar and Alamar on the coast, the Ciudad is a somewhat dismal place. The most imposing construction along this stretch of coast is the now sadly run-down **Estadio Panamericana** (*see p181*), built for the 11th Pan-American Games in Cuba in 1991. Its adjacent **Villa Panamericana** was once athletes' housing, but was later given to the voluntary workers who had built the stadium.

Cojímar

Set in a little cove at the mouth of the Río Cojímar is a small village of the same name, the shoreline of which still retains the air of a small traditional fishing community (in spite of ugly apartment buildings built here in the 1970s to deal with population overspill). The village was made famous by the fact that Ernest Hemingway docked his boat 'Pilar' here and could often be found at his favourite local **Bar-Restaurante La Terraza** (*see below*).

In 1962 locals erected the **Monumento a Ernest Hemingway** on the north-western corner of the cove. Myth has it that local fishermen melted down their propellers to make the bronze bust commemorating their legendary visitor. It consists of a pseudo-Greek rotundo, sheltering a bronze bust of the author, grinning and gazing out to sea. Across the street is the former **Fuerte de Cojímar**, a fortress now under military jurisdiction, but in 1762 the site where the British landed on their way to conquer Havana.

Bar-Restaurante La Terraza

Calle Real #161, esquina a Candelaria (939486).
Open 11am-11pm daily. **Main courses** $7-$34.
No credit cards.

A pleasant restaurant despite the tour groups. The walls are lined with black and white shots of Hemingway, many by famous Cuban photographers Raúl Corrales and Alberto 'Korda' Gutiérrez. Included are several images of the former skipper of Hemingway's boat, Gregorio Fuentes, the model for the fisherman in *Old Man and the Sea,* who passed away aged 104 in 2002.

Alamar

On the other side of the Cojímar river's drawbridge is **Alamar**, often dissed as a soul-destroying city of concrete. Housing reform in Cuba since the 1960s improved living conditions for many, but in some areas – and this is one – 'improvements' meant throwing aesthetic harmony to the wind. Nevertheless, this universe unto itself provides housing for 96,000 inhabitants and is the unlikely birthplace of some of the city's hottest culture.

Its active **Casa de Cultura** (5ta Avenida, esquina Avenida de los Cocos, 650624) is an energetic affair, while the affiliated **Fayad Jamis Centro de Arte y Literatura** is a gallery showing digital, erotic, graphic art and installations. The **Mundo de Gallo** (Calle 196 y 3ra, 656270) is a humorous and eccentric collection of welded art in an apartment block garden, created and overseen by resident 72-year-old Revolutionary hero and artist Héctor Gallo Portieles. The place is difficult to find, so be prepared to ask for directions. The **Cinema 11 Festival** (Avenida de los Cocos #16228, 651378) in the centre of Alamar is one of four headquarters for the Festival del Nuevo Cine Latinoamericano (*see p136*) held in Havana every December, while the amphitheatre on the western end is the site of the yearly **Festival de Rap Cubano Habana Hip Hop** (*see p134*). Behind it is a huge public swimming pool.

Playas del Este

See p246 & p247

One of the most logical options for beach getaways from Havana is often overlooked as all eyes are drawn further east to over-touted Varadero sands. The capital's eastern beaches, however, have beautiful creamy white sand and are just a 20-minute jaunt (by car) from Old Havana. To reach them, follow the (sometimes confusing) signs from the Vía Monumental and Vía Blanca, or take a cab ($10-$20). The Playas del Este are really a single, eight-kilometre (five-mile) stretch with changing names (from west to east): Tarará, El Mégano, Santa María del Mar, Boca Ciega and Guanabo. Several large resort hotels, mainly ghastly 1960s and '70s structures, are scattered between Tarará and Guanabo, with the majority at Santa María del Mar.

Tarará, a spacious, partially wooded beach and residential complex (with the well-equipped Marina Puertasol; *see p181*), and **Playa Mégano**, with coarser sand backed by pine trees and a long-abandoned domestic tourism complex, are the first. But easily the most popular of the eastern beaches are **Santa María del Mar**, **Boca Ciega** and **Guanabo**, a trio of creamy sands and crystalline turquoise waters, backed by coconut trees, pines and bluffs reaching to 80 metres (262 feet).

The most honky-tonk of all the eastern beaches is **Santa María del Mar**, whose busiest stretch is in front of the Hotel Tropicoco (*see p46*). Being a more touristy area, it has lodgings, restaurants, watersports hire, grocery stores and a pharmacy. Next along comes Havana's gay, lesbian and transvestite beach **Playa Mi Cayito** (*see also p152*). Then comes **Boca Ciega**, a lengthy strip with particularly soft, white sand stretching from the dilapidated wooden bridge crossing the Itabo river to Guanabo. Quieter than the other beaches, it is popular with Cuban families.

Last in line, but not least, is **Guanabo**, also popular with Cubans. Perhaps more interesting than the slightly poorer-quality sand is the strip of shops and snack bars (Avenida 5ta), which are far more varied (and less touristy) than those on the other eastern beaches. They include fast food outlets, an ice-cream parlour and a photo shop. The **Museo Municipal de La Habana del Este** (Calle 504, esquina 5taC, 962247, closed Mon), is a run-down wooden building at the eastern end of town, with an old whale skeleton and a few aboriginal relics. This neglected collection is saved only by a firm commitment to **Sibarimar**, the area's environmental watchdog project, currently administering 11 endangered areas. The environmentalists who run the project have just opened the **Rincón de Guanabo** (965697, $1), a tiny ecological haven for crabs and birds on a cove east of Peñas Altas after Guanabo, with a visitor centre and cafeteria.

Mundo de Gallo: art among the grass roots.

Textbook tropical terrain at **Playa Santa María del Mar**. *See p93.*

Eat, Drink, Shop

Eating & Drinking **96**
Shops & Services **116**

Features

The best Restaurants 96
Menu reader 98
Chinatown 102
Herbivore Havana 106
The best Bars 115
The best Shops 116
Peso shops 119
Rolling stock 122
Getting agro 126

Eating & Drinking

Fancy flavours are few and far between in Havana, but portions of homely, Creole fare abound.

Cuba is no gastro destination, let's get that straight. But in a country whose population still lives on food rations and suffers daily shortages of basic ingredients, this should come as no surprise.

As in all spheres where the tourist moves, Havana's restaurant scene is steadily changing with the influx of hard currency. The quality of food, even in the city's best restaurants, is unlikely to make a Parisian salivate, but the difference between a meal at a good *paladar* (private restaurant) and a bad state restaurant should not be underestimated. Eating out isn't cheap and, moreover, there is no guaranteed correlation between price and quality. Expensive, swanky restaurants aren't hard to come by these days in Havana's hotels and wealthier districts, but paying through the nose won't necessarily secure you decent food or efficient service. More often than not, you're paying for the location.

The real delight at many restaurants, in particular the smaller ones, is the atmosphere, and this Havana does have by the truckload. The best meals you will have will be in the privately owned *paladares*.

CUBAN CUISINE

Cuban food is hearty and uncomplicated, not as spicily hot as other Latin American or Caribbean fare, but not bland either. Ingredients such as orange and lime juice, olives, peppers, cumin, bay leaves, garlic and lots of onion are evidence of the mix of Spanish, African and Chinese influences that have created a vibrant, earthy cuisine.

Sometimes, though, you'd be forgiven for thinking that Cuban cuisine consists solely of rice and beans, with the odd bit of chicken or pork thrown in. But if you look hard, you may find the occasional traditional Cuban dish on the menu, such as *ajíaco* (stew), *tasajo* (dried cured beef) or *ropa vieja* (beef stew; the name means 'old clothes', on account of how the shredded beef looks). Other typical ingredients to try are *yuca* (cassava), *plátano* (plaintain) and *malanga* (taro).

STATE RESTAURANTS

The service in many state restaurants remains surprisingly poor – surprising because there is fierce competition to secure a job as a waiter in virtually any establishment where there's the opportunity to earn hard-currency tips (it can't be the average basic salary of around $10 per month that's the lure). But the link between good service and good tips has hardly permeated the service-industry mindset. Waiters tend to rely on tourists' goodwill to secure themselves a tip, rather than viewing tipping as a reward for work. If you come across appalling service (or food) in a state-run restaurant, ask to speak to *el gerente* (the boss). The personal touch is more usually found in a *paladar*.

PESO RESTAURANTS

These are restaurants where you can join the locals and pay in local currency. Eating in such establishments may confirm your worst suspicions about Cuban cuisine, but they're worth trying for the experience. Some peso restaurant proprietors will claim it is illegal for them to serve tourists. In fact, if the restaurant doesn't have a specific dollar menu, you should by rights be charged in pesos like the locals; however, the restaurants often get around this obstacle by offering a tailor-made menu priced in dollars ('just for you'). If you're not strapped for cash, pay the few extra dollars with a smile;

The best Restaurants

For trad Cuban cuisine

Casa Sarasua (*see p108*); **La Cocina de Lilliam** (*see p111*).

For fine wines

La Ferminia (*see p110*); La Bodeguita del Vino at **La Giraldilla** (*see p110*);

For dining with the in crowd

El Aljibe (*see p109*); **La Finca** (*see p110*); **La Giraldilla** (*see p110*); **La Guarida** (*see p105*).

For choice snacking

Cafetería El Rincón del Cine at the **Hotel Nacional** (*see p105*); **La Fontana** (*see p112*); **Pan.Com** (*see p111*).

For Italian

El Diluvio (*see p111*); **Piccolo** (*see p112*); **Pizza Nova** (*see p111*).

Rice, beans and a hunk of fried chicken are never far away.

the food served to you will usually be better than the peso fare and you'll be helping the waiters supplement their pitiful wages. If you're on a tight budget, stand your ground, agree on a peso price and check the bill carefully.

PALADARES

Cubans started welcoming paying diners into their houses to enjoy home-cooked food in the mid 1990s, as part of the government's introduction of limited private enterprise. Family members are the only employees at *paladares*, so there are plenty of domestic outbursts for you to enjoy while you eat. More importantly, at the best *paladares* the food is home-made, fresh and filling.

Try to give a healthy tip if you have a good meal at a *paladar*; as with *casas particulares*, the owners have to contend with high taxes and constant monitoring from Big Brother, so your contribution will be gratefully received. Some of the most successful *paladares* have been in operation for over five years, and some have evolved into high-class restaurants.

However, the high taxes also mean that *paladares* come and go all the time, either by their own choice or because they are closed down for violation of the rules. Rather farcically on occasions, *paladares* are only allowed to serve 12 customers at a time and they are not officially allowed to serve shellfish or steak. Some owners ignore these rules, and seafood may be available if you ask.

JINETEROS

A phenomenon that has grown in line with the increase in the number of visitors to Havana is that of the *jinetero/a*. Literally jockeys, they

Menu reader

BASICS
Carta/menú menu; **la cuenta** the bill; **desayuno** breakfast; **almuerzo** lunch; **comida** dinner; **entrante** entrée; **dulce/postre** dessert; **pan** bread; **agua** water (**con gas** fizzy; **sin gas** plain); **vino** wine (**tinto** red, **blanco** white, **rosado** rosé); **cerveza** beer; **café** coffee; **saladito** savoury snack; **trago** alcoholic drink or cocktail; **refresco** soft drink; **jugo de frutas natural** natural fruit juice; **guarapo** sugar cane juice; **limonada** lemonade; **bocadito** sandwich.

COOKING STYLES AND TECHNIQUES
A la parilla grilled; **asado** roasted; **frito** fried; **en cazuela/estofado** stewed; **rebozado** dipped in batter and deep-fried; **empanizado** coated in breadcrumbs and fried; **aporreado** shredded and stewed meat or fish; **fricase** stewed; **escabeche** pickled; **enchilado** stewed in wine and tomato sauce; **potaje** bean stew; **tortilla** omelette

MEAT AND POULTRY
Pierna de puerco pork leg; **jamón** ham; **chuleta** chop; **perrito** sausage/hot dog; **bistec** steak; **carnero** lamb; **chorizo** pork sausage seasoned with paprika; **conejo** rabbit; **pollo** chicken; **guanajo/pavo** turkey; **lechón** suckling pig; **tasajo** jerked beef; **pato** duck; **butifarra** white pork sausage; **res** beef; **palomilla de res** beef steak; **picadillo** minced beef; **chicharrones** fried pork skins and fat.

FISH AND SHELLFISH
Langosta lobster; **camarones** king prawns; **bacalao** salted cod; **atún** tuna; **pargo** red snapper; **cherna** grouper; **pulpo** octopus; **calamar** squid; **pez espada** swordfish; **cangrejo** stone crab.

VEGETABLES, RICES, PULSES AND CEREALS
Viandas refer to vegetables (often root vegetables) that are generally fried or boiled and seasoned with a garlic and lemon sauce. The following are considered *viandas*: **plátano** banana; **plátano macho** plantain; **yuca** cassava; **malanga** taro; **boniato** sweet potato; **papas** potatoes; **calabaza** pumpkin. **Quimbombó** okra; **frijoles** beans (**negros** black, **blancos** white, **colorados** red);

make their dollars in a variety of ways, ranging from prostitution to 'helping' tourists by 'guiding' them to *paladares* for the 'best meal in Havana'. *Jineteros* will have made a previous arrangement with the *paladar* owners (often their relations), in return for commission. You may get a decent meal by using the services of a *jinetero*, but bear in mind that the city's best *paladares* don't operate in this way and always agree on prices first: many an innocent tourist has parted with $40 per person for rice and beans in granny's kitchen.

OPENING TIMES
Opening times and days, like other information in Havana, should be taken with a large pinch of salt. Though the city is becoming more and more used to the demands of overseas visitors, *paladares* in particular sometimes close on a whim. So, if you're going out of your way to visit any of the places listed in this chapter, call ahead beforehand and make sure you go armed with a sense of humour as well as an appetite.

PRICES
Most restaurants and *paladares* charge in dollars. The golden rule is to check first. Be wary of those mystery menus with prices that alter as if by magic as soon as a foreigner enters the room. If anything on the menu is unclear, or if there isn't a menu at all, clarify all the prices in person (unless you like paying $6 for bread and butter). You could also apply the 'Cristal test' to give you a quick indication of how hard the bill will bite. In a cheap restaurant a local Cristal beer should cost about $1, rising to $2 in mid-range places and higher if it's an expensive restaurant. Ultimately, though, only the bill will tell you whether you've been ripped off, so scrutinise it very carefully. Note that service charges are beginning to creep on to bills in the most tourist-frequented places.

Note: pesos are sometimes designated by the $ sign; this is not as confusing as it sounds if you remember that restaurants generally charge in dollars (notable exceptions are certain restaurants in Chinatown and street stalls).

CREDIT WHERE CREDIT'S DUE
Cash is king in Cuba and only the top hotels and government-run restaurants accept plastic. Even if they do, they would much rather you paid in cash. Always double-check before you consume anything: although many places display the usual MasterCard and Visa stickers, the waiter may still go into a coma if actually asked to settle a bill with a credit card.

maíz corn; **arroz** rice; **garbanzos** chickpeas; **harina de maíz** cornmeal; **ajo** garlic; **pimiento** bell pepper (**maduro** red, **verde** green); **habichuelas** string beans; **pepino** cucumber; **aguacate** avocado; **tomate** tomato; **rábanos** radishes; **lechuga** lettuce; **col** cabbage; **cebolla** onion; **remolacha** beetroot; **acelga** swiss chard; **zanahoria** carrot; **berenjena** aubergine; **berro** watercress; **frijolitos chinos** soya bean sprouts.

FRUITS
Coctél de frutas fruit salad; **piña** pineapple; **limón** lime; **naranja** orange; **toronja** grapefruit; **fruta bomba** papaya; **guayaba** guava; **melón** watermelon; **plátano** banana; **coco** coconut; **maní** peanuts; **caña de azucar** sugar cane.

DESSERTS
Dulce de coco grated coconut cooked in syrup; **cascos de guayava en almíbar** guava halves cooked in syrup (this dessert is also prepared with orange or grapefruit skins); **pasta de guayaba con queso** guava fruit paste with cheese; **helado** ice-cream; **flan** caramel custard; **panetela** sponge cake; **señorita** millefeuille; **flan de calabaza** squash pudding; **arroz con leche** rice pudding; **buñuelos** fritters.

LOCAL SPECIALITIES
Ajiaco/caldosa pot au feu or stew; **congrí/arroz moro** rice cooked with black or red beans; **mojo** sour orange, garlic and oil sauce served with boiled tubers, like cassava and taro, and meats; **fritura** fritters (**de malanga** taro, **de maíz** corn, **de calabaza** squash); **tostones** fried plantains, **chicharritas de plátano** plantain chips; **croquetas** croquettes; **langosta mariposa** unshelled and grilled lobster; **enchilado de langosta/camarones** lobster/prawns in a wine and tomato sauce; **arroz con pollo a la Chorrera** rice cooked with chicken, peas and beer; **tamal en hojas** corn cakes; **tamal en cazuela** corn soup or purée; **masitas de puerco** fried pork squares; **picadillo a la habanera** stewed ground beef seasoned with raisins and olives; **ropa vieja** boiled, shredded and stewed beef; **aporreado de tasajo** boiled, shredded and stewed jerked beef; **pierna asada** roast leg of pork.

And, even if he does say 'that will do nicely', you may have to wait for 30 minutes while the telecommunication lines deal with your plastic. Therefore, always take enough dollars with you to cover the cost of your meal, and remember that no US credit cards, or even those issued by a bank associated with a US bank, are accepted.

Eating

La Habana Vieja

Old Havana is the epicentre of Havana's tourist trade, and some restaurants have become overly complacent as a result. However, it is possible to find a good meal, more often than not in charming colonial surroundings. Nearly all restaurants in Old Havana are operated by Habaguanex (www.habaguanex.com), the tourist company attached to the City Historian's Office that is responsible for restoring the city (*see p52* **Urban refit**). We list three that don't come under the Habaguanex umbrella: Gentiluomo, El Floridita and La Bodeguita del Medio.

Restaurants

El Baturro

Calle Egido #661, entre Merced y Jesús María (860 9078). **Open** 11am-11pm daily. **Main courses** $1.60-$21. **No credit cards**. **Map** p252 E14.

Careful here: there are two menus, the more expensive one (the one you will inevitably be given) posting combination platters at $15 and upwards, and a cheaper one (ask for the Spanish à la carte menu) offering practically the same combos for $3. Go figure. First opened in 1919 by a Spanish wine importer, authenticity still prevails at El Baturro, as with the hearty Asturian *fabada* (stew): the requisite broad beans, blood sausage, shoulder of pork, bacon and onion are all present, with just the right amount of saffron. El Baturro comprises a bar attached to the main dining room, a mezzanine and a private dining room. Take a look at the remains of the best-preserved section of the old city wall nearby.

Bodegón Onda

Calle Obrapía #53, esquina Baratillo (867 1037). **Open** noon-4pm, 7-10pm Mon-Sat; noon-4pm Sun. **Main courses** $10-$25. **Tapas** average $2. **Credit** MC, V. **Map** p252 E15.

Unmistakably a tapas bar, there are at least 15 Spanish finger foods at $3 or less, and a few expensive main courses, like the *churrasco*, a huge platter of beef with salad and fries ($25). A favourite with the lunch crowd from the Lonja del Comercio business office next door, the Bodegón's a real sleeper at night because it's more of less hidden away from the rest of Old Havana. Opened in 1999, the restaurant was the inspiration of two Spanish women – one of whom owned a restaurant in Santander. The cooking is pleasingly authentic: the tuna *empanada* is just as it should be and the Russian salad has all its components, bar green peas. A decent mid-range restaurant.

La Bodeguita del Medio

Calle Empedrado #207, entre San Ignacio y Cuba (338857). **Open** 10.30am-midnight daily. **Main courses** $9-$14. **Credit** MC, V. **Map** p252 D15.

Most *bodegas* (local grocery stores) in Cuba are on street corners for easy accessibility, but this one, opened by Angel Martínez in 1942, is in the middle of the street, hence 'del medio'. The abundance of photos of world celebrities, including former Beatles manager George Martin and Robert De Niro, on its walls should impress even the most urbane visitors but the fact that the best tables are reserved for dead people (Sammy Davis Junior et al) can grate. Unfortunately, the Bodeguita has allowed complacency to set in: the food is generally uninspiring and expensive, though the best bet is *picadillo habanero* at $9. By all means have a mojito with the squillions of tourists doing the same, but don't expect haute cuisine.

Cabaña

Calle Cuba #12, esquina Peña Pobre (860 5670). **Open** 10am-midnight Mon-Wed; 10am-2am Thur-Sun. **Main courses** $7-$18. **Credit** MC, V. **Map** p252 D15.

Cuban tourism workers are given meal vouchers to eat here, so you may see a bunch of blue-shirted bus drivers when you walk in. Originally opened at the end of the 19th century by a Spanish merchant who was in love with the wharf area, the old salt lived above his usually packed eaterie. These days, the food is tasty enough but priced rather beyond its station. The deliciously air-conditioned second floor has huge windows looking on to a portside street. A sound booth lies in wait for evening karaoke.

Café del Oriente

Calle Oficios #112, esquina Amargura (860 6686). **Open** 8.30am-midnight daily. **Main courses** $8-$30. **Credit** MC, V. **Map** p252 E15.

This is one of the best state-run restaurants in town for food, ambience and service. Photos of Spain's Queen Sofia dining here hint at the solvency of the average customer. One doesn't have to be rolling in it to eat here (try the $8 pasta with cheese, ham and broccoli), but it does help. The ritzy bar and deli downstairs has mouthwatering displays of chilled lobster, cured ham and pâté. Upstairs, the still more elegant restaurant – think chandeliers, crisp curtains and insignia plates – has appetisers such as eel and smoked salmon with caviar, or calf's brains with mustard and brandy cream sauce, accompanied, perhaps, by a $208 bottle of Dom Perignon. A ten per cent service charge is levied upstairs, but at least the service is unassailable.

Café Mercurio

Lonja del Comercio, Lamparilla #2, Plaza de San Francisco (860 6188). **Open** 8am-midnight daily. **Main courses** $7-$18. **Credit** MC, V. **Map** p252 E15.

Gleaming hardwoods and mirrored columns lend this restaurant – situated on the ground floor of the Lonja del Comercio – a polished air. The varied and reasonably priced menu takes in plenty of seafood and meat, and the house speciality of seafood rice reels you in with almost a whole lobster tail and plenty of peeled shrimp. Across the Plaza de San Francisco, in front of the basilica, is a statue of one of Havana's most loved and legendary figures, the homeless and good-hearted Caballero de París (*see p60* **Statuary rites**). Mercurio is a gem, particularly considering its fantastic location overlooking the *plaza*.

Café Taberna

Calle Mercaderes, esquina Brasil (Teniente Rey) (861 1637). **Open** 6am-10am daily. **Main courses** (noon-midnight daily) $2.50-$20. **No credit cards.** **Map** p252 E15.

Located on one corner of the Plaza Vieja, this venue was opened originally as a coffeehouse in 1772, and reopened in 1999 in homage to revered Cuban musician Beny Moré. There's a small mezzanine lounge and a sprinkling of outside tables at night, and there are long-term plans to build a grill on the roof. Among the best deals is the Taberna chicken at $7, although there are more exotic items such as *camarones a la salsa reglita* ($12) – shrimp with soy sauce, honey, ginger and brandy – for the more adventurous. Either way, the food tends to be three-star. The house dance duo gets things moving later on and there's an excellent magician. Apparently, the waiters did not read our last review because they are still chiselling customers: check your bill.

Cantabria

Calle Luz, esquina San Pedro (862 8000). **Open** *Lobby bar* 24hrs daily. *Restaurant* 7am-10pm daily. **Main courses** $4-$25. **Credit** MC, V. **Map** p252 F15.

Faithful to the Basque country, the restaurant serves a number of typical Cantabrian dishes, such as a Santander grand seafood platter ($23), consisting of lobster, shrimp, fish, squid and mussels. There are also a few creative mixes of Spanish and Cuban elements, such as calamaris stuffed with rice and beans. The bay provides a nice backdrop through the floor to ceiling windows and arches outside. There's a strong, mainly Spanish, wine list and comfortable roof terrace, and a bar and billiard table downstairs ($5 per hour).

El Castillo de Farnés

Avenida de Bélgica (Monserrate), esquina Obrapía (867 1030). **Open** *Bar* 24hrs daily. *Restaurant* noon-midnight daily. **Main courses** $4-$15. **Credit** MC, V. **Map** p252 E14.

This sometimes over-chilled Spanish restaurant – somewhat hidden behind the busy bar that's open 24 hours a day – is decorated with photos of Fidel, his brother Raúl and Ché Guevara eating here just after they occupied Havana in 1959; it was reputedly one of Fidel's preferred hangouts. It's a good place for a cheap breakfast, with egg dishes going for a buck or two, but doesn't make the grade for a formal dinner.

La Dominica

Calle O'Reilly #108, esquina Mercaderes (860 2918). **Open** noon-midnight daily. **Main courses** $5-$35. **Credit** MC, V. **Map** p252 E15.

A convent dining hall, then a meeting spot for Spanish politicos in the 19th century, La Dominica is now an Italian restaurant, and one of Havana's finest. The ceilings are kite high and though the decor is Venetian carnival-inspired, the restaurant remains a spot of subtle restraint: even the house band is discreet. Budgeteers should go for pizza deals on the pavement café; the more formal combination platters aren't for the tightfisted ($27-$35). Either way, the food is excellent and the pizzas some of the best you'll find. And a good wine list to boot.

Don Giovanni

Calle Tacón #4, esquina Empedrado (867 1027). **Open** 10am-midnight daily. **Main courses** $5-$22. **Credit** MC, V. **Map** p252 D15.

One of the best views of freighters slipping through the neck of Havana's pocket bay, and of the Morro lighthouse, will be available when the restoration of this Italian restaurant is complete. It hasn't let down clients in the meanwhile, though: the outdoor café is still thriving. Worth a trip for the grand mudéjar-style building alone.

Don Ricardo

Hotel O'Farrill, Calle Cuba #102, esquina Chacón (860 5080). **Open** noon-midnight daily. **Main courses** $7.50-$12. **Credit** MC, V. **Map** p252 D15.

The Don Ricardo restaurant at the newly restored Hotel O'Farrill can't rightly be called an Irish restaurant (it's mainly Cuban), but there is Irish stew at least. It seems the chefs have consciously appropriated the foreign genre by adding a tomato-based sauce. The St Patrick's week menu goes all out with dishes like coddle. Irish coffee, on the other hand, is available year round.

El Floridita

Calle Obispo #557, esquina Avenida de Bélgica (Monserrate) (867 1299). **Open** *Bar* 11am-midnight daily. *Restaurant* noon-midnight daily. **Main courses** $11-$42. **Credit** MC, V. **Map** p252 D14.

Opened in 1918, this elegant throwback to another era has a bar up front with the cordoned-off seat of former regular customer Ernest Hemingway. The occasional camera flash punctuates what is otherwise very subdued lighting. Unfortunately, the same restraint has not been used in the pricing of the menu, which offers such delicacies as lobster with cheese and béchamel sauce for a whopping $42. More of a monument than a place to eat, the ambience is nevertheless good, the place smells of class and there are some museum-piece dishes that must be unique to Cuba. Frogs' leg soufflé anyone?

Gentiluomo

Calle Obispo #557, esquina Bernaza (867 1300/1301). **Open** noon-midnight daily. **Main courses** $3-$18. **Credit** MC, V. **Map** p252 E14.

This Italian offshoot of El Floridita (*see above*) opened in 1991, and provides a tasty, competitive alternative to it. One of a trio of non-Habaguanex restaurants in Old Havana, it's had its ups and downs over the years, and is sometimes quiet. However, the fish fillet and lobster are the same as next door in the Floridita but half the price. The food is good: pizzas are nice and thin and the *tomate gratinado* is wonderful, with fresh tomatoes, melted gouda cheese and fresh basil.

Hanoi

Calle Brasil (Teniente Rey) #507, esquina Bernaza (867 1029). **Open** noon-midnight daily. **Main courses** $2.30-$8. **No credit cards**. **Map** p252 E14.

Forget the notion of savouring South-east Asia's finest cuisine, the fact of the matter is that this restaurant is plebian from the prices to the selection. The menu includes *chicharrones* (fried pork rinds) for 80¢, *manjúa* (a tiny crunchy fried fish appetiser for 40¢ and some down-home chef suggestions that don't exceed $6. A budget option through and through.

Jardín del Edén

Hotel Raquel, Calle Amargura, esquina San Ignacio (860 8280). **Open** *Breakfast buffet* 7am-10am daily. *Dinner* noon-11pm daily. **Main courses** $9-$12. **Credit** MC, V. **Map** p252 E15.

It's easy to get blasé about all the restoration work that has transformed Old Havana, but the Jewish-themed Hotel Raquel really is one of the must-sees. Typically Jewish items on the menu include gefilte fish – five delicious but small balls painstakingly crowned with cucumber – and vegetable kugel.

Al Medina

Calle Oficios #12, entre Obispo y Obrapía (867 1041). **Open** noon-midnight daily. **Main courses** $4-$22. **Credit** MC, V. **Map** p252 E16.

A former boys' school, this 17th-century building displays a Moorish influence so often found in colonial architecture – apt enough for a Middle Eastern restaurant. The menu is mainly Lebanese, with a large collection of meze dishes, plus grilled chicken and meat to follow if you've room. Al Medina is worth trying for something different, but ultimately it seems to fall between two stools: it doesn't score high on ambience, nor is the food exceptional. As far as we know, the small Middle Eastern grocer's and gift shop at the entrance are the only of their kind in Cuba.

El Mesón de la Flota

Calle Mercaderes #257, entre Amargura y Brasil (Teniente Rey) (863 838/862 9281). **Open** noon-midnight daily. **Main courses** $5-$18. **Tapas** $1-$5. **No credit cards**. **Map** p252 E15.

Chinatown

The first Chinese immigrants arrived in Cuba in 1847 to work on sugar plantations after the African slave trade ended. At the end of the 19th century, thousands more arrived from California – escaping US Chinese exclusion laws – and created Chinatown. Havana's *barrio chino* was once Latin America's biggest. A third wave of immigrants arrived in the early 20th century following the establishment of a republic in China.

The *barrio* was not set to thrive, however. Most of the city's Chinese community moved to San Francisco after the 1959 Revolution and Chinatown ground to a halt. Restaurants were allowed to open again in 1996 as a move to improve relations with communist China (and to create a tourist attraction), so Chinatown is back in business.

The main strip of Chinese restaurants is just off Calle Zanja on the Bulevar del Barrio Chino (or Cuchillo), which is decorated with red Chinese lanterns. Packed every night, waiters in smart silk uniforms beckon customers, menu in hand. Cubans and foreigners flock here for cheap, tasty meals – just don't come expecting textbook authenticity.

Chan Li Po

Calle Campanario #453, entre Zanja y San José (870 3686). **Open** noon-midnight daily. **Main courses** $2.50-$7.50.

Chan Li Po wins hands down for variety of food, as well as comfort levels – but it's still cheap enough to draw hordes of Cubans. Be prepared to wait in line in the street. Dishes run the gamut from paella to chop suey to pizza.

Chung Shan

Calle Dragones #311 altos, entre Rayo y San Nicolás (862 0909). **Open** noon-10.30pm daily. **Main courses** $1.50-$10.

On a backstreet one block from Zanja, this Chinese cultural association is named after a town in Guangdong province in southern China. Up a flight of stairs, the spacious, well-cooled Chung Shan has the best service in Chinatown, and is always full of Cubans. The dishes are good quality, and served piping hot.

La Muralla

Bulevar del Barrio Chino #12 (863 2081). **Open** 11am-midnight daily. **Main courses** $1.65-$5.

One of the few places that's not on a main square in Old Havana but that still manages to maintain a good atmosphere after dark. A former hangout for Havana's sailors, the Mesón has been serving wharf dwellers for more than 120 years. It reopened in 2000 with a maritime theme and a menu of well-prepared tapas, including anything from a classic Spanish omelette to Cuban-style *tamales*. The courtyard has hanging ivy, tropical plants and glazed ceramic tables, and four different house flamenco troupes stomp the floor from 9pm daily. One gripe: portions seem to have curiously shrunk since its opening.

La Mina

Calle Obispo #109, esquina Oficios, (862 0216). **Open** *Bar & café* 24hrs daily. *Restaurant* 10am-midnight daily. **Main courses** $4-$28. **Credit** MC, V. **Map** p252 E16.

Across the street from the Tong Po Laug, this clean and airy restaurant always seems to be empty. This is curious, since the food is good and cheap (lobster for $5). The lack of outdoor seating and slow service are discouraging.

Tien Tan

Bulevar del Barrio Chino #17 (861 5478). **Open** 11am-midnight daily. **Main courses** $2.30-$22.50.

Tien Tan is often billed as Chinatown's most authentic restaurant on account of its Chinese chef. It can be overpriced when it comes to seafood in comparison with its neighbours, and locals tend to shun the place. But it does do a decent job on sweet and sour dishes.

Tong Po Laug

Bulevar del Barrio Chino #10 (no phone). **Open** noon-1am daily. **Main courses** $2.50-$8.

Popular with locals and tourists, the Tong Po Laug has some of the lowest prices in the *barrio chino*, with a hearty meal costing under $5. Recently introduced dishes for vegetarians, such as omelettes and veggie stir-fries, have been a hit, and the outdoor area has been improved with a traditional wooden Chinese roof.

Los Tres Chinitos

Calle Dragones #357, entre Manrique y San Nicolás (863 3388). **Open** noon-midnight daily. **Main courses** $1.50-$7.

This maze-like restaurant has three dining rooms. One serves Chinese food, another typical Cuban *criollo* cuisine, while the upstairs area serves Italian food (although it sports Chinese-style stained-glass windows). The restaurant draws vast numbers of Cubans who line up outside, so get there early.

On one of Old Havana's loveliest squares (Plaza de Armas), La Mina complex – a sweet shop, bar, café, ice-cream parlour and restaurant – has an inside patio populated by roving peacocks, and pavement tables for a view of the square. The usual trilogy of pork, fish or chicken are all competently prepared for less than $8 and accompanied by congrí rice and chips. There are no less than six house bands, which rotate throughout the day.

El Patio

San Ignacio #54, Plaza de la Catedral (867 1034-1035). **Open** *Restaurant* noon-midnight daily. *Café* 24hrs daily. **Main courses** $9-$28. **Credit** MC, V. **Map** p252 D15.

This 18th-century colonial palace is one of Havana's most picturesque, with stained-glass windows, large arches and a pretty central courtyard. These days, it's probably the best place in Old Havana for people-watching, and there's usually an excellent band playing (supplemented by impromptu contributions from seasoned deadbeats). The restaurant inside is on two floors, and serves Cuban classics. The lowest prices are on the higher floor, an elegant 120-person grill restaurant. But wherever you savour the atmosphere, the food is unlikely to match the surroundings or the prices (a pepper steak is a staggering $20).

Puerto de Sagua

Calle Egido #603, entre Acosta y Jesús María (867 1026). **Open** noon-midnight daily. **Main courses** $2.50-$23.50. **Credit** MC, V. **Map** p252 E14.

The Sagua's a little out of the way, near Havana's main train terminus, but it's worth the hike. Opened in 1945, the space begins with a bar, complete with fish tanks. Further in is a good-value cafeteria and finally comes the elegant dining room with a larger aquarium. Expect very good-quality food for fair prices; there are six lobster dishes, all priced at $12.50. Upstairs (by special reservation) is an intimate *bodega*-style dining room for four.

El Rincón de Eleggúá

Calle Aguacate #257, entre Obispo y Obrapía (867 2367). **Open** noon-11pm Mon-Sat. **Main courses** $6-$10.50. **No credit cards**. **Map** p252 E15.

This family restaurant is named after the African deity Eleggúá – god of prosperity. Something must be working because it's still thriving after eight years. The ground floor has some pretty good Afro-Cuban decor, and is worth checking out for the low-key Cuban ambience. Upstairs is air-conditioned but not as charming. Servings can be undersized; the fried snapper ($10.50) consists of a small slab of fish, diminutive vegetable accompaniment and plain rice.

Santo Angel

Calle Teniente Rey (Brasil), esquina San Ignacio (861 1626). **Open** *Café* 8am-1am daily. *Restaurant* noon-11pm daily. **Main courses** $7-$28. **Credit** MC, V. **Map** p252 E15.

A high-class restaurant on the north-west corner of the beautifully restored Plaza Vieja. The café outside has cheapish sandwiches; inside there's a beautiful terrace and several large dining rooms. Prices are steep, but the presentation can include such wonders as a decorative rooster made from mashed potato, chive, fried plantain and pepper. The trademark pork with pineapple sauce is flavoursome. Mains dishes don't come with side dishes, which run from $1.50 to $2.50. Service is intermittently excellent (the rest of the time it's good).

La Torre de Marfil

Calle Mercaderes #115, entre Obispo y Obrapía (867 1038). **Open** noon-10pm daily. **Main courses** $3.50-$15. **Credit** MC, V. **Map** p252 E15.

Red Chinese lanterns hanging outside mark the entrance to this restaurant. Originally opened in 1983 a block away, it's been in its current spot since 1990. Inside, there's a red and gold theme going on, though massive wood beams are painted an astoundingly ill-chosen cerulean blue. The Chinese food's not great but prices make amends. There's a table for eight under a pagoda in the back, as well as a small interior courtyard. The absence of a house band and smoke-free air will be definite pluses for some, but the fact that it's often empty is something of a downer.

La Zaragozana

Calle Monserrate #33, entre Obispo y Obrapía (867 1040). **Open** noon-midnight daily. **Main courses** $5-$25. **Credit** MC, V. **Map** p252 D14.

This is a Spanish football bar (complete with flags, scarves and pictures of football players) fighting it out with something a little higher up the social scale. Happy hour (4-7pm) offers cheap food and drink specials every day; later on, exotic dishes such as salmon, squid or frogs' legs go for hard-to-justify prices. Don't miss the aphrodisiac soup, a light ginger-based broth with a couple of shrimp thrown in.

Paladares

La Casa Julia

Calle O'Reilly #506A, entre Bernaza y Villegas (862 7438). **Open** noon-11pm daily. **Main courses** $8-$10. **No credit cards. Map** p252 D15.

Opened a decade ago, the granddaddy of Old Havana *paladares* is still kicking. On arrival, note that the owners had to paint over the Bernaza side of their sign to save $100 per month on the licence. But the yellow Christmas-style lights are still there. The delicious large meat portions all come with white rice, with black beans on the side, plus fried or boiled veg and salad. The original velour painting of the topless jungle goddess with her lion and tiger still hangs.

Don Lorenzo

Calle Acosta #260A, entre Habana y Compostela (861 6733/863 4402). **Open** noon-midnight daily. **Main courses** $15-$20. **No credit cards. Map** p252 E15.

A 'yes' man through and through, accommodating owner Juan Carlos will serve whatever you want, within reason. This pricey little joint defies its neighbourhood, which could easily serve as a 'before' shot for Old Havana's restoration work. The food is fabulous; if you want the most traditional dish, go for the Cuban *arroz con pollo a la Chorrera*. Advise management if you're unaccompanied by a guide, as the menu prices drop.

Centro Habana

In addition to the following restaurants, Centro Habana is home to **Chinatown** (*see p102*), which has some lively and reasonably priced restaurants.

Restaurants

A Prado y Neptuno

Paseo de Martí (Prado), esquina Neptuno (860 9636). **Open** noon-midnight daily. **Main courses** $4-$12. **Credit** MC, V. **Map** p251 D14.

Occupied by a grocer's shop in the 19th century, this spot in the heart of the city has since housed various restaurants with such creative names as the Miami, Caracas and Budapest. Restored in 1998 as an Italian restaurant, the neo-classical building is now decked out with a snazzy contemporary interior, care of Italian architect Roberto Gottardi. This place has plenty of atmosphere, mostly deriving from its busy location, and the food is good if wallet-stretching.

Roof Garden

Hotel Sevilla, Calle Trocadero #55, entre Paseo del Prado y Agramonte (860 8560). **Open** 7-10pm daily. **Main courses** $6-$29. **Credit** MC, V. **Map** p251 D13.

This Spanish-Moorish-style hotel has one of Havana's most spectacular roof-top restaurants. If you want to enjoy breathtaking views over the city, go for breakfast in the magic light of morning or show up early for dinner before the sun sets. Prices are high (lobster stew with rum and cucumber clocks up a hefty $29) and quality has declined since the departure of the French chef who devised the menu, but the views make it an unforgettable experience all the same.

Paladares

Amistad de Lanzarote

Calle Amistad #211, entre Neptuno y San Miguel (863 6172). **Open** noon-11pm daily. **Main courses** $5-$6. **No credit cards. Map** p251 D14.

The simplicity of this basic *paladar* is compensated by the friendliness of its staff (who love to practise their English). Fish, chicken and pork are the main dishes – no surprises there – along with the usual side orders of salad and *congrí* in large quantities. The shelves on the walls show *santería* statues venerating the Yoruba deities.

Bellomar

Calle Virtudes #169, esquina Amistad (861 0023). **Open** noon-11pm daily. **Main courses** $10. **No credit cards. Map** p251 D14.

Situated in the midst of Centro Habana's considerable bustle, this authentic *paladar* is cramped, but makes up for it by being friendly and spotlessly clean. The tables are laid out in a corridor in a train-like fashion, and the decor is typical 1980s kitsch, with plastic flowers and tinted-glass tables.

The fish and meat dishes are substantial, though the side orders of *congrí* and fried plantain have been known to be unpalatable. Best go for an extra large salad instead.

La Guarida

Calle Concordia #418, entre Gervasio y Escobar (264 4940). **Open** noon-midnight daily. **Main courses** $15-$20. **Map** p251 D13.

Booking is recommended at Havana's most famous *paladar*, housed in the apartment where the Cuban film *Fresa y chocolate* was shot. Entering the crumbling mansion and climbing the marble staircase through what is today an apartment building, you may wonder if you came to the right address. Ring the third-floor doorbell, though, and you are welcomed into a trendy, dimly lit restaurant, crowded with foreigners. Among La Guarida's famed visitors are Jack Nicholson, Steven Spielberg and Queen Sofia of Spain (the chair she sat on is hung on the wall of the lobby). Paellas dominate the lunchtime menu, and at night it's nouvelle Cuban cuisine. The higher-priced dishes are well worth the value, from roast duck to the house speciality: pan-seared grouper. Service is fast and professional.

La Tasquita

Calle Jovellar #160, entre Espada y San Francisco (879 8647). **Open** noon-midnight daily. **Main courses** $6-$9. **Map** p250 C12.

This must be the smallest and most discreet *paladar* in Havana. Service is understated but attentive. The usual suspects – pork, chicken and fish – are well prepared; red snapper is usually on the menu. The decor is pretty kitsch.

Vedado

Out of action as this guide went to press was **La Torre** (553089), at the top of the landmark Edificio Focsa (*see p80*), which is currently being renovated. When the restaurant reopens, expect to enjoy fantastic views and spend at least $50 a head.

Restaurants

La Casona de 17

Calle 17 #60, entre M y N (553136). **Open** noon-midnight daily. **Main courses** $3.50-$40. **Credit** MC, V. **Map** p250 B11.

According to the management, Fidel's godparents lived here in the '40s and the man himself, of course, came to stay. Whatever its history, this painted, peach-coloured 1920s mansion is well worth a visit. Choose from two indoor colonial-style dining rooms, with impressive stained-glass ceiling lamps, and contemporary paintings. Private dining rooms (seating up to 20) are available for groups. Both the indoor eaterie and the outdoor grill restaurant, La Parillada, offer healthy-sized traditional Creole dishes. Takeaway service or home-delivery for an extra dollar.

El Conejito

Calle M, entre 17 y 19 (832 4671). **Open** noon-11pm daily. **Main courses** $3.50-$20. **No credit cards. Map** p250 B11.

This 1960s redbrick exterior belies a 17th-century Tudor mansion replica. During the first couple of years after the Revolution, Fidel and his powerful personal secretary Celia Sánchez used to take the walk from their government HQ in Hotel Havana Hilton (now the Habana Libre) to El Conejito to indulge in various rabbit dishes. Particularly recommended was, and still is, the mushroomy Conejo Financiera ($8), but better value is the pollo Gordon Blue ($5). The mixed salad, a plate of cabbage and slices of carrot, takes the term 'rabbit food' to a whole new level.

Hotel Meliá Cohiba

Paseo, entre 1ra y 3ra (333636/fax 334555/ www.solmelia.com). El Gran Añejo (ground floor). **Open** 7.30am-11pm daily. **Club sandwich** $11. *Habana Café* (ground floor) **Open** 8pm-2.30am daily. **Main courses** $11 minimum. *La Piazza* (1st floor) **Open** 1pm-2am daily. **Main courses** $7.50-$23.50. *El Abanico de Cristal* (1st floor) **Open** 7-11pm Mon-Sat. **Main courses** $8-$14. *Restaurante Plaza Habana* (1st floor) **Open** 7am-10am, 12.30-3pm, 7-11pm daily. **Buffet** breakfast $15, lunch $18, dinner $22. *All* **Credit** MC, V. **Map** p250 A9.

This huge imposing hotel offers a smorgasbord of eating options. La Piazza has a standard Italian menu; El Abanico de Cristal serves up an international à la carte menu; and the ground-floor El Gran Añejo does breakfasts and sarnies – a firm favourite being the *sandwich criollo*, with pork, ham, cheese and salad (not cheap at $11). Next door (but part of the hotel) is Habana Café, a wannabe Hard Rock-style place, though don't get your hopes up – the food is steeply priced and unimpressive, but then again even bad nachos might be a welcome change from beans and rice.

Hotel Nacional

Calle O, esquina 21 (333564/333567). Comedor de Aguiar **Open** noon-4pm, 7pm-midnight daily. **Main courses** $11-$36. *Buffet Veranda* **Open** 7-10am, noon-3pm, 7-10pm daily. **Main courses** $13 breakfast; $14 lunch; $20 dinner. *Cafeteria El Rincón del Cine* **Open** 24hrs daily. **Main courses** $6-$10. *La Barraca* **Open** noon-midnight daily. **Main courses** $8-$18. **Set menu** $11. *All* **Credit** MC, V. **Map** p250 B12.

You can spot this decadent monument from almost anywhere in Havana. Inside are four restaurants, offering food in different price brackets, but note that drinks prices are in keeping with the surroundings ($2.50 for a Cristal).

The **Comedor de Aguiar** is built on the site where Don Luis José Aguiar kicked the Brits' butts during the 1762 occupation. It's so elite that there's hardly ever anyone in it; possibly something to do with the slightly intimidating, immaculately dressed waiters guarding the doors. Starters, such as smoked salmon with capers and onions, start at $6, while mains (butterfly lobster, for example)

Herbivore Havana

Vegetarians are about as rare as snow is in Cuba, unless, of course, they happen to be foreigners, who cause quite some consternation among the locals when it is discovered that they willingly abstain from eating meat. Such conduct is unheard of in Cuba, and the majority of the population considers animal protein an essential part of any meal.

Indeed, all important occasions in Cuba are celebrated with the slaughter of a pig, and crackling (the skin of the pig sizzled in hot fat) is usually served as an aperitif. But despite health statistics – heart disease is a top three killer – Cubans are stubbornly resistant to change in their eating habits. Suggestions to eat more greens are often dismissed with 'I am not a rabbit/goat', or protests that fruit and vegetables are too expensive for the average wage-earner to buy on a regular basis. The latter argument is not entirely unfounded if you take into consideration that at the *agromercados* (farmers' markets) the cost of ingredients for a modest salad adds up to well over a day's wages. This is a problem that the government, to its credit, has addressed by providing an alternative source of veg in the shape of community market gardens.

As part of its drive to promote a healthier diet, the state-run **Vergel** chain opened seven vegetarian restaurants in Havana in 2002. Nearly all charge in Cuban pesos, meaning that a filling meal for two will cost the equivalent of $2. All this is good news for vegetarians bored with omelette after omelette and for vegans who can't face another plate of black beans. It's also good news for travellers whose choices are restricted by a low budget.

There are plans afoot to expand the Vergel menu, but it currently relies heavily on textured vegetable protein in the preparation of lasagne, 'meatballs' and croquettes, and dishes often lack imagination. Ingredients change with the seasons, but are fairly extensive at any time of the year, with typical veg including spinach, okra, sweet potato, aubergine, plantain, potato, beet, cabbage, maize, rice, taro, cauliflower and cassava.

All the restaurants listed below – with the exception of the **Eco-Restorán El Bambú** (known as El Bambú) – form part of the Vergel chain, which uses the slogan '*Más calidad de vida*' (A better lifestyle), a not-so-subtle warning to Cubans about their current dietary habits. The **Ecocheff**, before it closed for refurbishment, charged in hard currency but it's rumoured that it will reopen as a peso restaurant. Note that the following restaurants do not accept credit cards.

almost hit the $40 mark on occasions. Drinks add a further ouch factor. The quality is generally good, and the service slick.

Downstairs is the more relaxed, all-you-can-eat, self-service **Buffet Veranda**. (On the way down, look out for the cheesy photo of south London's finest: 'Naomi Campbell. Top Model.') The spread includes a good selection of fruit, salad and different sorts of bread. The buffet gains extra points for three different potato dishes (unbelievably rare in Cuba). Food can look jaded toward the end of the buffet session, so get there early.

Round the corner from the buffet is the cinema-themed **Cafetería el Rincón del Cine**. Here you can scoff down a full American brekky for $9.50, or choose from a selection of well-prepared and moderately priced burgers, pizzas and sandwiches. The large-screen telly turned up to the max will irritate those seeking peace and quiet.

Set in the picture-perfect tropical gardens is the new addition to the Hotel Nacional complex, **La Barraca**. This coolly shaded traditional *ranchón* (ranch) serves drinks in ceramic mugs and a succulent all-you-can-eat chicken menu. There's also pig-on-a-spit, cooked in an impressive outside clay oven.

Monseigneur

Calle O, esquina 21 (832 9884). **Open** noon-1am daily. **Main courses** $6-$17. **Credit** MC, V. **Map** p250 B12.

Monseigneur is an ice-cold, dimly lit world of fake marble, artificial flowers, kitsch statues, plus grand piano with a smiley pianist (who enjoys requests). Friendly, on-their-toes black-tie waiters dish out generous helpings of Franco-Cuban cuisine: try the prawn cocktail or red snapper, served with home-made rolls. This classic restaurant was made famous by Bola de Nieve (Snowball), the renowned Cuban jazz pianist who played here every night in the '60s. It's located opposite the main entrance to the Hotel Nacional (*see p42*).

La Plaza

Calle O #206, entre 23 y 25 (333740). **Open** noon-midnight daily. **Main courses** $5-$13. **Credit** MC, V. **Map** p250 B12.

Eco-Restorán El Bambú

Jardín Botánico, Carretera El Rocio 3.5km, Calabazar, Boyeros (549364/549159/ hajb@ceniai.inf.cu). **Open** 1-3pm Wed-Sun. **Buffet lunch** $12.

If you want to get out of the city and lunch in a more unusual setting, try this 'eco-restaurant'. All ingredients are organically cultivated and the buffet-style service allows you to eat all you want for $12. The choice is extensive, dishes are delicately flavoured with herbs from the surrounding gardens. Arrive early, especially at weekends, as this is a popular site for Cubans (who pay in pesos) eager to satisfy their curiosity about what it is like to eat 'herbs'.

El Biki

Calle San Lázaro, esquina a Infanta, Vedado (879 6406). **Open** noon-10pm daily. **Map** p251 C12.

El Carmelo

Calzada, esquina a D, Vedado (832 4495). **Open** noon-10pm daily. **Map** p250 A10.

Ecocheff

Avenida 3ra, esquina a 86, Miramar (206 1663). **Open** noon-10pm daily. **Map** p248 B1.

El Pekin

Calle 23 #1221, entre 12 y 14, Vedado (833 4020). **Open** noon-10pm daily. **Map** p249 C8.

This mirror-walled steakhouse (formerly known as Toro), on the first floor of Hotel St John's (*see p43*), offers a mix of traditional Creole culinary offerings and western cowboy cooking, with prices starting at $5. For the most exclusive meat dishes (tenderloin steak mixed grill, for example) the beef is imported from Canada. Each main dish is served with a jacket potato (a novelty in these parts) or rice and veg. A good choice of fresh fish and a healthy (so to speak) wine list keeps everyone happy. On Thursday to Sunday nights, *habaneros* queue patiently to enter the restaurant's all-night entertainment from 10pm.

El Polinesio

Hotel Habana Libre, Calle L, entre 23 y 25 (554011). **Open** noon-3.30pm, 7.30-11pm daily. **Main courses** $12-$22. **Set menu** $18. **Credit** MC, V. **Map** p250 B11.

This dimly lit Polynesian haven has a mid-priced oriental menu. Among the bamboo, canoes and lobster pots, look for the glass-screened room built to cook the house speciality: barbecued chicken. Wood is brought in from Pinar del Río to fire the barrel-like stone stoves, which results in pleasant, smoky flavours. Set meals ($18) include a starter, a main course and a not-very-Thai ice-cream dessert; add another $3 to $5 to the bill for a side order of rice. Value-for-money cocktails ($3.50) are served up in 'genuine' Polynesian goblets.

Primavera

Casa de la Amistad, Calle Paseo #406, entre 17 y 19 (831 2823/830 3114/3115). **Open** 11am-midnight daily. **Main courses** $6-$21. **No credit cards**. **Map** p250 B9.

Located in the Casa de la Amistad – a fine mansion built by the wealthy Catalina Lasa in the 1920s – Primavera has an endearing air of run-down opulence: check out the marble floor, central fountain, mirror wall and intricately designed iron-grill windows. The fare is standard but stay clear of the extortionately priced lobster – *paladares* serve it (albeit illegally) for a third of the price. There's a good selection of international wines for under $20. Make a night of it and enjoy traditional Cuban music on Tuesdays and Thursdays from 9pm ($5 cover charge). For music listings *see p153-p165*.

Restaurante 1830

Malecón #1252, esquina Calle 20 (553090/fax 334521). **Open** noon-midnight daily. **Main courses** $7.95-$36.55. **Credit** MC, V. **Map** p249 A7.

Old-world opulence meets Hollywood glamour in this Spanish colonial house. Guests are led down the red carpet to the two ornate dining rooms, one of which opens on to the sea. The ambience is stiff and formal, with waiting staff to match, but a trio of accomplished Cuban musicians lightens things up. The Cuban food has an international touch, with dishes such as lamb in guava sauce and beef in blue cheese, and there's an impressive choice of international wines starting at $13. Visit the elegant stained-glass Bar Colonial for a pre-dinner cocktail. Dinner guests can enjoy an open-air show (11pm Tue-Sun) free of charge.

La Roca

Calle 21 #102, entre L y M (334501).
Open noon-midnight daily. **Main courses** $3-$18. **No credit cards. Map** p250 B11.

Inside this fine art deco-style restaurant with multi-coloured glass windows, you can easily imagine the gangsters of old pouring in from the nearby ritzy casinos to grab a bite. Its name an abbreviation of Roberto Carnival (its founder), La Roca stands out from other state restaurants on account of its excellent black-tie service and spotless interior – though you do pay for these privileges with an automatic 10% service charge. If you can brave the ice-cold air-conditioning, you'll find the food is good, particularly sea bass (*cherna*) a safe, local bet. Enjoy a bottle from the plentiful wine list and a cigar from the humidor (surprisingly rare in Cuban restaurants). Be sure to book for Sunday lunch, as it's very popular with *habaneros*. The neon-lit bar alongside the restaurant is a classic (*see p115*).

Trattoria Marakas

Calle O #206, entre 23 y 25 (333740). **Open** noon-midnight daily. **Main courses** $4-12. **No credit cards. Map** p250 B12.

Heavy glass doors lead into this loud, bright American 1950s diner-style pizzeria, complete with small round tables, pistachio-coloured chairs and hanging garlic bulbs. This Cuban-Canadian joint venture is popular for its selection of 20 generously sized crispy pizzas for the ravenous, and five undersized pasta servings for the peckish.

Unión Francesa

Calle 17 #861, entre 4 y 6 (832 4493). **Open** noon-midnight daily. **Main courses** $2-$7. **No credit cards. Map** p250 B9.

Facing diagonally across from the John Lennon park this restaurant, one of Vedado's quieter areas, is a popular, relaxed spot. The best tables are upstairs on the spacious terrace, from where you have an impressive view of leafy-green Vedado. Waiters, who speak some English, are eager to please and service is fast. Pizza dishes (over ten varieties), sandwiches and the usual fish, chicken and pork are reasonably priced. We recommend the lobster, prepared in a rich tomato and herb sauce for under $7. With cocktails from $1.50 and the clear blue sky for a backdrop, we are fans.

Paladares

Casa Sarasua

Calle 25 #510, apto 1, entre H e I (322114).
Open noon-11pm Mon-Sat. **Main courses** $4-$8. **No credit cards. Map** p250 C11.

Comfy chairs await you on the balcony of this *paladar* overlooking leafy Calle 25, near the university. The owner, the last of his family left on this side of the Florida Straits, takes great pride in showing off his weaponry collection and is happy to recount his entire family history, before and after the Revolution. This *paladar* is an ideal spot for a low-budget, educational evening in a relaxed atmosphere. Trad Cuban fare is the order of the day – *frijoles, tostones* and big pork chops.

Gringo Viejo

Calle 21 #454, entre E y F (831 1946). **Open** noon-midnight daily. **Main courses** $6-$12. **No credit cards. Map** p250 B10.

This popular restaurant (booking recommended) has been dishing up Cuban and international food for the past eight years. Apparently, the owner was so proud of his resemblance to Kenny Rogers that he named the restaurant the 'old gringo' in tribute – you be the judge. Framed photos of smiling customers cover the walls inside – testimony to those who survived the freezing temperatures and the '80s soundtracks. But the food is good and the service friendly: try the Cuban speciality *ropa vieja* (meaning 'old clothes'; it's better than it sounds) for $8.

Le Chansonnier

Calle J #257, entre 15 y Línea (832 1576).
Open 6pm-midnight daily. **Main courses** $10-$12. **No credit cards. Map** p250 B11.

This majestic old colonial house, which also offers accommodation, has a charming front porch. Unfortunately, no meals are served outside, just drinks. Inside, an intimate candlelit dining room awaits, with grand chandeliers and a vast selection of antique plates on the walls. The French-style cooking is simple but food is always well prepared, and service friendly; the wine selection is limited. Le Chansonnier is exceedingly popular – book.

Decameron

Linea #753, entre Paseo y 2 (832 2444). **Open** noon-midnight daily. **Main courses** $6-$18. **No credit cards. Map** p250 B9.

In this particular case appearances do lie, so don't let the ugly brown brick exterior put you off. Inside is a cosy *paladar* with soft lighting and a collection of grandfather clocks (mercifully unwound), contemporary Cuban paintings, antiques and ceramic objects. The chef adds flair to tired old Cuban dishes, and care is taken in everything, from the smartly dressed table to the polite service and the French-style presentation. A stone's throw from Hotels Meliá Cohiba and Habana Riviera (*see p42 and p41*).

Doña Juana

Calle 19 #909, entre 6 y 8 (832 2699). **Open** noon-midnight daily. **Main courses** $5-$10. **No credit cards**. **Map** p249 B8.

This friendly *paladar* hides out in a newly painted but crumbling Vedado building. Make your way up to the first floor, traipse across the living room, down a long gloomy corridor to the kitchen and up to the roof terrace on a pretty steep spiral staircase. When you eventually get there, it's all worth it for the kitschly lit, quirkily decorated rooftop dining area. Try the huge breaded pork schnitzel ($5). Traditional Creole dishes abound in hearty, tasty portions.

El Hurón Azul

Calle Humbolt #153, esquina P (879 1691). **Open** noon-midnight daily. **Main courses** $7-$12. **No credit cards**. **Map** p250 B12.

Near the Hotel Habana Libre, this is one of Havana's finest *paladares* and very popular among the city's arty set. Fortes are stews, wine and desserts (including a great selection of tropical fruits). The interior decor isn't as charming as other *paladares* but top contemporary art compensates.

Las Mercedes

Calle 18 #204, entre 15 y 17 (831 5706). **Open** noon-midnight daily. **Main courses** $6.50-$17. **No credit cards**. **Map** p249 B8.

When you enter this subtly lit den – via the lush mini garden, complete with fish pond and wooden bridge – be careful not to tread on the house turtle that roams free. Cuban dishes are prepared with flare – you can order set menus starting at $15 or pick from the à la carte menu. The *brocheta* (kebab) is particularly recommended, as is the hearty swordfish with black beans and rice. To round off the meal, the jovial landlord may offer you a few stiff shots of dark rum.

Nerei

Calle 19 #110, esquina L (832 7860). **Open** 1pm-midnight daily. **Main courses** $13-$15. **No credit cards**. **Map** p250 B11.

This inviting patio, with four tables and a big barbeque on the side, is set back from the busy road by a narrow leafy garden. The food is traditional and a bit pricey, but includes a tender duck dish, which is a welcome surprise on a *paladar* menu. Don't be deterred by the chaos that seems to reign in the noisy kitchen – the results are good.

Las Tres Bs

Calle 21 #164, entre K y L (832 3085). **Open** 11am-midnight daily. **Main courses** $8-$10. **No credit cards**. **Map** p250 B11.

The entrance to 'Bueno, Bonito y Barato' (good, pretty and cheap) is a bit tricky to find since the sign disappeared, but don't get discouraged – many helpful neighbours are at hand. It's shabby rather than pretty, but in other respects it's a cosy *paladar* (situated opposite the famous Coppelia ice-cream parlour). The Alfonso family serves up generous helpings of Cuban staples, washed down with a couple of cold ones for a negotiable price. Bad-taste pictures and a chatting/singing parrot add to the ambience.

Miramar & the western suburbs

Miramar and the suburbs further west are the closest thing Cuba comes to an upper-class area, home to diplomats, expats and well-placed government types. The upmarket restaurants in Miramar reflect this, and tend to cater to more demanding diners. In addition to the restaurants listed below, **Club Havana** (*see p179*) has a sophisticated restaurant and a grill, and **Hotels Meliá Habana**, **Occidental Miramar** and **LTI-Panorama** (for all, *see p45*) all have an array of decent restaurants.

El Aljibe

Avenida 7na, entre 24 y 26 (204 1583-1584). **Open** noon-midnight. **Main courses** $12-$25. **Credit** MC, V. **Map** p249 B5.

Expats and nouveau riche Cubans gravitate here, and for good reason: El Aljibe is probably the only state-run restaurant in Havana that has managed to maintain consistently good food and service over the years. Expect some of the best Creole food around: the house speciality is roast chicken with sour orange sauce ($12) and beef brochette ($18) is another highlight. All dishes are served with masses of rice and creamy black beans, salad and fried plantains (unlimited portions). It now has a more intimate, air-conditioned wing.

La Cecilia

Avenida 5ta, entre 110 y 112 (204 1562). **Open** noon-midnight daily. **Main courses** $12-$25. **Credit** MC, V.

Though the service is still friendly and the menu still varied – including some traditional, hard-to-find dishes such as *tamal en cazuela* (creamed fresh corn with pork or chicken) and *ajiaco* (Cuban stew) – this restaurant unfortunately isn't what it used to be. The choice of open-air or air-conditioned eating is a bonus, but the entrance and the gardens are looking shabby and the enormous and once-beautiful outdoor cabaret adjacent to the restaurant has been shut down indefinitely. La Cecilia still maintains a good wine list by Cuban standards and you can choose from a wide range of classic meat and seafood dishes, as well as Cuban favourites such as *ropa vieja*. Avoid the busloads of tourists who arrive at lunchtime.

La Esperanza

Calle 16 #105, entre 1ra y 3ra (202 4361). **Open** 7-11pm Mon-Sat. **Main courses** $8-$13. **Map** p249 A8.

La Ferminia.

Decorated inside in art deco-gone-baroque style, this pretty *paladar* serves up a selection of creative, exquisitely prepared dishes. You are received by the owner in this well-kept house but his brusque manner won't be everyone's cup of tea. Prices are high: $30 for a starter and main (before wine), but food is prepared with loving care. If you make a reservation, be sure to arrive on time, otherwise you may get a telling off. There's no printed menu, so diners should be aware that while the main courses are reasonably priced, cocktails, starter and desserts inflate the bill.

La Ferminia

Avenida 5ta #18207, esquina 184, Siboney (336555). **Open** noon-midnight daily. **Main courses** $10-$28. **Credit** MC, V.

Set in the palatial former residence of one Doña Matilde Montalvo, the beautiful French decor, elegant dining rooms and the lush garden patio area at La Ferminia are quite breathtaking. Unfortunately, the food – from a classic French menu – doesn't quite match. La Ferminia doubles as Cuba's top cooking school: trouble is the apprentice waiters are slow and the food is often served on the cold side. Still, it's hard not to enjoy eating in what must have been one of pre-Revolutionary Cuba's most luxurious homes. In its favour, La Ferminia, unusually, has a vegetarian dining room, albeit with a rather limited choice of food. The wine cellar, on the other hand, is one of Cuba's best. On the patio there's an all-you-can-eat beef grill for $13, where lobster and seafood is also served.

La Finca

Calle 140, esquina 19, Cubanacán (208 7976). **Open** noon-midnight Mon-Sat. **Main courses** $14-$30. **Credit** MC, V.

Feel like splurging? The Farm should be able to help out. It's run by Cuba's gastronomic guru Tomás Erasmo, who, after opening El Tocororo (*see p111*) and El Rancho Palco (*see p111*; just across the street from La Finca), has now settled into this, his most ambitious culinary project to date. The atmosphere is elegant and romantic (think Tiffany lamps) but not overly formal and, best of all, you feel as though you are in a tropical paradise, surrounded by lush plants and trees. All dishes are beautifully presented, from the lobster thermidor or grill, to the fresh fish or the sizzling beef platter. Erasmo offers to make almost any dish you fancy if the ingredients are there; they're all fresh (except the beef, imported from Chile). La Finca is new, exclusive and expensive, but worth every penny.

La Giraldilla

Calle 222, esquina 37, La Coronela, La Lisa (330568). **Open** noon-midnight daily. *Macumba disco* 10pm-3am Tue-Sun. **Main courses** $5-$35. **Credit** MC, V.

This is the place for Havana's jet set. La Giraldilla is way off the beaten track – at least a 30-minute cab ride from Vedado – but it's well worth the trip. Despite its appalling title – 'Tourism Complex' – La Giraldilla is actually an enormous Spanish-style country estate on the outskirts of Havana. By day moneyed Cubans and business types do lunch, and after dinner it's something of a party zone. The main eating areas include the more informal **Patio de los Naranjos**, serving mostly Cuban food; the elegant, air-conditioned **Bistrot Gourmet**, which has by far the best food, including a delicious lobster au café ($25); and **La Bodega del Vino** (the wine cellar), where there's a short but sweet menu and wines take centre stage ($10-$400). If you spend more than $20 (impossible not to), you can go to the Macumba nightclub free of charge.

Pan.Com

Calle 7ma, esquina 26, Miramar (204 4232). **Open** 24hrs daily. **Main courses** 95¢-$3.95. **Credit** MC, V. **Map** p249 B5.

In a country where ham and cheese sandwiches are not only an institution but also the *only* meal you can buy involving bread, clean, efficient Pan.Com (meaning Bread.Com) successfully breaks the mould. With three types of bread (including fresh and crunchy baguette), fillings that include turkey breast, cream cheese and spiced sausage at reasonable prices, it's hardly surprising that this joint has become a favourite hangout. For a simple, open-air meal at any time of the day or night, Pan.Com can't be beaten.

Pizza Nova

Marina Hemingway (204 6969). **Open** 11am-1am daily. **Main courses** $3.75-$10.85. **Credit** MC, V.

Marina Hemingway is a hideaway for Americans who sneak into Cuba on their yachts, and for Cubans and expats who like to feel as if they are in another country. Pizza Nova is located alongside one of the marina's canals and has a charming outdoor patio with a huge rubber tree and a bar with a fresh ocean breeze. The pizza, served on a thin crust with plenty of sizzling cheese, comes with a choice of toppings that include lobster. There is also oven-baked pasta with cheese and fresh tomato and – often slightly overcooked – spaghetti. Still, the atmosphere is pleasant and the mojitos are delicious. Pizza Nova is a favourite hangout for families on the weekends.

El Rancho Palco

Calle 140, esquina 19, Cubanacán (208 9346). **Open** noon-midnight daily. **Main courses** $10-$25. **Credit** MC, V.

Another of chef Tomás Erasmo's creations, this is a favourite for large groups of diplomats and visiting Americans. With an outside eating area surrounded by lush vegetation, you almost feel you are eating in an upscale jungle (don't forget the insect repellent). There's also an air-conditioned area, live music and excellent food – fish is especially good. The Cuban food is excellent too. It all comes at a price, mind.

El Tocororo

Calle 18, esquina 3ra, Miramar (204 2209/4530/2998). **Open** noon-midnight Mon-Fri; 7pm-midnight Sat, Sun. **Main courses** $12-$35. **Map** p248 A5.

Once Cuba's most expensive – and only sophisticated – restaurant, El Tocororo (named after Cuba's national bird) was opened by Tomás Erasmo at a time when pork, rice and beans were all you could get. Lately it has been making an effort to become more accessible. The decor is heavy on the stained glass, with a distinct pre-Revolution bourgeois flavour, but it manages to pull it off. The speciality is meat and live lobster any way you like it. Service is excellent, and the food well presented and delicious, but there's no menu, which means you have to struggle with the waiters' often-broken English if your Spanish isn't up to scratch. At lunch there's a piano player and at night an excellent jazz and Cuban music band entertain while you eat. There is also a brand new tapas bar with live music open until 3am. The most exotic addition, though, is located at the left side of the main entrance: Tocororo's Japanese restaurant, the only one of its kind in Havana, serving delicious sushi, sashimi and tempura. The chef was trained by the Japanese ambassador's personal cook. Smart dress.

Paladares

La Cocina de Lilliam

Calle 48 #1311, entre 13 y 15, Playa (209 6514). **Open** noon-3pm, 7-10pm Mon-Fri, Sun. Closed 1st 2wks Aug, last 2wks Dec. **Main courses** $8.50-$12. **Map** p248 C4.

This is where the rich and famous (Jimmy Carter, the Rothschilds) go when in Cuba – though you don't have to be either to come here. What started as a humble family-run restaurant has turned into a mega-enterprise; an intercom asks if you have a reservation before opening the door electronically. Inside, Lilliam's beautiful garden restaurant shines, with the tables set in intimate corners of a large patio filled with tropical plants. The food is excellent: try the chicken mousse (minced chicken with a creamy cheese béchamel sauce), *ropa vieja* (here made with lamb) or stewed lamb. Portions are huge so you may want to share. There's a small, air-conditioned eating area upstairs. Unlike most state-run restaurants, the service is friendly, efficient and in most cases bilingual. Don't show up without a booking, as you'd be lucky to get a table.

El Diluvio

Calle 72 #1705, entre 17 y 19, Playa (202 1531). **Open** noon-2pm, 6.30pm-midnight daily. **Main courses** $7-$10. **Map** p248 D2.

The best thing about this place – besides the food, that is – is that it preserves the original concept and flavour of a *paladar*. El Diluvio (meaning 'the Flood') is strict about maintaining the rule of seating only 12 people at any one time, so be sure to reserve. The decor is stark but the service is excellent, and the food surprisingly good for an Italian restaurant in Cuba (it even has a home-made clay pizza oven). The menu changes according to what's available, but you can always find pizza made with real mozzarella and hand-made fresh pasta, served with sauces made with fresh tomatoes (almost unheard of in Cuba) and fresh basil. Don't pass up the lamb *chilindrón*-style (cooked with with tomatoes and peppers). The wine isn't so hot, so if you don't feel like roughing it, bring your own.

La Fontana

Calle 46 #305, esquina 3ra, Miramar (202 8337). **Open** noon-midnight daily. **Main courses** $8-$12. **Map** p248 B3.

Fast becoming one of the trendiest *paladares* for musicians, artists and intellectuals, La Fontana has a charming open-air terrace with large trees shading the tables. Grilled meat and seafood, including octopus, snails and fish, are the speciality, and you can see your food being prepared on the large open grill. The fish and seafood kebabs are outstanding; grilled, boneless chicken is lip-smackingly juicy. The wine list is small but adequate. In fact, the only minus (typical in Cuban restaurants) is that the music trio always pitches up when you are in the middle of an interesting conversation.

Eastern Bay & the Coast

Restaurants

Los XII Apóstoles

Below Castillo del Morro, Parque Histórico Militar Morro-Cabaña (863 8295). **Open** *Restaurant* noon-11pm daily. *Live music* 11pm-2am daily. **No credit cards. Main courses** $4-$28. **Map** p251 C16.

For trad Creole food and a fine view of the Malecón, the Twelve Apostles, situated at the foot of the lighthouse by the Morro Castle, is a good bet. A terrific meat platter, including beef, is yours for $15, though half a chicken will only set you back $5. At 11pm the place turns into a nightclub.

El Brocal

Avenida 5ta, esquina 498, Guanabo (962892). **Open** noon-midnight daily. **Main courses** $2-$12. **No credit cards. Map** p252 B30.

This 1930s house has a calmness about it, like a low-key Margaritaville, complete with painted wood clapboards and grass-filled well out front. The lofty ceiling inside shelters half a dozen tables, with six more on the porch, all surrounded by cowhide-covered chairs. The Mexican motif is being phased out, with Mariachis traded for a trad Cuban music trio, but the $1.50 tacos will remain, as will the cheap drinks.

La Divina Pastora

Near the Fortaleza de San Carlos de la Cabaña, Parque Histórico Militar Morro-Cabaña (860 8341). **Open** noon-11pm daily. **Main courses** $9-$28. **Credit** MC, V. **Map** p251 D/E16.

The high prices can't really be justified, nor is it suitable for an intimate experience, but La Divina Pastora really does have a fantastic view of the bay. Built as a gun carriage factory for cannons, La Divina Pastora is dominated by the splendid fortress directly behind, and its palm- and cannon-lined waterfront makes the hassle of finding it worthwhile. The food is nice enough, but doesn't turn up any real surprises. However, house band Septeto Caracol is excellent, dashing out *son*, *guaracha* and *bolero* with flair.

Paladares

Maeda

Calle Quebec #115, entre 476 y 478, Guanabo (962615). **Open** noon-midnight daily. **No credit cards. Main courses** $4.50-$8.75. **Map** p247 C23.

On a hilltop overlooking Guanabo, this tastefully decorated *paladar* is one of this seaside town's best-kept secrets. Specialising in grilled meat (but there's also pizza and pasta), quantity rules here, and the mixed grill platter is a fine deal at $6.75.

Piccolo

Avenida 5ta #50206, entre 502 y 504, Guanabo (964300). **Open** noon-midnight daily. **No credit cards. Main courses** $4-$8. **Map** p247 B25.

The open kitchen at the Piccolo, complete with wood-fired oven, turns out a fine focaccia. In fact, nearly all the food is very good, very Italian (even though the owners are Greek) and very good value.

Dos Hermanos
See p114.

Opus Habana: retro lounge. *See p115.*

The huge fruit and veg arrangement at the entrance is usually impressive, but on our last visit little of the produce was from the house's garden, which usually has basil, lettuce and beets.

Drinking

Bar life in Havana often disappoints tourists with grand expectations inspired by Ernest Hemingway, Graham Greene and the legendary decadence of the '40s and '50s. Periodic crackdowns by the police on undesirables and an emphasis on upmarket tourism, with prices that keep Cubans away, have not helped to create bars with real atmosphere. The classic Hemingway haunts – La Bodeguita del Medio and El Floridita – are particularly under-patronised by locals, and have become little more than photo opportunities. It is telling that on some nights, while the tourist bars in Old Havana are deserted at midnight, the Malecón is packed six deep with locals and there are large queues outside some nightclubs.

What Havana does have is a number of European-style patio bars in settings with rich architectural heritage. In Old Havana, each of the main squares (Plaza de la Catedral, Plaza de Armas, Plaza de San Francisco and Plaza Vieja) has bars providing a colonial-style ambience that's hard to beat for an afternoon or early evening drink. It's later on in the evening that Old Havana struggles to find a beat.

At the other end of the spectrum are the peso bars. These are cheap affairs where the draught beer has a potato taste and the rum comes from an unmarked old plastic bottle. As a tourist you will be an attraction here, though for a change more for conversation than dollars. The atmosphere is generally quite muted, which is why Cubans who can gravitate to dollar bars. But peso bars are well worth a look to see a different side of Cuba, though if you stay around to use the toilets, brace yourself. There are plenty of peso bars dotted around Calle Neptuno in Centro Habana.

Drinks are priced pretty universally at $1-$2 for a beer (imported beers can cost more) and $2-$5 for a cocktail (mojito, Cuba Libre and daiquiri are the most common Cuban cocktails). Cristal – a light lager – is the most-served Cuban beer, while Bucanero is a darker beer, and Hatuey and Mayabe are darker still.

La Habana Vieja

Bosque Bologna

Calle Obispo #460, entre Villegas y Aguacate (no phone). **Open** 11am-midnight daily. **No credit cards. Map** p252 D15.

One of the better of the new bars on Obispo, this joint (commonly known as 'Lázaro's bar') has a relaxed sit-down ambience and abundant greenery. It serves both an excellent mojito and a good chicken kebab: a strange combo, maybe, but definitely worth a stop.

Café del Oriente

Calle Oficios, esquina Amargura (860 2917). **Open** *Bar* 24hrs daily. *Restaurant* noon-midnight daily. **Main courses** $8-$30. **Credit** MC, V. **Map** p252 E15.

This is a high-class place. Outside, big tables are the ideal spot to appreciate the square without (for some unknown reason) being approached by hustlers. Inside, it's worth persevering with the snobby appearance and icy air-conditioning to appreciate some of the best service in Cuba, from waiters who perform with energetic efficiency and dignity.

Top tankards: Taberna de la Muralla.

Café de París

Calle San Ignacio, esquina Obispo (no phone). **Open** 8am-1am daily. **No credit cards. Map** p252 E15.

One of the busiest bars in Old Havana, it's a shame that the Café de París has become overrun with hustlers. Live music is provided every night until midnight by an excellent band (though, oddly enough, dancing is generally prohibited). For newcomers the attraction really is to bar-perch, and take in the comings and goings. The food and decor have improved recently, but both are still basic.

Café O'Reilly

Calle O'Reilly #203, entre Cuba y San Ignacio (no phone). **Open** 9am-midnight daily. **No credit cards. Map** p252 E15.

If only this were a real Irish pub. No matter, Café O'Reilly – split between two floors joined by a cast-iron spiral staircase – is nonetheless a relaxing Old Havana stop. The place to be is on the balcony.

Casa del Escabeche

Calle Obispo #503, entre Villegas y Bernaza (863 2660). **Open** 7am-11.45pm daily. **No credit cards. Map** p252 E15.

This unfeasibly small, unattractive looking place has a remarkably good reputation, mainly on account of the standard of its live music. Open wooden slats offer a good view in – check it out before going in.

El Castillo de la Real Fuerza

Plaza de Armas, esquina Avenida del Puerto (861 6130). **Open** 9am-midnight daily. **No credit cards. Map** p252 E16.

The rooftop terrace of this castle is a fine place to sip a cocktail during the day or early evening. The entrance, via the museum, ensures that there are never too many people spoiling your appreciation of the great view. Easily worth the $1 admission charge. Closed for renovation at the time of writing.

Dos Hermanos

Avenida del Puerto #305, esquina Sol (861 3514). **Open** 8am-midnight daily. **No credit cards. Map** p252 E15.

A port-style bar off the tourist track and with a rougher feel to prove it. While the music is too loud and no one has come in for a quiet drink, it's still worth a visit, but maybe not a detour.

Fundación Havana Club

Museo del Ron, Calle San Pedro #262, esquina Sol (8618051/862 3832). **Open** 10am-midnight daily. **No credit cards. Map** p252 E15.

The Rum Museum in the Fundación Havana Club is an apt setting for a bar, but unfortunately its museum location generally renders it a vacuum. A noticeable exception is when there's a Friday night party here (*see also p25*), and the Beautiful People descend.

Hotel Ambos Mundos

Hotel Ambos Mundos, Calle Obispo, esquina Mercaderes (860 9529-31). **Open** *Bar La Terraza* 7am-11pm daily. **Credit** MC, V. **Map** p252 E15.

The lobby bar struggles to maintain its elegant ambience but the rooftop bar is close to the action below but far enough away to enjoy your drink in peace.

La Lluvia de Oro

Calle Obispo #316, esquina Habana (862 9870). **Open** 8am-1am Mon-Thur; 8am-3am Fri-Sun. **No credit cards. Map** p252 E15.

Big on wood and space, this is the best bar on Calle Obispo on aesthetic grounds. But somehow it seems to miss out in the atmosphere stakes, and the service is generally slow. Take a quick look inside to see who's around and if the band is playing.

Taberna de la Muralla

Calle San Ignacio, esquina Muralla, Plaza Vieja (tel/fax 866 4453/www.habaguanex.com). **Open** noon-11pm daily. **Credit** MC, V. **Map** p252 E15.

This is one of the best bars in Cuba, newly established as a joint venture with an Austrian beer company. This explains its excellent draft Pilsen and Munich beer (both brewed on the premises). The bar has been beautifully restored as part of a wholesale renovation of the square, a sight best appreciated from the outside tables. Inside, long wooden tables bring to mind a revamped London pub. Service and food are both excellent.

Centro Habana

Bar Monserrate

Avenida de Bélgica (Monserrate) #401, esquina Obrapía (860 9751). **Open** 8.30am-3am daily. **No credit cards. Map** p252 D14.

Still one of the most consistent venues on the Old Havana bar scene. While maintaining much of its nostalgic appeal – multiple ceiling fans whir, surly waiters strut – Bar Monserrate is probably not the best place for a quiet drink. A phalanx of Cubans tends to descend on unsuspecting newcomers with offers to take them to the best disco in town/sell cigars/teach them tiddlywinks (you get the picture). The band that plays here may feature a bunch of OAPs, but they're pretty good.

Castropol

Malecón #107, entre Genios y Crespo (861 4864). **Open** 7pm-midnight Fri; 4pm-midnight Sun. **No credit cards. Map** p251 C15.

This social club is set in a marvellous (though run-down) building right on the Malecón. At press time, it was being renovated to include an upscale bar and restaurant. It's a lively and happening spot that, when the work is finished, is set to be one of the best places in town. It has a slightly rough atmosphere, ideal for visitors looking for a less formulaic bar experience. Excellent mojitos.

Hotel Inglaterra

Paseo de Martí (Prado) #416, esquina San Rafael (860 8595). **Open** *Bar Terraza* 6pm-1am Mon, Wed-Sun. **Credit** MC, V. **Map** p251 D14.

The veranda bar is a great spot for a pre-theatre drink, with the Gran Teatro next door. The roof bar (La Paradilla) has a wonderful view of Parque Central. but is more geared to copious drinking than it is to savouring the view. The band, typically good, is very loud: the only real solution here is to get up and dance.

Vedado

Cafetería Sofía

Calle 23 #202, esquina O (832 0740). **Open** 24hrs daily. **No credit cards. Map** p250 B12.

This is the local that everyone loves to hate. On quiet nights it may be the only bar in town that is really busy, which, given its unattractive decor and lack of sophistication, may come as a surprise. Its interest lies more in the tide of people drifting in and out. The all-female band seems to be carving out a home-made niche for itself.

Casa de la Amistad

Paseo #406, entre 17 y 19 (830 3114/3115). **Open** 11am-midnight Mon-Fri; 11am-2am Sat; 11am-6pm Sun. **Admission** $5 Tue, Sat; otherwise free. **No credit cards. Map** p250 B9.

A charming place for a drink, especially when there's a good band playing. The setting can't be beaten: the luscious green gardens of an old colonial mansion. The atmosphere is friendly and, for once, if you are asked to dance you won't have to think of increasingly exotic places you are from to throw persistent hustlers.

La Fuente

Calle 13, entre F y G (662514). **Open** 11.30pm-midnight Mon-Thur; 11.30am-1.30am Fri-Sun. **No credit cards. Map** p250 B10.

One of Havana's best bars, with greenery on all sides and a lovely fountain as the focal point. This is residential territory, so don't come expecting wild salsa dancing on tables, but rather to get an authentic look at a neighbourhood life. Shots and beers are cheap.

Opus Habana

3rd floor, Teatro Amadeo Rodán, Calzada #512, esquina D (324521). **Open** 8pm-3am daily. **Map** p250 A10.

This is a wonderfully kitsch 1970s joint (actually quite modern by Havana standards), where couples sit holding hands on the comfortable leather seats enjoying the happy tunes and fine view. Drinks are good and the service excellent. Food on offer is limited but if you're hungry at 1am there are certainly worse options.

La Roca

Calle 21, entre L y M (334501). **Open** noon-2am daily. **No credit cards. Map** p250 B11.

Perennially busy, La Roca serves good, relatively cheap food and cocktails, and has a dark, atmospheric feel. The building is fantastic, and the service is well above average. For restaurant review, *see p108*.

La Terraza del Hotel Nacional

Calle O, esquina 21 (333564/333567). **Open** 24hrs daily. **Credit** MC, V. **Map** p250 B12.

The Hotel Nacional conjures up images of grandeur that – with a palm-lined, spotlit driveway and smart doormen – are not far from being delivered. The magnificent terrace (straight through the lobby) is a perfect place for a pre-dinner drink – it's one of the very few places in Cuba with comfortable lounge seats, sea views and slick service.

Bars

For lounging

The **La Terraza del Hotel Nacional** (*see p115*) is the city's best chill-out zone. If you don't mind the tweety birds, that is.

For a retro vibe

La Roca (*see p115*) is art deco heaven, while **Opus Habana** (*see p115*) delivers on '70s retro.

For draft beer

Smart **Taberna de la Muralla** (*see p115*): Havana's only decent beerhall.

For venturing off the tourist trail

Castropol and **Dos Hermanos** (for both, *see p114*) for a non-sanitised bar experience.

Shops & Services

The dollar rules supreme in 21st-century Cuba, and it can buy you anything. Well, almost.

Although Havana still falls drastically short of being a shopping mecca, selling little that you can't get elsewhere, there's certainly been a dramatic change over the last decade. Until the 1990s, Cuba didn't have much more to offer its visitors than rum and cigars; these days a surprising number of brand names in clothes, shoes, sportswear, jewellery, perfume and electronics can be bought at the increasing number of shopping centres and boutiques that have sprung up throughout Havana (elsewhere on the island, pickings remain slim). It's all down to the power of the mighty dollar: its free circulation, along with the growth of the tourist industry, has led to a parallel expansion of the retail market.

DUAL ECONOMY

Almost everything of interest to the visitor in Havana will be charged in US dollars. The more adventurous traveller may want to obtain some Cuban pesos from the *cadecas* (exchange kiosks) scattered around town. Aside from the undesirable peso shops around the city (*see p119* **Peso shops**), the main things of interest available in Cuban pesos are flowers (from street stalls), fruit and vegetables from the city's markets (*see p126* **Getting agro**), street food and some second-hand books. Shops tend to change in either dollars or pesos, but rarely both.

You are more likely to poke your head into a peso shop out of cultural curiosity than to actually buy anything. In fact, foreigners can't purchase goods in *bodegas* (local grocery stores). They are strictly for Cubans on *libretas* (ration books). But the Cuban cigarettes sold in pesos and the dubious rum sold on the street and poured into the vessel of your choice may be of interest to the self-harming.

SHOPPING AREAS

Though the main commercial arteries of pre-1959 Havana are once again filling with shops, Havana has no Bond Street or Rodeo Drive. In La Habana Vieja, try in and around **Calle Obispo** for a range of shops; in Centro Habana, **Avenida de Italia** (Galiano) has a smattering of peso shops. But some of the best-stocked shops are to be found in hotels, and shopping malls in the **Miramar** suburb, and further west.

LEARNING THE RULES

Shopping in Havana can be an adventure or an ordeal, depending on your frame of mind. To start with, don't rely on credit cards, particularly if they are issued or backed by an American bank, as the embargo renders them invalid in Cuba. Other credit cards are be accepted in a limited number of venues, but cash is usually best. Even then, try to carry small denomination notes given that larger bills ($50 and $100) must be accompanied by a passport and, in any case, the shop may not be able to change them. Before entering the shop, you'll probably be required to deposit your bag in a *guardabolsos*, either at the entrance or just outside the premises. Remove your money and your passport, as security isn't guaranteed. On leaving the shop, be sure to keep your receipt, as guards at the door are obliged to check it against the goods.

The concept of refunds and exchanges is a fledgling one in Havana; returning electrical goods with guarantees shouldn't be a problem

The best Shops

Centro Comercial El Comodoro

Havana's shopping top-scorer, with full marks for design and layout. *See p118.*

Galerías de Paseo

The one-stop shop for everything from cars to plastic flower displays. *See p118.*

Habana 1791

Handmade colonial-style perfumes in customised containers. *See p128.*

Longina

For professional service and informed advice on Cuban music. *See p130.*

La Maison

Glamour and exclusivity without breaking the bank. *See p117.*

Palacio de la Artesanía

The place for variety and quality of *guayaberas* – pleated men's shirts with buttons. *See p128.*

but getting a refund on anything else is very hit and miss. To maximise your chances, bring the goods back with a receipt within 72 hours.

SOCIALIST SHOPPING VERSUS CAPITALIST COMPETITION

When you see something you really like, buy it on the spot. Don't delay because you're unlikely to find exactly the same item elsewhere, particularly in the case of clothes, craftwork, shoes and electrical goods. Availability is never guaranteed, and prices don't vary dramatically much across the city.

One of the biggest challenges for visitors shopping in Cuba is the contrast in standards of service. Cubans are only just learning how to deal with customers in accordance with international standards of etiquette, so don't be surprised if you are met with a poker-faced shop assistant who either ignores you entirely or responds without making eye contact, while painting her nails. Alternatively, you may be served by someone whose professionalism will make you wonder if you can be in the same country. So, prepare yourself for novel shopping situations, and try not to fall into the trap of continually comparing things to back home.

One-stop

Department stores

Casa Blanca

Avenida 1ra, esquina 36, Miramar (204 3941/ 3942). **Open** 10am-6pm Mon-Sat; 9am-1pm Sun. **Credit** MC, V. **Map** p248 B4.

Shoes, fabrics, clothes, food and drink are sold in this somewhat drab and run-down store. There are also electronics on the second floor.

La Época

Avenida Neptuno #359, entre Avenida Italia (Galiano) y San Nicolás, Centro Habana (669423/ 669692/669418). **Open** 10am-6.30pm Mon-Sat; 10am-1.30pm Sun. **Credit** MC, V. **Map** p251 D14.

This dated department store in the heart of Centro Habana wins the prize for having the rudest shop assistants in town. In addition, it offers toiletries, fashion label clothing, footwear, electrical goods, children's clothes, furniture and hardware. There's a supermarket in the basement.

Harris Brothers

Avenida de Bélgica (Monserrate) #305, entre O'Reilly y Progreso (San Juan de Dios), La Habana Vieja (861 1644/1615/2045). **Open** 9am-9pm Mon-Sat; 9am-7pm Sun. **Credit** MC, V. **Map** p251 D14.

This modern department store stocks a limited range of fashion, with labels including Benetton, along with a reasonable selection of sportswear, and a variety of toiletries.

The stylish setting of **Le Select**.

La Maison

Calle 16 #701, esquina 7ma, Miramar (204154/ 204258). **Open** 10am-6.45pm Mon-Sat. **Credit** MC, V. **Map** p249 B6.

Housed in an elegant mansion in Miramar, this collection of shops includes a good jewellery store, various clothing outlets fairly with reasonable prices, plus shops selling home accessories, sunglasses, footwear, a wide range of cosmetics and perfumes, and children's and baby clothes. There's also a gift store with an excellent selection of pure cotton and linen Cuban *guayabera* shirts.

Le Select

Avenida 5ta, esquina 30, Miramar (204 7410). **Open** 10am-6pm Mon-Sat. **Credit** MC, V. **Map** p249 B5.

This complex is set in a beautiful colonial building; the grand entrance hall, with chandeliers, marble statues and a vast mirror reveal something of the opulence of Havana of yesteryear. Many customers are from the diplomatic corps; in fact, the electrical goods shop on the first floor sells only to diplomatic staff and members of the foreign press. The once well-stocked delicatessen on the ground floor is now sadly depleted. Prices are high and much of the stock has passed its sell-by date. There are a couple of boutiques upstairs, along with a toiletries shop. Much of the time the staff are 'out'. Rumour has it that the whole place is going to be turned into an embassy residence. Watch this space.

Shopping centres

Casa Bella

Avenida 7ma #2603, esquina 26, Miramar (204 3566). **Open** 10am-7.30pm Mon-Sat; 10am-3pm Sun. **No credit cards. Map** p249 B5.
This palatial house contains a pharmacy, lingerie shop, shoe shop (for men and women) and perfumery.

Centro Comercial Náutico

Avenida 5ta, esquina 152, Naútico (208 0417). **Open** 10am-6pm Mon-Sat; 10am-1pm Sun. **Credit** MC, V.
Stores here include a mini supermarket, cafeteria, a dollar shop (Cuban equivalent of a pound shop), electrical goods shops and furniture stores. Perfumery, shoes and high-quality fashionwear are also sold.

Centro Comercial El Comodoro

Avenida 3ra, esquina 84, Playa (204 6178/ 61799). **Open** 10am-7.30pm Mon-Sat; 10am-2pm Sun. *Hairdresser* noon-7pm daily. **Credit** MC, V. **Map** p248 B1.
Situated in the grounds of the Hotel Comodoro and next to the Hotel Meliá Habana, this is arguably the best shopping complex in Havana, in terms of the quality of products, customer service and the stress-free nature of the environment. Stores include a mini supermarket, perfumery, jeweller's, two fashion-name sunglasses stores and photo developing outlets, plus an international pharmacy and shops selling children's clothes, electronic goods, sports equipment, shoes, bags and toys. Fashion concessions include Mango, Benetton and Versace. There's also a cigar shop across the road (look out for the crocodile statue), and a range of international magazines are stocked in the business centre.

Centro Comercial La Vigía

Avenida 5ta, esquina 248, Marina Hemingway, Jaimanitas (204 1151/1156). **Open** 10am-7pm Mon-Sat; 10am-4pm Sun. **Credit** MC, V.
Fear of boat thefts for illegal exits from Cuba have led to an intensive security presence at the Marina, where shops and restaurants cater mainly for yacht owners mooring at the nearby canals. The supermarket stocks some good but fairly expensive wines; there are also a couple of fashion boutiques, a good perfumery and cosmetics shop, plus footwear, sportswear, cigar, rum and coffee stores, a pharmacy and a souvenir shop (selling mainly T-shirts).

Centro de Negocios Miramar

Avenida 3ra, entre 76 y 80, Miramar (204 4437/4438 ext 114). **Open** 10am-6pm Mon-Sat; 10am-1pm Sun. **Credit** MC, V. **Map** p248 B2.
Shops in the Miramar Trade Center include boutiques, a sportswear store, a photography shop, shoe and jewellery outlets, plus a small supermarket.

Edificio FOCSA

Calle 17, entre L y M, Vedado (832 5532-9). **Open** 10am-7pm Mon-Sat; 10am-2pm Sun. **Credit** MC, V. **Map** p250 B11.
The key selling point of this collection of shops is that they are centrally located, at the base of the huge and strikingly ugly FOCSA building (though currently being renovated). The supermarket offers all the usual products, including bottled water at a fraction of the price it's sold at in nearby hotels. You may also want to duck into the downmarket clothes and shoe shops, and the perfumery.

Galerías Amazonas

Calle 12, entre 23 y 25, Vedado (831 9598). **Open** 10am-7pm Mon-Sat; 10am-3pm Sun. **Credit** MC, V. **Map** p249 C8.
This set of shops is devoted mainly to fashion, but also has fresh flowers and potted plants for sale in Cuban pesos. Top shops include the delicatessen, Tienda Brava for men's and women's fashion and Peletería Claudia (*see p125*) for shoes. Opposite is a well-stocked sports shop full of up to date gear, and a very good toiletries shop.

Galerías Cohiba

Hotel Meliá Cohiba, Avenida Paseo, entre 1ra y 3ra, Vedado (333636). **Open** 10am-6pm Mon-Sat; 10am-2pm Sun. **Credit** MC, V. **Map** p250 A9.
The Hotel Meliá Cohiba has a range of shops including car rental, a luxurious deli, the El Corojo cigar shop, a Benetton store and a number of other fashion outlets, as well as sports equipment shops. The souvenir shop is T-shirt territory.

Galerías de Paseo

Calle 1ra, entre Avenida Paseo y A, Vedado (553475). **Open** 10am-6pm Mon-Sat; 10am-2pm Sun. **Credit** MC, V. **Map** p250 A9.
Three floors of shops include one of the better supermarkets in town, furniture stores, fashion boutiques – with stylish Italian womenswear at reasonable prices – shoe shops, a photo developing shop, a delicatessen and a pet shop, as well as stores selling electrical goods, the Adidas label, toys, home accessories and artificial flowers. When you're done purchasing you can relax in the Jazz Café on the top floor (*see pp166-75*). Pretty good shopping – by Cuban standards.

Plaza de Carlos III

Avenida Salvador Allende (Carlos III), esquina Árbol Seco, Centro Habana (873 6370). **Open** 10am-7pm Mon-Sat; 10am-2pm Sun. **Credit** MC, V. **Map** p250 D12.
The cylindrical design of this well-known shopping centre in Centro Habana amplifies the noise and can induce a sensation of being trapped in a spin dryer, especially when it's busy at weekends. Carlos II features, among other things, downmarket clothes shops, places to get your photos developed, a sports shop, shoe shops, a supermarket, a cigar shop and a food court. Be prepared for a bit of push and shove.

Galería de Tiendas Internacionales

Hotel Habana Libre, Calle 25, esquina L, Vedado (554011). **Open** 9am-6pm Mon-Sat. **Credit** MC, V. **Map** p250 C11.

Peso shops

Many visitors leave Cuba confused by the country's so-called 'dual economy' – introduced to keep a failing economy afloat following the collapse of the Soviet Union. After all, everything seems to be priced in dollars. Once you know what to look for, though, it isn't hard to spot peso shops: they're generally dreary and drab, staff seem demoralised and the premises tend to be daunting in their emptiness, both in terms of customers and stock. Dollar shops, on the other hand, are (fairly) modern and nearly always crawling with customers. It's that simple.

Peso stores are depressingly limited in what they sell and much of the stock tends to look like '70s relics. You might find the odd bargain in second-hand clothing, cockroach poison or 1950s LPs. But if you're looking to fulfil your basic needs, you'll have a hard time. Despite the fact that most Cubans are paid in pesos, clothing, toiletries, furniture, hardware, electrical goods and many food items (including cooking oil, butter and canned goods) are available only in dollars – at prices well beyond the means of the average, and even above-average, wage earner. The prices–wages gap is now so wide that it really is an economic miracle that Cubans somehow manage to make ends meet. If you want to explore the peso sector, ask where the nearest *bodega* is. These 'grocery stores' are where locals use their ration books to obtain government-subsidised food.

There are a number of other peso stores dotted around Centro Habana that should satisfy your curiosity about goods that are sold in local currency.

Annet

Avenida de Italia (Galiano) #412, entre San José y San Rafael, Centro Habana (863 1780). **Open** 10am-5pm Mon-Sat; 10am-1pm Sun. **No credit cards. Map** p251 D14.

A surprisingly good selection of cassettes and CDs of Cuban music, together with second-hand clothes and classical sheet music.

Bazar Inglés

Avenida de Italia (Galiano) #352, esquina San Miguel, Centro Habana (863 2242). **Open** 10am-5pm Mon-Sat; 9am-1pm Sun. **No credit cards. Map** p251 D14.

New and used clothing for men and women, kept annoyingly out of reach of customers behind the counter.

Flogar

Avenida de Italia (Galiano) #402, esquina San Rafael, Centro Habana (863 1668). **Open** 9am-6pm Mon-Sat; 9am-1pm Sun. **No credit cards. Map** p251 D14.

Household products, clothes and shoes.

Eat, Drink, Shop

This very centrally located arcade attached to the Hotel Habana Libre includes an international pharmacy, a music store with a Cuban and international selection of sounds, a perfumery, fashion boutiques with well-known labels, plus a shoe shop, a cigar shop and a beauty parlour/hairdresser.

La Puntilla

Avenida 1ra, esquina A, Playa, Miramar (204 5209). **Open** 10am-6pm Mon-Sat; 10am-2pm Sun. **Credit** MC, V. **Map** p249 A7.

This newish, impressive-looking (but actually not very exciting) four-storey shopping centre in Playa has a grill restaurant on the top floor with fantastic sea views, plus a snack bar on the ground floor. Shops include a supermarket, a boutique stocking Givenchy and Ted Lapidus for men at reasonable prices, plus another clothing store, photo shop and the usual *Todo por un dollar* (everything for a dollar) shop.

5ta y 42

Avenida 5ta, esquina 42, Miramar (204 7070). **Open** 10am-6pm Mon-Sat; 9.30am-1.30pm Sun. **Credit** MC, V. **Map** p248 B4.

The centre belongs to the Cubalse chain (of which there are many branches throughout the city). There's quite a large array of shops here, and it's especially recommended for food, sportswear, clothing, kids' stuff, shoes, toiletries and hardware. There are always a few touts in the car park selling (at exorbitant prices) electrical goods that cannot be bought on the open market.

Supermarkets

Supermarkets throughout Havana don't vary much in their stock, which consists mainly of essentials: tins, butter, mayo, cereals, oil, frozen chicken, soft and alcoholic drinks and toiletries. The **Edificio FOCSA** complex (*see p80*) houses one of the city's most conveniently located supermarkets. The mother of all supermarkets – neon lighting and all – is probably the **Supermercado 5ta y 70** (Avenida 3ra, entre 68 y 70 Playa, 204 2198/2890). The recently opened **Centro Comercial El Palco** (Calle 188 y 5ta, Playa, 332168-72) is an excellent stop, stocking all the standard products, plus a number of luxuries (at luxury prices, naturally), a broad selection of wine, freshly baked bread and some of the best meat in town.

Antiques

Antique shops are a rarity in Cuba and you're more likely to see the impressive relics of the country's bourgeois past in government-owned mansions in the Vedado and Miramar neighbourhoods than in a retail outlet. However, there are a couple of stores in the city that are a delight to delve around in. If you see something you want to purchase, be aware that there are strict laws governing the export of items deemed to be of national and historic interest, so if you plan to make it further than the airport with your treasures (there's a room there bursting with confiscated items), make sure you buy them from authorised sources. These shops can provide a bill of payment and a further bill for customs purposes. If you're not given an export certificate when you buy the item, take it (or a photo if it's too large) to the **National Heritage Office** (Registro Nacional del Fondo de Bienes Culturales, Calle 17 #1009, entre 10 y 12, Vedado, 833 9658) between 8.30am and 11.30am from Monday to Friday. Many items over 40 years old may be subject to export regulations. Classic cars and paintings are the most strictly controlled, but furniture, stamp collections, coins, books and porcelain may also be restricted. At the time of writing, this office informed us that only contemporary paintings were currently allowed for export but, this being Cuba, rules may change.

In addition to the shops listed here, **La Maison** (*see p117*) sells antique tableware, jewellery and collectors' items. **Centro Comercial El Comodoro** (*see p118*) also sells a few antiques, although much of the stock is reproduction. **La Habanera** (*see p124*) also sells antique jewellery.

Casa de Antigüedades Dos Leones

Avenida Galiano #202, esquina Virtudes, Centro Habana (860 9661). **Open** 10am-5pm Mon-Sat. **Credit** MC, V. **Map** p251 D14.

Desks, rocking chairs, bedside tables and cabinets are crammed into this shop, together with an array of crystal chandeliers and art nouveau and art deco pieces. The marble statues and porcelain ornaments will catch your eye immediately.

La Vajilla

Avenida de Italia (Galiano) #502, esquina Zanja, Centro Habana (862 4751). **Open** 10am-5pm Mon-Sat. **Credit** MC, V. **Map** p251 D13.

Stock at La Vajilla can be erratic – on the one hand there are some excellent examples of late 19th- and early 20th-century furniture and household items, including some superb stained-glass lampshades, while other items are grotty and wood-wormed. This is an official antiques shop, so everything on sale has a certificate of export. Payment is set (officially) in Cuban pesos and prices are reasonable.

Books

Antique & second-hand

Look out for antique books among the goodies at the **crafts market** on the Malecón in Vedado (*see p129*). You're required to obtain special permission to take some older books out of the country; check the situation with the vendor (though bear in mind they may not know, or may tell you you don't need permission whatever the truth of the matter).

Librería Anticuaria 'El Navío'

Calle Obispo #119, entre Oficios y Mercaderes, La Habana Vieja (861 3283). **Open** 9am-7pm daily. **No credit cards. Map** p252 E15.

El Navío sells antique, rare, new, second-hand and collectable books, including first editions; there are also stamp collections, old photos, postcards and a collection of cigar bands. The shop itself is of architectural interest; it was built in the mid 16th century: a portion of the original wall is displayed under glass.

Plaza de Armas book market

Plaza de Armas, La Habana Vieja (no phone). **Open** 9am-6pm Wed-Sat; closed when raining/overcast. **No credit cards. Map** p252 E16.

This book market (*mercado de libros*) has numerous political tracts, books on Che Guevara and the Cuban Revolution, original Gabriel García Márquez novels, plus atlases, encyclopaedias and the odd book in English. You can also find wonderful 19th-century illustrated books and some great bindings. Feel free to bargain as the prices are high.

General

Note that international press is very hard to get hold of; you'll sometimes find Italian or Spanish newspapers in the **Galerías Cohiba** (*see p118*) and other hotels.

Centro Cultural Cinematográfico ICAIC

Calle 23 #1156, entre 10 y 12, Vedado (833 9278). **Open** 9am-5pm Mon-Sat. **No credit cards. Map** p249 C8.

If you don't make it to the cinema while you're in Havana, you might want at least to stop by the Cuban Film Institute for Cuban films on video (some with English subtitles), plus silkscreen posters (*see p143* **Post it**) and T-shirts.

Instituto Cubano del Libro

Calle O'Reilly #4, esquina Tacón, La Habana Vieja (863 2244). **Open** 10am-5pm daily. **No credit cards. Map** p252 E15.

The Cuban Book Institute houses two bookshops. One stocks a wide range of non-fiction and modern fiction, while the other (La Bella Havana to the left of the main entrance) covers the tourist market with guidebooks, postcards, music and some political-historical books on Cuba in English.

Librería La Internacional

Calle Obispo #526, esquina Bernaza, La Habana Vieja (861 3283/863 1941-4). **Open** 10am-5.30pm daily. **No credit cards. Map** p252 D14.

A fairly wide range of fiction and non-fiction books, CDs, cassettes, office supplies and postcards is stocked at La Internacional but, despite the name, there's actually very little that isn't in Spanish. Still, it's worth passing by if only to see the great mosaic inlay in the floor of the entrance.

Librería Rubén Martínez Villena

Paseo de Martí (Prado) #551, esquina Brasil (Teniente Rey), Centro Habana (861 5849). **Open** 10am-5pm Mon-Sat; 10am-1pm Sun. **No credit cards. Map** p251 E14.

Cuban and international literature fills the shelves at this *librería*. Well-known authors such as Isabel Allende and Alejo Carpentier are included among the fiction. Postcards and cultural journals also on sale.

Librería Rayuela

Casa de las Américas, Calle 3ra #52, esquina Avenida de los Presidentes (G), Vedado (552707-9/ www.casa.cult.cu). **Open** 8am-4pm Mon-Fri. **Credit** MC, V. **Map** p250 A10.

There are two bookshops on this site. On the right-hand side is a peso bookshop selling general literature and poetry books, while the larger shop on the left sells art books, international literature, videos of Cuban films (some have English subtitles), and CDs in dollars.

La Moderna Poesía

Calle Obispo #527, esquina Bernaza, La Habana Vieja (861 6983). **Open** 10am-8pm daily. **Credit** MC, V. **Map** p252 D14.

This spacious shop specialises in Cuban editions of fiction and non-fiction, posters, pens, paints, music, videos and items for children. In terms of non-Spanish books, you might find some political works in English, Cuban short stories and erotica.

Librería Ateneo Cervantes

Calle Bernaza #9, esquina Obispo, La Habana Vieja (862 2580). **Open** 10am-8.30pm daily. **No credit cards. Map** p252 D14.

A Cuban peso bookshop selling children's books, international literature and Cuban poetry, as well as postcards and posters.

Children's clothes & toys

Crafts markets (*ferias*) often stock interesting handmade toys. The department stores are also a good bet, in particular **Harris Brothers** (*see p117*), where there are lots of products for babies and smaller children on the third floor, including cuddly toys, bicycles, Chinese toys (admittedly of poor quality) and art products. Miramar's **5ta y 42** (*see p120*) sells children's clothes and shoes. **Centro Comercial El Comodoro** (*see p118*) houses shops selling good-quality children's clothing and shoes, plus the reasonable toyshop **La Juguetería**.

Casita de Piedra

Avenida 5ta, esquina 248, Marina Hemingway, Jaimanitas (204 1151 ext 147). **Open** 10am-7pm Mon-Sat; 10am-3pm Sun. **No credit cards.**

Rolling stock

Cuba is the country that historically produces the best tobacco in the world; and Cuban cigars reel in millions of tourists each year avid to buy at a fraction of the cost abroad. Of the major cultivating areas on the island of Vuelta Abajo (Villa Clara Province) and Vuelta Arribe (Pinar del Río) are considered to have the best *vegas* (small plots). Havana, however, is cigar city, home to the *habano*. This is where the *torcido* (rolling) takes place, transforming the tobacco leaves – already dried and aged – into *habano* cigars. Of the guided tours, the **Partagás** factory (Calle Industria #520, entre Dragones y Barcelona, Centro Habana, 338060, tour $10) is the best.

TIPS ON BUYING CIGARS

- There are two ways to know if a cigar is hand-rolled or machine-rolled: the price tag and the presence of an inscription on the bottom of the box that says *totalmente hecho a mano* (totally hand-rolled). Hand-rolled cigars are of a superior quality and are priced as such.
- Every cigar box has a code stamped on the bottom that indicates the factory where it was made. If you're interested in cigars made in a certain factory, ask the shop attendant. Factory of origin is important with some brands, such as Cohiba, where the best cigars are rolled at the El Laguito factory. In addition, the date of packaging is stamped at the bottom of the box – older packing can sometimes be a quality guarantee as the tobacco will be better aged.
- Choosing the size and flavour of a cigar is a matter of personal preference. The most prestigious brand of cigars – as the name suggests – is Cohiba Esplendidos. It was the first brand created after the Revolution and all the tobacco used in its production comes from the best *vegas* of Vuelta Abajo. Other, more recent brands include Cuaba, Vegas Robaina, Vegueros (made in Pinar del Río), San Cristóbal de La Habana and Trinidad. Pre-Revolutionary brands still going strong include Partágas, Montecristo (the best-selling brand), H Upmann, Romeo y Julieta and Punch.
- Each box of cigars must carry the government stamp, the *habanos* stamp and, in the near future, a holographic stamp will be added to guarantee authenticity. To take the cigars out of the country you need the purchase invoice and you will also need the holographic stamp once it becomes mandatory on the cigar boxes.
- Black-market cigars – on offer on almost any street corner in Havana – are usually fake and although they sell at half the price,

There are three shops in the complex cater for children – one has toys and swimming accessories, another sells children's clothes and the third has baby accessories.

Design & household goods

It's unusual to find much in the way of tastefully designed items in Havana. Of the department stores, **La Maison** (*see p117*) generally has the best selection of quality housewares. **Centro Comercial El Comodoro** (*see p118*) also has a decent selection of sheets, towels and hosts a tasteful Italian fancy goods shop. For fabrics and trimmings *see p124*.

Cuban craft products are often well made and are good value as purchases, but they generally have to be commissioned from the registered self-employed.

they don't offer even half the pleasure (unless, of course, you find smoking banana leaves a satisfying experience). The best places to buy real *habanos*, or even to while away an afternoon smoking them, are the **Casas del Habano** shops that are dotted throughout the city. This network of shops is licensed by the worldwide distribution company for *habano* cigars. The best branches are at the Partágas cigar factory (Calle Industria #520, La Habana Vieja, 338060), Club Havana (Avenida 5ta, entre 188 a 192, Playa, 204 5700) and at 5ta y 16 (Avenida 5ta, esquina a 16, Miramar, 204 7975). All accept credit cards.

Casa del Mueble La Flora

Calle 6, esquina 11, Miramar (203 6051). **Open** 9.15am-5pm Mon-Sat. **No credit cards**. **Map** p249 B6.

A variety of fairly ordinary furniture is on sale here, but there's also some stained-glass craftwork.

Colección Habana

Calle Mercaderes #13, entre O'Reilly y Empedrado, La Habana Vieja (861 3388). **Open** 9pm-6pm daily. **No credit cards**. **Map** p252 D15.

There's a wide variety of reproduction items in this tastefully decorated shop. Choose from china, glass, furniture, jewellery, materials, Cuban pottery, repro pistols, silk scarves, screens, mugs, dinner services and much more. Don't miss the garden complete with fountain and three huge turtles.

Galería Victor Manuel

Calle San Ignacio #56, entre Callejón del Chorro y Empedrado, Plaza de la Catedral, La Habana Vieja (861 2955). **Open** 10am-9pm daily. **Credit** MC, V. **Map** p252 D15.

This gallery stocks a wide variety of crafts, jewellery, paintings and sculptures to suit all tastes.

Galerías Manos (Asociación Cubana de Artesanos y Artistas)

Calle Obispo #411, entre Aguacate y Compostela, La Habana Vieja (666345). **Open** 10am-5pm Mon-Sat. **No credit cards**. **Map** p252 E15.

Cuban arts and crafts shop selling hand-woven tapestries (upstairs), lamps, handmade furniture, wooden carvings, paintings, musical instruments, shoes, bags and other assorted items.

Electronics

Many of the items for sale in electronics outlets in Havana are not actually available to Cubans. Goods in this category include microwaves, computers, air-conditioners, rice cookers, freezers, VCRs and video cameras. These restrictions are sometimes put down to fear of overloading the national grid. Cubans who want these items have no choice but to buy them second-hand or on the black market. In addition to the shops listed below, there are electronics outlets at the **Hotel Comodoro**, **Náutico** and **La Vigía** hopping complexes (for all, *see p118*).

Centro Video

Avenida 3ra, entre 12 y 14, Miramar (204 2469). **Open** 10am-6pm Mon-Sat. **No credit cards**. **Map** p249 B6.

This chain, with branches across Havana, sells electrical equipment and videos (plus sweets and toys). **Other locations**: throughout the city.

Dita

Calle 84, entre 7ma y 9na, Playa (204 5119). **Open** 10am-6pm Mon-Sat; 9am-1pm Sun. **Credit** MC, V. **Map** p248 C1.

Dita has two floors of electrical goods, including kitchen items, lighting, hi-fis, televisions, computers and computer components, telephones and fax machines – along with the requisite spare parts. Some of the stock is only available to diplomats or foreigners with special permission, but there's still a wide choice for the ordinary customer. There's a repair service on site.

Other locations: Miramar Trade Center, Avenida 3ra, entre 76 y 80, Miramar (204 0632).

Fabrics & trimmings

Colección Habana (*see p123*) stocks some beautiful fabrics and other trimmings. Try also **La Maison** (*see p117*).

Mercado del Oriente

Calle Mercaderes #111, entre Obispo y Obrapía, La Habana Vieja (863 9740). **Open** 10am-5pm daily. **Credit** DC, MC, V. **Map** p252 E15.

Situated next to the Museo de Asia, this Aladdin's Cave has a tempting array of oriental-style bedspreads, jewellery, carvings, tapestries and clothing.

La Muñequita Azul

Calle Obispo, esquina Mercaderes, La Habana Vieja (no phone). **Open** 9am-7pm daily. **No credit cards. Map** p252 E15.

Don't miss this little gem. There's not much in the way of material, but the Little Blue Doll has plenty of broderie trimmings, satins, zips and cotton thread. It also houses an 1886 Singer sewing machine.

Revert

Calle Obispo #403, entre Aguacate y Compostela, La Habana Vieja (no phone). **Open** 10am-7pm Mon-Sat; 10am-1pm Sun. **No credit cards. Map** p252 E15.

Imported fabrics, towels, sheets and bed linen are sold in this operation overseen by owner Mr Revert. Black and white photos show the shop some 50 years ago.

Fashion

The price of clothing tends to be high, certainly too high for the average Cuban, therefore *habaneros* have been forced to improvise in order to meet the high standards they have set themselves in terms of appearance.

Visitors on a budget also have the option of rooting around some of the fashion boutiques for reductions or exploring the second-hand clothes shops scattered around the city.

Places worth checking out for good-quality clothing include **Le Select** (*see p117*), **Galerías Amazonas** (*see p118*) and **Galerías Cohiba** (*see p118*). The **Centro Comercial El Comodoro** (*see p118*) has the most contemporary fashion outlets in Havana, including Benetton, Mango, Guess, Versace, Givenchy and YSL, and an attractive shoe store with accessories. It is also the best place in town for men's fashion. **La Época** (*see p117*) has some French labels at bargain prices, but otherwise you'll have to search hard to find anything of quality. Way out in front as the focal point for Cuban fashion is **La Maison** (*see p117*), which holds regular fashion shows.

Benetton

Calle Amargura, esquina Oficios, La Habana Vieja (862 2480). **Open** 10am-7pm Mon-Sat; 10am-1pm Sun. **Credit** MC, V. **Map** p252 E15.

The world-famous Italian brand also has concessions in Harris Brothers department store (*see p117*) and the Centro Comercial El Comodoro (*see p118*).

Novator

Calle Obispo #365, entre Compostela y Habana, La Habana Vieja (no phone). **Open** 10am-7pm Mon-Sat; 10am-7pm Sun. **No credit cards. Map** p252 E15.

Handmade hat shop, selling lovely straw hats for men, women and children.

El Quitrín

Calle Obispo #163, entre San Ignacio y Mercaderes, La Habana Vieja (862 0810/6195). **Open** 9am-5pm daily. **Credit** MC, V. **Map** p252 E15.

El Quitrín sells beautiful hand-made Cuban clothing in cotton and linen fabrics. The quality is better than you'll find at the markets (reflected in the higher prices). The famous *guayaberas* (traditional Cuban shirts) are a must for men and there are some chic dresses for women. Tablecloths and crocheted shawls are good buys too. Staff will make curtains to order.

La Sorpesa

Calle Obispo #520, entre Bernaza y Villegas, La Habana Vieja (863 1362). **Open** 10am-7pm Mon-Sat; 10am-1pm Sun. **No credit cards. Map** p249 D6.

This recently opened boutique sells a good selection of brand-name men's and women's clothing. Usually worth a rummage.

Tierra Brava

Galerías Amazonas, Calle 12, entre 23 y 25, Vedado (662437). **Open** 10am-7pm Mon-Sat; 10am-2pm Sun. **Credit** MC, V. **Map** p249 C8.

One of those boutiques where the real bargains can be found among cut-price clothing. Regular stock for both men and women includes fashion labels Lacoste, Levi's, Givenchy, Calvin Klein and Guess, plus there are hats, backpacks and swimwear.

Jewellery

Look out for fine handmade jewellery in most hotel shops. There are also very cheap handmade pieces to be found at the city's crafts markets (*see p129*).

La Habanera

Calle 12 #505, entre 5ta y 7ma, Miramar (204 2546/2648). **Open** 10am-6pm Mon-Fri; 10am-2pm Sat. **Credit** MC, V. **Map** p249 B6.

A well-kept secret, this very private antique jewellery store has fantastic pieces, including watches, pendants, rings, cameos, bracelets and tableware. The setting is hush-hush and conservative, which is rare in Cuba. Prices from $50 to exceedingly expensive.

Shoes & leather goods

The best selection of shoes and leather items can be found in the **Centro Comercial El Comodoro, Galerías Amazonas, Galerías**

Cohiba) and **La Vigía** (for all, *see p118*) and **La Maison** (*see p117*) shopping centres. All of these have some good shoes for women; the choice for men is more limited. For handmade leather accessories, head for the **crafts markets** on the Malecón or near the Plaza de la Catedral (*see p129*). Beware that the dye used on leather handbags for sale at these markets is not top quality and may run. Shoe repairers can be found in the streets in La Habana Vieja and Centro Habana; otherwise, there are repair shops opposite Frankfurt's at the corner of Calle 16 and Calle 23 in Vedado and at La Infancia, Calle 23, corner of 16, Vedado.

La Habana

Calle Obispo #415, esquina Aguacate, La Habana Vieja (no phone). **Open** 10am-7pm Mon-Sat; 10am-1pm Sun. **No credit cards**. **Map** p252 D15.
La Habana stocks shoes, bags and belts. The Novator branch has women's and men's hats.
Branch: Novator, Calle Obispo 375, entre Habana y Compostela, La Habana Vieja (861 5292).

Peletería Claudia

Calle 12, entre 23 y 25, Vedado (662437/662438). **Open** 10am-7pm Mon-Sat; 10am-2pm Sun. **No credit cards**. **Map** p249 5C.
This small shop stocks some fine shoes, plus good-quality luggage by Delsey.

Flowers & plants

It's only in the past few years that flowers have been widely available in Havana. After the Revolution, having flowers in the home was considered undesirably bourgeois, so Cubans had to make do with artificial flowers. Today peso flower stalls and flower carts (*floreros*) are a common sight on the streets of Havana. For a range of flowers and arrangements, try the stall opposite Galerías Amazonas on the corner of Calle 23 and Calle 12 near the Cementerio de Colón, which also sells potted plants, or the one at Calle D, #406, between 17 and 19 in Vedado. There are also fantastic flower arrangements (including vase) available for around $6 or so at the **Cuatro Caminos** market (*see p70*).

Jardín Wagner

Calle Mercaderes #113, entre Obispo y Obrapía, La Habana Vieja (669017). **Open** 9am-5pm daily. **No credit cards**. **Map** p252 E15.
If you're walking along Mercaderes, you're unlikely to miss the window at Jardín Wagner, which has water cascading down it. The shop stocks beautiful roses, fresh flowers and houseplants, plus artificial flowers. It also offers an Interflora service.

Tropiflora

Calle 12 #156, entre Calzada y Línea, Vedado (662332/830 3869/lineay12@ceniai.inf.cu). **Open** 8am-8pm Mon-Sat. **No credit cards**. **Map** p249 B8.
This shop stocks a wide variety of flowers, including many tropical varieties. It's responsible for the fantasy arrangements that decorate the world-famous Tropicana cabaret, as well as the lobbies and public rooms of many hotels and embassies. Tropiflora sells artificial plants and flowers and can provide arrangements for all kinds of occasions. Interflora service.

Food & drink

Most of the department stores and shopping complexes found across Havana house supermarkets for essential provisions (*see p120*). There are also small grocery shops in all Servi-Cupet petrol stations selling basic food, drinks and sweets. For fresh fruit and veg, *see p126* **Getting agro**.

Bread & cakes

As if to remind you that sugar is Cuba's main crop, excessive amounts of the stuff are used in cakes and pastries, and locals love it. Bread is generally poor in Cuba.

Bosque de La Habana

Hotel Meliá Habana, Avenida 3ra, entre 78 y 80, Miramar (204 8500/centro@clientes.mhabana.solmelia.cu). **Open** 24hrs daily. **Credit** MC, V. **Map** p248 B1.
This ice-cream parlour on the lower ground floor of this hotel sells the best cakes and pastries in town.

La Francesa del Pan

Calle 42, esquina 19, Miramar (204 2211). **Open** 8am-8pm daily. **No credit cards**. **Map** p248 C4.
This boulangerie sells very good bread and cakes.

Pain de París

Calle 25, entre Infanta y O, Vedado (873 3347). **Open** 24hrs daily. **No credit cards**. **Map** p250 B12.
The Pain de París chain is pretty expensive and the some of the products can look better than they taste. Still, at least there are branches across town. Some, but not all, are open 24 hours daily.
Other locations: throughout the city.

Panadería San José

Calle Obispo #161, entre Mercaderes y San Ignacio, La Habana Vieja (860 9326). **Open** 24hrs daily. **No credit cards**. **Map** p252 E15.
This bakery in the heart of La Habana Vieja is open 24 hours daily. Look out for the beautiful fresco above the shop entrance.

Pastelería La Francesa

Paseo de Martí (Prado) #410, entre Neptuno y San Rafael, Centro Habana (862 0739). **Open** 8am-11pm daily. **No credit cards**. **Map** p251 D14.
Good bread, croissants, sandwiches, coffee and cakes are served at this bakery-cum-café, located next to the Hotel Inglaterra.

Getting agro

Visiting the *agromercado* (farmers' market; shortened to *agro*) can be one of the simplest and cheapest pleasures of a stay in Havana. Firstly, because it's one of the rare activities in Cuba that brings the sense of satisfaction that comes with getting good value for money (spending in pesos), and secondly, because – as is the case the world over – a local market can offer a vivid 'slice of life' encounter. Stall-holders vie for attention with plenty of banter and social interaction, so come prepared with some vocabulary, *see p231*.

Pesos are the most important asset in any visit to the *agro*: although you can pay in dollars, you're far less likely to get ripped off it you pay in pesos, the way the prices are marked up. Mixing and matching between dollars and pesos is also quite acceptable. Pesos can be obtained from a Cadeca kiosk (normally located in or near the *agro* entrance). Don't forget your plastic bag (*java*), or look for the person selling them near the entrance. Even rice and beans are sold loose.

Produce varies hugely according to season and the vagaries of distribution. However, you'll usually find onions, cucumbers, cabbage, tomatoes, chillies, peppers, garlic and green beans, as well as seasonal produce like yucca or taro. Sweet potatoes are easier to find than the humble potato, which is only sold direct to ration-book holders. Note also the difference between sweet bananas and plantains (both called *plátanos*): the latter, used only for cooking, generally come in singles (*c/u*, or *cada uno*), while the fruit is usually sold '*a mano*' (in a bunch, literally a hand). In fact, when checking prices always take notice of whether the item is priced in pounds (*libras*) or singly (*cada uno*).

Other fruit can include oranges, pineapples, papaya (*fruta bomba*), watermelon, passion fruit, *mamay* and guavas. If you're in Cuba between May and September, you're smack in the middle of mango season. There's never much in the way of greens. You may find what is called spinach, but is actually more like chard, and the Cuban lettuce is a depressing item not worth the bother.

Coffee

Casa del Café

Calle Baratillo, esquina Obispo, La Habana Vieja (833 8061). **Open** 10am-6pm Mon-Sat; 10am-3pm Sun. **No credit cards. Map** p252 E16.
Cuban coffee of all sorts of roasts and grinds, plus every imaginable coffee accessory. There's an original bar from the 1900s and tourist souvenirs.

Luxury items

La Bodega del Vino

Complejo Turístico La Giraldilla, Calle 222, esquina 37, La Coronela, La Lisa (330568/ 330569). **Open** 10am-5am daily. **Credit** MC, V.
This tourist complex is a long way out of town, but you may be tempted to make the trip in order to visit the wine cellar, which, with over 200 wines, has the largest choice in Havana. It houses a decent restaurant too (*see p110*).

Galerías Amazonas

Calle 12, entre 23 y 25, Vedado (831 9598). **Open** 10am-7pm Mon-Sat; 10am-3pm Sun. **Credit** MC, V. **Map** p249 C8.
A large selection of rums is sold here and, in theory, a range of handmade chocolates from Spain and Belgium. The reality is more likely to be large quantities of Toblerone.

Rum

Aside from Bacardí, which was first made in Cuba but is now produced in the Bahamas, the most famous brand of Cuban rum is Havana Club, which, along with many other varieties

The failure to supply much greenery is testament to the fact that Cubans are big meat-eaters. *Agros* usually sell meat, both cured (rough chunks of ham and processed meat) and fresh (often entire legs or large slabs that are cut up into escalopes). The butchers are almost always intimidating and macho but don't be put off: pointing and sawing the air will usually get what you want. Very, very occasionally, you may find chicken at the market – the only time (short of buying a live one) that chicken can be seen whole.

WHERE TO FIND THE AGROS

The city's best and largest *agromercado* is the not-so-central **Cuatro Caminos** (Four Roads, *see p70*), at the junction of four of Havana's most populous districts. In Vedado, check out Calle 19 y B or the smaller Calle 17 y G. In Centro Habana, try Compostela, between Luz y Acosta. In Miramar, head for Calle 19 y 68 or Calle 42 y 19. A large market is held on the first Sunday of the month at Plaza de la Revolución (and on major *ferias* or public holidays).

(Mathusalem is often recommended by connoisseurs), is sold all over Havana. Rum is an ingredient for Cuba's most popular cocktails: white three-year rum is used for the famous mojito and Cuba Libre, while *añejo* is a fine digestif with a smooth, rounded taste.

Fundación Havana Club (Museo del Ron)

Calle San Pedro #262, esquina Sol, La Habana Vieja (861 8051/862 3832). **Open** *Museum & gallery* 9am-5.30pm Mon-Thur; 9am-4pm Fri, Sat; 10am-4pm Sun. *Bar* 10am-midnight daily. *Shop* 10am-9pm daily. **Credit** MC, V. **Map** p252 E15.

The Rum Museum has a bar and a shop next door decorated in 1930s style. It stocks only Havana Club products, including cocktail sets, T-shirts, caps and gift sets. *See also p56.*

Taberna del Galeón/Casa del Ron

Calle Baratillo, esquina Obispo, La Habana Vieja (338476/338061). **Open** 9am-5pm Mon-Sat; 9am-3pm Sun. **Credit** MC, V. **Map** p252 E16.

A brass galleon hanging in the entrance welcomes visitors into this old beamed building for free rum tasting and a good selection of bottles for sale.

Gifts

Apart from cigars and rum, standard purchases for visitors to Cuba, there's a growing crafts industry that offers some alternative souvenirs. Additionally, the big hotels have shops selling gold and silver jewellery (usually combined with black coral), T-shirts and posters. The iconic black and white shots of Fidel, Che and the Revolutionaries in the mountains – now made into posters, postcards and calendars – make good souvenirs. Some museums have tasteful gift shops selling silk scarves, CDs or books; the shops in the **Museo Nacional de Bellas Artes** (*see p69*) are particularly good. ICAIC film posters (*see p143* **Post it**) make striking gifts.

Casa del Abanico

Calle Obrapía #107, entre Mercaderes y Oficios, La Habana Vieja (863 4452). **Open** 9.30am-5pm Mon-Fri; 8.30am-noon Sat. **No credit cards**. **Map** p252 E15.

A beautiful shop choc full of fans, where you can have one hand-painted to order by the team of skilled fan-painters. Prices range from $2 to $150.

La Exposición

Calle San Rafael #12, entre Bélgica (Monserrate) y Agramonte (Zulueta), La Habana Vieja (863 8364). **Open** 9am-6pm Mon-Sat; 9am-1pm Sun. **No credit cards**. **Map** p251 D14.

Upstairs at La Exposición you'll find stationery, postcards, maps, *guayaberas* (traditional Cuban shirts for men) and pretty fans. Hidden away downstairs, meanwhile, and not even signposted, is a vast array of posters and reproduction prints of Cuban artwork at fantastically cheap prices. Framing service.

Palacio de la Artesanía

Calle Cuba #64, entre Cuarteles y Peña Pobre, La Habana Vieja (867 1118/1119/338072). **Open** 9am-7pm daily. **Credit** MC, V. **Map** p252 D15.

A great one-stop shop for gifts, this complex, located around a colonial-style courtyard, sells a large selection of cigars, rum, Cuban music and art, plus fashion and T-shirts for men and women, jewellery, watches, shoes, fans and books. A wide variety of good-quality cotton, linen and polyester *guayabera* shirts can be found in a shop on the ground floor.

Sede de Hermandad de Tejedoras y Bordadoras de Belén

Calle Obrapía #158, esquina Mercaderes, La Habana Vieja (861 7750). **Open** 10am-5pm daily. **No credit cards**. **Map** p252 E15.

This workshop, run by the Federation of Cuban Women (FCW), was founded in the early 1990s with the aim of rescuing dying traditions. Items on sale include attractive and brightly coloured handmade quilts, bags, clothing and tapestries.

Health & beauty

Beauty salons

Cuban women place a great deal of emphasis on their appearance and pay particular attention to their hands and feet. Unpainted nails are frowned upon by men and women alike, hence the infinite number of beauty salons offering a range of services for extremely low peso prices. If you decide to give one a go, keep an open mind as hygiene standards aren't always strictly enforced. If you want a wider range of treatments in more comfortable facilities, head for the salons at **La Maison** (*see p117*), **Palacio de la Artesanía** (*see above*) or at one of the larger hotels. Among the best are those at the **Galerías Cohiba** (*see p118*), **Meliá Habana** (*see p45*), Nacional (*see p42*) and **Habana Libre** (*see p41*).

Centro de Belleza 'Kalinka'

Avenida de Italia (Galiano), entre San Rafael y San Martín, Centro Habana (862 6951). **Open** 8am-6pm daily. **No credit cards**. **Map** p251 D14.

Hairdressing, facials, massages, pedicures and manicures are on offer here in Cuban pesos.

Salón Estilo

Calle Obispo #510, entre Bernaza y Villegas, La Habana Vieja (860 2650). **Open** 9am-9pm Mon-Sat. **No credit cards**. **Map** p252 E14.

This recently opened international cosmetics shop and beauty salon offers facials, massages, waxing and other hair removal techniques, as well as pedicures, manicures and hairdressing. The dollar prices are very reasonable.

SPA Club Comodoro

Hotel Comodoro, Avenida 3ra y 84, Playa (204 5049/spacomodoro@sermed.cha.cut.cu). **Open** 10am-7.30pm Mon-Sat; 9am-5pm Sun. **No credit cards**. **Map** p248 B1.

Well-equipped beauty parlour offering sophisticated techniques in massage therapy, facials, hair removal, peeling, weight reduction and chiropody.

Suchel

Calle Calzada #709, entre A y B, Vedado (833 8332). **Open** 8.30am-8pm Mon-Sat; 8.30am-3pm Sun. **No credit cards**. **Map** p250 A9.

This place has a gym, steam bath and hairdresser, and offers facials, massages and 'natural treatments' – all in Cuban pesos. There's also a second-hand clothes shop on the premises. Be prepared to queue, especially if you arrive after mid morning.

Cosmetics & perfumes

Cosmetics are sold in all the large hotels and perfumeries can be found in all the shopping centres, including **Centro Comercial El Comodoro**, **La Vigía** and **Náutico** (for all, *see p118*). If you are looking for something special, **La Maison** (*see p117*) has the widest selection of perfumes and cosmetics, while **Le Select** (*see p117*) has a very good range of hair products. Don't expect always to be able to try perfume in the shop.

Habana 1791 (Aromas Coloniales de la Isla de Cuba)

Calle Mercaderes #156, entre Obrapía y Lamparilla, La Habana Vieja (861 3525). **Open** 10am-6pm daily. **No credit cards**. **Map** p252 E15.

This beautiful shop is fascinating. It sells around ten varieties of original cologne, including a tobacco fragrance made from marinated tobacco leaves; customers are welcome to try out the ready-made colognes. You can also have a 'personal mixture' made up by the helpful shop assistants. The finished product is packed into a glass or ceramic bottle of your choice, which can be hand-painted to order, sealed with wax and sold in an attractive linen bag at reasonable prices. The shop also sells original silver pendants containing perfume, pot pourri and dried flowers. Next door is an array of toiletries imported from Europe. Just one criticism of the finished product: the aroma doesn't last long.

Opticians

Óptica El Almendares

Calle Obispo #364, entre Habana y Compostela, La Habana Vieja (860 8262). **Open** 10am-6pm Mon-Sat. **Credit** MC, V. **Map** p252 E15.

This recently opened shop sells a selection of fashionable frames, contact lenses and accessories.

Óptica Miramar/Casa Matriz

Avenida 7ma, entre 24 y 26, Miramar (204 2269/ 2990). **Open** 10am-6pm Mon-Fri; 10am-2pm Sat. **Credit** MC, V. **Map** p249 B5.

The friendly and professional Óptica Miramar sells a wide range of quite fashionable adult frames, plus contact lens fluids, sunglasses and children's frames. It also stocks some lenses, but doesn't always have a wide variety available. No appointment is required for the on-site optician (test $5).

Branches: Calle Neptuno #411, entre San Nicolás y Manrique, Centro Habana (863 2161); Plaza de Carlos III, Avenida Salvador Allende (Carlos III), esquina Árbol Seco, Centro Habana (873 6370).

Pharmacies

It's sad and ironic that although training standards for doctors in Cuba are high, the embargo has put a stranglehold on supplies, so pharmacies do not offer much choice and are often not fully stocked, not even with what we consider basics. If your ailment can be treated by natural remedies (anything from aloe vera lotions to various plant tinctures), the pharmacist (in peso outlets) will more than likely provide you with what you require from Cuban-made products. For international pharmacies, which stock a wide range of conventional medicines, *see pp218-33*.

Farmacia Taquechel

Calle Obispo #155, entre Mercaderes y San Ignacio, La Habana Vieja (862 9286). **Open** 9am-6.30pm daily. **No credit cards**. **Map** p252 E15.

Farmacia Taquechel is effectively a museum. It was first opened as a pharmacy in 1898 by Francisco Taquechel, and was reopened in 1995, completely restored to its original glory. The interior is beautifully decorated with intriguing gadgets, such as a century-old French porcelain water filter, a solar microscope and antique measuring pots. Nowadays, the shop sells a selection of natural products, including sponges, infusions, shark's cartilage, face creams, honey and red mangrove wine, Spirulina (a fortifier made from algae), ginseng and some essential oils. A brass flask hanging outside the pharmacy indicates the presence of this treasure trove.

Laundry & dry-cleaning

Most hotels offer dry-cleaning and laundry services, although these can be expensive and unreliable. To do it yourself head to one of numerous launderettes around the city.

Aster Lavandería

Calle 34 #314, entre 3ra y 5ta, Miramar (204 1622). **Open** 8am-5pm Mon-Fri; 8am-noon Sat. **No credit cards**. **Map** p248 B4.

Offers a very good, cheap and efficient dry-cleaning service. There are also self-service washing and drying machines available at reasonable prices.

Markets

Craft markets

Feria del Malecón

Malecón, esquina D, Vedado (no phone). **Open** 10am-6pm Mon, Tue, Thur-Sun. **No credit cards**. **Map** p250 A10.

Smaller than the crafts market (*feria*) near the Plaza de la Catedral (*see below*), this one near the Meliá Cohiba in Vedado has products including handmade shoes and sandals, clothing, bags, antiquarian books and stamp collections. It's a favourite place for locals to buy presents and is much more relaxed than its more tourist-orientated counterpart in Old Havana.

Feria (near the Plaza de la Catedral)

Calle Tacón, La Habana Vieja (no phone). **Open** 10am-6pm Wed-Sat. **No credit cards**. **Map** p252 E15.

The city's largest crafts market is held in a beautiful setting, close to the cathedral in the heart of La Habana Vieja. It's a hub of activity, and the ideal place to find souvenirs. Clothing includes a huge array of hats, from berets adorned with images of Che Guevara or a Revolutionary red star to straw hats and crocheted numbers. Other highlights include hand-woven hammocks, various musical instruments, papier mâché toys, mobiles, masks, hardwood sculptures, paintings and very inexpensive handmade jewellery. Also keep an eye out for *guayaberas* (traditional cotton shirts for men), embroidered cotton outfits for children, and a variety of leather shoes and accessories at reasonable prices. In short, there's something here for everyone. That includes pickpockets, so be on the alert.

Food markets

See p126 **Getting agro**.

Music

Cuban music has smashed through all frontiers and is now enjoying worldwide popularity. Internationally, the best-known Cuban music is salsa, but in the country itself you'll have access to other typical musical styles. CD prices tend to be higher than you might expect but you may also be offered bootlegs or 'home-made' versions by a band at a restaurant (quality isn't guaranteed).

Artex

Calle Oficios 362, entre Luz y Santa Clara, La Habana Vieja (862 3228/863 5392). **Open** 9am-5pm Tue-Sat. **Credit** MC, V. **Map** p252 E15.
Artex shops sell musical instruments, CDs and cassettes, some handicrafts, souvenirs and publications. There are about 25 branches around the city. Staff are particularly helpful at the Vedado branch (Calle 23, esquina L, 553162).

Casa de la Música de Miramar

Calle 20 #3308, entre 33 y 35, Miramar (204 0447). **Open** 10am-noon daily. **No credit cards. Map** p249 C6.
Musical instruments, sound systems and a wide variety of Cuban music in the form of CDs, tapes and sheet music. The Casa also houses a club for live music (*see pp153-65*).

Casa de la Música de Centro Habana

Avenida Galiano #255, entre Neptuno y Concordia, Centro Habana (862 4165). **Open** 10am-noon daily. **No credit cards. Map** p251 D14.
Cuba's top salsa bands perform here and you can buy their music in the adjacent shop, which sells an excellent selection of Cuban rhythms. *See pp153-65.*

Longina

Calle Obispo #360, entre Habana y Compostela, La Habana Vieja (862 8371). **Open** 10am-7pm Mon-Sat; 10am-1pm Sun. **No credit cards. Map** p252 E15.
This beautiful shop, with an art nouveau exterior and stained-glass features, has a wide choice of Cuban music, percussion instruments, cassettes and classic Cuban films on video. Service is first-class.

Tienda Tecmusic

Avenida 5ta, esquina 88, Miramar (204 8759). **Open** 10am-6pm Mon-Fri; 10am-1.30pm Sat. **No credit cards. Map** p248 C1.
A wide range of musical instruments, CDs and tapes.

Photographic services

Many hotels offer photo developing services, among them the **Nacional** (*see p42*), **Habana Riviera** (*see p41*) and **Comodoro** (*see p118*). Otherwise, look out for Photo Service outlets on the corner of Calle 23 and Calle O in Vedado (335031) and at **Galerías de Paseo** (*see p118*) and the **5ta y 42** shopping centre (*see p120*). Film processing is priced per photo (50¢ for developing, plus 30¢ per print).

Foto Prado

Paseo de Martí (Prado), esquina Virtudes, Centro Habana (863 4186). **Open** 9am-7pm Mon-Sat; 9am-1pm Sun. **No credit cards. Map** p251 D14.
Foto Prado sells film and offers a developing and photocopying service.

Fotografía Luz Habana

Calle Tacón #22, entre O'Reilly y Empredrado, La Habana Vieja (863 4263). **Open** 9am-7pm daily. **No credit cards. Map** p252 E16.
An attractive shop near the cathedral selling a good variety of cameras, accessories and binoculars. It also operates a one-hour film processing service.

Sport

Don't worry if you forget to bring your running shoes to Havana (mind you, you'd be mad to jog in this heat): you can buy everything from a pair of Nike trainers to a pool table here – you just have to know where to look. In addition to the places below, try the city's department stores and shopping centres. There's a sports shop selling baseball gear at the back of the **Estadio Latinoamericano** (*see p177*).

Adidas

Calle Neptuno, entre Campanario y Manrique, Centro Habana (862 5178). **Open** 10am-6pm Mon-Sat; 10am-1.30pm Sun. **Credit** MC, V. **Map** p251 D13.
The three-striped brand has a well-stocked two-storey shop here in Centro Habana. The ample range includes men and women's sportswear, plus running shoes, football boots, sunglasses, bags, towels and swimming hats.

Stationery & supplies

Papelería O'Reilly

Calle O'Reilly #102, esquina Tacón, La Habana Vieja (863 4263). **Open** 10am-6pm daily. **Map** p252 E15.
O'Reilly's sells some decent-quality pens, office equipment, fax paper, wrapping paper, children's books, as well as briefcases and a few items of luggage. Picture framing and photocopying services are also available.

Papelería San Francisco

Calle Oficios #52, entre Amargura y Brasil (Teniente Rey), La Habana Vieja (no phone). **Open** 9am-5pm Mon-Fri; 9am-1pm Sat. **No credit cards. Map** p252 E15.
Office equipment and stationery supplies.

Arts & Entertainment

Festivals & Events	**132**
Children	**137**
Film	**140**
Galleries	**145**
Gay & Lesbian	**150**
Music & Nightlife	**153**
Performing Arts	**166**
Sport & Fitness	**176**

Features

Digital art	135
Top five Cinemas	140
Post it	143
Don't miss Cuban films	144
Stu-stu-studio	149
Lesbian Havana	152
The best Venues	155
Generation rap	160
Bienvenue, willkommen, welcome	163
Havana laugh	168
Remember my name	173
High-density dance	174
Esquina caliente	177
The Blues	181

Festivals & Events

Havana's rich vein of well-attended cultural celebrations defies the laws of PR.

Ask any *habanero* what's on tonight and you'll likely be told '*no hay nada*' (there's nothing); locals are notoriously negative about there being anything to do. In fact, though, the Cuban calendar is stuffed full of festivals, fairs and events dedicated to dance, film, sport, theatre, music and even cigars. The tricky bit is finding out about them in the first place; information is scarce and often inaccurate – events may fail to materialise or people find out about them after they're over. Less now than before, however: with the advent of mass tourism and the ensuing flow of dollars, the majority of major festivals have become much better organised over the past few years and generally do take place at the projected time – some even have websites to prove it.

LISTINGS AND INFORMATION

Confusingly, there are two so-called listings publications that go under the name of *Cartelera*. One, the *Cartelera de la Habana*, is a weekly bulletin published on Thursdays (20 peso cents from newspaper kiosks; www.creart.cult.cu); the other, known as *Cartelera*, is also published weekly in English and Spanish but financed by advertising and distributed to hotels free of charge (published by JUGLAR; 553840). Don't expect exhaustive information from either but large cultural events are covered.

The **Buró de Convenciones**, based in the Hotel Neptuno-Tritón (Calle 3ra, esquina a 74, Miramar, 204 8273), produces a comprehensive calendar of events (pick one up from its offices free of charge) or on its website (www.cubameeting.org). The **Ministry of Culture** (Calle 2 #258, entre 11 y 13, Vedado, www.cubarte.cult.cu) also compiles a useful year-planner of festivals and events. If you're planning a trip based around a particular festival, check out both these websites before leaving computer-friendly shores.

The **Hurón Azúl** programme on national television gives a rundown of larger cultural events, while **Radio Taíno** (in both Spanish and English) broadcasts daily listings for live music events, and is probably the most accurate information available – shame that it's rattled off at such a pace that it's a hard to catch. Nevertheless, most publicity in Havana still travels by word of mouth, so be sure to ask at your hotel or *casa particular*.

Regular events

The **Casa de las Américas** (*see p79*) programme is always worth a look, as there is a steady stream of exhibitions, concerts and Latin American/Caribbean literary and cultural events.

Cañonazo

Fortaleza de San Carlos de la Cabaña, Parque Histórico Militar Morro-Cabaña, Carretera de La Cabaña, Habana del Este (620617/9). **Time** 9pm daily. **Map** p251 D/E16.

In memory of the curfew inviting citizens to return inside the (now-demolished) city walls, a cannon is fired from the ramparts of the castle across the bay from Old Havana at 9pm each night. The soldiers wear 18th-century costume and march solemnly along in a torch-lit file. It's a popular show, so get there early for a good view, but don't stand too close or you'll be deafened.

Spring

Festival de los Habanos

Information: Habanos SA (204 0443/0414/ aleal@habanos.cu). **Venues** Palacio de las Convenciones, Plaza San Francisco, Fortaleza de San Carlos de la Cabaña, Museo de Bellas Artes; visits to Pinar del Río. **Date** 1wk in 2nd half Feb, annual.

With its trade fair, seminars and trips to tobacco fields, this cigar festival caters to both business people and dedicated cigar aficionados. The highlight is the $400-a-head gala dinner where cigar-filled humidors autographed by Fidel are auctioned (the money goes to the Cuban health service), along with cigar-inspired artwork. Matt Dillon has been spotted several times…

Festival de Música Electroacústica Primavera en La Habana

Information: Laboratorio Nacional de Música Electroacústica, Calle 17 #260, esquina a I, Vedado (830 3983/icm@cubarte.cult.cu). **Venues** Sala-teatro Bellas Artes, Basílica Menor de San Francisco de Asís. **Date** 15-21 Mar 2004; 2nd half Mar, even-numbered years.

'Primavera' is organised by Juan Blanco, Cuba's most famous exponent of electro-acoustic music. International participants often include avant-garde US musical minimalists. From 2004, the festival will also experiment with DJs, techno and performance art.

Cuba's musical showpiece: **Cubadisco**.

Festival Internacional de Percusión

Information: Society of Percussionists of Cuba (PERCUBA), Calle 80 #1709 (interior), entre 17 y 19, Playa (203 8808/www.percuba.com). **Venue** Teatro Amadeo Roldán. **Date** 20-24 Apr 2004; late Apr, annual.

This percussionists' dream, founded by symphony percussionist Lino Neira, includes a competition, lectures, exhibitions of instruments and concerts.

Festival Los Días de la Danza

Information: Consejo Nacional de las Artes Escénicas (CNAE), Calle 4 #257 entre 11 y 13, Vedado (830 4126/351/cnae@min.cult.cu). **Venue** Teatro Mella. **Date** 2nd half of April, annual.

A showcase for Cuban dance companies of all genres and abilities, plus international dance groups. A good nine days of new talent spotting.

Primero de Mayo

Date 1 May.

May Day parades celebrating International Workers' Day are a must on any socialist country's calendar. The routine? Get up at the crack of dawn, apply sunblock, watch the stream of workers enter the Plaza de la Revolución, listen to Fidel's speech and wave a paper Cuban flag.

Festival y Concurso Internacional de Guitarra

Information: Instituto Cubano de la Música (ICM), Calle 15 #452, entre E y F, Vedado (830 3503-06/ 830 9972/832 0487/icm@cubarte.cult.cu). **Venue** Teatro Amadeo Roldán. **Date** 8-15 May 2004; 1st half May, even-numbered years.

Organised by Cuba's multi-talented composer and guitar maestro, Leo Brouwer, who is also conductor of the National Symphony Orchestra, this festival and competition has a large international following.

Feria Internacional el Disco 'Cubadisco'

Information: Instituto Cubano de la Música (ICM), Calle 15 #452 entre E y F, Vedado (830 3503-06). **Venues** PABEXPO, Teatro Mella, Parque Histórico Militar Morro-Cabaña, smaller venues. **Date** 23-30 May 2004; 2nd half May, annual.

Now in its seventh year, Cubadisco is the island's largest commercial musical event – both a fair and festival – and covers all musical genres within the Cuban music world. PABEXPO is the main venue but concerts by Cuba's best musicians take place all over the city. A daily programme is published.

Summer

Festival Nacional del Humor 'Aquelarre'

Information: Centro Promoción del Humor, Calle A #601 altos, entre 25 y 27, Vedado (830 3708/3914). **Venues** Teatro Mella, Teatro Nacional, Teatro Fausto, Teatro América. **Date** 1st half June, annual.

Cuban humour relies heavily on stereotypes – gay men, mother-in-laws, people from the east of the island – and slapstick. It can also be topical and cutting at times, but the delivery is so rapid and the understanding of Cuban life required so advanced that you'll miss a lot if you don't have excellent Spanish and local knowledge.

Festival Boleros de Oro

Information: UNEAC, Calle 17 #351, entre G y H, Vedado (832 0395/www.uneac.com). **Venues** Teatro América, Teatro Amadeo Roldán, Teatro Nacional, UNEAC. **Date** 2nd half June, annual.

A week-long event with performances by famous *bolero* singers, groups and orchestras of *filin* (literally 'feeling') from Cuba, Latin America and Spain, plus lectures and competitions. *Boleros* are famous for their lyrics of love and loss, so bring a hankie. Note that some events also take place in Santiago de Cuba.

Festival Cubarock Internacional 'Caiman Rock'

Information: Dirección Nacional de la Asociación Hermanos Saíz (AHS), Pabellón Cuba, Calle 23, entre M y N, Vedado (832 3511-13/ahsinternacional@ujc.org.cu). **Venues** Salón Rosado de La Tropical, Anfiteatro de Marianao, Patio de María. **Date** 1st half July, annual.

Cuba isn't usually associated with rock, but *roqueros*, as fans are known, are surprisingly numerous in Havana. Don't expect subtlety from bands with names like Agonizer and Zeus (though perhaps Rice and Beans offer a more nuanced performance). International input comes mostly from Latin American countries.

CubaDanza

Information: Danza Contemporánea de Cuba, Teatro Nacional, Avenida Paseo y Calle 39, Plaza de la Revolución (879 6410/www.cubarte.cult.cu). **Venue** Teatro Nacional. **Dates** 1st half Jan & Aug, annual. **Map** p250 D10.

A festival of modern dance classes, workshops and performances organised by Danza Contemporánea.

Encuentro Internacional de Casino

Information: Centro Nacional de Música, Calle 1ra #1010, entre 10 y 12, Miramar (203 7667/0923). **Venue** Plaza XIV Festival (Matanzas), Anfiteatro de Varadero. **Date** 26-29 Aug 2004; 4 days Aug, annual.

Casino – short for the *rueda de casino* (casino wheel) – is Cuba's true salsa, a street dance that, at its best, can take dancing in a circle to new heady heights, as the men change their partners in a series of ever more inventive turns at the call of the *salseros*. This new festival, organised by former Moncada percussionist Juan Gómez, began in 2003, attracting participants from as far away as Denmark and Indonesia, as well as celeb groups such as Los Van Van, Isaac Delgado and Pupy y Los Que Son Son.

Festival de Rap Cubano Habana Hip Hop

Information: Dirección Nacional de la Asociación Hermanos Saíz (AHS), Pabellón Cuba, Calle 23, entre M y N, Vedado (832 3511/3/ahsinternacional@ujc.org.cu). **Venues** Anfiteatro de Alamar, Casa de la Música (Centro Habana), Salón Rosado Beny Moré, Café Cantante (Teatro Nacional), Casa de la Música (Miramar), Museo de la Música. **Date** 1st half Aug, annual.

This festival was once a patchy affair but the word is out now and it has begun to attract an increasing number of hip hop artists from the United States, Latin America and Europe, as well as the cream of homegrown talent. Hip hop has hit the big time in Cuba in recent years, with over 1,000 outfits and an exuberant atmosphere surrounding performances. This popularity has attracted the inevitable government interest, and Cuban lyrics can only go so far. Some interesting raw expression does slip through, though – often in the chat of Cuba's fierce female rappers. The festival now includes DJs, graffiti artists, a colloquium at the Museo Nacional de la Música and a series of films. Organisers are hoping for a two-week tenth birthday celebration in 2004. *See also pp153-65.*

Carnaval de La Habana

Venue all over Havana. **Date** July/Aug, but varies.

'Life is a carnival,' sang Cuban singer Isaac Delgado. Less now than before, sadly – one of Havana's biggest attractions has become a bit touch and go. In 2002 the carnival was cancelled to channel money into schools; in 2003 it was postponed to coincide with the anniversary of the founding of Havana. The sad truth is that, even when it comes on time, it isn't the flamboyant spectacle it once was. Having disappeared during the Special Period, the carnival's latter-day reincarnation is but a shadow of the pre-1990s three-tier-float days, though the government has pledged improvements. If it does go ahead, expect cheap beer, smelly portaloos and brawls, and keep an eye on your belongings.

Autumn

Festival Internacional de Música Popular Beny Moré

Information: Dirección Provincial de Cultura de la Cuidad de La Habana, Centro Nacional de Música Popular, Calle G, entre Línea y 9, Vedado (831 1234/832 3503/icm@cubarte.cult.cu). **Venue** Teatro Mella. **Date** 10-14 Sept 2005; Sept, odd-numbered years.

Dedicated to the legendary 'Bárbaro del Ritmo' (Barbarian of Rhythm) – the man with the funny hat, crazy walk and intoxicating rhythms – this festival is organised by salsa darling Isaac Delgado. Concerts are also held in Beny Moré's home town, San José de las Lajas, Cienfuegos.

Festival de Teatro de la Habana

Information: Consejo Nacional de las Artes Escénicas (CNAE), Calle 4, #257, entre 11 y 13, Vedado (830 4126/cnae@min.cult.cu). **Venues** various theatres in Havana. **Date** 2nd half of Sept 2005; 12 days Sept, odd-numbered years.

If your Spanish is up to the challenge, this 12-day festival is well worth it, with performances from international groups, plus workshops and lectures. The poster is always striking, well designed and plastered all over town.

Festival Los Días de la Música

Information: Dirección Nacional de la Asociación Hermanos Saíz (AHS), Pabellón Cuba, Calle 23, entre M y N, Vedado (832 3511/3/ahsinternacional@ujc.org.cu). **Venues** various. **Date** Sept, annual.

Musicians under the wing of the Hermanos Saíz Association, the youth division of National Union of Writers and Artists (UNEAC), take the stage. It takes in a mix of musical genres, highlighting hip hop, rock and *nueva trova* in particular.

Digital art

With regular blackouts, some homes still without a phone, few personal computers and a fledgling internet culture, Cuba doesn't spring to mind as the host of a thriving, yearly digital art festival. In fact, if you've ever tried connecting to the internet at one of Havana's scarce cybercafés (with the intention of seeing more than ten webpages an hour, that is), you may come to the conclusion that checking your email is art enough in itself.

Yet, testament to Cuba's many perplexing paradoxes and eccentricities, the digital art festival has run uninterrupted since its 1999 inception and has generated much local and international attention.

Arts Minister Abel Prieto has gone on record as saying that computer technology offers low-cost possibilities for promoting art on an international scale. The organisers at the Centro Cultural Pablo de la Torriente Brau claim to have phenomenal levels of interest, and this is certainly backed up by the large number of foreign submissions in the 2003 festival, from 39 different countries (the majority from the US), adding to the island's 130 artists submitting in print and audio-visual categories. Exhibits fill various galleries and museums and, in some cases, are even on show in the street. In addition to the exhibitions, there are theoretical discussions, papers, talks and awards. There's even online 'interactive creation' between various countries, sponsored by Cuban telephone company ETECSA and its portal Cubasí. Just don't tell anyone who's been waiting years for a phone line.

And the quality of the work? It's a mixed bag: there are some stunningly constructed images and slick videos, but there's also a lot of self-indulgence, and organisers have pledged to be more selective in future. Check out the website: it's comprehensive, informative and – as one might expect – looks good, as does the festival catalogue.

International Salón de Arte Digital

Information: Centro Cultural Pablo de la Torriente Brau, Calle Muralla #63, entre Oficios e Inquisador, La Habana Vieja (666585/www.artedigitalcuba.cult.cu). **Venues** Centro Cultural Pablo de la Torriente Brau, Museo Nacional de Bellas Artes, Fototeca de Cuba, various galleries. **Date** late June, annual.

Dennis García's winning entry: *Confesiones de Freud.*

Festival de la Habana de Música Contemporánea

Information: UNEAC, Calle 17 #351, entre G y H, Vedado (553 3113/832 0194/www.uneac.com). **Venue** Teatro Amadeo Roldán. **Date** 1wk 1st half Oct, annual.

This 10-day contemporary music fest puts Cuba's salsa and Latin jazz-only image to rest. The works of contemporary Latin American and European composers are performed by the island's maestros, a pot pourri of soloists, choral and chamber groups, plus full orchestras.

Festival Internacional de Ballet

Information: Ballet Nacional de Cuba & Gran Teatro de la Habana, Calzada #510, entre D y E, Vedado (835 2948/bnc@cubarte.cult.cu). **Venues** Gran Teatro & other theatres. **Date** 19-28 Oct 2004; Oct, even-numbered years.

The Festival Internacional de Ballet is prima ballerina Alicia Alonso's baby, and features her own Cuban National Ballet, along with companies and soloists from around the world (the Washington State Ballet and Alvin Ailey have both attended). It also lures home Cuba's finest prodigals based abroad, such as Carlos Acosta and José Manuel Carreño. Premières, prizes, workshops and lectures make this one of Havana's best-attended events. Each festival has a specific theme.

Festival de Raices Africanas 'El Wemilere'

Information: Dirección Provincial de Cultura de La Habana (DPCCH), Calle 6, entre Línea y 9, Vedado (979776/dmcgboa@cubarate.cult.cu). **Venue** Guanabacoa. **Date** 2nd half Nov, annual.

If you've had a run of bad luck or desire something specific, Cubans will advise you to visit the little town of Guanabacoa. And it's worth the ferry trip across the bay to discover the pulse of Afro-Cuban religions too. Each year the week-long *Wemilere* (meaning 'party') is dedicated to a visiting country from the African diaspora, with live music, dance, workshops, lectures, art exhibitions and a craft fair. Some of the carnival-type dancing can border on the cheesy, but you can usually find plenty of real deal Afro-Cuban music and dance too. A friendly atmosphere surrounds the festival.

JO JAZZ

Information: Centro Nacional de Música Popular (CNMP), Avenida 1ra #1010, entre 10 y 12, Miramar (203 7667/mp@cubarte.cult.cu). **Venue** Teatro Amadeo Roldán. **Date** 26-30 Nov 2004; 2nd half Nov, annual.

Presenting the jazz stars of the future, JO JAZZ features the best of young (some extremely young) Cuban talent. There are several prizes to be won in the competition and one of the lucky musicians taking part gets a chance to cut an album with piano maestro Chucho Valdés. The 2003 festival included a British Council-sponsored visit from Anglo-Cuban jazz pianist Alex Wilson.

Bienal de la Habana

Information: Consejo Nacional de las Artes Plásticas, Avenida 3ra #1205, entre 12 y 14, Miramar (204 2744/www.cnap.cult.cu). **Venues** Centro de Arte Contemporáneo Wifredo Lam, Parque Histórico Militar Morro-Cabaña; various other galleries. **Date** 1 Nov-1 Dec, odd-numbered years.

This huge art festival has been rather erratic of late but it looks as if it's back on track. The Bienal gathers mostly Latin American and Caribbean artists, plus a sprinkling from the rest of the world, for exhibitions of contemporary art held all over Havana. Venues include the vast Parque Histórico Militar Morro-Cabaña complex. Installation and related dance, music and theatre events, plus special film seasons in the first few weeks, also feature. *See also pp145-9.*

Winter

Festival del Nuevo Cine Latinoamericano

Information: Casa del Festival del Nuevo Cine Latinoamericano, Calle 2 #411, entre 17 y 19, Vedado (552854-64/www.habanafilmfestival.com). **Venues** most cinemas. **Date** 2-12 Dec; 1st half Dec, annual.

This has to be Havana's best-known and best-organised festival. For the price of a pass ($40), you can buy into the island's most glamorous event, with competitions, lectures and parties, and – at the heart of it all – ten days of non-stop cinema. Most films and documentaries are made in Latin America, but there is work from independent US and European directors too. Social events and hobnobbing is based at Havana's flagship Hotel Nacional (*see p42*); sit in the beautiful gardens and peruse your daily programme. Essential viewing.

Festival Internacional de Jazz 'Jazz Plaza'

Information: ICM, Calle 15 #452 entre E y F, Vedado (830 3503-06/832 0487/icm@cubarte.cult.cu). **Venues** Casa de la Cultura de Plaza, Hotel Riviera, Jazz Café, Teatro Nacional, Teatro Amadeo Roldán, La Zorra y el Cuervo, UNEAC. **Date** 2nd half Dec, even-numbered years.

One of Havana's most famous music events, this jazz fest is organised by pianist Chucho Valdés. There's back-to-back music at several large venues (including the Teatro Nacional) and late-night improvisation at intimate smaller ones (such as La Zorra y el Cuervo). The festival attracts top international names (Roy Hargrove always appears), plus the best local jazzers. Spot the Hollywood film stars who usually make an appearance.

► Many of these events – and others – are also covered in chapters **Film**, **Music & Nightlife**, **Performing Arts** and **Sport & Fitness**.

Children

Not a Big Mac in sight, but plenty of old-fashioned fun.

Havana isn't tailored for visitors with children, at least not in the usual ways. The city lacks the amusements – malls, cinema multiplexes, McDonald's, theme parks – found elsewhere, but with careful planning and an open mind, Havana can be a wonderful family destination. For starters, aside from the risks of scrapes and sunburn, Havana is very safe. Plus, with children you're likely to see aspects of Cuban life you might otherwise miss. Approached in the right way, a trip to Cuba can give your kids the chance to experience a culture without junk food, mega-toy stores and mass advertising.

ACCOMMODATION

In hotels, children under 12 often have to pay half the adult room rate, but if no extra bed is required they can sometimes stay for free. Some offer formal babysitting (listed under hotel services), but if not, one of the chambermaids will usually look after the kids by arrangement if you want a child-free evening. A hotel with a pool offers a respite from the dust and the heat, but even if yours doesn't have one, many of the upmarket hotels, such as Hotels Meliá Cohiba, Meliá Habana, Novotel and Comodoro, charge a fee (usually $5) for non-guests. For more on swimming in Havana, *see p182*; for hotels, *see pp32-46*.

A *casa particular* (private home) is a good alternative for families, as there will often be two rooms available. Some *casas* may be slightly shabby, but they are invariably spotlessly clean and can usually provide hearty, home-cooked meals (hard to find in Havana's restaurants). They open a door to life in Cuba that tourists rarely see in hotels. The ideal is a *casa* with a yard where lizards, frogs and fruit trees provide children with hours of entertainment. For reviews of *casas particulares, see pp32-46.*

TRANSPORT

Avoid public buses (known as *guaguas*) – they are usually exceedingly hot, packed-in affairs. The most convenient way to get around Havana is by taxi but note that most don't have seat belts. A rental car is the best option if you plan on travelling outside of Havana and new cars with seat belts and airbags are available. Infant car seats are non-existent, so bring one with you. For short trips around town, bicycle rickshaws (*bici-taxis*) and yellow *cocotaxis* are fun, open-air options.

ADMISSION

Under-12s pay little or nothing to get into museums and other sights. Children are usually allowed into bars and restaurants with parents but discos are a no-no.

RISKS AND PRECAUTIONS

The heat in Havana at any time of the year can be hard on children, but the summer months are the hottest. Bring light, cotton clothing and avoid synthetic fabrics. Do your sightseeing in the morning and plan some down-time in the afternoon. Apply sunblock every day and make sure everyone gets lots to drink. Children should drink only sealed, bottled water and avoid eating uncooked food and food sold on the street.

Traffic is lighter in Havana than in most large cities but pedestrians do not have the right of way, so take extra precautions with little ones. Roads and pavements are often in a state of bad repair, so watch out for potholes.

There are very few public toilets in Havana and those that do exist are grim. Your best option is to duck into a nearby hotel or restaurant. Many toilets, even in restaurants, don't have toilet paper.

WHAT TO BRING

Pack a first aid kit with child-strength fever reducers, diarrhoea medicine, plasters and other medicines that are either not available or hard to find in Cuba. Basic baby necessities are available in Havana, but save yourself the hassle (and expense) by packing nappies and baby wipes. Pack plenty of sunblock and bring lightweight rain-gear as sudden, torrential downpours occur frequently between May and October. It's a good idea to take books, small toys, crayons and paper; these things can be hard to find in Havana and are often poor quality.

Days out

La Habana Vieja

Most of the renovated streets and squares of the old city are closed to car traffic, making this an excellent spot for families to explore on foot. Start in the **Plaza de Armas**, where the **Castillo de la Real Fuerza** (*see p51*) has good views from the tower and you can try a sustaining glass of *guarapo* (sugar cane juice) in the snack bar on the terrace. On the south side of the square, the recently modernised **Museo Nacional de Historia Natural** (*see p52*) has child-friendly displays on the plants and wildlife of Cuba. North of the museum, along Calle Tacón, wander through the **crafts market** (*see p129*). In nearby Parque José de la Luz y Caballero between Calle Tacón and Avenida Céspedes, children can ride ponies for three pesos on weekend afternoons. Further along Tacón is the **Parque Infantil la Maestranza**, with simple fairground rides.

The two museums worth taking in with children are the **Museo del Automóvil** (*see p54*), with its vintage cars, and the **Maqueta de La Habana Vieja** (Scale Model of Old Havana; *see p58*). On the nearby Plaza Vieja is the **Cámera Oscura** (*see p56*), an unusual roof-top observatory that uses reflectors to project the city on to a parabolic screen. After that, take a well-earned break at the **Taberna de la Muralla** (*see p115*), the beer hall opposite, while your kids run around the colonnades of the centuries-old buildings in the square. The nearby **Aqvarivm** (see *p55*) is a fresh-water aquarium featuring a riotous monthly (weekly in summer) children's event with Mamá Guajacona, a frenetic piscine puppet. At sunset, hire a horse-drawn carriage in **Plaza de San Francisco**.

Centro Habana

The **Museo de la Revolución** (*see p68*) is where older children can learn something about Cuba's extraordinary recent history. On display in the yard you'll find fighter planes and army tanks. On Espada y Vapor is the **Casa del Niño y la Niña**, a children's workshop with activities like music, chess, and trips to the beach. The Casa will lend out sports equipment too.

Vedado

In Nuevo Vedado to the west is the **Jardín Zoológico de La Habana** (*see p49*). The landscaping is attractive but the animals are confined to small cages, which may come as a shock to children used to first-world zoos. There are few tourists but lots of Cubans making a day of it, so bring a picnic and join in. Opposite the entrance to the zoo, Avenida Zoológico leads down to a bridge over the Río Almendares. Cross this to enter the **Bosque de La Habana** (*see p80* **Along Río Almendares**), a densely wooded park that stretches along the river. The jungle vegetation – including the *jagüey* (banyan or Indian) trees with their hanging aerial roots – is spectacular.

Miramar & the western suburbs

The **Maqueta de La Habana** (*see p84*), a vast and detailed scale model of the whole of Havana, gives a great sense of the layout of the city. A mezzanine gives a bird's-eye view that's useful for smaller children. Nearby, the **Acuario Nacional** (*see p83*) boasts a fine display of tropical fish and has dolphin and sea lion shows throughout the day. Several miles further down Quinta Avenida, **Marina Hemingway** (*see p181*) is a huge tourism complex where you'll find a bowling alley for kids over 12, a small amusement park and water games.

Cinecito. *See p139.*

The eastern bay & coast

Across the bay is the **Parque Histórico Militar Morro-Cabaña** (*see p88*). This vast military compound is a great place to learn about Havana's colonial history. The highlights are the lighthouse (Faro del Morro) and maritime displays at the Castillo de los Tres Reyes del Morro, plus the moats, ramparts and weaponry at the Fortaleza de San Carlos de la Cabaña. If you come in the late afternoon, stay on for the **Ceremonia del Cañonazo** (*see p132*), which takes place at 9pm every night, when soldiers dressed in the colours of the Spanish colonial army fire a cannon from the battlements.

THE BEACHES

The beach is the obvious place to go for a jaunt out of town with children, and there are plenty of them within a 20-minute taxi journey of the city. With its shallow waters, **Tarará** is one of the best for young swimmers (*see p93*).

Further south

If you've had enough of the city, consider spending a day in the huge parks on the south-western outskirts of Havana. You can get a taxi to take you but arrange for the cab to wait and agree on a fare before boarding. The immense **Parque Lenin** (*see p49*), about 20 kilometres (12.5 miles) from Old Havana, has a range of amusements, including an old-fashioned fairground, with merry-go-rounds and a miniature train. Ponies and horses are available for rides within the park, and look out for the **rodeo** (*see p178*) at the weekend. On the Embalse Paso Saquito, an artificial lake, you can rent a six-person rowing boat.

South of the park is the **Jardín Botánico Nacional** (*see p80* **Along Río Almendares**), which has a variety of tropical and subtropical plants. To the west of Parque Lenin is the **Parque Zoológico Nacional** (*see p49*), more of a safari park than a zoo. It can be visited by bus or, for an extra $5, you can have an English-speaking guide accompany you in your car. Watch out for Teresa the hungry elephant.

Sport & fitness

Children of all ages will find something to enjoy at **Club Habana** (*see p179*) in Siboney. Located on a stretch of beach, this former country club has a fitness centre, swimming pools, tennis courts and other activities. Day rates are $10 on weekdays, $15 on weekends or buy a *tarjeta de consumo* for a few dollars extra and have your meal and drinks included.

Entertainment

Musical shows, films, puppetry and clowns are presented at venues throughout the city at weekends (usually at 10am and 5pm) and often in the afternoons on other days too. Programme details are best obtained from the venues: **Teatro Nacional de Guiñol** for puppet shows; **Centro Cultural Bertolt Brecht**, **Teatro Fausto**, **Teatro Mella** and **Museo de Arte Colonial** for shows of all kinds. For all *see pp166-75*. Films for children are shown at **Cinecito**, **Cine Chaplin**, **23 y 12** and the **Fundación del Nuevo Cine Latinoamericano**. For all, *see pp140-44*.

The annual **Día de la Infancia** (third week in July) is celebrated with activities from street games to go-karting to concerts.

Shops

Don't expect to find anything here that you wouldn't rather buy back home. But if you need children's clothes or toys, you can find them at **Hotel Comodoro** (*see p118*), **La Puntilla** (*see p120*) and **Marina Hemingway** (*see p181*).

Feeding time

Most restaurants offer the typical Cuban meal: chicken or pork accompanied by rice, beans and shredded raw cabbage or sliced cucumbers. Other options commonly offered are french fries, hot dog, pizza or *bocadito de jamon y queso* (ham and cheese sandwich). In recent years, a few fast food chains have cropped up (Burgui, El Rápido), but children are welcome at most *paladares*, so skip the junk and take them to places offering home-cooked food in child-friendly environs.

If you are travelling with younger children, try to stock up on lightweight snacks and drinks. Soft drinks and bottled water are sold everywhere but, when available, try fresh tropical fruit juices. Most shops have a good range of natural (but long-life) Tropical Island juices in small cartons. In terms of milk, only UHT is available commercially.

At the **Supermercado Palco** (*see p120*) in Siboney, you'll find a well-stocked cold-cuts section with imported meats and cheeses, plus fresh baguettes, granola bars and other snacks. The **Pain de París** bakeries (*see p125*) are also a good source of bread, pastries and sandwiches. For a very Cuban experience, visit one of Havana's *mercados agropecuarios* (farmers' markets; *see p126* **Getting agro**), commonly known as '*agros*'. They are fun to visit and are the only place you'll find a wide variety of seasonal fresh fruit and vegetables.

Film

Serious film-going or Saturday nights out: despite dilapidated cinemas, *habaneros* just love the movies.

Going to the pictures is a way of life in Havana for both film buffs and noisy groups of young adolescents, no matter if the air-conditioning is conked out, the seats are broken or if there's a queue snaking down the street. Cinematic information is plentiful: analysis precedes films shown on TV; new releases (both homegrown and international) are covered in the dailies; and all major Cuban efforts receive a good deal of publicity. This, along with exposure to non-Hollywood movies, thanks to the US blockade, has produced a genned-up film-going audience.

Cuba's film industry has had a long and varied history, though the 1930s and '40s were marked by heavy American (and Mexican) influences. The pre-Revolutionary 1950s are best known for the bevy of Hollywood stars who visited the island (many captured in the Hotel Nacional Hall of Fame), swanking around Havana's nightclubs and casinos while their films were shown in the new cinemas springing up around Vedado.

COME THE REVOLUTION

When Revolutionary ideology kicked in in 1959 film aesthetics changed dramatically. The ICAIC (Instituto Cubano del Arte e Industria Cinematográficos) – responsible for production, exhibition and distribution – was founded just months into the Revolution, with a new emphasis on expressing Cuban identity, documentary making and creating a new type of more useful, less decadent cinema. In addition, US films fell out of favour. It took a couple of decades for Cuba to begin to open up culturally, and for Cubans to have the opportunity to see films made outside the Soviet bloc. Cinema-lovers now have the chance to see big international blockbusters from the previous years, albeit often on video projectors in special video rooms (*salas de video*).

Cinemas

Chaplin

Havana's No.1 cinema, with Dolby sound, good-looking audiences and the best programming in town. *See p141.*

La Rampa

Retro foyer, friendly staff and most films in original language. *See p142.*

Sala Glauba Rocha

State-of-the-art auditorium at the Fundación del Nuevo Cine Latinoamericano. *See p142.*

Trianón

Comfiest seats in Havana. *See p142.*

Yara

The big, noisy epicentre for all walks of Havana life. Popcorn nearly always on sale. *See p142.*

FAT YEARS AND LEAN YEARS

The years before the belt-tightening Special Period were a golden era for the Cuban film industry. The ICAIC nurtured some of Cuba's finest directors to date, such as its best-known filmmaker Tomás Gutiérrez Alea. His *Memorias del subdesarollo* (1968) and *Fresa y chocolate* (1993) were both groundbreaking films, the latter openly tackling the previously taboo subject of Cuban gay life. Other key directors flowering during this period were Humberto Solás with *Lucía* (1968) and *Cecilia* (1982). The '80s gave us Juan Carlos Tabío's delicious comedy *Plaff o demasiado miedo a la vida* (1988), plus Fernando Pérez with his debut fiction film *Clandestinos* (1987). The austerity of the Special Period meant less money for film-making, and market forces reared their head. The majority of recent Cuban films are co-productions with Spain and France. This has affected content to some extent; films have all too often become comedy versions of tropical kitchen-sink dramas, full of Cuban stereotypes and caricatures: *santería* trances, gossiping neighbours and crowded multi-family dwellings.

Luckily, though, the indomitable Cuban creative spirit continues to bob to the surface. Juan Carlos Cremata's award-winning *Nada* (2001) injected fresh comedy into the film scene, while Fernando Pérez's much-talked-about *Suite Habana* (2003) is the most recent hit to come out of Cuba. It has no dialogue as such, but its beautiful, plaintive orchestral score accompanies a moving insight into daily life.

But what of new talent? New directors to watch out for, all working in video, include Umberto Padron, Pavel Giroud, Esteban Insausti

Retro cinema: the 1950s interior of the **Acapulco**. *See p142.*

and Lester Hamlet. Funding is still a problem: these days ICAIC money has to be topped up by other sources. The 2003 Locarno Film Festival in Switzerland was dedicated to Cuban film, and a group of directors went to discuss funding for future projects. Hopefully, these young bloods will be able to rescue their film industry in one of those last-minute miracles Cuba is famous for.

RESOURCES

For analysis there's ICAIC's sporadic Spanish-language *Cine Cubano* magazine. The Institute itself sometimes carries it, but try bookshops or second-hand bookstalls for back copies. Visit www.cubacine.cu for a history of Cuban cinema. ICAIC (Calle 23 #1110, entre 8 y 10, Vedado) has an archive collection of films, currently in crisis due to lack of resources; alternatively, try the Latin American Video Archive (www.latinamericanvideo.org).

GOING TO THE CINEMA

Cinemas in Havana tend to be run-down, especially in Centro Habana and La Habana Vieja. Vedado has some of the best cinemas, such as the Riviera, La Rampa and the Chaplin, all on the main drag, Calle 23. There are no multiplexes in Cuba and all the cinemas will be showing one film at a time; that's not to say, however, that the same types of films are screened at all cinemas.

Cinemas in Havana can be roughly divided into three categories (a reflection of both film genres and clientele): the 'art house' **Chaplin** cinema (and to a lesser extent **La Rampa**), where audiences behave how you would expect film lovers to; the vast **Yara** and **Payret**, showing the latest releases and attracting groups of young courting couples from out of town in a lovely retro ritual; and the run-down neighbourhood picture houses.

Cuban film-goers generally prefer their foreign films subtitled rather than dubbed. However, outside the Chaplin and La Rampa cinemas, there can be no guarantee that films will be in their original language.

With the exception of the Chaplin and La Rampa, the relaxed atmosphere in Havana's cinemas seems to lead people to believe they're at home. So, be prepared for plenty of coming and going, and loud discussions about the film (sometimes this entertainment alone justifies the two-peso ticket). Note also that most cinemas and video rooms have air-conditioning, albeit sporadically. Cinemas charge in pesos and do not accept credit cards. Performances tend to start at 4.30pm and 9pm, with some late shows at weekends and children's films on Saturday and/or Sunday mornings.

Programmes usually change every Thursday, but check with individual cinemas. Each has a weekly city information sheet pinned up near the entrance, divided into districts. Opening times vary but cinemas are generally open every day of the week. Many – but not all – cinemas in Havana show films on a loop – you'll need to ask what time the showings are so as not to see the ending before the beginning. There's a 'no shorts, no flip-flops' dress code for men (which may or may not be enforced).

Major cinemas

Chaplin (Cinemateca de Cuba)

Calle 23 #1155, entre 10 y 12, Vedado (831 1011). **Map** p249 C8.

This well-tended cinema has a new Dolby sound system, an excellent range of films and appreciative audiences. Premières and presentations, daily programme changes, retrospective seasons, an art gallery and a counter selling books and videos make the Chaplin Havana's most interesting cinema.

Payret

Paseo de Martí (Prado) #503, esquina San José, Centro Habana (863 3163). **Map** p313 D14.

The Payret is the largest cinema in the area, screening popular films (be prepared for queues), often for up to a month. It's sadly run-down now but is still used as a main venue for the Latin American Film Festival. There's a dollar bar on the left-hand side that's seen better days, and a dank underground peso cafeteria. Continuous programmes start at 12.30pm. Late shows: midnight on Friday, Saturday, Sunday.

La Rampa

Calle 23 #111, entre 0 y P, Vedado (878 6146). **Map** p250 B12.

Named after both the street and the foyer's glamorous curved ramp, this still-attractive cinema dates back to the 1950s. La Rampa offers a newish film twice daily; the third showing is sometimes a retrospective of either someone from the cast or the director. Helpful staff, but if you get the usherette chatting you may miss half the film. Shows from 4pm.

23 y 12

Calle 23 #1212, entre 12 y 14, Vedado (833 6906). **Map** p249 C8.

Fairly comfortable but dark cinema catering mainly for children (*see p139*). Adult shows start at 8pm.

Yara

Calle L #363, esquina 23, Vedado (832 9430). **Map** p250 B11.

Built in 1949 by a long-fled TV mogul, this huge cinema (along with the street corner it fills) is one of Havana's landmarks. All walks of life converge here, and it's a favourite spot for people-watchers, peanut sellers, customers from the Coppelia ice-cream parlour opposite and habitués of the gay scene. It attracts a dolled-up, noisy Saturday night crowd (you might have to change your seat a few times) and tends to have a similar programme to the Payret (and looks equally run-down when the lights come up). There's a small art gallery in the foyer, plus a kiosk selling popcorn, drinks and Cuban videos – all in dollars. Continuous programme from 12.30pm. Late shows: midnight Friday, Saturday, Sunday.

Other cinemas

Acapulco

Avenida 26, entre 35 y 37, Nuevo Vedado (833 9573). **Map** p249 D7.

A little bit off the beaten track, this lovely '50s cinema is comfortable, in fairly good condition and boasts a huge wall-covering mirror in the foyer. Programming is a mix of international and Cuban films.

Actualidades

Avenida de Bélgica (Montserrate) #262, entre Ánimas y Neptuno, Centro Habana (861 5193). **Map** p252 D14.

Tucked away behind a slew of fancy hotels – Hotel Sevilla, Hotel Plaza, Hotel NH Parque Central – this rather functional-looking cinema has a complicated schedule of programmes with varied films that change three times a week (considerably more often than they clean the toilets). There's an intriguing bar of the same name next door. When the air-conditioning works it's really fierce.

Águila de Oro

Calle Rayo #108, entre Zanja y Dragones, Centro Habana (863 3386). **Map** p251 D13.

A few years ago the 'Golden Eagle', in the heart of Chinatown, only showed Chinese-language films. These days it shows the usual post-première movies instead. A visit here is not a particularly pleasant experience. No air-conditioning, but some noisy fans provide parallel dialogues.

Astral

Calzada de Infanta (Menocal) #501, Centro Habana (878 1001). **Map** p250 C12.

The recently renovated Astral has managed to rid itself of its reputation as Havana's smelliest cinema and is now very swish, thanks to a revamp after the state handed it over to the Young Communist League. It's used for occasional film premières, and is also a Latin American Film Festival venue.

Cinecito

Calle San Rafael #68, esquina Consulado, Centro Habana (863 8051). **Map** p251 D14.

The 'little cinema' shows films for children, starting at 4.30pm. Not as comfortable as its 23 y 12 counterpart, but good, noisy fun nonetheless.

Riviera

Calle 23 #507, entre Avenida de los Presidentes (G) y H, Vedado (830 9564). **Map** p250 B11.

The Riviera's distinctive lettering stands out like a beacon along a not very pretty stretch of Calle 23. Programming yields a mixed bag: dubbed US action (yep, Bruce Willis again) and run-of-the-mill films alternating with Yara leftovers. Audiences always seem to enjoy themselves though. Look out for the Monday Cine Caracol special showings, which have more interesting fare, and the occasional music concerts (hard rock, rap, salsa).

Sala Glauba Rocha

Fundación de Nuevo Cine Latinoamericano, Quinta Santa Bárbara, Calle 212, esquina 31, La Coronela, Marianao (271 8311/8141).

This modern cinema, one of the main venues for the Latin American Film Festival, is located in the grounds of poet Dulce María Loynaz's former family residence. It's the ultimate in comfort, with an independent programme of mainly Latin American films or retrospective seasons of Latin American directors. Showings are twice daily – call for times. There are weekend shows for children.

Trianón

Calle Línea #706, entre Paseo y A, Vedado (830 9648). **Map** p250 B9.

Comfortable seating and an intimate atmosphere make this one of Havana's more enjoyable cinematic

Post it

Everybody knows it's cool to have film posters on your walls (framed, of course), so why not add some genuine Revolutionary Cuban stock to your collection? Post-Revolutionary Cuban poster art is, after all, considered to be some of the richest in the world.

It wasn't until the ICAIC (the National Film Institute) was founded in March 1959, just months after Castro took Havana, that a new poster art form emerged. Pre-Revolutionary film posters had mainly depicted the usual Latino stereotypes of macho men and wild women, but the new poster art aimed at breaking traditional aesthetic patterns and took an anti-commercial, highly political stance. Influences: Eastern Europe, Japan and, of course, the new Revolutionary politics. Visuals: 51 x 76 centimeters (20 x 30 inches) format; blocks of dense colour or black and white only; silk screen technique, usually by anonymous designers, featuring only the name of the film and the main credits (representing the individual was considered a bad thing). Posters weren't initially restricted to Cuban films; any first-time-in-Havana movie warranted a poster.

Those in the know consider that the best and purest posters come from the pop-art-influenced '60s, and films such as *Lucía* or *Por primera vez.* Economic problems hit hard in the '70s but posters continued to be made – part of the state's effort to keep the population interested in culture (and the Revolution) in times of hardship. Come the 1980s, posters were restricted to Cuban films, with the real crunch coming during the '90s Special Period, when materials became scarce. Since 1999 new digital techniques have been in vogue, but it seems that modern poster artists find it hard to capture the impact and immediacy of the earlier posters.

The walls and ceiling of the ICAIC office's foyer (next door to the Chaplin cinema) are plastered with film posters. Some are available for sale (prices start at around $4). Alternatively, check out www.cubacine.cu for an online selection – the majority here are from the '80s. Prices range from $11 to $21. T-shirts are also sometimes available for $4-$5. Poster artists to look out for include Muñoz Bach (*Por Primera Vez*, 1967), Raúl Martínez (*Lucía*, 1968) and René Azcuy (*Besos Robados*, 1970).

experiences. The Trianón is also home to the El Público theatre group (*see p171*). A good mix of old and new, foreign and Cuban films.

Salas de video (Video rooms)

With notable exceptions, video rooms are always hot, humid and squashed, with postage stamp screens. Films are usually a mix of old and new.

Águila de Oro

Calle Rayo #108, entre Zanja y Dragones, Centro Habana (863 3386). **Map** p251 D13.
Chop-socky videos twice daily.

Alhambra

Paseo de Martí (Prado) #503, esquina San José, Centro Habana (863 3163). **Map** p313 D14.
Once located in the subterranean cafeteria, but now upstairs from the main theatre.

Centro Cultural Cinematográfico ICAIC

Calle 23 #1155, entre 10 y 12, Vedado (833 9278). **Map** p249 C8.
Havana's finest *sala de video*, facing the Chaplin cinema, with 32 supremely comfy seats, high-quality equipment and screen, plus a good selection of Cuban and Latin American features and documentaries.

Don't miss Cuban films

According to Fernando Pérez

Clandestinos, Madagascar, Hello Hemingway, La vida es silbar and now *Suite Habana*: with these few films, **Fernando Pérez** has built an international reputation for quirky and original flicks. Pérez tells us about three of his favourite Cuban films.

La Bella de la Alhambra (Enrique Pineda Barnet, 1989)

'A charming film with a magic touch. The director has given us a very lovely moment bringing together Cuban idiosyncrasies and Cuban music.'

Lucía (Humberto Solás, 1978)

'Seeing this film for the first time was a night of unforgettable emotion for me. Such dramatic images had never been seen in Cuban cinema. The photography and strong acting play out three stories of three eras of Cuban history.'

Memorias del subdesarollo (Tomás Gutiérrez Alea, 1968)

'One of the best films in the history of cinema, above all for its language, a language that breaks with all canons of narration and is very free, absolutely free.'

Screening information is displayed on a board inside the main entrance. 'El Centro' also houses a bar and a shop selling Cuban videos and books (all in dollars), plus the Videoteca del Sur, a project set up to promote Latin American cinema, and an art gallery.

Charlot

Chaplin cinema, Calle 23 #1155, entre 10 y 12, Vedado (831 1101). **Map** p249 C8.

Upstairs at the Chaplin. Videos are currently being shown on a TV screen, as the video projector is broken for the foreseeable future. The Charlot always shows interesting work, often complementing the main cinema's fare. Don't forget to tell the ticket seller you want the '*sala de video*'.

Museo Nacional de Bellas Artes

Edificio Arte Cubano, Calle Trocadero, entre Zulueta y Monserrate, La Habana Vieja (861 0241/3858). **Map** p252 D15.

The restored building housing the Cuban art collection has a small Sala de Audiovisuales showing art-house movies, plus another for children's films.

Yara A, B, C

Calle L #363, esquina 23, Vedado (832 9430). **Map** p250 B11.

The three 30-seaters upstairs rooms show a diverse selection of mainly US films. Arrive early and make sure you buy the right ticket. No air-conditioning.

Festivals

The annual Latin American Film Festival (**Festival del Nuevo Cine Latinoamericano**; *see p136*), held in December, began life in 1979 as a competition and showcase for the continent's films. Since then it has grown mightily in content and organisation and now features worldwide independent films and documentaries, retrospectives, seminars, directors' presentations, press conferences and a daily Spanish-language paper listing that day's and the next's films. Not to mention the heady atmosphere, the inevitable parties and the stars and directors in attendance (Francis Ford Coppola, Robert De Niro and Matt Dillon have all shown up in the past).

The Hotel Nacional (*see p42*) is the epicentre of activities surrounding the festival. Just $40 will buy a pass giving you access to a special mailbox in the foyer and entry to all cinemas and peripheral events; the catalogue is extra. The festival website (www.habanafilm festival.com) is a good source of information.

Cine Pobre is a recently initiated festival for low-budget films and documentaries. It takes place in Gibara, Holguín, but is organised from Havana by veteran Cuban director Humberto Solás. The annual **Festival de Nuevos Realizadores** in February gives young filmmakers the chance to show their mettle. In addition, the embassies of different European countries have organised mini festivals for the past few years, though their future hangs in the balance since the EU decided to halt a lot of cultural exchanges following the spring 2003 hijackers' executions and dissidents' trials. Check with ICAIC (Calle 23 #1111, entre 8 y 10, Vedado) for information on all of these events.

Galleries

With Cuba's new pseudo-private sector, the art scene is flourishing.

International interest in Cuban art is at an all-time high. The legalisation of the dollar in 1993 and the parallel introduction of tourism and limited forms of private enterprise have brought with them a surge of artistic productivity and creativity. Many artists are setting up commercial home studios (*see p149*), and the fruits are ripe for the picking. Visitors are, for the first time, travelling to Cuba with the precise intention of buying art, lured by the thought of uncharted territory (not to mention unmined gold). Art in 21st-century Cuba is no longer being made solely for the state, and its purpose has become less concerned with promoting the utopian dream and more concerned with the individual.

As with all creative spheres in Cuba, the Revolution had a big impact on art: the first national art school was founded, and technical artistic training was made free and widely available. But, some would argue, this came at a price; several years after the Revolution, Castro described the relationship between art and the new politics in the following enigmatic statement: 'Within the Revolution everything; outside the Revolution nothing.' The constraints of this statement were to be felt most heavily by artists in the grey years of the 1970s, when increased ideological censorship encouraged by the Soviet bloc led many to seek exile, unable to squeeze out creativity under such circumstances.

LISTINGS AND INFORMATION

Note that we have listed Havana's best-established and most important galleries, but galleries are a growth area, so ask around for new additions. This being communist Cuba, there is often a grey line between state-run and commercial galleries; we have listed a combination of key state-sponsored exhibition spaces and commercial galleries. For more information on Cuban art and artists visit www.cnap.cult.cu and www.cubart.net.

BIENAL DE LA HABANA

The most interesting time to visit Cuba to see art is during the **Bienal de la Habana** (*see p136*), which takes place on odd-numbered years (the next is set for November 2005). It is an international exhibition spear-headed by a team of curators from the Centro de Arte Comtemporáneo Wifredo Lam (*see p146*). Around 100 artists are selected to participate in this usually adventurous presentation of contemporary art, and many state-run institutions are used to house it. A lot of trading goes on among artists and curators at this time.

GETTING ART OUT OF CUBA

When buying art, antiques or collectibles make sure that you obtain the necessary permission and paperwork to leave with your items, or else they will be confiscated at the airport.

Making a point. Well, several. **Galería Habana**. *See p148.*

Cuba requires that you register your items at the National Heritage Office (*see below*) and obtain a *certificado de exportación*. You must pay a nominal fee of $10 for every five objects, which are entered into a database.

Art purchased from a state-run institution (such as Galería Habana, La Casona or even at the craft market) will usually already have its export stamp. When buying art directly from artists, make sure you buy at least two days before leaving the country, so that you or the artist can obtain the certificate (you may have to pick it up the following day). Bring the object and bill of sale (including title, date, medium) with you to the National Heritage Office.

The increase in art sales has made Cubans more sophisticated about arrangements for transporting very large objects, so ask about the options when you buy.

National Heritage Office

Registro Nacional de Bienes Culturales de la República de Cuba, Oficina Central, Calle 17 #1009, entre 10 y 12, Vedado (833 9658). **Open** 8.30am-11.30am Mon-Fri. **Map** p250 B8.

La Habana Vieja

Old Havana – particularly around Calle Oficios – is a hotspot for galleries and artists' studios. Permanent non-commercial exhibitions of art can also be found in **Casa de México**, **Casa Guayasamín** and **Casa Simón Bolívar** (for all, *see p58*).

Casa de Carmen Montilla

Calle Oficios #162, entre Amargura y Brasil (Teniente Rey) (338768). **Open** 9am-5pm Tue-Sat. **Map** p252 E15.

Venezuelan artist Carmen Montilla, with the support of the City Historian's Office, established this charming gallery in 1994. The building dates from the 18th century, but was damaged by fire in the 1980s, so considerable restoration work was necessary. Of particular note is an impressive ceramic wall mural by leading Cuban ceramicist Alfredo Sosabravo. The artistic focus is on contemporary art, plus Cuban and Latin American sculpure. Permanent and commerical exhibitions.

Casa de los Artistas

Calle Oficios #16, entre Obispo y Obrapía (639981). **Open** *Zaida del Río* 10am-4pm Mon-Sat. *Robert Fabelo* 11am-5pm Mon-Sat. *Ernesto Rancaño Vieites* 11am-6pm Mon-Sat. *Pedro Pablo Olivia* times vary. **Map** p252 E15.

Casa de los Artistas may be located above the tourist-filled La Mina restaurant on tourist-filled Plaza de Armas, but it is a serious arthouse. It houses the galleries-cum-workshops of four of the most famous contemporary Cuban artists alive today: Zaida del Río, Robert Fabelo, Ernesto Rancaño Vietes and Pedro Pablo Olivia. The works of these artists are some of the most visible and sought after in Cuba. Prices reflect this, generally starting at around $1,000.

Centro de Arte Contemporáneo Wilfredo Lam

Calle San Ignacio #22, esquina Empedrado (861 3419). **Open** 10am-5pm Mon-Sat. **Admission** $2; free under-12s. **Map** p252 D15.

This state-run cultural institution was inaugurated in 1983 for the study and promotion of the contemporary visual arts of emerging nations, and is now one of Cuba's most important galleries. Its profile is further raised by the fact that the Centro is responsible for the organisation of the Bienal de la Habana (*see p136*), Cuba's international art fair. The building houses a beautiful museum with a bookshop, café, library, galleries and an interior courtyard. The centre is named after one of Cuba's most famous modern painters (and friend of Pablo Picasso), Wildredo Lam (1902-1982). Though it carries a sizeable collection of Lam's lithographs and acrylic works, there are also temporary, often non-conventional, exhibitions of Cuban contemporary art and international travelling exhibitions.

Centro de Arte 'La Casona'

Calle Muralla #107, esquina San Ignacio (861 8544/8745/863 4703/www.galeriascubanas.com). **Open** 10am-5.30pm Tue-Sat. **Admission** free. **Map** p252 E15.

This prominent gallery, beautifully restored in 1979, is one of Havana's leading exhibition spaces. Under the direction of art entrepreneur Luis Miret Pérez, La Casona is devoted in the main to solo exhibitions, but also has catalogues of leading contemporary Cuban artists. Artwork is sold here for anything from $100 to $5,000, and La Casona is probably as close to a true commercial gallery as Cuba gets. It also houses a small shop selling serigraphy and the Galería Roberto Diago, specialising in contemporary engravings and Afro-Cuban art.

Centro de Desarrollo de las Artes Visuales

San Ignacio #352, esquina Brasil (Teniente Rey), Plaza Vieja (862 2611/avisual@cubarte.cult.cu). **Open** 10am-5pm Tue-Sat. **Map** p252 E15.

A state-run contemporary art centre on Plaza Vieja devoted mainly to exhibitions of young emerging Cuban artists, though there are occasional exhibits by international artists. The building is in dire need of renovation, but don't miss the top-floor gallery, if not only for impressive views of Old Havana and a dated fresco on the wall of the gallery. The Centro also houses a bookshop.

Centro Pablo de la Torriente Brau

Calle Muralla #63, entre Oficios e Inquisidor (666585/www.artedigitalcuba.cult.cu). **Open** 9am-5pm Mon-Fri. **Map** p252 E15.

Centro de Arte 'La Casona'. *See p146.*

A state-run art centre on pretty Plaza Vieja, devoted to new media and technology. The Centro Pablo, as it is locally known, organises a burgoening annual digital art festival each June (*see p137* **Digital art**).

Centro Provincial de Artes Plásticas y Diseño

Oficios #362, esquina Luz (862 3228/3295). **Open** 10am-5pm Tue-Sun. **No credit cards.** **Map** p252 E15.

This non-commercial art centre houses two galleries featuring paintings, ceramics and drawings by Cuban artists. The house dates to 1732; the owners once lived on the second floor, which has marble floors and mahogany woodwork, while the slaves' quarters were in the small, low-ceilinged mezzanine. The pretty interior courtyard and the view from the second-floor balcony are worth a peek.

Fototeca de Cuba

Calle Mercaderes, entre Muralla y Brasil (Teniente Rey), Plaza Vieja (862 2530/ fototeca@cubarte.cult.cu). **Open** 10am-5pm Tue-Sat. **Map** p252 E15.

The Fototeca is the capital's leading photographic centre. Exhibitions of the work of Cuba's photographic Revolutionary heroes – including Raúl Corrales, Alberto Korda, Osvaldo Salas, Ernesto Fernández and Mario García Joya – are the main reason for coming; however, there's also a shop selling postcards, photographic works and publications. If you're here to shop, head for Galería Joaquín Blez on the lower floor, which specialises in the sale of photos (especially black and white photos of the early Revolutionary days). The Fototeca houses one of Havana's scarce communal darkrooms, so is a good place to meet photographers.

Galería Forma

Calle Obispo #255, entre Cuba y Aguilar (862 0123). **Open** 9am-8pm daily. **Map** p252 E15.

A commercial gallery on lively Calle Obispo that sells pottery, sculpture and painting by Cuban artists across all artistic genres.

Galería Los Oficios

Calle Oficios #166, entre Amargura y Brasil (Teniente Rey) (863 0497/www.nelsondominguez.com). **Open** 10am-5pm daily. **Map** p252 E15.

This is the studio-gallery of the internationally renowned Cuban artist Nelson Dominguez. In keeping with an artist of this stature, his work, which usually includes painting, pottery, jewellery and sculpture, doesn't come cheap.

Galería Victor Manuel

Calle San Ignacio #56, esquina Callejón del Chorro, Plaza de la Catedral (861 2955). **Open** 9am-9pm daily. **Map** p252 D15.

Cuban art for sale, including wood carving, jewellery, paintings, pottery and crafts.

Museo Casa del Ron

Calle San Pedro #262, esquina Sol (862 4108/ 861 8051). **Open** 9am-5pm Tue-Sat. **Map** p252 E15.

This modern museum, one of the city's snazziest and most up-to-date, is dedicated to the making of rum. It houses a decent gallery that sells work by Cuban and international artists. The art seems to be bear no relation to that most quintessentially Cuban of tipples.

Taller Experimental de Gráfica

Callejón del Chorro #62, off Plaza de la Catedral (862 0979/www.cnap.cult.cu/instituciones/teg). **Open** 9.30am-4pm Mon-Fri. **Map** p252 E15.

Although printmaking in Cuba began in the 19th century, it wasn't until 1962 that this, Cuba's only engraving workshop, was established by Cuban artist Orlando Suárez. The small Galería del Grabado upstairs sells excellent, non-touristy prints, including etchings, lithographs, woodcuts and collagraphs.

At home with **Sandra Ramos**. *See p149.*

Centro Habana

The **Museo Nacional de Bellas Artes** (*see p68*), housed in two wings (Arte Cubano and Arte Universal), is the island's biggest and most impressive permanent art collection.

Galería Acacia

Calle San José #114, entre Industria y Consulado (861 3533/www.artnet.com). **Open** 10am-4pm Mon-Sat. **Map** p252 D14.

A high-end commercial gallery in Centro Habana dedicated to Cuban contemporary and avant-garde art. In the past, Acacia has sold a fascinating array of antiques, but seems now to be focused solely on Cuban painting.

Vedado

Other than the galleries listed below, the **Museo Nacional de Artes Decorativas** (*see p78*) houses an interesting permanent art collection, and the **Casa de las Américas** (*see p79*) has two galleries with both permanent and commercial exhibitions.

Espacio Aglutinador

Calle 25 #602, entre 6 y 8 (aglutsan@cubarte.cult.cu). **Open** 10am-8pm daily. **Map** p250 C9.

Espacio Aglutinador opened in 1994 as Cuba's first independent exhibition space, with a view to giving art in Cuba a fresh alternative perspective. It is still run by one of the co-founders, Sandra Ceballos, who also lives in the space with her designer/curator husband René Quintana. Though there are now other independent galleries in Havana these days, Espacio Aglutinador still plays a key role in showing artists left out of the official culture, as well as under-recognised older artists and internationally acclaimed artists. Recently awarded a grant from the Price Claus Foundation of the Netherlands to do major renovation.

Fundación Ludwig de Cuba

Calle 13 #509, piso 5, entre D y E (832 4270/9118). **Open** 10am-4pm daily. **Map** p250 B10.

Peter Ludwig of Germany founded this centre in 1995 to support young Cuban artists. Housed in the penthouse of a five-storey building, with a marvellous view of Vedado, it hosts regular exhibitions of works (for sale) by young Cuban and international artists, and has a permanent collection of contemporary Cuban art.

Galería Ciudades del Mundo

Calle 25 #307, entre L y M (832 3175/dppfach@ceniai.inf.cu). **Open** 8.30am-5pm Mon-Fri. **Map** p250 C11.

This gallery belongs to the Urban Planning Institute of Havana and specialises in artwork in the fields of architecture, urbanism and ecology.

Galería Habana

Línea #460, entre E y F (832 7101/habana@cubarte.cult.cu). **Open** 9am-5pm Tue-Sat. **Map** p250 A10.

A combination of state-run and commerical, Galería Habana has been in operation since 1962, making it one of Havana's best-established galleries. It exhibits the work of Cuban and international artists and has work for sale in the back room (ask Dalia González and her warm staff to show you through). Mercifully, the gallery handles all the necessary paperwork that allows you to leave the country with your new artwork. Prominent artists who have shown here include Sandra Ramos, Carlos Garaicoa, Carlos Estévez and Fernando Rodriguez. Prices range from $100 to $5,000.

Galería 23 y 12

Calle 23, esquina 12 (831 1810). **Open** 10am-6pm Tue-Sat; 10am-2pm Sun. **Map** p249 C8.

A state-run gallery that organises solo and group exhibitions of Cuban contemporary art. There's a small shop with prints, posters, engravings, photography, CDs and books.

Miramar & the western suburbs

Casa-Estudio de José Fuster

Calle 226, esquina 3A, Jaimanitas (271 2932/264 6052/fuster@cubarte.cult.cu). **Open** 9am-6pm daily.

Fuster has achieved international renown, but as a visitor to Jaimanitas you will see the artist on his home ground, the site of his most inspired work. A long way out of a town, but a fascinating excursion.

Galería Servando Cabrera Moreno

Avenida 1ra A, esquina 42 (203 7171). **Open** 10am-5pm Tue-Sat. **Map** p248 B3.

Commercial gallery in upmarket Miramar, with painting, photography, sculpture and installations.

Stu-stu-studio

Most artists living in Cuba have, out of necessity, combined their living and work spaces, so visiting an artist's home studio is one of the best ways of seeing what Havana has to offer in the way of contemporary art. Bear in mind that you are visiting a private home; it is important to make an appointment. The artists listed are some of the best in Cuba, often represented by commercial galleries outside Cuba, so prices are likely to be in line with international trends.

The best way to see artists' studios in Havana is to arrange a visit via **Ninart-Havana Bureau** (413906/rgmilian@hotmail.com/www.artcuba.com/ninart), a project that promotes contemporary art from Cuba. The Bureau, directed by Rolando Milian, will arrange visits to artists' studios, and can organise tours for individual collectors or groups. A ten per cent commission charge is levied on any art bought, but Ninart-Havana takes care of all the paperwork.

Lidzie Alvisa/ René Francisco

2096139/dupp@cubarte.cult.cu
Alvisa's creations, including works on paper and installations, explore personal and bodily themes. Her husband, René Francisco, is also an artist; his work offers an unusual commentary on the daily lives of Cubans.

Damian Aquiles

832 7806/damainaquile2000@yahoo.com
Damian Aquiles has lived both in Miami and Havana, and creates ususual artwork that explores the natural oxidation process.

Abel Barroso

830 4212/abelmeri@cubarte.cult.cu
Barroso is an accomplished printmaker who has exhibited internationally; his work often explores humour and irony through non-traditional forms, including installation.

Tania Bruguera

832 5108/tbruguera@aol.com
Tania Bruguera is an internationally known artist whose work takes in drawing, sculpture, installation, video and performance. Her current residence in Old Havana is in itself worth a visit. She also manages a performance programme at the ISA (*see p85*).

Angel Delgado

267 4090/delgado2003@myrealbox.com
Angel Delgado is known for having spent time in prisons in the early 1990s for creating a 'public scandal'. The performance piece in question consisted of him defecating on the national newspaper *Granma*. Delgado creates artwork from unconventional materials, including carved soaps and handkerchiefs, often based his experiences while encarcerated.

Aimée García/ Carlos Montes de Oca

264 3719/monte@cubarte.cult.cu
García creates paintings and installations based on Renaissance motifs combined with self-portraiture and has exhibited internationally. Her partner, artist Carlos Montes de Ocas, specialises in drawings.

Carlos Garaicoa

867 1231/garaicoa@cubarte.cult.cu
Carlos Garaicoa has created a name for himself internationally with works in photography, video, drawing and installation. Garaicoa has a studio in Old Havana, where he creates an array of ambitious and challenging art influenced by architecture, design and the city of Havana.

Luis Gómez

264 5212/legomeza@yahoo.com
Combining various working methods, including photography, sculpture and installation, Gómez is influenced by both African religions and conceptual work. He lives and works in the seaside town of Cojímar in eastern Havana.

Ibrahim Miranda

408077/ibrahimm@cubacel.net
Miranda often creates images made from collages of maps and topographical shapes. His imaginative collages of drawings, paper, fabric and ink often contain allusions to animals and the shape of the island.

Sandra Ramos

835 3027/sandraramos@cubarte.cult.cu
Well-known internationally for her sculptures and prints created during the Special Period and works based on themes of exile and longing, Ramos often combines self-portraiture with water imagery. The metaphysical space of living on an island is a recurrent theme.

Gay & Lesbian

Despite a history of intolerance to contend with, gay Havana is alive and kicking (more under the ground than over).

Cuba has had a bad rap on the international gay scene that can be traced back to overt oppression of homosexuals in the 1960s and '70s, as well as the island's much-maligned AIDS policy of the late '80s, which forced HIV patients into quarantine. More recently, the release of the anti-Castro, and arguably misleading, film *Before Night Falls* – about the life of gay Cuban writer Reinaldo Arenas – refuelled discussion about Cuba's treatment of homosexuals. Yet, in spite of (or perhaps because of) its past record, Cuba is now probably the most easy-going of all Latin American and Caribbean countries in terms of its acceptance of gay culture and lifestyle. While there is still plenty of social stigma attached to homosexuality, violence is not directed at gays and most people are happy to let others live their own sexual identity in a 'don't ask, don't tell' environment.

After attempting to turn gay men and long-haired hippies (who listened to – gasp! – the Beatles), along with all manner of 'objectors', into real men by sending them to work camps euphemistically called Military Production Support Units (Unidades Militares de Ayuda a la Producción), the Revolutionary government went through a period of self-reproof. Homophobic laws were one by one taken off the books, starting in 1975 with the overturning of the 1971 law preventing homosexuals from working in various professions, including education and the arts. This was followed in 1979 by the decriminalisation of homosexuality (the same year as Spain). Even Beatles music is back in favour, with Fidel himself inaugurating a statue of John Lennon in Havana in 2000 (*see p76* **Just like starting over**).

Castro now claims that he has 'never been in favour of, nor promoted, nor supported any policy against homosexuals'. Though this is little short of fabrication, homophobic rhetoric has now been all but eradicated from Cuban law (though the Public Scandal law is regularly subject to homophobic interpretation), and gay issues have made an entrance on to the public stage. The international success of Tomás Guttiérrez Alea's 1993 film *Fresa y chocolate*, about the attraction of an openly gay man for a young straight Revolutionary, did more for gay liberation in Cuba than anything else by breaking the taboo. Sonja de Vries's excellent 1994 documentary *Gay Cuba* recorded the ecstatic reactions of Cubans pouring out of the Yara cinema after watching the film ('What a friendship! I would love to have a friend like that!' – 'Are you gay?' – 'What me? No way! Straight! Pure macho!'). More recently, a *Juventud Rebelde* newspaper article described the remorse a couple were experiencing for rejecting their gay son, and a case study of six same-sex couples was recently published by the University of Havana commenting on the fact that they had – unsurprisingly – very similar issues that affect couples of any sexual make-up.

This is not to say that there haven't been homophobic reversals in Cuba. A year or so ago an unpleasant – and heavily criticised – editorial in local newspaper *Tribuna de la Habana*, openly attacked transvestites, and was responsible for the suppression of regular drag shows at the **Castropol** (*see p151*), and the temporary movement of the gay scene from the seafront Malecón to Calle 23 and Paseo. But everyone is back on the Malecón in force now.

Out and about, holding hands in public might be a little forward, but a kiss on the cheek no longer turns heads. Even transvestites and cross-dressers in full regalia can be seen out and about in public – a marked change from the old days, when they were confined to cabarets. In fact, one of the odd and contradictory aspects of macho culture in Cuba is the immense enjoyment of cross-dressing or transvestite shows. Until last year (*see above*) the **Castropol** specialised in drag shows but now hosts more staid lesbian nights twice a week.

The city of Santa Clara in the Central Provinces has a thriving gay scene, most of which is centred on the gay and lesbian nights at the Menjunje nightclub in the town centre. For information on **Santa Clara**, *see p198*.

WHERE THE PARTY'S AT

There are few specifically gay bars and clubs in Havana, and none that are state-backed. As a result, the gay scene is often played out on the street and at private parties. The **Yara** cinema (*see p142*) is the traditional night-time rendezvous point for gay men, although there have been efforts by the police to move people along when things get crowded around 11pm. The scene then moves down **La Rampa**

Who, me? Take a cruise on the **Malecón** – prime meeting and greeting territory.

(the section of Calle 23 from the junction of Calle L to the seafront) to the **Malecón** and settles on the sea wall, where gay men and lesbians openly hang out in large numbers until dawn.

On Fridays and Saturdays there is almost always a gay and/or lesbian party somewhere. Just show up at the Yara around 10pm and ask. There will be cars ready to take you to the action for $5 or so, or $2 apiece in a shared car. The gay *fiestas* used to be wild affairs held in anything from an old mansion in the middle of a wood to a 1950s beachside club, but things have changed of late due to a concentrated anti-drug campaign. The mere whiff of a joint can close a place down for good. Plus, the increase in male hustlers drives people away; the vast majority of the gorgeous men in their 20s at these parties are *jineteros*. It's fun to be around these stunners for a drink or two (on you), but remember it isn't always your fabulous body that's attracted them. The bulge in your trousers they're really after is probably the one made by your wallet.

LISTINGS AND LINGO

As with so many things in Cuba, and probably more so, the gay scene is prone to sudden change for no apparent reason; you should therefore be prepared for any of the following venues to be closed at short notice and for other information, such as admission prices, to fluctuate (they're nebulous at the best of times for any venue in Havana, let alone gay ones). Some, but not all, venues have air-con. In the ones that do, it's prone to break down or is turned up so high that your libido is seriously affected.

As well as the straightforward *homosexual* to denote a gay or lesbian, you may also hear the terms *maricón* or *pato* (poof), *pájaro* or *loca* (queen), and *tortillera* or *tuerca* (dyke). Best not use these terms casually, they may cause offence.

Bars, cafés & clubs

Many bars and cafés attract gay crowds without necessarily advertising themselves as gay. As always in Cuba, everyone's welcome. No credit cards are accepted in the following venues.

Cafetería La Arcada

Calle M, esquina 23, Vedado (832 0677).
Open 24 hrs daily. **Admission** free. **Map** p250 B11.
A pleasant place, smiliar to the Cafetería 23 y P but more downmarket, that has become a primarily male gay haunt.

Cafetería 23 y P

Calle 23, esquina P, Vedado (870 7631). **Open** 7am-3am daily. **Admission** free. **Map** p250 B12.
Close to the Yara cinema, this is a regular bar that has become a gay evening hangout simply because most of its clients happen to be, well, gay.

Castropol

Malecón #107, entre Genios y Crespo, Centro Habana (861 4864). **Open** 7pm-midnight Fri; 4pm-midnight Sun. *Dance shows* 7pm-midnight Fri; 4pm-midnight Sun. **Admission** free. **Map** p251 C15.
Once a drag-show cabaret, this popular nightspot features a small, outdoor patio filled with tables and chairs crowded together, and an inside dancefloor (house, salsa and Madonna). There's currently no air-con, so dress (or undress) accordingly as it gets very hot. There's occasionally a cabaret-style performance, which it won't hurt to miss. The crowd is friendly and, best of all, there's no hustling. At press time, Tuesday and Thursday nights were for a mostly lesbian crowd, although Cubans don't make a big deal about who is what. The place is about to undergo much-needed refurbishment that will mercifully include air-conditioning, a coat of paint and, we hope, a change of lighting to something more romantic than spotlight white.

Lesbian Havana

There are fewer hangouts for lesbians than there are for gay men in Havana, but a stroll along the Malecón close to La Rampa around midnight will reveal an increasing number of young women who are taking back a little of the street that the gay male population has overrun. Lesbian *fiestas* in Havana are less publicised affairs with news travelling by word of mouth. And unlike the male gay parties, they aren't riddled with hustlers. At press time **Castropol** (*see p151*) was also holding lesbian nights twice weekly.

Lesbians are far more 'out' in Cuba than almost anywhere else in Latin America. But this doesn't mean that they are as visible as Cuba's gay men, who are a cinch to spot. Butch dykes and femmes are around, of course, but lesbians tend not to dress to stereotype and blend in with their heterosexual counterparts. There are many older – and a few younger – lesbian couples living openly in Havana – although they'd be hard put to do the same in the provinces. Don't come expecting New York or London, but the lesbian scene in Havana is one of the most dynamic in Latin America.

Night Club Tropical

Calle Línea, esquina a F, Vedado (832 7361). **Open** 10pm-2am daily. **Admission** $4. **Map** p250 A10.

A small and smoky (but now air-conditioned, at least) cellar offering different nights for different patrons. Club Tropical often attracts young, gay fashion victims, but is less ostensibly gay these days. Before paying the cover, find out what kind of night is in store by checking out the crowd milling about outside.

San Lázaro #8A

San Lázaro #8A, entre Paseo de Martí (Prado) y Cárcel, Centro Habana (no phone). **Open** 11pm-4am Thur-Sun. **Admission** free. **Map** p251/252 C15.

This house, with courtyard, at the end of Prado at La Punta (the entrance to the Havana Bay), is the scene of regular Friday and Saturday night parties for a mostly young, male Cuban crowd. There's a drag show that can, erm, drag a little at one and a half hours. Drinks are $1 a pop, and food is cheap. Very hot and steamy but relatively few hustlers.

Cruising

Cuba's public scandal laws seek to dissuade sex workers and those looking for casual public sex. Although the police do not employ vice squads to entrap people into lewd conduct, police officers have ample room to interpret these ambiguous laws however they see fit. Thus, even picking someone up in a park can lead to hassle. Any Cuban involved is likely to be treated as a hustler (which is often the case).

It is certainly not illegal to meet and talk with someone in the street, but if you do this behind the bushes – even if your clothes are intact when a police torch lights up your evening – you will probably be taken down to the station and given a warning. Having said this, police intervention is rare, unless you're doing something particularly kinky. Cruising action abounds in the locales below. And Christmas Eve midnight mass at the Cathedral is another cruising opportunity.

At the ballet

Any good ballet (and in Cuba it's always good) attracts a large percentage of Havana's gay male population. You can find them in full force at the Sala García Lorca in the **Gran Teatro de La Habana** (*see p167*) in Centro Habana, and the intermissions offer great cruising opportunities. Prop yourself in the curve of the grand piano in the foyer, look gorgeous, cultured and uninterested, and wait.

At the beach

Playa Mi Cayito, some 30 minutes by car from Havana along the Playas del Este (*see p93*), offers a perfect backdrop: palm trees; blue, warm, clear water lapping on the shore; hour-glass fine sand; and plenty of same-sex couples sunbathing, with a plethora of bods to choose on weekends. The easiest way to get there is to take a taxi ($10-$15 each way) from anywhere in Havana. Be sure not to go at the wrong time of year, though: summer officially ends with August and few Cubans go to the beach after September.

At the cinema

Cine Payret (*see p142*), opposite El Capitolio in Centro Habana, offers the chance for old-fashioned back-row snogging. The film can be quite good, too.

On the street

Not the most romantic setting, but there's plenty of action along **Calle G** (from Calle Línea to 23, and from the José Miguel Gómez monument at 27 and to the School of Dentistry). The seafront by Hotel Neptuno-Tritón (corner of Avenida 3ra and Calle 72) in Miramar is active but some way out of town.

Where to stay & eat

Most establishments in Cuba are gay-friendly, but we'd particularly recommend the following *paladares*: **Le Chansonnier** (*see p108*), the **Decameron** (*see p108*), **La Esperanza** (*see p109*) and **La Guarida** (*see p105*). For a *casa particular*, try **Casa de Carlos y Julio** (*see p44*) in Vedado or **Casa de Eugenio y Fabio** in La Habana Vieja (*see p38*).

Music & Nightlife

Face the music? There's no getting away from it.

If religion is the opiate of the people, as Karl Marx famously wrote, then the drug of choice in Revolutionary Cuba is music. Music is everywhere in Havana, and locals joke that it's the only country in the world where you have to pay musicians not to play. Whether you're chasing a Buena Vista Social Club-fuelled nostalgia trip, the sounds of Havana's growing alternative music scene or a glitzy salsa extravaganza, Havana delivers, both in quantity and quality.

You simply can't escape music in Havana. The majority of bars and restaurants feature trios, quartets and septets; neighbourhoods are filled with the sounds of distorted radios blasting out hits, *toques de santo* (religious ceremonies with drumming, singing and dancing), spontaneous rumba sessions (*see p66* **Beat it**) or bands rehearsing. Even the bicycle taxis (*bicitaxis*) are often equipped with boom boxes powered by the driver's pedalling. At night the Malecón, Havana's communal living room, is rammed with young and old drinking rum and strumming guitars.

But most astonishing of all is that it is virtually impossible to hear bad music in Havana. The level of musical training is remarkably high and one of the unintended consequences of the US embargo is that, rather than being overrun by American pop, Cuba has nurtured its own unique blends of African and European rhythms – from rumba to *bolero*, cha cha chá to *timba* – and kept its levels of creativity high. The phenonmenal popularity of Cuban music, kick-started by the worldwide salsa craze and the impact of the extaordinarily successful Buena Vista Social Club project – has made music one of the country's leading exports, up there with rum, cigars and sugar.

INFORMATION

Havana is filled with bars and clubs for dancing, or just listening, and every night of the week you're guaranteed to find something of interest. The Spanish- and English-language *Cartelera* is one of the main sources for listings of cultural events in the city, but is patchy. Radio Taíno (FM 93.3) plays an interesting blend of Cuban and world music, and broadcasts regular updates in English on music events in the capital.

The best way to approach the plethora of live music available is – if you know what you're looking for – to go to where the best bands are playing, rather than wait for them to come to you. There is a regular rotation of bands among the premier clubs, namely the two **Casas de la Música**, the **Piano Bar Delirio Habanero** and **Café Cantante**. These four venues are all managed by EGREM, one of the three national recording labels (the other two are Unicornio and Bis Music), and have access to the very best bands. Look out for Los Van Van, Pupy y Los Que Son Son, Adalberto Alvarez y Su Son, Manolito Simonet y su Trabuco, Paulito FG, Isaac Delgado, NG La Banda, Klimax, David Alvarez y Juego de Manos, Arnaldo y su Talismán and Pedrito Calvo, among others. You can expect to pay more on the door for these top-tier musicians ($15-$25) but it's worth it. The main act will often not start until 11.30pm or later, but it's best to go early if you want a table. Note that you may have to endure a floor show for the privilege of a good seat.

Some of the most renowned *timba* and traditional music bands play in Havana's upmarket hotels. Buena Vista Social Club members Omara Portuondo, Ibrahim Ferrer, Amadito Valdés and Eliades Ochoa each play with their own ensembles, most commonly at the **Salón 1930 'Compay Segundo'** at the Hotel Nacional.

If your budget is tight head for one of the places that charges in Cuban pesos (*moneda nacional*), or take in a matinée (always cheaper) at one of the larger clubs, such as the two **Casas de la Música** and **Café Cantante**.

The Cuban government has also, in recent years, started to put on free concerts along the Malecón, just below the Hotel Nacional, and at la Tribuna Anti-Imperialista José Martí, adjacent to the US Interests Section. These open-air shows don't follow a regular programme but usually take place at weekends and begin around 9pm. The atmosphere is cheerful and safe in general but always keep your wallet close to your body and stay away from drunken, swaying crowds.

Be advised that clubs open and close with frequency in Havana, and that hours and cover charges change frequently, not to mention entire bills – what's touted on the advert is not always what ends up on stage. It's always best to call ahead to confirm who is performing and at what time. If you show up without a reservation and there is a crowd outside be sure to ask the doorman about the availability of space – don't just get in the queue. Keep in mind that these clubs exist to generate hard currency and they want you and your dollars inside. If it is a group you really want to hear, be persistent and patient and eventually you will be allowed in. The golden rule is to turn up early anywhere Los Van Van are playing, as their shows are pretty much guaranteed to be oversubscribed.

Finally, be advised that Cubans like to look smart when they go out and many places will not let in men dressed in shorts, sleeveless shirts or sandals. Women should dress up to the nines if they don't want to stand out.

CLASSICAL MUSIC

Classical music isn't exactly the first thing that comes to mind in connection with Cuba. Yet its history here goes back to the 19th century, when wealthy sugar barons brought chamber orchestras and opera companies from Spain and Italy to perform in Havana and other major Cuban cities. Italian tenor Enrico Caruso once sang at the Teatro Tomás Terry in Cienfuegos, a fact the locals are still proud to recount.

Cuban composers including Amadeo Roldán, Rodrigo Pratz, Ernesto Lecuona and Alejandro Garcia Caturla mastered traditional composition and brought their own distinctive Caribbean flavour to it. Roldán and Caturla are especially well regarded for having brought the influence of Africa into the music, creating a unique sound that is still enjoyed today.

Classical music fell out of favour after the Revolution of 1959 as it was considered part of the bourgeois legacy that needed to be shed. Things got so dire that the island had to import musicians and teachers from the Eastern bloc to keep its orchestras intact. Few young people wanted to take up the violin or the oboe. But with the collapse of the Soviet Union, large crowds began to turn out for symphony concerts even breaking down the doors of the Teatro Nacional in a crush to get into a concert of Bach's music. Classical music, overlooked for 30 years, reminded people of better days and simpler times. It became a source of solace amid the hardships of the Special Period. Young Cubans began to attend the conservatories again and the island now boasts six symphony orchestras, fully staffed with home-grown talent.

In Havana there are two major venues for classical music: the **Teatro Amadeo Roldán** (*see p162*) in Vedado, home of the National Symphony Orchestra; and the **Basílica de San Francisco de Asís** (*see below*) in Old Havana, home to Camarata Romeu, an all-female chamber ensemble. Other venues include **Iglesia de Paula** (*see p156*), home to prestigious ensemble Ars Longa.

It's also worth trying to catch one of the outdoor performances of the impressive Municipal Band of Havana, which plays the more popular end of Cuban and Hispanic classical music.

FESTIVALS

Cuba hosts a large number of music festivals – the odds are high that you'll catch one during your visit. *See pp132-6* **Festivals & Events** for listings and reviews. The main agents for Havana events are **Paradiso** (Calle 19, #560, esquina Avenida C, Vedado, 832 6928/9538) and Havanatur (*see p185*).

La Habana Vieja

There's a multitude of touristy bars and cafés churning out (albeit to a good standard) *Guantanamera* and the hits from the Buena Vista Social Club in and around Calle Obispo, Plaza de Armas and Calle Tacón. If you want to change the record – and it's well worth the extra initiative required – try visiting some of the venues listed below.

The **Museo de la Música** (*see p61*) has a small, narrow hall that sometimes hosts concerts by renowned Cuban musicians; the **Centro Pablo de la Torriente Brau** (*see p147*) on Plaza Vieja holds concerts in its pretty courtyard area, mostly involving the younger generation of Cuban *trovadores* (usually a singer with guitar); **Piano Bar Maragato** (Hotel Florida; *see p34*) has daily live shows. Some restaurants and bars in Old Havana have particularly good music. These include **La Mina** (*see p102*) on Plaza de Armas, **El Patio** (*see p103*) on Plaza de la Cathedral, **Café de París** (*see p114*) and **Bar Monserrate** (*see p114*).

Basílica Menor de San Francisco de Asís

Calle Oficios, entre Amargura y Churruca (862 3467). **Open** *Museum* 9am-6.30pm daily. **Concerts** 6pm Sat. Closed Aug. **Admission** $3-$10 tourists; 2 pesos Cubans. **No credit cards**. **Map** p252 E15.

This beautiful and peaceful basilica with fine acoustics has become an important classical music venue. In the picturesque square of the same name, the church has been lovingly restored and is now home to the wonderful Camarata Romeu, an all-female chamber ensemble founded in 1993, which has a brief to perform music by written by Cuban and Latin American composers. Many other excellent soloists (from home and abroad), groups and choirs also stage concerts here.

The best Venues

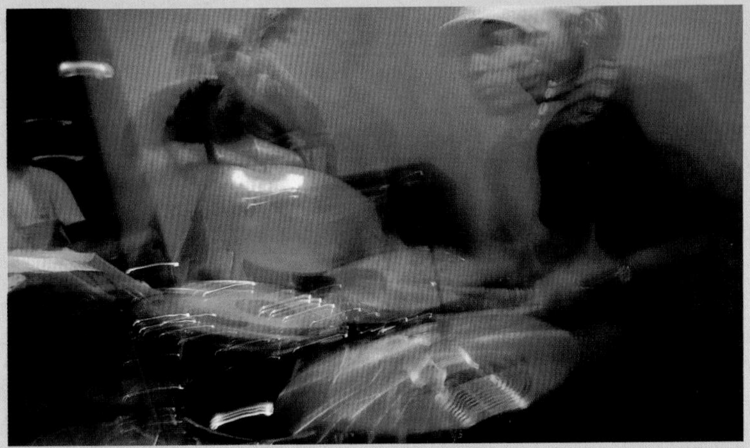

For *bolero*
El Gato Tuerto (*see p159*); **Hurón Azul/UNEAC** (*see p160*); **Salón Bolero** (*see p165*).

For *discoteca*
Club Ipanema (*see p164*).

For jazz
La Zorra y el El Cuervo (*see p162*; pictured); **Jazz Café** (*see 161*).

For rock
To find out what's on, pitch up at 23 and G, where the rock community tends to hang out at night. Or try the **Casa de la Cultura de Plaza** (*see p159*).

For *son*
Café Taberna (*see p155*); **Casa de la Amistad** (*see p159*).

For rumba
Hurón Azul/UNEAC (*see p160*); **Callejón de Hamel** (*see p156*); **Centro Cultural El Gran Palenque** (*see p159*).

For salsa
Casa de la Música (*see p157*).

For tango
Casa del Tango (*see p157*).

For traditional *trova*
Centro Habana's **Casa de la Trova** (*see p157*).

For state-of-the-art equipment
Teatro Amadeo Roldán (*see p162*); **Casa de la Música de Centro Habana** (*see p157*).

For an all-around good time
Anywhere **Los Van Van**, one of the world's best salsa bands, are playing. From the first note until the last the crowd is on their feet.

Café Taberna
Calle Mercaderes #531, esquina Brasil (Teniente Rey) (861 1637). **Open** 11am-11pm daily. **Admission** free. **Credit** (restaurant) MC, V. **Map** p252 E15.

This restaurant was the site of Havana's very first café, opened in 1777. It reopened after restoration in 1999 and is now a fine setting to enjoy some of the best *son* in town. The house bands are Son del Trópico, Sonido Son and the Septeto Matamoros (led by the grandson of the famous composer Miguel Matamoros). These groups are excellent and, better still, there is no cover charge. *See also p100.*

Casa de la Cultura de la Habana Vieja
Calle Aguiar #509, entre Brasil (Teniente Rey) y Amargura (863 4860). **Open** 8pm-midnight Tue-Sun. *Performances* phone for details. **Admission** 40 pesos tourists; 10 pesos Cubans. **No credit cards. Map** p252 E15.

Director Bertha Fernández is doing a fanastic job remodelling this large old structure, and it will be one of the top venues in Old Havana when the new patio is finished. In addition to classes and programmes for local residents, there are several shows

So *that's* where the Lady in Red steps out these days: **Cafe Taberna**. *See p155.*

each week of interest to visitors. Wednesdays feature *son*, usually care of the Orquesta Sonora Habana (8-11pm); Fridays *son* and salsa bands (9pm-midnight). The second and fourth Saturdays each month offer Afro-Cuban percussion and vocal groups from (6-9pm), while the first Saturday of the month is usually dedicated to rap music and the second and fourth Sundays to *boleros*. Foreigners and Cubans flock in equal numbers to this *casa,* and the open-air dancefloor is usually packed. Great value, and with consistently high-quality performers.

Iglesia de Paula

Avenida del Puerto, esquina Leonor Perez (860 4210). **Open** *Museum* 8.30am-6.30pm daily. **Concerts** phone for details. **Admission** $1 tourists; 1 peso Cubans. **Admission**: $5-$10. **No credit cards**. **Map** p252 F15.

The Iglesia de Paula is home to Cuba's prestigious early music ensemble Ars Longa. Small and recently spruced up, the church hosts concerts almost every weekend with two big events every year: September Baroque and the International Festival of Old Music Esteban Salas (February).

El Mesón de la Flota

Calle Mercaderes #257, entre Amargura and Brasil (Teniente Rey) (863 3838/862 9281). **Open** 11am-11pm daily. *Show* 9.30pm daily. **Admission** free. **Credit** MC, V. **Map** p252 E15.

If you've had it with *son* and salsa, drop by this restaurant for the daily flamenco show. The venue has a *tablao flamenco* (wooden stage) where dancers and musicians, such as the Havana Flamenco Company and Ecos, usually perform. *See also p102.*

Centro Habana

Other bars with live music in Centro Habana include La Paradilla rooftop bar at the **Hotel Inglaterra** (*see p38*), which has free concerts from 9pm to 11pm daily.

Cabaret Palermo

Calle San Miguel #252, esquina Amistad (861 9745). **Open** 10am-10pm daily. **Admission** phone for details. **No credit cards. Map** p251 E14.

This seedy dive is popular with Afro-Cuban youth due to the rap and other black music genres that dominate. But at the time of writing the Palermo was awaiting permission to resume live musical performances, so details were nebulous. Worth asking for the latest if you're in the neighbourhood. Features the largest circular bar in Havana.

Callejón de Hamel

Callejón Hamel, entre Hospital y Aramburu (878 1661). **Performances** 8.30pm-11pm last Fri of mth; 10am-noon Sat (children); noon-3pm Sun. **Admission** free (donations welcome). **No credit cards**. **Map** p250 C12.

Artist Salvador González has turned this alley into a shrine to both *santería* and the power of artistic vision. Brightly coloured murals, objects and kiosks celebrate Afro-Cuban religions with cheerful serendipity. It has become rather touristy in recent years but is nonetheless well worth a visit. The best rumba bands play here every week (in particular Clave y Guaguancó) and lots of the locals turn out to sing and dance. Come early to see the art and ask the genial MC Elias for a seat. *See also p66* **Beat it**.

Casa de la Cultura de Centro Habana

Avenida Salvador Allende (Carlos III), esquina Castillejo (878 4727). **Open** 8.30pm-1am daily. **Admission** 20-60 pesos (depending on group). **No credit cards**. **Map** p250 D12.

Centro Habana's Casa de la Cultura is a popular venue, with a varied cultural programme aimed primarily at neighbourhood residents. The large patio is sometimes the scene for concerts of reggae, rap and hip hop.

Casa de la Música de Centro Habana

Calle Galiano, entre Neptuno y Concordia (862 4165/860 8296-97). **Open** 10pm-3am Tue-Sun. *Shows* 11.30pm Tue-Sun; matinée (occasional) 4-8pm. **Admission** $10-$25; matinée $5. **No credit cards**. **Map** p251 D14.

Managed by record label EGREM, Havana's newest music venue has a spacious dancefloor, plus excellent sound and lighting systems. Such luxuries don't come cheap, but it is one of the best places to hear salsa in Havana. The club has a regular rotation of musicians, taken from the cream of the music scene, including Los Van Van, Isaac Delgado and Manolito Simonet. Arrive early for a table, as it's usually packed by 11pm. The matinée shows are very popular with locals and feature hip hop and rap, as well as *son* and salsa. It also houses a very well-stocked music store.

Casa del Tango

Calle Neptuno #309, entre Aguila y Italia (Galiano) (863 0097). **Open** 9.30pm-3am daily. *Performances* 10pm daily. **Admission** $3. **No credit cards**. **Map** p251 D14.

Owners Wilki and Adelaida have turned their home into one of the more eccentric venues in Havana, offering dance classes in tango and salsa, along with a floor show and dancing later on. The main room is a shrine to tango, packed with old posters, sheet music and other tango memorabilia. Hours depend on 'how things are going'.

Casa de la Trova de Centro Habana

Calle San Lázaro #661, entre Padre Varela (Belascoaín) y Gervasio (879 3373). **Open** 7-10pm Thur-Sun. *Performances* phone for details. **Admission** free. **No credit cards**. **Map** p251 C13.

This club has fallen on hard times but still features some very good soloists and small groups playing trad *trova*. Call first to check performance times.

Centro Andaluz en Cuba

Paseo de Martí (Prado) #104, entre Genios y Refugio (863 6745). **Open** 1pm-midnight daily. *Shows* 8.30-11pm Wed; 10pm-midnight Fri, Sat. **Admission** 60 pesos minimum consumption. **No credit cards**. **Map** p252 D15.

This former social club for descendants of Cuba's Andalusian population now specialises in flamenco, with peformances from homegrown troupes like Ecos and Habana Flamenca.

Club Oasis

Paseo de Martí (Prado) #256, entre Trocadero y Colón (863 3829). **Open** 6pm-2am daily (snack bar opens noon). *Show* 10.30pm daily. **Admission** $2 minimum consumption. **No credit cards**. **Map** p252 D14.

Located on El Prado, the grand avenue on the eastern edge of Centro Habana, this nightclub is on the ground floor of the Arabic Union of Cuba. A large, dimly lit room inhabited by a predominantly Cuban audience hosts a floor show, karaoke, comedians and salsa music.

Setentas Café

Hotel Deauville, Avenida de Italia (Galiano), entre Malecón y San Lázaro (338812/866 8812). **Open** 10pm-2am Tue-Sun. **Admission** $10 (7.30pm-9.30pm incl meal plus drink; after 9.30pm incl open bar). **No credit cards**. **Map** p251 C14.

This rowdy basement is popular with locals and features pop music from the '70s and '80s, plus karaoke. The $10 cover includes an open bar.

La Terraza

Hotel Lincoln, Avenida de Italia (Galiano) #164, esquina Virtudes (833 8209). **Open** 8pm-midnight Mon-Fri; 8pm-2am Sat, Sun. *Matinée* 4-8pm daily. *Café* 10am-noon, 2-8pm daily. **Admission** phone for details. **No credit cards**. **Map** p251 D14.

Pupy y Los Que Son Son, at **Casa de la Música de Centro Habana**.

Casa del Tango: more of a shrine than a house. *See p157.*

This open-air, rooftop venue on top of the Lincoln, one of Havana's oldest hotels, offers a fine view over Parque Central and the sea, but complaints from neighbours about the noise have limited performances to the daytime. A mixture of recorded music is played, aimed at the dancefloor, and there are daily live performances too; folkloric group Vocal Baobab popular regulars. Weekends here are particularly popular with Cubans, as prices for food and drink are reasonable and the hotel, which is run by the Islazul chain, is a favourite with those visiting from other parts of the island. The hotel also boasts the famous 24-hour Bar Tres Monitos.

Vedado

As befits the grander environs of Vedado, the music and nightlife in these parts tends to centre on major hotels, as well as the headquarters of several of the national cultural institutions, housed in several of the area's large, elegant former residencies and mansions. *See also p163* **Copa Room**, which has regular big-name concerts. Fans of synchronised swimming should head for the swimming pools at the **Hotel Habana Libre** (*see p41*) and the **Hotel Nacional** (*see p42*); both put on open-air aquatic shows that make for a surprisingly lively night out.

Amanecer

Calle 15, esquina O (832 9075). **Open** 9pm-2am daily. **Admission** $6-$10 (incl $4-$6 drinks). **No credit cards**. **Map** p250 B12.

This recently remodelled club has a large bar and dancefloor. It stages shows from 9pm daily, along with matinées from Wednesday to Sunday. Expect to see a variety show at midnight, sandwiched between danceable tunes either side. Admission is sometimes restricted to couples only.

Atelier

Calle 17, esquina 6 (830 6808). **Open** 11am-2am daily (music from 9pm). *Matinée* 4-9pm Sat, Sun. **Admission** 80 pesos per couple, incl 40 pesos drinks; matinée $1. **No credit cards**. **Map** p250 B9.

Live bands of varying quality play rock, reggae, pop and salsa at this cosy, neighbourhood club. Cover is in pesos, so there is usually a good contingent of Cubans dancing here. Weekends feature a matinée.

Cabaret Turquino

Habana Libre Hotel, Calle L, entre 23 y 25 (554011). **Open** 10.30pm-3am daily. **Admission** $15. **Credit** MC, V. **Map** p250 B11.

The management seems to have given up on offering a full-blown cabaret show here, but the fantastic views, some of the best in Havana, make up for it. Entertainment features a dance revue at midnight followed by live music, then a disco until 3am. Few top-name groups play here any more so the music is rarely first-rate. A popular spot for hustlers.

Café Amor 'Karabalí'

Calle 23, entre O y N (832 6757). **Open** 9pm-3am daily (show 11pm). **Admission** $5 (after 9pm). **No credit cards**. **Map** p250 B12.

A café by day, this new club opened on Valentine's Day 2003 (in keeping with the romantic name), offering a floor show and live music (usually *bolero* and *filin*) at 11pm. Diminutive stage and limited seating.

Café Cantante Mi Habana

Teatro Nacional de Cuba, Paseo, esquina 39, Plaza de la Revolución (879 0710). **Open** 10pm-3.30am daily. *Matinée* 4-8pm Sat, Sun. **Admission** $5-$10. **Map** p250 D10.

This is one of Havana's best, and most popular, clubs and it has been greatly improved thanks to a recent renovation that dazzles with brightly painted furniture and a starry ceiling. It's usually packed out in the afternoons, when locals pay 40 pesos (foreigners $5), and shows feature hip hop, salsa, rock, pop and traditional Afro-Cuban music. These afternoon sessions are a must for people who want to see up-to-date, often alternative, Cuban music. Days have different themes, so it is best to call ahead for details. At night, Café Cantante offers big-name salsa groups from 10pm, followed by a disco until 6am (cover $10).

Casa de la Amistad

Avenida Paseo #406, entre 17 y 19 (830 3114/ 3115). **Open** 9pm-midnight Tue, Thur; 9pm-1am Sat. **Admission** $5. **No credit cards. Map** p250 B9.

This beautiful 1920s mansion is now occupied by the Instituto Cubano de Amistad con los Pueblos, and boasts a lovely garden and a good dancefloor. The best night to go for live music under the stars is Tuesday (when the late Compay Segundo played), when old timers such as the Orquesta América and the Septeto Habanero take to the stage. Other shows are regularly offered on Mondays (*boleros*) and Saturdays (variety shows). Note the earlier start and finish times; this is an outdoor venue in the middle of a residential area. There has been a worrying trend emerging recently of staging a tacky cabaret before the bands play; we can only hope this is a temporary blip.

Casa de la Cultura de Plaza

Calle 7ma (Calzada), entre 6 y 8 (831 2320). **Open** phone for details. **Admission** phone for details; usually free. **No credit cards. Map** p249 A8.

The immense patio at this community centre plays host to live reggae, pop, rock, salsa and hip hop. A great place for a slice of local action but be sure to call first for details, as there's neither a fixed schedule nor prices. A venue for Havana's international jazz festival in December.

Centro Cultural El Gran Palenque

Calle 4, entre 5ta y 7ma (Calzada) (339075). **Shows** (Sábado de la Rumba) 3-5pm Sat. **Admission** $5. **No credit cards. Map** p250 A9.

Home to the world-renowned dance troupe Conjunto Folklórico Nacional de Cuba (*see p172*), El Gran Palenque's Sábado de la Rumba consitutes a fine way to while away a Saturday afternoon. Performances come from members of the Conjunto and invited guests, and take place in the large outdoor patio (with bar). The mixed bill changes regularly – if you're lucky you may even catch the Muñequitos de Matanzas – and the atmosphere is almost always hot. It attracts a strong, loyal crowd of Cuban regulars.

Centro Vasco

Calle 3ra, esquina 4 (833 9354/830 9836). **Open** *Bar* 10am–2am daily. *Restaurant* noon-midnight daily. *Show* (Taberna Don Sabino) 8pm-3am daily. **Admission** $5 (incl 1 drink). **Credit** MC, V. **Map** p250 A9.

Another of Havana's former Spanish social clubs that have now opened their doors to the general public, offering music and various shows daily, including comedians, fashion and special events. The basement venue (used at night) is pretty dingy. The street-level patio is also open for drinks and food during the day.

Club Imágenes

Calle 7ma (Calzada), esquina C (333606). **Open** 9pm-3am daily. **Admission** $5 minimim consumption. **Credit** MC, V. **Map** p250 A10.

This is a beautiful, very romantic piano bar, with subtle lighting and atmosphere. Try the house cocktail: *crema catalana* with Havana Club Reserva served in a champagne glass ($2).

Club Tikoa

Calle 23, entre N y O (830 9973). **Open** 9pm-2am Fri-Sun. *Matinée* 3-7pm Sun. **Admission** $3-$5; matinée 40-80 pesos. **No credit cards. Map** p250 B12.

Knots of young Cubans tend to hang around this La Rampa club, on account of the cheapish admission prices. The club features small groups playing *son* and salsa, plus a regular disco. The Sunday matinée, playing music from the '60s and '70s, is ideal for satisfying any cravings to hear Earth, Wind and Fire, the Eagles or Diana Ross.

El Cortijo

Hotel Vedado, Calle 25, esquina O (334072). **Open** 10.30pm-2am daily (incl open bar). Restaurant opens noon. **Admission** $8. **Credit** MC, V. **Map** p250 B/C12.

At this dimly lit basement club an $8 cover charge allows you unlimited drinks. But that is one of the few things to recommend it. A typical week takes in comedy shows (Mon-Wed) and magic shows (Thur-Sun). A disco follows the entertainment.

El Gato Tuerto

Calle O, entre 17 y 19 (836 0212). **Open** noon-3am daily. *Show* from 10pm daily. **Admission** $5 minimum consumption. **Credit** MC, V. **Map** p250 B12.

This intimate performance space is housed in a restored mansion just down the street from the plushy Hotel Nacional. The One-Eyed Cat used to be the place where young intellecturals and artists hung out in the early '80s. It reopened a few years ago, after 12 years of closure, restored, revamped and with pleasant, chic decor. This is a prominent venue for *bolero* and the bill usually features first-rate artists, who start at 11pm and play three sets with interludes until 4am. Light snacks are served and there's a restaurant upstairs (open noon-4am). The downstairs has a grand piano, a bar and seating for 80.

Habana Café

Hotel Meliá Cohiba, Paseo, esquina 3ra (333636). **Open** 8pm-2.30am daily. *Show* 9pm (main band at 11.30pm) Thur-Sun. **Admission** $10-$15. **Credit** MC, V. **Map** p250 A9.

The decor at Habana Café is distinctively American, with tables set among classic US cars (a Chevy, Pontiac and Buick grace the interior), along with

Generation rap

1999 was an important year for Cuban hip hop. It achieved state recognition when Abriel Prieto, the Cuban Minister of Culture, officially endorsed it as a form of artistic expression. The same year Orishas, Cuban hip hop's most famous group, released their debut album *A lo cubano* with EMI to worldwide critical acclaim and not inconsiderable commercial success. Cuban hip hop was getting to be big news, and the government, initially suspicious of the new genre, soon would have been naive to ignore it.

Hip hop is easily the fastest-growing music genre on the island, with a burgeoning festival to show for it, and is attracting some of Cuba's best young musicians. The current boom has been almost a decade in the making, as hip hoppers steadily forged a space for themselves in Cuba's contemporary musicscape. In the first place, Cuban hip hop was born – like US hip hop – underground. Coat-hanger radio antennae tuned into Miami stations such as WEDR (99 Jams), coupled with bootlegged copies of films such as *Beatstreet I* and *II* and *Wildstyle*, inspired a generation of Cuban breakers, and the rhythms of rap pioneers like the Sugarhill Gang, imported by visiting Cuban-Americans, started to take off.

But the birth of hip hop in Cuba was also the result of a particular set of social and economic circumstances. After the fall of the Soviet Union in 1989, Cuba fell into economic crisis, which created a need among the youth to vocalise what was happening in their neighbourhoods. One of Cuba's earliest rappers was Nilo MC (now in Madrid) who, between 1989 and 1992, could be found rapping in the streets, busking to the queues outside Coppelia ice-cream parlour or to crowds coming out of nightclubs.

Despite early stateside influences, Cuban hip hop soon began to carve itself an independent sound, tinged with many of the country's own rich rhythms. In fact, although the US blockade has hindered the formation of the necessary infrastructure to record the fruits of the rap scene, the fresh, raw sound of Cuban hip hop has also been nurtured by its isolation; its unique sound is a large part of its attraction.

It hasn't all been in a vacuum, though. In 1998, Black August – a New York-based collective of independent activists and members of the Malcolm X Grassroots Movement – came together with Cuban association Hermanos Saíz to arrange for Black Star to perform at the festival. This cultural interaction paved the way for further visits from international artists (Dead Prez, The Roots, Brazilian U-Afro and Bocafloja from Mexico). These cultural exchanges provided Cuban hip hop musicians with a vital sense of international community.

Most rap music produced in Cuba today can, for better or worse, only be seen live (self-recorded demos can be bought at shows). Within Havana, performances can usually be seen at **Atelier** (*see p158*) on Thursday nights, and **Café Cantante Mi Habana** (*see p158*) and **Parque Almendares** (*see p80*) on Saturday, but always phone to check before going out of your way. Cuba's hip hop culture magazine *Movimiento*, available at newsstands, is distributed by the Cuban Agency for Rap Music

pictures of Ernest Hemingway and pre-Revolutionary memorabilia. There's a floor show most nights before the major act begins. Thursday to Sunday offers renowned salsa names, such as Los Van Van, Bamboleo and Isaac Delgado. Attracts a tourist crowd in the main.

Hurón Azul/UNEAC

UNEAC, Calle 17, esquina H (832 4551-53). **Open** *Shows* 5pm Wed; 8.30pm-midnight Sat. **Admission** $5. **Credit** MC, V. **Map** p250 B11.

The home of the National Union of Artists and Writers is a grand old Vedado mansion, where the large veranda serves as a stage and its patio provides table seating. This is quite the place to be on Wednesday afternoons for La Peña del Ambia, named after its host and featuring rumba and emerging Afro-Cuban talent; on alternate Wednesdays *trova* and *son* are played. A meeting ground for artists and intellectuals, the Hurón Azul is jammed by starting time at 5pm (arrive by 4.30pm unless you want to stand). Saturday night from 8.30pm until midnight is given over to *bolero*, featuring the city's best soloists and ensembles.

Humor Club Cocodrilo

Calle 3ra, entre 10 y 12 (535305). **Open** 10pm-3am daily. *Show* 11.30pm. **Admission** $4 Mon-Thur, Sun; $5 Fri, Sat. **No credit cards**. **Map** p249 A6.

A warm intimate club for comedy, with distinctive decor. Not recommended unless your Spanish is excellent or you enjoy just watching other people laugh. A disco follows.

Jardines del 1830

Malecón, esquina 20 (553091/553092). **Open** 10pm-2am Tue-Sun. *Matinée* 4-8pm Fri, Sun. **Admission** $3-$4. **No credit cards**. **Map** p249 A7.

Obsesión.

and is a good source of information and discussion about Cuban hip hop. The agency was formed in 2002 as a government initiative to formally promote rap. It is hoped that, as a result, there will in the future be more recording, as well as coverage on TV and radio.

Following the raging success of the first rap festival in 1995, the **Festival de Rap Cubano Habana Hip Hop Festival** (*see p134*) has gone from strength to strength. The tenth anniversary festival in 2004 will cover an extended ten-day period and, it is hoped, will boast a star-studded bill. Rumour has it that Nas and Erykah Badu will perform.

Cuba's biggest names to look out for (other than Orishas, who reside in Paris; their second album *Emigrante* was a 2003 Latin Grammy award-winner) are: Obsesión, Doble Filo, Justicia, Anónmio Consejo, Papo Record, Las Crudas and Hermanos de Causa.

A beautiful outdoor garden, with a small stage and dancefloor, on the spot where the Almendares river flows into the ocean. Set behind an opulent restaurant, the club has fashion shows, dance reviews and live and recorded music from 10pm until 2am. Lately, reggae groups have been taking to the stage on Sundays (4-10pm). The loveliness of the setting is not usually matched by the quality of the entertainment, though sporadic Friday house nights are popular.

Jardines Teatro Mella

Calle Línea, entre A y B, Vedado (833 8696). **Shows** 6-8pm Wed. **Admission** *Show* 5 pesos. **No credit cards. Map** p250 A9.

Wednesdays afternoons (5-8pm) are given over to rumba in the open-air garden with Raices Profundas, one of the best Afro-Cuban ensembles in town. Teatro Mella itself is also one of the best venues in Havana for dance, theatre and music. *See also p66* **Beat it**.

Jazz Café

Galerías de Paseo, top floor, Calle 1ra, entre Avenida Paseo y A, Vedado (553475/553556 ext 121). **Open** noon-2am (show 11.30pm) daily. **Admission** $10 minimum consumption. **No credit cards. Map** p250 A9.

This is premier pianist Chucho Valdés's turf. It has a spectacular view of the sea, and programmes Cuba's best jazz musicians. Add in the minimum consumption entrance fee and you have one of the best deals in town. High-quality music, food, service and setting make it one of Havana's best night spots. There's usually a spot of dancing after the acts have finished.

Karachi Club

Calle K, entre 15 y 17 (832 3435). **Open** 9pm-2am daily. *Matinée* 4-9pm. **Admission** $3; matinée $1. **No credit cards. Map** p250 B11.

'El Karachi' offers an impressively diverse music programme (live and DJs). Salsa bands play on Mondays, Wednesdays and Saturdays and (usually very good) recorded music and karaoke on other nights. Weekend matinées take a trip back to the '60s and '70s.

La Madriguera

Quinto de los Molinos, entre Infanta and Jesús Peregrino (879 8175). **Performances** 8.30pm Sat, Sun (occasionally Fri). **Admisson** 5 pesos. **No credit cards. Map** p250 D11.

A dilapidated cultural centre that's home to the youth cultural association Hermanos Saíz (part of the League of Young Communists), La Madriguera is located in an oasis of greenery tucked between two busy thoroughfares where Vedado meets Centro Habana. The mission of Hermanos Saíz is to promote young artists (it also runs the annual rap fest; *see p134*), and there always seems to be music of some kind being played. This is the site of individual and group rehearsals for emerging artists, and shows are produced on an irregular basis, so most of the time you'll have to take a chance. Best to phone ahead.

El Pico Blanco

Hotel St John, Calle O, entre 23 y 25 (333740). **Open** 10pm-3am daily. **Admission** $10 (incl open bar). **Credit** MC, V. **Map** p250 B12.

Just another hotel dance room with live music daily and a disco afterwards. But it does have a smoke machine and good views of the bay and the city.

La Red

Calle 19, esquina L (832 5415). **Open** noon-9pm, 10pm-2am daily. **Admission** $6 (incl $3 drinks). **No credit cards. Map** p250 B11.

This small bar has a variety of shows daily at 10pm, including comedy, fashion shows, karaoke, with live music (pop, salsa, rap, rock) at weekends. This isn't somewhere to dance, but rather to hang out and listen to the show. Prices seem to vary at the whim of the doorman, so be sure to bargain.

Salón 1930 'Compay Segundo'

Hotel Nacional de Cuba, Calle P, esquina 21 (873 4701/333564). **Open** 9.30pm Sat (occasionally Fri). **Admission** $25 ($40 with dinner). **Credit** MC, V. **Map** p250 B12.

Booking is recommended at this elegant salon, now the venue for almost weekly concerts by members of the Buena Vista Social Club. Note that this usually means one of them with a pick-up orchestra, so don't be fooled into thinking you are going to see the entire original band. No matter, the music is excellent all the same. Booking recommended.

Salón Piano Bar 'Delirio Habanero'

Teatro Nacional de Cuba, Paseo, esquina 39, Plaza de la Revolución (879 0710). **Open** 10pm-6am daily. *Matinée* 4-8pm Sat, Sun. **Admission** $10; matinée 20-30 pesos. **No credit cards. Map** p250 D10.

This newly renovated – now all minimalist and with better facilities – bar atop the National Theatre has a splendid view of the Plaza de la Revolución and features top acts in an intimate setting. The weekend matinées feature mostly Afro-Cuban groups, such as Yoruba Andabo and Clave y Guaguancó. Some performances, especially matinées, are charged in pesos, which means there is usually a good mix of visitors and locals. In the evenings, the programme features *son*, smaller salsa bands, *trova* and vocal ensembles. The cover is $10 and drinks cost twice what they do in the afternoon. With record label EGREM running the joint, the quality of the music is very high. Note that the lift only goes to the 3rd floor and you will have to walk up the remaining two flights. Pay at the door to the club upstairs, so ignore the guy at the main entrance who may try to get you to pay him first.

Salón Rojo

Hotel Capri, Calle 21, entre N y O (333747). **Open** 10pm-3am daily. *Show* 11.15pm. **Admission** $20 (incl 2 drinks). **Credit** MC, V. **Map** p250 B12.

Hotel Capri – once an infamous mob hotel – was closed for renovations at the time of writing, but the former cabaret salon is scheduled to reopen at the end of 2003. It was one of the most popular discos in Havana before it shut down and should be again.

Teatro Amadeo Roldán

Calle 7ma (Calzada), esquina D, Vedado (832 4521). **Concerts** *Main hall* 5pm Sun (National Symphony Orchestra). *Sala Caturla* 6pm Thur-Sun. *Opus Bar* 3pm-3am daily. **Admission** $5-$10. **No credit cards. Map** p250 A10.

The National Symphony plays in the main hall here every Sunday, with a break in August. World-class guitarist and composer Leo Brouwer directs, and a concert here is a wonderful listening experience; Cuban pianist Frank Fernández is especially fine. The theatre has another, smaller, hall, the Sala Caturla. Both have excellent acoustics. There are various special concerts throughout the year – mainly classical music, but rock, *trova* and jazz ensembles also feature from time to time. The Opus Bar on the top floor is a popular spot for drinks before and after shows; if you prefer a mojito with your music you can watch the concert on the TV monitors in the bar. The main hall is used for several prestigious festivals, including the Festival Internacional de Percusión (*see p133*), the Festival Internacional de Jazz (*see p136*) and Cubadisco (*see p133*).

La Zorra y El Cuervo

Calle 23, entre N y O (662402/zorra@cbcan/cygt.cu). **Open** 9.30pm-2am daily. *Matinée* 2.30-7pm Sat, Sun. **Admission** $10; matinée $3 (incl $2 drinks). **No credit cards. Map** p250 B12.

This jazz club is an institution in Havana and a pleasant, intimate room for live music. The best Cuban jazz musicians perform here, and it is often the scene of jam sessions with visiting musicians. Weekend matinées called 'Afternoons of Remembrance' call on live bands, recorded music and videos to recall material from the '60s and '70s. One of the main venues for Havana's international jazz festival in December.

Bienvenue, willkommen, welcome

More Vegas than Berlin, Havana's *caberet-espectáculos* are song and dance variety shows performed by G-stringed *mulatas*. With the state aware of their huge popularity with foreign visitors, the primary function of cabarets these days seems to be to fleece tourists. Dress regulations apply in most cabarets: avoid shorts, sleeveless T-shirts and sandals.

Cabaret Nacional

Gran Teatro de la Habana, Paseo de Martí (Prado), esquina San Rafael, Centro Havana (863 0736). **Shows** 11.30pm daily (doors open 9pm). *Matinées* 3.30pm Wed, Sat. **Tickets** $5-$8; matinées $5 Wed, $10 Sat. **No credit cards. Map** p251 D14.

This dark, low-ceilinged, smoky venue is beneath the Gran Teatro on Central Park. It's not the top dance revue in town but you can't beat it on price at least. The best thing here are the matinée performances on Wednesdays (*danzón*) and Saturdays (*son, bolero, cha cha chá*), when lots of old timers turn out to dance to the music of their youth played by orchestras with an average age of 65. Drinks and light snacks are available, though you wouldn't come here for the food. Dance matinées are often full of teenagers, when it can get pretty crowded.

Cabaret Parisien

Hotel Nacional, Calle O, esquina 21, Vedado (873 4701 ext 129). **Shows** 10pm daily (doors open 9pm). **Tickets** $35 ($60 with dinner). **Credit** MC, V. **Map** p250 B12.

This beautiful, well-designed room is where Sinatra once sang for his mafia mates and molls. The show these days features a dance revue with a live band. The main company dances every day exceot Monday. Not half as good as the Tropicana, but half the price. Reservations recommended.

Cabaret Tropicana

Calle 72 #4504, Línea del Ferrocarril, Marianao (267 1717/0110). **Open** 8.30pm-1am daily (show 10-11.45pm). **Tickets** $65-$85 (incl bottle of rum & snacks). **Credit** MC, V. **Map** p248 F3.

Tucked away in the western neighbourhood of Marianao, this is the grandest of Havana's cabarets, with an outdoor theatre seating up to 800 and a smaller indoor space used when it rains. Opened in 1931 and hailed as the biggest nightclub in the world, the Tropicana has in its time played host to the likes of Beny Moré, Nat King Cole, 'Lucky' Luciano, Ernest Hemingway and Jack Nicholson. A spectacular, almost hallucinatory, revue is performed by over 200 dancers and singers, plus one of the best orchestras on the island. Sure, it's touristy as hell, but at least it's well executed. Make up your own mind as to whether the show is tackily sexist or infectiously sexy; it's pictured below.

Copa Room

Hotel Riviera, Malecón, esquina Paseo, Vedado (334051 ext 119). **Show** 10pm Mon, Wed-Sun (doors open 9pm). **Tickets** $10 Mon, Wed, Thur; $25 Fri-Sun. Includes open bar after 11.30pm. **Credit** MC, V. **Map** p250 A9.

The Riviera was the last hotel built by mobster Meyer Lanksy before the arrival of Revolutionaries in Havana. Aptly, the room looks a lot like Vegas. It was formerly the renowned Palacio de la Salsa, fondly mentioned in many a salsa song. Regrettably the show isn't up to scratch these days. Still, some of Havana's finest groups perform at the weekends; Paulito FG is a regular.

Wednesday rumba at **Hurón Azul/UNEAC**. *See p160.*

Miramar & the western suburbs

Casa de la Música de Miramar

Calle 20, esquina 35, Playa (204 0447/202 6147). **Open** 10pm-3am daily. *Matineé* 4-8pm Tue-Sun. **Admission** $10-$20; matineé $5 (tourists), 40 pesos (Cubans). **Credit** MC, V. **Map** p249 D8.

Housed in a beautiful Miramar mansion, Casa de la Música hosts the foremost stars of Cuban *son* and salsa. It's loud, fun and worth every penny. If you want to mingle with the locals, save some cash and catch the latest salsa moves, take in a matinée.

Club Ipanema

Hotel Copacabana, Calle 1ra y 54, Miramar (204 1037 ext 6131). **Open** 10pm-2am Fri; 5-9pm, 10pm-2am Sat; 7pm-midnight Sun. **Admission** $3 (incl 1 drink). **No credit cards. Map** p248 B3.

This agreeable club is part of the Hotel Copacabana complex. It draws a large crowd on Saturdays and Sundays for Club de los Tembas, featuring music from the '60s and '70s, and is hugely popular with Cubans in their 30s and upwards.

Macumba Habana

Complejo La Giraldilla, Calle 222, esquina 37, La Coronela, La Lisa (330568-69). **Open** *Shows* 10pm-4am Tue-Sun. **Admission** $10 Tue, Wed, Sun; $15 Thur-Sat. **Credit** MC, V.

Macumba Habana is a long way from the centre of town but is a beautiful space with a good sound system and plenty of room to move. It often hosts major acts, which are the only reason for making the trek. If you dine before the show at one of the complex's restaurants (*see p110*) the cover charge is waived. Be sure to phone ahead and check the programme to make sure that you don't go all that way for a fashion show or karaoke.

La Maison

Calle 16 #701, entre Avenida 7ma y 9na, Playa (204 1543/46/48). **Open** 10pm-3am daily. *Show* 10pm-1.45am daily. *Piano bar* 10pm-6am daily. **Admission** *Show* $10. *Piano bar* $5 (incl $3 drinks). **Credit** MC, V. **Map** p249 B6.

It's best known for its fashion shows, but La Maison also has a small cabaret act and live music. The piano bar is new and features comedians and karaoke.

Piano Bar Diablo Tun Tun

Calle 35, esquina 20, Playa (204 0447/202 6147). **Open** 11pm-6am Tue-Sun. **Admission** $10. **No credit cards. Map** p249 C6.

This new club, adjacent to the Casa de la Música, is smaller and quieter, and features some very good ensembles. There's a small dancefloor but this venue is much more geared toward listening.

Río Club

Calle A, entre 3ra y 5ta (209 3389). **Open** 9pm-3am daily. **Admission** $20 per couple (incl $6 food/drinks). **No credit cards. Map** p250 A9.

Situated on a tranquil if undistinguished spot on the banks of the Río Almendares, this pleasant venue is housed in a lovely 1950s building with a seated capacity of about 200. It's a popular joint with Cubans, and good for dancing. The disco starts at 9pm, followed by a live band at midnight.

Salón Bolero

Complejo Dos Gardenias, Calle Avenida 7ma y 26, Miramar (204 2353 ext 116). **Open** 10pm-3am daily. **Admission** $5. **Credit** MC, V. **Map** p249 B5.

This is Havana's best venue for *bolero* and *filin*, where some of the genres' greatest names have played, and still do. The complex is named after the beautiful song 'Dos Gardenias', by the late, great *bolero* singer and composer Isolina Carrillo, and made famous by the Buena Vista Social Club. Don't miss this classic venue, which reveals a very emotional and influential part of Cuban music. Dress up.

Salón El Chévere

Calle 49C y 28A, Reparto Kohly (204 4990/504 5162). **Open** *Salón* 10pm-3am daily. *Snack bar* 11pm-3am Thur-Sun. **Admission** *Salón* $10-$20 (incl open bar). *Snack bar* $5 (incl 1 drink). **No credit cards**. **Map** p249 D6.

An open-air disco nestling between vine-clad rocks and the Río Almendares, in the middle of the Bosque de la Habana, with a wide range of classy acts. Prices are steep – up to $20, depending on the band. A popular dance spot for locals, especially in summer.

Salón Rosado Beny Moré

Avenida 41, entre 44 y 46, Playa (203 5322/203 1281). **Open** 9pm-2am Mon, Fri, Sat. *Matinée* 4-8pm Wed-Fri; 1-8pm Sun. **Admission** $10 (foreigners), 5-25 pesos (Cubans). **No credit cards**. **Map** p249 D5.

This was once *the* place to go to dance salsa. Musicians called it 'the barometer' because if you could get the crowd dancing and cheering here you would have success anywhere. But it was also rowdy and at times dangerous, so after renovations it recently reopened in a subdued fashion with only one regular event: the 'grandparents' afternoon', on Sundays. The best of the classic ensembles play music from the golden era of the 1930s and '40s, though there are plans to expand offerings to include occasional salsa and rock shows. There is (unbelievably) a separate entrance and dancefloor for foreigners, with prices ranging from $5 to $20, but once inside you are welcome to go down to the Cuban section and mix it up.

Teatro Karl Marx

Calle 1ra, esquina 10 (203 0801-5). **Tickets** phone for details. **Admission** $10-$20. **No credit cards**. **Map** p249 A6.

This theatre has the largest audience capacity in Cuba (8,000), and although its cavernous space is rather cold and unattractive, it is probably one of the best-equipped venues in town. It's currently run directly by the state for special political events, but from time to time it hosts pop and rock concerts, when big names such as Carlos Valera and Pablo Milanés play to enthusiastic crowds. Notably, the Manic Street Preachers played in 2001. Be prepared to go and join the mother of all queues if a big name is on.

Glossary

Bolero Born in Santiago, this is a romantic, heart-felt genre, usually sung by a soloist or harmony duo in the form of a ballad.

Filin An evolution of *bolero* and *trova*, *filin* (a transliteration of 'feeling') started in 1940s Havana as a Cuban response to American jazz singers such as Sinatra and Fitzgerald.

Nueva trova This often politicised genre came about after the Revolution in 1959, when the government took several *filinista* singer-songwriters under its wing. Pablo Milanés and Silvio Rodríguez are the most famous exponents of this folk-tinged and emotionally charged genre, usually guitar based.

Rumba An umbrella term for various forms of Afro-Cuban song and dance. *See also p66.*

Salsa Something of a catch-all term, this transnational genre is descended from Cuban *son* but borrows heavily from other styles, especially American jazz. Salsa dancing is also influenced by other Afro-Cuban forms, particularly rumba (for example, 'casino-style').

Son The mother of all Cuban music genres, *son* originated in the 19th century in the rural eastern provinces, a merger between Spanish verse-and-chorus forms and African vocals and percussion – the *clave* (two wooden sticks that beat syncopated rhythms), the *güiro* (a long, hollow piece of wood with ridges that are scraped with a hard stick), the maracas and the bongos. What really defines *son* are the off-beat bass (*marimbula*) and the *tres*, a small guitar-like instrument with three sets of double steel strings, used with or instead of guitar. Septet formats later added in a trumpet; the genre continues to evolve.

Timba A contemporary development of Cuban *son*-derived salsa that has become one of the dominant sounds on the island today. Driven by the uniquely Cuban way of whole-body dancing, it draws on Afro-Cuban folkloric dances and rhythms, especially rumba, and more modern genres such as rap and reggae.

Trova Originating with the singer-songwriters (troubadours, hence 'trova') of the eastern part of the island, who, in colonial times, would go from house to house singing ballads about love, women and the motherland. The genre developed from the guitar-and-singer structure of the Spanish-influenced *canción*.

Performing Arts

The show must go on.

One of the first things you notice in Havana is how people look at each other – it's a city of unflinching stares, where people execute 180-degree pirouettes just to get a back view of someone; a city of keen spectators and, by extension, performers.

But what of established performance arts? Havana has a fertile, if underfunded, theatre and dance scene. Every weekend the capital's venues put on a diverse programme of plays, ballet, contemporary dance, folk dance, opera, concerts and comedy to satisfy most tastes.

Experimental and controversial theatre has had a long history in Cuba: the comically satirical *teatro Bufo* was developed here, gaining such popularity that on 22 January 1869 Spanish soldiers opened fire on spectators at the Villanueve Theatre for draping revolutionary Cuban flags around the auditorium, while actors and spectators shouted 'Viva Cuba!' Many were killed or wounded, and the date has now become National Theatre Day.

THE REVOLUTION AND THE ARTS

The Revolution triggered a boom in new companies and playwriting. While only 40 Cuban plays were performed in Havana between 1952 and 1958, 281 were staged in 1967 alone. One of the Revolution's first acts was to create different departments for the various arts, including theatre, dance and, for the first time, folkloric dance. Various foreign companies visited the island, including the Peking Opera, and writers such as Jean-Paul Sartre, and it was during these post-Revolutionary years that the performing arts were popularised, with the best companies touring the island, playing in schools, factories and sugar mills.

Then came the *años gris* (grey years) of the 1970s, when state policy was influenced by the military. Many artists were discharged during these anti-gay, dogmatic times, and it was joked that the Ballet Nacional de Cuba could become an all-female company. The end of the decade brought a turning point, though: the Ministry of Culture was created, and the arts began a period of recuperation. Prizes were instituted, people were returned to their posts (though some refused) and new theatre groups were created. Some of the previous momentum had gone, however: many artists had left the island and, after years of stagnation, it was hard to regain audiences.

Post-Special Period, Abel Prieto, the current minister of culture (and possibly the only government official to wear a mullet), has done much to put the performing arts back on their feet. There's still a heap of bureaucracy to contend with if you want to start a new group, and salaries and funds are minimal. Some companies receive extra support from foreign embassies, state companies like Cristal and Partagás, or from foreign investors, though donations tend to be show-specific. From an artistic point of view, restrictions on foreign travel have limited artists' horizons. Still, aspiring thespians get well taught at the Instituto Superior de Arte, and touring abroad is largely permitted these days, even with the risks of defections it entails (though enterprises can be sunk under the sheer weight of bureaucracy necessary to organise a foreign tour).

There's no denying that the intrusion of the state and its ideology into the arts imposes restrictions. Live performing arts are given more artistic freedom than recorded media like film and literature, but artists must still exercise a degree of self-censorship. Some artists have found this intolerable and have emigrated to develop their careers elsewhere.

WHAT TO SEE

The drawback facing tourists is that some plays are text-heavy, extremely contextual and hard to penetrate. But even if your Spanish isn't that hot, there are several companies worth catching for the beauty and daring of their stagings. **Teatro Buendía** is one: Flora Lauten's productions are unusual and often controversial. Also worth seeing is **Teatro El Público**, directed by Carlos Díaz, who manages to emphasise the erotic in any text he touches. A more popular writer/director, placing emphasis on the trials and tribulations of daily life, is **Hector Quintero** (his work is often performed at the **Teatro Fausto**); Cubans love his bitter-sweet portrayals and, even if you can't understand it all, it's still a good dramatic experience. Another interesting director is ex-Teatro Buendía member **Carlos Celdrán** at **Argos Teatro**. Look out also for anything written by the late Virgilio Piñero and also Antón Arrufat, who is regarded by many as Cuba's finest living playwrights, and winner of the 2000 Premio Nacional de Literatura.

The converted Greek Orthodox church that **Teatro Buendía** calls home. *See p170.*

LET'S DANCE

Dance in Cuba really is something special. The island has one of the world's most famous ballet companies (Ballet Nacional de Cuba), under ballerina extraordinaire Alicia Alonso, and has a rich, unique history of popular dance thanks to the island's Spanish and African roots. This mix gave birth to numerous popular dances: the *son, contra-danza, danzón, rumba, son, timba, cha-cha-chá, mambo, mozambique* and *pilón*.

Post-Revolutionary ballet and modern dancers have focused on capturing national and ethnic values and incorporating them into international dance codes, and thus thankfully providing themselves with government funding. Ramiro Guerra's **Danza Contemporánea de Cuba**, which fuses modern, popular and folkloric styles, has been largely responsible for the development of modern dance in Cuba. Another key group is the **Conjunto Folklórico de Cuba**, which was inaugurated by the state in 1962, thus giving African culture official status as a cultural expression.

So, what's new? Unfortunately, nothing much. The state policy of supporting new companies seems to have fallen by the wayside recently, the only newly recognised ones being **Danza Voluminosa** (*see p174* **High-density dance**) and Johanes García's **Compañía Folklórica Cubana JJ**. The economic situation can partly take the blame for this, but the interminable bureaucracy is also a major factor.

TICKETS AND INFORMATION

Telephone numbers are provided for all the theatres and companies, but box office operators are unlikely to speak English, and you should not rely on telephone reservations. Few theatres have advance booking facilities, and no box office accepts credit cards. The best way to acquire reliable information and guaranteed seats is to go to the theatre beforehand. Tickets for visitors are usually paid for in US dollars.

Listings can be found in the free English-Spanish monthly guide *Cartelera* (*see p132*), or on *Hurón Azul* on Thursday evenings at 10.30pm. Radio Taíno also has a cultural listings show every day at 1.30pm; the daily *Granma* also has information. Failing these options, enquire in hotel tourist offices. For general information on performing arts in Cuba, visit the state-run www.cubaescena.cult.cu.

Major venues

Gran Teatro de la Habana

Paseo de Martí (Prado) #458, entre San Rafael y San Martin (San José), Centro Habana (861 3077). **Open** *Box office* 9.30am-5pm Tue-Sun. *Performances* 8.30pm Thur-Sat; 5pm Sun. **Tickets** $5-$10 performances; $2 tour of theatre. **Map** p251 D14.

Havana's most prestigious theatre – and its loveliest – was built in the early 19th century by the megalomaniac Spanish governor Tacón, and was duly named the Tacón Theatre. The theatre, which seated 4,000 people and had 150 boxes, opened in 1846 with a season of Verdi operas. Between 1907 and 1914, it was remodelled by Austrian architect Paul Belau, financed entirely by the funds of Galicians who had emigrated to Cuba. The completed neo-baroque building opened with a spectacular production of *Aïda*. It now has various performance spaces, most importantly the 1,500-seater Sala García Lorca. Performers here have included actresses Sarah Bernhardt and Eleonora Duse, tenor Enrico Caruso and musicians Arthur Rubinstein and Sergei Rachmaninov.

The Gran Teatro is the performance space for the Ballet Nacional de Cuba, the Ballet Español de la Habana and the Teatro Lírico Nacional de Cuba. It's also the base for the Centro Pro Arte Lírico, formed in 1995 to unite the companies producing opera and *zarzuelas* (a popular musical-style theatre dating back to 17th-century Spain but later adopted in Cuba). The 120-seat Sala Antonin Artaud stages experimental works, while the 509-seater Sala Alejo Carpentier has a more diverse bill.

Teatro Nacional de Cuba

Paseo, esquina 39, Plaza de la Revolución, Vedado (870 4655/878 5590/873 5713). **Open** *Box office* 10am-6pm Tue-Sun. *Performances* times vary. **Tickets** $5-$10; 5-10 pesos. **Map** p250 D10.

Opened in June 1959, this was the first major building to be inaugurated after the Revolution. The layout is similar to London's Royal Festival Hall, and its brutalist use of concrete and glass makes it similarly ugly from outside. On the positive side, some of Cuba's best theatre and dance are performed here.

The 2,500-seat Sala Avellaneda is an impersonal space, used for large-scale dance and theatre productions. The 800-seater Sala Covarrubias was named after the playwright Francisco Covarrubias; now hailed as the founder of Cuban national theatre, he introduced the Cuban vernacular to the stage. It's used by a range of theatre companies. The Noveno Piso (Ninth Floor) is a warehouse-like flexible space that has become a centre for avant-garde productions of theatre and dance. The Salón Piano Bar 'Delirio Habanero' (*see pp153-65*), overlooking the Plaza de la Revolución on the third floor, was spruced up in 2000. In the basement, Café Cantante Mi Habana (*see pp153-65*) – managed by the state music label EGREM – stages musical shows in the afternoons and evenings. In addition, the tropical vegetation surrounding the theatre is sometimes used for children's shows, and there are rehearsal and teaching facilities.

Note: performances are sometimes cancelled due to demonstrations and events on the Plaza de la Revolución in front of the theatre.

Other venues

Casa de la Comedia

Calle Justiz #18, entre Baratillo y Oficios, La Habana Vieja (863 9282). **Open** *Box office* 1hr before performance. **Tickets** $2; 2 pesos. **Map** p252 E15.

Comedy was first performed here in 1778, but the mission statement of the Casa de la Comedia these days is to promote new Cuban plays. Also known as the Salón Ensayo (Rehearsal Room), it is the base for the company El Taller, directed by Dima Rolando. Afro-Cuban rituals are often held on its patio, and stand-up comedy shows are staged some Saturdays and Sundays at 7pm. This venue is at its most dynamic during theatre festivals.

Centro Cultural Bertolt Brecht

Calle 13, esquina I, Vedado (832 9359). **Open** *Box office* 1hr before performance. *Performances* 8.30pm Fri, Sat; 5pm Sun. **Tickets** $5; 5 pesos. **Map** p250 B11.

Founded in 1968, this cultural centre houses a 300-seat café-theatre and a smaller 150-seat space. In general, it has a conventional, author-led programme. Most interesting of the companies that work here is Teatro Mío, directed by Miriam Lezcano, which often focuses on the work of playwright Alberto Pedro Torriente; look out for *Weekend in Bahía* and *Manteca*. Other resident theatre groups are: Teatro Caribeño, directed by

Havana laugh

If you're expecting Ali G or Graham Norton from Cuban comedy, you'll be disappointed. In general, comedy in Havana just isn't funny to visitors. To start with, there's the language problem: you'll need an excellent understanding of Spanish to understand Cuban comedy. There's also a complex set of subtextual references to grapple with, the most common being gestures indicating a beard to portray Fidel. Then there's the political incorrectness. Jokes are often sexist (all women are whores or unfaithful wives), racist (stupid, thieving *negritos*), or homophobic (mincing fags, *maricones*, and devilish dykes, *tortilleras*). Finally, there's the ideology issue. The authorities have a decidedly narrow sense of humour. When artist Angel Delgado pulled his pants down and defecated on a copy of state newspaper *Granma*, the audience may have laughed, but he landed up in jail for a year.

If decoded and tolerated, however, humour in Havana is sophisticated and provides a crucial safety valve for the real frustrations of daily life. For this reason perhaps Fidel invented the anti-Fidelista jokes himself. (Example: What do Fidel and a strapless bikini have in common? No one knows how they stay up and everyone wants them to fall down.)

The best live comedy, mime and clown shows can be found in the **Festival Nacional del Humor 'Aquelarre'** (*see p133*) and at the Teatro Mella, Teatro América and the Teatro Fausto. Look out for Iván Camejo, an excellent stand-up comedian, whose company Humoris Cause is one of the best-known and risqué in Cuba. Another leading light is Mariconchi, who dresses up as a busy body woman to direct his acerbic wit on to contemporary Cuban reality. He performs regularly at Teatro America's comedy shows on Thursdays.

Eugenio Hernández Espinosa; Pequeño Teatro de la Habana, directed by José Milian; Grupo Pálpito, directed by Ariel Bouza; Teatro del Círculo, directed by Pedro Ángel Vera; and Teatro D'Dos, directed by Julio César Ramírez. Children's shows are held here on Saturdays and Sundays at 10am, and there are regular comedy nights.

Gaia

Calle Brazil (Teniente Rey) #157, entre Cuba y Aguiar, La Habana Vieja (862 0401/www.gaiahavana.com). **Open** phone for details. **Tickets** phone for details. **Map** p252 E15.

Gaia is an arts centre set up in 2000 as a not-for-profit collaboration between Cuban and British artists. The centre offers theatre and dance performances, classes, courses, workshops and exhibitions of works by young artists. Gaia Teatro, the centre's resident theatre company, has produced some interesting works since its inception: *Las cenizas de Ruth* was director Esther Cardoso's radical reinterpretation of the biblical story. In collaboration with the British Council, Gaia staged *Cooking with Elvis* in the Teatro Nacional, the first new British play performed in Cuba since *An Inspector Calls* opened in 1947.

Sala Teatro Adolfo Llauradó

Calle 11, entre D y E, Vedado (832 5373). **Open** phone for details. **Tickets** $5. **Map** p250 B10.

The new 120-seat home of the 45-year-old troupe Teatro Estudio, directed by the charismatic actress and director Raquel Revuelta, best known for her starring roles in classic Cuban movies *Un hombre de éxito*, *Cecilia*, *Soy Cuba* and *Lucía*.

Teatro América

Avenida de Italia (Galiano) #253, entre Concordia y Neptuno (862 5416). **Open** *Box office* 10am-4pm Tue-Sun. *Performances* times vary. **Tickets** $6-$10; 8 pesos. **Map** p251 D14.

In the 1950s this art deco building was one of the country's most glamorous theatres, hosting performances by Latin stars like Beny Moré, María Félix and Pedro Vargas. It had a facelift in 2001, and now stages vaudeville and variety shows at weekends, and comedy at 8.30pm on Thursdays.

Teatro Fausto

Paseo de Martí (Prado) #201, esquina Colón, La Habana Vieja (863 1173). **Open** *Box office* 2-8pm Tue-Sun. *Performances* 8.30pm Fri; 10am (children's show), 8.30pm Sat; 10am (children's show), 5pm Sun. **Tickets** $5; 5 pesos. **Map** p252 D14.

Directed by Armando Suárez del Villar, the Fausto offers variety and comedy shows, as well as children's theatre. Look out for shows by the flamboyant writer, director and actor Hector Quintero (who also presents at the Mella; *see below*).

Teatro Hubert de Blanck

Calle Calzada #657, entre A y B, Vedado (830 1011/833 5962). **Open** *Box office* 3-6pm Wed-Fri; 3-5pm Sat, Sun. *Performances* 8.30pm Sat; 5pm Sun. **Tickets** $5; 5 pesos. **Map** p250 A9.

The former home of the 19th-century Belgian musician Hubert de Blanck, who founded Havana's first music conservatory, was remodelled as a theatre in 1955 by his family. The long-running theatre group by the same name stages predominantly classics of the international theatrical canon, under the management of Orieta Medina. Talented director Bertha Martinez recently worked with the company on Lorca's *La zapatera prodigiosa*. The theatre is also the production house for Abelardo Estorino, Cuba's most prolifically performed living playwright.

Teatro Mella

Línea #657, entre A y B, Vedado (830 4987/tmella@cubarte.cult.cu). **Open** *Box office* 2hrs before performance. **Tickets** $5-$10. **Map** p250 A9.

Refurbished in 2000, this 1,500-seat theatre has a Gaudí-esque feel, and the interior comes complete with meringue-shaped balcony wrapping around the auditorium. It's used for dance, folklore (home to the Conjunto Folklórico Nacional de Cuba; *see p172*), circus and variety shows, and for seasons of comedy and dance.

Teatro Nacional de Guiñol

Calle M, entre 17 y 19, Vedado (832 6262). **Open** *Box office* 1hr before performance. *Performances* 3pm Fri; 5pm Sat; 10.30am, 5pm Sun. **Tickets** $3 adults; $2 children. **Map** p250 B11.

Due to reopen in early 2004 after major renovations, this is home to Cuba's leading children's theatre and puppetry company. As well as performing in this space, it presents shows in public squares and elsewhere in the country. Look out for performances of *El caballero de la mano de fuego* written by Javier Villafañe, and *La caperucita*, directed by Armando Morales.

Teatro El Sótano

Calle K, entre 25 y 27, Vedado (832 0630). **Open** *Box office* 5-8.30pm Fri, Sat; 3-5pm Sun. *Performances* times vary. **Tickets** $5; 5 pesos. **Map** p250 C11.

Home to the company Teatro Rita Montaner (named after one of the greatest Cuban divas of the 1950s), whose repertoire includes work by Valle-Inclán. Comedy shows take place on Thursday evenings.

Teatro Trianón

Línea #315, entre Paseo y A, Vedado (830 9648). **Open** *Box office* from 4.30pm Thur; from 7pm Fri, Sat; from 3.30pm Sun. *Performances* 8.30pm Fri, Sat; 5pm Sun. **Tickets** $5; 5 pesos. **Map** p250 B9.

The Trianón is a cinema during the week, and home to the company Teatro el Público (*see p171*), directed by Carlos Díaz, at the weekend. The venue doesn't have optimal conditions to host theatre at present but much-needed improvements are in the pipeline.

Theatre companies

Havana's principal theatre companies are listed below; note that others are mentioned under their relevant performance venues.

Argos Teatro

Calle Ayestarán 507A, esquina 20 de Mayo, Plaza de la Revolución, Vedado (information 878 1883/5551/www.cniae.cult.cu/Argos_Teatro). **Map** p250 E10.

Argos was formed in 1996 by Buendía graduate Carlos Celdrán with the intention of making dynamic theatre out of old stories. Celdrán is arguably the most exciting young director working in Cuba, and is widely considered to be the leader of Cuba's theatrical avant-garde. One of Argos's recent productions was *Roberto Zucco*, a disturbing portrait of a serial killer by Bernard-Marie Koltés. Celdrán's company has produced versions of August Strindberg's *Miss Julie*, a critically acclaimed version of Brecht's *Baal* and *La pequeña Oresteia*, based jointly on Euripides' *Oresteia* and Sartre's *Flies*. Look out for his explosive leading actress, Zulema Clares. Performances are at the former masonic lodge where the company rehearses, although it occasionally performs in the Noveno Piso at the Teatro Nacional.

El Ciervo Encantado

Information: Instituto Superior de Artes (ISA), Calle 120 #1110, entre 9 y 11, Miramar (208 8075). **Tickets** free.

Founded in 1996, the Enchanted Deer is directed by Buendía graduate Nelda Castillo. A gutsy challenger of the status quo, she seeks to create an exchange between actor and spectator. Highlights have been an expressionistic production of *Pájaros en la playa*, adapted from the eponymous novel by Severo Sarduy, and her witty use of cabaret and Cuban gestures in *¿De dónde son los cantantes?*, based on texts by Sarduy and the *enfant terrible* of Cuban letters, Guillermo Cabrera Infante. The company performs at the Facultad de Artes Plásticas at the ISA.

Estudio Teatral Vivarta

Information: Teatro Sótano, Calle K, entre 25 y 27, Vedado (832 0630). **Map** p250 C11.

Directed by upcoming actress Antonia Fernández, another daughter of the Buendía company, this small company received state backing in 2002. Fernández's *Muerte de amor en Verona* is an amusing adaptation of *Romeo and Juliet* in which Romeo is a dispossessed man on the fringes of society, played by a diminutive actor. This young group doesn't have its own space and relies on the goodwill of other, more established, groups. Recent productions have taken place in the Teatro Sótano.

Teatro Buendía

Calle 39, entre Loma y Bellavista, Nuevo Vedado (881 6689). **Open** *Box office* 2hrs before performances. *Performances* phone for details. **Tickets** call for details. **Map** p249 D8.

Buendía is probably the best known – internationally, at least – of Cuba's theatre companies. Flora Lauten, its director, is the fairy godmother of Cuban theatre; everything she touches turns to dramatic metaphor. Lauten, who was the last Miss Cuba before the Revolution, formed Buendía in 1985. It went on to become the most innovative, courageous and internationally successful Cuban theatre company of the 1990s. Committed to finding an autonomous voice, the company has benefited from contact with international masters such as Peter Brook, Enrique Buenaventura, Jerzy Grotowski, Santiago García and Eugenio Barba. The Buendía production of *Innocent Eréndira*, Gabriel García Márquez's tale of prostitution and rebellion, toured the world for five years, to great acclaim. Its version of *The Bacchae* was a sensual, polysemic production, winning the Critics' Prize of

Gran Teatro de la Habana. *See p167.*

2001 in Cuba. The company performs in a Greek Orthodox church that the actors converted themselves. The audience sits on hard, steeply raked benches – bring a cushion.

Teatro de la Luna

Teatro Nacional, Paseo, esquina Avenida Céspedes, Plaza de la Revolución (information 879 6011/870 4655/878 5590). **Map** p250 D10.

Works by Teatro de la Luna have strong sociopolitical references and require excellent Spanish to understand. The company is led by versatile young director, choreographer and actor Raúl Martín. A recent production, *El enano en la botella* by Abilio Estévez, explored the theme of resignation with delicate irony and lyrical restraint. Also in the company's repertory are Martín's version of Pirandello's *Six Characters in Search of an Author*, his adaptation of Virgilio Piñera's *Los siervos* and *Últimos días de una casa*, a monologue based on a poem by Dulce María Loynaz. The company tends to perform in the Teatro Nacional.

Teatro El Público

Teatro Trianón, Línea #315, entre Paseo y A, Vedado (830 9648). **Open** *Box office* 2hrs before performance. *Performances* times vary. **Tickets** $5; 5 pesos. **Map** p250 B9.

The company is directed by Carlos Díaz, who presides over an active repertory including gay-taboo-busting *wunderkind* poet Norge Espinosa's *Icaro* and international classics such as Fernando de Rojas's *La Celestina* and Tennessee Williams' *Glass Menagerie*. Carlos Díaz's stagings tend to be artistically controversial: the female lead in *The Crucible* was played by a man and there was plenty of over-the-top nudity in *La Celestina*.

Dance companies

Así Somos

Calle A #310, apto 7B, entre 3ra & 3raA, Miramar (203 4276/lorna@cubarte.cult.cu). **Map** p249 A7.

Lorna Burdsall – founder of Así Somos – was born in the US and trained at the Julliard in New York under Alfredo Corvino, Merce Cunningham, Martha Graham and Anthony Tudor. She fell for a Cuban Bacardí executive in New York and in 1955 moved back with him to Havana. After the Revolution, she was a founding member of Danza Nacional (now Danza Contemporánea) and helped introduce new techniques into Cuban modern dance, alongside Ramiro Guerra. In 1981 she founded Así Somos with a group of graduates from the National School of Arts.

Lorna is best described as an artistic magpie, assembling her work out of theatre, music, dance, masks and contemporary folklore. She uses flashlights for lighting, car-window cleaning cloths for costumes, Soviet army-surplus silk parachutes for backcloths, poetry by Lorca and José Martí, and musical sources ranging from Astor Piazzola to Chopin. Her work has been performed in all of Havana's theatres, and internationally too. These days, though, she prefers to stage performances in her living room, which fits 25 people.

Ballet Español de Cuba

Gran Teatro de la Habana, Paseo de Martí (Prado) #458, entre San Rafael y San Martin (San José), Centro Habana (861 3076/eduveiti@cubarte.cult.cu). **Map** p251 D14.

Founded in 1987 by Alicia Alonso, with the name Conjunto de Danza Española, direction of this Spanish dance company was subsequently assumed by Alonso's protégé, Eduardo Veitía. The company's main styles are flamenco and the *escuela bolera* (also known as the *baile de palillos*, dating back to the 18th century, and combining popular Andalusian dances with ballet). The company has worked with important figures in Spanish dance, such as Trini Borrul, Goyo Montero and Emilio Sagi. Recent premières have included *El fantasma*, inspired by Gaston Leroux's *The Phantom of the Opera*, and *Danzando sueños*, a tribute to Cuba's most renowned painter Wilfredo Lam (1902-82). Ballet Español tends to perform at the Gran Teatro de la Habana.

Ballet Nacional de Cuba

Calle Calzada #510, entre D & E, Vedado (552952/552953/www.balletcuba.cu). **Map** p250 A10.

A highlight of any trip to Havana is a performance by the Ballet Nacional de Cuba. The company's fusion of tropical passion, extraordinary physical power and Soviet discipline has made it as technically accomplished as any other. Ballet in Cuba was an entirely European notion until the mid 20th century. But in 1948 Cuban ballerina Alicia Alonso teamed up with her brother and brother-in-law to open a company in Havana, the Ballet Alicia Alonso, which in 1961 became the Ballet Nacional de Cuba. Most celebrated for her role as Giselle, Alicia Alonso left her mark in many of the great theatres of the world. She is also Cuba's most important choreographer to date. In late 2003 the Ballet Nacional had a whopping 89 works in repertory, of which 12 were choreographed by Alicia. Recent productions have suggested a deterioration in standards, however: *Viaje a la luna* and *Tula* were disappointing. Other choreographers have worked with the Ballet Nacional: look out for the smouldering *Tierra y luna* choreographed by Spaniard María Rovira, and inspired by Lorca's poetry.

The interior of the Gran Teatro competes with the world's great ballet stages, although the orchestra pit resembles the *Marie Celeste* because a decision has been made to cut costs by using recorded music for ballet. Ballet performances are the only ones that start punctually in Cuba, so turn up on time. It's also possible to watch rehearsals during the week.

Codanza

Calle Fomento #202, entre Arias y Agramonte, 8010, Holguín (information 2442234/fax 244 2517/sethlg@tauronet.cult.cu).

Catch this Holguín-based company if you can. Founded in 1992 and directed by Marisel Godoy, it uses a ballet base to build a style that mixes popular rhythms with theatre and comedy. It toured Spain in 2000, and performs during dance festivals in Havana.

Compañía de la Danza Narciso Medina

Cine Teatro Favorito, Calle Padre Varela (Belascoaín), esquina Peñalver, Centro Habana (878 2650). **Performances** 3pm Sat, Sun. **Tickets** $2-$4. **Map** p250 E12.

Founded in 1993 by Narciso Medina, this contemporary dance group includes oriental and martial arts dance and movement in its performance style. The company has toured in the US, France and Japan, where it received the Grand Prix at Saitama for its best-known work, *Metamórfosis*. The company's most recent show, *Génesis para un carnaval*, was ill-received by local critics.

Compañía Folklórica Cubana JJ

Information: 313467/bradman@infomed.sld.cu.

This company was founded by Johanes García, once the lead dancer of the Conjunto Folklórico Nacional de Cuba. It stages anything from large-scale productions to duets, and seeks to reflect Cuba's various cultural influences. No fixed performance space.

Conjunto Folklórico Nacional de Cuba

Calle 4 #103, entre Calzada y 5ta, Vedado (830 3939/3060/833 4560/folkcuba@cubarte.cult.cu). **Open** *Box office* 2pm onwards on performance days. *Performances* 3pm Sat. **Tickets** $5; 5 pesos. **Map** p250 A9.

The Conjunto is one of Cuba's largest (over 100 performers) and best-known dance companies, and has toured to London, Lyon and Greece in the past few years. Founded in 1962, its current director, Juan García Fernández, is a former dancer with the company. Co-director (and founding member) Rogelio Martínez is a noted Afro-Cuban academic and writer/poet, responsible for much of the dramaturgy. The CNC is the flagship of the Revolution's missionary strategy to preserve the racial and traditional roots of Afro-Cuban culture. The company has a repertory of over 70 productions, representing the full spectrum of Afro-Cuban dance and music, primarily the dances representing the Yoruba deities, as well as dances of Haitian origin and the full range of Cuban social and popular dances. It usually performs at Teatro Mella, with occasional outdoor spectaculars. Rumba is played every Saturday at 2.30pm ($5) in El Gran Palenque, the courtyard attached to the company's home.

DanzAbierta

Information: c/o Conjunto Folklórico de Cuba, Calle 4 #103, entre Calzada y 5ta, Vedado (information 830 3939/3060/833 4560/folkcuba@cubarte.cult.cu). **Map** p250 A9.

DanzAbierta (meaning 'open dance') is probably Cuba's foremost contemporary dance ensemble, as far as international exposure goes in any case. Director Marianela Boan, former dancer/choreographer with Danza Contemporánea, has evolved as Cuba's answer to postmodernism in dance theatre. She innovatively mixes the gestures of everyday life with social and political comment and techniques. Emerging as a counterpoint to mainstream contemporary dance in the 1980s, Boan was one of the main leaders of a new avant-garde, forming her own company in 1988, pioneering investigations into gesture, corporeality and Cubanness to create what she called 'contaminated dance' – a hybrid form integrating dance, song, acting and dramaturgical rigour. DanzAbierta's first productions revealed scrupulous research, a wide

Remember my name

Carlos Acosta is Cuba's very own Ronaldo. Critics from St Petersburg to New York, London to Havana, have hailed him as the greatest ballet dancer performing today.

Something of an icon at home, Acosta is an intriguing cultural phenomenon. He is one of the world's first black ballet superstars; that says a lot even in racially diverse Havana, where there are still very few black faces in the Ballet Nacional's lines of white swans. He is also the first Latin American ballet superstar since Alicia Alonso. But most importantly, he is a phenomenal dancer: his jumps are stratospheric; his spinning-top pirouettes slow sensually to total stillness; and he effortlessly knots and un-knots his legs mid-leap. The combination of his athletic upper body and the falcon-like grace of his movements have justifiably earned him comparisons with his two heroes, Rudolph Nureyev and Mikhail Baryshnikov.

Acosta's life-story is a classic rags-to-riches tale. Born in 1973, the son of a truck driver and the youngest of 11 children (most of them with different mothers), Acosta grew up in Los Pinos, a poor neighbourhood in southern Havana. Carlos's father sent him to ballet school at the age of nine, but Acosta played truant much so that the school expelled him – twice. At the age of 13, after seeing the Ballet Nacional perform for the first time, he was inspired. He studied hard at a dance school in Pinar del Río and, aged 15, returned to the Escuela Nacional de Danza, leapfrogging the corps de ballet, as a principal. Three years later he joined the prestigious Ballet Nacional de Cuba, and they packed him straight off to Italy to gain experience with the Turin Ballet.

Soon after winning the prestigious 1990 Prix de Lausanne, the English National Ballet contracted him, and his career seemed to be poised for take-off. But London weather and society jarred with Carlos, who soon became nostalgic for Cuba. After years of to-ing and fro-ing, he currently divides his dancing time between the Royal Ballet in London, the American Ballet Theatre in New York and Havana.

Having conquered all the great classical roles, Acosta choreographed his first show, *Tocororo* (pictured), in 2003. It premièred in front of Fidel Castro in the Gran Teatro and went on to play at Sadler's Wells in London. Named after Cuba's national bird, the production loosely tells Acosta's own life story, mixing an array of forms – Afro-Cuban dance, musical theatre, ballet, *teatro Bufo*, breakdance, rumba and contemporary dance. Critics in Britain and Havana were as complimentary about Acosta's lead performance as they were damning of his choreography.

Acosta says his heart is in Cuba, where his parents and siblings still live. He has built on Alicia Alonso's legacy in helping to destroy *machista* prejudices about ballet dancers, raising their status close to that of footballers in other Latin American countries. Acosta returns regularly to Cuba to perform, usually in the Gran Teatro, in collaboration with Danza Contemporánea (*see p174*). He is writing an autobiography that he hopes will inspire a new generation of Cuban dancers. He has also spoken of his desire to set up his own company in Havana – so, watch this space.

High-density dance

Remember Mr Creosote from Monty Python's *Meaning of Life*? Now imagine him in a tutu and ballet slippers, dancing on pointes. That's the unique selling point of **Danza Voluminosa**: the dancers are all unashamedly fat.

The company's mission is to create a radically unconventional new aesthetic that plays on the way the dancers' physical volume moves in space. The company's use of corpulence smashes the conventions of beauty that dance has traditionally imposed on performers' physiques. Portly as porpoises, performers use moves and techniques from classical dance. Danza Voluminosa as performed in the Gran Teatro and the Teatro Mella, but its usual performance spaces are squares, museum courtyards and the streets of Old Havana. Disposing of the need for traditional stages, the company also eschews fixed scripts in favour of spontaneous improvisation.

The brainchild and star of the company is trained classical dancer Juan Miguel Más, weighing in at 16 stone (101 kilograms). After ten years working in contemporary dance, he founded Danza Voluminosa in 1996. The average weight of the troupe's performers is 15.5 stone (98 kilograms), and the heaviest woman is 24 stone (152 kilograms). Applicants don't need prior dance experience. The only criteria for joining the company, Más says, are that 'they must be fat and prepared to express themselves through movement'. The performers' weight does impose certain restrictions, though. They avoid high jumps because of possible damage to the heel, and lifts must be performed from the middle of the body in a way distinct from traditional lifts. Instead, dancers work from the ground, using a different centre of gravity, and making full use of the arms to draw shapes in the air.

field of cultural reference and an effusively free style. Her best pieces in recent years have been *Chorus perpetuum*, which opened to critical acclaim in 2003 and has toured extensively; *El pez de la torre nada en el asfalto*, a witty reflection on the absurdities of the Special Period; and *El árbol y el camino*, in which five naked dancers use coat-hangers like branches to portray a mythical tree, which was presented at the 2001 Edinburgh Festival fringe.

Danza Combinatoria

Calle Consulado #302, esquina Virtudes, Centro Habana (information 862 8255/878 6765/ rcrw@cubarte.cult.cu). **Map** p251 D14.

Founded in 1971, this small but well-established company takes a sensual, sculptural form of surrealism to the stage. Director Rosario Cárdenas applies mathematical principles to dance – permutation, combination and variation. She also applies the principles of painting composition, and borrows from Eugenio Barba's work and occasionally from the Abakuá religion. Cárdenas's best work to date is *María Viván*, based on a poem by Virgilio Piñera. *Dador* is also inspired by poetry, that of José Lezama Lima; it toured Spain in 2003. Look out for new show *Oroborus*.

Danza Contemporánea de Cuba

Information: Teatro Nacional, Paseo, esquina 39, Plaza de la Revolución, Vedado (879 2728/6410). **Map** p250 D10.

The powerhouse of Cuban contemporary dance – directed by former dancer Miguel Iglesias – has been losing steam over the last few years. Nevertheless, this company remains a must-see for modern dance fans. Among its more recent shows are *El soñador* by Jorge Abril and *Compás* by the Dutch choreographer Jan Linkens. The company was founded in 1959 by Ramiro Guerra, who initiated the evolution of a particularly Cuban approach to contemporary dance, drawing heavily on Afro-Cuban dance movement and rhythm, as well as popular Cuban dance forms. No doubt due to Cuba's isolation and the lack of international touring opportunities, the company's work isn't always innovative, but what it lacks in choreographic interest it makes up for in sheer energy, with strong dancers (Carlos Acosta, for example; *see p173*),

Más cites Colombian painter and sculptor Fernando Botero, famous for his big-bellied portraits, as a major influence on his work. Más has directed and taken the transvestite lead in a production of *¿Fedra?*, an acid-humoured parody of *Phaedra*, the Greek tragedy, in which all the characters destroy each other out of destiny or passion. The highlights of the show, which was produced on a budget of $1,000, are a *Full Monty*-style striptease by Hippolytus, played by opera singer E Valenti Figueredo. The production was jointly choreographed by Más and Ramiro Guerra, and performed at the Teatro Mella to huge audiences. 'The laughter we give is like what Charlie Chaplin did,' Valenti says. 'You laugh at first, and then you see the serious intention and the professional work behind it.'
For more information on Danza Voluminosa, call 879 6410.

combining classical ballet with Cuban popular dance and international contemporary influences. Lidice Nuñez is the company's most exciting ambassador of cosmopolitan choreography, making use of space and gesture to explore the traumatic experience of being young in an old system. Performances are in the Gran Teatro, and the Nacional and Mella theatres.

Danza Teatro Retazos

Calle 82 #1317, esquina 15, Miramar (204 9986/ retazos@cubarte.cult.cu). **Map** p248 D2.
Founded in 1987, Retazos is led by Ecuadorean choreographer Isabel Bustos, who creates a sensual, disciplined chaos of unusual physicalities. She describes her work as 'intimist', that is, founded on an aesthetic of intimacy and emotion. Bustos makes imaginative choices of performance spaces and of music.

Festivals

April is a good month for performing arts festivals. The annual week-long street dance festival **La Habana Vieja: Ciudad en Movimiento** sees over 500 artists from various countries perform in inner courtyards of colonial mansions, such as the Casa Guayasamin and the Casa Bolívar, or in the Plaza Vieja. Also starting in April is the festival **Los Días de la Danza** (*see p133*); the **Festival de Academias de Ballet**, with shows by students at the international ballet school; and the **Festival Elsinore**, with theatre and dance productions by students from the ISA (*see p85*).

The **Festival de Teatro de la Habana** (*see p134*) takes place in odd-numbered years in September, and the **Festival Internacional de Ballet** (*see p136*) in even-numbered years from the end of October. **Mayo Teatro** is a new festival of Latin American drama that takes place in May in even-numbered years, organised the Casa de las Américas. **CubaDanza** (*see p134*) is a festival of modern dance classes, workshops and performances organised by Danza Contemporánea every even-numbered year in January and August.

Sport & Fitness

Impressive competitive clout in forte fields but run-down public facilities.

Sport is a huge focus of national pride and passion for Cubans, but while western sports stars have seen their salaries rise to the stratosphere, Cuba quixotically defends the principle of amateurism. State money has been poured into sport over the years, creating an impressive level of participation and achievement – and showing the US that this small thorn in its side is a force to be reckoned with.

Since the Revolution, all sport in Cuba has been government supported, as well as exclusively amateur. The National Institute for Sport and Recreation (INDER) was formed in 1961 and today some 1.2 million Cubans practise sport. In total, there are almost 40 accredited disciplines, each with a governing federation affiliated to INDER.

POLITICAL UNDERCURRENTS

The Cold War and US-Cuban relations have often taken a toll on Cuba's participation in international sporting events. In the 1984 Olympics, held in the US, Cuba didn't send any participants as a demonstration of its solidarity with Eastern European teams, who pulled out on account of security fears. Cuba boycotted the 1988 Olympics because they were held in Seoul instead of jointly in North and South Korea. On a more positive note, 1999 saw a historic match in Cuba between the Baltimore Orioles baseball team and the Cuban national team – the first time a major league US baseball team had competed in Cuba. Many hope that such sports encounters can slowly bring the two countries closer.

Defection is a big problem for Cuban sport. Sportsmen and women are frequently lured abroad, where celebrity and wads of cash await. Baseball pitchers René Arocha, José Contreras and Osvaldo 'El Duque' Hernández, cyclist Michel Pedroso and swimmer Gunter Rodríguez are among the more famous cases. And in 2001 there was a mass defection by (most of) the men's national volleyball team.

LOOKING TO THE FUTURE

After withdrawing from the Central American and Caribbean Games in El Salvador, nominally on grounds of security (though some say it was lack of funds), the government decided to stage the first **Cuban Olympiad** in November 2002. Conceived to provide the island's athletes with a competitive stage at home, thousands flocked to stadiums in six provinces.

The second Cuban Olympiad is slated for April 2004, in advance of the Olympic Games of Athens 2004. Cuba will be entering the Olympics with a fresh army of young athletes and players, some of them still in their teenage years, but eager to prove they can make it. Cubans hope the 2003 Pan-American Games in Santo Domingo will be a taste of things to come: the national team was placed second of 42 nations in the final medal table – not bad when you consider the size and resources of some of the competition.

INFORMATION

For official information about a particular sport, contact the following federations: **athletics** (952101/972101); **baseball** (8781682/8786882); **basketball** (577156); **boxing** (577047); **cycling** (953776); **judo** (411732); **tae kwon do** (545000-4 ext 184); **tennis** (972121); **volleyball** (445394/445392); **wrestling** (577344). You can also contact the press and information department of INDER on 577144. **Cubadeportes** (Calle 20 #705, entre 7 y 9, Miramar, 204 0947/545021/sports programme 545026) publishes an annual list of sporting events, but it isn't geared to taking queries from tourists. The website www.cubasports.com/ has general information and history about sports in Cuba.

Spectator sports

For general information and help with obtaining tickets for events, the tourist desks or PR (*relaciones públicas*) department of major hotels are useful places to start. The best sources of information are *Juventud Rebelde* (www.jrebelde.cubaweb.cu) and *Granma* (www.granma.cubaweb.cu). INDER (www.inder.co.cu) administers a website with a yearly schedule of events, athletes' profiles and the online paper *Jit*. You can also try the sports pages of www.radiococo.cu and www.radiorebelde.co.cu. Foreigners normally pay for tickets in dollars (rather than pesos) at a one-to-one rate (still remarkably cheap). No credit cards are accepted.

Baseball

Forget the usual scene: here there are no luxury boxes, no mammoth electronic scoreboards and no plastic-grass outfields. And definitely no spoiled-rotten million-dollar ballplayers. A visit to a Cuban ballpark during the Serie

Nacional de Béisbol or for the post-season series in April and May is a relaxing escape into baseball's innocent past.

The Serie Nacional season lasts from late October until May, during which 16 teams play 90 league matches followed by the play-offs. Matches usually take place all over Cuba on Tuesday, Wednesday, Thursday and Saturday at 8.30pm and Sunday at 1.30pm, with a week's break for New Year and another before the All Star game between East and West in the middle of the season. During the season, check the back pages of *Granma* or ask at your hotel for details of matches. Due to the sheer number of games, tickets are usually easy to get hold of either directly from the stadium or by asking your hotel tour desk. *See also p181* **The Blues**.

Estadio Latinoamericano

Calle Pedro Perez #302, entre Patria y Sarabia, Cerro (870 6526-9/8175). **Games** 8.30pm Tue-Thur, Sat; 1.30pm Sun. **Tickets** $3 boxes, $1 stands. **Map** p250 F10.

Basketball

The national basketball league (Liga Superior de Baloncesto – LSB) runs from September to November and consists of just four teams. The Havana team is the Capitalinos; they can be seen in action at the **Coliseo de la Ciudad Deportiva** and the **Sala Polivalente Ramón Fonst**. Although basketball doesn't inspire the same mass following as baseball, the games can be intensely fought and great fun to watch. In 1999 several of Cuba's best male basketball players defected, and it may take several years for the sport to recover. The women's team, meanwhile, is doing substantially better, winning gold in the 2003 Pan-American Games.

Coliseo de la Ciudad Deportiva

Vía Blanca, esquina Avenida Boyeros (545000/ boxing department 577047). **Open** 8am-5pm Mon-Fri. **Tickets** $1-$3. **Map** p249 F7.

Sala Polivalente Ramón Fonst

Avenida de la Independencia, entre Bruzón y 19 de Mayo, Plaza de la Revolución, Vedado (820000/881 4196). **Games** 8.30pm Mon-Sat; 3pm Sun. **Tickets** $1. **Map** p250 D10.

Esquina caliente

A unique aspect of Cuban baseball culture is the '*esquina caliente*' (literally 'hot corner'). In the Parque Central in Old Havana (or at the corner of 23 and 12 in Vedado), you will see a group of men of all ages arguing and gesticulating excitedly. From a distance it's easy to confuse this commotion with a social disturbance. However, when you get closer, you will discover that it's simply Cuban baseball fanatics gathering to argue fervently about their sport, the recent performance of their favourite teams and the inside scoop on the players. Often several people are yelling at the same time, puffing up their chests and trying to tower over their debating opponents, creating a cacophony of voices and waving arms. Never does it come to blows, though. Rather, it's testament to the place that baseball holds in the hearts of Cubans.

Boxing

Cuba has proved to be a fertile ground for producing great boxers, both during the professional years before 1962 and since the adoption of amateur rules thereafter. Cuba has been the overall champion of the boxing competition at every Olympic Games since Munich in 1972 (with the exception of Montreal '76). Its most recent of many crowns was at the Pan-American Games 2003. The amateur nature of the sport in Cuba means that, despite their brilliance, Cuban boxers are not well known on the international stage. Within Cuba, however, former and current stars of the ring, such as Kid Chocolate, Maikro Romero and Teofilo Stevenson are national heroes. Boxers to look out for these days are Mario Kindelan, Yudel Johnson and Guillermo Rigondeaux. The Girardo Córdova Cardín International Tournament is Cuba's most prestigious competition, held in a different Cuban city every April or May.

In Havana, the **Sala Polivalente 'Kid Chocolate'**, a multipurpose sports facility opposite the Capitolio, stages local and national boxing matches. International championships are held at the much bigger **Coliseo de la Ciudad Deportiva** (*see above*). For a glimpse behind the scenes, you can see budding Stevensons training and fighting at the **Arena Trejo**, Cuba's oldest boxing gym and arena (you may be charged a couple of dollars).

Arena Trejo

Calle Cuba #815, entre Merced y Leonor Pérez (Paula), La Habana Vieja (862 0266). **Open** 8am-5pm Mon-Fri. **Tickets** $1. **Map** p252 F15.

Sala Polivalente 'Kid Chocolate'

Paseo de Martí (Prado), entre San Martín y Brasil, Centro Habana (862 8634/863 5834). **Open** varies. **Tickets** $1. **Map** p252 E14.

Cycling

The **Velodromo Reinaldo Paseiro** is a purpose-built facility in eastern Havana constructed for the Pan-American Games in 1991. Major events include the **Vuelta de Cuba** (Tour of Cuba) every February; call the cycling federation (*see pp214-7*) or the velodrome for events.

Velodromo Reinaldo Paseiro

Avenida Monumental km4.5, Villa Panamericana, Habana del Este (information 953776). **Open** 8am-6pm Mon-Fri. **Tickets** usually $1.

Football

Football, the most universal of sports, isn't a strong discipline in Cuba. In the past two years the quality of Cuban football has risen, though it's still light years away from the standard of the top South American teams, and has never made it past the preliminary qualifying matches of the World Cup. This lack of success is frustrating for a demanding Cuban public, eager to see their 11 do better. Nevertheless, fans follow every major international tournament on TV, regardless of whether the national team is taking part. In an effort to improve the quality of football on the island, the Cuban federation has hired a Peruvian coach, and for the first time ever the team qualified for the quarter finals at the Golden Cup 2003 in the US.

The Havana team, Ciudad Habana, nicknamed Los Rojos ('the Reds'), have improved over the years and have reached the national semifinals and finals in the past three seasons. Games are held at the **Estadio Pedro Marrero**.

Estadio Pedro Marrero

Avenida 41 #4409, Marianao (203 4698). **Matches** 3pm Sat, Sun. **Tickets** 1 peso.

Martial arts

Cuba has achieved impressive results in the martial arts, taking home six judo medals, five wrestling medals and two tae kwon do medals from the Sydney Olympic Games in 2000.

In Havana, you can watch martial arts at the **Sala Polivalente 'Kid Chocolate'** or the **Sala Polivalente Ramón Fonst** (for both, *see p177*). Some recent events, though, have taken place at the **Sala San Isidro** in Old Havana. Several Chinese societies have started to include martial arts events and sessions among their activities. For more information, visit the **Wucho Centre** in Chinatown (Calle Manriquez #507, entre Zanja y Dragones, Centro Habana).

Sala San Isidro

Calle San Isidro, La Habana Vieja (861 7242). **Open** 8am-6pm Mon-Fri. **Tickets** $1. **Map** p252 F14/15.

Rodeo

Rodeos are held twice a month on Sundays at the stadium in **Parque Lenin** (*see p49* **The beautiful south**). There are also fairs featuring rodeo action in the park in July, November and February. The lively **Feria Agropecuaria de Boyeros** (Boyero Cattle Fair), very close to Havana's José Martí Airport, holds rodeos once a month.

Feria Agropecuaria

Avenida de la Independencia (Rancho Boyeros) #31108, Boyeros (683 4536). **Open** 10am-10pm daily. **Admission** $5. **Tickets** vary.

Parque Lenin

Calle 100, esquina Cortina de la Presa, Arroyo Naranjo (443026). **Open** *Winter* 9am-5.30pm Wed-Sun. *Summer* 9am-5.30pm Tue-Sun. **Tickets** vary.

Estadio Panamericano. *See p181.*

Volleyball

Volleyball was quick to develop in Cuba. The national male team rose from nowhere to win the bronze medal at the Olympic Games in Montreal in 1976, while the women's team were crowned world champions two years later, and have enjoyed continued international success ever since. Called Las Morenas del Caribe (rough translation: the Wonderful Caribbean Brown Sugars), the team hold every major international title and won the Olympic title for the fourth consecutive time at the 2000 Games in Sydney.

Unfortunately Cubans rarely get to see the women's team play at home, but they do pack the **Coliseo de la Ciudad Deportiva** (*see p177*) to admire the men's team in action in the Liga Mundial de Voleibol (World Volleyball League), held every year in the spring. For schedule details, and information on tickets, contact the Coliseo or ask at your hotel. Sometimes matches are held at the Sala Polivalente Ramón Fonst (*see p177*).

Following the defection of most of the men's team in 2001, many feared the end of Cuba's prominence in men's volleyball; however, a younger generation of players has filled the team's roster, and it's looking as if Cuba will regain its international ranking soon.

Active sports

Although they are not up to North American or European standards, public sports facilities in Havana are relatively plentiful. However, if you are eager to play team sport with Cubans the best option is to join in with locals playing informal games of baseball, football or basketball. On any given afternoon, especially at weekends, you can find Cubans playing on public courts or fields throughout the city. If you bring your own basketball, football or gloves and bats, you are almost guaranteed to attract a group of willing players. Some of the popular sites are 23 and D in Vedado, Avenida 5ta and Calle 60 in Miramar, Centro Saborit (5ta and 90, Miramar) and the Ciudad Deportiva (*see p177*).

Visitors can also pay to use **Club Habana**, a luxurious private members' club on the coast to the west of the city, where facilities include tennis courts, a large swimming pool, a lovely beach, yacht hire, scuba-diving excursions and other watersports facilities. In addition, some upscale hotels offer sports and fitness facilities to non-guests.

Club Habana

Avenida 5ta, entre 188 y 192 (204 5700).
Open 7.30am-10pm daily. **Admission** *Monthly membership* $150. *Daily rate* $20 Mon-Fri; $30 Sat, Sun; free under-14s.

Cycling

During the petrol shortages of the worst days of the Special Period, bikes became a necessity and Havana's streets are still full of bikes. If you fancy getting out of the city, contact the **Club Nacional de Cicloturismo Gran Caribe**, which organises cycling trips in the countryside, and also promotes ecological bike tours. For more information on cycling in Havana, including details of bicycle hire and repair services, *see pp218-230*.

Club Nacional de Cicloturismo Gran Caribe

Information: Transnico, Lonja del Comercio, Calle Amargura #2, esquina Oficios, La Habana Vieja (669954/330170). **Open** 9am-5pm Mon-Fri. **Map** p252 E15.

Fishing

Fishing fanatics flock to Cuba to try their luck with the huge number of fish that swim the Gulf Stream just off the coast of Havana. The country hosts numerous major fishing competitions, the most famous of which is the **Ernest Hemingway International Marlin Tournament** held annually in May or June. Other important international competitions include the **Currican Tournament** in April and the **Blue Marlin Tournament** in August or September. For information, contact Náutico Internacional Hemingway at Marina Hemingway (204 6653/1689).

You can charter a boat for sport fishing at all times of year from Marina Hemingway (*see p181*) and Marina Puertosol Tarará (*see p182*), both of which also offer many other facilities. If you prefer to fish in the peaceful waters of lakes, reservoirs or rivers, the **Agencia de Viajes Horizontes** tourist agency should be able to give you details of excursions to rich inland fishing spots such as Maspotón in Pinar del Río province, the Laguna del Tesoro (Treasure Pond) in Ciénega de Zapata and Yarigua in Cienfuegos. In fact, large mouth bass fishermen come from around the world to fish in Lake Hanabanilla in the Escambray mountains, near Tope de Collantes (*see p204*). Jardines de la Reina, a string of keys off the south coast, offers some of the best year-round fishing for bonefish in the Caribbean.

However, the most typical way to fish *habanero* style is to bring your rod, line and hooks, arm yourself with bait and find yourself a spot on the Malecón for hours of fishing alongside the locals. Bear in mind that to go ocean fishing you have to bring your passport and check out with the coastguard and immigration at Marina Hemingway. It's also important to inquire into what kinds of ocean fish can be eaten; it's quite common for barracuda to be contaminated with a highly venomous coral toxin.

Agencia de Viajes Horizontes

Calle 23 #156, entre N y O, Vedado (662161/662160/www.horizontes.cu). **Open** 8am-5.30pm Mon-Fri. **Map** p250 B12.

Fitness

To find out whether a hotel has a gym or health club on the premises, check the list of hotel services given for every hotel (*see pp32-46*). Three of the best gyms are in hotels **Meliá Habana, Meliá Cohiba** and **NH Parque Central. Club Havana** (*see p179*) also has gym facilities.

Outside hotels, Havana has plenty of gyms and sports centres that offer fitness classes at reasonable rates. Cuban fitness instructors are generally highly trained and the facilities are usually good, if not state-of-the-art. (It's advisable not to wear your expensive white lycra attire unless you want it stained with machine grease.) Strictly speaking, the gyms below are for Cubans only but if you show up staff can usually arrange an informal price of $1-$2.

Gimnasio Integral Bioamérica

Calle 17, esquina E, Vedado (832 9087). **Open** 8am-8pm Mon-Fri. **Map** p250 B10.

Gimnasio Monte

Calle Monte, entre Suárez y Revillagigedo, La Habana Vieja (861 7748). **Open** 8am-8pm daily. **Map** p251 E13.

Gimnasio de la Villa Panamericana

Calle A y Avenida Central, Edificio #20, Habana del Este (951010). **Open** 8am-8pm daily.

Golf

Cuba boasts one excellent golf course and another good one. The best is the 18-hole **Varadero Golf Club** (*see pp191-195*); the other is the **Havana Golf Club** (built by the British in the 1930s), a 20-minute drive from central Havana, near Boyeros. The club has a nine-hole course, plus tennis courts, a pool, bar and restaurant. There are plans to construct international-standard golf courses at resorts on Cayo Coco and other tourist centres.

Havana Golf Club

Calzada de Vento km8, Capdevila, Boyeros (338918/338919). **Open** 8.30am-8pm daily. **Fees** *Non-members* $20 for 9 holes; $30 for 18 holes. **Club hire** $10. **Caddie hire** $5 for 9 holes. **Lessons** $10 for 30mins.

Horse riding

The **Centro Ecuestre** (also known as the Club Hípico) offers riding lessons and pony rides in the expansive, grassy surroundings of Parque Lenin. Riding lessons are also available at the **Feria Agropecuaria de Boyeros** (Avenida de la Independencia #31108). If you're in Playas del Este, ask at the **Hotel Club Atlántico** (Avenida de las Terrazas, Santa María del Mar, 971085) about hiring a horse. If you've got small kids, more leisurely riding is available at **Parque de Anfiteatro** (*see p60*) in La Habana Vieja.

Centro Ecuestre

Parque Lenin, southern Havana (441058). **Open** *June-Aug* 9am-5pm daily. *Sept-May* 9am-5pm Wed-Sun. **Rides** $13-$15 per hr.

The Blues

When you hear locals in Havana talking passionately, often with exaggeratedly expressive gestures (*see p177* ***Esquina caliente***), about 'Los Azules' (the Blues), they're referring to the Industriales, the city's long-established baseball team, founded in 1963. The most successful 'nine' in the Cuban National League, it's the team to beat and the team that everyone – even the fans of its die-hard rivals – wants to see in action.

In 38 seasons, the Blues have achieved 1,541 wins and 857 losses, an all-time national record. Since the introduction in Cuban baseball of the play-off structure in 1986, the Blues have qualified 14 times for the post-season series with a 57-46 win-loss balance. For more stats and information on the Industriales check www.radiococo.cu.

Some of Cuba's best players of the past 40 years have worn the Industriales jersey, including infielders Pedro Chávez, Urbano González, Antonio 'Tony' González, Lázaro Vargas, Juan Padilla, outfielders Antonio 'Ñico' Jiménez and Javier Méndez; and pitchers Manolo Hurtado, Santiago 'Changa' Mederos, Osvaldo 'El Duque' Hernández and René Arocha. After defecting, El Duque and René Arocha succeeded as Big Leaguers in the US. El Duque, a former New York Yankees star pitcher – now with the Montreal Expos – holds the second-best pitching record in post-season games while Arocha contributed wins for the St Louis Cardinals. (Arocha holds the all-time record for any Cardinal rookie hurler, with five wins in a row in his first five starts.)

Baseball is widely acknowledged to be Cuba's national pastime, but in reality it amounts to a national obsession. And never is this more clear than at the huge Estadio Latinoamericano, most commonly referred to as 'El Latino', the field on which all Cuban ballplayers aspire to play. It's the home park of the Blues, who share it with the 'Metropolitanos' (or 'Los Metros'), Havana's other team, which came into existence when the Cuban League expanded in the late '70s. When one team is on the road, the other provides the entertainment.

When the Blues emerge on to 'El Latino's' 55,000-seat diamond, the ballpark acquires an intense, pressure-cooker atmosphere and the cheering crowd erupts.

Running

The Comisión Marabana organises a schedule of road races and other competitive events throughout the year: key running events include the International Terry Fox Race (5km/3 miles) every February, which raises funds for cancer research; the Ultra Marabana (98km/62 miles) in April; the Mother's Day Race (5km/3 miles) and the Clásico Internacional Hemingway race (10km/6 miles) in May; the Olympic Day Mini Marathon (4km/2.5 miles) in June; and the Marabana (Havana Marathon) in November.

Serious runners can use the track at the **Estadio Panamericano**, **Estadio Pedro Marrero** (*see p178*) or at the **Ciudad Deportiva** (*see p177*). But a far more pleasant way to stretch your legs while enjoying the scenery is to follow the Malecón around the bay, or along Avenida 5ta in Mirama. Mind the potholes. **Parque Lenin** (*see p49*) to the south is another attractive jogging option.

Comisión Marabana

Ciudad Deportiva, Vía Blanca, esquina Avenida Boyeros, Apartado 5130 (545022).

Estadio Panamericano

Carretera Vieja de Cojímar, esquina Doble Vía, Habana del Este (974140). **Open** 8.30am-5.30pm Mon-Sat. **Admission** $1.

Sailing & boating

Marina Hemingway offers mooring for up to 100 yachts in four parallel, six-metre-deep, specially designed waterways that are protected against strong waves and currents. Services include electricity hook-ups, weather reports and boat repairs. Boat owners who are planning to moor their vessels at the marina aren't required to make reservations (though it's advisable). Arriving vessels should call the control tower on VHF16, VHF72 or VHF77 to announce their arrival. The marina authorities organise an international amateur sailing regatta, the **Regata Corona Internacional**, usually held in June and open to all. Yachts and motorboats can be rented out from Náutica Puerto y Marlin at the marina. Other services available include sailing and boat rides along the shore (around $22 an hour), and trips with snorkelling, swimming, fishing, and lunch included ($45-$60).

To the east of the city, **Marina Puertosol Tarará** has 50 berths (1.5 metres deep), each with water and electricity hook-ups. Although the facilities are not as good as those at the Marina Hemingway, the surroundings are nicer. The marina has a variety of vessels for hire, including live-in motorboats (from $2,100 per week). Yachts can be rented by the day ($250) and Hobiecat dinghies and pedal boats are available ($4 for 30 minutes).

Note that Cuban citizens are not allowed to accompany a foreigner on motor yachts or sailing boats, regardless of the length of voyage. The only exception to this rule is the Corona sailing regatta where the authorities relent and allow Cubans on to sailing boats.

Marina Hemingway

Calle 248, esquina 5ta, Santa Fe (204 1150). Recreación Base Náutico, Puerto Marina Hemingway (204 6848/209 7928).

Marina Puertosol Tarará

Vía Blanca km19, Playa Tarará (971462).

Scuba diving

Cuba's crystal blue waters and beautiful coral reefs entrice divers from across the world. Among the tour operators, **Puertosol** (204 5923) and **Horizontes** (662160/1/662004) offer attractive packages at good prices. Try also **Club Habana** (*see p179*) and the **Copacabana** and **Comodor** hotels (*see p46 and p45*). However, most deals involve excursions to sites a good distance from Havana, such as Pinar del Río province and the Isla de la Juventud, and in particular El Colony.

There are some diving opportunities close to the city. Shipwrecks can be explored off the Barlovento shore to the west of Havana, or at a series of dive sites known as the 'Blue Circuit' (*Circuito azul*), which extends east from Bacuranao to the Playas del Este. (The western beach at Tarará is a particularly good spot for diving and snorkelling.) *See pp88-93.*

Equipment is good quality and instructors are trained to international standards. To take part in a diving trip, all divers require an international scuba licence. Lessons and initiation dives for beginners are also available.

La Aguja Centro de Buceo

Marina Hemingway, Avenida 5ta, esquina 248, Jaimanitas (204 1150 ext 2119). **Open** 10am-4pm daily. *Dives* 10.30am, occasional afternoons (phone for details). **Rates** (1-2 dives, incl equipment, instructor & boat) $25-$40.

Buceo Marina Puertosol

Calle 7ma, entre 3ra y Cobre, Tarará, Habana del Este (961508). **Open** 9am-5pm Mon-Fri.

Swimming

Some of the best pools in Havana are found in the upscale hotels, such as the Meliá Cohiba, Meliá Habana, Novotel, Nacional and Copacabana (for all, *see pp32-46*). The latter has both a freshwater pool and a natural saltwater ocean-fed pool. Visitors can also make use of the facilities at **Club Habana** (*see p179*). The large pool and stretch of beautiful beach at this private members' club offer some of the best swimming in the city. Other alternatives include the **Centro Turístico La Giraldilla**, and the pool at the **Marina Hemingway** (*see p181*).

A word of warning: do not be tempted to join the local kids who swim in the sea off the Malecón; the water is badly polluted here and there are sharp rocks beneath the surface.

Centro Turístico La Giraldilla

Calle 222, esquina 39, La Coronela, La Lisa (204 6062). **Open** 11am-7pm daily. **Admission** $5; $2 concessions; free under-6s.

Tennis & squash

Cuba is now pushing to develop tennis at a higher level. The Cuban tennis team train at the six tennis courts (*canchas de tenis*) at the **Complejo Panamericano** (*see p181*) in eastern Havana, which arranges exchange matches between Cuban players and foreign tennis clubs. The tennis federation (*see p176*) can help co-ordinate accommodation and transport at decent rates.

The following hotels have tennis and/or squash courts that can be used by non-guests; contact the hotels directly for details of rates: **Copacabana** (squash, tennis; *see p46*); **Meliá Habana** (tennis; *see p45*); **Nacional** (tennis; *see p42*); **Occidental Miramar** (squash and tennis; *see p45*). The courts at the **Complejo Panamericano** are also for hire, as are the excellent courts at **Club Habana** (*see p179*). Note that tennis balls and strings are very hard to procure in Havana, so bring your own supply. At Club Havana and Novotel you can get lessons from a tennis pro for around $5 per hour. Alternatively, head out to the **Havana Golf Club** (*see p180*), which has five tennis courts.

Watersports

In addition to sailing, diving and snorkelling, the coast near Havana has facilities for other watersports such as jetskiing, kayaking and water-skiing. Try **Club Habana** (*see p179*), **Marina Hemingway** (*see p181*), **Marina Puertosol Tarará** (*see above*) and the hotels in the Playas del Este.

Beyond Havana

Getting Started 184
Pinar del Río 186
Varadero 191
The Central Provinces 196
Santiago de Cuba 206

Features

Paradise islands 198
Don't miss Santiago 206
Hotter than July 210

Maps

Map: Santa Clara 197
Map: Cienfuegos 201
Map: Trinidad 203
Map: Santiago de Cuba 207

Getting Started

A long and winding road.

To many, Havana is Cuba and Cuba is Havana. Yet beyond the capital there are cities, villages and rural areas not yet transformed by mass tourism. Houses, farms and mountain slopes remain much as they were decades ago. Their inhabitants may not be as suave as the *habaneros* but are also unlikely to be so jaded when it comes to welcoming foreign visitors.

Cuba is made up of huge, diverse landscapes and it would take weeks, if not months, to cover the country in its entirety. In the following chapters we offer key excursions from the capital.

One of the most manageable, and probably the most common, trips from Havana is to Pinar del Río Province, in particular to the charming village of **Viñales**, famed for its *mogotes* (limestone rock formations) and lush landscape. The rest of the province is poorly served by public transport, but if you have a car, **María La Gorda**, on Cuba's western tip, is scuba heaven.

Beach resort **Varadero**, a two-hour drive east along the Vía Blanca, is a cinch to get to from Havana. A long strip of white sand, lined with large all-inclusive hotels, awaits. Those wanting to meet local people or explore Cuban culture won't find much to keep them in Varadero, but it's ideal for a spot of hassle-free luxury beach time.

Trinidad, a small, perfectly preserved colonial town about 350 kilometres (220 miles) south-east of Havana in the Central Provinces, is an essential stop on any tour of Cuba. On the down side, the small town is gradually becoming overrun by camera-wielding tourists and tour buses, and less and less of the town's authentic feel is seeping through.

Santa Clara and **Cienfuegos**, on the way to Trinidad, are not as impressive architecturally but do offer manageable insights into life in a provincial town. Santa Clara has a vibrant, friendly feel, while Cienfuegos is a bigger, more industrial – but still attractive – port city. A visit to Santa Clara or nearby sleepy **Remedios** has the advantage of easy access to the northern keys – strings of mini-islands with white sands and turquoise sea – connected by a causeway.

The big trip, though, is without a doubt **Santiago de Cuba**, Cuba's second city, at the eastern end of the island. It's a long way from Havana, however you tackle it, but is worth it for its vibrant music and dance scenes and impressive mountain scenery.

For a map of Cuba, *see p240.*

LISTINGS

Note that most museums charge $1-$2, and that only admission fees over $3 appear in the listings. Few establishments outside the large, more upmarket hotels accept credit cards.

Travelling around Cuba

As with everything else in Cuba, expect the unexpected when it comes to public transport. Petrol shortages and breakdowns can create last-minute problems, though the Víazul bus network is generally very reliable.

By rail

There are daily departures from the central train station in Havana (Estación Central de Ferrocarriles; *see p214*) to all Cuba's major towns. Tickets can be bought in dollars in person at least an hour before your train departs, or before 7pm if you're travelling at night. For details of the electric train between Havana and Matanzas, *see p89.*

By bus

Tourists are encouraged to use the big Víazul buses, which are kitted out with air-conditioning, video screens and refreshments. You pay in dollars (one-way only) but prices are reasonable (for example: $5 Havana to Matanzas, $10 to Varadero, $51 to Santiago). (The Astro company serves the same destinations and will always sell a few dollar seats to foreigners, but tickets are only slightly cheaper and the old buses are generally uncomfortable and inclined to break down.) You can pick up Víazul buses where they originate at the terminal in Nuevo Vedado. For Havana's bus stations, *see p215.*

By air

Most domestic flights within Cuba leave from Terminal 1 of José Martí International Airport. **Cubana** (officially Cubana de Aviación) covers many destinations within Cuba, including Cienfuegos, Santiago de Cuba and Varadero. However, its flights, while usually the cheapest available, are prone to delays, don't have a good safety record and provide little comfort. Cubana's most central office is on La Rampa in Vedado

The hills are alive, around Trinidad.

(Calle 23, #64, entre P e O, Vedado/331986-9/ 334446-9, www.cubana.com). A generally more expensive but more comfortable option is **Aero Caribbean**, which leaves from Terminal 5 and covers Holguín, Santiago de Cuba, Trinidad and Varadero. Its office is in the Cubana office in Vedado (833 3621).

Tourist agencies

The following state-run tourism companies variously offer excursions, activities and hotel and tour bookings around Cuba, including full packages out of Havana. If you don't have the time to roll with the uncertainties of independent travel – of which there are many here – you'd do well to arrange a trip in advance. Most of these organisations also have branches around the country for making local arrangements.

For sources of tourist information, *see p227*.

Asistur

Paseo de Martí (Prado) #208, entre Trocadero y Colón, La Habana Vieja (338527/24hr service 866 4499/www.asistur.cu). **Open** 9am-5pm Mon-Fri. **No credit cards**. **Map** p252 D14.

Services include medical care, legal help, travel documents, air and hotel reservations.

Cubamar

Calle 3, entre 12 y Malecón, Vedado (832 1116/831 0008/www.cubamarviajes.cu). **Open** 8.30am-5.30pm Mon-Sat. **Credit** MC, V. **Map** p249 A8.

Specialist youth and nature tourism, with campsites, villas and nature trails.

Cubanacán

Calle 17A, entre 174 y 190, Siboney, Playa (208 8666/www.cubanacan.cu). **Open** 8am-5pm Mon-Fri. **Credit** MC, V.

Runs hotels and restaurants, three marinas, scuba centres, health tourism facilities and a travel agency.

Gaviota

Avenida del Puerto #102, piso 3, entre Justiz y Obrapía, La Habana Vieja (666 7737/8/www.grupo-gaviota.com). **Open** 8am-5pm Mon-Fri. **Credit** MC, V. **Map** p252 E16.

As well as owning hotels, marinas, restaurants and shops, Gaviota also runs a travel agency.

Havanatur

Edificio Sierra Maestra, Avenida 1ra, entre 0 y 2, Miramar (554082/554883/www.havanatur.cu/www.havanatur.co.uk/www.havanatur.com). **Map** p249 A7.

Havanatur's main reservations office, offering full travel services including tailor-made packages.

Horizontes

Calle 23 #156, entre N y O, Vedado (334090/www.horizontes.cu). **Open** 8.30am-8pm daily. **Credit** MC, V. **Map** p250 B12.

Some 50 hotels nationwide, plus travel agencies.

Infotur

Calle Obispo #524, entre Bernaza y Villegas, La Habana Vieja (862 4586/www.infotur.cu). **Open** 8.30am-1pm, 2-8.30pm daily. **No credit cards**. **Map** p252 D14/15.

Excursions, hotel bookings, museums, sale of maps and posters, plus an internet, fax and postal service.

Rumbos

Calle 0 #108, entre Avenidas 1ra y 3ra, Miramar (24hrs 204 3688/204 4439/www.rumboscuba viajes.com). **Open** 8.30am-5.30pm Mon-Sat. **Credit** MC, V. **Map** p249A7.

Rumbos specialises in à la carte holidays.

Transtur

Calle J #210, esquina 19, Vedado (reservations 835 0000/553990/www.transturcuba.com). **Open** 8am-5pm Mon-Fri. **Credit** MC, V. **Map** p250 B11.

The largest tourism transport company in Cuba, Transtur offers cars, buses and taxis for hire, and possesses a broad and diverse fleet of vehicles. Sales offices throughout the country.

Pinar del Río Province

Some of Cuba's finest flora and fauna, just a short foray from the capital.

For those with only a short time in Cuba and looking for a change from Havana's hurly-burly, Pinar del Río lies beckoning to the west. For some reason, perhaps because many *pinareños* are descendants of Canary Islanders and not mainland Spaniards, they have become the butt of *habaneros*' humour: they're the stupid ones in all the jokes. Indeed, they can be very different to their capital city counterparts in that they're friendly, courteous and generous.

The province's many rivers make it very green and fertile: tobacco, coffee, sugar cane, rice, citrus and other fruits are among its agricultural products. More recently, environmental tourism has been added to the area's economic activities, with two biosphere reserves. Unfortunately, the area was badly affected by two hurricanes ten days apart in 2002; many homes were lost or damaged and the tobacco crop suffered badly.

GETTING THERE

There's a good six-lane *autopista* leading to the province that terminates in the provincial capital, Pinar del Río.

Alternatively, there's the even more scenic route along the Carretera Central (CC) which stretches throughout the province. Or else the Circuito Norte (CN) travelling inland along the coast west of Havana. If you've time, stop off en route at **Artemisa** in Havana Province (59 kilometres, 37 miles, from the capital) and pay tribute to the many who died in the 1953 attack on Moncada Garrison by visiting the Museo de Historia and the Mausoleo de los Mártires.

Both the Víazul and Astro bus companies go to Pinar del Río city (fares $11 and $7 respectively; journey time 3hrs), arriving at Calle Adela Azcuys, one block north of Calle José Martí. A train leaves the Old Havana train station once every other day; the five- to six-hour journey costs $6.50.

All hotels and tour operators have excursions and tours to places of interest throughout Pinar del Río; the two bus companies also run services to the larger towns.

Las Terrazas

Just beyond Havana Province, 80 kilometres (50 miles) from the capital, approachable from both the *autopista* (km 51) and the CC, is the first of Pinar del Rio's biosphere reserves – **Las Terrazas**. Tucked away within the valley of the Sierra Rosario mountains this is a rural community project and tourist complex that takes its name from the terraces dug out of the hillsides during the late 1960s when the area was the focus of a huge reforestation and resettlement programme. As well as restoring the ecosystem – damaged by years of deforestation by 19th-century French coffee planters – the project aimed to provide the impoverished local *campesinos* with access to better housing, education and medical services. From 1971 to 1974 a 1,000-strong rural community was moved here. Some 50 per cent of those now living in Las Terrazas are involved in tourism.

The Rancho Curujey information office and Ecology Research Centre within the complex has a large map explaining the layout. There's a huge amount to see and do: swimming under the cascades of the San Juan river, boating on the lake, hiking, guided nature walks, cycling, horse riding, visiting the ruins of the coffee plantations. The project is centred around the eco-friendly **Hotel Moka**, built around a carob tree, which now grows out above its roof.

The complex also contains a lakeside cottage where Las Terrazas' most famous contemporary son, the late singer Polo Montañez, lived. It's now called the Peña de Polo and displays his gold and platinum discs on the walls; his music blares out from the stereo system and his brother greets visitors. Wandering among the cottages, peeking in at the artists' studios and workshops could make you think that you were in any little village in Cuba. Perfect. Or too perfect? There are those who find something reminiscent of *The Prisoner* in Las Terrazas.

Flights of fancy aside, the hard facts are that this is a successful project and one-third of the income from visitors is reinvested in its upkeep. There's also a small museum with photos of the project's first stages and the skeleton of a *cimarrón* (runaway slave), plus a library and a cinema. UNESCO designated the area as a biosphere reserve in 1985. Its stunning flora is home to the *zunzuncito* (the world's smallest humming bird); Cuba's national bird, the red, white and blue *tocororo*; the planet's tiniest frog, about the size of a thumbnail, and a huge variety of trees, flowers, and ferns. There are various charges for day visitors to Las Terrazas: it's $2 to swim in the lake; $4 for a

Camouflaged **El Bambú** at rural community project and tourist complex Las Terrazas.

tour of the entire area and a swim in the San Juan river, with additional charges for hiring boats and so on.

It's worth a slight detour to visit **Buena Vista**, a restored coffee plantation abandoned by its French owners and now a living museum. The colonial mansion has wonderful views across hills on all sides, and also houses a restaurant.

Where to stay & eat

The 26-roomed 'ecological' **Hotel Moka** (Carretera de la Candelaría km51, 082 778555, doubles $90-$105) is interestingly designed and rather swish. The hotel has a restaurant serving international food and grill bar. There's a $3 cover for non-residents using the swimming pool. The newish bar-café **El Bambú**, built into the hillside, is definitely worth a stop. There are three other restaurants in the village: **La Fondita de Mercedes** serves Creole food in a patio setting; close by is **Casa de Campesino** with a similar menu, plus **El Romero**, a new vegetarian restaurant. .

Soroa

Some 80 kilometres (50 miles) west of Havana and close to Las Terrazas is Soroa, located in the small valley of the Manatiales river. Founded as a French colonial coffee plantation in the 19th century, it was originally famous for its orchid gardens, waterfall and medicinal baths.

In the 1940s Tomás Felipe Camacho, a lawyer from the Canary Islands living in Havana, decided to turn his Soroa summer residence into a shrine to his youngest daughter, Pilar, who had died in childbirth. Completed in 1951, this 35,000 square-kilometre (13,500 square-mile) park on the slopes of the Guaniguanico mountain range is home to 6,000 species of ornamental plants, trees and flowers, including an **orchid garden** ($3, photos $1, video $2) with 700 species of orchids, 110 of them indigenous to Cuba. The best time to visit is between November and March, but the area's microclimate ensures that there are always some orchids in bloom. An international event on growing and tending orchids is held in March (even-numbered years; contact emujica@vrect.upr.edu.cu for details).

Cross the road and follow the path, which eventually becomes stone-stepped, down to the 22-metre (73-foot) high **Arco Iris** waterfall ($3, free for guests of nearby hotels). There's a marvellous view of the valleys and sea from the top of the waterfall, and a pool for swimming. Nearby are medicinal baths (smell the sulphur) offering mud treatments and massage.

Nature and bird lovers' walks (look out for the hummingbird and the nightingale) take in visits to coffee plantation ruins, the Loma de Vigía observation point, the charcoal makers' pit and the slaves' stone mine. The hotel can arrange guided walks and horse riding.

Where to stay & eat

Hotel & Villas Horizontes Soroa, (Carretera de Soroa km8, Candelaría, 085 2122/2041, doubles $43-$55), has a 49-cabin air-conditioned complex set in the grassy area around a swimming pool. Non-residents can use the pool for $3. There are also some self-catering villas with swimming pools close to the orchid garden (double $68-$78) plus a five-bedroon mansion close to the Castillo de las Nubes restaurant (mains $4-$8, double $85-$92). **La Caridad** (no phone) campsite is located in the woods close by, and is very basic.

Further west

About eight kilometres (five miles) along the road from Soroa is the *paladar* **El Trebol** (also known as El Ranchón). You can't miss it as it's on a main junction, set back slightly from the road. It offers basic Cuban fare in generous portions, all in Cuban pesos.

There are also a few *casas particulares* scattered along the way. Moving westwards, 120 kilometres (80 miles) from Havana is the **Balneario San Diego de los Baños**, a natural spa for the relief of arthritis, rheumatism and skin problems. Legend has it that its fame spread after the mineral springs cured a slave of his leprosy. In fact, its waters have been used since 1700; the Spanish developed it into a spa in 1891 and a small town grew up around it. In the 1980s it was developed into a resort for health tourism offering various medicinal treatments with mud, massage, hydromassage and acupuncture. It's looking a little worn these days.

Around five kilometres (three miles) west along the CC is **Parque Nacional La Güira**, a 22,000 hectare park that once belonged to the Cortina estates. Now sadly neglected, it's worth a visit just to wander among the ruins of a once-handsome mansion with sculpted gardens and pagodas in the grounds. Cross the bridge and descend through the forest to the lake and river. Apart from the birds it shelters (migratory species passing through, as well as native birds), the forest is also the habitat of the Creole deer, a species on the verge of extinction.

At La Güira's northern edge, 16 kilometres (ten miles) from the CC and located among the pine groves is the **Cueva de los Portales** where Che Guevara made his headquarters during the 1962 October Missile Crisis. The cave contains the original furniture and some of Che's belongings.

Where to stay and eat

The **Hotel Mirador** (Calle 23 final, 082 778338, doubles $32-$38) is located near the spa. Built in 1948, it was refurbished in 1994 and hosts birdwatchers as well as spa users. Rooms have new furniture but are cluttered; the pool area is small and has little greenery. The hotel serves an adequate buffet ($8) and also has a grill restaurant and snack bar.

Pinar del Río

Located 162 kilometres (77 miles) south-west of Havana, this bustling city of some 124,000 inhabitants is currently undergoing a facelift due to the influx of tourists. At first glance it doesn't seem to have much to offer beyond some pretty traditional-style terraces with tiled roofs, and a small historic centre. But there's some interesting eclectic architecture here and the government is keen to promote the area as a cultural destination.

The **Museo de Ciencias Naturales Sandalio de Noda** (Calle Martí Este #202, esquina Avenida Pinares) is housed in the former Palacio de Guasch – built in an interesting eclectic style, and the province's first concrete building. The exhibits are old-fashioned and there's an uninspiring collection of stuffed animals (don't miss the *zunzuncito* and *tocororo*).

The **Museo de Historia Provincial** (Calle Martí Este #58, entre Colón y Isabel Rubio) gives a historical perspective on the province, with paintings and some lovely colonial furniture. It also hosts temporary exhibitions. The **Casa de Antonio Guiteras Holmes** (Calle Maceo Oeste #52) pays tribute to this 1930s revolutionary leader.

Located around the small Parque de Independencia square is the **Museo de Artes**

Visuales and, more interestingly, the **Casa-Taller de Pedro Pablo Oliva** (closed Fri-Sun), a very smart gallery-cum-studio showing the work of this successful *pinareño*. On the opposite side of the square is the **Centro Hermanos Loynaz**, a restored building dedicated to the famous artistic family from Havana. For film buffs, a visit to the 19th-century neo-classical **Teatro Milanés** – featured in Cuban film *La Bella de la Alhambra* – is essential.

If you want a taste of the local Guyabita liqueur, tours and tastings are available at the **Guyabita del Pinar factory** (Isabel Rubio Sur #189, esquina Ceferino Fernández y Frank País, closed Sat, Sun). Founded in 1892, the factory is the only place in the world where this liqueur (which comes in two strengths: strong and a bit stronger) is made.

At the time of writing the **Fábrica del Tobaco Francisco Donatién** was closed for renovation, though the **Casa de Habanos** is open for buying cigars. There's also an open-air **Casa de la Música** a few doors down from Café Pinar (*see below*).

Where to stay and eat

The **Hotel Pinar del Río** (Calle Martí, entre final y Autopista, 082 755070-4, doubles $34-$38), with restaurants, four bars, disco and shops, is the decent option in central Pinar. That said, attempts to make the place look more hospitable have been limited by the soulless concrete-block design. Part of the newly renovated **Hotel Vueltabajo** should be finished by April 2004. This early 20th-century building (esquina San Juan y Martin) will provide an attractive option for city-centre accommodation.

A short drive in the direction of Viñales brings you to the **Villa International Aguas Claras** (Carretera a Viñales km7.5, 082 778426/778427, doubles $24-$32). Set in unspoilt grounds where chickens and pigs run free, complete with Monet-style lily pond and bridge, the complex has 50 double rooms in individual cabins, a swimming pool and bar. The rustic restaurant is inexpensive (mains $2-$6).

There are several places to eat in and around the city. **Café Pinar** (Calle Velez Caviedes #34) is a snack bar with a basic restaurant attached. At 9pm the café's courtyard becomes a nightclub (entrance $2). **La Casona** (Calle Martí s/n, esquina Colón) looks attractive from a distance but the menu is very limited. A better bet is the small attached bar where shots cost from 30¢ upwards. The restaurant-cabaret **Rumayor** is a kilometre north of the city on the CC to Viñales. It opens at midday for Creole food and hosts a cabaret (from 11pm Tue-Sun).

At the time of writing there were only two legal *paladares* in Pinar: **El Mesón** (Calle Martí #205, esquina Comandante Pinares y C Pacheco, 082 762867, mains $4-$5); the food tends to be a little more adventurous than the average *paladar*. The other is **Nuestra Casa** (Calle Colón, esquina Frank País y Primero de Enero, mains $4); just three tables are arranged on the roof (the narrow metal staircase is not for the faint-hearted).

The inescapable fact remains, though, that Pinar is no gourmet haven. In fact, it may be a good idea to bring some fresh food with you.

Valle de Viñales

This valley lies 25 kilometres (15 miles) north of Pinar del Río along the 241, a sound but winding and narrow road. The valley and its town are nestled among the **Sierra de los Organos**, the mountain range lying west of the Sierra Rosario, with breathtakingly verdant landscapes, featuring *mogotes* – tree-covered limestone knolls. The limestone bedrock has been steadily moulded by underground rivers, creating huge caverns in the area. UNESCO has declared the area a Natural World Heritage Site and, catching a view of the scenery, it's easy to understand why. The two best viewing points are from **Hotel Jazmines** and **Hotel La Ermita** (for both, *see p190*).

There are plenty of opportunities to enjoy the area's natural beauty close-up too. You can hike up **Dos Hermanos**, the area's most famous *mogote,* five kilometres (three miles) west of the town of Viñales. There are also guided tours around several caves in the vicinity. Five kilometres north of the town is the **Cueva de los Indios**, where for $5 you get to explore the first 400 metres (1,300 feet) on foot, then take a 20-30 minute boat ride along the underground river (9am-6pm daily).

Not far away is the 140-metre (467-foot) long **Cueva de San Miguel**; it takes about ten minutes to explore, is a bit slippery (wear sensible shoes) and costs $1 to enter. The entrance area has a bar and a late-night show every Saturday. The Palenque restaurant and Afro-Cuban show lie in wait at the cave's exit.

The other tourist attraction in Viñales is the **Mural de la Prehistoria**. Apparently, Che Guevara was responsible for commissioning Cuban painter Leovigildo González (one of Diego Rivera's pupils) to execute the huge mural on the cliff face in 1961. It costs a dollar to see the mural at close quarters.

But just as pleasant is meandering around the pretty little village of **Viñales**, with its wooden church (built around 1878), bookshop, craft shop, art gallery, museum and Casa de Cultura (with nightly events).

Where to stay and eat

Hotel Los Jazmines (Carretera a Vinales km25, 08 796205 doubles $61-$71) is probably the area's best-known hotel, with lots of facilities (restaurants, two bars, poolside grill bar, disco, shops, sports facilities, guided walks, horseback trekking). The down side is the tacky souvenir stalls. Food in the first-floor restaurant is adequate (mains $4.50-$7).

For somewhere more tranquil, **La Ermita** (Carretera de La Ermita, km0.5, 08 796121/071/072, doubles $58-$65) is pleasant, clean and only 20 minutes' walk from town, with tennis courts and a swimming pool. Its sloping grounds have 63 rooms in two-storey blocks with red-tile roofs. The restaurant serves Creole food (mains $5-$20).

The Rumbos chain has two smallish houses opposite the Cueva de los Indios: **Las Magnolias** (doubles $25) has three double rooms with all mod cons and air-con; **Finca Campesina** (doubles $25) has two double rooms.

There are 198 *casas particulares* in Viñales village. Recommended are Mario Arteaga's **Villa Tita** (Calle Salvador Cisnero, Edificio Colonial #1, apto 9, 08 793222/796192). Or try **María Luisa** at No.142 on the same main street (08 793390, doubles $15); she has two lovely colonially furnished rooms with air-con. Next door is the **Restaurant Casa de Don Tomás** (mains $5-$12), a beautiful colonial house built in 1889 by María Luisa's grandfather. It has a good atmosphere, tasty food and friendly service.

Seven kilometres (4.5 miles) north of Viñales village, quite close by the Cueva de los Indios, is **Hotel Rancho San Vicente** (Carretera Puerto Esperanza km33, 08 796201/796221/2, doubles $43-$48). This spa and ecotourism complex has 53 rooms in pine cabins built on stilts and bungalows set in grassy grounds around a swimming pool. Natural therapies and walking tours are offered. The restaurant (mains $5-$8) is small and tasteful.

Some of the area's caves have restaurants attached. **La Cueva de los Indios** (mains $4-$5) serves à la carte Creole fare. The Cueva de San Miguel's **Palenque de los Cimarrones** (mains $5-$8) is an Afro-Cuban theme restaurant with 'folkloric' entertainment. Cuban favourites chicken and pork are served.

Cayo Levisa

With five kilometres (three miles) of unspoiled beaches, sand banks, coral reefs and crystal waters, Cayo Levisa is pretty much paradise – and official policy is to keep it that way. Take the road leading northwards from Viñales to **Palma Rubia** (or, if you're coming from Havana, take the Circuito Norte through Bahía Honda and la Palma). A ferry leaves for Cayo Levisa at 10am (and at 11am in high season). The fare (return trip only), including cocktail, costs $15 ($27-$40 with lunch). The ferry returns at 5pm, but speed boats can take you back at other times for a $10 fee. The key has a diving centre, which offers courses, plus facilities for kayaking, sailing and snorkelling. Cayo Levisa has accommodation in the shape of bungalows or wooden cabins (doubles $71-$81). The restaurant serves Cuban and international food, with candlelit dinners three times a week. Very good news is the fact that Cayo Levisa attracts few mosquitoes.

Excursions to other keys in the Gulf of Mexico include **Cayo Jutías**, which has a small seafood restaurant.

Península Guanahacabibes and María La Gorda

The Guanahacabibes nature park, along the westernmost point of the peninsula, is a biosphere reserve and the country's largest forested area. It's home to a profusion of flora and fauna – including turtles, wild deer and migratory birds – plus underground caverns and over a hundred lakes. Stop at the reserve's **Estación Ecológica** for information on guided walks. **María La Gorda**, on the far western tip of the island, is known for the amazing diversity of the sealife in the surrounding reefs, but also for its quiet isolation. Divers happily drive from Havana to reach this pristine destination. The **María La Gorda Diving Centre** offers diving courses, equipment hire, snorkelling, excursions for non-divers and other sports facilities.

Where to stay & eat

Opposite the park's ecology station, in front of the meteorological headquarters, are four double rooms ($9). For further information call 082 75600. There's also a small café opposite the ecology station.

María La Gorda has 56 rooms spread over several locations, including recently built beautiful pine cabins set in woodland (doubles $50-$56). The restaurant is expensive, with lobster at $39 (though the buffet is $15). This area's charm lies in its isolation, so remember to bring anything you may need. Rooms get booked up, but staff will always give you a hammock.

Getting there

It's a three-hour drive from the city of Pinar del Río, along the Carretera San Juan, taking in the Oyos de Monterey tobacco fields and the town of San Juan y Martínez.

Varadero

All-inclusive hotel heaven (and/or hell).

Varadero is the biggest resort complex in the Caribbean, equipped with over 14,000 hotel rooms – an ever-increasing figure – and an extraordinarily perfect beach. Varadero, in Matanzas Province, marks the western end of the Hicacos Peninsula, a 22-kilometre (14-mile) finger blessed with fine white-sand beaches and crystal-clear aquamarine waters. The northern, sea-facing side is lined to the last inch of sand with hotels of varying degrees of luxury; the side facing the Bahía de Cárdenas is where the majority of the local population lives.

Although Cubans have been spending beach holidays in Varadero since the 19th century, things really took off in the 1930s, when American tycoon Irénée Dupont decided he had found paradise, bought a huge chunk, and began to build: a mansion, golf course, air strip and so on. Others followed suit, and the area soon became to Havana what the Hamptons are to New York. The proliferation of large-scale hotel development has continued relatively unabated since the 1970s, and Varadero today is more akin to somewhere on the Spanish Costa del Sol than anywhere in the Hamptons.

The majority of visitors come to Varadero on all-inclusive package holidays, so the town isn't particularly well tailored to independent travellers. If your main stay is in Havana, you can visit Varadero on a one-day excursion (it's two and a half hours from the capital). However, sunrise and sunset are both spectacular enough to make it worth staying a night.

The gulf between tourists and Cubans is never more pronounced than in Varadero. Vast sections of beach – generally the best ones – are the preserve of hotel guests, and there's little intercultural mingling except with hotel staff.

Check weather reports if you plan to visit during hurricane season (September to November). Varadero was heavily affected by Hurricane Michelle in November 2001, causing some hotels to close temporarily.

GETTING AROUND

Varadero peninsula isn't very walkable, due to its long, thin shape, and the distances involved. The main road is the Autopista del Sur, which extends from the bridge connecting the mainland to the peninsula's eastern arm and runs the length of its southern shore. The main drag in Varadero town is Avenida Primera, which runs from one end of town to the other. The shorter western end of the peninsula is accessed from the town by Avenida Kawama.

Taxis can be pricey, running at roughly 50¢ per kilometre (**Transgaviota** 045 619761/2, **Turitaxi** 045 613763/377, **Taxi OK** 045

612827), and you've no virtually no chance of getting a peso cab here. The easiest place to pick up a cab is at one of the many hotels. Most hotels also hire bicycles and scooters. The cheaper option for getting around is to catch the open-top double decker bus that runs up and down the length of the peninsula. The bus (9am-9.30pm) takes roughly an hour to complete its circuit. A day pass costs $2 and entitles the holder to unlimited rides. Or for $10 per person you can ride in a horsedrawn coach all over Varadero, with the coachman pointing out spots of interest.

Sightseeing

Varadero is all about the beach, but if being a full-time beach bum isn't your idea of fun, you won't be totally at a loss. One of the most pleasant places in town for those who have had enough of blue and white is the lush green of **Parque Josones**, at the corner of Primera Avenida and Calle 56. It's a spacious, well-trimmed park, with tree-shaded paths, an artificial boating lake (50¢ per person per hr), a large swimming pool ($3, incl $2 refreshments) and some excellent restaurants (*see below*).

Casa Villa Abreu (Calle 57, entre 1ra y Playa, 045 613189), Varadero's museum, is charming if unextensive. It's set in an old wood-frame house, with architecture reminiscent of that of the southern United States in the 19th century. The history section has artefacts from the pre-Columbian period to the present, and there's a display of local sports exhibits.

The **Delfinario** (Autopista Sur km12, 45 668031, closed Mon, $10) holds several dolphin shows a day. Cubans pride themselves on training the animals with loving care, and keeping them in a natural setting.

One of the most unusual and enjoyable excursions from Varadero is to the easternmost end of the Hicacos Peninsula, known as Punto Francés, or **Varahicacos**. The local authorities have set aside 295 hectares as an ecological reserve, and from ancient cave writings to 500-year-old cactus trees, what they have preserved is a national treasure. Trails through the reserve are well marked, but you will need the help of the multilingual guides to get the most out of your visit. If you go early in the morning or just before sunset, you will see a variety of birds. As well as the native species, in winter visitors can see numerous migratory birds from Canada, the US and Cuba's northern cays.

One trail leads to the Cuevas de los Musulmanes, where an indigenous burial ground was found. Another cave, with distinctive geological formations, is today filled with hundreds of bats (none are considered dangerous). Varahicacos also lays claim to the oldest cactus tree in Cuba – perhaps in Latin America – and the only completely natural beach in Varadero. The sand along this 900-metre (3,000-foot) stretch is brought in by the currents and is a light golden colour. (All the other beaches are made of fine white sand that has been brought in from nearby cays.)

Note: no hotels, stalls or other man-made constructions mar the area, so bring your own picnic lunch if you plan to spend the day here.

Sports

Though Varadero doesn't have much to offer in the way of architecture or history, it is one of the best spots in Cuba for watersports, with several smart marinas and diving clubs. Most hotels offer their own aquatic sports, boats, equipment and instructors. But if yours doesn't, or you're on a day trip, **Marina Gaviota** (Autopista Sur, 045 667755), **Marina Chapelin** (Carretera Las Morlas km12, 045 667550), Puertasol's **Acua Diving Centre** (045 668064) and the **Barracuda Diving Centre** (Avenida 1ra y Calle 58, 045 613481) all offer snorkelling trips out on the keys, deep sea fishing and diving. (Diving is cheaper if you have your own equipment or are in a group.)

Jungle Tour (Marina Chapelin, Carretera Las Morlas km12, 045 668440, www.jungletour-cuba.com, $39 per person) lets you pilot your own Aqua-Ray on a two-hour adventure. **Varasub** (Avenida Playa, entre 36 y 37, 045 667027, £25) offers a 90-minute trip on a semisubmerged sub, so you can gawp at the colourful sea life without getting wet.

Varadero is also home to the best golf club in Cuba; the **Varadero Golf Club** (Carretera Las Américas km8.5, Autopista Sur, 045 667388, www.varaderogolfclub.com, prices) is the country's only 18-hole course.

Where to eat

Except for the all-inclusives, most hotels have decent restaurants and snack bars open to the public. The town itself is also sprinkled with restaurants and fast food joints. The town's main restaurants are located around the Parque Josones (*see above*): **El Retiro**, once the home of the family that built the park in the 1940s, is an elegant, traditional restaurant for anyone who wants to eat out in style. **La Campana**, an old stone building which was once a guest house, serves typical Cuban food in a more relaxed atmosphere. The food is well prepared and the service good. **Dante** is considered the best Italian restaurant in Varadero (some say in Cuba) and has a lovely, outdoor setting on a small piece of land jutting into the park's lake.

Parque Josones: when you don't want to be beside the seaside. *See p192.*

Shopping & entertainment

As well as checking out the complexes within the hotels, shoppers can trawl the boutiques at the **International Conference Centre** or try the **crafts fare** outside the Coppelia ice-cream parlour on Calle Playa (esquina 46). **Plaza Américas** (Autopista Sur km11.5) is a handy mall with shops, banks and travel agencies.

In keeping with all-inclusive life, most hotels in Varadero have their own disco. To venture out try **La Rumba** (Carretera las Americas, km4, 045 668210), one of Varadero's longest running nighclubs.

Where to stay

Varadero's Hicacos Peninsula has over 40 hotels; choosing the right one is key to getting the most out of your stay. Nearly all are on or very close to the beach. The quieter (and more upmarket) hotels are situated towards the eastern end of the peninsula up to ten kilometres (6.2 miles) from Varadero's town centre. Conversely, the broadest stretches of sand at the western end of the peninsula are often busier owing to their proximity to Varadero town and denser hotel development.

Nearly all hotels in Varadero are billed as 'all-inclusive' or 'ultra all-inclusive' (and other variations on the theme), but it's best to check beforehand to find out what this actually includes, besides room, meals, beach and pool. For example, some include all nautical sports, others only the non-motorised ones. Most include a wide variety of entertainment, sports and other activities. Some even include excursions. Note that in low season some hotels can be quite empty, so the hotel disco may close early, and some of the activities advertised in the brochure may be cancelled.

We haven't listed rates here, since prices vary hugely according to season, availablilty and what facilities are included. Most double rooms cost between $150 and $300; the nicest hotels don't necessarily charge the highest prices, so it's worth doing some research.

RESORTS

Meliá Paradisus (Rincón Francés, 045 668700, www.solmelia.com) sets the standard for luxurious ultra-all-inclusive style and service. The rooms, which are spacious, comfortable and tasteful, are arranged in small blocks and surrounded by well-tended gardens. A maze-like network of paths connecting the different areas of the hotel ensures that a quiet corner of green shade is never far away.

Sandals Royal Hicacos (Autopista Sur km15, 045 668844), which opened in late 2002, is Varadero's newest all-inclusive hotel. Close to Paradisus both geographically and in terms of exclusivity, and with an equally impressive range of activites, Royal Hicacos differs by operating a strict couples-only policy (but not same sex). Raised walkways pass over a system of mini canals and shallow pools to give a floating feeling. Rooms are low-rise, and none offer sea views, owing to the sand dunes between the hotel and the beach. In keeping with the hotel's rarefied romantic ambience, all bathrooms contain twin-sized bath tubs.

Meliá Las Américas (Carretera de las Morlas, 045 667700, www.solmelia.com,

Meliá Paradisus (*p193*), and a guest a-pier-ance on the Varadero sands.

$180-$290) is the only hotel in Varadero offering a half-board and B&B options on a five-star range of facilities, including five swimming pools. The hotel is particularly popular with golfers, as it offers direct access to the golf course (with discounts for guests).

At the time of going to press, Superclub's newest addition to its **Grand Lido** chain of resorts was in the final stages of construction at the far eastern end of the Hicacos Peninsula. Word has it that this will become the most luxurious all-inclusive on the peninsula.

German-managed **LTI Varadero Beach Resort** (Carretera Las Morlas, Punta Hicacos, 045 668822) has a reputation for good value among its mainly British visitors. Family groups are welcome, and there are good discounts for young children. Rooms are clean, comfortable and tasteful, and service friendly and efficient. In August 2003, sand was dredged from the sea bed to provide a much-needed extension to the beach, but the new sand is still rather coarse and will need time to soften up. LTI has announced a merger with fellow German hotel group Maritim, under whose name the hotel will soon be rebranded.

Beaches Varadero (Carretera Las Morlas km14, 045 668470) is run by Sandals Resorts. Although it's a poorer sister to Royal Hicacos, potential visitors should not be deterred by the worrying mustard-coloured exterior; once inside, the lobby area is pleasant enough, the gardens are well tended and the swimming pool a good size. Accommodation is split between the five-storey main building and two-storey garden villas. The hotel boasts an especially ample range of entertainment programmes, including feeding nursing sharks lurking in a garden pool (generally not advertised until guests have safely checked-in and drunk their welcome cocktail). Over-16s only.

Tryp Peninsula Varadero (Parque Natural Punta Hicacos, 045 668800, www.solmelia.com) is Meliá's latest bid to dominate the Varadero monopoly board, and provides dependably high standards. The accommodation is in three-storey balconied blocks, whose green gable roofs and understated colonial-style features provide relief from the school of eyesore design to which most modern beach resorts conform. Paths through the large resort run anywhere and everywhere but staff seem to know where they are going, generally on electrical buggies. Work is being undertaken to conserve a lagoon that borders the hotel's western edges. So, if it was pink and flew, you probably saw a flamingo.

Sports are a strong feature at **Hotel Superclub Breezes Varadero** (Carretera las Américas km3.5, 045 667030, www.superclubs cuba.net), with four floodlit tennis courts and good guest rates at the adjacent golf course. The 270 rooms are pleasant, but the furnishings are now a bit worn around the edges (the hotel is almost ten years old). To make up for it, it has Varadero's prettiest hotel gardens. Eight hotel bars might help clients not to feel too self-conscious if they choose to participate in the toga party, a weekly highlight in Breezes' busy activities programme. Over-16s only.

The preponderance of older, well-dressed (mainly Spanish) guests at **Meliá Varadero** (Carretera de la Morlas, 045 667013, www. solmelia.com) creates a sense of slightly unrelaxed decorum. Rooms are arranged along the arms of a huge seven-pronged star. The highlight is probably the cavernous seven-storey central atrium filled with lush tropical vegetation, with a domed roof; glass lifts glide smoothly up and down one side. The pleasant sound of falling water is marred only by orchestral muzak. The main buffet is excellent, as are the other à la carte restaurants. Situated atop a low rocky headland, the pool and gardens have terrific sea views.

Mercure Coralia Cuatro Palmas (Avenida 1ra, entre 60 y 61, 045 667040), a decent mid-range option, is located at the eastern end of Varadero town. The main hotel facilities, together with bed and breakfast and half-board accommodation, are provided in buildings located to the north of Avenida 1ra, with direct access to the beach. All-inclusive guests are housed separately in three blocks to the south of the road (although known as Coralia Las Palmas, these form part of the same hotel). The hotel has been managed by French group Accor since 1998, and was renovated in 2000, so the level of service and standards of accommodation are relatively high (standards are lower in the all-inclusive section, which Accor have downgraded to three-star). There's a gym, sauna and nautical centre but no scuba diving. Varadero's best area for restaurants and bars (between calles 43 and 53) is within walking distance, as is the crafts market.

Hotel Superclubs Puntarena (Avenida Kawama y Final, 045 667120-29) consists of two unsightly twin towers at the far western end of the peninsula. This resort's reputation has faded in recent years, and it's not hard to see why. The buffet is unexciting, while the Chinese restaurant's aspirations don't stretch much further than a bottle of soy sauce. The furniture in the rooms is worn, communal areas aren't impermeable to tropical rainstorms and the garden and pool areas suffer from an over-zealous application of concrete. On a more positive note, the beach at this end of the peninsula is fabulous, with large, empty stretches of fine white sand, and the upper rooms have panoramic views.

Brisas del Caribe (Carretera Las Morlas km12, 045 668030) is operated by Cubanacán, and is one of the few hotels in Varadero that isn't foreign-managed. In early 2003, long-overdue refurbishment work was carried out. The food has also improved, but still lacks quality and variety. Adequately furnished, the rooms are also rather basic. Still, this all-inclusive hotel retains its cheerful demeanour, and is a popular and cheaper all-inc option.

Technically speaking, **Sol Sirenas Coral** (Calle K y Avenida de las Américas, 045 668070/667240) consists of two hotels. However, they were recently amalgamated to make one enormous complex, and uniform rates were established. Standards of accommodation and catering make it a reasonable mid-range option.

Approximately half of the 407 rooms at **Sol Palmeras** (Carretera de las Morlas, 045 667008, www.solmelia.com) are housed in a small village of independent bungalow units of varying size, particularly good for family accommodation. Hotel staff vaunt the range and quality of activities on offer to all age groups, children in particular.

BUDGET OPTIONS

For those with less to spend on a beach break, cheaper alternatives are easy to find among the older and smaller Cuban-managed hotels, particularly those situated near to or in Varadero town. Note that owners of private houses in Varadero town are not permitted to rent rooms to foreigners (though some still do).

Two good budget options are **Villa la Mar** (Avenida 3ra, entre 28 y 30, 045 614515/613910, doubles $33-$78) across the road from the beach, where all rooms have cable and air-con; and **Mar del Sur** (045 612246, doubles $52-$62), a peach and blue hotel, with a triangular pool and scattered small gazebos.

Tourist information

Rumbos

Calle 13, esquina Avenida 1ra (045 612384).
Open 8am-5pm Mon-Fri.

Getting there

By bus

The Vía Blanca dual carriageway goes directly from Havana to Varadero ($2 toll at the entrance for cars and motorbikes). Buses arrive at the small **Terminal de Omnibuses** on Calle 36 and Autopista Sur (Víazul 045 614886; Astro 045 612626). Astro buses to Havana ($6) leave once a day (8.30am) and Víazul buses to Havana ($10) leave three times a day (8am, 4pm, 6pm): both take around 3hrs. There are also direct bus links with Trinidad and Santa Clara.

By rail

The nearest railway stations are in Cárdenas, 18km (11 miles) to the south-east, and Matanzas, 42km (26 miles) to the west, making train connections with Havana impractical.

By air

Varadero's **Juan Gualberto Gómez airport** (045 613016) lies 25km (16 miles) to the west of Varadero, but add a further 20km (12.5 miles) if you are at the easterly end of the peninsula. There's a bus costing $10 per person from the airport to hotels on the strip. There are domestic flights from Baracoa, Cayo Coco, Cayo Largo, Havana, Holguín and Santiago de Cuba. A flight to Havana from here costs just $36, although overall it's much less convenient than the bus.

The Central Provinces

Pockets of prime colonial architecture in the midst of lush tropical scenery.

Villa Clara Province

Santa Clara & around

The most important town in Villa Clara Province – and by far the most lively – is its capital city, Santa Clara, known as 'Che's city'. Ernesto 'Che' Guevara was the leader of the rebel column that took the city in 1958, the event that effectively spelt the end of Batista's rule in Cuba.

A huge statue of the guerrilla leader, the **Monumento a Che Guevara**, towers over the entrance to the city at Avenida de los Desfiles on **Plaza de la Revolución**. The statue is inscribed with an emotionally charged letter from Che to Fidel when he left Cuba, which makes interesting reading for Spanish speakers. This is where most visitors to Santa Clara come to pay tribute to Guevara. Below the statue is the hero's mausoleum, which also houses the remains of the other Latin American guerrillas who died with him, and the **Conjunto Escultórico Comandante Ernesto Che Guevara** (042 205878, closed Mon, free). The museum contains displays on Che's involvement in the Revolution, and some of his personal belongings. You will come across other shrines to Che as you walk around the city, such as **El Che de los Niños**, a bronze statue by Casto Solano showing Che holding a young child. This can be found on the outskirts of Santa Clara.

El Che de los Niños.

Monumento a la Toma del Tren Blindado (no phone, closed Mon) makes a fascinating stop; it is the spot where on 28 December 1958 18 guerillas (led by Che Guevara) attacked one of Batista's trains containing 408 heavily armed troops with a bulldozer. Four carriages – now containing related displays – of the derailed train and the bulldozer have been preserved.

Like most colonial-era cities, Santa Clara's municipal life is centred around a public square. The **Parque Leoncio Vidal** is named after a hero of the 19th-century independence war against Spain. It is edged by Calles Vidal and Abreu; the latter is named after one of the heroines of that same struggle, Marta Abreu. The park is bordered by buildings housing government offices, the public library and cultural centres, as well as the Hotel Santa Clara Libre (*see below*). However, in contrast to the squares in most cities of the period, this park is not overlooked by a church.

Where to stay & eat

Other than plenty of peso pizzerias (around five pesos a pizza) and the **Coppelia** ice-cream parlour (Calle Colón #9, entre Mujica y San Cristóbal, 042 206426, closed Mon), the best feeds are to be had at the city's *paladares*. One of the best is **La Bodeguita del Centro** (Calle Villuendas #264, 042 204356). **La Marquesina**, a 24-hour café on the square itself, next to Teatro la Caridad, is ideally placed for refreshment.

The 1950s **Hotel Santa Clara Libre** (Parque Vidal #6, entre Marta Abreu y Tristá, 042 207548-51, doubles $29-$36), the only hotel in the city centre, is conveniently placed on the central square. It's not the most pleasant stay in the area, though; the building is run-down and there are often problems with the water supply.

The only other city-centre accommodation comes in the form of Santa Clara's many *casas particulares*. One of our favourites is mint-green

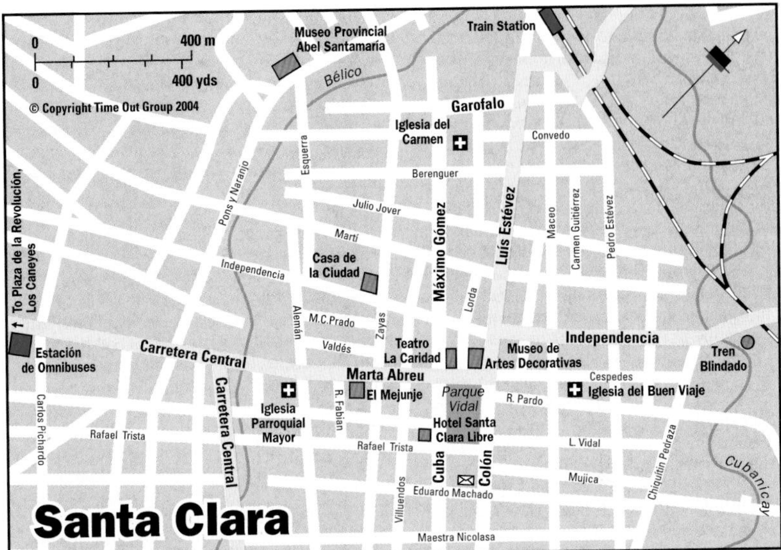

Casa Mercy (San Cristobál #4, entre Cuba y Colón, 042 216941, www.casamercy.com), with two clean rooms and friendly hosts, just a block off the square. Even closer to the square is **Casa Orlando Cordero Rodríguez** (Calle Rolando Pardo #16, entre Maceo y Parque, 042 206456, o_cordero2003@yahoo.com), which has a roof terrace that affords privacy. *Casas particulares* cost around $20-$25 per double per night.

The best accommodation, however, lies on the outskirts of town. **Los Caneyes** (Avenida de los Eucaliptos y Circunvalación, 042 218140-43, $38-$48) consists of 91 attractive thatched cabins in a peaceful woody area just outside town. The rooms are modern, and there's a swimming pool, jacuzzi and shops. You'll need your own transport or a taxi to get to the city centre, two kilometres (1.25 miles) away.

Another similarly attractive place a little further out is Cubanacán's **Villa La Granjita** (Carretera a Maleza km2.5, 042 218190/218191, recep@granjita.vyt.cyt.cu, doubles $38-$50), with 75 rooms. It combines natural-looking cabins with modern indoor conveniences, and has a swimming pool, a restaurant and horses.

Nightlife

Santa Clara is pretty lively after dark. On weekend nights, the square becomes the social hub for both young and old. There are a handful of nightclubs around the city centre, but they change their clientele, opening hours and music regularly, so ask around for what's hot and what's not. **Club Mejunje** (Marta Abréu #107, entre Alemán y Juan Bruno Zayas, no phone, $1-$5) is a cultural centre with a bohemian feel, and is the focus of Santa Clara's thriving gay scene.

Tourist information

Havanatur

Calle Máximo Gómez #13, entre Boulevard y Alfredo Barreras (042 204001). **Open** 8.30am-5pm Mon-Fri; 8.30am-noon Sat.

Getting there

By bus

Astro and Viazul buses arrive at the **Terminal de Omnibuses Nacionales** (042 292113/292114), which is located on the corner of Carretera Central and Oquendo, in the west of the city (a short taxi ride). **Astro** buses ($15) to Havana leave at 6.30am, 9.30pm and 9.40pm and take over 4hrs. **Víazul** buses ($18) leave at 9.30am, 3.30pm and 8pm.

By train

Santa Clara's **railway station** (042 203256/202896) is on the Parque de los Mártires in the northern part of town, but you have to go across the park to Calle Luis Estévez Norte #323 to book. Two departures daily for Havana ($10).

Remedios

North-east of Santa Clara is the sleepy historical town of San Juan de los Remedios. Founded in 1513 as Santa Cruz de la Sabana, it was the second town to be settled by the newly arrived Spanish conquistadors, and was maintained as a feudal fiefdom by Spanish nobleman Vasco Porcallo de Figueroa (whose principal claim to fame was to have reputedly fathered 300 children during his lifetime). He was named mayor of Remedios in 1545.

Piracy, which was the bane of many Spanish settlements in Cuba, was the main form of economic sustenance for Remedios. The town's inhabitants earned their living from smuggling, and actual raids by pirates were infrequent. Far from the two earliest Spanish capitals (Santiago and Havana), the territories of Remedios, Sancti Spíritus and Trinidad in the central regions lay outside the jurisdiction of Spanish governors.

Even more than its early friendly links with the pirates, Remedios owes its mystique to legends about devils and exorcisms. In 1682, the story goes, a priest was called upon to exorcise the devil from a local woman. The devil threatened to unleash his evil legions on the people unless they abandoned their village. Eighteen families (comprising some 200 people) decided to heed the devil's warning, and left Remedios. It was these 18 families who founded the city of Santa Clara, on 15 July 1689.

Two years later the inhabitants of Santa Clara set fire to Remedios to rid the area of the devil's curse; this 'holy war' was only ended in 1694 by order of the Spanish government. (Other accounts say the inhabitants of Santa Clara were angry at the collaboration of the people of Remedios with the pirates who continued to plague Cuba.) In any case, under the Crown's protection, Remedios continued to grow. It is now a relatively large town, with a population of 18,000, although if you wander around its streets, you may well feel you have gone back several centuries in time. It has all the colonial charm of Trinidad with very little of its tourism.

Some of the area's history is marked with annual events held in Remedios. The **Parrandas** festival, held in the last week of December, features colourful floats and fireworks, traditional dancing, and plenty of beer and rum to create an exciting end-of-year ritual. Since 1820 the parishes of San Salvador and del Carmen have taken part in what was initiated by the local priest as a means of waking people up for midnight mass to improve attendance. If you happen to be in town during the festival, look out for the neighourhood's two symbols: San Salvador's rooster and Carmen's sparrowhawk. The low-key **Museo de las Parrandas Remedianas** (Calle Máximo Gómez #71, entre Alejandro del Río y Andrés del Río, no phone, closed Mon) gives a glimpse of the history of the festivals.

Many visitors find that wandering around the backstreets of Remedios is interesting enough in itself, but if you're looking for sights, seek out **Plaza Martí**. This typically Spanish central park is shaded by royal palm trees and

Paradise islands

Villa Clara Province has some blissful keys (*cayos*) within easy reach of the mainland. These miniature islands come complete with powdery white sand and blue curaçao water, providing ample space for living out your Bounty advert tropical dreams in relative isolation. But maybe not for long. As part of Cuba's push to save itself from economic collapse through tourism, many of the isolated keys around Cuba's coast have been developed into luxurious all-inclusive resorts. A cluster of keys off the north coast of Villa Clara Province is set to be next in line.

A 48-kilometre (30-mile) causeway (*pedraplén*) was built between 1989 and 1999 out of the small port of Caibarién to the Archipiélago de Sabana-Camagüey, with a view to developing the keys. Somewhere in the region of 100,000 hotel rooms are to be spread between Cayo Santa María, Cayo Ensanchos, Cayo Las Brujas and Cayo Francés. After ecological problems were inflicted by the Cayo Coco causeway further along the coast, the causeway out of Caibarién has been built differently to allow the free movement of tidal waters.

Though hotel construction work continues apace (a five-star Meliá Santa María is due to open in spring 2004), at the time of writing there were just two hotels in this cluster of keys. Cayo Santa María has the 300-room **Hotel Sol Cayo Santa María** (042 351500, www.solmelia.com, $180-$190), an all-inclusive resort with 11 kilometres (seven miles) of white sand beaches.

For a more subtle – and cheaper – resort, Gaviota-operated **Villa Las Brujas** (042 204199, $60-$70) on Cayo Las Brujas comes recommended. Attractively designed modern cabanas are arranged along a ridge with sea views. There's a restaurant and a quiet stretch of sandy beach unusually free of music.

dotted with marble and wrought-iron benches. One side is dominated by the **Iglesia de San Juan Bautista** (0422 395683), which was built in 1692 and is one of Cuba's oldest churches. The church has been restored, revealing some of the ornate splendour inside. The carved cedar altar is inlaid with gold leaf, and the Moorish-style ceiling is made of mahogany. Various down over the pews.

If you like colonial architecture and furnishings, visit the equally pretty church of **Nuestra Señora del Buen Viaje** (no phone, closed for renovation at the time of writing) at Alejandro del Río #66 and the bright pink **Teatro Rubén M Villena** (Camilo Cienfuegos #30, 0422 395364, closed Sat, Sun).

One of the town's most informative museums (for Spanish speakers) is **Museo de Música Alejandro García Caturla** (Parque Martí, no phone, closed Mon) on the north side of the square, dedicated to one of Cuba's foremost composers. Caturla was only 14 when he began writing music in 1920, and was influenced by both the sounds of Africa and the classical music of Stravinsky. Caturla defied the traditions of the Spanish ruling class in many ways, particularly by his marriage to a black woman. He also studied law, and became a municipal judge, with a reputation for incorruptibility. In 1940 he was assassinated by a policeman who was due in court the next day accused of beating a woman to death.

A few minutes' walk from Plaza Martí, at Calle Antonio Maceo #56, between Fe del Valle and General Carrillo, is a colonial home housing the **Museo de Historia Francisco Javier Balsameda** (no phone, closed Mon). The museum traces the history of the area.

Where to eat & stay

Once viewed as solely a place to visit from Santa Clara, Remedios is becoming an increasingly popular overnight stay. The town's only hotel – the ten-room **Hotel Mascotte** (Calle Máximo Gómez #114, 0422 395481, $38-$44) – sits in pole position on Parque Martí, with pleasant 19th-century decor. The front five rooms are considerably better than the others, and overlook the square.

In general the standard of *casas particulares* is streets behind that of nearby Santa Clara. However, modern, pastel-coloured **Hospedaje El Chalet** (Brigadier González #29, 0422 395331) is an exception to the rule, with two spotless rooms decorated to a high standard.

There are no *paladares* in Remedios, and the only places to eat are **El Louvre** on the square and the restaurant inside the **Hotel Mascotte** – both have uninspiring menus.

Nuestra Señora del Buen Viaje, Remedios.

Getting there

By bus

The bus station is six blocks south of the Plaza Martí, along Independencia. Buses run to Santa Clara several times a day. The alternative is a private taxi.

By car

From Santa Clara or Remedios, head toward Caibarién. Fifteen kilometres (9.5 miles) north of Caibarién, you will come to a 24-hour toll booth (peaje) at the entrance to the causeway, where you show your passport and pay $2 per car.

By air

A small airport (042 350009) on Cayo las Brujas was not operating at the time of writing. There are other airports at Cayo Coco and Santa Clara.

Cienfuegos Province

Cienfuegos

Though a fortress was built in the early 18th century, Cienfuegos wasn't founded until 1819. Set on a beautiful bay, the city was subject to pirate attacks and periodic battles for dominance among the European powers of the 17th and 18th centuries.

Unlike the rest of the island's towns, it was founded by French settlers, rather than Spanish conquistadors or their British competitors. Its

The ornate and Moorish-inspired **Palacio de Valle**, Cienfuegos.

French background, combined with direct influence from the United States, gives Cienfuegos its unique characteristics. In terms of architecture, the French influence has left the city with attractive neo-classical buildings.

Wander around the beautiful downtown area, centred around **Parque Martí**. Bordering this main square are numerous important buildings, among them the **Catedral de la Concepción Inmaculada** (043 525298). Founded in 1869, the cathedral boasts lovely stained-glass windows, brought over from France during the time of the Paris Commune. Also on the square are the **Teatro Tomás Terry,** one of the city's cultural landmarks, the **Museo Histórico**, the **Ayuntamiento** (City Hall), the **Casa de la UNEAC** and the **Fondo de Bienes Culturales**, which displays and sells art.

There are two unique cemeteries on the outskirts of town: the Tomás Acea and La Reina; both can be visited independently or on a guided tour. Some 20 kilometres (12.5 miles) east of the city centre is Cienfuegos's famed **Jardín Botánico** (043 451115, $2.50). The garden covers an area of nine square kilometres (3.5 square miles) and contains more than 2,000 species of plants.

If you only have time for one sight, make it the intriguing **Palacio del Valle** (043 551226) at the very tip of Punta Gorda to the south. It was built in 1917 and has an incredibly ornamental look and a Moorish style. Don't leave without having a cocktail in the roof bar gazing out to sea. It also houses a restaurant.

Another popular trip is the **Castillo de Jagua** (no phone), at the mouth of the Bahía de Cienfuegos. The 17th-century fortress can be reached by ferry from the wharf in Cienfuegos at Calle 25, esquina 46 (remember to check return ferry times). **Rumbos** (*see p201*) can provide a boat trip around the bay and several of the keys, for swimming and snorkelling.

Where to eat & drink

The elegant **1869 restaurant** in the Hotel Unión (*see below*, mains $6-$25), housed in Hotel Unión, is one of Cienfuegos's most pleasant restaurants. The **Club Cienfuegos** complex towards Punta Gorda is housed in the swankily restored former Yacht Club and has a range of bars and restaurants. The seafront terrace is ideal for sipping mojitos. One of the most romantic spots for dining is the pricy restaurant at **Palacio del Valle** (*see above*). **El Criollito** (Calle 33 #5603, entre 56 y 58, 043 525540, mains $7-$10) is a decent, if pricey, *paladar*.

Nightlife

Club El Beny (Avenida 54 #2904, entre 31 y Parque, 043 551105, closed Mon, $3) is a smart central nightclub. **Casa de la Música** (Calle 37, entre 4 y 6, Punta Gorda, 043 552320, closed Mon, $1-$5) gets going at about 10.30pm with live music, comedy and dance shows.

Where to stay

The beautifully restored, and well-located, **Hotel Unión** (Calle 31, esquina 54, 043 451020, www.cubanacan.cu, doubles $65-$85) is by far and away the best place to stay in central Cienfuegos. It has 36 rooms, 13 suites, a beautiful swimming pool, plus a gym and restaurant. Gran Caribe's **Hotel Jagua**

(Calle 37 #1, entre 0 y 2, 043 551003, reservas@jagua.co.cu, doubles $80-$95) at Punta Gorda has 143 air-conditioned rooms and 13 poolside *cabañas*. It has plenty of facilities (swimming pool, restaurants, tourism bureau) but not a lot of character.

Out of town there's **Hotel Rancho Luna** (Carretera Racho Luna km16, 043 548012 doubles $70-$80), popular with Canadian tour groups, and the smaller, more stylish **Hotel Faro Luna** (Carretera Rancho Luna km18, 043 548030, doubles $55-$65), with decent rooms and a pool on the water's edge.

Otherwise there's the aesthetically challenged concrete block that is **Hotel Pasacaballos** (Carretera Rancho Luna, km22, 043 548013, doubles $30-$38) overlooking the bay, used mainly by Cubans.

Tourist information

Havanatur

Avenida 54 #2906, entre 29 y 31 (043 551613/ 551393). **Open** 8.30am-5.30pm Mon-Sat.
Excursions, hotel booking, car hire and air tickets.

Rumbos

Calle 37, esquina 48, Punta Gorda (043 551379/ 551174). **Open** 10am-6pm Mon-Fri.
For trips to the surrounding countryside, including El Nicho (*see below*), and local boat trips.

Getting there

By bus

All buses arrive at the bus station on Calle Gloria, between 56 and 58 (043 515720). **Astro** buses to Havana ($14) leave four times a day (6.15am, noon, 4.15pm and 7.30pm) and take 5hrs. **Víazul** buses ($20) leave twice a day (8.15am, 1pm) and take about 4hrs.

By train

The railway station is across the road from the bus station (043 525495). In theory the service to Havana ($16) runs once a day, but it's not very reliable.

The rest of the province

It's hard to choose between the province's many spectacular sites, but if you have time for only one, visit **El Nicho** in the Escambray mountain range. Havanatur or Rumbos (*see above*) can

arrange this for you, or if you have a sturdy car and a good map, you can try it yourself. Hiring a guide helps. The trek around El Nicho is outstanding, taking in babbling brooks and streams, waterholes for swimming and a pristine cave (El Calvo). A tour here may last eight or nine hours; Cubamar arranges overnight trips.

For a taste of the coast, head 20 kilometres (12.5 miles) south of Cienfuegos to **Playa Rancho Luna**, a pleasant sandy beach.

Sancti Spíritus Province

Trinidad

Trinidad was founded as the Villa de la Santísima Trinidad on the site of a small Indian settlement in 1514. The city, with its red-tiled roofs, cobblestone streets, stained-glass arches and intricately designed wrought-iron grated windows, was declared a World Heritage Site by UNESCO in 1988. It is now one of Cuba's premier tourist attractions, and tourists flock to see this intact relic of Spanish colonial times.

There are disputes over whether the first mass here was celebrated by Franciscan Father Juan de Tesin, or by the equally renowned Father Bartolomé de las Casas, who was a great defender of the indigenous peoples on the island. The cross, however, was frequently accompanied by the gun, and the area also served as a recruiting ground for Hernán Cortez, when he set out on his expedition to conquer Mexico in 1519, gathering horses, men and supplies here.

For the next two centuries Trinidad was mostly a quiet valley where Spanish settlers raised cattle and grew tobacco. But its proximity to the sea also made it a home for *contrabandistas* and slave traders from the British-controlled isles of the Caribbean. It wasn't until the 19th century that sugar cane became an important crop here. The slave rebellion in Haiti had a marked impact on the region, as French colonial settlers fled to Cuba in droves. By 1827 they had set up more than 50 small sugar mills in the valley near Trinidad, thus earning it the name Valle de los Ingenios (Valley of the Sugar Mills), and making Trinidad one of the most prosperous cities on the island. Sugar soon became its most important product and the commercial boom this created enabled the newly wealthy landholders to build the fine homes that have lasted to this day.

The Wars of Independence against Spain (1868-78, 1895-8) took a heavy toll on this area, and by the time they were over, neighbouring Cienfuegos and Matanzas provinces had become the hub of the sugar trade. Trinidad remained in a time warp. No longer a bustling commercial centre, it has maintained its charm and elegance through the centuries.

The city's museums and churches are concentrated around the delightful **Plaza Mayor**. Here you can sit on one of the park benches, in the shade provided by a canopy of bougainvillea, and watch the daily life of the town. As tourism takes a hold over this small town, hustlers are increasing in numbers and persistence, and it can be a drain on the visitor.

The **Iglesia Parroquial de la Santísima Trinidad** (0419 3368) on the north-east side of Plaza Mayor was the main parochial church of Trinidad until 1814, when it was destroyed by a storm. The church was rebuilt in 1892 and resumed its former role. Today, it is important for the relics it contains, such as the 1713 Cristo de la Vera Cruz (Christ of the True Cross).

As befits a historic city, Trinidad has a number of museums, housed in the former homes of the landed aristocracy. On the Plaza Mayor itself, the Palacio del Conde Brunet (Calle Echerrí, esquina Simón Bolívar) is now the **Museo Romántico** (0419 4363, closed Mon); the former home of Sánchez Iznaga has become the **Museo de Arquitectura** (Calle Respalda #83); and the mansions of Alderman Ortiz and Don Juan Andrés Padrón have been combined as the **Museo Arqueológico Guamuhaya** and the **Museo de Ciencias Naturales Alexander von Humboldt** (Calle Simón Bolívar #457, esquina Villena; people refer to them by either name; closed at time of writing for refurbishment). Within these museums you can still see the opulence with which the sugar barons and traders lived off the sweat of their African slaves. If you only have time for one, make it the Museo Romántico, which contains a collection of antique furniture, arranged in beautifully restored rooms.

The **Museo Municipal de Trinidad** (0419 4460, closed Fri) is located a block below the square, at Calle Simón Bolívar #423, on the corner of Callejón de Peña, in a mansion that once belonged to the Borrell family. The highlight of this museum is the tower with picture-postcard views. The **Museo Nacional de la Lucha Contra los Bandidos** (Calle Fernando Echerrí, esquina Piro Guinart, 0419 4121, closed Mon) portrays the history of the five-year-long battles between local rebel forces and counter-Revolutionary insurgents (*bandidos*) hiding out in the surrounding Escambray mountains after 1959. Exhibits include photos, authentic objects and parts of a US U-2 spy plane that was shot down in the area. The museum is housed in the former San Francisco de Asís

convent, a block north of Plaza Mayor. The bell tower of the convent, something of a symbol of the town, is often open to the public. From here you will have a breathtaking view over Trinidad, taking in the city's oldest church, now in ruins, **Nuestra Señora de la Candelaria de la Popa** to the north-east. While you're at the top, have a look at the bells and the machinery that operates them. Close inspection will reveal that they were made in Boston.

Another interesting square is the **Plaza Santa Ana** at the corner of calles Santo Domingo and Santa Ana. In addition to the remains of the **Iglesia Santa Ana**, the square is the location of the former Cárcel Real (Royal Prison). This fortress-like structure is now home to a key cultural and commercial centre. In its broad, sun-drenched courtyard, the Trinidad Folk Ensemble perform Afro-Cuban dances and music for visitors. Inside the building is an art gallery, a handicrafts bazaar and a ceramics shop. There's also a bar, cafeteria, coffee shop and restaurant.

Where to eat

Considering its size and villagey feel, Trinidad has a surprising number of restaurants, often in fine colonial mansions. One of these is **El Jigue** (Calle Villena, entre P Guinart y P Piz Girón, 0419 6476, mains $7-$17); it has a beautiful setting but is let down by mediocre food. Nearby, **Taberna La Chanchánchara** (0419 6403, mains $5-$23), one block up on Calle Villena, is one of the oldest buildings in Trinidad, combining architectural styles from the 18th, 19th and 20th centuries. It's a lively place, with music and dancing, and serves a speciality cocktail made of rum, honey, lemon and water, which is named after the tavern.

The **Trinidad Colonial** (0419 6473, mains $5-$23) on the corner of Calles Maceo and Colón is a more formal restaurant, with a decent international menu. The restaurant mimics the rich elegance of the 19th century. Nearby **Las Begonias** café (corner of Calles Gutiérrez and Simon Bolívar, no phone) serves up cheap snacks and has internet access. It's something of a social hub for young locals and travellers.

Better prices – and almost always better cuisine – can be found in the city's *paladares*, and if you stay in a *casa particular*, your hosts may prepare meals for you. The best *paladar* in town is **Sol y Son** (Calle Simón Bolívar #283, entre Frank País y José Martí, mains $5-$8), offering professional service and excellent food. **La Coruña** (Calle José Martí #430, entre Piro

Guinart y Santiago Escobar, mains $8) serves up hearty portions but is rather cramped.

Nightlife

Probably the most unusual nightclub in town (if not in Cuba) is the **Discoteca Ayala** (0419 6133, closed Mon, $10). Known locally as La Cueva, it occupies a huge cave (with stalactites and all). Head up the path behind the cathedral, off Calle Juan Manuel Márquez (Amargura).

Hotspots for live music include the **Casa de la Música** (Calle F J Zerquera #3, 0419 6622, $1-$3), as well as the small open-air plaza halfway up the steps to the venue. The **Casa de la Trova** (Calle F H Echerrí #29), a block east of the Plaza Mayor, hones a more traditional, folky vibe. Nearby, the courtyard at the **Ruinas de Segarte** (Calle José Menéndez y J M Márquez, $1-$3) has a mixed bill of traditional music and Afro-Cuban dance.

Where to stay

Although the tiny city of Trinidad has no major hotels (though construction is under way of a five-star on the Parque Céspedes), it is full of *casas particulares*. It is worth taking the time to visit a few of these private homes before taking your pick. Make sure you choose one with a blue and white emblem, which means it's licensed. Visitors arriving at the bus station may be met by an intimidating wall of eager hosts and *jineteros*.

Other accommodation options in the town centre include the basic but friendly **Hotel La Ronda** (Calle José Martí, entre Colón y Lino Pérez, 0419 4011, doubles $22), which has internet access in its lobby and a bar, and the newly opened rooms at **Casa Regidor** (Simón Bolívar #424, 0419 6572/3, doubles $38-$48), just half a block from the Plaza Mayor. The four rooms have a rustic feel with terracotta tiled floor, bright blue shutters, air-conditioning, TV and en suite bathrooms. This place is a good budget alternative to a *casa particular*, with considerably more privacy.

One of the most comfortable places to stay in Trinidad, on a hill on the outskirts of town, is **Motel Las Cuevas** (Finca Santa Ana, 0419 6133, www.horizontes.cu, doubles $69-$79). This pleasant complex of small bungalow-style rooms has a pool and two restaurants.

Tourist information

Rumbos

Calle Gloria #101, esquina Simón Bolívar (0419 6198). **Open** 8.30am-5pm Mon-Sat. Excursions, hotel bookings, scooter and bicycle hire.

Getting there

By bus

Buses from other provinces arrive at the bus terminal (0419 4448) on Calle Piro Guinart #224, between Maceo and Izquierda. **Astro** buses leave every other day for Havana ($21) and take six hours. **Víazul** buses go twice a day ($25); journey time around five hours.

By train

The railway station (0419 3348) is located on the south-western edge of town, on Calle Antonio Maceo, although it only serves destinations in the nearby area, such as the Valle de los Ingenios (*see below*).

By air

Aeropuerto Alberto Delgado (0419 616393) is two kilometres south-west of the city centre. The airport is was closed for renovation at the time of writing.

Around Trinidad

If you're short of time, choose between the deserted sugar mills of the Valle de los Ingenios, the beaches of the Ancón peninsula, with their excellent snorkelling and scuba-diving sites, and the forested mountains that shelter the Topes de Collantes natural health spa and hotel.

Just two kilometres from Trinidad, **Mirador Cerro de la Vigía** provides a rare view of the entire city of Trinidad, with its labyrinth of streets. The red-tiled roofs of its mansions and the wrought iron of doors and balconies glitter brilliantly in the sunshine. Moving higher up into the clouds, **Mirador La Loma del Puerto**, at 192 metres (640 feet), provides a panoramic view of the entire valley.

Valle de los Ingenios

Sweeping through the hills north-east of Trinidad, towards Sancti Spíritus, the **Valle de los Ingenios** (Valley of the Sugar Mills) was the most important sugar-producing area in colonial Cuba, and has been declared a UNESCO Cultural Heritage Site. Its 65 archaeological plots include the remains of numerous mills, with parts of their machinery and many tools and utensils still intact. You will also find the remains of manor houses, a slave hamlet, warehouses, infirmaries and a bell tower.

A key site within the Valley is the **Manaca Iznaga**, one of the most important sugar mills during the 19th century. The best-preserved parts of the complex are the slaves' quarters, the buildings that served as warehouses, and the 43.5-metre (145-foot) Manaca Iznaga tower, which you can climb for a view of the entire valley. The old mansion of the Iznaga family has been fitted out with a bar and restaurant.

The most interesting way to see the valley is on the delightful 1919 steam train that runs between Trinidad and Guachinango ($10; reservations Rumbos). The train stops at the ruins of the **Magua** mill, and again for lunch at Manaca Iznaga. The train departs at 9.30am and comes back at 3pm. The regular train costs a fraction of the price.

Topes de Collantes

Twenty kilometres (12.5 miles) north of Trinidad – and surrounded by a totally different type of landscape filled with giant ferns, moss, lichens, pine and eucalyptus trees – the road winds up the mountains of the Escambray to the **Topes de Collantes** health resort. This isn't the highest peak of the Escambray range: Pico San Juan (1,156 metres, 3,793 feet) and Pico de Potrerillo (931 metres, 3,054 feet) both beat the 771-metre (2,530-feet) elevation of this resort. Topes de Collantes opened as a tuberculosis sanatorium in 1954. The main structure was rebuilt in 1984, with additional, smaller buildings erected among the towering trees and ferns. Initially the spa catered primarily to Cubans, who had been referred here by their doctors for specific treatments or rehabilitation. Today, the resort has joined the tourist drive. The huge **Kurhotel** (042 540180, rates $38-$48), offers natural therapies, **Los Helechos** (042 540330-5, doubles $32-$42) and the bungalows of **Villa Caburní** (042 540330, doubles $32-$42) are all open to foreigners. The whole complex has a rather jaded air, and is hardly the luxury health farm many visitors might be expecting.

Treks, available to non-residents for a $6.50 fee, are the highlight of a visit to the area. The most popular trail is to the 62-metre (207-foot) waterfall known as **Salto del Caburní**, with a small pool suitable for bathing. The path is challenging (allow three hours, plus swimming time), but well signposted, and worth the sweat for the lush green scenery. Avoid the path after rain. Note that the resort is only accessible by car or private taxi from Trinidad.

Península de Ancón & the keys

South of Trinidad – a short taxi ride from the centre of town – the Península de Ancón is caressed by the warm blue-green waters of the Caribbean, and is a good spot for watersports.

The 271-room **Hotel Ancón** (0419 6120-9, doubles $100-$116) is right on this sandy stretch. This concrete hotel, built in the 1980s, isn't pretty but the rooms aren't bad inside. Staff can arrange watersports, including sailing, snorkelling and scuba diving around the sunken ships along the coast.

Plaza Mayor, Trinidad. *See p202.*

The newest addition to Playa Ancón is the swanky **Hotel Brisas Trindad del Mar** (0419 6507, reservas@brisastdad.co.cu, doubles $130-$160), an all-inclusive resort in pseudo-colonial style, decked out in bright colours. It even has a miniature version of Trinidad's Plaza Mayor – a little pointless, perhaps, when the real thing is just a few miles away.

Alternative accommodation can be found next door at **Hotel Costasur** (0419 6174-8, doubles $45-$54) on Playa María Aguilar, further down the coast. Built in 1975, it has 111 rooms in the main building and two newer extensions, plus 20 rooms in duplex bungalows. There is a pool and a sandy beach.

Off the white sand beaches of Playa Ancón is **Cayo Blanco de Casilda**, with its own beautiful beach and reefs that are ideal for snorkelling. Just off its western tip, at a depth of 18 to 40 metres (59 to 131 feet), scuba divers can view the largest black coral grove in Cuba. At the edge of the island shelf, you can swim among red snappers, bass, turtles, lobsters and a variety of multicoloured tropical fish. The **Marina Cayo Blanco**, next to the Hotel Ancón, provides catamarans, water scooters and surfboards, plus scuba diving and snorkelling gear.

Santiago de Cuba

Cuba's second city is hot. And we're not just talking about the weather.

Cuba's second largest, and third oldest, city sways to its own rhythm: even the local Spanish has its own musical lilt. Located some 950 kilometres (600 miles) from Havana in the south-eastern part of the island, Santiago is a thriving cultural and industrial centre, home to half a million inhabitants.

The city started life in 1515 at the mouth of the Río Paradas, as the third *villa* built by Diego Velázquez (*see p6*). The settlement soon moved to its present location and became Cuba's capital city, until it was replaced by Havana in 1607. Due to its location at the exteme south-east of the island, Santiago was the recipient of various waves of immigration. The first African slaves in Cuba were brought here; French colonists fleeing from neighbouring Haiti settled here, and Jamaicans often made the short trip between the islands. As a result Santiago de Cuba has a more diverse ethnic blend than in other areas of Cuba, a fact reflected in its vibrant music and dance scenes.

In its history, Santiago has often been an incubator of revolution, having played a key role in the revolutions of both 1898 and 1959. Two major historical attractions of the revolution that brought Fidel to power are located here, the **Cuartel Moncada** (Moncada Barracks, *see p207*), where Castro first attacked the Batista regime on 26 July 1953 (the origin of all the Julio 26 signs throughout the country) and the **Granjita Siboney** (*see p208*), a farmhouse where the Revolutionaries stayed before the attack. Both sites have now become national museums.

The city is noted for its hospitality and the warmth of its people and has a very different and relaxed, villagey feel to it than bustling, hard-edged Havana. It also has a beautiful setting in the Sierra Maestra mountains. Unfortunately, it has become a prime hustling spot in recent years, so keep a strong hold on your belongings and just keep walking.

The colonial centre is most easily explored on foot. However, some central areas are hilly. Admission to the museums listed is under $2, unless indicated otherwise. All museum labels are in Spanish.

Don't miss Santiago

Casa de la Trova

Santiago's premier music venue is nothing short of an institution. *See p209.*

Castillo de Morro

The views from this clifftop fort will take your breath away. *See p208.*

El Cobre

A small mining town, home to a religious shrine to **La Virgen de la Caridad**. *See p208.*

Moncada Barracks

Site of the first stirrings of Revolution in 1953, when 100 rebels attacked Batista's troops. *See p207.*

Sightseeing

Parque Céspedes and around

Parque Céspedes is the city's main square, located east of the Bahía de Santiago. Its eclectic architecture runs from the colonial to the modern. On the west side of the square, at the corner of Aguilera, is the oldest house in Cuba: begun in 1516 and completed in 1530, it belonged to the city's first governor, Diego Velázquez. The site is now known as the **Museo de Ambiente Histórico** (no phone), which gives an excellent insight into colonial wealth in Cuba between the 16th to 18th centuries. Velázquez lived on the top floor, while the ground floor was used as a dealing house and smelting room for gold. Visitors can wander freely through the rooms.

On the south side of the park is the provincial cathedral, the white **Catedral Primada Metropolitana Nuestra Señora de la Asunción** (entrance on Calle Félix Peña). A building with an unlucky past, it has been rebuilt four times due to a series of distasters from earthquakes to pirate attacks; the current structure dates from 1818. On the north side of the square is the **Ayuntamiento**, the town hall, a 1940s reconstruction of a 1783 design. Fidel Castro gave his victory speech from the balcony on 2 January 1959, after the defeat of Batista.

Walk two blocks up Calle Aguilera to the east, at the corner of Pío Rosado, for the **Museo**

Emilio Bacardí (0226 28402), the second oldest museum in Cuba, which houses the personal collection of the famous industrialist Emilio Bacardí Moreau, founder of the rum dynasty. The museum boasts an extraordinary collection of weapons, as well as an art gallery on the second floor.

Calle Heredia & south

Calle Heredia runs along the southern side of Parque Céspedes behind the cathedral, and is lined with craftspeople and artists selling painting, woodwork and musical instruments. It is also home to numerous cultural sites, the most famous of which is the **Casa de la Trova** at No.206 (*see p209*), a long-standing symbol of Santiago's deep-rooted musical culture. The **Museo del Carnival** (0226 26966, closed Mon), at the corner of Pío Rosado, traces the history of Santiago's famous carnival (*see p210* **Hotter than July**), and is full of costumes and musical instruments. Folkloric dance performances often take place here at 4pm. Further west on Heredia, you'll come across the office of the **UNEAC**, the artists' and writers' union, with a small art gallery. A few doors down is the **Casa Natal de José María Heredia**, the house where Santiago's most famous poet was born in 1803. There's a **museum** (no phone) dedicated to his life, and the place is also being turned into a cultural centre.

South-east of Parque Céspedes, on Calle Rabi, is the **Museo de la Lucha Clandestina** (0226 24689, closed Mon). This beautifully restored yellow colonial building was once a police station and is now devoted to telling the story of underground leader Frank País and other local Revolutionaries. Don't miss the nearby **Padre Pico Escalinata**, Santiago's famous stairway.

Back toward Parque Céspedes, proceed one block east of Padre Pico to Bartólome Maso, where you'll find the **Balcón de Velázquez** fortification (7am-8pm daily, free), with spectacular views of the bay, the city and surrounding mountains.

Cuartel Moncada & around

No visit to Santiago is complete without a visit to the **Cuartel Moncada** (Moncada Barracks), where Fidel launched his first (and unsuccessful) attack on the Batista regime on 26 July 1953. The building now houses a school but part of it has been turned into the **Museo Histórico 26 de Julio** (Avenida de los Libertadores, 0226 20157, closed Mon). It's located a few blocks north of the

Catedral Nuestra Señora de la Asunción. *See p206.*

Coppelia ice-cream stand. The museum provides insight into the pre-Revolutionary period in Cuba from 1953 to 1959. English-speaking tour guides on request.

Further north

General Antonio Maceo, one of the foremost revolutionaries of the 19th-century wars of independence, is honoured at the **Plaza de la Revolución**, at the junction of Avenida de los Libertadores and Avenida de las Américas. The monument consists of a gargantuan bronze statue of the general on horseback, surrounded by huge iron machetes rising from the ground at different angles. Maceo's birthplace is at Calle Maceo #207, between Corona and Rastro. The **Museo de Holografía** (0226 43768) is housed below the Maceo monument, and features holograms of artefacts from the War of Independence and the Revolutionary War.

The main draw of **Cementerio Santa Ifigenia**, north-west of the city on Avenida Crombet, is **José Martí's mausoleum**. It is a huge structure with a statue of Martí inside, built in a circular design so shafts of sunlight enter all day from different directions.

East of the centre

The former high-class neighbourhood of Vista Alegre has the **Centro Cultural Africano Fernando Ortiz** (Avenida Manduley #106, entre Calle 3 y 5, 0226 42487). Also known as Casa de Africa, it depicts the rich African heritage of Cuba. The area also has the **Museo de la Religión** (Calle 13 #206, 0226 43609), with displays on religious practice in Cuba, especially *santería*.

Castillo de Morro

Some 14 kilometres (8.5 miles) south of the centre is the impressive **Castillo de Morro** (0226 91569, $4) atop the bluffs over the entrance to Santiago Bay. Perhaps the best part of the tour is a visit to the **Museo de Piratería** inside the castle, which explores the pirate attacks made on Santiago in the 16th century. A cannon-firing ritual, similar to the one in Havana (*see p132*), has recently started every evening at sunset. The view of the bay, with the sun setting over the mountains and sea, makes it an ideal time to visit.

Further afield

The **Gran Piedra** is a pleasant one-day excursion from Santiago. This vast boulder sits on top of a mountain in the Baconao reserve, at the tip of the Cordillera de Gran Piedra mountain range, about 20 kilometres (12.5 miles) east of the city. From its summit, 1,214 metres (3,983 feet) above sea level, there are fantastic views of the valley below and the Caribbean Sea. To reach the top, visitors need to climb dozens of steps carved into the rock. A taxi from central Santiago will cost around $35.

Two kilometres south of the Gran Piedra turning, coming from Santiago, is **Granjita Siboney** (022 39119, closed Mon). This historic farmhouse is where Fidel Castro and the other rebels gathered before launching their attack on the Cuartel Moncada in 1956. It is now a museum with Revolutionary exhibits; the road leading to it is lined with monuments commemorating the attack.

One of the most visited places near Santiago is the unassuming mining town of **El Cobre**, west of the city, named after the copper mines that once flourished in the area. It would probably never have entered the history books, had it not been for a religious miracle that took place on the nearby coast in 1628. Three fishermen found a wooden board inscribed with the words 'I am the Virgin of Charity', and a statue of a mulatta Virgin carrying a brown-skinned baby Jesus, floating in the sea. They brought the statue to El Cobre, where it can be seen in the basilica (022 36118). The site is visited by thousands every year, many of whom leave offerings.

Arts & entertainment

Music

The music scene in Santiago is world-class. Most major venues are within a 15-minute walk from the main square, and cover charges are cheap ($1-$3), so if you don't like what you're hearing you can simply get up and head to the next place. Much of what you will hear around town is *son* music, the style that originates from the countryside around Santiago, made famous first by the late Miguel Matamoros and more recently by the Buena Vista Social Club.

The **Casa de la Trova** (Calle Heredia #208, no phone) is the city's premier music venue. There are usually several shows daily, starting at 11am with the best old-timers ($1), followed by performances outside on Patio Virgilio until around 7pm ($1); at 8pm there's another show, then at 10pm the upstairs salon is opened for high-energy, younger performers ($3). All spaces have room to dance and the quality of musicianship is high. Across from the Casa de la Trova is **La Cocinita** (Calle Heredia #254, closed Mon, 0226 27804), a popular watering hole, with often very good bands playing for tips. A beer costs only ten pesos.

Hotel Casa Granda (*see p210*) has a veranda overlooking the main square and is a fine place to people-watch. Early evenings feature live music with some very good groups performing everything from *son* to doo wop. Drinks are a tad expensive but you're in pole position on the square. The roof terrace has panoramic views and hosts occasional concerts.

The **Patio de la Trova** (Calle Heredia #266, 0226 55814/27037), across from the Museo del Carnival on Calle Heredia, is a favourite haunt for young *santiagueros* with hip hop, rap, rumba and salsa concerts, as well as folkloric dance shows. There seems to be no regular schedule of events but announcements are posted out front on the day of the show.

ArtEx (Calle Heredia #304, live music from 10pm daily, $2) is based in the small courtyard of a restored colonial building. The dancefloor is tight but it's a beautiful spot to listen to music under the open sky. Nearby **Coro Madrigalista** (no phone), in the alleyway between Calle Heredia and Aguilera, is a funky community club (named after the choir that rehearses here) offering music from 9pm Monday to Saturday. The quality of performers is uneven but admission is only $1. Look out for the rumba group Kazumbi that appears here on occasions. Events are posted outside.

Everyone knows Patio de la Música Tradicional Cubana as **Los Dos Abuelos** (Pérez Carbo #5, Plaza Marte, 0226 23302/23267, $2). It's a lovely colonial-style music club – an open-air venue with seating for 40, and excellent mojitos – featuring many of the same groups that appear at the Casa de la Trova. Half a block from Parque Céspedes, there's more open-air fun to be had at **Bar Claqueta** (Calle Felix Pena #654, $2 live music), which is open 24 hours.

Casa de las Tradiciones (Calle Rabi #154, entre Princesa y San Fernando, $1) is a true neighbourhood haunt. This venerable club in the Tivolí area is open from 9pm and features nothing but *son* and *trova*, with some very good bands and plenty of guest artists sitting in. Being a little off the main tourist circuit saves this small venue from being overrun with foreigners. Definitely worth the trek.

The **Casa de la Música** offers top-notch programming. It was closed following complaints about noise at the time of writing, but when it reopens in a new location (sometime in 2004) it's bound to be one of the best venues in town. Ask at the UNEAC or at hotels.

One other musical event of note is the annual **Festival de la Trova** (cpmusica@cultstgo.cult.cu), held in mid March, hosted by Eliades Ochoa of Buena Vista Social Club fame, and his own touring band Cuarteto Patria.

When it comes to clubbing, the most popular venue in the city is **Club Tropical Company Gallo** (Tropicana, 0226 41031, closed Mon, $5 per couple), where the DJs play a lively mix of salsa, reggae and techno. The local authorities have shut the place down on occasions on account of sex tourism, hence a couples-only rule. You'll have to negotiate the scrum at the gate, but be persistent and you'll eventually be admitted – though you may need to make up a 'couple' with one of the young Cubans waiting in line. Meanwhile, young Cubans who like their music loud and flashy head for **Disco La Iris** (Aguilera #617, closed Tue, $6-$10), just off Plaza Marte. It's a throwback to the early days of the disco era, with strobe lights and pounding beats. The downstairs café is open 24 hours.

Hotter than July

Ask almost any *santiaguero* what their favourite month is and most will say July, the month when the entire city gets consumed by one huge party. Rum flows in rivers, and the city throbs with music and dancing on the streets and in the parks. Some of the most famous music and dance groups from around the island come to Santiago to play, along with all the local favourites.

What began in the 19th century as a religious celebration linked to Easter has become a secular holiday moved to the middle of the summer. Carnival was originally the one time of the year when slaves were allowed to give free rein to their drumming and dancing, and the festivities were led by secret societies that mirrored those of Africa. These *carabalí*, as they came to be known in Cuba, existed in every neighbourhood and would compete each year to create the most original and dazzling *comparsas* (dance groups). This tradition is preserved, as viewing stands are set up on Avenida Jesús Menendez and each *barrio* competes with its costumes, music and dancing before judges to win bragging rights for the year. The competition is serious business and the quality of the music and dancing is very high.

Dance

The world-renowned Ballet Folklórico Cutumba, considered by many to be the island's best folkloric dance company, has its home at **Casa del Estudiante** (Calle Heredia #204, 0226 27804). The colonial building hosts occasional performances, plus rumba and salsa events at odd times during the week. **Casa del Caribe** (Calle 13 #154, 0226 42285), a cultural centre in Vista Alegre, also puts on interesting Afro-Cuban folkloric events, generally on Thursday nights and Sunday afternoons. It's best to call ahead to see what's cooking but it's nearly always worth attending. A different kind of dance experience is to be had at **Cabaret Tropicana** (Autopista Nacional km1.5, 0226 42579/46573, closed Mon). This popular open-air venue has seating for up to 800 people and fills to capacity in high season. Choreographer Ernesto Arminan has created a panorama of Cuban history through music and dance. The costumes are exquisite, the dancing exciting and the house band excellent. Worth the steep admission ($20-$30).

Baseball

If you happen to be in town between January and May, be sure to catch a baseball game at the **Guillermon Moncada stadium** (0226 42640, $2) on Avenida de las Américas, just north of the Hotel Santiago. This is a baseball-crazy town, home to the national champions in 1999, 2000 and 2001. There's an electric atmosphere at the games and, as you would expect in Santiago, a slick rhythm section that plays whenever the home team gets something going.

Where to stay

Santiago isn't noted for the excellence of its accommodation. In fact, it is better equipped with *casas particulares* than hotels.

One of the city's two top hotels, the **Meliá Santiago** (Avenida de las Américas, 0226 87070, www.solmelia.com, doubles $112-$115), is a little way out of town. It has a variety of restaurants, a pool and spa, and several small stores, including a pharmacy, an internet centre and several bars. The **Casa Granda**

During Carnival, the whole city of Santiago is filled with the rhythm of the drums and the piercing sound of the Chinese trumpet. The Carnival party stretches over a week towards the end of July and is timed to coincide with the national celebration of 26 July – the date of Castro's attack on the Moncada Barracks in 1953 (*see p207*). Indeed, the original attack by Fidel and his companions was set on this date because they believed that the soldiers guarding the building would be in no shape to defend it due to their participation in Carnival.

There's also a pre-Carnival party of some renown in Santiago: the **Festival del Fuego** is held every year in early July. Hosted by the Casa del Caribe, this event honours the cultural traditions of a different Caribbean country each year, with concerts, lectures, poetry readings and dances. For more information about the Festival del Fuego, contact the Casa del Caribe on 0226 641998 or caribe@cult.stgo.cult.cu. For more information about the Santiago Carnival contact Rumbos, Cubatur or any other tour operator.

(Parque Céspedes, esquina Calle Heredia, 0226 53021-4, doubles $96-$112), on the other hand, is bang in the heart of the city on the town's central square. This four-star hotel (run by Gran Caribe) has good service and above-average rooms. The main restaurant is good though pricey.

Other hotels in the town centre include the **Gran Hotel** (Enramadas #317, esquina San Felix, 0226 53028, $32). Opened in 2003, it's not run by a major chain, which can make it difficult to make a reservation from outside Santiago. It's clean and comfortable, but the main attraction is the price, though rates don't include breakfast. The hotel also has an inexpensive restaurant. The **Hotel Libertad** (Aquilera #652, Plaza Marte, 0226 28360/28394, doubles $34-$38) is an attractively decorated, 16-room establishment with lobby and rooftop bars, 24-hour internet access, a disco and a reasonably priced restaurant. Plaza Marte is a very noisy part of the city – ask for a room at the back.

The **Hotel Las Américas** (Avenida de las Américas, 0226 42011, doubles $56-$67) has comfortable – if not spectacular – rooms and a decent pool. The hotel is a popular late-night drinking and dining spot, and internet access is cheaper than average. The **Hotel San Juan** (Avenida Siboney y Calle 13, 0226 87200, doubles $40-$60) is in the Vista Alegre neighbourhood (a $3 cab ride from the city centre). The 112 rooms were recently spruced up and are quite large and comfortable. There's a games room with mini bowling lanes and pool table and a large pool. Also on the outskirts of town is **Hotel Versalles** (Alturas de Versalles, Carretera del Morro, 0226 91016/91504, doubles $50-$60) a 60-room hotel near the airport and the Morro Castle. Fifteen rooms have unrivalled views of the city, the bay and the Sierra Maestra mountains. There's a large pool, a disco, plus basketball and volleyball courts. Ten smaller, single rooms surround the pool ($25 per night). Around ten kilometres (six miles) out of town is the lovely **Villa Marquete** (Hacienda El Caney, doubles $53-$63), a secluded six-room hotel with pool. **Motel Rancho Club** (Altos de Quintero, Carretera Central km4.5, 0226 33202, doubles $32) is a more modest establishment on the site of a former farm, overlooking the city and the bay. The rooms are comfortable but the hot water can be unreliable and this part of the city is prone to power cuts. The pool is a popular weekend hangout for local families, and there's live music several nights a week.

Casas particulares

Renting out rooms in private homes (*casas particulares*) is a growth industry in Santiago and there are plenty to choose from, both in the centre of town, and the Vista Alegre and Sueño neighbourhoods, where many of the nicer homes are located. Ask any cabbie and he'll gladly take you to several (for commission, of course). The key is not to feel pressured to take something you don't like – the exception being during Carnival in July, and the end of the year, when you'll probably have to take what you can get.

Prices are generally $20 a night for the better houses, though you can bargain if you are staying for a few days. Breakfast is generally offered (not included) and it's a good idea to accept, as few places besides hotels serve food before noon.

A few blocks from Parque Céspedes, **Gisela and José** (Calle Pío Rosado/Carniceria #409, entre San Francisco y San Gerónimo, 0226 25176) have two upstairs rooms with a terrace, each with private bath and air-con. **Señora Lourdes González** (Calle Joaquin Castillo Duany #253 (Santa Lucia), entre Lacret y Félix Pena, 0226 24944) is the gracious hostess at a comfortable home just three blocks from Parque Céspedes.

In Sueño, try the newly remodelled rooms in the house of **Juan Teodoro Florentino**

(Calle J #61, entre 2ra y 3ra, 0226 24797); he can arrange percussion or dance classes. Or go next door to see **Aidé Haber Menedez** who rents a two-room apartment that will accommodate up to four people (Calle J #65, entre 2da y 3ra, Reparto Sueño, 0226 25186).

Further out in Reparto Vista Alegre is the home of **Esmeralda Gonzalez** (Avenida Pujol #107, esquina 5ta, 0226 46341), where a spacious, comfortable room comes with parking and a separate entrance. In the area of Santa Bárbara (near Vista Alegre), **Margarita Rodiles** (Calle 13 #3, esquina 10, 0226 41611) rents out rooms.

Where to eat & drink

Santiago is no place for foodies, but there are a few decent restaurants, and at least the mediocre ones don't charge too much. All the hotels have restaurants, the best of which are at the **Meliá Santiago** and **Casa Granda** (for both, *see p210*).

Plaza Dolores (known as Búlevar by locals) is a crowded square ringed with restaurants of varying quality. The best are the ever-buzzing **Café Matamoros** (0226 52205) on Calle Calvario and its neighbour the **Mar-Init** (0226 53602), which specialises in seafood. It's best to avoid **La Perla del Dragón** and **La Terracina** – both are pricey and geared to tourists. **El Bodegón** (formerly Taberna Dolores, and known as both), on the corner of Aguilera and Reloj, is another popular spot for locals, with prices in both dollars and pesos. There's often live music in the courtyard, the food is hearty and you can eat for under $2.

Santiago 1900 (San Basilico #354, entre Pío Rosado y Hartmann, 0226 23507) is one of the best places in town on account of its setting (the former Bacardí family mansion), ambience and low prices. The premises comprise an air-conditioned room with a baby grand piano, a patio and several upstairs rooms. Food features the usual suspects (pork, rice and beans), plus pizza.

Vista Alegre is home to the fanciest restaurant in town, complete with wine list and doormen; **ZunZún** (Avenida Manduley #159, entre 5ta y 7pta, 0226 41528, mains $2.50-$25) is set in the former residence of an Arab oilman who fled after the Revolution; there are several formal dining rooms and tables on the veranda. Also on Avenida Manduley, **La Maison** (#52, at Calle 0226 41117) has an elegant restaurant in the rear and a cheaper café out front.

Just outside the Morro Castle is the excellent **Restaurante El Morro** (0226 91676, mains $3-$30). The food is good and the setting – overlooking a twinkling Caribbean Sea – is even better. It's only open until 9pm (5pm in low season), but it will stay open later for groups that have a reservation.

If you fancy lunch on a tropical island, take the ferry from Marina Merlin to Cayo Granma ($3 return, and worth it for the trip alone). There the charming seafood restaurant **El Cayo** (0226 90109, mains $10-$30) awaits, complete with waterside balcony.

By far the best *paladar* in town – well, on the outskirts of town – is the **Salón Tropical** (Calle Fernández Marcane, entre Calle 9 y 10, 0226 41161, mains $5-$15) in the Reparto Santa Barbara. It's best to call for reservations and be sure to ask for seating on the terrace. The house speciality is barbecued chicken for $8. Downtown is **Las Gallegas**, one block away from Parque Céspedes (Calle San Basilio #305, entre San Félix y San Pedro, mains $6-$10), serving well-prepared Creole fare.

Finally, no trip to Santiago is complete without a cup of coffee at **Café La Isabelica** (Aguilera y Valiente, no phone), at the edge of Plaza Dolores. Cheap and lively, it's a fave with Santiago's bohemian set.

Tourist information

All the big hotels have tour company desks for flights and further hotel reservations.

Rumbos

Calle Heredia #969, esquina Parque Céspedes (622843/622222).

Cubatur

Avenida Victoriano Garzón, entre 3ra y 4ta, Reparto Santa Barbara (0226 52560).

Getting there

By air

International and domestic flights come into **Aeropuerto Internacional Antonio Maceo** (0226 91053), located 5km (3 miles) south of the city. There are 14 flights a week to Havana ($100) and the journey takes 1-2.5hrs.

By bus

Interprovincial buses arrive at the **Astro** terminal (0226 23050) on Carretera Central and Yayaró, near Plaza de la Revolución. Tourist buses pull into the **Víazul** (0226 28484) next door. Both companies run daily services to Havana. The journey takes about 15hrs (Astro $42; Víazul $51).

By rail

The new **railway station** (0226 2836) is on Avenida Jesús Menéndez, north-west of the city centre. Standard trains to and from Havana run every other day ($30). There is also a deluxe train, Locura Azul (also known as the *tren francés*), departing on alternate days for $42. The journey takes around 14 hours.

Directory

Getting Around **214**
Resources A-Z **218**
Further Reference **232**
Index **234**

Features

Specialist package holidays 226
Average temperatures 230
Travel advice 218
US citizens travelling to Cuba 228

Directory

Getting Around

Arriving & leaving

By air

Flights to Havana arrive at **Aeropuerto Internacional José Martí** (switchboard 266 4644/ 335577/information 266 4644/335 777/ 333179). The airport is 25 kilometres (16 miles) south-west of central Havana and has five terminals, with no interconnecting transport apart from taxis. Domestic flights use Terminal 1; charter flights from Miami and New York arrive at Terminal 2; most other international flights arrive at the large, modernised Terminal 3 (flight information 266 4133/335754/335666); Terminal 4 serves the military; and Aerocaribe flights come into Terminal 5.

Terminal 3 has a 24-hour tourist information desk with English-speaking operators (266 4133/335754/ 335666), though they can seem to spend more time away from the phones than answering them. There is also a bureau de change and several car rental desks (*see p216*).

There is no public transport directly to and from the international terminals but taxis can always be found right outside the terminal buildings. The journey into town takes 30 minutes and costs around $12-$15. Note that the taxis that use the rank outside Terminal 3 are the most expensive. Cheaper rates can be found by calling or picking up a Panataxi or other tourist taxi (*see p215*). Some tourist agencies run minibuses into town for tour groups, which independent travellers can often use for a charge.

Public buses (*see p215*) run from the domestic terminal to Vedado and Parque Central but, due to the distances between terminals, this service is useful only if you have arrived on a domestic flight at Terminal 1.

There are direct flights to Havana from Europe, Canada, the Caribbean and Central and South America, many of which are run by the national airline **Cubana de Aviación**. Cubana flights are sometimes the cheapest available but they can be unreliable and are often heavily overbooked, so be sure to confirm your return flight at least 72 hours in advance of departure time. Cubana scheduled flights to Havana depart from London Gatwick once a week. Other options include **Iberia** via Madrid (in the UK 020 7830 0011/ www.iberia.com; in Havana 204 344445/fax 204 3443), **Air France** via Paris, (in the UK 0845 0845 111/ www.airfrance.fr; in Havana 662642/ fax 662634), **Air Jamaica**, often direct (www.airjamaica.com; in the UK 020 8570 9171/fax 020 8577 2995; in Havana 662447 ext 48/fax 662449), **Martinair** (www.martinair.com; in the UK 0870 6062444; in Havana 833 3730/3729/fax 833 3732) and **Air Europa** (www.air-europa.com; in the UK 0870 2401501; in Havana inside the Hotel Habana Libre 666918).

There are no direct flights from the USA (the planes coming in from Miami, Los Angeles and New York are not for tourists, they are for licensed travellers and Cuban Americans), Australia or New Zealand to Cuba. Cubana runs scheduled services from Toronto and Montreal in Canada, from Cancún and Mexico City in Mexico and from several Caribbean, Central and South American airports. Nassau in the Bahamas is a handy stopover for people connecting from the US. From the Caribbean, try **Air Jamaica** (www.airjamaica.com) or **Aerocaribe** (www.aerocaribe. com.mx), and from Mexico, try Aerocaribe or **Mexicana de Aviación** (www.mexicana.com.mx).

All foreign visitors departing from Cuba on international flights are charged a $25 departure tax. This must be paid at either of the designated counters between the check-in areas and passport control. For details of customs regulations in and out of Cuba, *see p219*.

If you need to change your departure date, you must go in person to the relevant agency. Most charge a fee for this, depending on the type of ticket, starting from $100. Check regulations with your booking agency before you leave Cuba, and if you are told you have a flexible ticket, bring a letter with you, if possible, to confirm this.

Cubana de Aviación

Havana office *Calle 23 #64, entre P e O, Vedado (331986-88/334446-49/fax 662021/www.cubana.com).* **Open** 8.30am-4pm Mon-Fri; 8.30am-noon Sat. **Map** p250 B12.

London office *49 Conduit Street, London W1R 9FB (020 7734 1165/ fax 020 7437 0681).* **Open** 9.30am-5.30pm Mon-Fri.

By sea

There are no international scheduled ferry services to Havana and, due to the US embargo, few cruise ships visit Cuba as part of their itinerary. Cruise ships that do call in at Havana dock at the **Terminal Sierra Maestra** (Avenida San Pedro #1, La Habana Vieja, 336607/336524/336093).

By rail

There are daily departures from the central train station in Havana to all major towns in the country (and vice versa). Tourists must pay for tickets in US dollars. The regular train from Havana to Santiago, for example, costs $30 single (you can never buy return tickets on buses or trains) and takes about 12 hours. Conditions are basic: no air-conditioning, no café, bad toilets, but spacious carriages and a friendly, bustling atmosphere.

The *rápido* train is faster (although only by about an hour), has air-conditioning (take something warm to wear as temperatures can be less than tropical), better toilets and fewer people. Take plenty of food and drink with you and be prepared for delays. Unfortunately, although train journeys are a great way to see the country, many rail lines are old and dilapidated and Cuba does not have a particularly good rail safety record.

Reserve tickets by phone or go in person at least one hour before departure and before 7pm if you're leaving during the night. Don't forget you'll have to show your passport for any type of travel transaction. For details of the national rail network and services, *see p184*. For information on the Hershey electric train that runs between Havana and Matanzas, *see p89*.

Estación Central de Ferrocarriles

Calle Arsenal y Egido, La Habana Vieja (861 2959/862 1920). **Map** p252 F14.

By bus

Modern, relatively luxurious, long-distance **Víazul** (www.viazul.cu) buses, and the sometimes older and less reliable **Astro** buses, depart from the national bus station (*see below*), as well as from the Víazul terminal in Nuevo Vedado for destinations around the country. For general information on bus travel in Cuba, *see p184*.

You can book with Víazul by phone, but always arrive one hour before departure time. The buses are very punctual. Astro doesn't have a booking system for foreigners. Only two places are reserved for tourists on each bus so get there at least an hour prior to departure time.

Fares are reasonable; for example, Havana–Viñales, by Astro, takes around four hours and costs $8. The same journey by Víazul takes three hours and costs $12.

There are also a number of well-organised tourist bus agencies including **Transmetro** (830 4000/6584/fax 830 4091), **Panatrans** (881 1013) and **Panautos** (553298), which run excursions and trips for tourists. These buses can also be hired for group travel. Contact major hotels for further information.

Terminal de Ómnibuses Nacionales

Avenida de la Independencia (Rancho Boyeros) #101, Vedado (870 9401/879 2456/Astro 24hrs 870 3397/Víazul 870 3397). **Map** p250 D10.

Víazul

Avenida 26, esquina Zoológico, Nuevo Vedado (811413/815652/811108/fax 666092). **Open** 24hrs daily. **Map** p249 E7.

Getting around Havana

Buses

Before the Special Period, Havana's buses (*guaguas*, pronounced 'wa-was') efficiently served the whole city. But fuel shortages, lack of spare parts and general inefficiency during the 1990s left the whole system on the brink of collapse. The situation has improved a lot in the last few years, but most buses are still subject to massive overcrowding, which can make even the shortest journey a daunting undertaking. During rush hours (7-9am and 4-6pm), the struggle to get on and the crush of passengers can be hard work. Unless you're travelling long distances, it's usually quicker and more pleasant to walk, although bussing around is very cheap as all fares, even for tourists, are in fractions of a peso.

Transmetro rents out charter buses to companies to ferry their employees, although they do sometimes pick up individuals.

Ómnibus Metropolitanos is the main provider. Its *ruteros* (standard city buses, 40 centavos flat rate, and *taxibuses*, one peso) run non-stop services between the city and the bus and train stations. Much of the system's overload is carried by the *metrobuses*, lumbersome converted articulated trucks that have two humps, hence their more common name: camels (*camellos*). *Camellos* carry up to 300 passengers and cover marginally longer distances. *Habaneros* call them X-rated buses because they often contain 'bad language, violence and sex'. The 'violence' is usually nothing more than pushing and shoving, while the 'sex' is usually limited to a spot of groping, made easy by the extreme proximity of fellow passengers. It's an uncomfortable way of travelling and is not for the delicate or fainthearted.

Contrary to appearances, queues (*colas*) operate religiously at most bus stops (*paradas*), so it is very important to ask for *el último* (the last in the queue) and board the bus directly after that person. Once on the bus, keep a very close eye on your belongings (crowded buses are fertile ground for pickpockets) and, importantly, make your way to the exit at the back of the bus as soon as possible to avoid missing your stop.

Most buses run at least hourly during the day and slightly less often between 11pm and 5am. The more popular routes (the P1 and P4, for example, *see below*) run every 15-30 minutes, sometimes even more frequently. There are special night buses, less frequent, between midnight and 5am. There are neither route maps nor timetables for local buses but the front of each bus normally displays the route number and destination. (*camellos* are prefixed by the letter M). Many of the *camellos* converge on Parque de la Fraternidad in La Habana Vieja. Other useful places to pick up buses are Parque Central in Centro Habana and La Rampa (Calle 23) in Vedado.

Two examples of popular routes, useful for longer journeys, are the P1 and P4. The **P1** runs from Miramar to the San Miguel del Padrón district, along Calle 3ra via Línea and Paseo in Vedado, to Infanta and Avenida Salvador Allende (Carlos III) in Centro Havana. The **P4** runs from the roundabout on Avenida 5ta and Calle 140 in Playa (called El Padadero de Playa) via Calles 23 and 26 in Vedado, and Reina and Galliano in Centro Habana and finally to La Habana Vieja.

Taxis

Although much of Havana (and especially La Habana Vieja) is best explored on foot, taxis are a very useful and relatively cheap way to travel between neighbourhoods. There are plenty to choose from, although they are harder to find in less-visited areas. Just stand by the side of the road and flag one down. There are so many and various options, however, it can be very confusing.

Official tourist taxis (*turistaxis*) are modern cars with the taxi signs on the roof. The cheapest rates are offered by **Panataxi** (*see p216*), which can be reliably booked by phone. Rates within the city are not negotiable and meters start at $1, with each kilometre charged at 60¢-80¢ (night-time rates are about 20% higher). Prices for long distances can be negotiated, and, depending on the type and size of car, can compare favourably to the cost of hiring a car. The second cheapest tourist taxi service is **Habanataxi** (*see p216*).

Cheaper than the tourist taxis are the black and yellow Ladas of the **Empresa Provincial de Taxi**. These vehicles are state-owned but privately operated and they are not permitted to take foreigners. If you are on your own and don't look too obviously like a tourist, you might be able to flag one down, but phone bookings are only accepted for Cubans going to and from hospital. If they are running on a set route (on a main road from one area to another), you will normally pay ten pesos for any destination along that route, but if you want to go off-route or door to door you will need to negotiate a price before you get in the taxi.

Many of the large 1950s US-made vehicles with a cardboard 'taxi' sign on the dashboard are licensed in pesos and are not permitted to take tourists. The rate is fixed at ten pesos for set routes with negotiable prices for anything else. They travel a set route and can be found rumbling along Avenida 3ra in Playa, along Línea or Calle 23 in Vedado, mostly going to and from La Habana Vieja. They are also found at specific places (such as bus terminals), where they set off only when they have a full load.

There are also numerous illegal taxis, often driven by underpaid Cuban professionals, trawling the streets and waiting outside hotels. Both permit-holding and illegal drivers can usually be hired for half a day for about $20. Drivers may be fined if caught with a foreigner in the car as the government wants to net tourist dollars for the state economy, but many drivers are keen enough to get the dollars to take the risk.

With any non-metered taxi always agree the price before you get in and don't be afraid to bargain a little, although don't be insensitive about this, as taxis are generally relatively cheap and it is seen as bad manners for a foreigner to barter just for the sake of it.

Aside from all the normal tourist taxis you can hail a **cocotaxi**, a small three-wheeled scooter that looks like a scooped-out orange, with a bright yellow cab. These fun taxis are now found as far out as Miramar and charge 50¢ per kilometre (though check approximately how much your journey is going to cost beforehand as they don't have meters). You can order a *cocotaxi* by phone (873 1411) and they can also be hired to ferry you around for between $7-$8 an hour, all in.

For another uniquely Cuban experience look out for the beautifully maintained, pre-Revolution classic American cars used as official tourist taxis throughout the city. **Gran Car** (417980/335647/tel/fax 577378) has a fleet of period models in tip-top condition. These gorgeous convertibles can be hired either as taxis for specific short runs in the city, or with a driver by the hour ($18) or the day ($110), with fixed prices for trips out of town (one-day return to Viñales costs $261, and the same to Varadero beach costs $192. Contact Gran Car or the main hotels for details.

Tourist taxi companies

Fénix 8604317
Habanataxi 539086/539090
Micar 204 2444/204 5555
OK Taxis 204 9518-19
Panataxi 555555
Rex (limousine service, most expensive) 339160
Transgaviota 339780
Transtur/Turistaxi 336666

Other forms of transport

Rickshaw-style tricycles, known as *bicitaxis*, are a very pleasant way of roving the streets of La Habana Vieja and Centro Habana. They are cheaper than taxis and a far more relaxing way of covering short distances. Expect to pay a dollar per ride within the old city but always agree this before mounting.

Horse-drawn carriages can be picked up at various tourist spots in La Habana Vieja for a 50-minute, 56-key-sight colonial tour of the city or a 50-minute tour of 'New Havana' (includes Revolution Square). You can find them from 10am onwards outside of hotels Inglaterra and Parque Central, in the Plaza de San Francisco and in front of the Capitolio among other locations. Each trip normally costs $30 for two people or $40 for four people. The *cochero* (driver) will also provide a normal taxi service to wherever you want to go. For reservations and further information contact FENIX SA (861 9380).

Driving

Traffic travels on the right. Speed limits, which are rigorously enforced, are 20kph (12.5mph) in driveways and car parks; 40kph (25mph) around schools; 50kph (31mph) in urban areas; 60kph (37mph) in rural areas; 90kph (56mph) on paved highways; and 100kph (62mph) on the motorway. Any traffic fines you incur (from $5 to $30 depending on the infringement) must be paid within 15 days. Check details with your car rental agency.

Driving can be useful for venturing out of the city, but isn't recommended in Havana itself. As well as missing out on the pleasure of walking the streets or being driven in the back of a classic American car, visiting drivers are likely to find themselves horribly confused by the city's warren of one-way streets. The volume of traffic is increasing all the time and Havana now has noticeable rush-hour traffic, as well as numerous and dangerous potholes.

Many *habaneros* drive quite recklessly and are inclined to make unpredictable manoeuvres. The use of indicators and brake lights isn't particularly widespread, so watch out for surprise stops (sometimes breakdowns), often in the middle of the road, and unannounced turns in fast-moving traffic. Cyclists present a further hazard as they observe few rules of the road and often ride two or three (and an electric fan) per bike. Avoid driving around La Habana Vieja, much of which is pedestrianised.

Due to its serious transport problems, Cuba has become a country of hitchhikers, so if you're driving in or outside Havana it is much appreciated if you stop to give lifts to the many and varied people who wait at traffic lights in the city or on the motorways in the country. Just be careful to keep your belongings in sight, as some might be tempted.

Car hire

None of the international car hire companies has offices in Cuba so visitors are reliant on the national providers (*listings below*). For quality, security and comfort choose **Rex**, then **Habanautos**. But the cheapest is **Micar**, then **Habanautos**.

With the rise in tourism, the demand for hired cars in Cuba sometimes outstrips the supply. In high season (December to April) it may be wise to reserve a car before you arrive, although this can only be done 15 days in advance. Once in Havana, most hotels have a car hire desk or can at least help you make arrangements. The main car rental companies have offices all over the city and also in the arrivals area of Terminal 3 at the airport. Some of these are open 24 hours daily.

To rent a car, you must be at least 21 years old, with one year's driving experience, and must hold a valid national driving licence or an international driving permit.

Renting a car is the easiest way to see the country, but it's not cheap. Unless you're looking for a long-term hire, prices don't vary much. Most companies charge between $55 and $100 per day, plus a deposit of $200 to $300. The fee and deposit must be paid in advance by cash, credit card (not one issued by a US bank) or travellers' cheques. Rates include unlimited mileage, but insurance, fuel and parking are extra. On hiring the car you'll be charged $1.10 a litre (cash) for a tank of petrol (check that it's full) but don't expect a refund for any fuel remaining in the tank when the car is returned. You'll be offered insurance (payable in cash) either covering accidents but not theft (policy A; $10-$12 per day) or covering all risks except loss of radio and spare tyre (policy B; $15 per day). Any additional drivers are normally charged a flat fee of $10-$15 each or $3 per day. If you don't fancy driving yourself around, some companies also provide chauffeurs, for which you'll pay a daily rate, plus room and board if you're away overnight. Keep your hire agreement with you until you return the car or you'll be charged a $50 penalty.

If you are involved in an accident or have something stolen from your car, you'll need to obtain a police report (*una denuncia*) in order to make an insurance claim. Make plenty of time to do this as police work can be extremely slow.

Hire cars are sometimes poorly maintained, so try to get a new vehicle and always check it carefully. A test drive is a good idea. Make it clear if you want seat belts in the back as many cars don't have them.

Cubacar 332277/fax 330760/ www.cubacar.cubanacan.cu
Havanautos 203 9658/9805/9347/ www.havanautos.cubaweb.cu
Micar 204 2444/3437/fax 204 8349/micar@colombo.cu
Panautos 553298
Transtur 669806/335551/335541/ fax 335542

Breakdown services

Your car hire company should deal with all breakdowns and repairs. Check that your hire contract includes this information, plus emergency numbers, and ring them first in case of any accident or emergency. In addition to this, repair services, but not recovery services, are provided by a branch of **Oro Negro** at Avenida 5ta #12001, esquina 120, Playa (208 6149), between 8am and 7pm Monday to Saturday. There are other branches at Avenida 7ma, esquina 2, Miramar (204 1906) and Avenida 13, esquina 84, Playa (204 1938).

If your broken-down car needs towing, call the very professional, 24-hour **Agencia Peugeot** (666650/577533), which will charge 50¢ per kilometre to get to the car and $1 per kilometre to tow it to wherever you want to go.

Fuel stations

Servi-Cupet (SC) and **Oro Negro** (ON) both have several 24-hour petrol stations in the city (ON at Almendares, by the tunnel, Avenida 7ma, Miramar; SC at Malecón and Paseo, Vedado). Various grades of petrol are sold. Note that it is illegal to put anything but *especial* in hired cars (currently priced at 90¢ per litre). Do accept and abide by this otherwise you may get the petrol pump attendant into trouble and damage the car. Local petrol stations, which require special vouchers and charge in pesos, often run out of fuel and don't carry *especial*. Avoid buying black-market fuel from individuals on the street – it not only damages the car but puts you and other people at risk.

Parking

There are no parking meters on the streets of Havana and, although you have to avoid places where the pavement is painted yellow, it is unusual – thanks to the relatively low numbers of vehicles – to have difficulties finding a parking space. Car theft can be a problem so it's advisable to use designated hotel car parks (*parqueos*) with a guard (*custodio*). These charge from 50¢ an hour, with overnight fees of $1 (for non-hotel guests). There are car parks opposite the hotels **Sevilla**, **Nacional**, **Habana Libre**, **Meliá Cohiba**, among others. For all, *see pp32-46*. Beware: illegally parked cars are subject to fines and may be towed away.

Campervans

For a Cuban-style Route 66 experience, hire yourself a big, new, luxurious campervan and take to the open road. One week in this six-person roadster will set you back $1,155, $36 for a full tank of petrol and a $400 refundable deposit. The price includes insurance and if your budget won't stretch for the week, the daily cost is $165 all in.

Campingcar

Calle 3ra, entre 12 y Malecón, Vedado, or outside the Capitolio (tel/fax 8337558/cubacamper@enet.cu). **Map** p249 A8.

Cycling

Cycling became a necessity due to the fuel shortages during the Special Period and remains a very common mode of transport, despite widespread potholes, copious fumes and the perils of sharing the road with the average *habanero* motorist. Most Cubans use cumbersome Chinese bikes, although mountain-style bikes are becoming more common.

Punctures are inevitable given the state of the roads and repair workshops are numerous throughout the city (look for the '*Ponchera*' sign). A puncture repair job costs ten pesos. There are scores of bicycle parking places (*parqueos*) where you pay one or two pesos to leave your bike in the charge of an attendant. You should still secure it well. These *parqueos* are crucial as you can never safely leave your bike on the street, even if you have a good lock. Spare parts and tools are scarce, so bring whatever you might need with you if you are travelling with your own bike. Contact the **Federación Cubana de Ciclismo** (973776/953885/953661/panaci@enet.cu) for further information.

If you are travelling to the eastern side of the bay or to the eastern beaches (*see pp88-93*), you can take the **Ciclobus**, which transports you and your bike through the tunnel from Parque El Curita in La Habana Vieja. The fare is 40 centavos one way.

Bicycle hire

Although you can very easily arrange to borrow a bike from a Cuban for a few days (expect to pay around $2-$3 a day), there are now a limited number of places to hire bicycles. Try the innovative, two-year-old Canadian-Cuban project **Bicicletas Cruzando Fronteras**, which trains bicycle mechanics (especially women) and brings in much-needed spare parts. Bike hire, including helmet and locks, costs $2 an hour or $12 for 24 hours, $8 a day for 2-7 days, $5 a day for between 8-15 days and $2 a day for more than 16 days. You are required to leave your passport, a credit card or $250 as a guarantee. Also try major hotels for bike hire.

Your alternative is to pick up a second-hand bike from the Cuatro Caminos market (*see p70*) for somewhere between $20-$40, which could end up being cheaper than hiring one.

The Club Nacional de Cicloturism Gran Caribe (*see p179*) will provide bikes for those taking part in one of its cycling tours. For spectator cycling events, *see p178*.

Bicicletas Cruzando Fronteras

Edificio Metropolitano #412, Calle San Juan de Díos, esquina Aguacate, La Habana Vieja, 860 8532/fax 669546/cfenix@ohch.cu). **Open** 8.30am-5pm Mon-Fri; 8.30am-4pm Sat. **Map** p252 D15.

Motorbikes/scooters

Groovy little scooters can now be hired from **Rumbos** outlets; they are a great way to get around the city. You can find branches in Parque Central, Calle Galiano #401 at the corner of San Rafael, Centro Habana (338634) or on Avenida 3ra at the corner of 30, Miramar (204 5491). Most major hotels also have outlets. Prices are around $10 for an hour, $13 for two hours to $15 for three hours. If you hire for a number of days or weeks, prices drop significantly. Take good care on the roads, watch out for heavy downpours, patches of oil, potholes and the unpredictable manoeuvres of Cuban drivers.

Walking

As a pedestrian, keep a lookout for *bicitaxis* and *cocotaxis* when you cross the street, as they tend to come whizzing out of nowhere. Otherwise, walking is one of the most pleasant ways of enjoying Havana, especially in the city's denser areas, such as La Habana Vieja or Centro Habana, where walking is more practical. Distances between areas in Havana are relatively large.

Walking along the Malecón – the city's seaside promenade, connecting La Habana Vieja, Centro Habana and Vedado – makes for a pleasant walk.

Resources A-Z

Addresses

In Cuba (and in this guide), addresses state first the street name, then the number (often designated by a # sign), followed by the two cross streets (*entrecalles*) between which the building is situated. Thus, the restaurant La Mina, Calle Oficios #6, entre Obispo y Obrapía, will be found on Calle Oficios, between Calle Obispo and Calle Obrapía. If a building is on the corner (*esquina*) of two streets, both streets are given, but the street where the entrance is located tends to be given first. So the Museo del Automóvil, Calle Oficios #13, esquina Jústiz will be on Calle Oficios at the corner of Calle Jústiz. (Note that this address could also be given in a shorter form, as Calle Oficios y Jústiz). A street name followed by '*s/n*' indicates that the building has no street number. Residential addresses sometimes specify *altos* (upper floor), *bajos* (ground floor) or *sótano* (basement) in their address, or use *primer piso* (first floor), *segundo piso* (second floor) and so on.

Some street names in the city centre were changed after the Revolution, but *habaneros* are inclined to use the old and new names indiscriminately, which can be very confusing for the unsuspecting visitor. To make matters worse, the words *calle* (street) and *avenida* (avenue) are often omitted entirely in directions or an address; even *habaneros* sometimes confuse the two, and in some cases even they don't know if a street is officially a *calle* or an *avenida*. Hence, Cubans often give directions that refer to well-known landmarks rather than streets.

In this book we have given the official/new name of each street with the old name in brackets. Most maps also follow this practice. Below is a list of streets with two names, with old names in brackets: **Agramonte** (Zulueta); **Aponte** (Someruelos); **Avenida Antonio Maceo** (Malecón); **Avenida de las Misiones (northern half)** (Monserrate); **Avenida de Bélgica (southern half)** (Egido); **Avenida Carlos Manuel de Céspedes** (Avenida del Puerto); **Avenida de España** (Vives); **Avenida de Italia** (Galiano); **Avenida Salvador Allende** (Carlos III); **Avenida Simón Bolívar** (Reina); **Brasil** (Teniente Rey); **Capdevila** (Cárcel); **Leonor Pérez** (Paula); **Máximo Gómez** (Monte); **Padre Varela** (Belascoaín); **Paseo de Martí** (Paseo del Prado); **San Martín** (San José).

Attitude & etiquette

Cubans are generally very warm and friendly, and usually well disposed towards tourists. As a foreigner you will often be expected to pay for Cuban friends if you go out eating or drinking with them as they simply won't have the money to pay or chip in. If you want to pay, you can help avoid an uncomfortable situation by saying *yo invito* (it's my treat), which can then be accepted or refused. Of course, many Cubans assume that foreigners are rich (which relatively speaking, they are). However, many others find this situation intensely embarrassing and like to help pay whenever they can. A good thing to do together is to go to the movies (two pesos), the theatre (five-ten pesos) or to take a trip by bus (40 centavos).

While Cubans often address those whom they don't know as *Compañero/Compañera* (comrade), it's more appropriate for foreigners to use *Señor/Señora/Señorita* with strangers. When you don't know an adult always use *usted* rather than *tu* (meaning 'you'). Both women and men greet females and children, even those they don't know well, with one kiss on the cheek and much affection. Men tend to shake hands with other men.

Everyday life for a Cuban demands an enormous amount of patience. As a tourist you may easily feel frustrated by things that don't work (*no funciona*), that take a very long time, or aren't in stock (*no hay*), as well as the pandemic lack of customer service. Try to relax, and remember that people are struggling. It pays to be firm in some situations, but losing your temper will usually make things worse here. A charm offensive is the strategy that succeeds most often. Cubans are known for their laid-back ways of dealing with difficulties, so unless you want to end up seriously stressed out, your best bet is just to adapt and go with the flow.

Note that tourists of darker skin are more likely to suffer harassment from the police. Visitors who are black or of Latin appearance are often taken for Cuban and so might be asked to show their passports to gain access to hotels or other places where Cuban citizens might not normally be allowed.

You will also note if you are staying or moving around in La Habana Vieja (men and women alike) that you will often be approached by persistent people selling cigars, promoting restaurants or rented rooms, or by young people working as prostitutes. These are known as *jineteros* (literally 'jockeys', 'riding' on the backs of tourists). While this is almost never aggressive, it can be extremely wearing. Moreover, you could leave Cuba with a very one-sided impression indeed. Life is tough here, for some more than others, and necessity, unfortunately, breeds all manner of behaviour. Try to get out to the less touristy areas in order to leave Cuba with a more balanced impression.

Travel advice

For up-to-date information on travel to a specific country – including the latest news on safety and security, health issues, local laws and customs – contact your home country government's department of foreign affairs. Most have websites packed with useful advice for would-be travellers.

Australia
www.dfat.gov.au/travel

Canada
www.voyage.gc.ca

New Zealand
www.mft.govt.nz/travel

Republic of Ireland
www.irlgov.ie/iveagh

UK
www.fco.gov.uk/travel

USA
www.state.gov

Business

Cuba remains politically committed to socialism and the state continues to control all but some very small businesses. However, opportunities in Cuba abound and increasing numbers of suppliers and investors come to do business here every year (*see p86*). Joint ventures have meant the development of big business, especially in the fields of tourism, mining, power generation and biotechnology.

In the past, many business visitors have entered Cuba on tourist visas. Now, if you are coming to research business opportunities, you need to apply to the Cuban embassy in your country and ask for an A7 visa (in theory this can be issued on the spot). If you're actually coming to do business, on a business visa (*visa de negocio*), it will theoretically take between seven and ten days to process. You can apply independently, although it's more usual to opt for sponsorship or partnership through an appropriate Cuban government organisation. Bear in mind that visa regulations can change at short notice, so it's always crucial to check with the Cuban embassy in your country of origin with plenty of time before setting off.

Those visiting Havana for any purpose should remember that annual trade fairs and international summit meetings, as well as the usual peak tourist season, can make it hard to book flights and hotels for the dates you require. *See p230* **When to go**.

Business services & facilities

There are several hotels offering facilities for the business visitor, including meeting rooms, internet facilities and some secretarial or translation services. These include Hotels Meliá Cohiba, Nacional, NH Parque Central or Meliá Habana (*see pp32-46*).

Representatives at your embassy can usually advise on commercial services available locally, and fax services may be available there for a small fee. If you need Spanish-language support during your stay, **ESTI** (Centre for Translation and Interpreting Services) can provide a translation and/or interpreting service. For more on internet access, *see p222*.

Esti *Línea #507, entre D y E, Vedado (832 7586/fax 333978/ montoto@esti.cu)*. **Open** 8.30am-5pm Mon-Fri. **Map** p250 A10.

Customs

Things are always changing in this department so check if in doubt. Incoming visitors over the age of 18 are permitted to bring the following items into Cuba: unlimited money (though you must declare any amount over $5,000); personal effects; gifts worth up to $50; ten kilograms of medications; two litres of alcoholic drink; 200 cigarettes or 50 cigars or 250 grams of tobacco. The import of food, plant and animal products and telecommunications equipment is subject to restrictions. Banned items include narcotics, obscene publications, explosives, weapons (except for licensed hunting weapons) and video recorders. Coming in with a laptop and/or mobile phone will not be a problem but don't consider bringing a computer and/or other telecommunication equipment. Officials may suspect that you intend to sell them in Cuba, and they could be held in customs until your departure.

Departing visitors can export cigars up to the value of $2,000 (with a sales invoice); 50 cigars (without a sales invoice); six bottles of rum; and up to $5,000 in cash. For restrictions on the export of art and antiques, *see p120*, and for allowances for US citizens, *see p228* **Travel by US citizens to Cuba**.

For more detailed information, go to www.aduana.islagrande.com, contact the Cuban embassy in your country or contact your embassy in Havana.

Disabled

Havana is not an easy place for disabled travellers. There are very few amenities or services for people with physical disabilities, and the potholed streets and pavements make moving around very challenging for travellers in wheelchairs or with mobility difficulties. A few hotels (the most expensive ones) claim to have proper facilities, maybe even a room or two adapted for disabled guests; however, these may not meet international standards.

Drugs

There are some recreational drugs available in Havana, but penalties for illegal drug use are very severe. In response to evidence of trafficking by tourists, there has been a widespread clean-up and a fervent anti-drug campaign, which includes keeping a special eye on suspicious tourists. Most foreigners in Cuban jails are there for drug-related offences.

Electricity

The national grid operates on 110-volt, 60AC, as in the USA and Canada. However, European-managed hotels may have a 220-volt system, or even a combination of both, so check the voltage before plugging in your appliance. Two-pin plugs of the American flat pin type and screw-type light fittings are used. Visitors from the UK and the rest of Europe will require an adaptor to run any British electrical appliances in Cuba, but keep such items to a minimum because they could be confiscated at the airport.

Despite some recent improvements in the electricity supply, Havana is still subject to unexpected and sometimes quite lengthy electricity blackouts (*apagones*), so do pack a good pocket torch along with some spare batteries, as well as candles and a lighter. Also, bear in mind that faulty wiring and dodgy sockets are common. Bigger hotels tend to have their own back-up generators.

Embassies & consulates

Australia and New Zealand do not have diplomatic or consular representatives in Cuba, so the interests of those countries are represented by the Canadian and British embassies respectively. In the absence of an embassy, the USA is officially represented by the US Interests Section in Havana, under the protection of the Swiss embassy.

British Embassy

Calle 34 #702-4, entre 7ma y 17, Miramar (204 1771/consular fax 204 8104/commercial fax 204 9214/ embrit@ceniai.inf.cu). **Open** 8am-3.30pm Mon-Fri. **Map** p248 B/C4.

Canadian Embassy

Calle 30 #518, esquina 7ma, Miramar (204 2516/fax 332044). **Open** 8.30am-5pm Mon-Thur; 8.30am-2pm Fri. **Map** p249 B5.

United States Interests Section

Calzada, entre L y M, Vedado (333551-4). **Open** 8.30am-5pm Mon-Fri. **Map** p250 A11.

Emergencies

In emergencies, **Asistur**, the 24-hour assistance agency for tourists, is a good first contact. In serious cases contact your embassy (*see above*).

Asistur

Calle Prado #208, entre Colón y Trocadero, Centro Habana (office 866 4499/emergency 338527/ 338339/fax 338087/www.asistur.cu). **Open** *Office* 8.30am-5pm daily. *Emergency phone lines* 24hrs daily). **Map** p251 D14.
Asistur deals with insurance claims, arranges replacement documents and helps with financial problems.

Emergency numbers

Ambulance (Clínica Cira García) 204 2811-4
Ambulance (Red Cross) 405093-4
Fire Brigade 867 5555
Poison Control Centre (Centro Nacional de Toxicología) 260 1230/ 8751
Police 867 7777/882 0116

Health

The public health system is rightly held up as one of the Revolution's greatest achievements. Statistically, the number of doctors, dentists, clinics and hospital beds per capita is impressive, although due to lack of funds, the condition of much of the equipment and facilities has been deteriorating badly in recent years. What is lacking in equipment and medicines, though, will often be more than made up for by the care shown by most hospital and neighbourhood health centre staff.

At 73 years for men and 78 years for women, life expectancy in Cuba is on a par with that of the US. Many tropical diseases have been eradicated, including typhoid, diphtheria, tetanus, polio and hepatitis A. Mosquitoes are not malarial but can be a nuisance, so bring plenty of repellent with you. There have also been occasional outbreaks of mosquito-carried dengue fever in Cuba; the last was recorded in 2002. At the time of writing, houses were being fumigated once again, a sign that dengue is present. However, Cuba's health system has proved itself competent to deal with cases that occur efficiently.

Random checks have been carried out by some of the embassies and the results apparently confirm that the city's water supply is safe to drink. However, many Cubans boil their water as giardia and other parasites are very common. You are highly advised to do the same (ten minutes minimum) or stick to bottled water, which is readily and cheaply available in restaurants, *paladares* and shops. Avoid street food or drink containing water, such as soft drinks with ice cubes or ice-cream. In remote areas, it's a good idea to carry water-purifying tablets or a drinking bottle fitted with a filtration system.

Accident & emergency

In a medical emergency, call your neighbours, a taxi and all the ambulance numbers, as, for whatever reason, emergency services (*see above*) have been known not to answer. Minor accidents can be dealt with at the city hospitals that cater for foreigners (*see below*).

Before you go

You're only required to have a yellow fever vaccination if you're arriving in Cuba directly from South America. Otherwise, no other vaccinations are strictly required for travel to Cuba so most people don't bother. However, the UK Department of Health recommends vaccinations for hepatitis A, polio and typhoid. You might also want to consider a hepatitis B vaccination if you are a frequent traveller or intend to stay overseas for a long period. All travellers should have had booster injections for tetanus and diphtheria within the last ten years, and ensure that their measles, mumps and rubella immunisation is complete. Tuberculosis is rare in Cuba; however, children under 12 should be immunised as a precaution. Check with your doctor before you go. Pregnant women should also check with their doctors which vaccines are safe before being immunised.

Note that some vaccinations require you to have an initial injection, then a follow-up shot a few weeks later, so make sure you leave enough time for both before your trip; a vaccination course should be started no later than six weeks before travel.

For further information on health issues, consult the **Travel Doctor** website, www.traveldoctor.com.au.

Complementary medicine

The impact of the US blockade on medical supplies, together with the sudden end to Soviet aid in the early 1990s, meant that Cuba was practically forced to develop alternative medicine (known as *medicina alternativa* or *medicina verde*) and complementary techniques. These are now used in practically all health centres and hospitals and are hugely popular. There is particular interest in acupuncture, acupressure, massage and suction treatment, as well as the so-called *medicina verde*: herbalism, homeopathy and honey remedies.

Alternative remedies are available from **Farmacia Ciren** (Calle 216, esquina 13B, Playa, 336777-8) and **Farmacia Las Praderas** (Calle 230, entre 15a y 17, Siboney (337475-9/271 0825). These outlets also provide information on practitioners of complementary therapy. There are also two homeopathic pharmacies in Vedado: Calle 23, esquina Calle M, and Línea, esquina Calle 14. The international pharmacies (*see p221*) all carry a modest selection of herbal remedies. Most neighbourhoods also have a herb shop (*yerbero*), which sells a wide variety of herbs for medicinal and religious use.

Contraception & abortion

Condoms (*preservativos*) are widely and very cheaply available, but they're mostly Chinese in origin, unreliable and about as sensual as a rubber glove. It's advisable to bring your own condoms or any form of contraceptives you might need during your stay. Abortion rates are high.

Dentists

Dental treatment at any of the hospitals for foreigners (*see below*) is of a good standard and no more expensive than it would be in the private clinic in Britain.

Doctors

In addition to the doctors at the international hospitals, all four- and five-star hotels tend to have a 24-hour doctor on site. First consultations cost between $15 and $25, according to the grade of the hotel. Follow-up consulations are between $10 and $20.

Hospitals & clinics

Havana has a large number of hospitals, mostly reserved for Cubans, although some are designed to attend to foreign patients as well. The last ten years have also seen the development of a network of hospitals and clinics catering exclusively to foreigners and charging in dollars. Most of these are concentrated in and around Havana. In addition to emergency care, they offer advanced treatment in practically every sphere of health: orthopaedic surgery, neuro-rehabilitation, dentistry, cancer treatment, cardiology, hypertension, basic and comprehensive medical check-ups, eye surgery (laser correction, glaucoma and cataracts), geriatric conditions and plastic surgery. Some have achieved international recognition, such as CIREN, where groundbreaking work has been done on Parkinson's disease, nervous system conditions and spinal injuries affecting both adults and children.

As well as offering emergency and specialist treatment, some clinics are aimed at relatively healthy (and wealthy) people who simply want to improve their quality of life. The four-star **La Pradera**, for example, is specifically promoted as a hotel-cum-health resort.

English-speaking staff are available at most institutions dealing with foreigners. Nevertheless, language can sometimes be a barrier, and a few words of Spanish or a fluent friend with you will always help.

Centro Internacional de Restauración Neurológica (CIREN)

Avenida 25 # 15805, entre 158 y 160, Cubanacán (336003/271 6999/336356/fax 336302/332420/www.ciren.cubaweb.cu/cineuro@neuro.sld.cu).
The International Centre for Neurological Recovery (CIREN) treats patients with multiple sclerosis, Parkinson's disease and other injuries or conditions affecting the nervous system. Additionally, it offers dental services and a full range of plastic surgery, together with holistic treatments.

Centro Internacional de Salud La Pradera

Calle 230, entre 15a y 17, Siboney (337473-85/fax 337198/337199/www.softcal.cubaweb.cu/praderas).
This clinic offers a wide-ranging health and beauty programme, including aerobics, massage, laser therapy, anti-cellulite treatment, anti-stress therapy, general medical check-ups, dentistry and specialist care for multiple sclerosis, neurological and orthopaedic conditions. In 2000 its most famous patient was Diego Maradona, who checked in to recover from his cocaine addiction.

Clínica Internacional Cira García

Calle 20 #4101, esquina Avenida 41, Miramar (204 2811-14/fax 204 2640/www.ciracubanacan.cu).
Map p249 B6.
Exclusively for foreigners, this state-of-the-art clinic offers a broad programme of treatment that includes some 41 types of plastic surgery (full nose job, $1,710). It's also the best place to seek emergency treatment. Generally speedy, efficient and attentive treatment.

Hospital Cimeq

Avenida 216, esquina 11B, Siboney (271 5022/336497).
Rather grim-looking, but above-average hospital where ministry officials, some other Cubans and foreigners are treated.

Hospital Hermanos Ameijeiras

Padre Varela (Belascoain), esquina San Lázaro, Centro Habana (877 6072-76/fax 873 3167/www.hha.sld.cu). **Map** p251 C13.
This hospital is for Cubans, but has designated areas for dollar-paying patients, offering a large range of treatments.

Pharmacies

Local pharmacies open either on *turnos regulares* (8am-6pm Mon-Fri; 8am-noon Sat) or *turnos permanentes* (24 hours daily). You'll find these all over Havana but unless you have a very simple complaint their poorly stocked shelves may not be of much use. There are also several international pharmacies in Havana, which supply a comprehensive range of medication in dollars. Note that the Hotels Plaza, Comodoro, Habana Libre, Meliá Cohiba, Nacional, Parque Central, the Cira García Hospital and Marina Hemingway all have small pharmacies, and there is another at the airport (Terminal 3). For complementary medicine supplies and homeopathy, *see p220.*

Centro Internacional de Retinosis Pigmentaria Camilo Cienfuegos *Calle L #151, esquina 13, Vedado (333599).* **Open** 8am-8pm daily. **Map** p250 A/B11.

Farmacia Casa Bella *Avenida 7ma # 2603, esquina 26, Miramar (204 7980).* **Open** 8am-8pm daily. **Map** p249 B5.

Farmacia CIREN *Avenida 25 # 15805, entre 158 y 160, Cubanacán* (336777/336778, ext 116). **Open** 9am-5pm Mon-Fri; 9am-noon Sat.

Farmacia del Clínica Internacional Cira García *Ground floor, Clínica Internacional Cira García, Calle 20 #4101, Miramar (204 2880).* **Open** 9am-9pm daily. **Credit** MC, V. **Map** p249 C6.
This pharmacy is well stocked and open 24 hours a day. It's located in an impressive hospital for foreign patients.

Farmacia Internacional Miramar *Avenida 41 # 1814, esquina 20, Miramar (204 2051).* **Open** 9am-8.45pm daily. **Credit** MC, V. **Map** p249 C6.

Prescriptions

Due to the relative difficulty in getting hold of medication in Cuba, be sure to bring with you any prescription drugs you may need during your stay, plus aspirins and usual holiday medications.

STDs, HIV & AIDs

STDs such as herpes and gonorrhoea are fairly common in Cuba, but syphilis and AIDS are rare. Bring condoms from home (bearing in mind the inferiority of the locally available kind) and be sure to use them.

Cuba's initial radical programme for treating HIV-positive Cubans – essentially quarantining them in sanatoria – was widely criticised as repressive and despotic. In its defence, the government had at least taken steps to control a disease about which little was known, while others dithered with dire consequences, and the sanatoria themselves provided good levels of care. Policies are very different today: the sanatoria still provide optional housing for people living with HIV and AIDS, but also operate as outpatient clinics and support centres. The island now has labour legislation protecting HIV/AIDS carriers, education in schools and safe sex advertising on radio and television. Cuba currently has one of the world's lowest infection rates.

Lineayuda

830 3156. **Open** 9am-9pm Mon-Fri.
This anonymous helpline is an important source of information about sexually transmitted diseases and especially AIDS.

ID

Visitors should carry a photocopy of their passport around with them at all times. You'll need the passport itself when you want to change money, use travellers' cheques, draw out cash using a credit card, or pay for with a $50 or $100 bill.

Insurance

Visitors are highly recommended to take out private travel insurance for their trip to Cuba. A good policy should cover flight cancellation, theft, loss of life and medical charges. Health insurance is particularly advised, since the cost of medical services adds up quickly, even in Cuba. Make sure you are covered for hospitalisation, nursing services, doctor's fees and repatriation.

Internet

Although still developing and with some way to go, public internet facilities (in hotels, main post offices, press centres) have become much more widely available, though usually expensive and slow. The public facilities are very popular as neither the majority of Cubans nor foreign visitors have access to home computers. This means *colas* (queues), and sometimes horribly long ones. In view of this, and frustratingly slow connections, allow plenty of time and *paciencia* (patience). The good news is that if you're a night bird some of the outlets are open 24 hours. And now, if you come with a laptop, the more modern hotels have facilities that allow you to link up to the net directly from your room. Cuba's phone company, **ETECSA**, has two subsidiary internet service providers: **Ceniai** (862 6565/863 5209) and **Infocom** (204 4444).

Internet access

Cibercafe Capitolio (Capitolio building, La Habana Vieja, 860 3411/ 861 1519, $6 per hr) is very central and one of the less expensive venues, as is **Infointernet** (Calle 15, #551, entre C y D, Vedado, 554501, $6 per hr).

The telecommunications company ETECSA has internet access at the **Centro de Prensa Internacional** (Calle 23, entre N y O, Vedado, 554701, $3 per 30mins) and in Calle Habana #406, esquina Obispo, La Habana Vieja. Both also offer use of PCs and fax.

In addition to the above, almost all mid-range to upmarket hotels have internet access (usually available to non-guests). Try Hotels Meliá Cohiba, Inglaterra, Nacional, Habana Libre, NH Parque Central and Meliá Habana (*see pp32-46*). Hotel internet centres usually have shorter queues (if any), but you pay for the privilege, with prices up to $12 per hour. One of the cheapest is Hotel Inglaterra, at $2.50 per 30 minutes.

If you're a temporary or permanent resident you can get a much better deal with companies like **Colombus** (204 1170), which offers, for example, 15 hours of email-only access for $20. This can last months as you're only ever connected to send and receive. Internet access is more expensive at $20 for five hours. Also check out other new and ever-changing deals available with **ETECSA**, **Infocom** (204 4444) or **Ceniai** (862 6565/863 5209).

For a review of useful websites about Cuba, *see pp233*.

Language

For Cuban-Spanish words and phrases, *see p231*.

Legal assistance

As a first point of call, visitors should contact **Asistur** (*see p220*) or their consulate (*see p219*). The **Consultoria Jurídica Internacional** also specialises in legal help for foreigners.

You can also visit **Bufetes Internacionales** (Avenida 5ta #16202, esquina 162, Playa, 666824/204 6749) or **Bufete Especializado de la Notaria del Ministerio de Justicia** (Calle 23, Edificio #501, sótano esquina J, Vedado, 832 6024/6813). All these services are very professional, but go early as queues tend to form at the crack of dawn.

Consultoria Jurídica Internacional

Calle 16 #314, entre Avenidas 3ra y 5ta, Miramar (204 2490/fax 204 2303/cji@cji.get.cu). **Open** 8.30am-noon, 1.30-4.30pm Mon-Fri. **Map** p249 B6.

Libraries

If you're hoping to improve your knowledge of Cuba by visiting one of the local libraries, you're likely to be disappointed. Most of the libraries are poorly stocked and international books are thin on the ground. Note that libraries of whatever size, national or local, only offer reference and not lending services. Even then, take your passport with you.

Biblioteca Nacional de Cuba 'José Martí' *Avenida Independencia y 20 de Mayo, Plaza de la Revolución, Vedado (881 5013/555442-4/ www.bjm.cu).* **Open** 8.15am-6.15pm Mon-Fri. **Map** p250 D9/10.
Havana's main library occupies 16 floors. Consulting a book is a complicated business. Bring as many documents as you can in the way of diplomas, certificates, and proof of educational qualifications.

Biblioteca 'Rubén Martínez Villena' *Calle Obispo #59, entre Oficios y baratillo, Plaza de Armas, La Habana Vieja (862 9037-9).* **Open** 8.15 am-7.45pm Mon-Fri; 8.15am-4.15pm Sat. **Map** p252 E16.
This library has recently been renovated and now has multimedia facilities, making it easily Cuba's most modern library.

Instituto de Literatura y Linguística *Avenida Salvador Allende (Carlos III) #710, esquina Castillejo, Centro Habana (878 6486).* **Open** 8am-4.30pm Mon-Fri; 8am-1pm Sat. **Map** p250 D12.
Probably the best source of novels and non-Spanish texts in Havana.

Lost property

Lost property is *objetos perdidos/ extraviados* in Spanish. Airport Terminal 3 has a *reclamaciones* counter that is open 24 hours daily. If you leave something in a taxi, call the taxi office as soon as possible and be persistent in asking staff to try and track it down (still unlikely).

Media

Unfortunately, and rather depressingly, it is not what is said, but what is not said, in Cuban press, television and radio that allows us to get a better grasp of how the country operates. Supporters of the government argue that in the face of external threat from the north it is only prudent to aim for maximum consensus at home. The result is censorship, or to be more precise, self-censorship, which has created silences and gaps and ruled out the possibility of unbiased and accurate reporting. What is read, seen and heard tends to be trite and mediocre, so divorced from everyday experience that it can be wildly unrealistic.

Television

The above is particularly the case with television. Evening news broadcasts on foreign affairs are frequently negative: everything happening abroad is bad, while in contrast all things local are good. Coverage of domestic crime, including murder, rape and theft, not to mention 'dissident activity' is almost non-existent. Cubans have to rely on word of mouth, otherwise known as 'Radio Bemba' for information about what is really going on in the country.

Even within these rigid boundaries, some of the more outstanding intellectuals and journalists manage to excel in their ability to analyse in a public forum. Round table discussions focusing on world and national developments have been broadcast since the time of the Elián affair in 2000. These are often, but not always, the tedious exchanges that you might expect.

You may not get a chance to see Cuban television as most hotels don't receive local channels. Viewing for tourists is limited to **CNN** (Spanish and English), **HBO** and perhaps international versions of Spanish, German or French channels. Beyond the hotels, however, there is a choice of three channels: **Cubavisión**, **Telerebelde** and **Canal Educativo**; the latter was inaugurated in 2002 and to date is currently only broadcast in Havana. Cubavisión has a mix of programmes but its highest ratings are undoubtedly the nightly soap operas. Telerebelde specialises in sport and documentaries, while the Educational Channel offers Open University-style classes for children and adults on a wide variety of subjects.

Press

The two main national dailies, *Granma* and *Juventud Rebelde* comprise only four sheets of paper (eight pages) each. A cursory glance reveals that views opposing the official line are not published.

If a genuine forum for critical debate exists within the written press then you are most likely to find it in journals and periodicals. **Bohemia**, **Unión**, **Revolución y Cultura**, **Temas**, **Unión** and **Tricontinental** are cultural and semi-intellectual publications that provide the kind of in-depth reporting and analysis on matters that are not generally covered in the daily press.

If you do want to keep up with current events during your stay in Cuba, then some of the larger hotels, such as the Habana Libre, Nacional, Meliá Cohiba and Comodoro, stock some international press, though not usually English-language newspapers.

Bohemia Articles on literature, politics, culture, science, economics and sports.

La Gaceta de Cuba Complements *Unión* and covers theatre, photography, cinema and the arts.

Granma *www.granma.cubaweb.cu.* The news bulletin for the Central Committee of the Cuban Communist Party. Turgid and often self-righteous in tone. Weekly versions are available in English, French and Portuguese.

Juventud Rebelde *www.jrebelde.cubaweb.cu.* The Young Communist League (UJC) daily. Has more room for manoeuvre than Granma, consequently some of the articles have some spark. The Sunday edition often publishes work by well known international writers such as Gabriel García Márquez, James Petra and Eduardo Galeano.

Orbe *www.prensa-latina.cu.* This weekly features some well-written articles on international affairs, science, economics, culture and sports.

Tribuna de La Habana *www.islagrande.cu.* News and events in Havana.

Trabajadores *www.trabajadores.cubaweb.cu.* A weekly published by the CTC, the Central Trade Union co-ordinating body. Dull, to say the least.

Tricontinental *www.tricontinental.cubaweb.cu.* This quarterly is published in Spanish and English by OSPAAAL, the Organisation for Solidarity with the Peoples of Asia, Africa and Latin America. Articles tend to be well written and focus on political matters related to the three aforementioned continents.

Música Cubana This UNEAC (Cuban Union of Writers and Artists) publication comes out quarterly and carries articles on the leading figures and trends within Cuban music.

Unión Also published by UNEAC, this bi-monthly journal comprises articles on Cuban and foreign writers, poets and artists.

Radio

Radio has traditionally been something of a hot potato in Cuban politics. Fidel, Che and their Revolutionaries launched Radio Rebelde in 1957 from the mountains of the Sierra Maestra to lambaste Fulgencio Batista's regime and publicise their own cause. These days the only voice of opposition on the airwaves comes from **Radio Martí**, the unabashed voice of the Miami anti-Castro throng. There are some 70 radio stations currently operating in Cuba.

Radio Rebelde *www.cuba.cu/rrebelde.* Broadcasting music, sports, news and nightly programmes.

Radio Habana Cuba *www.radiohc.cu.* Broadcasts worldwide in nine languages on the shortwave and covers current affairs and cultural events from a strictly Cuban government perspective. See the website for frequencies.

Radio Enciclopedia *www.radioenciclopedia.co.cu.* Plays mostly instrumental music.

Radio Reloj *www.radioreloj.cu.* Offers round-the-clock news bulletins (broadcast in a deadpan voice) on national and international events to the accompaniment of a highly irritating clock ticking and beeping away in the background.

Radio Progreso offers music and light entertainment.

Radio Taíno targets mainly tourists and is broadcast in Spanish and (phoney American) English. The tone is reminiscent of the worst commercial radio you can think of, but without the commercials.

Money

Cuba has three currencies in circulation: the US dollar; the Cuban peso; and the *peso convertible*. However, despite this triple currency system, dollars rule, and virtually every transaction you make in Cuba will be in dollars. Make your life simple and come with dollars in cash and with a Visa or Mastercard credit card (not issued by a US bank). Travellers' cheques are only changed in international banks and can make life very difficult. Although it is risky to carry large amounts of cash on you, your stay will be less frustrating if you can limit the number of times you have to seek out a bank. The US dollar became legal tender in Cuba in 1993, and since then it has flooded the market. Every Cuban needs dollars as they are the only means of buying 'luxury' consumer goods and of achieving a more comfortable standard of living.

Although peso prices are often very cheap, foreign visitors paying in dollars tend to leave surprised by how much money they end up spending in Cuba. Moreover, unlike many Latin American countries, there is not really a bargaining culture in Cuba; you may be able to negotiate on long-distance taxi fares, or the price of objects sold in crafts markets, but elsewhere you will be expected to pay the quoted price.

Recently, European suppliers operating in Cuba have started to quote prices in euros. Use of the currency is limited at present to the big tourist resorts, such as Varadero and Guardalavaca, but is likely to become more widespread.

Dollar currency

Each dollar is divided into 100 cents (¢). Coins range from copper pennies (1¢) to silver nickels (5¢), dimes (10¢) and quarters (25¢), plus rarer half-dollar and one-dollar coins. Notes come in denominations of \$1, \$5, \$10, \$20 and \$50. In Cuba, dollars are known as *dólares*, or *divisa* (the slang term is *fula*). However, to get you even more hot and bothered, many people say pesos when they mean dollars. If in doubt, double check whether they are referring to *pesos cubanos* or *dólares*. To add to the confusion, the dollar symbol ($) is often used to denote the peso and the *peso convertible* (as well as the dollar). In these instances, the context should tell you whether a price is in dollars or pesos. Carry dollars in low denominations, as many places will not be able to give change, and take your passport (or a photocopy) if you intend to pay with a $50 or $100 note in all but the most upmarket places. Note that coin change from dollar bills is always given in *pesos convertibles* as US coins are not legal tender in Cuba.

Pesos cubanos

The Cuban peso, known as the peso, or *moneda nacional* (national currency), at press time had an exchange rate of 26 pesos to a dollar. This varies but not massively. Each peso is divided into 100 centavos. Notes are available in denominations of one, three, five, ten, 20 and 50 pesos; coins start at one centavo, followed by five centavos, ten centavos, 20 centavos, one peso and three pesos.

Although you'll pay for nearly everything in the city in dollars, it's always useful to have a handful of pesos for use on buses, in taxis and at street stalls, fruit and vegetable markets (*agromercados*), peso restaurants and cinemas. You'll probably use pesos more if you spend time outside Havana. Note that the export of Cuban pesos is prohibited (although customs officials are unlikely to be bothered by a few coins; in fact, the handsome three-peso coin with Che's image makes a fine souvenir).

Pesos convertibles

The convertible peso was introduced in 1995 and has the same value as the dollar. You may be given *pesos convertibles* in change, even if you've paid in dollars. It's not a problem; just spend them or change them at a bank before you leave as they are useless currency outside the country. The currency circulates as notes of one, five, ten, 25, 50 and 100 pesos, and coins of five, ten, 25 and 50 centavos.

ATMs

You can use the main credit cards (Visa, Mastercard) but you will not be able to use a US card in Cuba. There are now many more holes in the wall in Havana. Key locations include:

Vedado J and 23; 23 and P; Línea and M; Edificio FOCSA (*see p80*); Hotel Habana Libre (*see p41*).

Centro Habana Padre Varela (Belascoaín) and San José; Centro Comercial Carlos III (*see p118*); San José and Monserrate; Infanta and Manglar.

La Habana Vieja Aguiar and Empedrado; Brasil (Teniente Rey) and Oficios; Cuba and O'Reilly; O'Reilly and Compostela.

Miramar Avenida 5ta and Calle 112.

If you have any problems you can go to the **National Card Centre** (FINCIMEX, Centro Nacional de Tarjetas de Créditos, Calle 23 y M Vedado). Here, staff offer a friendly and efficient service; they will ring your card centre free of charge and even access your current statement.

Banks

Banks in Havana will exchange foreign currency into dollars and are the only places that cash travellers' cheques, but beware of paying commission when you buy and being charged again when you cash the cheques. Life is much simpler in Cuba with a credit card and cash. Branches of the Banco Financiero Internacional, Banco Internacional de Comercio and Banco Metropolitano will also let you withdraw cash against a credit card (as long as the card was not issued by a US bank). You can also now use credit cards at some *cadecas* (*see below*) and at the big hotels.

Bureaux de change

Cadeca (short for *casa de cambio*) exchange offices are found throughout Cuba – in tourist areas, shopping centres and next to many *agromercados* (food markets). The rates are usually in line with those at the banks, service is reliable, and, because there are so many branches, the queues are often shorter. Use the *cadecas* to change your dollars for pesos and to break larger dollar bills so that you have smaller cash for tipping. You can withdraw dollars using your credit card in the following *cadecas*:

Vedado 23 and L; Hotel Nacional (*see p42*); Hotel Habana Riviera (*see p41*; Línea and Paseo.

La Habana Vieja Lonja del Comercio (*see p54*); Obispo and Compostela.

Aeropuerto Internacional José Martí Terminal 3.

Most hotels will also change your money, even if you aren't a guest, but note that most hotels cash up their tills at 6pm.

Credit cards

Credit cards issued by US or affiliated banks are not accepted anywhere in Cuba. Non-US credit cards are accepted in a few shops and restaurants and in almost all tourist hotels. Credit card withdrawals can be made at some banks between 9am and 7pm Monday to Saturday (be prepared to queue). Alternatively, the bank at the Hotel Nacional de Cuba (*see p42*) is open 8am-8pm daily and you seldom have to wait.

Opening hours

Like everything else in Havana, opening hours are variable; the times given below are only intended as guidelines. As a basic and very important rule, if you have to get something done, do it in the morning, and allow plenty of time.

Banks 8.30am-3pm Mon-Fri.
Government offices 8.30am-12.30pm, 1.30-5pm Mon-Fri.
Fruit & vegetable markets (*agromercados*) 8am-6pm Tue-Sat; 8am-noon Sun.
Shops 10am-5.30pm Mon-Sat; 10am-1pm Sun. Some close on Sunday.

Police stations

All crimes should be reported immediately, in person, to the **Policia Nacional Revolucionaria** (PNR). There is a police station in every district and, it sometimes seems, a policeman on every street corner. The headquarters of the PNR is on Calle Tacón, opposite the Parque Arqueológico, in La Habana Vieja, but for information call 867 7777 or 882 0116.

Postal services

Cuba's postal service (Correos de Cuba) is still snail-slow, unreliable and petty theft within it is rife. Letters posted in Cuba can arrive in Europe any time between two weeks later and never; the rule is, if you really want something to arrive at its destination, don't post it. It's best to rely on people you know travelling in and out of Cuba to carry letters and parcels for you. This is also the safest way to receive mail, as there are no reliable poste restante services. If you do want to send a letter from Cuba (and don't include any money or anything else inside the envelope), it costs 0.75 pesos from a local post office.

Urgent communications should be sent as emails from hotels as sometimes faxes aren't always reliable. Packages or documents can be sent by the costly but reliable

DHL courier service (Calle 26, esquina 1ra, Miramar, 204 1578/fax 204 0999/ comercial@dhl.cutisa.cu). A small package (up to 50 grams) costs $30 to the United States, Canada and Mexico, or more to the rest of the world.

Telegrams

Go to any post office and fill in a form; the words will be counted and you pay in pesos. A few words to the UK will cost the equivalent of around a dollar and your message will arrive in two or three days.

Religion

Since the early 1990s, freedom of religion has been part of the Cuban constitution. Notionally, the majority of those who practise religion in Cuba are Roman Catholics. In reality, however, many Cuban Catholics are actually followers of the Afro-Cuban religion *santería*, which combines Catholicism with Yoruba beliefs. For more on Cuba's religious practice, *see p91* **Keeping the faith**.

Islam

Unión Arabe de Cuba

Calle Oficios #16, entre Obispo y Obrapía (861 5868). **Open** 9am-4.30pm Mon-Sat; 9.30am-12.30pm Sun. **Admission** free. **Map** p252 E15.
This museum has Cuba's only mosque. *See p54.*

Judaism

Casa de la Comunidad Hebrea

Calle I, entre 13 y 15, Vedado (832 8953/beth_shalom@ent.cu). **Open** 9.30am-5pm Mon-Fri. *Services* phone for details. **Map** p250 B11.

Sinagoga Adath Israel de Cuba

Calle Acosta #357, esquina Picota, La Habana Vieja (861 3495/ adath@enet.cu). **Open** 8am-7.30pm Mon-Sat; 8am-10am Sun. *Services* (Tora) 9am Mon, Thur, Sat. **Map** p252 E14.

Protestant

Catedral Episcopal de La Santísima Trinidad

Calle 13 #876, esquina 6, Vedado (833 5760/episcopal@ip.etecsa.cu). **Open** 11am-3pm Mon-Wed, Fri; 11am-7pm Thur. *Services* phone for details. **Map** p250 B9.

Primera Iglesia Presbiteriana-Reformada de La Habana

Calle Salud #222, entre Campanario y Lealtad, Centro Habana (862 1219/1239/www.prccuba.org). **Open** 9am-noon, 2-5pm daily. **Services** 9am, 10.30am Sun. **Map** p251 D13.

Safety & security

A few years ago, La Habana Vieja was notorious for petty theft from tourists, but the increased presence of police on many street corners in this area, as well as in Vedado and some of Centro Habana, has greatly diminished the problem.

Nevertheless, pickpockets are still about; don't flash cameras, jewellery or wallets. Violent crime against tourists is very rare, though not unheard of. If you are the victim of a robbery, you should contact the police immediately (*see p224*). You will need a police statement in order to make an insurance claim.

Smoking

Smoking is tolerated in most public places and no-smoking areas are rare. Despite a fairly vigorous campaign by the government, smoking remains popular, with cigarettes available for Cubans on the *libreta* (ration book).

Study

Just as Cuba has become a hip holiday destination, so studying here is also a growing market. However, the bureaucracy of arranging to study in Cuba can be very difficult. One way to ease your passage through the bureaucracy is to find someone who has gone through the maze and come successfully out the other end. In most cases the red tape is best left to specialist organisations. If you do choose to enrol directly while you're in Cuba, the choice of courses on offer can be wider and, in some cases, cheaper than at home.

You can start by going directly to a number of schools and institutions, depending on your study interest. Good places include the **Universidad de La Habana** (*see p226*), **Instituto Superior de Arte** (ISA; *see p226*), **Escuela Internacional de Cíne y Televisíon** in San Antonio de los Baños (Apartado Aereo 4041, Finca San Tranquilino, Carretera Vereda Nueva km4, 0650 3152), and **Escuela Nacional de Ballet** (Calle 120 #1110, entre 9na y 13, Cubanacán, Playas, 210288).

Student visas

Study in Cuba is possible with a tourist visa (*see p229*), but you'll have to leave the country every two months and re-enter with a new visa, which can be a drag and expensive. If you want to stay in Cuba for longer, you'll need to apply for a student visa. Do this as quickly as possible as paperwork can take an age. If you're exceedingly organised and enrol on a course at a well-established institution before you arrive in Cuba, the school will do the paperwork for you and you'll be able to apply for a student visa from the Cuban consulate in your home country. More often than not, however, students will have to do all the paper-pushing themselves once they are in Cuba, before their tourist visa runs out.

Student visas are issued by the educational institution's Department of International Relations, or by the Dirección de Posgrado in the case of the University of Havana. For your application you will normally need six passport photos, $80, a valid tourist card, a valid passport and a copy of the licence certificate of your residence in Havana. To obtain a student visa, foreign students must live either in university accommodation (limited availability) or in a *casa particular* that has an official dollar licence. Don't be tempted to live in an unlicensed place as both you and the landlords could find yourselves in trouble.

Once you've got a student visa, remember that you must give two week's notice to International Relations and pay a fee of $25-$45 before leaving the country. In an emergency it's possible to leave at shorter notice and this will involve a bit more cash (normally $50).

Long-term study

If you'd rather save your time and mental energy for academic rather than bureaucratic challenges, the easiest route is to enrol at a university in your home country that offers a year in Cuba as part of the study programme. For some years, universities such as Essex, Wolverhampton and North London (in the UK) and Ohio Wesleyan University (in the USA) have offered interesting study programmes in Cuba in the fields of language, business and culture.

Cuba has also become a popular destination for medical students.

Specialist package holidays

Dance

The best dance holidays package tuition with visits to clubs where you can dance the night away to the best of Cuba's salsa or *son* orchestras. The following British outfits organise dance packages: **Salsa Caribe** (020 8985 1703/www.salsacaribe.co.uk); **Key to Cuba** (020 8533 3605/www.key2Cuba.com); **Dance Holidays** (Carefree Travel, Zurich House, East Park, Crawley, West Sussex RH10 6AJ/ 01293 527722/www.danceholidays.com).

Spanish language

Language learning can often be combined with other activities. **Caledonia Languages Abroad** (The Clockhouse, Bonnington Hill, 72 Newhaven Road, Edinburgh EH6 5QG/ www.caledonialanguages.co.uk) offers Spanish and salsa holidays in Santiago, with home-stay half-board accommodation, and other dancing and cultural trips. From 2004 the company is offering Spanish and walking holidays based in the Sierra Maestra and Trinidad. Its long-established Spanish courses, for all levels, operate in Santiago and Havana all year round. The Faculty of Modern Languages at the **Universidad de la Habana** (*see p226*) also runs various Spanish courses, some with music and culture modules (flights and board not included).

Music & culture

The Conjunto Folklórico Nacional de Cuba (*see p172*) in Havana, runs **FolkCuba**, a course offering a selection of modules in Afro-Cuban and popular dance and percussion twice annually – in the last two weeks in January and the first two weeks of July.

British-based **La Timbala** runs workshop courses on Afro-Cuban percussion and culture (www.afrocubaweb.com/timbala/latimbala).

Miscellaneous

London-based **Capitolio Travel** (020 7359 9995/www.cubaspecialtours.com) organises tailor-made packages, and also liaises with specialist holiday companies. Trips have included birdwatching and photography, walking and cultural packages.

Despite the constant shortage of medicines, students are attracted to Cuba by its excellent healthcare reputation and the hands-on teaching methods. Cuban medical students are thrown right in at the deep end and deal with patients from the second year of their course, in contrast to most European medical students. Note that excellent Spanish is required for studying medicine in Cuba.

Language courses

One of the more popular ways to study Spanish in Cuba is to enrol at the University of Havana, which offers language and grammar courses for all levels, plus classes on Cuban culture and film. To enrol, simply turn up at the Postgraduate Department on the first Monday of the month. You'll need to do an introductory test and courses run for two to four weeks ($200/$250 respectively), with classes daily from Monday to Friday. Longer courses are also available.

If you're after more flexible schedules, try the **Instituto Superior de Artes**. This music and art college has a very dedicated Spanish language faculty and will do its utmost to find a course to suit the language needs and length of stay of every potential student. Prices average about $9 per three-hour class. Foreign art, music, drama and dance students at all levels are also accepted on a short-term basis at this prestigious college. Foreign students interested in a full-time course ($2,500 per year) must sit an entrance examination. *See also above* **Specialist package holidays**.

Instituto Superior de Artes (ISA)

Calle 120 #110, entre 9na y 13, Cubanacán, Playa (208 8075/208 9771/fax 336633/vrri@isa.cult.cu).

Universidad de La Habana

Postgraduate Department/ International Relations, Calle J, entre 25 y 27, Vedado (832 4245/ 831 3751/fax 552192/dpg@comuh.uh.cu). **Open** *Sept-July* 8am-3.30pm Mon-Fri. *Aug* 8.30am-1.30pm Mon-Fri. **Map** p250 C11.

Telephones

The phone system has been greatly improved in Havana since digitalisation, but the incidence of wrong numbers, crossed or dead ines (usually when it rains), phones being out of order and other problems is still frustratingly high. Many *habaneros* do not have a phone, but then it's customary to take the number of a neighbour who will either yell for the person you want or take a message. Foreigners living longer term in a *casa particular* and sharing the phone line with their landlords will need to organise a very clear system of answering and taking messages as the latter is not a Cuban speciality. Phone charges are still very cheap on peso lines and Cubans are used to talking extensively by phone. People may also simply pick up the phone in someone else's house and make a call.

Dialling & codes

To call Havana from overseas, first dial your international access code (0011 from Australia; 011 from Canada; 00 from New Zealand; 00 from the UK; 011 from the USA), followed by 53 (for Cuba), 7 (for Havana), and finally the five- or six-digit number.

We've checked the phone numbers in this guide, but numbers are very prone to change. ETECSA normally provides a recorded message for three months after a number change. If you are unsure of a number change, ask a friend, ring 0 for the operator or 113 for directory enquiries; the lines are usually busy but maybe you'll be lucky and get through to information services.

Making a call

To call a number outside of Havana, first dial 0, followed by the city code. You can find city codes in any telephone directory and they are also included in the listings in this guide.

You can make an international call from a private phone but only through the international operator (bilingual, dial 09) and by reversing the charges. Then you can speedily (it's expensive) get your family or friends to phone you back.

To make a direct international call you will need to go to a hotel (a very expensive option) or, more economically, to the staffed dollar phone kiosks (*see also below*, public phones). International codes include: Australia 43; USA 1; New Zealand 64; UK 44 (after the international code, drop the initial zero of the area code). Dial 119 first to get an outside line. The cost of international calls is high, starting at around $2.50 per minute to North America and going up $4-$5 per minute for much of the rest of the world. Foreign charge cards cannot be used in Cuba.

Cuban area codes

(dial 0 first if you're inside Cuba)
Holguín 24
Matanzas 45
Pinar del Río 82
Sancti Spiritus 41
Santa Clara 42
Santiago de Cuba 22
Trinidad 419
Varadero 45
Viñales 8

Cuban operator services

Directory enquiries 113
International enquiries 09
National operator 0
Repairs 114
Wake-up call 870 2511

Public phones

There are four kinds of public telephone in Havana: dollar coin phones, peso coin phones, dollar card phones and peso card phones. They are found all over the city, but trying to make a call can be an irritating experience. The most widespread are dollar phones, which charge 15¢ for a three-minute call. Peso phones charge just five centavos for three minutes, but are not that common in tourist areas, are very often out of order and don't offer an international service.

You can make local, national and international calls and buy both the peso and dollar phone card at staffed ETECSA cabins. The peso cards cost five or ten pesos, the dollar cards (also available in hotels and some shops) cost $10, $25 and $45.

Telephone directories

The Havana phone directory is updated every year, although numbers can change rapidly. Many entries are only listed by category, which can make looking for individual venues problematic. You may look for a restaurant under *restaurante*, for example, when it's actually been classed as a *cafetería*. Note, too, that while private domestic numbers are listed in the directory, private enterprises, such as *paladares*, are not.

Mobile phones

There are two mobile phone companies in Cuba. **Cubacel** (www.cubacel.cu) is an analogue system (only US or triband handsets will work) and **C_Com** (www.ccom.cu) is a digital system, hence European handsets should be compatible (however, at the time of writing, coverage was limited to Havana and the Matanzas area). Both companies have roaming agreements with other country networks and both have offices at José Martí Airport (Terminal 3), so you can sort a phone out on arrival. Some of the larger hotels can arrange a deal through their business offices. Cubacel also has an office at Calle 28 #510, entre Avenidas 5ta y 7ma, Miramar (880 2222).

As a visitor you have two options: to use your own phone if your network has a roaming agreement with Cuba; or, if you are planning a longer visit, to open a temporary account to obtain a Cuban SIM card, using C_Com (unless you have a tri-band or US-compatible handset).

Be warned, though, that the cost of using a mobile phone in Cuba is phenomenally high, starting with a flat fee of $120 (though you can find cheaper offers) to activate the phone, followed by a monthly fee of $40 or a pre-paid card costing from $20 upwards. Calls are charged on top of this at a rate of 40¢ per minute within Cuba (30¢ at night), $2.40 per minute to North America, and around $5 per minute to Europe. If you run out of credit on your phone, you'll have to call the office to arrange for more before being reconnected.

Faxes

Faxes can be received in most of the big hotels for only $1 (sometimes less) per page but are costly to send to Europe, at around $4 per minute.

Time

Cuba is five hours behind Greenwich Mean Time and therefore equivalent to Eastern Standard Time (New York and Miami). Daylight saving time runs from May to October.

Tipping

All tourists are relatively wealthy compared to the average Cuban, so if you get good service, tip accordingly. Tip five to ten per cent in restaurants and cafés unless a service charge is included in the bill. In hotels leave a dollar on the pillow every morning if you can, or, if you are in a *casa particular*, hand over a few extra dollars when you leave if you have been satisfied with the service. Alternatively, you can leave hard-to-come-by items such as toiletries. Porters who help you with your luggage and tourist taxi drivers usually get a dollar.

Toilets

Forget public toilets; they are wretched places, and few and far between. Fortunately, most hotels and restaurants will let you use theirs. Some have attendants who should be tipped from 10¢ to 25¢ before you leave. Although some offer toilet paper, most don't.

Tourist information

Before you go

Tourism in Cuba is governed by the **Ministerio de Turismo** (Calle 19 #710, Vedado, 833 4202/0545/www.cubatravel.cu). A number of state tourist agencies such as Cubanacán, Cubatur and Havanatur (for all, *see p184*) represent Cuba abroad. US citizens should contact the Canadian representatives of these organisations in Toronto or Montreal.

US citizens travelling to Cuba

Contrary to popular opinion, the US government does allow its citizens to travel to Cuba. The 'travel ban' is technically an economic ban, a component of the embargo. The problem is not travel as such, it is the spending of money. The US government's takes a strong stance against Cuba, aggressively supports the economic ban and pursues violators.

The current regulations regarding travel to Cuba stem from a confusing mosaic of additions and subtractions to the laws covering the embargo. Recent legislation has included the Cuban Democracy Act of 1992, granting the US Treasury Department the authority to impose fines of up to $50,000 on those who violate the ban. This was followed in 1996 by the Cuba Liberty and Democracy Solidarity Act (known as the Helms-Burton law), which required all travel to Cuba be licensed by the Office of Foreign Assets and Control (OFAC), a division of the US Treasury Department.

Two categories of visitor don't require an OFAC licence: Cuban nationals are allowed to visit close family members once a year; and those on a 'fully hosted' trip, where a third party not subject to US jurisdiction pays for all expenses, are also exempt. US Customs officers have the authority to ask US citizens for proof that they didn't pay for anything on their trip.

An OFAC licence enables a US citizen to spend money on the island, as long as it's not for a commercial purpose. OFAC regulations have two categories of licences, 'general' and 'specific'.

People travelling to Cuba under a 'general license' do not require written government permission. Those entitled to travel this way are journalists, government officials and certain professional researchers.

More Americans travel to Cuba under 'specific license'. To obtain this licence potential visitors must apply in writing to OFAC. Only those attached to educational institutions, private foundations and research facilities are eligible. In 2003 President Bush eliminated a whole category of 'specific licenses', namely those granted for 'people-to-people' exchange, by which museums, alumni associations, religious groups and cultural organisations could sponsor trips open to the population at large around a specific educational theme. Now, the only type of educational exchanges permitted are those by students enrolled in a degree programme at an accredited institution.

Be that as it may, Americans are travelling to Cuba in record numbers, many going illegally (without a licence), leaving from a third country. Customs officers in Cuba are aware of the situation and will generally not stamp American passports. The Bush administration is on to this and not at all pleased. If you do travel illegally, don't immediately board a flight home after returning from Cuba to a third country. US Customs officials have been known to visit airports in Canada and observe who transfers from flights from Cuba on to US-bound flights. Since Bush took office well over 1,200 Americans have received letters from OFAC threatening fines of up to $50,000, a rather hefty sum for a holiday in the sun. If such a letter lands on your doorstep, write back within 30 days and request a hearing.

Note that the Cuban government require US citizens to obtain a visa. *See p229.*

Useful addresses

Center for Constitutional Rights

666 Broadway 7th floor, New York, New York 10012 (212-614-6464/info@ccr-ny.org).
This organisation has a Cuba Travel project and a clearing house for legal information about the ban. It also distributes a publication called *Advice for Travelers to Cuba.*

Marazul

800-223-5334/marazulcharters.com.
This company has branches in New Jersey and Miami and operates charter flights from Miami and New York. It can also assist in obtaining a Cuban visa.

National Lawyers Guild

143 Madison Avenue 4th floor, New York, New York 10016 (212-679-5100/ nlgo@nlg.org).
This group has a Cuba sub-committee, part of whose work is to campaign against the ban. It also has a lawyer referral network.

OFAC

US Department of Treasury, 1500 Pennsylvania Avenue NW, Treasury Annex, Washington DC, 20220 (202 622 2480/ www.treas.gov/ofac).

Cuban Tourist Board *154 Shaftesbury Avenue, London WC2H 8JT (020 7240 6655/fax 020 7836 9265/cubatouristboard.london@virgin.net).*

Bureau de Tourisme de Cuba *Suite 1105, 440 Boulevard Rene Levesque Ouest, Montreal H2Z 1V7 (514 875 8004/fax 514 875 8006).*

Cuban Tourist Board *Suite 705, 55 Queen Street East, Toronto M5C 2R6 (416 362 0700/fax 416 362 6799).*

In Havana

The government tourist bureau, **Infotur**, runs tours in Havana and to other parts of Cuba. It has three or four information offices in the city. In addition, most hotels have a tourist information desk where staff arrange package tours and provide information and maps. The desk in the lobby of the Hotel Habana Libre (*see p41*) is particularly good.

In general it can be difficult to get clear, precise information on events and venues in Cuba. For publications on festivals and events in Cuba *see p132*.

Agencia de Viajes San Cristóbal

Oficios #110, entre Lamparilla y Baratillo, La Habana Vieja (866 9585). **Map** p252 E15.

The official cultural travel agency for Habaguanex, the commercial wing of the City Historian's Office, can make bookings for Habaguanex hotels and organises some of the best guided tours. It can also arrange specialised tours beyond Havana.

Infotur

Calle Obispo #524, entre Bernaza y Villegas, La Habana Vieja (862 4586/tel/fax 333333/obispodir@cubacel.net). **Open** 10am-6pm daily. **Map** p252 D14/15.

Branches: Terminal 3, Aeropuerto Internacional José Martí (366 6112); Avenida 5ta, esquina 112, Miramar (204 7036).

Visas & immigration

Tourist cards & visas

All foreign visitors to Cuba require a passport (valid for at least six months beyond their departure from Cuba), an onward or return air ticket and a tourist card (*tarjeta de turista*). Tourist cards will be issued automatically if you book a package tour. Independent travellers can buy tourist cards from the travel agent or airline when they purchase their ticket or at the check-in desk before they board the plane to Cuba. The Cuban consulate in London will also issue a tourist card for £15 on presentation of a photocopy of your passport and booking confirmation from a travel agent. As a last resort you can buy the card when you land at José Martí Airport, although this is not recommended because you're likely to get charged more and it could be a hassle. Some airlines won't allow passengers without a tourist card to board the plane in the first place.

On arrival, immigration officials will stamp your tourist card with the date of your arrival and it's then valid for four weeks from that date.

Hang on for dear life to your tourist card, as you'll need it to leave the country. A replacement costs $25 (this can be a lot of hassle) and in addition to the cost you may be delayed by some bureaucratic wrangling, problematic if your flight is about to depart. You're expected to give details on the tourist card of your intended address for at least the first two nights of your stay in Cuba. Enter the name of a state hotel or a licensed *casa particular* where you are staying. Certainly do not leave this section blank, or you could have your passport confiscated until you have booked approved hotel accommodation at the airport tour desk.

If you intend to stay in Cuba for a longer period, or you're travelling on business or for journalistic purposes, you'll need a special visa. Applications should be made through a Cuban consulate at least three weeks in advance of your trip.

Extending your stay

If you want to extend your stay in Cuba beyond the four weeks designated on your tourist card, you have to go in person to the immigration office (Control de Extranjeros) with your passport and tourist card, before your first tourist card runs out. It's now the only place to do this and it's best to go there as near to 8.30am as you can. If you go later in the morning, expect a long queue. Take evidence of your official holiday residence or, if you are on the move, tell the visa officials that you are travelling around the island. You'll rarely encounter any problems getting an extension, although it will cost you $25 and must be paid using stamps of the same value. The stamps are available from branches of Banco de Comercio or Banco Financiero Internacional found all over Havana (*see* **Banks**).

Control de Extranjeros

Ministerio del Interior, Calle Factor y Final, Tulipan, Nuevo Vedado. **Open** 8.30am-noon Mon-Fri. **Map** p249 E8.

Cubans & naturalised citizens

As far as the Cuban government is concerned, anyone who was born in Cuba is Cuban, even if they have since become a naturalised citizen of another country. Visitors who fall into this category require an entry permit (*autorización de entrada*) to re-enter the country and can also apply to the nearest Cuban diplomatic office for a Vigencia de Viaje, which allows them to visit Cuba as often as they like within a two-year period.

US visitors

For details of regulations governing US visitors to Cuba, *see p228* **Travel by US citizens to Cuba**.

Weights & measures

The metric system (kilometres, metres and centimetres; kilograms and grams) is compulsory in Cuba. However, fruit and veg is sold by the pound in *agromercados*. Temperature is given in Celsius (ºC).

What to take

Clothes

Lightweight, loose-fitting clothes, preferably made of cotton, will help to keep you cool and fresh in the heat and humidity. Don't forget, though, that the temperature can drop considerably in the winter, so pack a warm sweater and a light jacket too. The former is also crucial for those arctic air-conditioner moments. Pack a sun-hat to protect you from the strong sun and an umbrella for regular tropical downpours. Cubans like to dress up when they go out for the evening, so ladies, remember your heels and something glamorous for Havana's nightlife.

Medical supplies

Many day-to-day medical supplies are not readily available in Cuba. In addition to prescription medicines, you should bring the following:

Antihistamine tablets/cream
Antiseptic wipes and cream
Aspirin/paracetamol
Bandages/Band Aids
Contraceptive pills/condoms

Diarrhoea preparation
Multi-vitamins
Rehydration salts

Other essentials

Adaptor
locks for luggage
Mosquito repellent
Photocopies of documents
Sun-cream
Torch and spare batteries
Lighter
Ear plugs.

Useful extras

Candles
Cigarette papers/rolling tobacco
Dictionary (English-Spanish)
Envelopes
Pens and pencils
Pen-knife (bury it in your hold luggage)
Cotton buds
Sanitary towels (these are available, but you won't be able to choose which brand you buy) or tampons;
Teaspoon
Umbrella.
Water-puifying tablets.

When to go

High season in Cuba lasts from November to April and July to August. During this time hotels are at their busiest and most expensive, with most places fully booked at Christmas, New Year and Easter. Room rates tend to be 20 to 40 per cent lower at other times of year, but as most Cubans take their holidays in July and August, beaches are packed in high summer. Many hotels in Havana are fully booked for the Día de Rebeldía Nacional 25-27 July and also during trade shows such as the Feria Internacional de La Habana (FIHAV) in early November. If you want to visit the city at these times, book flights and hotels as early as possible.

Public holidays

On the following days most shops, museums and businesses are closed.
Día de la Liberación (Liberation Day) 1 Jan
Día de los Trabajadores (May Day) 1 May
Día de Rebeldía Nacional (Celebration of the National Rebellion) 25-27 July
Inicio de la Guerra de Independencia (Anniversary of the start of the First War of Independence) 10 Oct
Navidad (Christmas) 25 Dec

Climate

Cuba is located in the tropics and has two distinct seasons: summer (May to October), which is hot and wet, and winter (November to April), which is slightly cooler and drier. Gulf Stream currents warm the waters around the island, while the north-east trade wind known as *la brisa* cools the city throughout the year. Humidity rarely falls below 70 per cent and can reach an enervating 90 per cent. Two-thirds of the annual rainfall (132cm; 52in) falls between May and November, usually as short, sharp showers but also during occasional heavy and prolonged storms. Some years, Cuba is subjected to a dry period (*la sequía*) lasting three to five months. Otherwise, December, February, March and April are the driest months of the year. There is an average of eight hours of sunshine per day throughout the year. *See also below* **Average temperatures**.

Bear in mind that from May to October the weather is very hot and humid indeed, with the very hottest period usually being August and September.

Hurricanes occasionally occur between September and November, but are usually well forecast. If an electrical storm brews up while you are out and about, most likely during the summer months, keep away from the royal palm trees, which tend to attract lightning. For weather information, pick up a copy of *Granma* (*see p223*), which prints a daily weather forecasts. There are also regular weather reports in Spanish on Cuban TV.

Average temperatures

	High (C/F)	Low (C/F)
Jan	25/78	17/63
Feb	26/79	17/63
Mar	27/82	18/66
Apr	28/84	20/68
May	30/87	21/71
June	31/88	23/74
July	31/89	23/74
Aug	31/89	23/74
Sept	31/88	23/74
Oct	29/85	21/71
Nov	27/82	20/69
Dec	26/79	18/65

Women

Although it's a macho country, Cuba is, on the whole, much safer for women than many other Caribbean countries. However, a woman of whatever age, travelling on her own, should be prepared to cope with stares, *piropos* (comments) and even proposals of marriage. Some Cubans want to escape the harsh conditions of the island and would marry you tomorrow in order to do so. If it bothers you, wear a ring on your wedding finger and if necessary invent a tall, dark and fictional husband.

Although many Cuban women wear short skirts and a lot of lycra, some foreign women prefer to wear less revealing clothes in an attempt to avoid unwanted attention. If you are harassed by a Cuban man, make it clear if you're not interested and he will usually get the message. Flirting is a national pastime and is normally very playful.

If you do need help or advice, contact the **Federación de Mujeres de Cuba** (Paseo #260, entre 11 y 13, Vedado, 552771/ fmccu@ceniai.inf.cu). Originally set up to implement the equality laws of the Revolution, the Federación now promotes the interests of women.

Working in Havana

If you plan to work in Cuba, you can apply for a visa from the Cuban consulate in your home country (*see p219*). You'll need to know the name and details of the business or organisation that is sponsoring your stay and allow at least three weeks for your application to be processed. Journalists and students (*see p225*) require special visas to enter the country; these are also available from the local consulate.

Vocabulary

Like other Latin languages, Spanish has different familiar and polite forms of the second person (you). Many young people now use the familiar *tú* form most of the time; for foreigners, though, it's always advisable to use the more polite *usted* with people you don't know, and certainly with anyone over 50. In the phrases listed here all verbs are given in the *usted* form. Cuban Spanish is notably different from Castillian Spanish in some of its vocabulary (such as *carro* rather than *coche* for car), and also in its tendency to drop final letters of words and also the 'd' from the final 'ado' of words. It's rare to come across a Cuban who speaks fluent English, though many, in Havana at least, speak a few words. For food- and drink-related vocabulary, *see p98*.

Pronunciation

c before an **i** or an **e** is soft, like **s** in **s**it.
c in all other cases is as in **c**at.
g, before an **i** or an **e**, and **j** are pronounced with a guttural **h**-sound that does not exist in English – like **ch** in Scottish lo**ch**, but much harder.
g in all other cases is pronounced as in **g**et.
h at the beginning of a word is normally silent.
ll is pronounced almost like a **y**.
ñ is like **ny** in ca**ny**on.
z is always the same as a soft c, like s as in **s**it.
A single **r** at the beginning of a word and **rr** elsewhere are heavily rolled.

Basics

hello *hola*; **hello** (when answering the phone) *hola, diga*
good morning, good day *buenos días*; **good afternoon, good evening** *buenas tardes*; **good evening** (after dark), **good night** *buenas noches*
goodbye/see you later *adiós/hasta luego*
please *por favor*; **thank you** (very much) *(muchas) gracias*;
you're welcome *de nada*
do you speak English? *¿habla inglés?*
I don't speak Spanish *no hablo español*
I don't understand *no entiendo*
what's your name? *¿cómo se llama?*
speak more slowly, please *hable más despacio, por favor*
wait a moment *espere un momento*
Sir/Mr *señor* (*sr*); **Madam/Mrs** *señora* (*sra*); **Miss** *señorita* (*srta*)
excuse me/sorry *perdón*
excuse me, please *oiga* (to attract attention; literally 'hear me')
OK/fine/(or to a waiter) **that's enough** *vale*
where is... *¿dónde está…?*
why? *¿porqué?*; **when?** *¿cuándo?*; **who?** *¿quién?*; **what?** *¿qué?*; **where?** *¿dónde?*; **how?** *¿cómo?*
is/are there any... *¿hay…?*
very *muy*; **and** *y*; **or** o
with *con*; **without** *sin*
open *abierto*; **closed** *cerrado*
what time does it open/close? *¿a qué hora abre/cierra?*
pull (on signs) *tirar*; push *empujar*
I would like... *quiero…* (literally, 'I want…'); **how many would you like?** *¿cuántos quiere?*
I like *me gusta*;
I don't like *no me gusta*
good *bueno/a*; **bad** *malo/a*; **well/badly** *bien/mal*; **small** *pequeño/a*; **big** *gran, grande*; **expensive** *caro/a*; **cheap** *barato/a*; **hot** (food, drink) *caliente*; **cold** *frío/a*
something *algo*; **nothing** *nada*
more/less *más/menos*
the bill/check, please *la cuenta, por favor*
how much is it? *¿cuánto es?*
do you have any change? *¿tiene cambio?*
price *precio*; **free** *gratis*
discount *descuento*
bank *banco*; **to rent** *alquilar*; **(for) rent, rental** *(en) alquiler*; **post office** *correos*; **stamp** *sello*; **postcard** *postal*; **toilet** *los servicios*

Getting around

airport *aeropuerto*; **railway station** *estación de ferrocarriles*; **car** *carro* or *coche*; **bus** *guagua* or *rutero* (general terms for a city bus); *autobús* (air-conditioned tourist bus), *camello* (pink articulated bus); **train** *tren*
a ticket *un billete*; **return** *de ida y vuelta*; **bus stop** *parada de autobús*;
the next stop *la próxima parada*
excuse me, do you know the way to...? *por favor, ¿sabe como llegar a...?*
left *izquierda*; **right** *derecha;*
here *aquí* or *acá*; **there** *allí*
straight on *recto*; **to the end of the street** *al final de la calle*;
as far as *hasta*; **towards** *hacia*
near *cerca*; **far** *lejos*

Accommodation

do you have a double/single room for tonight/one week? *¿tiene una habitación doble/para una persona para esta noche/ una semana?*
where is the car park? *¿dónde está el parking?*
we have a reservation *tenemos reserva*
an inside/outside room *una habitación interior/exterior*
with/without bathroom *con/sin baño*; **shower** *ducha*
double bed *cama de matrimonio*; **with twin beds** *con dos camas*
breakfast included *desayuno incluído*
air-conditioning *aire acondicionado*; **lift** *ascensor*; **swimming pool** *piscina*

Time

morning *la mañana*; **midday** *mediodía*; **afternoon/evening** *la tarde*; **night** *la noche*; **late night/early morning** (roughly 1-6am) *la madrugada*
now *ahora*; **later** *más tarde*
yesterday *ayer*; **today** *hoy*;
tomorrow *mañana*; **tomorrow morning** *mañana por la mañana*
early *temprano*; **late** *tarde*
delay *retraso*; **delayed** *retrasado*
at what time...? *¿a qué hora…?*
in an hour *en una hora*
the bus will take 2 hours *el autobús tardará dos horas*
at 2 *a las dos*; **at 8pm** *a las ocho de la tarde*; **at 1.30** *a la una y media*
at 5.15 *a las cinco y cuarto*;
at 22.30 *a veintidós treinta*
Monday *lunes*; **Tuesday** *martes*; **Wednesday** *miércoles*; **Thursday** *jueves*; **Friday** *viernes*; **Saturday** *sábado*; **Sunday** *domingo*
January *enero*; **February** *febrero*; **March** *marzo*; **April** *abril*; **May** *mayo*; **June** *junio*; **July** *julio*; **August** *agosto*; **September** *septiembre*; **October** *octubre*; **November** *noviembre*; **December** *diciembre*
spring *primavera*; **summer** *verano*; **autumn/fall** *otoño*; **winter** *invierno*

Numbers

0 *cero*; **1** *un, uno, una*; **2** *dos*; **3** *tres*; **4** *cuatro*; **5** *cinco*; **6** *seis*; **7** *siete*; **8** *ocho*; **9** *nueve*; **10** *diez*; **11** *once*; **12** *doce*; **13** *trece*; **14** *catorce*; **15** *quince*; **16** *dieciséis*; **17** *diecisiete*; **18** *dieciocho*; **19** *diecinueve*; **20** *veinte*; **21** *veintiuno*; **22** *veintidós*; **30** *treinta*; **40** *cuarenta*; **50** *cincuenta*; **60** *sesenta*; **70** *setenta*; **80** *ochenta*; **90** *noventa*; **100** *cien*; **1,000** *mil*; **1,000,000** *un millón*.

Further Reference

Books

Fiction & literature

Bush, Peter (editor) *The Voice of the Turtle: a collection of Cuban short stories translated into English.* The short story is a strong genre in Cuba and this collection gives a good overall picture, spanning over a century.

Cabrera Infante, Guillermo *Tres Tristes Tigres* (*Three Trapped Tigers*). A sharply comic novel of pre-Revolutionary Havana in which the hedonistic city itself is a protagonist.

Carpentier, Alejo *Los pasos perdidos* (*The Lost Steps*). It is in this novel that the great Cuban writer develops his theory of Magic Realism.

García, Cristina *Dreaming in Cuban* (1992). The young Cuban-American writer explores the theme of families divided by politics and the Florida Straits through three generations.

Greene, Graham *Our Man in Havana* (1958). Set on the very eve of Castro's Revolution, the darkly comic novel evokes Havana in the 1950s through the misadventures of a vacuum-cleaner salesman turned reluctant spy.

Guillén, Nicolás Guillén was the Revolution's official poet and has been widely translated. Apart from his political poems, Guillén is best known for his very rhythmical Afro-Cuban works, which have often been set to music.

Gutiérrez, Pedro Juan *Dirty Havana Trilogy (2002)*. Interlinked stories from Havana's underground. Strong, unforgiving language makes it a powerful read.

Hemingway, Ernest *The Old Man and the Sea* (1952). This tale of a local fisherman's epic struggle won Hemingway the Nobel Prize for Literature in 1954. Hemingway lived in Cuba for many years and donated the prize to the Virgen de la Caridad del Cobre, Cuba's patron saint. Try also *Islands in the Stream* (1970), based on the author's experiences hunting Nazi submarines during World War II, and *To Have and Have Not* (1937), an exciting account of illegal trade between Havana and Florida.

Hijuelos, Oscar *The Mambo Kings Play Songs of Love.* Cuban-American novel about the world of Cuban musicians playing in New York in the 1950s.

Iyer, Pico *Cuba and the Night* (1995). An ambivalent love story set in the dark days of 1980s Havana.

Lezama Lima, José *Paradiso* (*Paradise*). Lezama Lima is the giant of 20th-century Cuban literature. This, his only novel, gives a richly detailed picture of Havana through the eyes of a sensitive young protagonist growing up in the city.

Piñera, Virgilio Best known as a playwright, particularly of absurdist drama, Piñera is one of Cuba's most important writers, although not much of his work has been translated.

Sarduy, Severo *¿De dónde son los cantantes?* (*From Cuba with a Song*). This patchwork novel explores Cuba's identity through Spanish, African and Chinese roots. Sarduy left Cuba and lived in Paris for many years before he died of AIDS in 1993.

Non-fiction

Arenas, Reinaldo *Antes que anochezca (Before Night Falls).* The autobiography of the Cuban dissident and homosexual. Arenas was persecuted and imprisoned in Cuba and finally abandoned the island in 1980 for New York. Suffering from AIDS, Arenas committed suicide in 1990.

Anderson, John Lee *Che Guevara: A Revolutionary Life* (1997). A weighty and exhaustive biography of the Revolutionary hero.

Barclay, Juliet *Havana: Portrait of a City.* A well-written history, with photos and illustrations, of the development of Havana from the early 16th century to the late 19th century.

Block, Holly *ArtCuba: The New Generation (2001).* A beautifully presented review of contemporary Cuban art by over 60 artists.

Cabrera Infante, Guillermo *Mea Cuba.* Banned in Cuba for its strong condemnation of Castro, this collection of essays and memoirs presents a personalised account of the literary/political scene during the early years of the Revolution.

Fuentes, Norberto *Hemingway in Cuba* (1984). A key account of the author's life in Cuba, with ample illustrations.

González-Wippler, Migene *Santería: The Religion* (1994). Plenty of interesting information on Afro-Cuban religion.

LaFray, Joyce *¡Cuba Cocina!* (1994). Cuban cooking served up in all its glory.

Martí, José Anyone hoping to understand Cuba needs some knowledge of Martí's poems, essays and letters. Martí wrote prolifically and his works are collected in over 30 volumes, most of which have been translated into English.

Matthews, Herbert *Revolution in Cuba* (1975). A sympathetic analysis by the *New York Times* journalist.

Miller, Tom *Trading with the Enemy: A Yankee travels through Castro's Cuba* (1992). Part travelogue, part social analysis, Tom Miller's astute comments on Cuba in the 1990s is one of the best recent books about the island.

Roy, M *Cuban Music* (2002). Comprenhensive exploration of the origins, politics and key figures of Cuban music.

Smith, Stephen *The Land of Miracles* (1998). Tales of touring Cuba in an American car.

Szulc, Tad *Fidel: A Critical Portrait* (1986). An excellent, revealing biography of the Revolutionary leader.

Thomas, Hugh *Cuba, or the Pursuit of Freedom 1726-1969* (1971). Historian Hugh Thomas's scholarly history of the island is over 30 years old now, but is still probably the standard work on Cuba's history. Try also Thomas's more recent and equally definitive *The Cuban Revolution* (1986).

Film

Buena Vista Social Club (Wim Winders 1998). Nostalgic documentary focusing on the elderly stars of the phenomenally successful album by the same name.

Comandante (Oliver Stone 2003). Oliver Stone interviews Fidel Castro with intriguing (but not groundbreaking) results.

Fresa y chocolate (Strawberry and Chocolate; Tomás Gutiérrez Alea and Juan Carlos Tabío 1993). Taboo-breaking film about the trials and tribulations of a homophobic Revolutionary student.

Lista de espera (Waiting List; Juan Carlos Tabío 1999). Tabío's debut, this comedy drama follows a group of travellers waiting at a run-down Cuban transit station for the next bus.

Memorias del subdesarrollo (Memories of Underdevelopment; Tomás Gutiérrez Alea 1968). Based on a novel by Edmundo Desnoes, it follows a man whose family flees to Miami in 1961. A seminal work within the Spanish-speaking world.

Miel para Oshún (Honey for the Goddess; dir. Humerto Solas 2001). The tale of a Cuban who was taken to the US as a child and returns decades later to look for his mother.

La muerte de un burócrata (Death of a Bureaucrat; Tomás Gutiérrez Alea 1966). A black comedy about the absurdities of Cuban bureaucracy.

Suite Habana (Fernando Pérez 2003). Powerful, moving silent film following the lives of several *habaneros*.

Music

Artists

Buena Vista Social Club *Buena Vista Social Club* (1997). The Ry Cooder-backed album featuring a group of Cuban old-timers, which became nothing short of an international sensation. Members of the group can often be seen playing venues in Havana and internationally. A slick production.

Clave y Guaguancó *Noche de la Rumba* (1999). Cuba's foremost group to specialise in Afro-Cuban group has been around for over 50 years.

Delgado, Issac *Con ganas* (1993). An early album from Cuba's salsa/timba superstar, known as 'El Chévere de la Salsa'.

Milanés, Pablo *Serie Millennium 21* (1999). A double compilation CD set of classics from the famous *nueva trova* singer.

Papa Noel & Papi Oviedo *Bana Congo* (2002). Slick, highly listenable collaboration between veteran Congolese singer Papa Noel and Cuban *tres* player Papi Oviedo.

Orishas *A lo cubano* (2000); *Emigrante* (2003). One of the hottest groups to come out of Cuba in recent years, Orishas blend hip hop, harmonies and percussion to impressive effect.

Rodríguez, Silvio *Días y flores; Unicornio; Rabo de Nuve*. One of Cuba's most prolific singer-songwriters on the *nueva trova* scene. A specialist in emotionally intense lyrics and moving ballads, Rodríguez's early acoustic albums are considered to be his best. Songs are often loaded with pro-Revolutionary ideology.

Segundo, Compay *Antología* (1995). This compilation of 30-odd of Compay's greatest songs is a good way of getting acquainted with one of Cuba's all-time greats, who died in 2003. Compay was part of the famed Buena Vista Social Club project.

Los Van Van *Llegó… Van Van* (2000). This multi-piece orchestra is one of Cuba's most popular long-standing groups. Inventors of the *songo* rhythm, Los Van Van won a Grammy in 2000 for best salsa group.

Yusa *Yusa* (2003). Up-and-coming singer with a soulful contemporary Cuban flavour.

Los Zafiros *Bossa Cubana* (reissued 1999). A pop sensation in the 1960s, with their rich harmonies and doo-wap choruses. *Bossa Cubana* contains some irresistible tunes.

Compilations

Antología del Bolero – Collecion Tributo
This CD provides an excellent introduction to the complexities and variety of *bolero* music.

Fiesta Cubana: El Bolero
Another compilation CD, this one contains some of the giants of Cuban *bolero* music, including Beny Moré, Frank Domínguez and Bola de Nieve.

Rapsodia Rumbera
This compilation of rumba music includes works in all the major styles (yambú, guaguancó, rumba-columbia). Many of the great rumba musicians are featured on the CD, including Chano Pozo, Malanga, Nieve Fresneda and Tio Tom.

Cantos de Santería
A fascinating and mystical CD, this is one of the only recordings available dedicated to the religious music of *regla de ocha* or *santería*, the Christian/African synthesis religion still practised in Cuba and South America.

Vivencias – Charanga Típica de Guillermo Rubalcaba
A rich and complex recording of the music of the piano virtuoso Guillermo Rubalcaba, this CD combines internationally known orchestral works with waltz classics and a selection of more intimate pieces.

Websites

www.afrocubaweb.com
This up-to-date site draws together a vast array of information on themes such as culture, politics, literature, music, dance and theatre to celebrate the influence of African culture on Cuban life.

www.cubaliteraria.cu
An extensive website, dedicated to Cuban authors and literature.

www.cubatravel.cu
Cuban portal for tourism in English, listing tour operators/agencies, embassies and tourist offices, including addresses and phone numbers.

www.cubaweb.cu
A good general portal for information and links to resources relating to Havana and Cuba, Cubaweb covers topics including news, tourism, business, the internet, government, trade, culture and events. The site is produced in both English and Spanish – so doubles as a study aid.

www.cubaweather.org
Climate statastics and commentary, plus weather forecasts for Cuba in English.

www.cult.cu
The Cubarte site, in English and Spanish, is a key resource for the traveller interested in the cultural and artistic life of the island. It contains extensive information on cinema, dance, music, books, prizes and events.

www.discuba.com
The website for the Cuban Music Shop offers a wealth of information on all styles of Cuban music and discographies of the major artists. Info on upcoming events, performances and concerts as well as information on cinema and video releases. Offers online shopping.

www.dtcuba.com/eng/
English and Spanish language website called the *directorio turístico de Cuba* (Cuban directory). Health, marinas, embassies, nightclubs, restaurants and more besides are covered in this comprehensive website.

www.granma.cu/ingles
The website for the official newspaper of the Cuban Communist Party, Granma provides state-approved news in five languages: Spanish, English, French, German and Portuguese.

www.islagrande.cu
This crowded site provides a search engine for websites related to Cuba. Spanish language.

www.prensa-latina.cu/
Prensa Latina is a news agency with English-language information and articles about Cuba.

www.uscubacommission.org
For the traveller who likes their holidays to be liberally laced with politics, the US-Cuba Commission's site gives up-to-the-minute information on the latest developments in US-Cuba political relations.

Index

Note: numbers in **bold** indicate key information on a topic; *italics* indicate photographs.

a

abakuá 91
abortion 220
accommodation 32-46
  best 32
  by price
    budget 37, 40, 43, 46
    mid-range 36-37, 40, 42, 45-46
    expensive 34-36, 38-40, 41-42, 45
  casas particulares 37-38, **39**, 41, 44, 46
  chains 32
  child friendly 137
  disabled visitors 34
  gay-friendly 152
  Habaguanex hotels 35
  peso hotels 33
  security 33
  see also p238 accommodation index
Acosta, Carlos 173
Acuario Nacional de Cuba 83
addresses 218
Agencia de Viajes San Cristóbal 54, **229**
agromercado 126-127
Aguja Diving Centre, La 87, 182
air travel 184
airport & airlines 214
Alamar 92-93
Alarcon, Ricardo 30
Albemarle, Earl of 9
Almendares, Río 80-81
antiques 120
Antonelli, Juan Bautista 88
aquariums 55, 83
Aqvarivm 55
architecture, colonial 25, 35
Argos Teatro 170
art 145-149
  and the Revolution 145
  exporting 145-146
  see also galleries
Artemisa 186
Así Somos 171
ATMs 224
Azules, Los 181

b

ballet 172-173
Ballet Español de Cuba 171
Ballet Nacional de Cuba 172
Bances, María Teresa 81
banks 224
Bar-Restaurante La Terraza 92
bars 113-115
  best 115
  gay 151-152
  see also p238 bar index
baseball 176, 177, 181
Basílica de San Francisco de Asís 154
Basílica Menor y Convento de San Francisco de Asís **54**, **55**, 60
basketball 177
Batista, Fulgencio **13**, **14**, 15, 206
Bay of Pigs 16
bayside Havana **89-91**, 241
beaches 92-93, 191-194, 198
  with children 139
Beatles, the **76**, 78
beauty salons 128
Biblioteca Nacional 74
bicitaxis 216
bicycle hire 217
Bienal de la Habana 136, 145
biosphere reserve 186
boating 181
Bodeguita del Medio, La 59, **100**
Bolívar, Simón 57
book market 51, 121
book shops 120-121
books, reference 232
Bosque de La Habana 81
boxing 177
bread shops 125
breakdown services 217
Buena Vista 187
Buena Vista Social Club 153, **233**
Burdsall, Lorna 171
bureaux de change 224
buses 184, **215**
Bush George W 19, 228
business 219

c

Caballero de París, El 54, **60-61**
cabaret 163
cafés *see* bars
Café Cantante Mi Habana 153, **158**
Café Taberna 155, *156*
'Caiman Rock' 134
cake shops 125
Calle 23 75-77
Calle Línea 79-81
Calle Mercaderes 56-58
Calle Obispo 61-62
Calle San Lázaro 71
Calle Tacón 59-61
Callejón de Hamel 67, 156
Cámara Oscura 56
camello bus *23*, 26
campervans 217
Cañonazo 132
Capitolio, El 64, *65*
car hire 216
Cárcel de la Habana 66
Carnaval de la Habana 134
carnival, Santiago 210-211
Carpentier, Alejo 59
Casa Alejandro de Humboldt 55
Casa de Africa 57
Casa de Benito Juárez 57, 58
Casa de la Amistad 78, **159**
Casa de la Comedia 54, **168**
Casa de la Cultura de la Habana Vieja 155
Casa de la Obra Pía 57, 58
  Casa Oswaldo Guayasamín 57, 58
Casa de la Tinaja 51
Casa de la Trova, Santiago 206, **209**
Casa de las Américas 79
  Casa de Asia 58
Casa de las Brujas 82
Casa de los Árabes 54
Casa de los Artistas 53, **146**
Casa de Obispo 54
Casa del Habano 83
Casa Natal de José Martí 63
Casablanca 89
Casa-Museo Abel Santamaría 72-73
Casa-Museo de Arquitectura y Mobiliaria 77
Casa-Museo Dulce María Loynaz 78
Casa-Museo Máximo Gómez 74
Casa-Museo Simón Bolívar 57, 58
Casas de la Música 153, 157, 157
casas particulares 37-38, **39**, 41, 44, 46
Casona, La 56, 145-149
Castillo de la Real Fuerza 7, **50**, **51**
Castillo de Los Tres Reyes del Morro 7, 88
Castillo de Morro 206, **208**
Castillo del Principe 73
Castillo San Salvador de La Punta 7, 49, **65**, **67**
Castro, Fidel *13*, **14**, **15**, 16, 17, *19*, 20, **28**, 29, *30*, 85, 206
Castro, Raúl 28, 29, *30*
Castropol 150, 151, 152
Catedral de La Habana 58, 59
Catholic church 18
Caturla, García 199
Cayo Hueso 71
Cayo Levisa 190
Celdrán, Carlos 166, 170
Cementerio Chino 77
Cementerio Colón 77
cemetery, Espada 70
cemetery, Jewish 90
censorship 166
Central Provinces 196-205
Centro Cultural Bertolt Brecht 80, **168**
Centro de Arte Contemporáneo Wilfredo Lam 59, 145, **146**
Centro de Estudiso Martianos 81
Chaplin 140, 141
Che Guevara *12*, 14, 15, 188, **196**, *196*
  mausoleum 196
  monument 196
  statue 74
children 137-139
  accommodation 137
  advice 137, 139
  restaurants 139
  shops 121-122
Chinatown 71, **102-103**
Churchill, Winston 44, 72
Cienfuegos, Camilo *13*, 15
Cienfugos 184, **199-201**
cigars 122-123
  factories 69, 70, 77
  festival 132
  shops 69, 70, **122-123**
Cine Pobre 144
Cinema 11 Festival 93
cinema see film
climate 230
clothes shops 124-125
Club Habana 86, *87*, **179**
clubs
  gay 151-152
  see also music & nightlife
Cobre, El 206, **208**
coffee shops 126
Cojímar 92
Cold War 16
Colina Lenin 89, 90
Coliseo de la Ciudad Deportiva **177**, 179
Columbus, Christopher 6
Columbus, Diego 6
comedy 168
Communist Party 13

Conjunto Folklórico Nacional de Cuba 172
consulates 219
contraception 220
Convento e Iglesia de La Merced 63
Convento e Iglesia de Nuestra Señora de Belén 62, 63
Convento e Iglesia de Santa Clara 62, 63
Convento e Iglesia del Sagrado Corazón de Jesús e Ignacio de Loyola 70, 71
Convento y Capilla de la Immaculada Concepción 71
Cortés, Hernán 7, 202
credit cards 98, 116, **224**
cruise ships 214
Cuartel Moncada 206, **207**
CubaDanza **134**, 175
'Cubadisco' 133, *133*
Cuban Olympiad 176
Cubanacán 84-86
Cueva de los Portales 188
cuisine, Cuban 96, **98-99**
customs 219
cycling 178, 217

d

dance **166-167**, 174
 companies 171-174
 festivals **133-136**, 175
 holidays 226
Danza Contemporánea de Cuba 174
Danza Voluminosa 174-175
DanzAbierta 172
Delgado, Gisela 29
dentists 220
department stores 117
design shops 122-123
Días de la Danza, Los **133**, 175
digital art 135
disabled travellers 219
 hotels 34
diving 87, **182**
doctors 220
dollar currency 25, **223-224**
Don Giovanni 59, 101
driving 216-217
drugs, illegal 219
dry-cleaning 129

e

economy
 1960s 17
 dollar economy 25
 dual economy 119
 modern **21**, **25**, 82, 86
 foreign investment 16
 post Cold War 16
 US embargo 15, 29, 228
Edificio Bacardí 62
Edificio Fosca 80
electricity 219
electronic shops 123
embargo, US trade 15, 29, 228
embassies 219
emergencies 219-220
emigration 18
Encuentro Internacional de Casino 134
Espada cemetery 70
esquina caliente 177
Estadio Latinoamericano 177
Estadio Panamericano 92, *179*, **181**
Estadio Pedro Marrero 178
Estadio Universitario Juan Abrahantes 73
Estatua Cristo de la Habana 89
etiquette, Cuban 218
Expo Cuba 48

f

fabric shops 124
Factoría 7, 9
Farmacia Sarrá 62
Farmacia Taquechel 62
farmers' market 126-127
fashion shops 124-125
faxes 227
Feria Internacional el Disco 'Cubadisco' *133*, 133
festivals & events **132-136**
 digital art 135
 film 136, 144
 listings & information 132
 music 93, **132-136**
 in Santiago 210-211
 theatre & dance **133-136**, 175
Festival Boleros de Oro 133
Festival Cubarock Internacional 'Caiman Rock' 134
Festival de Academias de Ballet 85, 175
Festival de la Habana de Música Contemporánea 136
Festival de los Habanos 132
Festival de Música Electroacústica Primavera en La Habana 132
Festival de Nuevos Realizadores 144
Festival de Raices Africanas 'El Wemilere' 136
Festival de Rap Cubano Habana Hip Hop 93, **134**, 161
Festival de Teatro de la Habana **134**, 175
Festival del Nuevo Cine Latinoamericano 136, 144
Festival Elsinore 85, 175
Festival Internacional de Ballet **136**, 175
Festival Internacional de Jazz 'Jazz Plaza' 136
Festival Internacional de Música Popular Beny Moré 134
Festival Internacional de Percusión 133
Festival Los Días de la Danza 133
Festival Los Días de la Música 134
Festival Nacional del Humor 'Aquelarre' **133**, 168
Festival y Concurso Internacional de Guitarra 133
film 140-144
 best cinemas 140
 cinema tips 141
 Cuban directors & films 140, **144**, **232**
 festivals 136, 144
 information 140
 posters 143
 salas de videos 143
fishing 180
Floridita, El 62
florists 125
food shops 125-127
football 178
Fortaleza de San Carlos de la Cabaña 88
Fototeca de Cuba 56, **147**
fuel stations 217
Fundación Havana Club 55
Fuster, José 86

g

Gabinete de Arqueología 60, 61
Gaia 169
Galería Habana 81, *145*, **148**
galleries 145-149
 information 145
 studios 149
gangsters 44
gay & lesbian **150-152**
 bars & clubs 151
 beaches 93, 152
 cruising 152
gift shops 127
Girona, Mario 72
golf 180
Gómez, José Miguel 73
Gómez, Máximo 66, 74
González, Elián 19, 22, 23
Gran Teatro de La Habana 65, **167**, *171*
Guanabacoa 90-91
Guanahacabibes, Península 190
Guananahatabey people 6
Guantánamo Bay 11, 13
Gutiérrez-Menoyo, Eloy 30
gyms 180

Habaguanex hotels 35
Habana, Centro 64-71
 accommodation 38-41
 with children 138
 galleries 148
 music & nightlife 156-158
 restaurants 104-105
Habana del Este 92-93
Habana Vieja, La 50-63
 accommodation 34-38
 bars 113-115
 with children 137-138
 galleries 146-147
 music & nightlife 154-156
 restaurants 99-104
 Southern 62-63
habaneros, contemporary 25-27
Havana Golf Club 180
health 220-221
 shops 128
Helms-Burton law 18
Hemingway, Ernest 61, 62, 86, *90*, 92, 181
Hershey, Milton 89
hip hop 160-161
history 6-20
 Cuban missile crisis **16**, 88
 key events 20
 organised crime 44
 propoganda 140
 Revolution, 1959 **14-15**, 22, 44
 and the Arts 145, 166
 'Special period' **18**, 68
HIV & AIDS 221
holidays, public 230
holidays, package 226
horse riding 180
Hospital Materno Eusebio Hernández 87
hospitals 220-221
Hostal Conde de Villanueva **34**, 57
Hotel Ambos Mundos **34**, 61
Hotel Florida **34**, 62
Hotel Habana Libre 41, 72
Hotel Inglaterra **38**, 64
Hotel Nacional de Cuba 42, **72**, *73*
Hotel Presidente 79
Hotel Santa Isabel **36**, 51
Hotel Sevilla **39**, 65
hotels *see* accommodation
household goods shops 122-123
housing, local 26
Humboldt, Alejandro de 55
Hurón Azul 160

i

ID 221
Igelsia de Jesús de Miramar 83, 84
Igelsia de San Antonio de Padua 83, 84
Iglesia de Nuestra Señora de Regla 89, 90
Iglesia de Ortodoxo Griego 54
Iglesia de San Francisco de Asís 56
Iglesia de San Francisco de Paula 63
Iglesia de Santa Rita de Casia 83, 84
Iglesia del Espíritu Santo 62
Iglesia del Santo Ángel Custodio 60
Iglesia del Santo Cristo del Buen Viaje 62
Iglesia Nuestra Señora Caridad del Cobre 71
immigration 229
Instituto Cubano de Amistad con los Pueblos (ICAP) 77
Instituto Cubano del Arte e Industria Cinematográficos 77
Instituto Cubano del Libro 52
Instituto Superior de Arte (ISA) 84, 85
insurance 221
Internacional Salón de Arte Digital 135
international relations 15-19
  Europe 22
  sporting events 176
  USA 23
internet 222
investment, foreign 16
Islam 225

j

Jaimanitas 86-87
Jardín Botánico Nacional 48
Jardín Diana de Gales 54
Jardines de La Tropical 81
jewellery shops 124
Jewish centre 80
jiniteros 97-98
JO JAZZ 136
Jusdaism 225

k

Krushchev, President 16

l

Lage, Carlos 30, *30*
Laguito, El 85
language 231
  courses 226
  holidays 226
  menu reader 98-99
Lansky, Meyer 44, 72
laundry 129
leather goods shops 124
legal assistance 222
Lennon, John **76**, 78
lesbian Havana 152
  see also gay & lesbian
libraries 222
libretas see ration books
Lisa, La 87
lost property 222
Loynaz, Dulce María 78
lucha, la 26

m

Maceo, Antonio 10, *17*
Machado, Gerardo 13
Madriguera, La 74
Magoon, Charles 12
Malecón 71, **151**, *151*
Mambí 55
Manaca Iznaga 204
mansions 7, 85
Manuel de Céspedes, Carlos 50
Maqueta de La Habana 83, 84
Maqueta de la Habana Vieja 58
María La Gorda 184, **190**
Marianao 87
Mariel boatlift 15, 18
Marina Hemingway *84*, 86, **181-182**
markets 70, 116, **126**, **129-130**
Márquez, Claudia 29
Martí, José 10, 29, 60, **74-75**
  birthplace 63
  museum 71
  statue 64
  study centre 81
martial arts 178
Más, Juan Miguel 174
Mayo Teatro 175
media 222-223
medical students 65, 70
medical supplies 229
medicine, complementary 220
Mella, Julio Antonio 73
memorials
  Ethel & Julius Rosenberg 77
  José Martí 74, 75
  Julio Antonio Mella 73
  víctims of the Maine 79
menu reader 98-99
Mercado Cuatro Caminos 70
Mexican War, 1847 9
Ministry of Culture 132
Miramar 82-87
  accommodation 45-46
  with children 138
  galleries 148
  music & nightlife 164-165
  restaurants 109-112
Miramar Trade Center 83, 83
missile crisis, Cuban **16**, 88
mobile phones 227
money 223-224
Monroe, President James 9
monuments
  Ernest Hemingway 90, 92
  José Miguel Gómez 73
  Máximo Gómez 66
Morro, El 88
motorbikes 217
Mundo de Gallo 93, *93*
murallas, las 64
Museo Antropológico Montané 73, 74
Museo de Arte Colonial 59
Museo de Ciencias Naturales Felipe Poey 73, 74
Museo de la Ciudad 50, 51
Museo de la Educación 55
Museo de la Orfebrería 51
Museo de la Revolucion **68**, 79
Museo del Aire 87
Museo del Automóvil 54
Museo del Chocolate 57
  Museo del Naipe 56
Museo del Ministerio del Interior 82, 84
Museo del Ron 55
Museo del Tabaco 58
Museo Fragua Martiana 71
  Museo José Martí 75
Museo Municipal de La Habana del Este 93
Museo Municipal de Regla 89, 90
Museo Nacional de Alfabetización 87
Museo Nacional de Artes Decorativas 78
Museo Nacional de Bellas Artes 68, *69*
Museo Nacional de Historia de las Ciencias Carlos J Finlay 56
Museo Nacional de Historia Natural 50, 52
Museo Nacional de la Cerámica Cubana 50, 51
  Museo Nacional de la Danza 80, 81
Museo Nacional de la Música 60
Museo Nacional del Deporte 75
Museo Napoleónico 73, 74
Museo Numismático 54
  Museo de los Orishas 70
Museo Postal Cuba 75
museums
  anthropology: Museo Antropológico Montané 73, 74
  arts & architecture: Casa de Africa 57; Casa de las Américas 79; Casa de Asia 58; Casa de Benito Juárez 57, 58; Casa de la Obra Pía 57, 58; Casa Oswaldo Guayasamín 57, 58; Casa-Museo de Arquitectura y Mobiliaria 77; Museo de Arte Colonial 59; Museo Nacional de Artes Decorativas 78; Museo Nacional de Bellas Artes 68, 69; Museo Nacional de la Cerámica Cubana 50, 51; Museo Nacional de la Danza 80, 81; Museo Nacional de la Música 60
  Castro: Casa-Museo Abel Santamaría 72-73
  history: Casa-Museo Simón Bolívar 57, 58; Museo de la Ciudad 50, 51; Museo Napoleónico 73, 74; Museo Postal Cuba 75
  local: Museo Municipal de La Habana del este 93; Museo Municipal de Regla 89, 90
  literacy: Museo de la Educación 55; Museo Nacional de Alfabetización 87
  revolutionary: Museo del Aire 87; Museo Fragua Martiana 71; Museo José Martí 75; Museo del Ministerio del Interior 82, 84; Museo de la Revolucion **68**, 79
  science: Museo de Ciencias Naturales Felipe Poey 73, 74; Museo Nacional de Historia de las Ciencias Carlos J Finlay 56; Museo Nacional de Historia Natural 50, 52
  specialist: Museo del Chocolate 57; Museo del Naipe 56; Museo Numismático 54; Museo de los Orishas 70; Museo del Ron 55; Museo del Tabaco 58
  transport: Museo del Automóvil 54
music & nightlife 153-165
  best venues 155
  cabarets 163
  classical music 154
  Cuban artists 233
  festivals 132-136
  glossary 165

hip hop 160-161
information 153
package holidays 226
rumba 66-67
in Santiago 209
shops 130

National Heritage Office 146
National Union of Writers and Artists of Cuba (UNEAC) 78, 79
newspapers 223
Nicho, El 201

Oficina del Historiador de la Ciudad 52
Olympics 176
opening hours 98, **224**
Operation Mongoose 17
opticians 129
orishas 91

Pabellón Cuba 72
PABEXPO 85
'Padilla Affair' 11
Padilla, Herberto 11
palacios see mansions
Palacio de Domingo Aldama 69
Palacio de Gobierno 55
Palacio de la Artesanía 60
Palacio de las Convenciones 85
Palacio de Valle, Cienfuegos 200, *200*
Palacio del Segundo Cabo 50, 52, *53*
paladares 96, **97**, 104, 108, 109, 111, 112
Palma, Tomás Estrada 11
palo monte 91
parking 217
parks 48-49
Parque Alejandro de Humboldt 55
Parque Almendares 81
Parque Central 64-65
Parque Cervantes 59
Parque Céspedes 50
Parque de la Fraternidad 69
Parque de los Enamoradoros 66
Parque de Simón Bolívar 56
Parque Histórico Militar Morro-Cabaña 88
Parque Lenin 48, 178
Parque Lennon **76**, 78
Parque Maceo 71
Parque Metropolitano de la Habana (PMH) 80
Parque Prado 83
Parque Rumiñahui 57
Parque Zoológico Nacional 49
Parroquia del Vedado 81
Paseo del Prado 64
Patio, El 59, **103**
Paya, Oswaldo 29, 30
performing arts 166-175
comedy 168
dance 167, 174
companies 171-174
holidays 226
festivals **133-136**, 175
major venues 167-168
and the Revolution 166
theatre companies 169-171
tickets & information 167
Peniñsula de Ancón 205
pesos convertibles 224
pesos cubanos 224
peso hotels 33
peso prices 223-224
peso restaurants 96
peso shops 116, **119**
pharmacies 129, **221**
Philip II 7
photographic services 130
Piano Bar Delirio Habanero 153, **162**
Pinar del Rio 184, **186-190**
piracy 198
Platt Amendment 11, 13
Playa Mi Cayito 93, 152
Playa Santa María del Mar *92*, 93
Playas del Este 93
accommodation 46
restaurants 112
with children 139
Plaza de Armas 49, **50-53**
Plaza de la Catedral 58-59
Plaza de la Revolucion 74-75
Plaza de San Francisco 54-56
Plaza del Cristo 62
Plaza Finlay 87
Plaza Organopónico 74
Plaza Vieja 56, 57
police stations 224
Pope John Paul II 19, *19*
postal services 224
'Prado, El' 64
prescriptions 221
Primero de Mayo 133
Protestant churches 225
Punta, La 65-68

q

Quinta Avenida 82
Quinta de los Molinos 73
Quintero, Hector 166

radio 223
Rampa, La 72-73, *73*
ration books 26, 116
Reagan, Ronald 18
Real Fábrica de Tabacos La Corona 68, 69
Real Fábrica de Tabacos Partagás 49, **70**
regla de ocha 91
Regla 89-90
reglas congas 91
religion 91, **225**
Reloj de Quinta Avenida 82
Remedios 184, 197-199
restaurants **96-112**
best 96
child-friendly 139
Chinatown 102-103
credit cards 98
Cuban cuisine 96, 98-99
jineteros 97-98
menu reader 98-99
opening times 98
paladares 96, **97**, 104, 108, 109, 111, 112
peso restaurants 96
prices 98
vegetarian 106-107
see also p238 restaurants & paladares index
restoration, urban 52
Revolution, 1959 **14-15**, 22, 44
and the Arts 145, 166
Reyes, Blanca 29
Río Almendares 80-81
rodeo 178
Rosenberg memorial 77
rum shops 126
rumba 66-67
running 181

s

sailing 181
Sala Polivalente 'Kid Chocolate' 64, **177**
Sala Polivalente Ramón Fonst 75
salas de videos 143
Salón 1930 'Compay Segundo' 153
Salón Bolero 165
Sancti Spíritus province 202-205
sanctions 17
Santa Clara 184, **196-197**
santería 91
Santiago de Cuba 206-212
best sights 206
carnival 210-211
casas particulares 211
music & dance 209-210
scooters 217
scuba diving 182
security 225
Seminario de San Carlos y San Ambrosio 60
shoe shops 124
shopping & services **116-130**
best shops 116
children's 139
department stores 117
farmers' markets 126-127
peso stores 119
tips 116-117
shopping centres 118
Sibarimar 93
Siboney 86-87
Siboney people 6
sightseeing 47-93
best sights 49
tips 48
slave trade 9, 10
Soroa 187
Soviet Union 15, 16
Spanish-American War 11
'Special period' **18,** 68
sport & fitness 176-182
baseball 176, 177, 181
for children 139
information & tickets 176
shops 130
squash 182
stationery shops 130
STDs 221
study 225-226
sugar industry 10, 25, 202, 204
supermarkets 120
swimming 182
synagogue 62, 80

Taíno people 6, 7
Tarará 93
taxis 215
Teatro Amadeo Roldán 154, 162
Teatro América 169
Teatro Buendía 166, *167*, **170**
Teatro el Público 166, **171**
Teatro Fausto 65, **169**
Teatro Mella 169
Teatro Nacional de Cuba 74, 153, **168**
telegrams 225
telephones 226-227
television 222
Templete, El 50, 53
Ten Years War 10, 50
tennis 182
Terrazas, Las 186-187
theatre 166-171
companies169-171
festivals 175
and the Revolution 166
venues 167-169
tickets
sport 176
theatre 166
time difference 227
tipping 227
toilets, public 227
Topes de Collantes 205
Torreón de San Lázaro 71
Torreón de Santa Dorotea de Luna de La Chorrera 81

tourist agencies 185
tourist industry 25
tourist information 227-229
toy shops 121
trains 184, **214**
electric 89
transport, public 26, **214-215**
air 214
buses 215
trains 214
around Cuba 184
with children 137
travel advice 218
travel ban 228
Tren Eléctrico de Hershey 89, *89*
Tribuna Anti-Imperialista 79
Trinidad 184, **202-205**

u

UNEAC 78, **79**, 160
Unión Francesa de Cuba 78
United States Interest Section 79, 219
Universidad de La Habana 73, 74, 75
University & area 73-74
US citizens 228
USS *Maine* 11
memorial 79

vaccinations 220
Valle de los Ingenios 204
Valle de Viñales 189-190
Varadero 184, **191-195**
Varela Project 29
Varela, Félix 29, 60
Vedado 72-81
accommodation 41-44
bars 115
central Vedado 77-79
with children 138
galleries 148
music & nightlife 158-163
restaurants 105-109
Velázquez, Diego 6
Villa Clara islands 198
Villa Clara province 196-199
Viñales 184, **189**
visas 229
student 225
vocabulary 231
volleyball 179

walking 217
walls, city 64
watersports 182
weather 230
websites, useful 233
Weerth, Georg 70
weights & measures 229
women travellers 230
Wood, General Leonard 11
working in Havana 230
World War I 12

Yara cinema 140, **142**, 150

Zanja Real 55
zoo 49

Hotels & *casas particulares*

Casa Belkis 44
Casa de Ana 44
Casa de Carlos y Julio 44
Casa de Dr José Ma Parapar de la Riestra 46
Casa de Esther Fonseca 44
Casa de Eugenio y Fabio 37
Casa de Evora Rodríguez García 41
Casa de Gladys Cutido 41
Casa de Irma 44
Casa de Jésus y María 37
Casa de María del Carmen Villafaña 41
Casa de Marta 46
Casa de Mayra 46
Casa de Mercedes 41
Casa de Migdalia Carabelle Martín 38
Casa de Raúl Diaz Macaya 41
Casa del Científico 40
Hostal Conde de Villanueva 34
Hostal del Tejadillo 34
Hostal el Comendador 36
Hostal Los Frailes 37
Hostal Valencia 37
Hotel Ambos Mundos 34
Hotel Armadores de Santander 33, 34
Hotel Beltrán de Santa Cruz 37
Hotel Capri 43
Hotel Caribbean 40
Hotel Comodoro 45
Hotel Copacabana 46
Hotel Florida 34
Hotel Habana Libre 41
Hotel Habana Riviera 41, 43
Hotel Inglaterra 38
Hotel Lincoln 40
Hotel Meliá Cohiba 41
Hotel Meliá Habana 45
Hotel Mirazul 46
Hotel Nacional de Cuba 42, 45
Hotel Occidental Miramar 45
Hotel Park View 40
Hotel Plaza 38
Hotel Presidente 42
Hotel Raquel 35
Hotel San Miguel 35
Hotel Santa Isabel 36
Hotel Sevilla 36, 38
Hotel Sevilla 38
Hotel St John's 43
Hotel Telegrafo 38
Hotel Tropicoco 46
Hotel Vedado 43
Hotel Victoria 43
LTI-Panorama 45
Mesón de la Flota 37
NH Parque Central 39
Palacio O'Farrill 36
Rafaela y Pepe 38
Raúl Campos Alfonso 46
Residencia Académica 37
Villa Los Pinos 46

Restaurants

A Prado y Neptuno 104
Al Medina 101
Aljibe, El 109
Baturro, El 99
Biki, El 107
Bodegón Onda 99
Bodeguita del Medio, La 100
Brocal, El 112
Cabaña 100
Café del Oriente 100
Café Mercurio 100
Café Taberna 100
Cantabria 100
Carmelo, El 107
Casona de 17, La 105
Castillo de Farnés, El 100
Cecilia, La 109
Chan Li Po 102
Chung Shan 102
Conejito, El 105
Divina Pastora, La 112
Dominica, La 101
Don Giovanni 101
Don Ricardo 101
Ecocheff 107
Eco-Restorán El Bambú 107
Esperanza, La 109
Ferminia, La 110, 110
Finca, La 110
Floridita, El 101
Gentiluomo 101
Giraldilla, La 110
Hanoi 101
Hotel Meliá Cohiba 105
Hotel Nacional 105
Jardín del Edén 101
Mesón de la Flota, El 102
Monseigneur 106
Murralla, La 102
Pan.Com 111
Patio, El 103
Pekin, El 107
Pizza Nova 111
Plaza, La 106
Polinesio, El 107
Primavera 107
Puerto de Sagua 103
Rancho Palco, El 111
Restaurante 1830 108
Rincón de Elegguá, El 103
Roca, La 108
Roof Garden 104
Santo Angel 103
Tien Tan 103
Tocororo 111
Tong Po Laug 103
Torre de Marfil, La104
Trattoria Marakas 108
Tres Chinitos, Los 103
Unión Francesa 108
XII Apóstoles, Los 112
Zaragozana, La 104

Paladares

Amistad de Lanzarote 104
Bellomar 104
Casa Julia, La 104
Casa Sarasua 108
Chansonnier, Le 108
Cocina de Lilliam, La 111
Decameron 108
Diluvio, El 111
Don Lorenzo 104
Doña Juana 109
Fontana, La 112
Gringo Viejo 108
Guarida, La 105
Hurón Azul, El 109
Maeda112
Mercedes, Las 109
Nerei 109
Piccolo 112
Tasquita, La 105
Tres Bs, Las 109

Bars

Bar Monserrate 113
Bosque Bologna 113
Café de París 114
Café del Oriente 114
Café O'Reilly 114
Cafetería Sofía 115
Casa de la Amistad 115
Casa del Escabeche 114
Castillo de la Real Fuerza, El 114
Castropol 114
Dos Hermanos 112, 114
Fuente, La 115
Fundación Havana Club 114
Hotel Ambos Mundos 114
Hotel Inglaterra 114
Lluvia de Oro, La 115
Opus Habana 113, 115
Roca, La 115
Taberna de la Muralla 115
Terraza del Hotel Nacional, La 115

Bars (gay)

Cafetería La Arcada 151
Cafeteria 23 y P 151
Castropol 151
Night Club Tropical 152
San Lázaro #8A 152

Legend	
Place of Interest and/or Entertainment	
Railway Station	
Park	
College/Hospital	
Beach	
Steps	
Area Name	VEDADO
Church	
Information	
Post Office	

Maps

Cuba 240
Havana Overview 241
Street Index 243
Playas del Este 246
Miramar & the Western Suburbs 248
The City 250
La Habana Vieja 252

Cuba
Gulf of Mexico
Straits of Florida
Andros Island
BAHAMAS
Cat Island
San Salvador
Great Guana Cay
Rum Cay
Great Exuma
Long Island
Samana Cay
Crooked Island
Long Cay
Ragged Island
Acklins Island
Anguila Cays
Archipiélago de Sabana
Varadero
Havana
Mariel
Matanzas
Cárdenas
Viñales
Artemisa
See p241
Pinar del Río
Golfo de Batabanó
Golfo de Guanahacabibes
Bahía de Cortés
María la Gorda
Cayos de San Felipe
Nueva Gerona
Isla de la Juventud
Península de
Archipiélago de los Canárreos
Cayo Largo
Cayo Las Brujas
Cayo Coco
Cayo Santa María
Archipiélago de Camagüey
Remedios
Santa Clara
Cienfuegos
CUBA
Trinidad
Sancti Spíritus
Ciego de Ávila
Cayo Sabinal
Camagüey
Golfo de Ana María
Cayo Grande
Jardines de la Reina
Yucatan Basin
Las Tunas
Holguín
Great Inagua
Golfo de Guacanayabo
Bayamo
Manzanillo
Baracoa
Guantánamo
Santiago de Cuba
La Gran Piedra
Windward Passage
Cayman Islands
Cayman Brac
Little Cayman
Grand Cayman
CARIBBEAN SEA
Cayman Trench
Jamaica Channel
JAMAICA
Kingston
HAITI
0
100 miles
0
100 km

Havana Overview

Street Index

0 – P249 A7/B7
1, Avenida – P249 A5-7
1ra – P250 E9
1ra, Avenida – P249 A8
1ra, Avenida – P250 A9
2 – P249 A7/B7
2 – P250 A9-D9
2da – P250 E9
3, Avenida – P249 A6-7/B5
3ra – P250 E9
3ra, Avenida – P249 A8
3ra, Avenida – P250 A9-10
4 – P249 A6/B6
4 – P250 A9-D9
5, Avenida – P248 B2-4
5, Avenida – P249 B5-6
5a, Avenida – P248 B2-4
5b – P248 B2-3
5ta, Avenida – P249 A8
5ta, Avenida – P250 A9-10
6 – P249 A6/B6
6 – P250 A9-C9
7 – P250 A9-10
7, Avenida – P248 B3-4/C1-3
7, Avenida – P249 B5-6
7a – P248 C2-3
7b – P248 C2-3
7c – P248 C3
8 – P249 A6/B6
8 – P249 A8/B8
8 – P250 A9-C9
9 – P248 C1-3
10 – P249 A6/B6
10 – P249 A8-C8
11 – P248 C1-4
11 – P249 B7-8
11 – P250 A10-11/B9-10
12 – P249 A6/B6
12 – P249 A8-C8
13 – P248 C2-4/D1
13 – P249 B7-8
13 – P250 B9-11
14 – P249 A6/B6
14 – P249 B8/C8
15 – P248 C3-4/D1-2
15 – P249 B7-8
15 – P250 B9-11
16 – P249 A5/B6
16 – P249 B8/C8
17 – P248 C3-4/D1-2
17 – P249 B7-8
17 – P250 B9-12
18 – P249 A5/B5/C6
18 – P249 B8/C8
19 – P248 C4\D1-3
19 – P250 B9-12
19 de Mayo – P250 D10
20 – P249 A5/B5/C5-6
20 – P249 B7-8/C8
20 de Mayo, Avenida – P250 E10
21 – P248 C4/D1-3
21 – P250 B9-12
22 – P249 B5/C5-6
22 – P249 B7/C7
23 – P248 C4/D1-3
23 – P250 B10-12/C9/10
24 – P249 B5
24 – P249 B7/C7
24 – P249 D7
25 – P248 C4/D2-4
25 – P248 F1
25 – P249 C7
25 – P250 C9-12
26 – P249 B5/C5-6
26 – P249 B7/C7
27 – P248 C4/D2-4
27 – P249 C7
27 – P250 C9-12
28 – P249 B5
28 – P249 B7/C7
28 – P249 C6
28 – P249 D7
29 – P248 D3-4/E2-3
29 – P249 C7
29 – P250 C10
29b – P248 E1
29c – P248 E1-2
29e – P248 E1-2
29f – P248 F1-2
29g – P248 F1-2
29h – P248 F1-2
30 – P248 B4
30 – P249 C5
30 – P249 D7/E7
31 – P248 D4/E2-3
31 – P248 D4/E3/F1-2
31 – P249 C5
31 – P250 C9
32 – P248 B4
32 – P249 D7/E7
32 – P250 C9
33 – P248 E2-3
33 – P249 C5-6/D5
33 – P249 D7
34 – P248 B4/C4
34 – P249 C5
35 – P248 E2-3
35 – P248 F1
35 – P249 C5-6/D5
35 – P249 D7
35 – P250 D9
36 – P248 B4/C4
36 – P249 C5/D5
36a – P248 B4
37 – P249 C5-6/D5
37 – P249 D7
37 – P249 D7-8
37 – P250 D9
38 – P248 B4
38 – P249 E6
39 – P249 D5
39 – P249 D7-8
39 – P250 D9
39a – P249 D5
40 – P248 B4
40 – P249 E6
40a – P248 B3-4
41 – P248 F2-3
41 – P249 D5
41 – P249 D7
41 – P250 D9
42 – P248b3-4/C4
42 – P249 C5/D5
42 – P249 E6
42a – P249 D5
43 – P249 D6
43 – P249 E7
44 – P249 D5
44 – P249 D5
45 – P249 D6
45 – P249 E7
46 – P249 D5
47 – P248 F3
47 – P249 D6
47 – P249 E7
48 – P249 D5
49 – P249 D5-6
49 – P249 D6
49a – P249 D6
49b – P249 D6
49c – P249 D6
50 – P248 D4
51 – P249 E5
52 – P248 D4
54 – P248 D4
56 – P248 D4/E4
58 – P248 D4/E4
60 – P248 B3-D2/E4
60a – P248 D3
62 – P248 C3-E3
62a – P248 D3
64 – P248 C3-E3
64a – P248 D3/E3
66 – P248 C3-E3
66a – P248 D3/E3
68 – P248 C3-E3
68a – P248 D3
70 – P248 B2/C2/D3/E3
70a – P248 D2-3
72 – P248 C2/D2-3/E3
72a – P248 D2
74 – P248 C2-E2-3
74 – P248 F3
74a – P248 D2
76 – P248 F3
76 – P248c2-E2
78 – P248 C2/D2

78 – P248 F3-4
80 – P248 C2/D2
80 – P248 F3
82 – P248 C1/D1-2
82 – P248 F2-3
84 – P248 B1-D1
84 – P248 F2-3
86 – P248 C1/D1
86 – P248 F2-3
88 – P248 F2-3

A – P249 A7
A – P250 A9-C9-10/D10
Acosta – P251 E14-15/F15
Agramonte – P251 D14/E14
Aguacate – P251 D15/E15
Aguiar – P251 D15/E15
Aguila – P251 D14/E13/F13
Almendares – P250 D11
Amargura – P251 E15
Amenidad – P250 E11
Amistad – P251 D14
Angeles – P251 D13/E13
Ánimas – P251 C13/D14
Apodaca – P251 E14
Aramburú – P250 C12/D12
Aranguren – P250 D10
Árbol Seco – P250 D12/E12
Armas, Plaza de – P251 E16
Arroyo – P250 E11-12
Auditor – P250 E10/F10
Ayestarán, Calzada de – P250 E10
Ayuntamiento – P250 E9

B – P249 A7
B – P250 A9/B9-10/C10
Barcelona – P251 D14
Bélgica, Avenida de – P251 D14/E14
Benjumeda – P250 D11/E11-12
Bernal – P251 D14
Bernaza – P251 D14/E14
Borrego – P250 F11
Brasil (Teniente Rey) – P251 E15
Bruzón – P250 D11

C – P249 A7
C – P250 A10-C10
C. Protestantes – P250 D9
Cadiz – P249 F8
Cádiz – P250 F11
Calzada Del Cerro – P249 F8
Campanario – P251 C14/D13/E13
Cárcel – P251 D15
Cárdenas – P251 E14
Carlos Manuel de Céspedes, Avenida – P250 D9-10/E9
Carlos Manuel de Céspedes, Avenida – P251 D15
Carmen – P250 E12
Castillejo – P250 D12
Castillo – P250 F12
Catedral, Plaza de La – P251 D15
Cerro, Calzada del – P250 F9-10
Chacón – P251 D15
Chávez – P251 D13
Churruca – P249 F8
Churruca – P251 E15
Cienfuegos – P251 E14
Clavel – P250 E11-12
Clavel – P250 E9-10
Colón – P249 F8
Colón – P251 D14-15
Colón, Avenida de – P249 D8-P250 D9
Compostela – P251 D15/E15
Concepción de La Valla – P250 E12
Concordia – P250 C12-P251 C13/D13-14
Condesa – P251 E13
Consulado – P251 D14
Corrales – P251 E13-14
Cristo – P251 E14
Cuarteles – P251 D15
Cuba – P251 D15/E15
Cuchíllo – P251 D13

D – P250 A10-C10
Desagüe – P250 D11/E12
Desamparado – P251 E14-15
Diaria – P251 F13-14
Dragones – P251 E14

E – P250 A10-C10
Economía – P251 E14
Egido – P251 E14/F14
Empirio – P249 E7
Enrique Barnet (Estrella) – P250 D11-12
Ermita – P250 E9-10
Escobar – P250 E12
Escobar – P251 C13/D13
Espada – P250 C12
España, Avenida de – P251 F13
Esperanza – P251 F13
Estancia – P250 E9
Este – P249 E8
Estévez – P250 F11-12

F – P250 A10-C10
Fábrica – P251 F13
Factor – P249 E8
Factoria – P251 E14/F14
Falgueras – P250 F9-10
Fernandina – P250 F11-12
Figuras – P250 E12
Franco – P250 D12/E12

General E. Núnez – P250 E10
Genios – P251 D15
Gervasio – P251 C13/D13
Gloria – P251 E13-14

H – P250 A10/B11
Habana – P251 D15/E15
Hamel – P250 C12
Hidalgo – P249 D8/E8-P250 D9
Hornos – P250 C12
Hospital – P250 C12/D12
Humboldt – P250 B12

I – P250 A11/B11
Independencia, Avenida de La – P249 E8/F7-8-P250 E9
Industria – P251 D14
Infanta – P249 F8
Infanta, Calzada de – P250 C12/D11/E11
Italia, Avenida de – P251 D14

J – P250 A11-C11
Jesús María – P251 E14/F15
Jesús Peregrino – P250 D12
Jovellar – P250 C12
Julia Borges – P250 D9

K – P250 A11/B11

L – P250 A11-C11
L. Ferrocarril – P250 E10
La Rosa – P250 E9/F9
La Torre – P249 D7
Lagunas – P251 C13-14
Lamparilla – P251 E15
Lealtad – P251 C13/D13/E13
Leonor Pérez – P251 E14-15
Lindero – P250 E12
Línea – P249 B7-8
Línea – P250 A9-10/B9/B11-12
Lombillo – P249 D8/E8-P250 E9/F9
Lugareño – P250 D11
Luz – P251 E14-15

M – P250 A11-C11
M. Abreu – P250 E10
Malecón – P249 A8-P250 A9-11/B12
Malecón (Ave de Maceo) – P251 C13-15
Maloja – P251 E13
Manglar – P250 E12
Manrique – P251 C14/D13-14/E13
Marianó – P250 E9-10/F9
Marino – P250 E9
Marquéz González – P250 C13/D12/E12
Masón – P250 E10
Matadero – P250 F12
Máximo Gómez – P251 E13/14/F12
Merced – P251 F14-15
Misión – P251 E14
Misiones, Avenida de Las – P251 D15
Morro – P251 D15

N – P250 B12/C12
Neptune – P250 C12
- P251 D13-14
Nueva del Pilar – P250 E12

O – P250 B12/C12
Obispo – P251 E15
Obrapía – P251 E15
Oficios – P251 E15-16
Omoa – P250 F12
Oquendo – P250 C12-E12-P251 C13
O'Reilly – P251 D15/E15

P. Vidal – P250 E11
Padre Varela – P250 D12-E12-P251 C13/D13
Panchito Gómez – P250 E10
Panorama – P250 D9
Paseo – P250 A9-D9-10
Paseo de Martí (Prado) – P251 D14-15
Patria – P250 E10/F10
Pedro Pérez – P250 E10/F10
Pedroso – P250 E10-11
Peña Pobre – P251 D15
Peñalver – P250 D11-12-P251 E13
Pezuela – P249 F8
Pila – P250 F12
Pinera – P250 E9/F9
Pje. Vista Hermosa – P250 E10
Plasencia – P250 D11-12
Pocito – P250 D12
Prensa – P249 F8
Preseverancia – P251 C13/D13
Presidentes, Avenida de Los – P250 A10-C10
Primelles – P249 F8
Príncipe – P250 C12
Puerta Cerrada – P251 F13
Puentes Grandes, Calzada de – p249 F6/7
Puerto, Avenida Del – P251 F13-14

Rancho Boyeros, Avenida – P250 D10/E9-10
Rastro – P250 E12
Rayo – P251 D13/E13
Recurso – P249 E7
Refugio – P251 D15
Retiro – P250 D11-12
Revillagigedo – P251 E13/F13
Revolución, Plaza de La – P250 D9-10
Rizo – p249 E5
Romay – P250 F11

Salud – P250 D12
Salvador Allende, Avenida – P250 D11-12
San Carlos – P250 D12/E12
San Cristobal – P249 F8
San Francisco – P250 C12
San Ignacio – P251 D15/E15
San Isidro – P251 E14-15
San Joaquín – P250 F11
San Juan de Dios – P251 D15
San Lázaro – P250 C12-P251 C13-14
San Martín – P250 C12/D12/E11
San Miguel – P250 C12-P251 D13-14
San Nicolás – P251 D13-14/E13
San Pablo – P250 E10/F10
San Pedro – P250 E9/F9
San Pedro – P251 E15
San Rafael – P250 C12/D12-P251 D13-14
Santa Catalina – P250 F9-10
Santa María – P249 F7
Santa Marta – P250 E11-12
Santa Rosa – P250 F11-12
Santa Teresa – P249 F8
Santiago – P250 D12
Santo Tomás – P250 E11-12
Simón Bolívar, Avenida – P251 D13/E13
Sitio – P250 D12/E12
Sol – P251 E14-15
Soledad – P250 C12
Suarez – P251 E14/F14
Subirana – P250 D12/E12

Tenerife – P250 E12-P251 E13
Territorial – P250 E10
Trocadero – P251 D14-15
Tulipán – P249 D8/E8-P250 E9/F9

Unión Y Ahorro – P250 F10-11
Universidad Campos – P250 F11

Valle – P250 C11-12/D12
Vapor – P250 C12
Velazco – P251 E14-15
Vía Monumental – P251 B16
Villegas – P251 E14-15
Virtudes – P251 C13/D13-14
Vista Hermosa – P250 F9-10

Washington, Avenida – P250 B12

Xifré – P250 D11

Zaldo – P250 E11
Zanja – P250 D12
Zapata, Calzada de – P250 C9-10
Zequeira – P250 F11
Zoológico, Avenida -p249 E6/7
Zulueta – P251d14-15

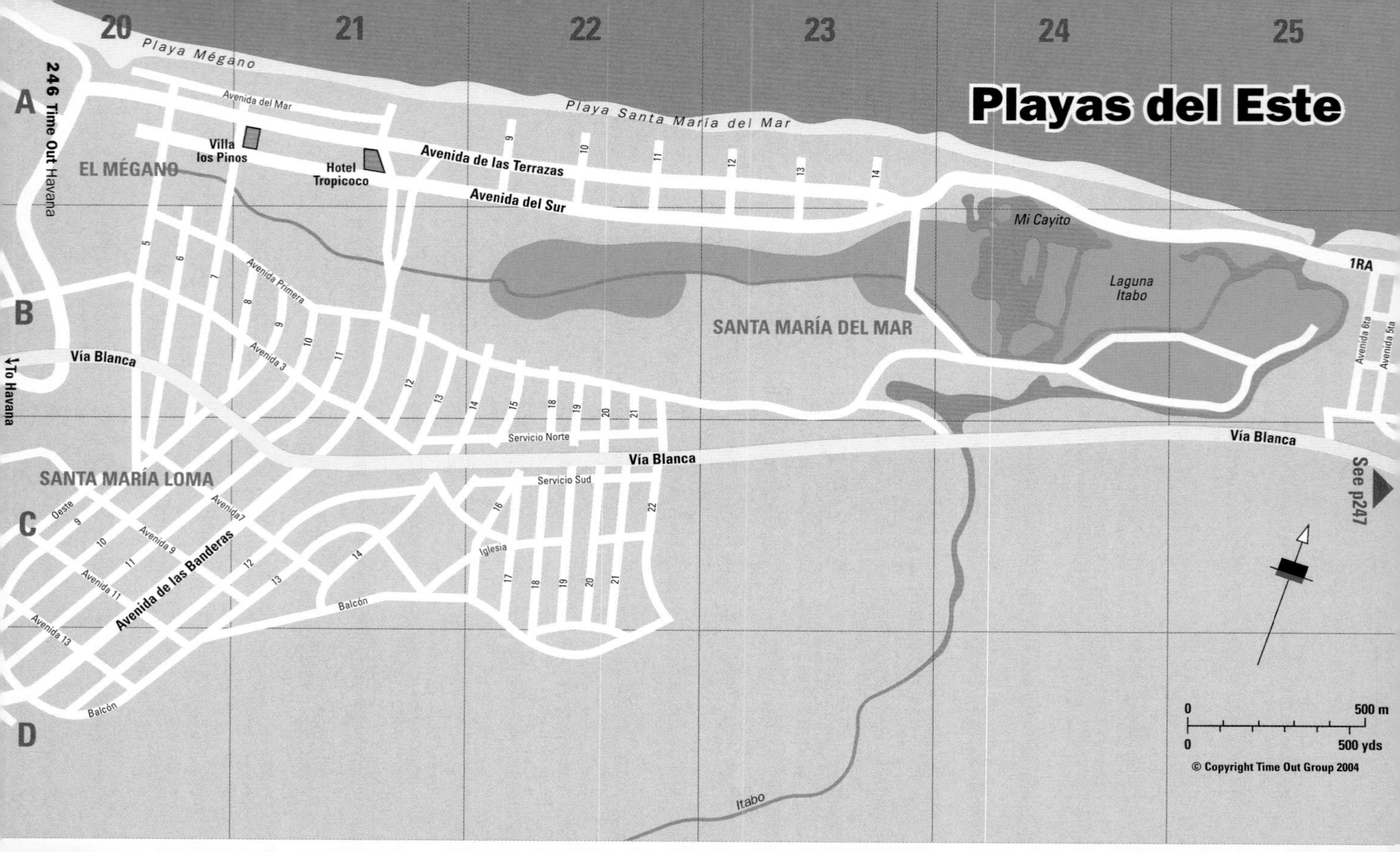

To Havana
See p247

Playas del Este (continued)

See p246

Miramar & the Western Suburbs

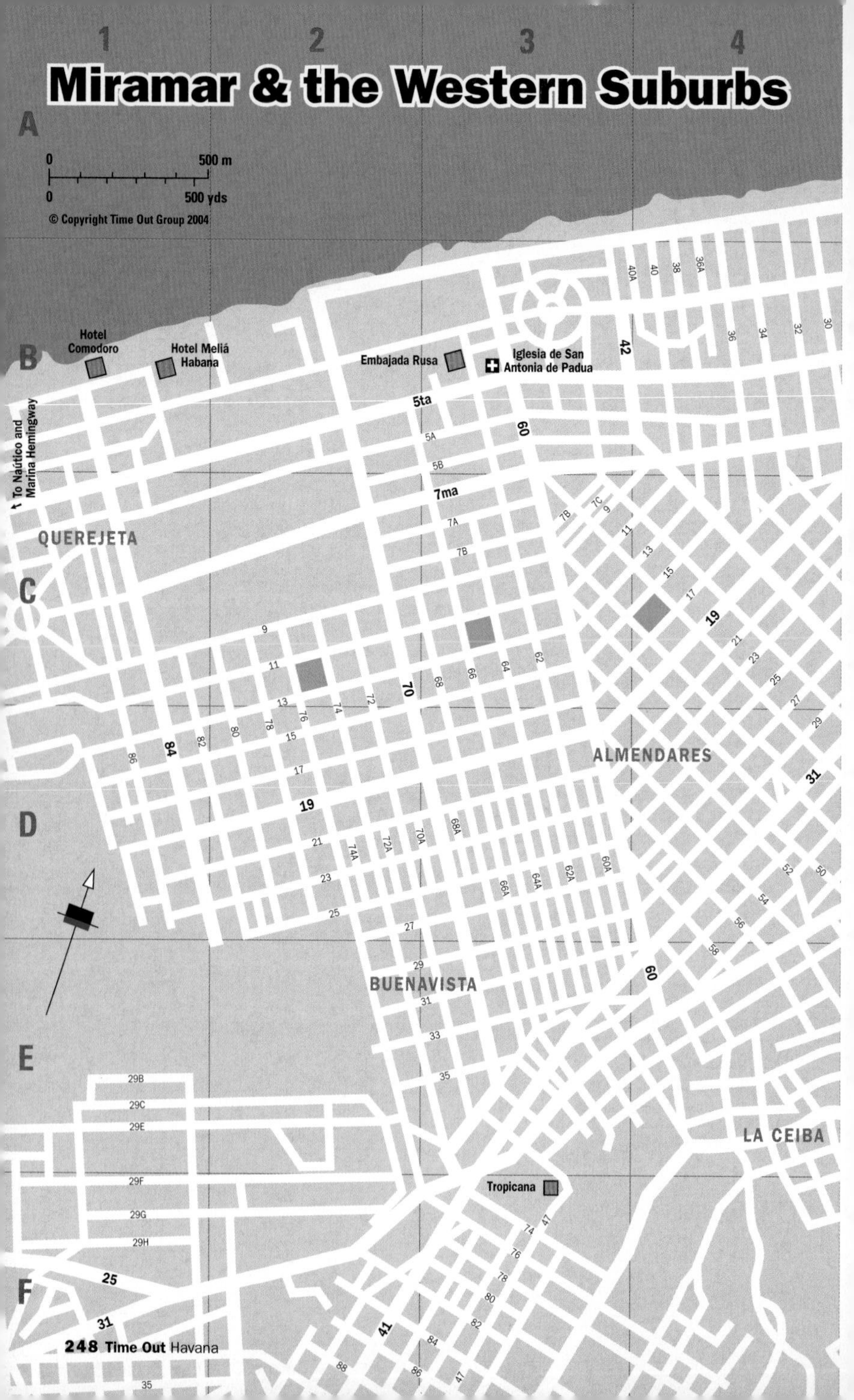

1
2
3
4
A
B
C
D
E
F
0
500 m
0
500 yds
© Copyright Time Out Group 2004
Hotel Comodoro
Hotel Meliá Habana
Embajada Rusa
Iglesia de San Antonia de Padua
To Naútico and Marina Hemingway
5ta
7ma
QUEREJETA
ALMENDARES
BUENAVISTA
LA CEIBA
Tropicana

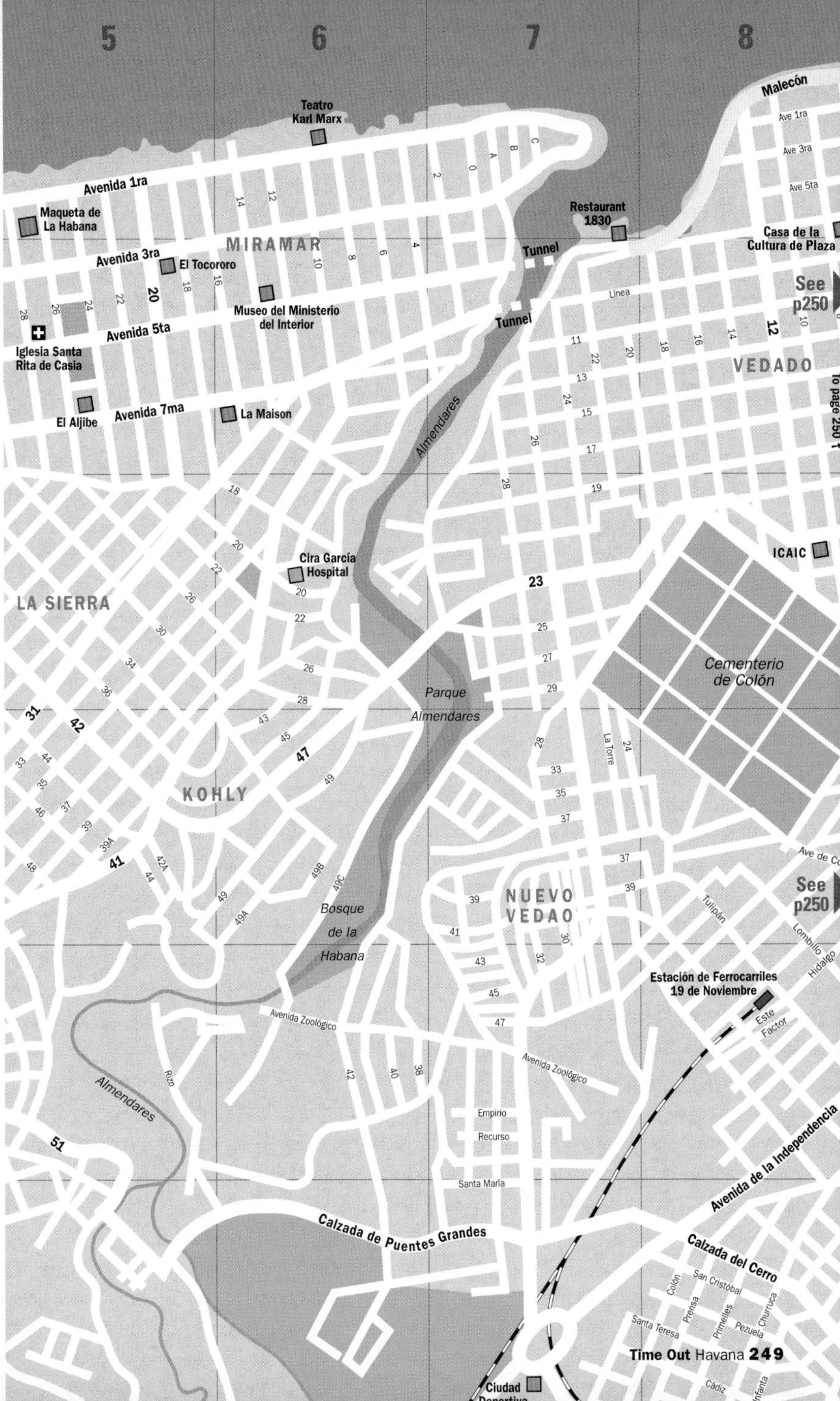

5
6
7
8
Malecón
Teatro Karl Marx
Ave 1ra
Ave 3ra
Ave 5ta
Avenida 1ra
Maqueta de La Habana
MIRAMAR
Restaurant 1830
Casa de la Cultura de Plaza
Avenida 3ra
El Tocororo
Tunnel
Museo del Ministerio del Interior
Línea
See p250
Iglesia Santa Rita de Casia
Avenida 5ta
Tunnel
VEDADO
El Aljibe
Avenida 7ma
La Maison
To page 250
Almendares
ICAIC
Cira García Hospital
LA SIERRA
Cementerio de Colón
Parque Almendares
La Torre
KOHLY
Ave de Colón
NUEVO VEDAO
See p250
Tulipán
Bosque de la Habana
Lombillo
Hidalgo
Estación de Ferrocarriles 19 de Noviembre
Este
Factor
Avenida Zoológico
Avenida Zoológico
Rizo
Almendares
Empirio
Recurso
Avenida de la Independencia
Santa María
Calzada de Puentes Grandes
Calzada del Cerro
San Cristóbal
Colón
Prensa
Primelles
Churruca
Santa Teresa
Pezuela
Cádiz
Infanta
Ciudad Deportiva

9
10
11
12
A
B
C
D
E
F
Hotel Habana Riviera
Feria del Malecón
Monumento a Calixto García
Hotel Meliá Cohiba
Casa de las Américas
Malecón
Estadio José Martí
Galerías de Paseo
Teatro Amadeo Roldán
(Calzada)
Hotel Presidente
Teatro Mella
Iglesia del Sagrado Corazón de Jesús
Línea
Museo Nacional de la Danza
VEDADO
Avenida de los Presidentes
Avenida Washington
Edificio Focsa
Monumento al Maine
Museo de Artes Decorativas
UNEAC
Hotel Victoria
Hotel Nacional
Parque Lennon
Casa de la Amistad
Agromercado
Cine Yara
Pabellón Cuba
Coppelia
See p249
Paseo
(G)
Hotel St John's
Humboldt
(La Rampa)
Hotel Habana Libre
Casa Museo Abel Santamaría
Cine la Rampa
Hotel Vedado
Príncipe
Vapor
Jovellar
Universidad de La Habana
Museo de Historia Natural Montané
Calzada de Infanta
San Lázaro
Hamel
Concordia
Neptuno
Museo Napoleónico
Calzada de Zapata
Castillo del Príncipe
Cementerio de Colón
San Francisco
Espada
Soledad
Oquendo
San Miguel
San Rafael
Valle
Hospital
Aramburú
San Martín (San José)
C. Protestantes
Quinta de los Molinos
Zanja
Salud
Jesús Peregrino
Castillejo
CENTRO
Teatro Nacional
Lugareño
Avenida Salvador Allende (Carlos III)
Julia Borges
Ministerio del Interior
Terminal de Omnibuses Interprovinciales
Casa de la Cultura de Centro Habana
Bruzón
Pocito
Aranguren
Almendares
Panorama
Avenida Carlos M. de Céspedes
Paseo
Plaza de la Revolución
19 de Mayo
Desagüe
Xifré
Enrique Barnet (Estrella)
Santiago
(Belascoaín)
Avenida de Colón
Museo Postal José Luís Guerra Aguiar
Benjumeda
Retiro
Memorial y Museo José Martí
Arbol Seco
Convento & Iglesia del Sagrado Corazón de Jesús
Hidalgo
Calzada de Infanta
Plasencia
Subirana
Franco
Palacio de la Revolución
Peñalver
Sitio
Estancia
Avenida Rancho Boyeros
Territorial
Desagüe
Oquendo
Marqués González
San Carlos
Padre Varela
Escobar
Marino
Calzada de Ayestarán
Ave. 20 de Mayo
P. Vidal
Benjumeda
Concepción de la Valla
Ave de la Independencia
Ermita
Panchito Gómez
Santo Tomás
San Pedro
Masón
(Zaldo)
Clavel
Figuras
Lombillo
M. Abreu
Santa Marta
Estadio José M. Pérez
General E. Núnez
San Martín
Carmen
La Rosa
Ermita
3ra
2da
1ra
Ayuntamiento
Arroyo (Manglar)
Tulipán
Auditor
L. Ferrocarril
Nueva del Pilar
Lindero
San Pablo
San Pedro
Clavel
Amenidad
Rastro
Tenerife
CERRO
Pje. Vista Hermosa
Manglar
Padre Varela
Pedroso
Pedroso
Mariano
Vista Hermosa
Pedro Pérez
Patria
Universidad Campos
Pinera
Estadio Latinoamericano
Matadero
See p249
Lombillo
Falgueras
Estévez
Estévez
Santa Rosa
Santa Catalina
Máximo Gómez (Monte)
Unión y Ahorro
Cádiz
Zequeira
Omoa
La Rosa
Borrego
San Joaquín
Romay
Fernandina
Pila
Tulipán
Calzada del Cerro
Castillo
To Southern Havana

13
14
15
16
The City
0
500 m
0
500 yds
© Copyright Time Out Group 2004
Estrecho de la Florida
B
C
D
E
F
El Morro (Castillo de los Tres Reyes del Morro)
Vía Monumental
Torreón de San Lázaro
Monumento a Antonio Maceo
Convento Capilla de la Inmaculada Concepción
Malecón (Ave de Maceo)
Castillo de San Salvador de la Punta
Tunnel
Malecón
Estudiantes de Medicina
Máximo Gómez
Canal de Entrada
Fortaleza de San Carlos de la Cabaña
Ave Carlos Manuel de Céspedes
Real Fábrica de Tabacos La Corona
Memorial Granma
Museo de la Revolución
Museo Nacional de Bellas Artes
HABANA
BARRIO CHINO
Hotel Inglaterra
Gran Teatro
Parque Central
Capitolio
Edificio Bacardí
El Floridita
Catedral
Plaza de la Catedral
LA HABANA VIEJA
Iglesia Nuestra Señora Caridad del Cobre
Real Fábrica de Tabacos Partagás
Palacio de Domingo Aldama
Parque de la Fraternidad
Dragones
Cuchillo
Máximo Gómez (Monte)
Plaza de Armas
Casa de la Cultura
Basílica Menor y Convento de San Francisco de Asís
Convento e Iglesia de Nuestra Señora de Belén
Convento de Santa Clara
Estación Central de Ferrocarriles
San Pedro
Bahía de La Habana
Desamparado
Muralla de La Habana
Avenida del Puerto
Castillo de Atarés
Ensenada de Atarés
See p252

La Habana Vieja
14
15
16
D
E
F
Máximo Gómez
Real Fábrica de Tabacos La Corona
Museo de la Revolución
Palacio de la Artesanía
Parque Antiteatro
Memorial Granma
Museo Nacional de la Música
Museo de Bellas Artes (Arte Cubano)
Hotel Inglaterra
Parque Central
Edificio Bacardí
Centro de Arte Contemporáneo Wilfredo Lam
Catedral
Parque Céspedes
Plaza de la Catedral
Gran Teatro
El Floridita
Capitolio
Museo de Bellas Artes (Arte Universal)
Museo de Arte Colonial
Palacio del Segundo Cabo
Castillo de la Real Fuerza
Farmacia Taquechel
Museo de la Ciudad
Plaza de Armas
El Templete
Hotel Santa Isabel
Museo Numismático
Museo Nacional da Historia
Casa de la Obra Pía
Casa Benito Juárez
Casa de los Arabes
Iglesia del Santo Cristo del Buen Viaje
Casa de la Cultura
Museo Ciencias Carlos J Finlay
Lonja del Comercio
Aqvarivm
Plaza Vieja
Basílica Menor y Convento de San Francisco de Asís
Casa Alejandro de Humboldt
La Casona
Palacio de Gobierno
Convento e Iglesia de Nuestra Señora de Belén
Convento de Santa Clara
Estación Central de Ferrocarriles
Casa Natal de José Martí
Convento e Iglesia de la Merced
Muelle de Luz
Muralla de La Habana
Canal de Entrada
Bahía de La Habana
Ave Carlos Manuel de Céspedes
Colón
Aguila
Trocadero
Bernal
Amistad
Industria
Consulado
Genios
Refugio
Cárcel
Morro
Paseo de Martí (Prado)
Zulueta (Agramonte)
Ave de las Misiones
Peña Pobre
Cuarteles
Chacón
Tejadillo
Tacon
San Ignacio
Cuba
Aguiar
Habana
Compostela
Aguacate
Empedrado
San Juan de Dios
O'Reilly
Obispo
Villegas
Bernaza
Avenida de Bélgica (Monserrate)
Agramonte
Lamparilla
Obrapía
Amargura
Brasil (Teniente Rey)
Jústiz
Pía
Baratillo
Oficios
Cristo
Muralla
Economía
Corrales
Sol
Churruca
Apodaca
Egido
Gloria
Misión
Santa Clara
Luz
Acosta
Jesús María
Mercaderes
Merced
Leonor Pérez (Paula)
San Isidro
Velazco
San Pedro
Desamparado
0
300 m
0
300 yds